Network+™
Certification Study Guide

Second Edition

COMPUTING TECHNOLOGY INDUSTRY ASSOCIATION

Network+™
Certification Study Guide

Second Edition

Syngress Media, Inc.

McGraw-Hill Osborne

New York   Chicago   San Francisco   Lisbon   London   Madrid
Mexico City   Milan   New Delhi   San Juan   Seoul   Singapore   Sydney   Toronto

McGraw-Hill/Osborne
2600 Tenth Street
Berkeley, California 94710
U.S.A.

To arrange bulk purchase discounts for sales promotions, premiums, or fund-raisers, please contact **McGraw-Hill**/Osborne at the above address. For information on translations or book distributors outside the U.S.A., please see the International Contact Information page immediately following the index of this book.

Network+™ Certification Study Guide, Second Edition

1234567890 DOC DOC 019876543210

Book p/n 0-07-213180-2 and CD p/n 0-07-213179-9
parts of ISBN 0-07-213181-0

Publisher Brandon A. Nordin	**Editorial Director** Gareth Hancock	**Series Design** Roberta Steele
Vice President & **Associate Publisher** Scott Rogers	**Associate Acquisitions Editor** Timothy Green	**Cover Design** Greg Scott
VP, Worldwide Business **Development** **Global Knowledge** Richard Kristof	**Acquisitions Coordinator** Jessica Wilson **Project Manager** Jenn Tust	**Editorial Management** Syngress Media, Inc. **Production and Editorial** Apollo Publishing Services
	Technical Editor Michael Cross	

This book was published with Corel VENTURA™ Publisher.

9000 Regency Parkway, Suite 500
Cary, NC 27512
1-800-COURSES
www.globalknowledge.com

From Global Knowledge

Global Knowledge supports many styles of learning. We deliver content through the written word, e-Learning, Classroom Learning, and Virtual Classroom Learning. We do this because we know our students need different training approaches to achieve success as technical professionals. This book series offers each reader a valuable tool for Network+ Certification.

Global Knowledge is the world's largest independent IT trainer. This uniquely positions us to offer these books. We have trained hundreds of thousands of students worldwide. Global Knowledge captured those years of expertise in this series. The quality of these books shows our commitment to your lifelong learning success.

For those of you who know Global Knowledge, or those of you who have just found us for the first time, our goal is to be your lifelong training partner. Global Knowledge commits itself daily to providing all learners with the very best training.

Thank you for choosing our training. We look forward to serving your needs again in the future.

Warmest regards,

Duncan Anderson
President and Chief Executive Officer, Global Knowledge

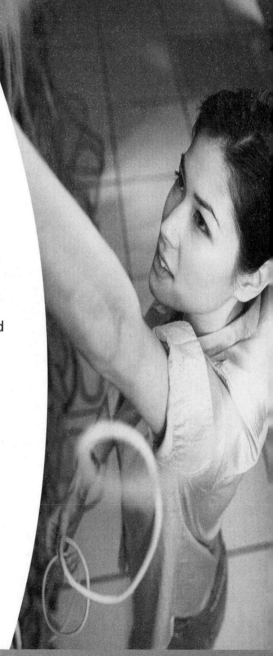

CompTIA Authorized Quality Curriculum

The contents of this training material were created for the CompTIA Network+ exam covering CompTIA certification exam objectives that were current as of January, 2002.

How to Become CompTIA Certified: This training material can help you prepare for and pass a related CompTIA certification exam or exams. In order to achieve CompTIA certification, you must register for and pass a CompTIA certification exam or exams.

In order to become CompTIA certified, you must:

1. Select a certification exam provider. For more information please visit http://www.comptia.org/certification/test_locations.htm.

2. Register for and schedule a time to take the CompTIA certification exam(s) at a convenient location.

3. Read and sign the Candidate Agreement, which will be presented at the time of the exam(s). The text of the Candidate Agreement can be found at http://www.comptia.org/certification.

4. Take and pass the CompTIA certification exam(s).

For more information about CompTIA's certifications, such as their industry acceptance, benefits, or program news, please visit http://www.comptia.org/certification.

CompTIA is a non-profit information technology (IT) trade association.

CompTIA's certifications are designed by subject matter experts from across the IT industry. Each CompTIA certification is vendor-neutral, covers multiple technologies, and requires demonstration of skills and knowledge widely sought after by the IT industry.

To contact CompTIA with any questions or comments:
Please call + 1 630 268 1818
email: questions@comptia.org

About Syngress Media

Syngress Media creates books and software for Information Technology professionals seeking skill enhancement and career advancement. Its products are designed to comply with vendor and industry standard course curricula, and are optimized for certification exam preparation. You can contact Syngress via the Web at www.syngress.com.

Authors

Jarret W. Buse (Network+, A+, MCT, MCSE+I, CCNA, CNA) is a technical trainer and consultant specializing in Microsoft products. He has worked in the computer field for nine years and instructs students in the use of various Microsoft products as well as different computer certifications. With a degree in programming, Jarret is actively working towards his MCSD.

Contributors

Cameron Brandon (MCSE + Internet, CNE, A+, Network+) is a network engineer/administrator living in Portland, Oregon. His networking specialty is Windows NT with BackOffice Integration. Cameron participated in the Intel migration to Windows NT in Oregon, the largest migration of its kind in history. He completed his MCSE, CNE, CNA, MCPS: Internet Systems, and A+ certifications in just five months, and just received his Network+ certification.

Ralph Crump (MCSE, CNE3, CNE4, CNE5) is an architecture and design engineer in Atlanta, Georgia, with a major telecommunications company. He specializes in Windows NT and BackOffice applications including Exchange and SMS and Novell NetWare solutions. He could not have done this without the support of his wife and daughter.

Brian Frederick (Network+, MCSE, CNE4, CNE5, Compaq ASE) is a Systems Engineer with Entre Information Systems, Inc. in Iowa. Brian has been implementing and designing small and large networks for more than five years, with over 10 years general computer experience. He is married with two children and has written a variety of other titles for Syngress Media.

Mike Kendzierski (MCSE) Director of Internet Services at USWeb/CKS has extensive experience deploying complex client/server and Internet systems. Mike is also a regular speaker at technical conferences, such as Microsoft Explorer, on topics ranging from E-Commerce Systems to Lowering the Total Cost of Ownership.

Mike is a published technical author with several titles, including Windows NT and BackOffice technologies, such as Microsoft Site Server and Internet Information Server. When he's not deploying E-Commerce Systems, he can be found roaming Manhattan searching for a local Starbucks.

Technical Editor

Michael Cross (Network+, MCSE, MCP+I, CNA) is an Internet Specialist and Programmer, who has also served as a Network Administrator for the Niagara Regional Police Service. He is responsible for designing and maintaining their public Web site at www.nrps.com, as well as their Intranet and a second version of the Intranet accessed by officers in police cars. In addition, he programs applications that are used to maintain licensing, summons for court, monitor the resale of items that may be stolen, and various other purposes. As Network Administrator, he was responsible for network security and administration, and continues to assist in this regard. He has been consulted and assisted in computer-related/Internet criminal cases, and is part of an Information Technology team that provides support to a user base of over 800 civilian and uniform users.

Michael also owns KnightWare, a company that provides Web page design, consulting, programming, networking, and various other services. You can visit his site at www.knightware.ca. He has served as an instructor for private colleges and technical schools in London, Ontario Canada. He has been a freelance writer for several years, and published over three dozen times in numerous books and anthologies. He currently resides in St. Catharines, Ontario Canada with his lovely wife Jennifer, and two slightly neurotic cats.

Series Editor

D. Lynn White (MCPS,MCSE,MCT,MCP+Internet, CTT) is President of Independent Network Consultants, Inc. Lynn has more than 16 years in programming and networking experience. She has been a systems manager in the mainframe environment, as well as a software developer for a process control company. She is a technical author, editor, trainer and consultant in the field of networking and computer-related technologies. Lynn has been presenting mainframe, Microsoft official curriculum and other operating systems and networking courses in and outside the United States for more than 14 years. Her latest certification has been to receive her CTT (Certified Technical Trainer) by the Chauncey Group International. Lynn would like to extend thanks to her son Christopher for providing the foundation for all her life's endeavors.

ACKNOWLEDGMENTS

We would like to thank the following people:

- Richard Kristof of Global Knowledge for championing the series and providing access to some great people and information. In addition, David Marini, Duncan Anderson, Julie Ungaro, Rich Thompson, Richard Cleveland, and Ronda Swaney.

- All the incredibly hard-working folks at **McGraw-Hill**/Osborne: Brandon Nordin, Scott Rogers, Gareth Hancock, Tim Green, and Jessica Wilson for their help in launching a great series and being solid team players.

CONTENTS AT A GLANCE

1   Basic Concepts   1

2   The Physical Layer   69

3   Data Link, Network, and Transport Layers   115

4   TCP/IP Fundamentals   163

5   TCP/IP Suite Utilities   221

6   Remote Connectivity   287

7   Wide Area Network Technologies   341

8   Network Security   379

9   Network Implementation   433

10 Administering the Change Control System   481

11 Maintaining and Supporting the Network   535

12 Identifying, Assessing, and Responding to Problems   573

13 Troubleshooting the Network   603

A   About the CD   657

B   About the Web Site   663

    Index   665

CONTENTS

Foreword .... *v*

About the Contributors .... *xi*

Acknowledgments .... *xv*

Preface .... *xxxv*

Introduction .... *xxxix*

1 Basic Concepts **1**

Understanding Basic Network Structure 2

    Bus Topologies 3

    Exercise 1-1: Installing Cabling in a Bus Network 5

    Star Topologies 6

    Mesh Topologies 7

    Ring Topologies 7

    Wireless Topologies 9

    Segments and Backbones 11

Network Operating Systems 14

    Microsoft Windows NT 14

    Exercise 1-2: Creating a Startup Boot Disk 15

    Novell NetWare 17

    UNIX 19

Network Protocols 20

    IPX/SPX 21

    TCP/IP 21

    NetBEUI 22

    Exercise 1-3: Determining Which Protocol
to Implement 22

Fault Tolerance and High Availability 23

Mirroring 24

Duplexing 25

Striping With and Without Parity 26

Exercise 1-4: Creating a Stripe Set with Parity on a

Windows 2000 Server 27

Volumes 27

Tape Backup 28

The OSI Model 29

Protocols 30

Services 33

Functions That Pertain to Each Layer 33

Exercise 1-5: Communicating Between Two PCs 37

Networking Media and Connectors 39

Cabling 39

Exercise 1-6: Understanding Cable Types and

Applications 41

Media Connectors 43

Network Elements 48

Full and Half Duplexing 48

WANs, LANs, MANs, and VLANs 48

Servers, Workstations, and Hosts 49

Server-Based Networking and Peer-to-Peer Networking 49

Cables, NICs, and Routers 52

Broadband and Baseband 52

Gateways 53

Exercise 1-7: Networking Solutions 53

✓ Two-Minute Drill 56

Q&A Self Test 59

Lab Question 63

Self Test Answers 64

Lab Answer 68

2   The Physical Layer **69**

Network Interface Cards 70

The Computer Bus 71

Installing a NIC 74

Exercise 2-1:   Installing a Network Interface Card 75

Configuring a NIC 80

Troubleshooting NICs 84

Resolving Hardware Resource Conflicts 86

Network Components 88

Hubs 88

Multistation Access Units 90

Switching Hubs 90

Exercise 2-2:   Determining the Network Device to Use . . . 92

Repeaters 94

Transceivers 94

Wireless Access Points 97

✓   Two-Minute Drill 101

Q&A   Self Test 103

Lab Question 107

Self Test Answers 109

Lab Answer 113

3   Data Link, Network, and Transport Layers **115**

Data Link Layer Concepts 116

MAC Addresses 117

Exercise 3-1:   Determining Your Local Machine's

MAC Address 117

Bridges 120

802 Project Model 121

IEEE 802 Categories 122

Network Layer Concepts 125

Unique Network IDs 126

Routing 126

Router and Brouter Differences 127

Routable and Nonroutable Protocols within the

    Network Layer 128

Static and Dynamic Routing 131

Default Gateways and Subnetworks 133

Exercise 3-2:   Determining Your TCP/IP Configuration .. 136

Transport Layer Concepts 136

Connection-Oriented Communication 137

Connectionless Communication 138

Name Resolution 140

Exercise 3-3:   Editing the HOSTS File 146

Protocols within the Transport Layer 147

✓   Two-Minute Drill 150

Q&A   Self Test 153

Lab Question 157

Self Test Answers 158

Lab Answer 162

4   TCP/IP Fundamentals **163**

TCP/IP Fundamentals 164

IP Addresses 164

Dynamic Host Configuration Protocol 165

Exercise 4-1:   Configuring TCP/IP to Use DHCP 170

Boot Protocol 171

Network Address Translation 172

Domain Name Service 173

Internet Domain Name Server Hierarchies 175

Resolving Host and Domain Names 176

Windows Internet Naming Service 178

HOSTS Files 180

The Main Protocols of the TCP/IP Suite 181

TCP/IP Addressing 188

A, B, and C Classes of IP Addresses and Their Default

Subnet Masks 188

Class A Addresses 189

Class B Addresses 190

Class C Addresses 190

Class D Addresses 191

Class E Addresses 191

Subnetting 192

Special Internet Addresses 193

Exercise 4-2: Configuring TCP/IP to Use DHCP 194

Port Numbers (HTTP, FTP, and SMTP) 194

TCP/IP Version 6 196

TCP/IP Configuration Concepts 196

Configuration Parameters for a Workstation 196

Exercise 4-3: Changing the NetBIOS Name 203

✓ Two-Minute Drill 207

Q&A Self Test 210

Lab Question 214

Self Test Answers 215

Lab Answer 219

5   TCP/IP Suite Utilities **221**

ARP 222

How ARP Works 223

Exercise 5-1: Using ARP to See Your Local ARP Cache . . . 226

RARP 227

Troubleshooting Duplicate IP Address Problems 228

Telnet 229

How Telnet Works 229

Using Telnet 229

Troubleshooting with Telnet   231

Exercise 5-2:   Connecting to an Exchange Internet
Mail Service   232

NBTSTAT   233

How NetBIOS over TCP/IP Works   233

Using NBTSTAT   234

Exercise 5-3:   Using NBTSTAT to Determine the Services
Available on a Local PC   235

Tracert   237

Exercise 5-4:   Using Tracert to Determine Internet Paths . .   238

How Tracert Works   238

Using Tracert   239

Netstat   241

How Netstat Works   242

Exercise 5-5:   Using Netstat to Determine Open
Connections to Other Systems   242

Netstat Options   243

Troubleshooting with Netstat   245

IPCONFIG/WINIPCFG   247

IPCONFIG   248

WINIPCFG   249

Exercise 5-6:   Using IPCONFIG or WINIPCFG   250

FTP   251

How FTP works   251

Using FTP   252

Exercise 5-7:   Using FTP to Display a Listing of Available
Files   252

Troubleshooting with FTP   255

TFTP   255

Ping   256

How Ping Works   256

Exercise 5-8:   Using PING   257

Troubleshooting with Ping 258

NSLOOKUP 259

How NSLOOKUP Works 260

Exercise 5-9: Starting the NSLOOKUP Utility 261

Troubleshooting with TCP/IP Utilities 263

Connectivity Problems 264

Name Resolution Problems 267

✓ Two-Minute Drill 273

Q&A Self Test 276

Lab Question 280

Self Test Answers 282

Lab Answer 286

6 Remote Connectivity **287**

Remote Connectivity Concepts 289

Serial Line Internet Protocol and Point-to-Point Protocol . . . 289

Exercise 6-1: Creating a PPP Dial-Up Connection in
Windows 9x 294

Exercise 6-2: Enabling the Log File for a PPP Dial-Up
Networking Connection for Windows 9x 296

Point-to-Point Tunneling Protocol 298

Exercise 6-3: Setting Up Windows NT as a PPTP Client . . 301

Integrated Services Digital Network and the Public
Switched Telephone Network 303

Dial-Up Networking 313

Exercise 6-4: Installing Dial-Up Networking 313

Modem Configuration Parameters 314

Unimodem 318

Telephony API 320

Requirements for a Remote Connection 321

Terminal Services 322

Advantages of Terminal Services 323

Disadvantages of Terminal Services 323

Protocols 324

Exercise 6-5: Installing a Windows 32-bit ICA Client 325

✓ Two-Minute Drill 329

Q&A Self Test 332

Lab Question 336

Self Test Answers 337

Lab Answer 340

7 Wide Area Network Technologies **341**

Packet-Switching versus Circuit-Switching Networks 342

Exercise 7-1: Packet-Switching Network Exercise 345

Asynchronous Transfer Mode 347

Exercise 7-2: ATM Network Exercise 348

Synchronous Optical NETwork/Synchronous Digital Hierarchy 349

Exercise 7-3: SONET Network Exercise 351

Optical Carrier Level-X 353

Frame Relay 354

Exercise 7-4: Frame Relay Network Exercise 355

Fiber Distributed Data Interface (FDDI) 358

Tx/Ex-Carrier 362

CSU/DSU 363

Exercise 7-5: FDDI Network Exercise 363

✓ Two-Minute Drill 369

Q&A Self Test 371

Lab Question 375

Self Test Answers 376

Lab Answer 378

8 Network Security **379**

Selecting a Security Model—User-Level and Share-Level 381

Windows NT Security Subsystem 381

User-Level Security 384

Exercise 8-1: Creating a New Share Using User-Level
Security 391
Share-Level Security 392
Domains and Workgroups 392
Securing the Registry 395
Password Practices and Procedures 396
Password Policies 396
Username and Password Guidelines 398
Exercise 8-2: Auditing Setup 402
Data Encryption and Protecting Network Data 406
Defining Data Encryption 406
Exercise 8-3: Encrypting Data Files with Windows 2000 . . 410
Common Encryption Programs 412
Uses of a Firewall 412
Firewall Architecture 413
Exercise 8-4: Setting Up Filtered Ports 418
✓ Two-Minute Drill 422
Q&A Self Test 425
Lab Question 429
Self Test Answers 430
Lab Answer 432

9 Network Implementation **433**
Installing the Network 434
Administrative and Test Accounts 436
Passwords 439
Exercise 9-1: Changing Your Password on a
Windows 2000 System 441
IP Addresses 442
IP Configurations 445
Name Resolution 446
WINS 446

DNS   447

Relevant Standard Operating Procedures   447

Environmental Factors that Affect Computer Networks   449

Cables   449

The Network Operations Center   450

Minimizing Electrical Interference   451

Computer Chassis   451

Error Messages   452

Exercise 9-2:   Generating the "Deleting Files"
Error Message   452

Common Peripheral Ports and Network Components   454

Network Interface Cards   454

Network Connection   455

Network-Attached Storage   455

Serial Ports   456

Parallel Ports   457

Universal Serial Bus   457

Small Computer System Interface   457

Interrupts   457

Print Servers   458

Peripherals   458

Bridges   459

Hubs   459

Switches   460

Routers   461

Gateways   462

Exercise 9-3:   Determining Ports on a PC   463

Compatibility and Cabling Issues   465

Incompatibilities with Analog Modems and a Digital Jack . . .   465

Uses of RJ-45 Connectors with Different Cabling   466

Patch Cables and Length of Cabling Segment   466

✓ Two-Minute Drill   468

Q&A   Self Test 471

Lab Question 476

Self Test Answers 477

Lab Answer 480

10 Administering the Change Control System **481**

Documenting Current Status 482

Exercise 10-1:   Running WINMSD on a Windows 9*x*

System or Later 483

Returning a System to Its Original State 484

Exercise 10-2:   Returning a System to Its Original State ... 485

Backup Techniques 486

Tape Backup 487

Replicating a Folder to a Network Drive 488

Exercise 10-3:   Backing Up Data to a Network Drive 489

Removable Media 489

Multigeneration 490

Removing Outdated or Unused Drivers after a Successful Upgrade ... 491

Exercise 10-4:   Using Windows Update on a

Windows 2000 System 493

Effects on the Network Caused by Local Changes 494

Version Conflicts 494

Overwritten DLLs 495

Exercise 10-5:   Setting Options for File Protection 496

Drive Mapping 497

Exercise 10-6:   Mapping a Network Drive through the

Graphical Utility with Windows 95/98 and NT 497

Printer Port Capturing 499

Exercise 10-7:   Mapping a Network Printer 500

Changing or Moving Equipment 502

Exercise 10-8:   Checking the Hardware

Compatibility List 502

Adding, Deleting, or Modifying Users 503

Exercise 10-9: Disabling a User Account on a PC

as a Workgroup 504

User and Group Management 505

Exercise 10-10: Creating a Group Account and Adding

Users to the Group 505

Profiles 507

Rights 508

Procedures/Policies 509

Administrative Utilities 511

Login Accounts and Groups 512

✓ Two-Minute Drill 518

Q&A Self Test 521

Lab Question 526

Self Test Answers 528

Lab Answer 533

11 Maintaining and Supporting the Network **535**

Test Documentation 536

Vendors' Software Patches 537

Exercise 11-1: Downloading a Patch from Novell 538

Upgrades 540

Hardware Upgrades 540

Network Maintenance 543

Standard Backup Procedures and Backup Media

Storage Practices 543

Periodic Application of Software Patches and Other Fixes

to the Network 548

Installing Anti-Virus Software on the Server and

Workstations 549

Update Virus Signatures 556

Exercise 11-2: Downloading and Installing a Virus

Signature 557

✓ Two-Minute Drill 561

Q&A Self Test 563

Lab Question 566

Self Test Answers 567

Lab Answer 571

12 Identifying, Assessing, and Responding to Problems .. 573

Handling Network Problems 574

Information Transfer 575

Handholding 579

Exercise 12-1: Checking for a Resource Kit 579

Technical Service 581

Documentation 583

Prioritizing Network Problems 586

High-Priority Problems 587

Low-Priority Problems 588

✓ Two-Minute Drill 591

Q&A Self Test 593

Lab Question 597

Self Test Answers 598

Lab Answer 602

13 Troubleshooting the Network 603

Managing Network Problems 604

Does the Problem Exist Across the Network? 604

Workstation, Workgroup, LAN, or WAN Problem? 605

Is the Problem Consistent and Replicable? 607

Standard Troubleshooting Methods 607

Exercise 13-1: Checking Device Manager 608

Troubleshooting Network Problems 609

Establish the Symptoms 611

Identify the Affected Areas 612

Establish What Has Changed 614

Select the Most Probable Cause 615

Implement a Solution 615

Test the Result 616

Recognize the Potential Effects of the Solution 616

Documenting the Solution 617

Sample Troubleshooting Situations 617

System or Operator Problems 619

Checking Physical and Logical Indicators 620

Link Lights 620

Collision Lights 621

Power Lights 621

Error Displays 621

Error Logs and Displays 622

Exercise 13-2:   Checking Event Viewer 623

Performance Monitors 624

Network Troubleshooting Resources 624

TechNet 625

Manufacturer Web Sites 625

Resource Kits and Documentation 626

Trade Publications and White Papers 626

Telephone Technical Support 626

Vendor CDs 627

Other Symptoms and Causes of Network Problems 627

Recognizing Abnormal Physical Conditions 627

Isolating and Correcting Problems in the Physical Media 631

Checking the Status of Servers 632

Checking for Configuration Problems 633

Checking for Viruses 635

Checking the Validity of the Account Name and Password .. 635

Rechecking Operator Logon Procedures 636

Selecting and Running Appropriate Diagnostics 636
Network Tools 637
    Crossover Cables 638
    Hardware Loopback 638
    Tone Generators 638
    Time Division Reflectometers 639
    Oscilloscopes 639
    Network Monitors and Protocol Analyzers 639
Selecting Appropriate Tools to Resolve
Network Problems 639
    ✓ Two-Minute Drill 643
    Q&A Self Test 646
        Lab Question 651
        Self Test Answers 652
        Lab Answer 656

A   About the CD **657**
Installing CertTrainer 658
    System Requirements 658
CertTrainer 658
ExamSim 659
    Saving Scores as Cookies 659
E-Book 660
CertCam 660
DriveTime 661
Help 662
Upgrading 662

B   About the Web Site **663**
    Get *What* You Want *When* You Want It 664

Index **665**

PREFACE

This book's primary objective is to help you prepare for and pass the required Network+ exam so you can begin to reap the career benefits of certification. We believe that the only way to do this is to help you increase your knowledge and build your skills. After completing this book, you should feel confident that you have thoroughly reviewed all of the objectives that CompTIA has established for the exam.

In Every Chapter

- ■ Each chapter begins with the **Certification Objectives**—what you need to know in order to pass the section on the exam dealing with the chapter topic. The Certification Objective headings identify the objectives within the chapter, so you'll always know an objective when you see it!

EXERCISE

- ■ **Certification Exercises** are interspersed throughout the chapters. These are step-by-step exercises. They help you master skills that are likely to be an area of focus on the exam. Don't just read through the exercises; they are hands-on procedures that you should be comfortable completing. Learning by doing is an effective way to increase your competency with the language and concepts presented.

exam
Ⓦatch

- ■ **Exam Watch Notes** call attention to information about, and potential pitfalls in, the exam. These helpful hints are written by authors who have taken the exams and received their certification; who better to tell you what to worry about? They know what you're about to go through!

- ■ S & S sections lay out specific scenario questions and solutions in a quick and easy-to-read format.

SCENARIO & SOLUTION

I want to connect two LAN segments that use Ethernet and Token Ring.	Connect the two network segments with a switch. Switched ports are cheap, and they do a great job. Using a standard hub allows no separation of the two LAN segments.
I want to connect two LAN segments in different geographical locations.	To connect LAN segments in different geographical locations, you need a router. A router can find the destination address of a packet and send the packet accordingly.

■ The **Certification Summary** is a succinct review of the chapter and a re-statement of salient points regarding the exam.

■ The **Two-Minute Drill** at the end of every chapter is a checklist of the main points of the chapter. It can be used for last-minute review.

■ The **Self Test** offers questions similar to those found on the certification exam. The answers to these questions, as well as explanations of the answers, can be found in Appendix A. By taking the Self Test after completing each chapter, you'll reinforce what you've learned from that chapter, while becoming familiar with the structure of the exam questions.

Some Pointers

Once you've finished reading this book, set aside some time to do a thorough review. You might want to return to the book several times and make use of all the methods it offers for reviewing the material:

1. *Re-read all the Two-Minute Drills,* or have someone quiz you. You also can use the drills as a way to do a quick cram before the exam.

2. *Re-take the Self Tests.* Taking the tests right after you've read the chapter is a good idea, because it helps reinforce what you've just learned. However, it's an even better idea to go back later and do all the questions in the book in one sitting. Pretend you're taking the exam. (For this reason, you should

mark your answers on a separate piece of paper when you go through the questions the first time.)

3. *Complete the exercises.* Did you do the exercises when you read through each chapter? If not, do them! These exercises are designed to cover exam topics, and there's no better way to get to know this material than by practicing.

4. *Check out the Web site.* Global Knowledge invites you to become an active member of the Access Global Web site. This site is an online mall and an information repository that you'll find invaluable. You can access many types of products to assist you in your preparation for the exams, and you'll be able to participate in forums, on-line discussions, and threaded discussions. No other book brings you unlimited access to such a resource. You'll find more information about this site in Appendix B.

The CD-ROM Resource

This book comes with a CD-ROM that includes test preparation software and provides you with another method for studying. You will find more information on the testing software in Appendix A.

How to Take the CompTIA Network+ Certification Examination

Good News and Bad News

If you are new to certifications, we have some good news and some bad news. The good news is that a computer industry certification is one of the most valuable credentials you can earn. It sets you apart from the crowd and marks you as a valuable asset to your employer. You will gain the respect of your peers, and certification can have a wonderful effect on your income.

The bad news is that certification tests are not easy. You may think you will read through some study material, memorize a few facts, and pass the examinations. After all, these certification exams are just computer-based, multiple-choice tests, so they must be easy. If you believe this, you are wrong. Unlike many "multiple-guess" tests you have been exposed to in school, the questions on certification examinations go beyond simple factual knowledge.

The purpose of this introduction is to teach you how to take a computer certification examination. To be successful, you need to know something about the purpose and structure of these tests. We will also look at the latest innovations in computerized testing. Using *simulations* and *adaptive testing*, the computer industry is enhancing both the validity and security of the certification process. These factors have some important effects on how you should prepare for an exam, as well as your approach to each question during the test.

We will begin by looking at the purpose, focus, and structure of certification tests, and we will examine the effect these factors have on the kinds of questions you will face on your certification exams. We will define the structure of examination questions and investigate some common formats. Next, we will present a strategy for answering these questions. Finally, we will give some specific guidelines on what you should do on the day of your test.

Why Vendor Certification?

The CompTIA Network+ certification program, like the certification programs from Microsoft, Lotus, Novell, Oracle, and other software vendors, is maintained for the ultimate purpose of increasing the corporation's profits. A successful vendor certification program accomplishes this goal by helping to create a pool of experts in a company's software, and by "branding" these experts so that companies using the software can identify them.

Vendor certification has become increasingly popular in the past few years because it helps employers find qualified workers, and it helps software vendors, such as Microsoft, sell their products. But why vendor certification rather than a more traditional approach, such as a college degree in computer science? A college education is a broadening and enriching experience, but a degree in computer science does not prepare students for most jobs in the IT industry.

A common truism in our business states, "If you are out of the IT industry for three years and want to return, you have to start over." The problem, of course, is *timeliness*; a specific computer program that a first-year student learns about will probably no longer be in wide use when he or she graduates. Although some colleges are trying to integrate computer certification into their curriculum, the problem is not really a flaw in higher education, but a characteristic of the IT industry. Computer software is changing so rapidly that a four-year college just can't keep up.

A marked characteristic of the computer certification program is an emphasis on performing specific job tasks rather than merely gathering knowledge. It may come as a shock, but most potential employers do not care how much you know about the theory of operating systems, networking, or database design. As one IT manager put it, "I don't really care what my employees know about the theory of our network. We don't need someone to sit at a desk and think about it. We need people who can actually do something to make it work better."

You should not think that this attitude is some kind of anti-intellectual revolt against "book learning." Knowledge is a necessary prerequisite, but it is not enough. More than one company has hired a computer science graduate as a network administrator, only to learn that the new employee has no idea how to add users, assign permissions, or perform the other day-to-day tasks necessary to maintain a network. This brings us to the second major characteristic of computer certification that affects the questions you must be prepared to answer: real-world job skills.

CompTIA's Network+ certification program will be testing you on current network implementations in wide use today, including network-related hardware and software. The job task orientation of certification is almost as obvious, but testing real-world job skills using a computer-based test is not easy.

Computerized Testing

Considering the popularity of CompTIA's certification, and the fact that certification candidates are spread around the world, the only practical way to administer tests for the certification program is through Prometric or VUE testing centers. Typically, several hundred questions are developed for the new CompTIA certification examination. The questions are first reviewed by a number of subject matter experts for technical accuracy, and then are presented in a beta test. The beta test may last for several hours, due to the large number of questions. After a few weeks, CompTIA uses the statistical feedback from the beta exam to check the performance on the beta questions.

Questions are discarded if most test takers get them right (too easy) or wrong (too difficult). A number of other statistical measures are taken of each question. Although the scope of our discussion precludes a rigorous treatment of question analysis, you should be aware that CompTIA and other vendors spend a great deal of time and effort making sure their examination questions are valid. In addition to the obvious desire for quality, the fairness of a vendor's certification program must be legally defensible.

The questions that survive statistical analysis form the pool of questions for the final certification examination.

Test Structure

The kind of test we are most familiar with is known as a *form* test. For the CompTIA certification, a form consists of 72 questions and allows for 90 minutes to complete.

The questions in a CompTIA form test are equally weighted. This means they all count the same when the test is scored. An interesting and useful characteristic of a form test is that you can mark a question you have doubts about as you take the test. Assuming you have time left when you finish all the questions, you can return and spend more time on the questions you have marked as doubtful.

CompTIA, like Microsoft, may soon implement *adaptive* testing for the Network+ exam. To develop this interactive technique, a form test is first created and administered to several thousand certification candidates. The statistics generated are used to assign a weight, or difficulty level, for each question. For example, the questions in a form might be divided into levels one through five, with level one questions being the easiest and level five the hardest.

When an adaptive test begins, the candidate is first given a level three question. If he answers it correctly, he is given a question from the next higher level; if he answers it incorrectly, he is given a question from the next lower level. When 15–20 questions have been answered in this manner, the scoring algorithm is able to predict, with a high degree of statistical certainty, whether the candidate would pass or fail if all the questions in the form were answered. When the required degree of certainty is attained, the test ends and the candidate receives a pass/fail grade.

Adaptive testing has some definite advantages for everyone involved in the certification process. Adaptive tests enable the test center to deliver more tests with the same resources, because certification candidates often are in and out in 30 minutes or less. For CompTIA, adaptive testing means that fewer test questions are exposed to each candidate, which enhances the security, and therefore the validity, of certification tests.

One possible problem you may have with adaptive testing is that you are not allowed to mark and revisit questions. Because the adaptive algorithm is interactive, and all questions but the first are selected on the basis of your response to the previous question, it is not possible to skip a particular question or change an answer.

Question Types

Computerized test questions can be presented in a number of ways. Some of the possible formats are used on CompTIA certification examinations, and some are not.

True/False

We are all familiar with True/False questions, but because of the inherent 50 percent chance of guessing the correct answer, you will not see questions of this type on your Network+ certification exam.

Multiple Choice

The majority of Network+ certification questions are in the multiple-choice format, with either a single correct answer or multiple correct answers. One interesting variation on multiple-choice questions with multiple correct answers is whether or not the candidate is told how many answers are correct.

EXAMPLE:
Which networking protocols are routable? (Choose two.)

Or

Which networking protocols exist in the Network Layer of the OSI model? (Choose all that apply.)

You may see both variations on CompTIA certification examinations, but the trend seems to be toward the first type, where candidates are told explicitly how many answers are correct.

Graphical Questions

One or more graphical elements are sometimes used as exhibits to help present or clarify an exam question. These elements may take the form of a network diagram or pictures of networking components on which you are being tested. It is often easier to present the concepts required for a complex performance-based scenario with a graphic than it is with words. Expect to see some graphical questions on your Network+ exam.

Test questions known as *hotspots* actually incorporate graphics as part of the answer. These questions ask the certification candidate to click a location or graphical element to answer the question. As an example, you might be shown the diagram of a network and asked to click on an appropriate location for a router. The answer is correct if the candidate clicks within the *hotspot* that defines the correct location. The Network+ exam has a few of these graphical hotspot questions, and most are asking you to identify network types, such as a bus or star network. As with the graphical questions, expect only a couple of hotspot questions during your exam.

Free Response Questions

Another kind of question you sometimes see on certification examinations requires a *free response* or type-in answer. This type of question might present a TCP/IP network scenario and ask the candidate to calculate and enter the correct subnet mask in dotted decimal notation. However, the CompTIA Network+ exam most likely will not contain any free response questions.

Knowledge-Based and Performance-Based Questions

CompTIA Certification develops a blueprint for each certification examination with input from subject matter experts. This blueprint defines the content areas and objectives for each test, and each test question is created to test a specific objective. The basic information from the examination blueprint can be found on CompTIA's Web site at http://www.comptia.com/certification/networkplus/index.htm

Psychometricians (psychologists who specialize in designing and analyzing tests) categorize test questions as knowledge based or performance based. As the names imply, knowledge-based questions are designed to test knowledge, and performance-based questions are designed to test performance.

Some objectives demand a knowledge-based question. For example, objectives that use verbs such as *list* and *identify* tend to test only what you know, not what you can do.

EXAMPLE:
Objective: Explain the following Transport Layer concepts.
Which two protocols are connectionless-oriented network protocols? (Choose two.)

    A. FTP

    B. TCP

    C. TFTP

    D. UDP

       Correct answers: C, D.

The Network+ exam consists of mostly knowledge-based multiple-choice questions that can be answered fairly quickly if you know your stuff. These questions are very straightforward, lacking a complex situation to confuse you.

Other objectives use action verbs such as *install, configure,* and *troubleshoot* to define job tasks. These objectives can often be tested with either a knowledge-based question or a performance-based question.

EXAMPLE:

Objective: Configure a Windows 98 workstation for NetBIOS name resolution.

Knowledge-based question:

Where do you configure a Windows 98 workstation to use a WINS server for NetBIOS name resolution?

A. Start | Settings | Control Panel | Network | WINS Configuration

B. Start | Settings | Control Panel | Network | TCP/IP | Properties | WINS Configuration

C. My Computer | Control Panel | Network | WINS Configuration

D. My Computer | Control Panel | Network | TCP/IP | Properties | WINS

Correct answer: B.

Performance-based question:

You want to ensure you have a reliable tape backup scheme that is not susceptible to fire and water hazards. You are backing up three Windows NT servers and would like to completely back up the entire systems. Which of the following is the most reliable backup method?

A. Configure the backup program to back up the user files and operating system files: complete a test restore of the backup; and store the backup tapes offsite in a fireproof vault.

B. Configure the backup program to back up the entire hard drive of each server and store the backup tapes offsite in a fireproof vault.

C. Copy the user files to another server; configure the backup program to back up the operating system files; and store the backup tapes offsite in a fireproof vault.

D. Configure the backup program to back up the user files and operating system files and store the backup tapes offsite in fireproof vault.
Correct answer: A.

Even in this simple example, the superiority of the performance-based question is obvious. Whereas the knowledge-based question asks for a single fact, the performance-based question presents a real-life situation and requires that you make a decision based on this scenario. Thus, performance-based questions give more bang (validity) for the test author's buck (individual question).

Testing Job Performance

We have said that CompTIA certification focuses on timeliness and the ability to perform job tasks. We have also introduced the concept of performance-based questions, but even performance-based multiple-choice questions do not really measure performance. Another strategy is needed to test job skills.

Given unlimited resources, it is not difficult to test job skills. In an ideal world, CompTIA would fly Network+ candidates to a test facility, place them in a controlled environment with a team of experts, and ask them to plan, install, maintain, and troubleshoot a network. In a few days at most, the experts could reach a valid decision as to whether each candidate should or should not be granted Network+ status. Needless to say, this is not likely to happen.

Closer to reality, another way to test performance is to use the actual software and create a testing program to present tasks and automatically grade a candidate's performance when the tasks are completed. This *cooperative* approach would be practical in some testing situations, but the same test that is presented to Network+ candidates in Boston must also be available in Bahrain and Botswana. Many testing locations around the world cannot run 32-bit applications, much less provide the complex networked solutions required by cooperative testing applications.

The most workable solution for measuring performance in today's testing environment is a *simulation* program. When the program is launched during a test, the candidate sees a simulation of the actual software that looks and behaves just like the real thing. When the testing software presents a task, the simulation program is launched and the candidate performs the required task. The testing software then grades the candidate's performance on the required task and moves to the next question. In this way, a 16-bit simulation program can mimic the look and feel of 32-bit operating systems, a complicated network, or even the entire Internet.

Simulation questions provide many advantages over other testing methodologies, and simulations are expected to become increasingly important in the computer certification programs. For example, studies have shown that there is a very high correlation between the ability to perform simulated tasks on a computer-based test and the ability to perform the actual job tasks. Thus, simulations enhance the validity of the certification process.

Another truly wonderful benefit of simulations is in the area of test security. It is just not possible to cheat on a simulation question. In fact, you will be told exactly what tasks you are expected to perform on the test. How can a certification candidate cheat? By learning to perform the tasks? What a concept!

Study Strategies

There are appropriate ways to study for the different types of questions you will see on a CompTIA Network+ certification examination.

Knowledge-Based Questions

Knowledge-based questions require that you memorize facts. There are hundreds of facts inherent in every content area of every Network+ certification examination. There are several tricks to memorizing facts:

- **Repetition** The more times your brain is exposed to a fact, the more likely you are to remember it. Flash cards are a wonderful tool for repetition. Either make your own flash cards on paper or download a flash card program and develop your own questions.

- **Association** Connecting facts within a logical framework makes them easier to remember. Try using mnemonics, such as "All People Seem To Need Data Processing" to remember the seven layers of the OSI model in order.

- **Motor Association** It is often easier to remember something if you write it down or perform some other physical act, such as clicking on a practice test answer. You will find that hands-on experience with the product or concept being tested is a great way to develop motor association.

We have said that the emphasis of CompTIA certification is job performance, and that there are very few knowledge-based questions on CompTIA certification exams. Why should you waste a lot of time learning file names, IP address formulas, and other minutiae? Read on.

Performance-Based Questions

Most of the questions you will face on a CompTIA certification exam are performance-based scenario questions. We have discussed the superiority of these questions over simple knowledge-based questions, but you should remember that the job task orientation of CompTIA certification extends the knowledge you need to pass the exams; it does not replace this knowledge. Therefore, the first step in preparing for scenario questions is to absorb as many facts relating to the exam content areas as you can. In other words, go back to the previous section and follow the steps to prepare for an exam composed of knowledge-based questions.

The second step is to familiarize yourself with the format of the questions you are likely to see on the exam. You can do this by answering the questions in this study guide, or by using practice tests. The day of your test is not the time to be surprised by the complicated construction of some exam questions.

For example, one of CompTIA Certification's favorite formats of late takes the following form found on Microsoft exams:

Scenario: You have a network with...
Primary Objective: You want to...
Secondary Objective: You also want to...
Proposed Solution: Do this...
What does the proposed solution accomplish?

   A. It achieves the primary and the secondary objective.

   B. It achieves the primary but not the secondary objective.

   C. It achieves the secondary but not the primary objective.

   D. It achieves neither the primary nor the secondary objective.

This kind of question, with some variation, is seen on many Microsoft Certification examinations and will be present on your Network+ certification exam.

At best, these performance-based scenario questions really do test certification candidates at a higher cognitive level than knowledge-based questions do. At worst, these questions can test your reading comprehension and test-taking ability rather than your ability to administer networks. Be sure to get in the habit of reading the question carefully to determine what is being asked.

The third step in preparing for CompTIA scenario questions is to adopt the following attitude: Multiple-choice questions aren't really performance-based. It is all a cruel lie. These scenario questions are just knowledge-based questions with a little story wrapped around them.

To answer a scenario question, you have to sift through the story to the underlying facts of the situation and apply your knowledge to determine the correct answer. This may sound silly at first, but the process we go through in solving real-life problems is quite similar. The key concept is that every scenario question (and every real-life problem) has a fact at its center, and if we can identify that fact, we can answer the question.

Exam Blueprint

The Network+ exam is divided into four major categories called *domains*. Media & Topologies, Protocols & Standards, Network Implementation and Network Support. Each category or domain is broken down into several exam objectives with a percentage applied reflecting the amount each objective relates to the entire Network+ exam.

You can find detailed information on each domain at http://www.comptia.com/certification/networkplus/index.htm

Signing Up

Signing up to take the CompTIA Network+ certification examination is easy. Please check the CompTIA Web site at www.comptia.org for pricing information and further updates concerning the Network+ exam.

There are, however, a few things you should know:

1. If you call to register during a busy time period, get a cup of coffee first, because you may be in for a long wait. The testing centers do an excellent

job, but everyone in the world seems to want to sign up for a test on Monday morning.

2. You will need your social security number or some other unique identifier to sign up for a test, so have it at hand.

3. Pay for your test by credit card if at all possible. This makes things easier, and you can even schedule tests for the same day you call, if space is available at your local testing center.

4. Know the number and title of the test you want to take before you call. This is not essential, and the operators will help you if they can. Having this information in advance, however, speeds up the registration process.

Taking the Test

Teachers have always told you not to try to cram for examinations, because it does no good. If you are faced with a knowledge-based test requiring only that you regurgitate facts, cramming can mean the difference between passing and failing. This is not the case, however, with many certification exams. If you don't know it the night before, don't bother to stay up and cram.

Instead, create a schedule and stick to it. Plan your study time carefully, and do not schedule your test until you think you are ready to succeed. Follow these guidelines on the day of your exam:

1. Start out with a good night's sleep. The scenario questions you will face on your Network+ certification examination require a clear head.

2. Remember to take two forms of identification—at least one with a picture. A driver's license with your picture, and social security or credit cards are acceptable.

3. Leave home in time to arrive at your testing center a few minutes early. It is not a good idea to feel rushed as you begin your exam.

4. Do not spend too much time on any one question. If you are taking a form test, take your best guess and mark the question so you can come back to it if you have time. You cannot mark and revisit questions on an adaptive test, so you must do your best on each question as you go.

5. If you do not know the answer to a question, try to eliminate the obviously wrong answers and guess from the rest. If you can eliminate two out of four options, you have a 50 percent chance of guessing the correct answer.

6. For scenario questions, follow the steps we outlined earlier. Read the question carefully and try to identify the facts at the center of the story.

Finally, I would advise anyone attempting to earn computer certifications to adopt a philosophical attitude. Even if you are the kind of person who never fails a test, you are likely to fail at least one certification test somewhere along the way. Do not get discouraged. If certifications were easy to obtain, more people would have them, and they would not be so respected and so valuable to your future in the IT industry.

1

Basic Concepts

CERTIFICATION OBJECTIVES

1.01	Understanding Basic Network Structure
1.02	Network Operating Systems
1.03	Network Protocols
1.04	Fault Tolerance and High Availability
1.05	The OSI Model
1.06	Networking Media and Connectors
1.07	Network Elements
✓	Two-Minute Drill
Q&A	Self Test

I n the world of computing today, the knowledge of how computers communicate in a network is very important to being a good network technician. This chapter introduces you to the basics of what makes a network tick.

You should refer to this chapter often as you read the rest of this book. We will look at the various topologies, network operating systems, and common terminology. Some pieces of this chapter are very brief. That is because the material in this chapter serves as the foundation for the following chapters. Be sure to get a basic understanding of the material in this chapter. Once you understand it, the following chapters will be easier to understand and learn.

CERTIFICATION OBJECTIVE 1.01

Understanding Basic Network Structure

Using computers in a professional setting without any kind of network is unthinkable these days. From the dial-up connection of a consultant's laptop to the company information distributed on an intranet, networks are essential to a company's success. Network technicians must know the essentials of a network so that they can fulfill the responsibilities of maintaining and troubleshooting their own networks.

A *network* is made up of two basic components: the *entities* that want to share information or resources, such as servers and workstations, and the *medium* that enables the entities to communicate, which is a cable or a wireless medium. The entities are usually workstations, and the medium is either a cable segment or a wireless medium such as an infrared signal.

Various topologies make up computer networks. Topology is the physical layout of computers, cables, and other components on a network. Many networks are a combination of the various topologies that we examine in this book:

- Bus
- Star
- Mesh
- Ring
- Wireless

Bus Topologies

A *bus topology* uses one cable to connect multiple computers. This might sound a little strange, but the fact is, it is very easy to set up and install this type of network. The cable is also called a *trunk*, a *backbone*, or a *segment*. A bus topology is configured in a couple of common ways. Most of the time, as shown in Figure 1-1, *T-connectors* are used to connect to the cabled segment. They are called T-connectors because they are shaped like the letter *T*. You will commonly see coaxial cable used in bus topologies. Exercise 1-1 shows you how to install a bus network.

Only one computer at a time can transmit a packet on a bus topology. Computers in a bus topology "listen" to all traffic on the network but accept only the packets that are addressed to them. Broadcast packets are an exception because all computers on the network accept them. When a computer sends out a packet, it travels in both directions from the computer. This means that the network is occupied until the destination computer accepts the packet. The number of computers on a bus topology network has a major influence on the network's performance.

Another key component of a bus topology is the need for termination. If the cable isn't terminated, the packet (which is an electronic signal) will bounce back and forth along the cable and bring down the whole network. To prevent packets from bouncing up and down the cable, devices called *terminators* must be attached to both ends of the cable. A terminator absorbs an electronic signal and clears the cable so that other computers can send packets on the network. If there is no termination, the entire network fails.

FIGURE 1-1

In a bus topology, all computers are connected on one linear cable

A bus is a *passive* topology. That means that the computers on a bus topology only listen or send data. They do not resend or regenerate data. So, if one computer on the network fails, the network is still up.

If you are familiar with daisy chaining, you will have no problem getting an idea of what the bus topology is like. The bus topology daisy chains computers on a cable segment in which one PC or device is connected to the next PC or device and so on.

Advantages of the Bus Topology

One advantage of a bus topology is cost. The bus topology uses less cable than the star topology or the mesh topology. Another advantage is the ease of installation. With the bus topology, you simply connect the workstation to the cable segment, or *backbone*. You need only the amount of cable to connect the workstations you have. The ease of working with a bus topology and the minimal amount of cable required make this the most economical choice for a network topology. Most important, if a computer fails, the network stays functional.

Disadvantages of the Bus Topology

The main disadvantage of the bus topology is the difficulty of troubleshooting it. When the network goes down, it is usually due to a break in the cable segment. With a large network, this problem can be tough to isolate. Figure 1-2 shows a cable break between computers on a bus topology, which would take the entire network down. Another disadvantage of a bus topology is that the heavier the traffic, the slower the network.

Scalability is an important consideration with the dynamic world of networking. Being able to make changes easily within the size and layout of your network can be important in future productivity or downtime. The bus topology is not very scalable.

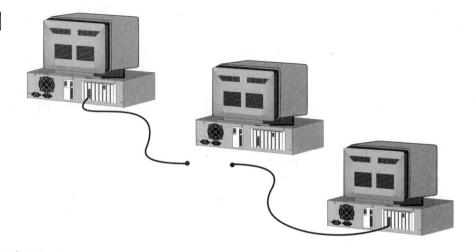

FIGURE 1-2

A bus topology
with a break in a
segment, which
would take down
the entire
network

EXERCISE 1-1

Installing Cabling in a Bus Network

In this exercise, you will learn how to install the cabling in a bus topology. Do the
following:

1. Have all PCs in place with network card that have a BNC connector.

2. Run cable between all PCs in a line so that the cable length is no more
    than 185 meters (606 feet).

3. Use a crimping tool to place a BNC connector on all ends of the cables.

4. Place a T-connector on all the BNC network interfaces.

5. Connect an end of each cable to an end of the T-connector (from one
    computer to another).

6. Place a terminator on the two PCs that are on the ends of the bus that
    have an empty socket on the T-connector.

Star Topologies

In a *star topology*, all computers are connected through one central hub or switch, as illustrated in Figure 1-3. This is a very common network scenario.

The term *star topology* originated in the days of mainframe systems. A mainframe system had a centralized point where the terminals connected.

Advantages of the Star Topology

One advantage of a star topology is the centralization of cabling. In a hub, if one link fails, the remaining workstations are not affected, as they are with other topologies, which we examine in this chapter.

Centralizing network components can make an administrator's life much easier in the long run. Centralized management and monitoring of network traffic can be vital to network success. With a star configuration, it is also easy to add or change configurations because all the connections come to a central point.

Disadvantages of the Star Topology

On the flip side, if the hub fails in a star topology, the entire network, or a good portion of the network, comes down, too. This is, of course, an easier fix than trying to find a break in a cable in a bus topology.

Another disadvantage of a star topology is cost: To connect each workstation to a centralized hub, you must use much more cable than you do in a bus topology.

FIGURE 1-3

Computers in a
star topology are
all connected to
a central hub

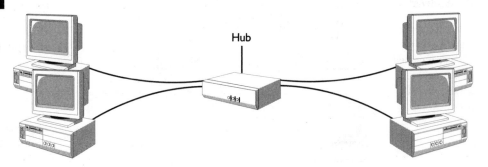

Hub

Mesh Topologies

A *mesh topology* is not very common in computer networking, but you must understand the concept for the exam. A mesh topology is more commonly seen with something like the national phone network. In a mesh topology, every workstation has a connection to every other component of the network, as illustrated in Figure 1-4.

Advantages of a Mesh Topology

The biggest advantage of a mesh topology is *fault tolerance*. That means that if there is a break in a cable segment, traffic can be rerouted. This fault tolerance means that the network going down due to a cable fault is *almost* impossible. (We stress *almost* because no matter how many connections you have in a network, the network can still crash.)

Disadvantages of a Mesh Topology

A mesh topology is very hard to administer and manage because of the numerous connections. Another disadvantage is cost. With a large network, the amount of cable needed to connect and the interfaces on the workstations can be very expensive.

Ring Topologies

In a *ring topology*, all computers are connected via a cable that loops around. As shown in Figure 1-5, the ring topology is a circle that has no start and no end. Terminators are not necessary in a ring topology. Signals travel in one direction on a ring while

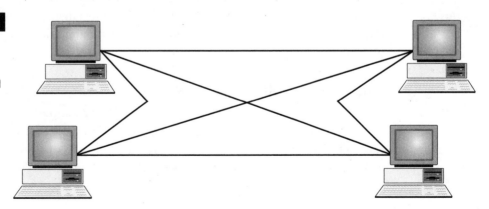

FIGURE 1-4

Computers in a mesh topology are all connected to every other component of the network

FIGURE 1-5

Signals travel in
one direction in
a ring topology

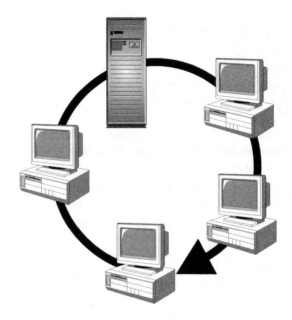

they are passed from one computer to the next. Each computer checks the packet for
its destination and passes it on as a repeater would. If one of the computers fails, the
entire ring network goes down.

Advantages of a Ring Topology

The nice thing about a ring topology is that each computer has equal communication
access on the network. (With bus and star topologies, only one workstation can
communicate over the network at a time.) A ring topology provides good performance
for each workstation. This means that busier computers that send out a lot of
information do not inhibit other computers from communicating. Another advantage
of the ring topology is that signal degeneration is low.

Disadvantages of a Ring Topology

The biggest problem with a ring topology is that if one computer fails or the cable
link is broken, the entire network could go down. With newer technology, however,
this isn't always the case. The concept of a ring topology is that the ring isn't broken
and the signal hops from workstation to workstation, connection to connection.

Isolating a problem can be difficult in some ring configurations. (With newer technologies, a workstation or server will put out a beacon if it notices a break in the ring.) Another disadvantage is that if you make a cabling change to the network or a workstation change, such as a move, the brief disconnection can interrupt or bring down the entire network..

on the
Job

In many environments, you will see a couple of these topologies integrated into the same network. One example is a school that had both Token Ring and Ethernet segments. The server was running NetWare and had three network cards installed; it acted as a router for all the segments. The main thing about this scenario was that administrators had to make sure they understood how logical and physical cable segments work. Each network card determined a segment. There were two Token Ring network cards and one Ethernet network card installed in the server. This was not an ideal solution, but they had the old Type 1 Token Ring along with the newer Token Ring using standard RJ-45 patch cables. This scenario made things complicated when moving equipment around. Thankfully, they upgraded and eventually went to one topology; now they are all running Ethernet.

Wireless Topologies

A *wireless topology* is one in which few cables are used to connect systems. The network is made up of transmitters that broadcast the packets using radio frequencies. The network contains special transmitters called *cells*, which extend a radio sphere in the shape of a bubble around the transmitter. This bubble can extend to multiple rooms and possibly floors in a building. The PCs and network devices have a special transmitter/receiver, which allows them to receive broadcasts and transmit requested data back to the cell. The cell is hooked by a physical cable to a central cable network, which is also hooked to the servers and other cells. A wireless network is shown in Figure 1-6.

Another option for wireless networks is the use of a radio antenna on or near the building, which allows one cell to cover the building and the surrounding area. This approach is best in a campus-type arrangement, where you find many buildings in a close geographical area that need to be included in the cell. This setup does not easily allow you to connect the buildings by a backbone and physical cables and then to each building containing the required cells for all its PCs and devices.

FIGURE 1-6 Wireless topology

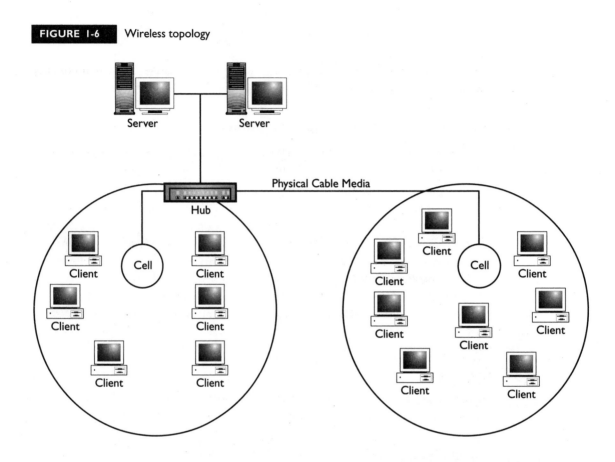

Wireless networks can also consist of infrared communications, similarly to a remote control TV, but this type of communication is slow and requires a direct line of sight as well as close proximity for the communication to work. Infrared is mainly used only between two systems. Infrared is not often used as a complete networking solution and should not even be considered as an option for a whole network; it is useful only between laptops and even a laptop and a printer.

Advantages of a Wireless Topology

The nice thing about wireless networks is the lack of cabling. The wireless network requires only base backbone segments to which to connect the wireless cells. Once these are set up, the PC and network devices also need the special transmitter/

receiver network interface cards to allow the PCs and devices to communicate with the cell and then through the cell to the servers.

Troubleshooting failed devices and cells is very easy and makes failed components easy to find and replace.

Disadvantages of a Wireless Topology

One disadvantage of wireless networks is that there is a greater chance of interference and blockage. Other devices and machinery that emit radio frequencies or "noise" can cause interference and static, which can disrupt the bubble of communication around the cell. Another source of noise is lightning during storms. This noise is the same static you hear when lightning strikes while you are speaking on a phone.

Blockage can occur in structures that are made of thick stone or lots of metal, which do not allow for radio frequencies to pass through easily. This drawback can usually be somewhat overcome by changing the frequency used by the devices to a higher frequency. You can determine early if this is going to be a problem in your building by trying to use a radio inside the building to pick up some radio stations. If the radio will not pick them up, the building material is too thick to allow radio frequencies to pass through the walls. This problem can be overcome by installing a cell in each room where a PC or network device will be placed.

exam

ⓌatchWatch

For the Network+ exam, you need to be able to visually recognize these topologies from a diagram of a logical network.

Segments and Backbones

With the various topologies we've looked at, you have seen the words *segment* and *backbone* mentioned a couple of times. To make clear what the word *segment* means as it relates to networks, we have to look at it two ways. The first is an actual physical cable segment. A physical cable segment can be a 6-foot piece of twisted-pair CAT5 cable. Networking also involves a logical segment that contains all the computers interconnected on the same network. Figure 1-7 shows six different logical segments on a Transmission Control Protocol/Internet Protocol (TCP/IP) network. Even though the computers are physically connected, they are on six different logical segments due to the different addressing. Addressing determines your logical cable segment. The physical cable segment contains the physical cables connecting the various logical segments.

FIGURE 1-7 Six different logical cable segments on a TCP/IP network

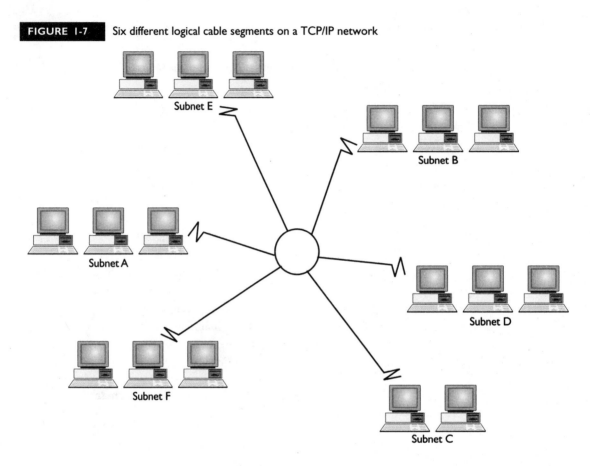

We also saw the word *backbone* mentioned a few times. A backbone is the main cable segment in the network. In a bus network, you might see a cable that has smaller cables connected to it that links the workstations at the other end of the cable. Figure 1-8 shows a Thick Ethernet backbone with Thin Ethernet drops coming off it.

Another global example of a backbone is a satellite linking geographically dispersed local area networks (LANs), making a wide area network (WAN). Such a backbone is an example of a wireless communications network, whereas the previous examples all used cable as the medium.

FIGURE 1-8

FIGURE 1-8

A thick Ethernet
backbone with
thin Ethernet
drops

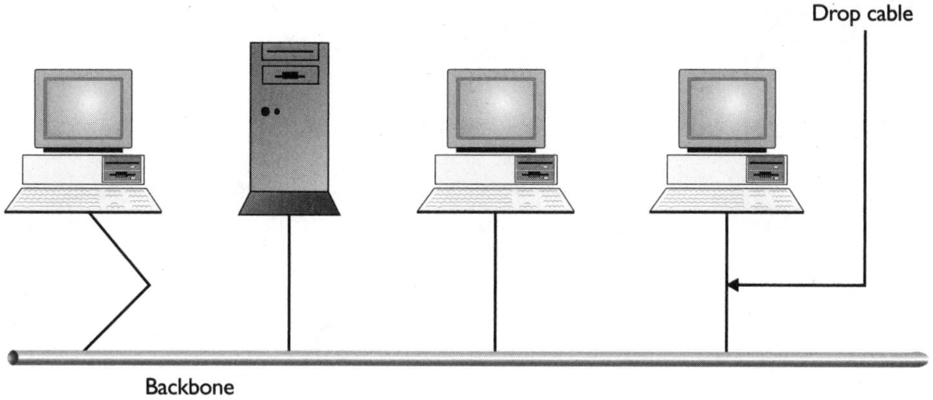

Drop cable

Backbone

Now that you understand some of the basics of topologies, let's examine a few
real-world scenarios and their possible solutions.

SCENARIO & SOLUTION	
I am an engineer. I want to have a network with a single cable to which all computers attach with drop cables. Which type of network should I use?	Use a bus topology.
I want to have a central hub that connects all the various computers via patch cables. Which topology should I use?	Use a star topology.
As a network technician, I want all my computers to have multiple redundant links to ensure minimal downtime. Which topology would I use to achieve this goal?	Use a mesh topology.
I want to have a logically circular base for connecting all computers, with no ending point. Which topology should I use?	Use a ring topology.
I want to have a network with little or no physical cabling in the areas around the employees and their PCs. Which topology should I use?	Use a wireless topology.

Network Operating Systems

Now that you have a general idea of the layout or topology of networks, let's look at the *network operating system (NOS)*. We focus on the three most widely used network operating systems available:

- Microsoft Windows NT/Windows 2000
- Novell NetWare
- UNIX

NOSs can operate in two fashions. In a *peer-to-peer* environment, each workstation on the network is equally responsible for managing resources. Each individual workstation can share its resources with other systems on the network. Configuring this type of network can be challenging because nothing is centralized.

A *client/server* environment, on the other hand, takes a centralized approach to the NOS. If, as an administrator, you identify one machine as the network server, you can centralize network resource sharing. Clients then access the server. Examples of server operating systems are Windows NT Server 4.0 and Windows 2000. Possible clients for these OSs include Windows XP Professional, Windows 2000 Professional, Windows NT Workstation 4.0, Windows ME, Windows 98, Windows 95, Windows for Workgroups, Windows 3.1, and even MS-DOS Client.

Microsoft Windows NT

Developed from the VMS platform many years ago, Microsoft Windows NT has grown into a very popular NOS with a new and different interface, which has also been used in the later versions of Windows, such as Windows 2000 and Windows XP. The graphical interface and the look and feel of the other operating systems in the Windows family made Windows NT very popular among users and network administrators. Figure 1-9 is a screen shot from Windows NT Server 4.0. The interface looks like that of Windows 95 or Windows 98 but has some differences in the utilities installed to manage the server. Exercise 1-2 shows you how to create a startup disk so that you can experience this interface for yourself.

FIGURE 1-9

Windows NT
Server 4.0
enables you to
manage a NOS
as a client/server
environment

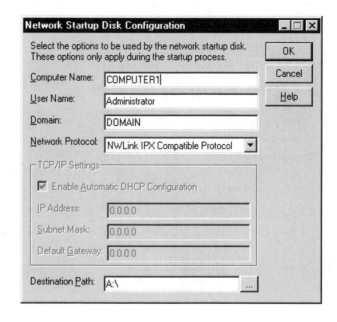

EXERCISE 1-2

Creating a Startup Boot Disk

This exercise shows you how to create a startup boot disk to install client OS, such
as Windows 95, on client PCs from a network server. Do the following:

1. Copy the Windows 95 source files to a directory on the server and share
   the directory as **Windows95**.

2. On the Windows NT 4.0 Server, go to **Start | Programs | Administrative
   Tools (Common) | Network Client Administrator**.

3. This sequence of choices opens the Network Client Administrator window,
   which allows you to select **Make Network Installation Startup Disk**. Then
   press the **Continue** button.

4. Select the last option, **Use Existing Shared Directory**, and specify the server
   name and share name of the directory (Windows95).

5. Select the **OK** button.

6. The next window prompts for the path to the diskette on which to create the boot copy. Select either the button for a **3.5" floppy in Drive A:** or the button for a **5.25" floppy in Drive A:**.

7. Select the Network Client (**Windows 95**) in the next section.

8. In the Network Adapter box, select the **network adapter type** located in the client PC, and select the **Next** button.

9. The last screen is used to specify the account to use to log in to the server and download the client OS. Specify the Computer Name, User Name, Domain, and Network Protocol. Once you select Network Protocol, other choices might appear at the bottom of the window to specify protocol settings.

10. The Destination Path option at the bottom of the window lets you specify where the boot files should be copied to. This should be left at the default, A:\.

11. Make sure a diskette is in drive A: and is DOS-bootable, then press the **OK** button.

12. Once the copying process is completed, remove the disk and place it in the client PC and boot the PC using the new boot disk. This should connect the PC to the server, download the Windows 95 installation files, and install Windows 95.

Clients and Resources

A major component of successful networking with a NOS is the client software. Whether the workstations are in a workgroup environment (peer to peer) or a client/server relationship, you need client software. Client software has the proper drivers, software, and configuration to communicate with other computers across a network medium. Some examples of client software are Windows XP Professional, Windows 2000 Professional, Windows NT Workstation 4.0, Windows 95, and Windows for Workgroups.

One reason Windows NT and Windows 2000 have been so successful is that they supports many different clients. Windows NT can communicate with MS-DOS Network Client 3.0, Windows ME, Windows 98, Windows 95, Windows 3.11 for

Workgroups, Windows NT Workstation 4.0 Windows 2000 Professional, Windows XP Professional, OS/2, LAN Manager, Macintosh, NetWare, and UNIX clients.

In a centralized environment, one computer must be the master of the network. The computer that serves all other computers on the network is known as the *server*. The word *server* comes from the fact that this computer serves the needs of other computers on a centralized network.

Windows NT Server 4.0 and Windows NT Workstation 4.0 are very similar on the surface, as are Windows 2000 Server and Windows 2000 Professional. Windows NT Server 4.0 and Windows 2000 Server are designed to be powerful machines that serve other machines' needs, whereas Windows NT Workstation 4.0 and Windows 2000 Professional are designed to run on a client machine on a network.

Windows NT Server 4.0 and Windows 2000 Server are geared to the server role. The software is designed to be a server that isn't used as a workstation but simply provides resource management and control to the network. Server software is really designed only for administrator use. The average user would not need to use even half the features included with server-side software. The main components of server software provide network control, tracking, error control, and user management.

Directory Services

With Windows NT, the primary server that holds security account information is called a *domain controller*. A domain controller manages user access to the network. When a user logs on to a workstation on the network, the user password is validated by one of the domain controllers. Domain controllers often serve as directory service servers as well. Directory service servers enable users to locate, store, and secure data on the network.

Directory services are also used with Windows 2000 and Windows XP domains but are referred to collectively as Active Directory (AD). AD is a hierarchical structure that allows for larger domains and provides for all servers to be equal in the hierarchy, unlike Windows NT domains.

Novell NetWare

It started as a college project for one individual many years ago; now Novell NetWare is used in more businesses than any other NOS in production today. NetWare has evolved into a very powerful network operating system. The major difference between

Windows NT and NetWare is at the server. Until NetWare 5, the server in NetWare was truly a text-based network operating system, with many of the administrative tasks done at a client workstation. You could manage certain administrative items from the server console, but the main part of the user administration—file system administration—was done from a workstation while logged in to the server. Figure 1-10 shows a screen shot from a remote session with a Novell server.

Clients and Resources

NetWare 5 supports a wide variety of clients. The main ones, of course, are the Windows platform of operating systems. In the versions of NetWare prior to NetWare 5, IPX/SPX had to be used as the protocol. Now NetWare 5 gives you the capability to use pure IP on a NetWare network. Novell client software can be added to many operating systems to allow for connection to NetWare servers. This software can be downloaded from the Novell Web site at www.novell.com.

on the **job**

For Windows operating systems to have full access to a 32-bit NetWare server, they should have the Novell Client32 client software installed.

| FIGURE 1-10 | With Novell NetWare, you can access the server remotely, from a workstation |

```
MS-DOS Prompt - RCONSOLE                                        _ □ ☒

 8 x 12 ▾  [ ]  🗎 🖺  🔲  🖻 🖨  A

   Version 5.00b    July 1, 1996
   (C) Copyright 1994-1995, Novell, Inc. All rights reserved.
   Patent Pending--Novell, Inc.
SPXS.NLM
   SPX/SPXII Protocol for NetWare 3.x & 4.x
   Version 5.00o    August 8, 1996
   (C) Copyright 1992-1995 Novell, Inc.
   All Rights Reserved.
SMDR.NLM
   NetWare SMS Data Requestor
   Version 4.10    July 2, 1996
   (C) Copyright 1991-1996 Novell, Inc. All Rights Reserved.
TSA410.NLM
   NetWare 4.10 Target Service Agent
   Version 4.14    July 23, 1996
   (C) Copyright 1990-1996 Novell, Inc.  All rights reserved.
AVENGINE.NLM
   Anti-Virus Scanning Engine Library v22.05
   Version 22.05    January 28, 1998
   (C) Copyright 1995-1997 Iris Software. All Rights Reserved.
TUI.NLM
   Textual User Interface MPR31A.PTF
   Version 1.04a    March 13, 1996
   Copyright 1992-1994 Novell, Inc.  All rights reserved.
NHCLCNWFS:_
```

Directory Services

One of the driving features of NetWare since version 4 has been Novell Directory Services. The directory tree is a hierarchical grouping of objects that represent resources on the network, as shown in Figure 1-11. The objects on the tree can be users, printers, volumes, and servers, as well as workstations.

The Directory Services built into NetWare make administration easier because everything is organized and centralized within one utility. Maintenance and network upkeep are easier and more cost effective because less time is required to use one utility rather than multiple utilities.

UNIX

Originally developed by Bell Labs, UNIX is becoming a very popular operating system for powerful networking and database management. UNIX boasts three key features that make it powerful: multitasking, multiusers, and networking capabilities.

UNIX is a very powerful multitasking operating system that can run many processes in the background while enabling users to work in the foreground on an application. The multiuser feature enables many users to use the same machine. The last feature,

FIGURE 1-11

The NetWare Administrator directory tree shows resources on the network

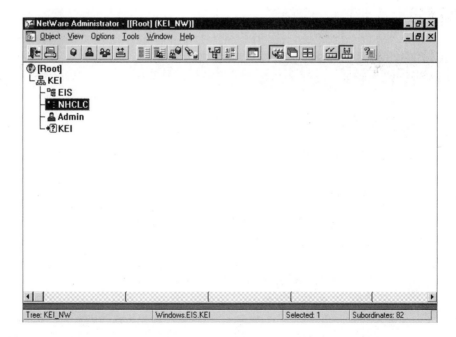

networking capability, is becoming standard in operating systems developed since 1995. UNIX has been the leader in several powerful and diverse utilities that have ported over to other operating systems.

Clients and Resources

Most UNIX systems use a terminal to access the main computer. With a Windows 95 machine, you can use a terminal emulation program to access a UNIX box. Most UNIX activity is command-line driven. UNIX is one operating system that takes time to learn. The main thing to know is that UNIX is still accessed via terminal session, whether it is on a terminal itself or run through an operating system, such as Windows 95 or later, with a terminal emulator. The terminal emulator can be a third-party terminal emulator or the terminal emulator that comes with the Windows operating system.

Directory Services

The UNIX file system is similar to the DOS file system in that it has a directory structure. In UNIX, users are assigned permissions to directories and files, enabling them to access certain parts of the Network File System (NFS). NFS drives the access and security of UNIX. We look at NFS a little more closely later in this chapter.

CERTIFICATION OBJECTIVE 1.03

Network Protocols

Packets and protocols are the fundamental building blocks of data transmission over a network. All data that is transmitted across a network is put into *packets* containing information about the source and destination of the data. These packets are created using standards, or *protocols*. Because there are many different network configurations, there are many different protocols, from which you can choose the one that best fulfills your network's needs.

You can think of a protocol as a language your computer speaks to communicate with other computers on the network. Just as there are different languages in the human world, there are different protocols in the computer world. If two computers use different protocols to communicate on a network, they will not be able to communicate with each other. Think of it as similar to two people who speak different languages trying to talk to each other: No real communication occurs. The information can be passed, but the receiving person or computer cannot understand that information due to the different language or protocol.

IPX/SPX

Internetwork Packet Exchange/Sequenced Packet Exchange (IPX/SPX) is the protocol most commonly used with Novell NetWare versions 4.11 and before, whereas later NetWare versions use TCP/IP by default. IPX/SPX, a routable protocol, is a very fast and highly established protocol, but it is not used on the Internet. Novell developed IPX/SPX for use in NetWare. The protocol NWLink IPX/SPX that is shipped with Windows 95 and Windows NT was written by Microsoft and is fully compatible with the Novell IPX/SPX protocol.

e x a m
ⓦ a t c h

IPX/SPX is the fastest routable network protocol suite available.

TCP/IP

Transmission Control Protocol/Internet Protocol (TCP/IP) is the most common protocol used today. A routable protocol, TCP/IP is the protocol on which the Internet is built. TCP/IP is very robust and is commonly associated with UNIX systems.

TCP/IP was originally designed in the 1970s to be used by the Defense Advanced Research Projects Agency (DARPA) and the U.S. Department of Defense (DOD) to connect systems across the country. This design required the capability to cope with unstable network conditions. Therefore, the design of TCP/IP included the capability to reroute packets.

The Network+ exam focuses on administering TCP/IP and knowing the protocol suite. In this book we look at how TCP/IP fits into the Open Systems Interconnect (OSI) model and how to configure and administer the IP addressing scheme. One thing you must gain from this book is a clear understanding of TCP/IP. Not only will such an understanding prove vital for the exam, but you will need it for your career as well. Most networks today use some form of IP. TCP/IP drives the Internet, and the Internet is driving computing.

o n   t h e
Ⓙ o b

With the Internet using only TCP/IP and its popularity ever increasing, it is wise for all administrators to understand TCP/IP as well as possible. Note that Chapters 4 and 5 of this book go into more detail on TCP/IP but do not cover all aspects of TCP/IP.

NetBEUI

NetBios Extended User Interface (NetBEUI) is a transport protocol commonly found in smaller networks. NetBEUI was first implemented with LAN Manager products. It is not frequently used in large networks and will become even less frequently used in the future because it is not a routable protocol. A nonroutable protocol is unable to go across a router, which means it cannot be used in a WAN. NetBEUI is an extremely quick protocol with little overhead because of its inability to route packets.

exam
ⓦatch   ***NetBEUI is a nonroutable protocol.***

EXERCISE 1-3

Determining Which Protocol to Implement

This scenario-based exercise allows you to determine the appropriate protocol to use in a real-world scenario:

A company wants access to the Internet but on its internal network uses a protocol that is unusable on the Internet. This setup allows for security so that no Internet hackers can readily access the company network and access server data anywhere on the WAN. Which protocol can the company use that will continue protecting its internal network but allow access to the Internet? (*Note:* This exercise might require some network devices to achieve the requirements.)

1. The first requirement is that TCP/IP not be used on the internal network since this is the protocol used on the Internet.

2. The second requirement is that the Internet be accessible, which will require a gateway to change the internal protocol to TCP/IP when sending data to the Internet and change the TCP/IP packets from the Internet to the internal protocol when data is sent back from the Internet.

3. The scenario mentions a WAN, which most likely signifies routers, so a routable protocol must be used. This leaves out NetBEUI, so we must use IPX/SPX on the internal network.

SCENARIO & SOLUTION

I have a Novell NetWare 4.11 server on my network. What protocol is required by default for me to connect workstations to the server?	You need IPX/SPX.
My supervisors want to ensure that the company employees can access the Internet. Which protocol should I use?	Use TCP/IP.
Which two common protocols can I use if my network uses routers?	You can use IPX/SPX and TCP/IP.
What is the fastest protocol I can use on a small, nonrouted network for my workgroup?	You can use NetBEUI.

CERTIFICATION OBJECTIVE 1.04

Fault Tolerance and High Availability

Possibly the biggest concern of any company today is ensuring that its data stays intact. Companies can lose millions upon millions of dollars if the data that drives their businesses becomes corrupted or disappears.

A technology called *Redundant Array of Inexpensive Disks (RAID)* minimizes the loss of data when problems occur in accessing data on a hard disk. RAID is a fault-tolerant disk configuration in which part of the physical storage contains redundant information about data stored on the disks. Standardized strategies of fault tolerance are categorized in RAID levels 0–5. Each level offers various mixes of performance, reliability, and cost. The redundant information enables regeneration of data if a disk or sector on a disk fails or if access to a disk fails. RAID 0 has no redundant information and therefore provides no fault tolerance. Table 1-1 shows the common RAID levels.

There are several ways to ensure that the integrity of data is kept intact. We look at five of these—mirroring, duplexing, striping with parity, volumes, and tape backup (the most common)—to get a better understanding of how they work and their advantages.

| TABLE 1-1 | RAID Levels |

RAID Level	Description
RAID 0	Disk striping.
RAID 1	Disk mirroring.
RAID 2	Disk striping across disks. Also maintains error-correction codes across the disks.
RAID 3	Same as RAID 2 except the error-correction information is stored as parity information on one disk.
RAID 4	Employs striping data in much larger blocks than in RAID 2 and 3. Parity information is kept on a single disk.
RAID 5	Disk striping with parity across multiple drives.

Mirroring

One of the more common ways to have an online backup copy your data is to create a *mirrored* copy of the data on another disk. The mirroring system utilizes a code that duplicates everything written on one drive to another drive, making the data on the two drives identical. (As outlined in Table 1-1, this is RAID 1.) Figure 1-12 shows an example of two mirrored disks.

| FIGURE 1-12 |

Disk mirroring writes data to two separate disks

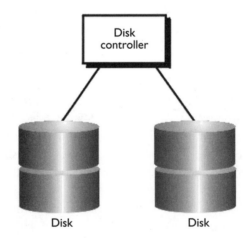

The best way to incorporate disk mirroring is at the hardware level with what is known as an *array controller*. An array controller is an interface card that connects to both drives via a SCSI cable and has the configuration information on the logical drive that is created. Today's network operating systems also allow for software-level mirroring of two drives. Windows NT and Novell each offer a software-level mirroring configuration.

·The cost of mirroring is a drawback to using this RAID implementation. Two drives are used, but only the space of one drive is actually used for storing data. The other drive is just a copy of the same data and is not available to store different data.

Duplexing

Duplexing ensures fault tolerance—not just with your data but also with your disk controller. With traditional mirroring, there is one disk controller. If the controller fails, the hard drive is down until that component is replaced. Duplexing gives you a second controller. There can be a mirror with this type of configuration, but each drive is connected to its own controller. If a controller fails, you still have an intact configuration. This can also speed up response time when you are writing to disk. Figure 1-13 shows an example of disk duplexing with multiple controllers.

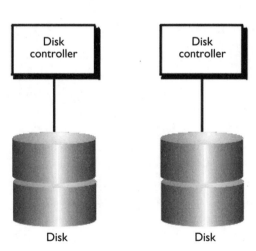

FIGURE 1-13

Disk duplexing provides fault protection for your data and disk controller

Striping With and Without Parity

Striping is becoming more and more popular. The striping of data is a way to spread the data out across the disks. This technique can improve performance. To do striping properly, you need a minimum of three hard disks. Three or more different drives all acting to get a piece of the data make input/output (I/O) faster. Striping also gives you the option of adding parity to the drive set.

RAID 5, also known as *disk striping with parity*, provides the performance of RAID 0 but with fault tolerance. Disk striping consists of data being written in stripes across a volume that has been created from areas of free space. These areas are all the same size and spread over an array of 3 to 32 disks. The primary benefit of striping is that disk I/O is split between disks, improving performance, although improvements do not exceed the I/O capabilities of the disk controllers. Fault-tolerant functionality is added to disk striping with the addition of parity information in one of the stripes. The parity stripe is the exclusive OR (XOR) of all the data values for the data stripes in the stripe. If no disks in the stripe set with parity have failed, the new parity for a write can be calculated without having to read the corresponding stripes from the other data disks.

on the **()** o b

It should be noted that if more than one disk should fail, all data is lost. The more drives implemented in a stripe set, the better the chances of having more than one disk fail and lose all data.

With stripe set with parity, disk utilization increases as the number of disks increases, thus providing a lower cost per megabyte. Disk read operations can occur simultaneously, resulting in better disk performance. However, the system or boot partition cannot be located on a stripe set with parity. Furthermore, if a disk that is part of the stripe set fails, read operations for data are substantially slower than that of a single disk. Because a stripe set with parity works with the operating system, it requires more memory than a mirrored set.

Again, some vendors sell disk subsystems that implement RAID technology completely within the hardware. Some of these hardware implementations support hot swapping of disks, which enables you to replace a failed disk while the computer is still running.

Windows NT Server 4.0 and Windows 2000 Server provide software support for two fault-tolerant disk configurations: mirroring and stripe sets with parity, as described. The Disk Management utility configures mirror sets and stripe sets with parity, as shown in Exercise 1-4, and regenerates the volume when a disk fails. Here are some points to consider:

- Hardware fault tolerance is faster.
- Software fault tolerance is less expensive.
- The capability to swap a failed disk while the system still runs is available only with hardware fault-tolerant equipment.

exam
ⓦatch *Make sure you understand the various implementations of RAID, especially RAID 0, 1, and 5.*

EXERCISE 1-4

Creating a Stripe Set with Parity on a Windows 2000 Server

This exercise shows the steps in creating the software implementation of a RAID 5 stripe set with parity on a Windows 2000 server to allow for fault tolerance of user data:

1. Select **Start | Programs | Administrative Tools | Computer Management**.

2. In the Computer Management window, select **Disk Management** in the left pane, under Storage.

3. Select a disk that has been unallocated in the right pane, and right-click it, then select **Create Volume**.

4. A wizard starts and guides you through the process, allowing you to choose three volumes and make them a RAID 5 implementation.

Volumes

A *volume* is a part of a hard disk used to store information. You can think of a volume as a partition or what is referred to as a *drive letter*. If you have a RAID 5 implementation using five hard disks, the partition across all five disks will be seen as a single drive letter and is one volume.

Most network servers are set up with various volume configurations. Usually you will see at least two volumes on a server: a system volume, called SYS on a NetWare server; and a data volume, sometimes called VOL1 on a NetWare server. The system volume holds the network operating system files to make the server work. Separating the two volumes helps ensure that the server does not run out of disk space on the system volume. If this were to happen, the server would probably crash.

Tape Backup

Tapes are a feasible means of storing data backups. Tapes are much less expensive than an array of disks and are reliable. A *backup set* is a group of files, directories, or disks selected for a single backup operation. A *family set* is a collection of related tapes containing several backup sets. Information describing the backup sets stored on the tape is collectively called a *catalog*. A catalog for a family is located on the last tape.

Tape backups are *offline storage*, meaning the data is copied to tape cartridges stored external to the computer and the data is not readily accessible. The data must be copied from the tapes back to the hard disk to be accessible.

Backup Strategies

A *normal backup*, also called *full backup*, copies all selected files and marks each file as having been backed up. With this type of backup, you can restore files easily because the most current files will be on the last tape.

An incremental backup backs up only files that have been created or changed since the last full or incremental backup and marks them as being backed up. To restore files when both full and incremental methods were used, start with the last full backup and then work through all the incremental tapes.

A *differential backup* copies files that have been created or changed since the last full backup. It does not mark files as having been backed up. To restore files when both full and differential methods were used, only the last full backup and the last differential backup are needed. *Note:* In differential backups, files are not marked as backed up, so if two differential backups are performed in a row, the files backed up during the first backup will be backed up again, regardless of whether or not the files have changed since the first differential backup.

A *daily backup* copies all selected files that have been modified the day the daily backup is performed and does not mark them as having been backed up.

Tape Logs

You can generate a log file of the backup operations, in the form of a text file, during the backup process. These are options available for logging:

- **Summary Only** Logs only major operations such as loading a tape or starting a backup.
- **Copy Full Detail** Logs information for all operations, including the names of all the files and directories that are backed up.
- **Don't Log** No information is logged.

CERTIFICATION OBJECTIVE 1.05

The OSI Model

The Open Systems Interconnect (OSI) protocol suite is a group of standards for protocols that have been standardized into a logical structure for network operations. This structure contains seven layers that are commonly referred to as the *OSI model*. The seven layers of the OSI model, from highest to lowest, are Application, Presentation, Session, Transport, Network, Data Link, and Physical. Network communication starts at the Application layer of the OSI model and works its way down through the layers step by step to the Physical layer. The information then passes along the cable to the receiving computer, which starts the information at the Physical layer. From there it steps back up the OSI layers to the Application layer, where the receiving computer finalizes the processing and sends back an acknowledgment, if needed. Then the whole process starts over. Figure 1-14 shows an example of packets being transmitted down through the OSI layers, across the medium, and back up the OSI layers.

The OSI model is conceptual in nature, meaning that it is not followed exactly by every protocol. In fact, many protocols span layers or can be associated with more than one layer. Table 1-2 shows the layers and the protocols that reside at each layer.

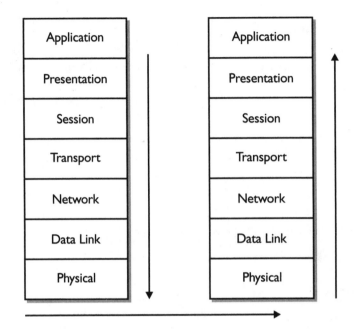

FIGURE 1-14

In the OSI model, data is transmitted down through the layers, across the medium, and back up through the layers

Protocols

Different protocols work at different levels of the OSI model. Here we look at a few of the main protocols for this exam, apply them to the OSI model, and see how they fit in the OSI model's seven layers.

TABLE 1-2   Osi Model Protocols, Services, Methods, and Layers

OSI Layer	Protocols, Services, Methods, and Layers
Application	FTP, SMTP, Telnet
Presentation	JPEG, GIF, MPEG
Session	NFS, RPC
Transport	TCP, UDP, SPX
Network	IPX, IP
Data Link	Ethernet, Token Ring
Physical	Twisted pair, Thinner coax, AUI, Network interface card

IPX

IPX is an extremely fast, streamlined protocol that is not connection oriented. IPX can be used for a Windows NT network and is fairly common due to its widespread use on Novell NetWare. The primary responsibility of IPX is handling broadcast issues. IPX is a routable protocol that is located in the Network layer of the OSI model. IPX is capable of being run over both Ethernet and Token Ring networks using the appropriate network interface card (NIC) drivers, which are provided by the NIC manufacturer. For a number of years, IPX over Ethernet was the default use of NICs.

TCP/IP

TCP/IP is one of the most popular protocol suites. TCP/IP is actually a combination of two different protocols, TCP and IP, working together at different layers of the OSI model to build a foundation for other applications and protocols on the upper layers. Since TCP/IP is two different protocols, it is actually located in two different layers of the OSI model. TCP is located in the Transport layer, and IP is located in the Network layer. TCP breaks the data into manageable packets; IP tracks information such as the source and destination of the packets. TCP/IP is fully capable of running over either Token Ring or Ethernet networks, as long as an appropriate NIC is used. IP over Ethernet is the most common implementation in networking today because Ethernet is much less expensive than Token Ring and because TCP/IP is widely used on the Internet.

NFS

Network File System (NFS) is a protocol for file sharing that enables a user to use network disks as thought they were connected to the local machine. NFS was created by Sun Microsystems for use on Solaris, Sun's version of UNIX. NFS is still frequently used in the UNIX world and is available for use with nearly all operating systems. NFS is a protocol that is universally used by the UNIX community. Vendor and third-party software products enable other operating systems to use NFS. It has gained acceptance with many companies and can be added to nearly any operating system. In addition to file sharing, NFS enables you to share printers. NFS is located in the Application layer of the OSI model and is considered a member of the TCP/IP protocol suite. The primary reason to use the NFS protocol is to access resources located on a UNIX server or to share resources with someone working on a UNIX workstation.

SMB and Novell NCP

Server Message Block (SMB) and Novell NetWare Core Protocol (NCP) are protocols that are implemented in redirectors. A *redirector* is software that intercepts requests, formats them according to the protocol in use, and passes the message to a lower-level protocol for delivery. Redirectors also intercept incoming messages, process the instructions, and pass them to the correct upper-level application for additional processing.

SMB and NCP are primarily used for file and printer sharing in Microsoft and Novell networks, respectively.

SMTP

Simple Mail Transport Protocol (SMTP) is the protocol that defines the structure of Internet mail messages. SMTP uses a well-defined syntax for transferring messages. An SMTP session includes initializing the SMTP connection, sending the destination e-mail address, sending the source e-mail address, sending the subject, and sending the body of the e-mail message.

FTP and TFTP

File Transfer Protocol (FTP) is a standardized method of transferring files between two machines. FTP is a connection-oriented protocol, which means that the protocol verifies that packets successfully reach their destinations.

Trivial File Transfer Protocol (TFTP) has the same purpose and function as FTP except that it is not a connection-oriented protocol and does not verify that packets reach their destinations. By not verifying that data is successfully transferred to its destination and therefore requiring less overhead to establish and maintain a connection, TFTP is able to operate faster than FTP.

DECnet

DECnet is a proprietary protocol developed by Digital Equipment Corporation for use primarily in WANs. You can run DECnet on an Ethernet network, but it is done infrequently. DECnet is a routable protocol.

DLC

Data Link Control (DLC) is not a common protocol. DLC, a nonroutable protocol, is sometimes used to connect Windows NT servers to printers.

exam
ⓦatch

*TCP/IP, IPX/SPX/NWLink, AppleTalk, and DECnet are routable protocols;
NetBEUI and DLC are not.*

Services

The NOS has a series of responsibilities to make sure that the workstation or server functions as needed. With Windows networking, many different services run in the background and have key responsibilities of their own. One example of a service you will read about is the browser service, which controls the network browsing features in Windows NT. With Windows NT or Windows 95, you can use Network Neighborhood, and with Windows 2000 you can use Network Places to find other computers on the network. The browser service enables this operation to function properly. Other services within Windows NT are responsible for certain other actions.

Functions That Pertain to Each Layer

Each layer has specific functions that it defines. Some functions (such as error control and flow control) are defined in more than one layer. Although this seems redundant, it does not mean that these functions must be implemented at both layers. Don't forget that the OSI is a *model.* One designer may use error control at one layer, another may use it at a different layer. It all depends on the designer's goals.

It is very easy to memorize the various layers of the OSI model from top to bottom, but it is easier to learn what these layers *do* by taking a bottom-to-top approach.

The Physical Layer

The bottom layer of the OSI hierarchy is concerned only with moving bits of data onto and off the network medium. The Physical layer does not define what that medium is, but it must define how to access it. This includes the physical topology (or structure) of the network, the electrical and physical aspects of the medium used, and encoding and timing of bit transmission and reception. Since this layer deals with electrical signals, this is the layer that corresponds to the repeater. The repeater boosts the electrical signals.

The Data Link Layer

The Data Link layer handles many issues for communicating on a simple network. (The Network layer discussed in the next section performs the functions necessary to communicate beyond a single physical network.) The Data Link layer takes apart the frames generated by the upper layers for transmission. When receiving messages from the network, this layer reassembles this information back into frames to send to the upper layers. This layer actually does a lot more than just break apart and put together frames.

The 802 model (discussed later in this chapter) breaks the Data Link layer into two sublayers: Logical Link Control (LLC) and Media Access Control (MAC). The LLC layer starts and maintains connections between devices. When you send data from your workstation to a server on the same network segment, it is the LLC sublayer that establishes a connection with that server. The MAC layer enables multiple devices to share the media. Most LANs have more than one computer (of course!), and the MAC sublayer determines which computer may speak and when.

Another important job of the Data Link layer is physical device addressing. The MAC sublayer maintains physical device addresses (commonly referred to as *MAC addresses*) for communicating with other devices. Each device on the network must have a unique MAC address; otherwise, the network will not know exactly where to send information when a node requests it. For example, how would the postal service know where to send your bills without your address?

Most NICs in a computer provide the MAC address as an address burned into the interface card. Some older network cards even required an administrator to set the address manually using switches. Even with a permanent MAC address burned into the card, some protocols enable you to define this address via software, although this capability is unusual.

The MAC address is used to communicate only on the local network. When transmitting to a server on the same LAN segment, the protocol uses the MAC addresses to communicate between the two computers. If the server is located on another network segment across a WAN, the MAC address of the nearest router (discussed later in this chapter) is used to send the information, and it is up to the router to send the data further on.

Finally, the Data Link layer manages flow control and error correction between devices in a simple network. In more complex internetworks, it is up to the Network layer and other upper layers to perform these functions. This layer is similar to the bridge that operates at this layer of the OSI model. A bridge deals with MAC addresses only to permit packets to pass through the bridge to another segment.

The Network Layer

The Network layer is one of the most complex and important ones. The Network layer manages addressing and delivering packets on a complex internetwork. Internetworks are joined by devices known as *routers*, which utilize routing tables and routing algorithms to determine how to send data from one network to another.

The most obvious example of an internetwork is the Internet. The Internet is very large, covering the entire globe, and consists of almost every conceivable type of computer, from palmtop to mainframe.

In order to operate on an internetwork, each network that participates must be assigned a network address. This address differentiates each network from every other network that forms the internetwork. When sending data from one network to another, the routers along the way use the network addresses to determine the next step in the journey.

The Network layer also enables the option of specifying a service address on the destination computer. All modern operating systems, such as UNIX, Windows NT, and OS/2, run many programs at once. The service address enables the sender to specify for which program on the destination the data is being sent. Service addresses that are well defined (by networking standards, for example) are called *well-known addresses*. Service addresses are also called *sockets* or *ports* by various protocols.

Table 1-3 summarizes the devices that operate at each layer of the OSI model.

TABLE 1-3   Devices that Operate at the OSI Model Layers

OSI Layer	Device(s) That Operate at the Layer
Application	Gateway
Presentation	Gateway
Session	Gateway
Transport	Gateway
Network	Router, gateway
Data Link	Bridge, gateway
Physical	Repeater, gateway

You need to remember the layers at which each device operates. You also need to remember that a gateway can be used at any layer, and any device that operates at any layer will also operate at all layers under it.

The Transport Layer

The Transport layer works hard to ensure reliable delivery of data to its destinations. The Transport layer also helps the upper layers (Application, Presentation, and Session) communicate with one another across the network while hiding the network's complexities.

The Transport layer also interacts with the Network layer, taking on some of the responsibilities for connection services. One of the functions of the Transport layer is segment sequencing. Sequence switching is a connection-oriented service that takes segments that are received out of order and resequences them in the right order.

Another function of the Transport layer is error control. It commonly uses acknowledgments to manage the flow of data between devices. Some Transport layer protocols can also request retransmission of recent segments to overcome errors.

The Session Layer

The Session layer manages dialogs between computers. It does this by establishing, managing, and terminating communications between two computers. The Session layer uses three types of dialogs: simplex, half duplex, and full duplex.

Simplex dialogs enable data to flow in only one direction. Since the dialog is one way, information can be sent but not responded to or even acknowledged. An example of a simplex dialog is a public announcement (PA) system in a large building. Announcements can be made, but the PA system doesn't enable any response or acknowledgment from the listeners.

Half-duplex dialogs enable data to flow in two directions but only one direction at a time. With half-duplex dialogs, replies and acknowledgments are possible, but this isn't always the most efficient communication method. If an error is detected early in transmission, for example, the receiver must wait for the sender to finish before any action can be taken. A citizens' band (CB) radio is an excellent example of a half-duplex dialog.

Full-duplex dialogs enable data to flow in both directions simultaneously. This method provides more flexibility but also requires more complex communication methods. A telephone is a prime example of full-duplex communication.

When a session is established, three distinct phases are involved. In *establishment* the requestor initiates the service and the rules for communication are established. Once the rules are established, the *data transfer* phase may begin. Both sides know how to talk to each other, the most efficient methods, and how to detect errors, all because of the rules defined in the first phase. Finally, *termination* occurs when the session is complete and communication ends in an orderly fashion.

The Presentation Layer

It is up to the Presentation layer to make sure that data sent by the Application layer and received by the Session layer is in a standard format. As discussed earlier, different types of computers can interpret identical data differently.

A network standard defines the proper format for any data as it is transmitted. When the Presentation layer receives data from the Application layer to be sent over the network, it makes sure that the data is in the proper format. If it is not, the Presentation layer converts the data. On the flip side, when the Presentation layer receives network data from the Session layer, it makes sure that the data is in the proper format and once again converts it if it is not.

The Application Layer

The Application layer provides a consistent, neutral interface to the network. Many people confuse the Application layer with an actual software package, such as a word processor. This is not the case. The Application layer provides consistent ways for an application to save files to the network file server or print to a network printer. An example is how Windows 95 makes it just as easy to print to a network printer as it is to print to a locally attached printer. This is the Application layer in practice.

The Application layer also advertises a computer's available resources to the rest of the network.

EXERCISE 1-5

Communicating Between Two PCs

Now that you have read the information about the OSI model, you can apply this information in the following scenario-based exercise. Let's assume that you want to download a file from an FTP server on the Internet. Can you explain the process that occurs on your PC to initiate the file transfer between the PCs? The process occurs as follows:

1. The FTP interface is opened, and the remote PC to connect to is selected from the interface.

2. The FTP interface is running on the Application layer and submits information to the Presentation layer, which converts the requests to the proper format that the other PC will understand.

3. The requests are sent from the Presentation layer to the Session layer, where the connection is made and communication configurations, such as using half or full duplex, are decided. (*Note:* The communication is half or full duplex since the protocol being use is FTP, which is connection oriented and requires acknowledgments for the data packets received.)

4. The data packets are sent to the Transport layer, where the route is determined between the two PCs. The Transport layer also segments the packets if needed for transmission on the network media.

5. The data packets are sent to the Network layer next, where the determination is made as to where the data packets should be sent—usually to the default gateway.

6. The next stop is the Data Link layer, which supplies the physical addressing of the destination of the data packets, such as the MAC address of the default gateway.

7. Finally, the data packets are sent to the Physical layer, where the data is changed to electrical signals and transmitted on the network media. The network media could also be a phone line, over which the data is converted to analog signals by the modem.

8. The data packets are routed to the FTP server to which you are making a file request. The data packets are processed in reverse order on the FTP server, and then the file is sent back to your PC in the same order listed in Steps 1–7. As the data is received, your PC performs the same steps in reverse order until the FTP application has received the whole file that was requested.

CERTIFICATION OBJECTIVE 1.06

Networking Media and Connectors

Cabling is the LAN's transmission medium. LANs can be connected together using a variety of cable types. Each cable type has its own advantages and disadvantages, which we examine here.

Cabling

Three primary types of physical media can be used at the Physical layer: coaxial cable, twisted-pair cable, and fiber-optic cable. Transmission rates that can be supported on each of these physical media are measured in millions of bits per second (Mbps).

Coaxial Cable

Coaxial, or coax, cable looks like the cable used to bring the cable TV signal to your television. One strand (a solid-core wire) runs down the middle of the cable. Around that strand is insulation. Covering that insulation is braided wire and metal foil, which shield against electromagnetic interference. A final layer of insulation covers the braided wire. Coaxial cable is resistant to the interference and signal weakening that other cabling, such as unshielded twisted-pair (UTP) cable, can experience. In general, coax is better than UTP cable at connecting longer distances and for reliably supporting higher data rates with less sophisticated equipment.

Just because TV cable is coax does not mean it will work with computer networks. Network coaxial cable has very specific requirements, such as gauge, impedance, and attenuation.

Thinnet refers to RG-58 cabling, which is a flexible coaxial cable about ¼-inch thick. Thinnet is used for short-distance communication and is flexible enough to facilitate routing between workstations. Thinnet connects directly to a workstation's network adapter card using a BNC T-connector and uses the network adapter card's internal transceiver. The term *10Base2* refers to Ethernet LANs that use Thinnet cabling.

Thicknet coaxial cable can support data transfer over longer distances better than Thinnet can and is usually used as a backbone to connect several smaller Thinnet-based networks. The diameter of a Thicknet cable is about ½ inch; this cable is harder to work with than Thinnet cable. A transceiver is often connected directly to Thicknet cable using a connector known as a *piercing tap*. Connection from the transceiver to the network adapter card is made using a drop cable to connect to the adapter unit interface (AUI) port connector. The term *10Base5* refers to Ethernet LANs that use Thicknet cabling.

Cat3 Cable

CAT3 is a grade of cable that enables networking, but CAT5 is the better way to go. The key thing about CAT3 is that it already exists in most office buildings and homes. CAT3 is a voice-grade cable used in phone networks. It can be used for networking up to 10 Mbps.

Cat5 Cable

Most UTP cable in today's networks is CAT5. CAT5 is a standard that enables up to 100 Mbps data transmission. This is the standard UTP or STP cable type. CAT5 is the highest rating of the UTP cabling.

Fiber-Optic Cable

Optical fibers carry digital data signals in the form of modulated pulses of light. An optical fiber consists of an extremely thin cylinder of glass, called the *core*, surrounded by a concentric layer of glass, known as the *cladding*. There are two fibers per cable— one to transmit and one to receive. The cylinder can also be an optical-quality plastic. The cladding can be made up of gel that reflects signals back into the fiber to reduce signal loss.

Fiber-optic cable supports up to 1000 stations and can carry the signal up to and beyond 2 miles. Fiber-optic cables are also highly secure from outside interference such as radio transmitters, arc welders, fluorescent lights, and other sources of electrical noise. On the other hand, fiber-optic cable is by far the most expensive of these cabling methods, and a small network is unlikely to need these features. Depending on local labor rates and building codes, installing fiber-optic cable can cost as much as $500 per node.

Two electrical phenomena can disrupt your network: cross-talk and outside electrical noise. *Cross-talk* is caused by electrical fields in adjacent wires inducing false signals in each wire. Outside electrical noise comes from lights, motors, radio systems, and many other sources. Fiber-optic cabling is immune to these types of interference.

UTP Cable

Unshielded twisted-pair (UTP) cables are familiar to you if you have worked with telephone cable. The typical twisted-pair cable for network use contains three or four pairs of wires. Each pair of wires contained in the cable is twisted around the other. The twists in the wires help shield against electromagnetic interference. The term *10BaseT* refers to Ethernet LANs that use UTP cabling.

UTP cable uses small plastic connectors designated as RJ-45. These are similar to the phone connectors except that instead of four wires, as found in the home system, the network RJ-45 contains eight contacts.

UTP cable is easier to install than coaxial because you can pull it around corners more easily. Twisted-pair cable is more susceptible to interference than coaxial, however, and should not be used in environments containing large electrical or electronic devices.

STP Cable

Shielded twisted-pair (STP) cable differs from UTP in that it uses a much higher-quality protective jacket for greater insulation. Thus, it is less subject to electrical interference and supports higher transmission speeds over longer distances than UTP.

To better understand all the cable types and when to use some specific types, see Exercise 1-6.

EXERCISE 1-6

Understanding Cable Types and Applications

A company wants to hire you to design a cable installation based on its specifications. The firm has three buildings that are all similar in size. The buildings each have four floors; each floor has 8-foot ceilings and roughly 75 users. The dimension of each building is 100 meters by 200 meters. The company requires high bandwidth and wants to have 100 Mbps network speed using a cable that will possibly be usable for faster speeds later.

One issue that must be overcome is that a radio station has a broadcast tower two blocks away that causes interference on all electrical signal devices in the area. The buildings are all in close proximity, since they each cover one block and are all at the same intersection, as shown in Figure 1-15. The wire closet is in the center of the building on each floor.

How would you go about solving this problem?

One possible solution is as follows:

1. Each building should be joined by fiber-optic cable, Building 1 to Building 2 and Building 2 to Building 3. It can be feasible to connect Building 1 and Building 3 to allow for redundant paths.

2. A router can be placed on the top floor of each building to connect the fiber-optic cables.

3. A switch will be placed on each floor in the wire closet and connected to the router on the fourth floor.

FIGURE 1-15

Diagram of company layout for Exercise 1-6

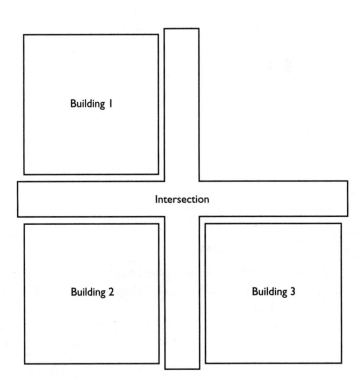

4. Each floor will then use STP cable to eliminate the radio frequency interference (RFI) generated by the radio station. STP cable will also be used to connect the switches to the router in each building. (*Note:* With the maximum distance being 100 meters from the switch to the most distant PC, it is possible to use a higher-grade cable to allow for a distance of more than 100 meters. The cables should be a minimum of Category 5, but higher grades do exist, such as Categories 6 and 7.)

Media Connectors

We've looked at some of the types of connectors that can be used in networking. With transmission types come distance limitations. In this section we look at various 10Mb (megabit) connection types, 100Mb connection types, and BNC connectivity.

10Base2, 10Base5, and 10BaseT

With 10 Mbps connections, three types of cabling schemes carry different distance limitations. Table 1-4 shows the differences between 10Base2, 10Base5, and 10BaseT. 10Base2 and 10Base5 are seen more in coax environments; 10BaseT refers to twisted pair.

100BaseT, 100VGAnyLan, 100BaseTX, and 100BaseFX

Connectivity of 100 Mbps increases the performance of LANs and WANs for better throughput with more bandwidth than 10 Mbps connections. The use of 100BaseT using CAT5 twisted pair to transmit at 100 Mbps with NICs and devices rated for 100Mb transfer speeds is referred to as *Fast Ethernet.* Cable distance limitations are the same as for 10BaseT when using CAT5 cable. 100BaseTX cables use two sets of two pairs, or eight wires, which are standard with CAT5.

TABLE 1-4   Distances of Various 10Base Cabling

Cable Media	Maximum Distance Per Segment
10Base2 (Thinnet)	185 meters
10Base5 (Thicknet)	500 meters
10BaseT (twisted pair)	100 meters

100VGAnyLAN is an Ethernet and Token Ring specification using four pairs of CAT3, CAT4, or CAT5 cable. This technology was developed by Hewlett-Packard and is not compatible with Fast Ethernet.

100BaseFX is an Ethernet standard that uses fiber-optic cable to connect network systems and devices. Fiber-optic cable is usually used as a backbone to connect buildings; Fast Ethernet is most likely then used within the buildings. The distance of 100BaseFX is the same as the limits on fiber-optic cable: 2 miles.

Gigabit

Gigabit networks are fiber-optic networks that operate at 1,000 Mbps, or 1 gigabit per second (Gbps). This is sometimes known as "gigabit to the desktop" and is extremely expensive to implement for large networks. This type of cabling is usually employed only as a backbone between buildings if Fast Ethernet connection between the buildings might cause a bottleneck.

BNC, RJ-11, and RJ-45

The BNC connector is used to connect IEEE 802.3 10Base2 coaxial cable to a hub. The BNC connector looks like a connector you would plug into your television. Figure 1-16 shows a T-connector that can connect to the workstation and join to physical cable segments. A special crimping tool is used to put the connector on the end of the wire. The actual wire runs down the middle and must make contact with the end of the connector shown in the middle.

The RJ-45 connector is used with twisted-pair cables. It looks like a telephone connector but is wider. There are eight pins, hence there are eight wires. Ethernet can use only four of the wires or possibly all eight. If only four wires are used, the pins you should know are 1, 2, 3, and 6. Figure 1-17 shows an RJ-45 connector. A special crimping tool is also needed to make contact between the pins and the cable inside.

The RJ-11 connector is a telephone connector. There are four pins, hence there are four wires. Again, a special crimping tool is needed to make contact between the pins and the cable inside. RJ-11 connectors can be used with cables of Categories 1 through 5 but use only four of the wires if the cable has more than four wires.

FROM THE CLASSROOM

Unraveling the Ethernet Name Jargon

The jargon used to describe the various Ethernet types is easily explained. Ethernet types are given as *##BaseXX* and are designated as follows:

1. *##* stands for the speed of the network.

2. *Base* stands for *baseband*; this could be *Broad* to stand for *broadband communications*, which are discussed in a later section of this chapter.

3. *XX* stands for the cable type or media.

4. Initially the cable media 5 was to represent Thicknet due to the maximum length being 500, or 5 x 100, meters. *2* represented Thinnet or its maximum length of 200 meters, or 2 x 100 meters (actually, 185 meters).

5. *T* stands for *twisted-pair cabling* and can be further used to show the number of pairs; for example, 10BaseT4 requires four pairs of wires from a twisted-pair cable.

6. *F* is for *fiber-optic cable.*

7. *X* represents a higher grade of connection, and 100BaseTX is twisted-pair cabling that can use either UTP or STP at 100 Mbps. With fiber-optic cable such as 100BaseFX, the speed is quicker than standard 10BaseF.

8. *VG* is used for the VGAnyLan specification.

—*Jarret W. Buse, MCSE+I, MCT, CCNA, CNA, A+, Network+*

FIGURE 1-16

The BNC T-Connector, used to connect IEEE 802.3 10Base2 coaxial cable to a hub

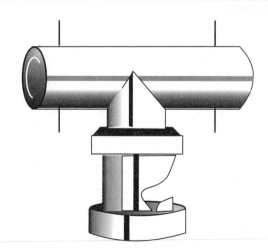

The RJ-45
connector, used
with Twisted-pair
cables

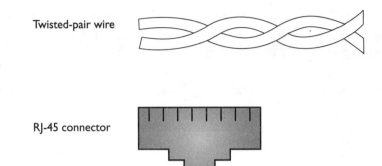

Twisted-pair wire

RJ-45 connector

Fiber-Optic Connectors: SC and ST

Fiber-optic cables can use many types of connectors, but the Network+ exam is concerned only with the two major connector types: the straight-tip (ST) connector and the subscriber (SC) connector. The ST connector is based on the BNC-style connector but has a fiber-optic cable instead of a copper cable. The SC connector is square and somewhat similar to an RJ-45 connector.

Regardless of the connector type, the fiber-optic cable still functions at the same speed. The only thing that you need to worry about is that the connector matches the device to which it is being connected, since the two connector types are not interchangeable (Table 1-5).

TABLE 1-5   Fiber-Optic Connectors

Cable Media	Cable Type	Maximum Distance	Connector Type
10Base2	Coax	185 meters	BNC
10Base5	Coax	500 meters	BNC, AUI
10BaseT	UTP	100 meters	RJ-45
100BaseT	UTP	100 meters	RJ-45
100BaseTX	UTP	100 meters	RJ-45
10BaseF	Fiber	2 miles	SC, ST
100BaseFX	Fiber	2 miles	SC, ST

FROM THE CLASSROOM

The Role of Network Topology, Cabling, and Connectors

Just as network topology, cabling, and connectors are important in passing your Network+ exam, they are important in your role as a network professional. A strong understanding of how network topology, cabling, and connectors coexist is a very valuable skill set to possess. This is especially the case if you are a network engineer who must design and implement a network from the ground up. You must know the characteristics of each network topology and apply them in each unique situation you encounter.

For example, let's say that you are designing a network for a small investment firm with 10 users and a minimal budget. Instantly you should be thinking, "Bus topology," which is relatively inexpensive and the easiest to implement for smaller networks such as this one.

Your choice of network topology also dictates your choice of cabling. In our example, we have implemented a bus topology, which is conducive to the coaxial cable. Coaxial cables are connected from the network backbone, which is most likely another coaxial cable, to each workstation with a BNC T-connector, which leads us to our last specification: the network connector. Just as the network topology dictated the choice of cabling, it dictated our choice of connector. The BNC connector is the cornerstone of coaxial cabling.

Although the preceding demonstration seemed easy, the secret lies in understanding the limitations of each network, such as the maximum cable length and number of workstations per segment. What will truly set you apart as a network professional is your ability to understand the features and limitation of each network type. This will also come in handy during your Network+ exam, which will test your knowledge of these very rules.

—*Cameron Brandon, MCSE+Internet, CNE, A+, Network+*

CERTIFICATION OBJECTIVE I.07

Network Elements

In this section, we review some of the common terminology that is used in networking environments. We've already defined and used some of these terms in the chapter; they are repeated here to make sure you have a clear understanding of each one for the exam. You could see any of these terms on the exam in a variety of questions or scenarios.

Full and Half Duplexing

When data travels across a medium, it of course travels in a certain direction. With the newest of network adapters, hubs, and switches, we have a term that determines how the data travels in regard to direction. This term is *duplex*. We can use either half duplex or full duplex. In *half-duplex communication*, data travels both ways on the medium but in only one direction at a time. In *full-duplex communication*, you can have data travel in both directions simultaneously.

WANs, LANs, MANs, and VLANs

In case you aren't clear on the differences between a wide area network (WAN) and a local area network (LAN), you should know that a WAN spans multiple geographic locations and a LAN is confined to a single building or a college campus, for example.

The term *metropolitan area network (MAN)* is not often used anymore, it refers to a network that spans a single city or metropolitan area. A *virtual local area network (VLAN)* creates a small grouping of PCs that are required to communicate with one another only on a larger network. This is accomplished by specifying the network addresses of the PCs on the VLAN as members of the VLAN on all network devices connecting the network together, such as switches. The switches limit the VLAN members to communicating only with other PCs within the same VLAN. A VLAN can be implemented on a LAN, a MAN, or a WAN.

Let's take a look at some scenarios and solutions related to these concepts.

SCENARIO & SOLUTION

I have a network that spans three buildings within the same block. What type of network is this?	A LAN.
My company has four offices within Chicago. The headquarters are located centrally in Chicago, and an office is located on each of the north, south, west, and east sides of Chicago. What type of network is this?	You have a MAN.
My company has three offices, which are connected by satellite links to create a network. One office is in New York, another in Los Angeles, and the third in St. Louis. What type of network is this?	This is a WAN.
I work as an administrator for a bank. I need to place a special auditing team on a separate network from the rest of the employees. How can this be accomplished without running new network cables?	You can install a VLAN.

Servers, Workstations, and Hosts

In networking today, you must have workstations. A workstation used to be called a *terminal;* it is the device from which the user accesses applications and data. The user logs in and connects to various resources via a workstation.

The user does not directly use the server. The server *serves* the workstations and users. Usually, the server is not directly used with its local keyboard or mouse. Administrators remotely manage the server from a workstation.

Hosts are computers or devices that are connected to a network and that use a unique ID to be accessed by another system. A host can be a server or any PC that is sharing a file or device, such as a printer. A printer with its own NIC connected to the network will be its own host.

Server-Based Networking and Peer-to-Peer Networking

Different organization sizes, structures, and budgets need different types of networks. A local newspaper needs a different approach for its network than a multinational company. Networks can be divided into peer-to-peer and server-based networks. The difference between the two is explained in the following sections.

Peer-to-Peer Network

A *peer-to-peer network* has no dedicated servers. There are no hierarchical differences between the workstations in the network. The user at each workstation can decide which resources are shared on the network. In a peer-to-peer network, all workstations are clients and servers at the same time. Of course, this situation creates some restrictions for the properties of the network.

The size of a peer-to-peer network or workgroup is usually limited to 10 workstations. It is technically possible to connect more workstations and to let them share data; however, it is not advisable. Because there is no centralized administration in a workgroup, the security level is low, and it is very hard to keep an overview of the shared resources on the network.

It is fairly simple to implement a peer-to-peer network. All users get a computer on their desks. The workstations are connected with a simple and visible cabling system. The users can then administer their own computers and the resources they want to share on the network. Because all users in a workgroup are administrators of their own computer, they need to be trained in order to function properly on the network.

Security is an issue on a peer-to-peer network. Anybody on the network can access any shared resource as long as he or she knows the password for that resource. Too often, though, the resources don't require passwords, so if you have a network on which a lot of sensitive data is stored and processed or you have other reasons to want high security, a peer-to-peer network is not the way to go.

Most of the modern operating systems for standalone computers already have built-in workgroup networking capabilities. Because there is no need for server-level security and performance, you can operate a peer-to-peer network on operating systems such as Windows for Workgroups, Windows NT Workstation 4.0, Windows 2000, Windows XP, Windows 98, Windows ME, and Windows 95.

Server-Based Networks

When your network environment grows beyond 10 users, you might need a server-based network to ensure the security of your files and directories and to organize your resources efficiently, which the server will allow for centralized administration. As your network traffic increases, you'll need more servers to spread their tasks so that they all can be performed in the most efficient way. That is the point at which you introduce specialized servers such as the following:

- File and print servers
- Application servers

- Domain controllers
- Directory services

File and print servers control and share printers and large amounts of data. These servers are typically high-powered computers that are built specifically for the purpose of moving files between disk and network as quickly as possible. File servers often have the following characteristics:

- Large amounts of memory
- Fast hard disks
- Multiple CPUs
- Fast I/O buses
- High-capacity tape drives
- Fast network adapters
- Redundant power supplies
- Hot-swappable hard disks and power supplies

File and print servers also check the access control list (ACL) of each resource before enabling a user to access a file or use a printer. If the user or a group to which the user belongs is not listed in the ACL, the user is not allowed to use the resource. A good definition of a file and print server is that it can only send complete files to the client and cannot find or process data within those files.

Application servers enable users to access the server side of client/server applications. Application servers store vast amounts of data that is manipulated, extracted, or otherwise used by the clients. For example, the salary administration of a large organization typically occurs on an application server. The server enables the users to do searches for people's names, add new data, and do calculations on it. These are some applications that you might find on an application server:

- SQL Server
- Oracle
- Exchange Server
- Lotus Notes

A server can be both a file and print server as well as an application server. A good definition of an application server can be seen when a client requests that the server find and/or manipulate data and return only the results. Servers require specialized knowledge to install and configure the operating system. Servers also allow for LAN expansion and WAN implementation.

Cables, NICs, and Routers

Networking would not work without at least two of the following three items: cables, NICs, and routers. The cable, of course, is the most common medium for connecting components in a computer network. The various types of cable that we have looked at in this chapter include untwisted pair, coaxial, and fiber and can even include no medium (in wireless communication devices).

The NIC, or network interface card, is the key component that makes a workstation or computer communicate with the rest of the network. It is literally the interface to the network and how the workstation gets its information on the medium. A NIC has a transceiver of some sort to connect to the cable.

A router is a necessity in the WAN. It would not be possible to connect multiple sites if it were not for routers. Routers make the Internet what it is, bringing together all the various high-speed backbones in one large network. A router is a computer in and of itself that controls and routes the data on a large or small WAN-style communications solution.

Broadband and Baseband

Broadband LANs are the exception rather than the rule, although many cable companies are now offering Internet services at extraordinary transmission speeds. These networks differ from their baseband counterparts in that they use coaxial or fiber-optic cable to carry multiple channels of data. A single cable can carry five or six separate communications channels. A broadband network is analogous to cable TV: One cable brings in many "channels" as well as networking services.

Broadband systems use analog signaling and a range of frequencies. With analog transmission, the signals employed are continuous and nondiscrete. Signals flow across the physical medium in the form of electromagnetic or optical waves. Broadband technologies use amplifiers to bring analog signals back up to their original strength.

Most LANs are baseband. A baseband network uses only one channel on the cable to support digital transmission. Signals flow in the form of discrete pulses of electricity or light. With baseband transmission, the entire capacity of the communication channel is used to transmit a single data signal.

As the signal travels along the network cable, it gradually decreases in strength and can become distorted. If the cable length is too long, resulting in a signal that is weak or distorted, the received signal could be unrecognizable or misinterpreted. As a safeguard, baseband systems sometimes use repeaters to receive an incoming signal and retransmit it at its original strength and definition to increase the practical length of a cable segment.

Gateways

A *gateway* is used with increasing frequency in networking because of the Internet. A gateway connects dissimilar network operating systems. When UNIX wants to talk to NetWare, for example, there must be a gateway through which the two can communicate. A gateway is like a translator between two systems that are different from each other. The most common example of this communication occurs on the Internet. Everyone who connects to the Internet, whether through a dial-up connection or through a LAN, must have a default gateway to which his or her workstation points.

Now that you have read all the information for this objective, work through Exercise 1-7 and determine its solution.

EXERCISE 1-7

Networking Solutions

A company's managers want to hire you to design a strategy for them to set up their network to meet the organization's needs. The company has purchased another business and plans to make some changes. The existing company has a Novell NetWare server, version 4.11. The cabling is all Category 5 and is set up as 100 Mbps between all PCs. The following requirements must be met:

■ The company plans to also implement a Windows 2000 server, and all users must be able to access both servers until the Novell NetWare server can be removed and all data moved to the Windows server.

■ There is a special department that does not need access to the servers and must be inaccessible to all other PCs. The department will manage these eight PCs and perform all maintenance on these systems. Administration on these PCs does not need to be centralized.

■ The special department also requires access to the Internet to allow posting of information to specialized Web sites as well as being able to check postings by other businesses.

How would you implement this network to meet the requirements? Possible ways to implement this network are as follows:

1. To meet the first requirement, a gateway needs to be installed to allow for communication between these two NOSs.

2. The special department should be set up as a peer-to-peer network to allow for no centralized administration.

3. To allow access to the Internet from the special department, you can either implement a physically separated network or a virtual LAN.

CERTIFICATION SUMMARY

This chapter plays a key part in this book. It serves as an introduction to all the various components of networking. Understanding the basic network structure takes a little knowledge of computing and information sharing. First, remember that for a network to exist, we need to have two things: the entities that want to share information or resources; and the medium that enables the entities to communicate (a cable, such as coaxial or unshielded twisted pair) or a wireless network made up of infrared signals. In this chapter we looked at the various topologies that exist in networks: bus, star, ring, mesh, and wireless. These topologies have their own strengths and weaknesses. We also looked at the difference between segments and backbones.

You learned about some of the network operating systems for client/server networks: Windows NT, Windows 2000, Novell's NetWare, and UNIX.

A network needs rules to govern how communication will happen. These rules are known as *protocols,* and we looked at some of the protocols that make network communication possible: IPX/SPX from Novell; TCP/IP, which drives the Internet today; and NetBEUI, which is a nonroutable protocol.

With networking, we need to ensure that we will not lose data; this takes fault tolerance. The more uptime and availability on a network, the better the return in investment a company receives. Some methods of fault tolerance are drive mirroring, disk striping with parity, disk duplexing, and tape backup.

With networking, you will notice that standards are followed throughout different operating systems. Many standards flow from one operating system to another. The OSI model is a seven-layer approach to a network operating system. In this chapter, we looked at each layer and what it does. An easy way to remember the layers (Application, Presentation, Session, Transport, Network, Data Link, and Physical) is with the sentence, "All people seem to need data processing."

We also looked at the various networking media and connectors. Knowing the various grades of cable can be important for the exam, as well as knowing what a connector looks like. The most common are RJ-45 and coax connectors.

We reviewed some basic terminology in the last part of the chapter. From duplexing to WAN and LAN, there are many terms with which you need to become familiar for the exam. If there is one thing that networking gives you, it is acronyms, and you should know them for the exam.

TWO-MINUTE DRILL

Understanding Basic Network Structure

❑ A network is made up of two basic components: the entities that want to share information or resources and the medium that enables the entities to communicate.

❑ Topology is the physical layout of computers, cables, and other components on a network.

❑ Many networks are a combination of these topologies:

  ❑ Bus

  ❑ Star

  ❑ Mesh

  ❑ Ring

  ❑ Wireless

❑ A bus topology uses one cable to connect multiple computers.

❑ In a star topology, all computers are connected through one central hub or switch.

❑ With the mesh topology, every workstation has a connection to every other component of the network. This type of topology is more commonly seen with something like the national telephone network.

❑ In a ring topology, all computers are connected via a cable that loops around.

❑ In a wireless topology, radio frequencies are used instead of physical cables.

❑ The physical cable segment contains the physical cables connecting the various logical segments.

❑ A backbone is the main cable segment in the network.

Network Operating Systems

❑ The three most widely used network operating systems available are:

  ❑ Microsoft Windows NT/2000/XP

  ❑ Novell's NetWare

  ❑ UNIX

Network Protocols

❑ Packets and protocols are the fundamental building blocks of data transmission over the network.

❑ Internetwork Packet Exchange/Sequenced Packet Exchange (IPX/SPX) is the protocol most commonly used with Novell NetWare.

❑ IPX/SPX is the fastest routable network protocol suite available.

❑ Transmission Control Protocol/Internet Protocol (TCP/IP) is the most common protocol used today. TCP/IP, a routable protocol, is the protocol on which the Internet is built.

❑ NetBios Extended User Interface (NetBEUI) is a transport protocol commonly found in smaller networks.

❑ NetBEUI is a nonroutable protocol.

Fault Tolerance and High Availability

❑ RAID is a fault-tolerant disk configuration in which part of the physical storage contains redundant information about data stored on the disks.

❑ The mirroring system utilizes a code that duplicates everything written on one drive to another drive, making the contents of the drives identical.

❑ Duplexing ensures fault tolerance—not just with your data, but also with your disk controller.

❑ The striping of data is a way to spread the data out across the disks.

❑ Usually you will see at least two volumes on a server: a system volume and a data volume, sometimes called VOL1.

❑ Tapes are a feasible means of storing data backups.

The OSI Model

❑ The Open Systems Interconnect (OSI) protocol suite is a group of standards for protocols that have been standardized into a logical structure for network operations.

❑ The seven layers of the OSI model, from highest to lowest, are Application, Presentation, Session, Transport, Network, Data Link, and Physical.

❑ Different protocols work at different levels of the OSI model.

❑ TCP/IP, IPX/SPX/NWLink, AppleTalk, and DECnet are routable protocols; NetBEUI and DLC are not.

Networking Media and Connectors

❑ Cabling is the LAN's transmission medium.

❑ Three primary types of physical media can be used at the Physical layer: coaxial cable, twisted-pair cable, and fiber-optic cable.

Network Elements

❑ In half-duplex communication, data travels both ways on the medium but in only one direction at a time. In full-duplex communication, you can have data travel both directions simultaneously.

❑ Networks can be divided into peer-to-peer and server-based networks.

❑ The NIC, or network interface card, is the key component that allows a workstation or computer communicate with the rest of the network.

❑ A router is a computer in and of itself that controls and routes the data on a large or small WAN-style communications solution.

❑ Broadband systems use analog signaling and a range of frequencies.

❑ A baseband network uses only one channel on the cable to support digital transmission.

❑ A gateway connects dissimilar systems.

SELF TEST

The following questions will help you measure your understanding of the material presented in this chapter. Read all the choices carefully because there might be more than one correct answer. Choose all correct answers for each question.

Understanding Basic Network Structure

1. Which of the following is an example of a network?

   A. A computer attached to a printer and a scanner to input and output information

   B. A computer sharing a communication medium to communicate with peripherals or other computers to share information

   C. Several printers connected to a switch box going to a single terminal

   D. Several diskettes holding information for one workstation

2. The physical layout of computers, cables, and other components on a network is known as which of the following?

   A. Segment

   B. Backbone

   C. Topology

   D. Protocol

3. Which topology has a centralized location in which all the cables come together to a central point, similar to a mainframe, and if this point fails, it brings down the entire network?

   A. Bus

   B. Star

   C. Mesh

   D. Ring

   E. Wireless

4. Which topology has a layout in which every workstation or peripheral has a direct connection to every other workstation or peripheral on the network?

   A. Bus

   B. Star

C. Mesh

D. Ring

E. Wireless

Network Operating Systems

5. Which network operating system was developed from the VMS platform?

A. NetWare

B. UNIX

C. Windows 95

D. Windows NT

6. Which operating system was originally developed by Bell Labs and has multitasking, multiuser, and built-in networking capabilities?

A. UNIX

B. Windows NT

C. Windows 95

D. NetWare

7. Which of the following are network operating systems and not simply operating systems that will communicate on a network? (Choose all that apply.)

A. Novell NetWare

B. Microsoft Windows 3.1

C. Microsoft Windows 9X

D. Microsoft Windows NT

Network Protocols

8. What do networks use to communicate with each other that is sometimes known as a language that networked computers use?

A. NIC

B. Segment

C. Protocol

D. Cable

9. Which network protocol was developed by Novell for use in its network operating systems?

    A. IPX

    B. TCP/IP

    C. NetBEUI

    D. DLC

10. Which protocol is used on the Internet to give each computer a unique address?

    A. IPX

    B. TCP/IP

    C. NetBEUI

    D. DLC

Fault Tolerance and High Availability

11. Which of the following are methods of ensuring fault tolerance with data on a network? (Choose all that apply.)

    A. Disk mirroring

    B. Disk striping without parity

    C. Disk striping with parity

    D. Tape backup

    E. Disk duplexing

12. When multiple disk controllers are used in a drive-mirroring scenario, it is known as which of the following?

    A. Disk multiplexing

    B. Disk duplobuilding

    C. Bidirectional disking

    D. Disk duplexing

The OSI Model

13. Which of the following is *not* a layer in the OSI model?

    A. Physical

    B. Transport

C. Network

D. Data Transmission

Networking Media and Connectors

14. Which of the following is *not* a common type of medium used in networking?

A. Coaxial cable

B. Twisted-pair cable

C. Fiber-optic cable

D. RJ-45

15. What is the distance limitation on 10Base2, or Thinnet?

A. 100 meters

B. 185 meters

C. 250 meters

D. 500 meters

Network Elements

16. When data is able to travel in both directions on a cable, it is known as which of the following?

A. Fault tolerance

B. Half duplex

C. Biduplex

D. Full duplex

17. In what type of network is there no dedicated server and each node on the network is an equal resource for sharing and receiving information?

A. Client/server

B. Peer-to-peer.

C. Windows NT Server 4.0

D. Novell IntraNetWare 4.x

18. In order for differing networks to communicate with each other, we need to use a which of the following to translate between the networks?

A. Protocol

B. Medium

C. Gateway

D. Bridge

LAB QUESTION

Your company wants to implement a fast network architecture that will use the most standard type of network cabling as well as network devices and interface cards. The managers want the network to be able to allow employee access to the Internet. The network must be expandable to one day cover a large geographical area, but for now it needs to cover only a single building. The supervisors also want to implement a way to allow the server to be able recover from a hard drive failure or other hardware failure within the storage subsystem but only require two hard disks. Your job is to design the basic network requirements and explain the purpose that the requirements meet. What do you come up with as a plan?

SELF TEST ANSWERS

Understanding Basic Network Structure

1. ☑ **B.** A computer sharing a communication medium to communicate with peripherals or other computers to share information is a network. The entities are usually workstations, and the medium is either a cable segment or a wireless medium such as an infrared signal.

    ☒ **A, C,** and **D** are incorrect because a network, by definition, is two or more computers connected to share information. These three choices do not allow two or more PCs to share information; they are only setups of several connected devices or a PC connected to a peripheral device.

2. ☑ **C.** Topology is the physical layout of computers, cables, and other components on a network. Many networks are a combination of the various topologies.

    ☒ **A** is incorrect because a segment is a part of a LAN that is separated by routers or bridges from the rest of the LAN. **B** is incorrect because a backbone is the main part of cabling that joins all the segments together and handles the bulk of the network traffic. **D** is incorrect because a protocol is a set of rules governing the communication between PCs; a protocol can be thought of as similar to a language.

3. ☑ **B.** In a star topology, all computers are connected through one central hub or switch. A star topology actually comes from the days of the mainframe system. The mainframe system had a centralized point at which the terminals connected.

    ☒ **A** is incorrect because a bus topology uses one cable to connect multiple computers. **C** is incorrect because the mesh network has every PC connected to every other PC and can resemble a spider's web. **D** is incorrect because a ring topology resembles a circle or ring. **E** is incorrect because there is no physical cabling to represent the topology; it is represented by a bubble or cell.

4. ☑ **C.** A mesh topology is not very common in computer networking, but you have to know it for the exam. The mesh topology is more commonly seen with something like the national telephone network. With the mesh topology, every workstation has a connection to every other component of the network.

    ☒ **A** is incorrect because a bus topology uses one cable to connect multiple computers. **B** is incorrect because a star topology is made up of a central point or hub with cables coming from the hub and extending to the PCs. **D** is incorrect because this topology resembles a circle or ring. **E** is incorrect because there is no physical cabling to represent the topology; it is represented by a bubble or cell.

Network Operating Systems

5. ☑ D. Developed from the VMS platform many years ago, Microsoft Windows NT has grown into a very popular network operating system with a new and different interface.
☒ A, B, and C are incorrect. The graphical interface and look and feel of the other operating systems in the Windows family made Windows NT very popular among users and network administrators. Windows 95 was simply a great enhancement of Windows of Workgroups. NetWare and UNIX were not based on VMS.

6. ☑ A. Originally developed at Bell Labs, UNIX is becoming a very popular operating system for powerful networking and database management. UNIX boasts three key features that make it powerful: multitasking, multiuser, and networking capabilities.
☒ B, C, and D are incorrect. Windows 95 and NT were developed by Microsoft; NetWare was developed by Novell.

7. ☑ A and D. Novell NetWare and Microsoft Windows NT are NOSs. NetWare is in more businesses than any other NOS in production today; it has evolved into a very powerful network operating system. The major difference between Windows NT and NetWare is at the server.
☒ B and C are incorrect. Windows 3.1 had no native networking integrated with the OS. Windows 9x has built-in networking services, but they are for use as client operating systems and not as true servers.

Network Protocols

8. ☑ C. You can think of a protocol as a language your computer speaks to communicate with other computers on the network. Just as there are different languages in the real world, there are different protocols in the computer world. If two computers use different protocols to communicate on a network, they will not be able to communicate with each other.
☒ A is incorrect because a NIC is the device used to place the data on and receive data from the network medium. B is incorrect because a segment is a part of a network that is separated from the other segments within the LAN. D is incorrect because it is actually the medium on which data is transferred.

9. ☑ A. IPX/SPX—Internetwork Packet Exchange/Sequenced Packet Exchange—is the protocol most commonly used with Novell NetWare. IPX/SPX, a routable protocol, is a very fast and highly established protocol, but it is not used on the Internet. Novell developed IPX/SPX for use in NetWare.

☒   B, C, and D are incorrect. TCP/IP is a standard that is used by the Internet and companies connecting to the Internet. NetBEUI was created by Microsoft as a nonroutable protocol for use by peer-to-peer workgroups. DLC was developed by IBM for communication between PCs and mainframes.

10.   ☑   B. Transmission Control Protocol/Internet Protocol, or TCP/IP, is the most common protocol used today. A routable protocol, TCP/IP is the protocol on which the Internet is built. TCP/IP is very robust and is commonly associated with UNIX systems. The Internet uses only the TCP/IP protocol, so all other choices are incorrect.
☒   A, C, and D are incorrect because TCP/IP is the only protocol used on the Internet.

Fault Tolerance and High Availability

11.   ☑   A, C, D, and E. All but disk striping without parity (RAID 0) are fault tolerant and help ensure that data is not lost. Without the parity information, there is no ability to recover from a hard disk failure.
☒   B is incorrect because disk striping without parity does not offer the ability to recover from a hard disk failure, so it does not guarantee fault tolerance.

12.   ☑   D. Disk duplexing ensures fault tolerance—not just with your data, but also with your disk controller. With traditional mirroring there is one disk controller. If the controller fails, the server is down until that component is replaced. Duplexing gives you a second controller.
☒   A, B, and C are incorrect because they are all nonexistent.

The OSI Model

13.   ☑   D. Data Transmission is not an OSI layer. The seven layers of the OSI model, from highest to lowest, are Application, Presentation, Session, Transport, Network, Data Link, and Physical. Network communication starts at the Application layer of the OSI model and works its way down through the layers step by step to the Physical layer.
☒   A, B, and C are incorrect because they are all OSI layers.

Networking Media and Connectors

14. ☑ **D.** RJ-45 is not a common network medium. Three primary types of physical media can be used at the Physical layer: coaxial cable, twisted-pair cable, and fiber-optic cable. Transmission rates that can be supported on each of these physical media are measured in millions of bits per second (Mbps). RJ-45 is a connector type for twisted-pair cabling.

 ☒ **A, B,** and **C** are incorrect because they are all common network media.

15. ☑ **B.** 10Base2 (Thinnet) has a distance limitation of 185 meters. 10Base5 (Thicknet) has a distance limitation of 500 meters, and 10BaseT (twisted-pair) has a distance limitation of 100 meters.

 ☒ **A, C,** and **D** are incorrect because these are not the distances covered by Thinnet.

Network Elements

16. ☑ **D.** In full-duplex communication, you can have data travel in both directions simultaneously.

 ☒ **A, B,** and **C** are incorrect. Fault tolerance is the ability to recover from a failure; biduplex does not exist. In half-duplex communication, the NIC can only send or receive at one time.

17. ☑ **B.** A peer-to-peer network has no dedicated servers. There are no hierarchical differences between the workstations in the network. The user at each workstation can decide which resources are shared on the network. In a peer-to-peer network, all workstations are clients and servers at the same time.

 ☒ **A** is incorrect because this network type has a dedicated server. **C** and **D** are incorrect because a Windows NT Server 4.0 and Novell IntraNetWare 4.x constitute the server portion of the client/server network.

18. ☑ **C.** A gateway is like a translator between two systems that are different from each other. The most common example of this communication occurs on the Internet. Everyone who connects to the Internet, whether through a dial-up connection or through a LAN, must have a default gateway to which his or her workstation points.

 ☒ **A** is incorrect because most networks use different protocols that require a gateway to translate the protocol from one type to another. **B** is incorrect because this is the cable or media over which the data is transferred. **D** is incorrect because a bridge is used to connect similar networks to actually keep them separated and cut down on network traffic.

LAB ANSWER

To implement a fast network using common standards, you should implement a Fast Ethernet network using Category 5 cabling. To access the Internet, the network should use the TCP/IP protocol, especially if the network is expanded using routers to make a WAN.

For the server to recover from a hard disk failure or other storage subsystem failure, the server should implement RAID 1, or mirroring with disk duplexing, in case of a hard disk controller failure. RAID 1 requires only two hard disks.

2

The Physical Layer

CERTIFICATION OBJECTIVES

2.01	Network Interface Cards
2.02	Network Components
✓	Two-Minute Drill
Q&A	Self Test

I n Chapter 1, you learned the basic components of networking. A computer needs some sort of interface to the rest of the network. This interface is accomplished through the use of a network interface card (NIC). You can integrate a NIC into the system at purchase time or install it at a later time. The NIC prepares information from the computer for transmission across the network medium. It also translates signals from the network medium into information the computer can use. This process involves converting the data stream on the computer bus, which is a parallel data stream, to a serial data stream that can travel along the network medium. Of course, this process is reversed when the communication is reversed.

In this chapter, you will learn about NICs—from installation and configuration to troubleshooting. You will learn the specifics of the different types of NIC, including features that some cards have and others do not. You will look at interrupt requests (IRQs), diagnostics, erasable programmable read-only memory (EPROM), and other things you will need to know for the exam. You will learn how NICs communicate with each other using their unique MAC or hardware addresses.

You will also learn more detail about other components that were introduced in Chapter 1, including hubs, switches, repeaters, and transceivers. These networking components directly interact with the NIC.

CERTIFICATION OBJECTIVE 2.01

Network Interface Cards

The NIC is an add-on component for a computer, much like a video card or sound card. On some systems the NIC is integrated into the system board. On others it must be installed in an expansion slot. Here we discuss both types and what it takes to configure or replace them.

NICs are known by a variety of names, including *network adapters, network cards, network adapter boards,* and *media access cards.* Regardless of what you call them, they function by enabling computers to communicate across a network. NICs are often defined by the following criteria:

- The type of Data Link protocol they support, such as an Ethernet adapter or a Token Ring adapter

- The type of media to which they connect
- The data bus for which they were designed

The computer must have a software driver installed to enable it to interact with the NIC, just as it must for any other peripheral device. These drivers enable the operating system and higher-level protocols to control the functions of the adapter. The NICs that exist in the various workstations on a network communicate with each other using their own unique addresses. The hardware address, or *MAC address,* as it is commonly called, is unique on each network card on a network. You might wonder how a manufacturer can ensure uniqueness among all the network cards in the world. No doubt there are network cards that have the same address, but each manufacturer is assigned a range of addresses by the various network standards organizations, and the manufacturers use only the ranges assigned to them. Within its assigned range, a manufacturer could have duplicate addresses, but the duplicates are so spread out that it is almost impossible for a network, small or large, to have the same network address on two network cards.

The Media Access Layer (MAC) address, or hardware address, is a 12-digit number consisting of digits 0 through 9 and letters A through F. It is basically a hexadecimal number assigned to the card. The MAC address consists of two pieces: The first signifies the vendor it comes from, the second is the serial number unique to that manufacturer. For the exam you will not need to know how these numbers break down; you just need to know what the MAC address is. You will learn more about MAC addresses later in this book.

The NIC performs the following functions:

- It translates data from the parallel data bus to a serial bit stream for transmission across the network.
- It formats packets of data in accordance with protocol.
- It transmits and receives data based on the hardware address of the card.

The Computer Bus

A *computer bus* is the term used for the speed and type of interface the computer uses with different types of interface cards and equipment. The bus is actually a combination of wires, chips, and components that enable all the individual pieces to interact and make a computer what it is. The computer bus is an internal communication channel the computer uses to communicate between devices. Different computers have different bus types. Let's look at two of the more common bus types in computers today: ISA and PCI.

Industry Standard Architecture

Industry Standard Architecture (ISA) was implemented on the earliest computers. The ISA bus started in the IBM PC/XT and PC/AT models in the early 1990s. Almost every computer today contains ISA expansion slots. The ISA architecture is a 16-bit interface.

Peripheral Component Interconnect

The Peripheral Component Interconnect (PCI) bus, on the other hand, is a 64-bit bus, but it is implemented as a 32-bit bus, making it faster when it comes to communicating between the system and the interface cards. PCI was developed by Intel. Most newer personal computers contain a combination PCI/ISA bus, meaning that they have both kinds of slots. PCI slots are short, and usually the connectors on the motherboard are white or ivory in color. The 16-bit ISA bus, on the other hand, has a longer slot, which is brown on the system board. The interface cards come ready to fit these slots. The PCI cards are short and not sectioned the way an ISA card could be.

Microchannel Architecture

Recognizing the speed limitations of the 16-bit bus, both IBM and other companies released new bus architectures in 1988. IBM's 32-bit data bus was called Microchannel Architecture (MCA). It was released with IBM's PS/2 product line and was a totally new architecture that was not backward compatible with ISA cards. MCA adapters were predictably more expensive and offered higher performance than the ISA adapters. IBM has since phased out MCA, and these types of adapters have become increasingly difficult to obtain.

Extended Industry Standard Architecture

Extended Industry Standard Architecture (EISA) is an alternate 32-bit bus architecture that was designed by a consortium of companies, including Hewlett-Packard and

Compaq. It was designed to be backward compatible with ISA devices and is the data bus of choice for PC servers in non-IBM environments for high performance and throughput. EISA cards are also higher in terms of cost and performance than ISA cards.

PC Card

The PC Card bus, formerly known as PCMCIA for the Personal Computer Memory Card Industry Association, is an architecture designed primarily for laptops and other portable computers. Adapters for this bus are sometimes called credit card adapters after their size and shape, which is roughly equal to the size of a credit card. Because of their small size, most have a receptacle to which an external adapter must be connected for attachment to the media. These NICs are also sometimes combined with a modem in a single card, called a combo card.

exam
ⓦatch

It is very important that you know these types of slots and their abilities as far as the bus width (or bits) the slot can handle.

SCENARIO & SOLUTION

I have a system that supports only 16-bit cards. What type of bus does my computer have?	It has ISA.
I am implementing a server for my company, and I want to implement only 64-bit network cards and peripherals. What type of bus should be implemented in my server?	Use a PCI bus.
I have an old IBM PS/2 computer. What type of interface cards should I purchase?	You need MCA.
I need to buy a new computer in which I can use some of my old 16-bit interface cards as well as buying newer 32-bit cards. What type of bus do I require?	You need EISA.
I have a laptop computer with no docking station in which I need to add a network interface card and modem. What type of interface cards do I need?	You need PC Cards (PCMCIA).

Installing a NIC

Installing a NIC is like installing any other interface card in a computer. You must determine the slot it will go in and have the right tools to remove the expansion slot cover and to remove and insert screws. Newer computers do not require any tools, even screwdrivers. The ability to work on a computer with your hands free of tools is making technicians' jobs easier. The Network+ exam will challenge you to know what to do in certain situations. In this section you learn several troubleshooting techniques and how to recognize the common issues that you will face as you work with NICs.

The Installation Process

Before you begin the physical installation of the NIC or network adapter, be sure to address the following issues:

- Ensure that the adapter is compatible with the data bus, the protocol, the media, and the network operating system. In the case of Windows NT, the hardware compatibility list (HCL) details adapters that have been verified for use with NT.

- Ensure that there is an open bus slot on the machine in which you want to install the adapter.

- Ensure that there are system resources, including an IRQ level, base I/O address, and direct memory access (DMA) channel, available to be assigned to the adapter. Choose and record parameters from available settings, unless the adapter is configured automatically through Plug and Play.

- Ensure that the adapter includes all items necessary for installation, including external transceivers or adapters, a T-connector for a thinwire Ethernet adapter, and product documentation.

- Ensure that the software, including the network driver and utilities for testing and configuring the adapter, is included. If a software driver is not provided, a driver might be included with operating system installation media. If not, drivers and driver updates could be available for download from the adapter manufacturer via the Internet or a bulletin board service.

- Remember that the NIC cannot do any useful work until high-level protocols and network services have also been installed and configured.

The installation process is really straightforward. If you have never installed an interface card in a computer before, you need to get some hands-on experience before you go much further. Exercise 2-1 takes you through the process of installation.

Installing a Network Interface Card

In this exercise, you will learn how to remove the cover, assign a slot, and install a NIC. To help ensure no electrostatic damage is done to the computer, be sure to wear an antistatic strap on your wrist or ankle or use an antistatic floor map to ground yourself. Disconnect any power cables to the computer. Now do the following:

1. Review the installation instructions included in the documentation to help you avoid unnecessary problems and make the installation more efficient.

2. If necessary, configure selected settings on the network adapter, using either jumper plugs or DIP switches. If this is required, make sure that all settings are completed before installing the card or you will have to remove the card and start over. With a software-configurable adapter, this configuration occurs after the physical adapter is installed.

3. Put the computer on a work surface that is at a good working height and with enough room to rotate the computer. Refer to the manufacturer's instructions and remove the case of the unit. This might require removal of screws or simply pressing a couple release levers or buttons.

4. Locate the expansion slots and, on the rear of the computer, you should see corresponding openings. Do the slots have covers on them? If the slots have covers, go to Step 5. If the slots do not have covers, go to Step 6.

5. You must remove the covers from the expansion slots before you can install the interface card. Determine the slot in which you want to install the interface card. (Remember that there is a difference between PCI Cards and ISA cards, so take this difference into consideration before choosing a slot.) You might need a screwdriver to remove the slot cover, or you might simply need to flip up a holder to remove the cover. Refer to your manufacturer's documentation to see how your machine's covers are removed.

6. You are ready to install the card. Grasp the card *only* on the edges. (Touching the components on the interface card could damage them.) Hold the card next to the slot cover and the upper-front corner, and with even pressure, insert the card into the slot. The card will not click, but there should be a noticeable feeling of insertion.

7. Secure the card in its slot by replacing the screw or putting the holder back into place. This completes the physical installation of the interface card.

Installing Drivers

When you install a new device in a computer system, you must also install the corresponding software driver for that device. The following paragraphs describe the steps necessary to complete the network adapter driver installation. They also explain the parameters that you need to set on the driver software.

To install the network adapter driver, you need to copy files to the appropriate location on the system hard disk and make the operating system aware of the adapter and its drivers. You can accomplish this task using a setup utility provided by the adapter manufacturer, or you can use the operating system configuration utilities, such as the Network applet on the Control Panel in Windows 95 and Windows NT.

If you use a vendor-provided setup program, it is normally invoked from a command line. The setup program goes through various steps to prompt for parameter input, to check the card, and to load the required files.

To manually install a network driver in Windows 95/98 or Windows NT, open the **Control Panel** and double-click the **Network** icon. The Network dialog box opens. At this point, the dialog boxes diverge for the various operating systems. In Window 95/98, click the **Add** button and then select **Adapter** from the list. The Select Network Adapters dialog box appears, as shown in Figure 2-1. Select the appropriate manufacturer from the Manufacturers list, and then select the appropriate network adapter from the Network Adapters list.

Adding an adapter in Windows NT 4.0 is a little different, even though the main graphical user interface (GUI) is the same as Windows 95 and Windows 98. You go to the same initial place to configure the networking components, but the window is different because each component of the network is on a separate tab. In Windows

FIGURE 2-1

To add a network adapter in Windows 98, select the appropriate manufacturer and network adapter from the lists

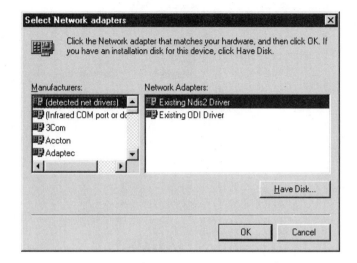

95 and Windows 98, the protocols, adapters, and other components are shown in one area. Figure 2-2 shows the Windows NT Network Properties window.

Testing

If there is one thing you will do often, it is testing to be sure any updates or changes you made are working properly. Once your network card is installed, you have to connect the cable to it. Some network cards will have multiple transceivers on them. You must connect the appropriate cable for the network.

Once the cable is connected, you can check a couple of things to see if the card is operating properly. The first of these is the link light on the back of the card. Some NICs do not have this feature, but if yours does, you should see a light next to the transceiver. Some 10 Mbps cards have an activity light and a connection light. Some 10/100 Mbps cards have both a 10Mbps light and a 100 Mbps light, along with the activity light, which tells you the speed at which you are connected. The operating system needs to be configured with the appropriate protocols and any configuration the protocol requires.

The second thing you need to do to determine if there is connectivity is the most important. When the card is completely configured, try logging in to the server and accessing various network resources. With Windows 95 and Windows 98, you will

FIGURE 2-2

Windows NT
network
properties

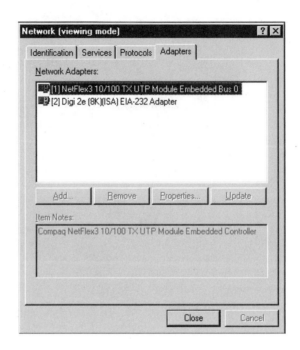

not see the same login screen when you are connected to the network as you do when you are not connected to the network. When you are not connected to the network, you will simply get the Windows login screen, which asks you for a username and password. The username and password do not authenticate you, they simply determine your Start menu icons and desktop layout if you have user profiles in place. Another option is to use PING to determine if you are actually able to communicate on the network.

Drivers

When you install a network card in a Windows 95 or Windows 98 machine, usually Plug and Play recognizes and configures the hardware by loading the appropriate driver. A *driver* is a piece of the operating system that enables the operating system to communicate with the device. There are different types of drivers for modems, sound cards, and just about any other component in a computer.

The manufacturer provides the driver, and usually the driver has its own configuration program to set up and install the network adapter. This is usually a SETUP.EXE, INSTALL.EXE, or INSTALL.BAT file. If this isn't the case, and

Plug and Play finds the network adapter but no default driver exists, you will have the opportunity to change to the appropriate drive and directory and update the driver.

From time to time, you might want to update the drivers for your various devices. Manufacturers update their drivers if problems are found in current versions. You can update the driver for your network card in a couple of ways. Since most workstations have Windows 95 or 98 on them, let's look at some examples from those operating systems.

The easiest way to update your driver in Windows 95 or 98 is to find your device on the Device Manager page of the System Properties dialog box. Either right-click the **My Computer** icon on your desktop and select **Properties** from the pop-up menu, or select **Start | Settings | Control Panel** and double-click the **System** icon. The System Properties dialog box appears. Click the **Device Manager** tab to bring it to the front. The Device Manager page lists all the devices installed on your machine. Select your network adapter from the list and then click the **Properties** button. A screen similar to Figure 2-3 is displayed.

Click the **Update Driver** button to install the new driver. The driver can usually be downloaded from the manufacturer's Web site. You should see some information

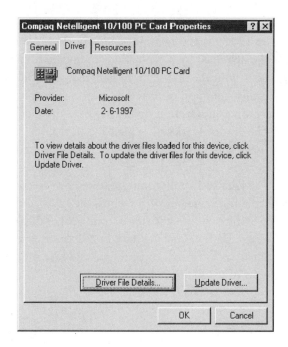

FIGURE 2-3

To obtain your network card properties, select your network adapter on the device manager page

on what to do to install the driver or at least what directory holds the appropriate files for your operating system. A good rule of thumb is to always check the README file on the update. Even though it takes time to review the file, the information it contains will save you time down the road.

Configuring a NIC

Depending on the network operating system or the workstation, you could need to do some configuration of the NIC. This is definitely the case if you have a DOS or Windows 3.1 workstation. The DOS-level drivers have either a configuration for (C.G.) file or an initialization (IN) file that determines how the card functions.

Other components involved in configuration include software located in the chips on the interface card. This software is known as an erasable programmable read-only memory, or EPROM. There could also be jumpers that determine settings for the card.

Erasable Programmable Read-Only Memory

Every interface card, whether a network card, a video card, or a sound card, comes with EPROM, which is a set of software instructions built into the interface card to perform its functions.

An EPROM is sometimes *flash able*. This means that the software in the EPROM can be upgraded by downloading an update from the manufacturer and then using a utility to write the update to the flash memory. Different EPROMs do different things. The most common of these on a network card is the boot PROM. The boot PROM boots the workstation if there is no hard drive or disk from which to boot.

The dustless workstation is a concept that has been around for some time. Designed for use in fairly large environments, it originally had two goals. The first was to enhance security on the network by removing local storage from the end user and requiring that all data and applications be stored on servers. By managing user access to this information via server permissions, the LAN administrator can more effectively control the environment. The second goal of dustless workstations was the cost of mass storage. By removing the cost of local storage, particularly as workstation populations increased, companies could save money. This has become less an issue as the cost of mass storage has declined.

The challenge of using dustless workstations lies in booting them. Normally, a system at startup looks for a hard disk that is bootable in order to start the operating system. This specifically involves looking for a master boot record that tells the system where to find the boot files. In the case of a dustless workstation, no disk is available to perform this function, because all storage is accessed through the network adapter.

You can add a remote boot PROM to a network adapter to enable the system to boot using files stored on the network. An adapter capable of booting remotely has an empty socket that can be populated with a boot PROM. Once installed and configured, this boot PROM directs the system to the network location of the boot files.

on the
Job

In some cases, you will work with very old equipment when your clients or employers have a small budget. If you are forced to work with workstations that have no hard disks, you will have to appropriately configure not only the workstations but the server.

A client of mine was a school in a small town. They were holding off until the following school year to upgrade their computers. They had 30 or so dustless workstations with old IBM Token Ring network cards and a boot PROM. I had to configure the server to enable the network cards to connect to the server and to use a file that is a copy of a boot disk to load the appropriate DOS files, as though the workstation were booting up. Then the workstation went through the normal login process.

Because these were legacy machines, I had to research the proper configuration. In the school's Novell environment, it took some time to get everything to work properly. I learned from this experience that research sometimes is required to properly implement a solution for a client when unusual circumstances are involved. Once the appropriate research is done, the solution must be implemented and tested—and tested again. As a network-savvy person, you will learn to test yet again to make triple-sure everything is working as it should be.

Jumpers

As we mentioned, some network cards have jumpers on them to change the configuration. A *jumper* is a plastic piece that connects two metal posts on the card. Figure 2-4 shows an example of jumper blocks; the black areas represent the locations of the jumpers.

FIGURE 2-4

Interface card and
jumpers

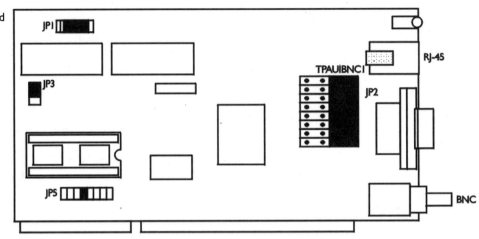

The jumpers on an interface card can do many different things. The most common things that they do are set the IRQ and the I/O address. If you are not familiar with these components, don't worry—we will look at them later in this chapter. For now, you need to know that jumpers configure a card that is not software configurable.

Jumpers can also determine which transceiver is being used on the network interface. Some NICs have multiple connection options, so setting the jumpers determines the transceiver to which to hook the cable. Some NICs have jumpers to set the speed of the card, if it handles multiple speeds. For exam purposes, the point here is, of course, that jumpers can configure just about any setting for an interface card. NICs differ in terms of jumper settings and configurations, so refer to the documentation supplied by your NIC's manufacturer.

Plug and Play Software

With the introduction of Windows 95 came the Plug and Play operating system. Plug and Play has been around for a while. Windows 95 was the first operating system to take advantage of it. The Plug and Play operating system and the Plug and Play BIOS work hand in hand to configure expansion components such as NICs. The premise behind Plug and Play software is to make configuration by the end user minimal if not nonexistent.

FROM THE CLASSROOM

Installing and Configuring Network Interface Cards

From experience, I can urge you to verify that your network adapters are installed and configured correctly. These settings are easy to overlook if you are in a hurry. However, it is in your best interest to make sure that you have these NICs configured correctly, or havoc might ensue. You could learn the hard way the same lesson I did at my first networking job several years ago.

I was building a new Windows NT server. We were in the process of upgrading the hubs from 10 Mbps to switched 100 Mbps, so we were installing new network cards in the servers. These network cards were capable of 100MB per second; however, they needed to be configured for 10 Mbps, the settings of our hubs at that time. After I installed the network card, I began installing Windows NT Server as usual. I was talking with the other network administrator when my phone rang. A user said he no longer had access to a database. I asked him a few questions and then thought it would be better to visit his workstation and fix the problem. On the way there, I saw that many users were standing outside their cubicles wondering what was going on. By this time I knew that the caller's downed database was not an isolated incident.

I retreated to the server room, and sure enough, the hub was not responding. This was not the only hub in the company, but it was the most important hub. Every Windows NT database, application, and file server in the server room was connected directly to this hub. The primary domain controller and all backup domain controllers were also connected to this hub. We got out the documentation for the hub to find out why it was locked up. We reset the hub and powered it off and on, but nothing was working. It was panic time because everything had come to a complete stop.

The other network administrator asked what I had done, and I told him I didn't do anything. Luckily, he asked me specifically what I was doing before the crash, and I said, "Just configuring this server." "What were you configuring?" he asked me, and I told him: the network card. Of course, he realized what had happened. He pulled the network cable off the server and the hub lights began flickering with activity. When he plugged it back in, the network activity ceased. He loaded up the network card diagnostics, and sure enough, the network card was set for 100 Mbps.

One false move had rendered the entire company's network useless. This is a great example of the fragility of networks. You need to understand what you are working on, and make sure you spend the time needed to do the job correctly. I would hate for the same thing to happen to you. Watch those network card settings!

—*Cameron Brandon, MDSE.+Internet, ONE, A+, Network+*

Troubleshooting NICs

If there is one thing a network administrator spends time doing, it is troubleshooting. Troubleshooting can seem like a difficult task. Networks can seem overwhelming sometimes. But if you take a structured approach to troubleshooting, it will be very easy to solve problems you encounter on a daily basis.

When you are troubleshooting network problems, it is important to follow a logical troubleshooting methodology. The first step is to determine which areas of the network are affected. For example, you need to determine if the problem is with one protocol, if it is with everything on one side of a router, or if all the machines are connected to the same cable. No matter what, the affected areas will always have something in common. The affected areas could, of course, be your entire network, but that is something that they have in common.

Second, identify any differences between the affected areas and the unaffected areas. For example, if you are unable to get a network connection with all your workstations that are connected to a thinwire coax cable, but all other workstations are functioning, more than likely your problem resides in that thinwire coax cable.

Third, restart the affected hardware. This is probably the most common solution to network outages. By restarting all affected hubs, routers, and switches, you can often clear up the problem.

Fourth, segment the affected area—divide the area in half. The best example of this practice is in thinwire coax. Determine the midpoint of the cable and place a terminator on each end. One-half the cable should now be working and is obviously not your problem. Repeat this step until you find the problem.

Fifth, if you are still unable to find the problem, it's time to get out some tools. They can range from technical databases to diagnostics. We focus on the diagnostic side of troubleshooting for purposes of this exam.

Network Card Diagnostics

One other option is to use a diagnostic program to run a series of tests on the network adapter. You can use generic diagnostic programs or vendor-supplied diagnostics. Many diagnostics must be run without the network drivers loaded. Figure 2-5 shows a diagnostic and testing program for a 3Com card.

Diagnostic programs run a variety of tests. Some test communication, others test communication in and out of the card with the use of a loopback plug.

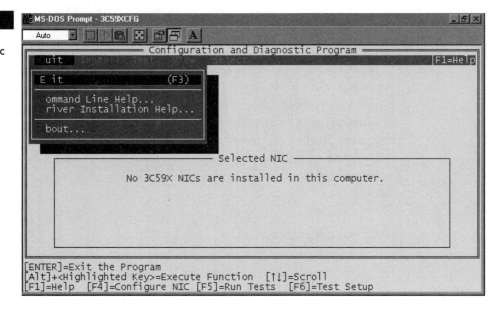

FIGURE 2-5

Use a diagnostic program, such as this 3Com program, to troubleshoot a NIC

Loopback Test

The *loopback test* is one that tests communication in and out of the card. A stream of data is sent out and loops back around into the card. The input is then compared to see if the data received is the same as that sent.

Some cards can run an internal loopback test. Others must have a loopback adapter that plugs into the card. This way the data is actually sent out of the card and loops around and comes back into the card as though it were received from another device. Sometimes this is a more accurate and realistic test of the card.

Vendor-Supplied Diagnostics

If you use the general diagnostic programs, you should take a look at the vendor-supplied diagnostics that are available. The manufacturer designs specific tests that can be better than the generic tests run by general diagnostic applications. All the major manufacturers have diagnostic programs available. Check the manufacturer's Web site for the latest programs.

Resolving Hardware Resource Conflicts

Today's computers have many different devices installed. Each device must be able to communicate with the processor or other components within the computer. Sometimes you will see that two or more devices are trying to communicate across the same channels or the same link.

There are three main ways for a device to communicate with components in a computer. The first and most commonly configured way is the IRQ, or interrupt request. The second is the DMA, or direct memory access. The third is the I/O address, which is a specific memory address. Here we look briefly at each of these methods.

Interrupt Requests

A device uses IRQs to interrupt the processor and request service. There are sixteen IRQ lines, many of which are routinely committed to devices such as the disk controllers and serial and parallel ports. A common configuration for a network card uses IRQ 3 (which is also used by the serial port COM2), IRQ 5, or IRQ 10. Like the I/O address, the IRQ must be chosen so that the card does not conflict with another device. Table 2-1 lists some common IRQ settings.

exam
ⓌatcH

You must know these IRQ settings for the A+ exam. You should know them equally as well for the Network+ exam.

Direct Memory Access

DMA is a process whereby some devices can directly access memory on the system, without the intervention of the CPU. This capability removes the processor from handling these data transfers and speeds the transfer process. Any device with DMA capability has a DMA channel, which it uses to control direct memory access. Since many hardware devices do not use this feature, there is more flexibility in configuring this setting.

I/O Base Address

The *I/O base address* is the starting address for a series of registers used to control the card. A common I/O address for a network card is 300h. Care must be taken to ensure that this address is not already in use by another device, or the adapter will fail.

TABLE 2-1	Common IRQ Settings
IRQ Setting	**Common Usage**
1	Keyboard
2	Cascaded controller with IRQ 9; commonly used for VGA display
3	COM2 or COM4
4	COM1 or COM3
5	Sound/parallel port 2
6	Diskette
7	Parallel port/LPT1
8	Real-time clock
9	Redirected IRQ 2; sometimes available
10	Open
11	Open/SCSI
12	Open/PS/2 port
13	Coprocessor/math processor
14	Primary IDEA
15	Secondary IDEA

Transceiver Type

The *transceiver type* setting is required for network adapters that are capable of attaching to more than one media type. Typical cards of this nature include Ethernet cards that have both twisted-pair and coaxial connectors. One of the more common oversights in configuring a NIC, this setting renders the card nonfunctional if configured for the wrong media connection. To alleviate this problem, some cards of this type have an auto setting that causes the card to search for the transceiver that has media connected to it. We look at this topic in more detail later in this chapter.

on the
job

In the real world, you always want to leave the transceiver type set to Auto, just in case the network is later upgraded and the cabling is changed. I have seen networks upgraded from coaxial to twisted-pair and, since the transceiver type was set to Auto, it was only a matter of changing the cabling and connecting it to the NIC.

CERTIFICATION OBJECTIVE 2.02

Network Components

NICs must interact with other devices on the network. You were briefly introduced to some of the common network devices in Chapter 1. Here you will learn in more detail some of the common network components.

Computers are linked via various connectivity devices. These devices include hubs, multistation access units (MASS), switches, repeaters, transceivers, and wireless access points (WAS).

Hubs

Hubs are one of the most important components of a network. They are the central locations to which all cabling must connect in most topologies. You can easily remember the layout of a hub if you think of a wheel and picture how the spokes radiate out from the hub of the wheel. In a network, each spoke is a connection, and the hub of the wheel is the hub of the network, where all the cables come together.

The Role of Hubs in Topologies

Most network topologies can use a hub in one way or another. Figure 2-6 shows an example of a hub with five workstations attached to it. This diagram helps you visualize where the hub fits into the network. The most prominent user of hubs is the 10BaseT topology. 10BaseT is entirely dependent on hubs for its infrastructure.

Passive Hubs

The function of a *passive hub* is simply to receive data from one port of the hub and send it out to the other ports. For example, an eight-port hub receives data from port 3 and then resend that data to ports 1, 2, 4, 5, 6, 7, and 8. It is as simple as that.

A passive hub contains no power source or electrical components. There is no signal processing. It simply attaches the ports internally and enables communication to flow through the network.

FIGURE 2-6

A network hub is like the hub of a wheel; the spokes are the connections to workstations

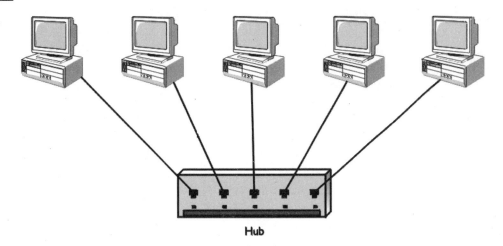

Hub

For the exam, remember that a passive hub does not act similarly to a repeater, as the active hub does, so the cable distance between two PCs is the total cable length and not PC-to-hub length, as with active hubs.

Active Hubs

An *active hub* provides the same functionality as a passive hub, with an additional feature. Active hubs repeat the data while receding it to all the ports. Using active hubs, you can increase the length of your network. It is important to remember that UTP Category 5 cabling can be run a maximum of 100 meters. With an active hub, you can run this type of cable 100 meters on each side of the hub. An active hub has a power source and built-in repeaters to boost the signal. Extra electronics built into an active hub allow for signal regeneration.

When exam time comes, remember the difference between an active hub and a passive hub: An active hub contains electronic components to boost the signal; a passive hub contains no power source or electronic components.

Hybrid Hubs

A *hybrid hub* is a hub that can use many different types of cables in addition to UTP cabling. A hybrid hub is usually cabled using thinwire or thickwire Ethernet, which is discussed later in this chapter. A hybrid hub is the most common type of hub. Hybrid hubs are used to interconnect hubs that are farther than the 100-meter limitation of 10BaseT.

Multistation Access Units

A *multistation access unit (MAU)* is a device to which multiple workstations are connected in order to communicate on a Token Ring network. Sometimes a MAU is also referred to as a hub. Be careful not to confuse a MAU with a UTP hub; their actual functions are quite different.

A MAU typically has eight ports and uses either IBM Data or RJ-45 connections. A MAU looks a lot like a hub at a glance, but it the words *MAU* or *Token Ring* will be printed on it. A MAU is typically not powered, but I have seen them powered with various lights for connectivity and activity.

MASS provide network fault tolerance by not using a port if the PC attached to that port is powered off or nonfunctioning or if the cable connecting the PC to the port is damaged or missing. The only possible point of failure is if the MAU itself malfunctions.

e x a m
ⓦ a t c h

Remember that the MAU allows for a physical star topology but is logically a ring topology because it cycles through all ports in order to simulate a ring.

Switching Hubs

Switches have become an increasingly important part of our networks today. As network usage increases, so do traffic problems. As a systems engineer, you will be faced with this reality on an almost continuous basis. A common solution to traffic problems is to implement switches. Figure 2-7 shows how traffic travels in a switched environment.

Multiport Bridging

Switches, also referred to as *multiport bridges*, automatically determine the MAC addresses of the devices connected to each port of the switch. The switch then examines each packet it receives to determine its destination MAC address. The switch then determines for which port the packet is destined and sends it out to that port only.

Network Performance Improvement With Switching

The primary benefit of implementing switching technology is to improve network performance. It is important to note that if you are not having traffic problems on your network, adding a switch will probably not change your network's performance. If your network is having traffic problems, switching—when implemented properly—can greatly increase your performance.

Switching is a fairly involved process. For example, Computer A transmits a packet to Computer C. The packet enters the switch from Port 1 and then travels a direct route to Port 3. From Port 3 the packet is transmitted to Computer C. During this process, Computer B is unaware of the traffic between Computers A and C because there is a direct path within the switch and no shared bandwidth.

FIGURE 2-7

A network with a switching hub

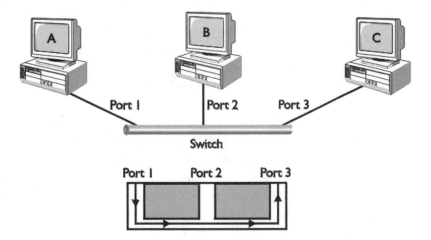

on the **!** **O**ob *It is a best practice to use switches whenever possible because of the increase in performance over a standard hub. The bandwidth with a standard hub is shared by all users connected to the hub; however, with a switch, all users get the full network bandwidth. For example, a 10 Mbps network with an eight-port hub and eight PCs allows each user to have (10 ÷ 8) Mbps bandwidth, but with a switching hub, each user would have a full 10 Mbps bandwidth.*

Now that you have an understanding of some of the network components, let's work through an exercise that will allow you to think about how these devices are used.

EXERCISE 2-2

Determining the Network Device to Use

This exercise consists of three scenarios. Choose the network device to use or replace an existing device with another:

1. A company has a problem with its network; an IT employee finds the central connection device of the ring network is faulty. He sends another, newly hired IT employee to a local electronics store to find a similar device to replace the device that failed. The new IT employee does not take the existing device, but she does notice that it is nonpowered and has 24 RJ-45 ports on it. She returns with a device that is nonpowered and has 24 RJ-45 ports. The device is installed and all PCs powered back on, but the network is still not functioning. What is the problem, and how can it be fixed?

2. Recently, a company's central network device failed. They sent a salesperson to purchase a replacement that would be inexpensive. The salesperson returned with a new device, and it was installed. It cost about half the price of some other devices at the store and had the same number of ports and port types. After the device was installed, some PCs functioned fine on the network, while others were unable to access any network resources. It was determined that the PCs that could not access the network resources were located further from the central connection device than the PCs that did work properly. What is the problem?

3. A company has recently purchased a new building that is 2.5 blocks from the existing headquarters. The company wants to have the two buildings joined by fiber-optic cables to allow the buildings to be on the same network. The IT department contracts with a company to run the fiber-optic cables between the buildings, and the IT staff have purchased two routers to place in each building that have fiber-optic connectors on them. The routers were placed on back order due to low stock at the manufacturer. Meanwhile, the fiber-optic cable has been run between the buildings, and the cable ends are left hanging the two server rooms for the routers to be hooked to them. When the routers finally arrive, they are installed by a technician who places the routers in the appropriate building and connect the cables to them. Immediately the staff notices that the two buildings cannot connect to one another. A router specialist is contracted to verify that the routers are configured correctly. The two buildings are still unable to communicate with one another. What can possibly be wrong if the fiber-optic cables have been installed correctly between the two buildings?

The answers for the three scenarios are as follows:

1. The employee apparently purchased a passive hub that has 24 RJ-45 ports, not a 24-port MAU. The passive hub needs to be replaced with a MAU, or the Token Ring NICs need to be replaced with Ethernet NICs.

2. The hub that was purchased was working fine, but it was apparently not an active hub and therefore did not regenerate the data signals and caused the usable cable distance to be cut in half. This caused any PCs that were farther than 100 meters from each other by cable distance not to be able to communicate. The active hub allows each cable length from the hub to the PC to be 100 meters via Category 3 or higher cable.

3. The fiber-optic cable ends have been placed in the routers incorrectly. With fiber-optic cables, there are two cables. One cable is for transmitting data one way, and the other cable is for transmitting in the opposite direction. This system allows for full-duplex communication. If the transmit cable from one building is placed in the transmit port at the other building, the data will not be received by either end. The cables need to be switched at one building.

Repeaters

Repeaters can be used in the Ethernet coaxial cable environment the same way they are used for UTP. Thickwire can normally transmit a distance of 500 meters, which can be extended by introducing repeaters. Thinwire can normally transmit a distance of 185 meters and can be extended by use of a repeater. This, of course, is the advantage of using a repeater. If your network layout exceeds the normal specifications of cable, you can use repeaters to build your network. This extension allows for greater lengths when planning your cabling scheme.

Transceivers

A *transceiver* is that portion of the network interface that actually transmits and receives electrical signals across the transmission media. A transceiver is also the part of the interface that actually connects to the media. Transceiver types can be classified as either onboard or external.

SCENARIO & SOLUTION

I need an inexpensive way to connect a network in a star topology using Ethernet standards. What type of device do I need?	You need a hub.
I need an inexpensive way to connect a network in a star topology using Token Ring standards. What type of device do I need?	A MAU will do the trick.
I need a star network using Ethernet standards with enhanced performance. What type of network device do I require?	You need a switching hub.
I need to extend the distance of a cable drop to almost twice the allowed length for the cable type. What type of network device should I use to be able to extend my allowable cable length?	A repeater will handle the task.

Onboard Transceivers

Onboard transceivers are built onto the network interface card. With these types of transceivers, the media connector is built right on the back of the NIC. Common examples of this type include RJ-45 receptacles for twisted-pair cable and BNC connectors for thinwire coaxial cable.

External Transceivers

With an external transceiver, the actual media connection is made external to the NIC using a small device that attaches to the NIC via an extension cable. These types of connections use an adapter unit interface (AUI) connector, also called a Digital-Intel-Xerox (DIX) connector, on the back of the NIC. The AUI connector is a female 15-pin D-connector that looks very much like a joystick port. An AUI connector enables a network card to be used with multiple types of media. A common implementation is to use this configuration for an Ethernet card that can be attached to twisted-pair, thickwire, or thinwire coax by simply changing the external transceiver type. Figure 2-8 shows what an AUI connector looks like.

The types of transceivers and media that can be served by a NIC determine the appropriate connector. Each media type has a typical connector type or connection method.

Thickwire Coax

Thickwire, or standard Ethernet coax, uses a connection method that typically involves an external transceiver connected to the adapter's AUI port. This external transceiver has a connection called a *vampire tap.* To attach a thickwire transceiver to the media, you must drill a hole in the cable using a special drilling jig that

FIGURE 2-8

An AUI connector enables a network card to be used with multiple types of media controls the depth of the hole. This jig prevents the drill from drilling through and severing the center conductor.

The vampire tap consists of a pin that is inserted into the hole drilled in the cable and a clamp that holds the tap onto the cable. One of the challenges of this type of connection is to position the tap so that it contacts the center conductor without shorting to the shield surrounding it. These difficulties, as well as the cost and size of thickwire cable, have rendered it largely obsolete, although it could occasionally be found in existing installations.

Thinwire Coax

Thinwire coax can be attached directly to an adapter if an onboard transceiver is used. In this case, a connector called a BNC, or barrel connector, on the network card attaches to a T-connector. The T-connector has a female fitting that attaches to the card as well as two additional male fittings that attach to cable segments or a terminator.

Each end of a thinwire Ethernet segment must be terminated, so the last node on each end could have a terminator attached to the side of the T-connector opposite the inbound cable. All other nodes use T-connectors with cable segments attached to both sides, just like holiday tree lights. A thinwire segment cannot be attached directly to the BNC connector on the network adapter; it must use a T-connector.

An alternative connection method can use the AUI connector with an external thinwire transceiver. In this case, the cable attachment to the transceiver is still made through a T-connector.

Twisted-Pair Wiring

The typical connector for a twisted-pair connection is called an *RJ-45 connector*. The RJ-45 connector looks like an oversized phone connector. The reason for the difference in size is that a phone connector has either a four-wire connector or a six-wire connector. RJ-45 has an eight-wire connector.

An RJ-45 patch cable can be plugged directly into the back of a twisted-pair network adapter, or less commonly, it can be attached to an external transceiver. The patch cable usually runs to a wall receptacle, which is wired back to a patch panel and ultimately back to a wiring hub.

Fiber-Optic Cabling

Fiber-optic adapters generally have two connectors, one each for incoming and outgoing fiber cables. The mechanical connectors that join the cable, called *ST connectors*, are designed to pass light seamlessly across the joined fiber segments. For this reason, these connectors must be made with great precision. Fiber-optic runs are generally made back to a concentrator that performs a hub function.

In many situations, fiber-optic cabling is used to connect high-speed computers and provide a high-speed backbone to which slower LANs are attached. The LANs might connect copper media, such as twisted-pair or coaxial cable, to a set of hubs that are then bridged to the fiber-optic backbone for high-speed data transfer between LANs.

Configuration

The transceiver type configuration is set using jumpers, DIP switches, or configuration software, in the same way that the I/O base address and other parameters are set on the card. Most cards have at most two types of transceiver. During configuration, these transceivers can be referred to in the following ways:

- **Internal vs. external**   The card has an AUI port and an onboard twisted-pair or coaxial connector.

- **DIX or AUI**   The card uses an external transceiver.

- **Coax, 10Base2, or BNC**   The card has an onboard thinwire Ethernet connection.

- **TP, UTP, or 10BaseT**   The card has an onboard twisted-pair connection.

The Auto setting might be available if the card can autosense the connected media.

Wireless Access Points

Wireless access points (WAS) are the cells for the wireless network topology discussed in Chapter 1. These are devices which transmit and receive radio frequencies and are used to send and receive data to and from the PCs and network devices with the wireless transmitters connected to them. The WAP devices are also connected to a physical cable which connects the WAP device to the rest of the network. The servers and main PCs will be connected by physical cables and the WAP devices will be

connected to this physical network cable system and will allow for transmissions to
and from the servers.

WAP devices will usually allow for the administrator to change frequencies of the
WAP device to allow for multiple WAP devices to work in close proximity of one
another in the case that the radio frequency bubble that is the area of coverage is
overlapped by another WAP device.

SCENARIO & SOLUTION

I have to explain how the network adapter converts the data for transmission on the network medium. What are the two types of data streams used in conjunction with the computer bus and the network medium?	Parallel, serial
I am troubleshooting a communication problem and I have to know the address of the network card that was assigned at the factory when it was made. What address am I looking for?	MAC or hardware
I am configuring my network adapter in a non-Plug and Play environment. What four things do I need to know to configure the adapter and ensure I can communicate on the network medium and not conflict with any other device in the system?	I/O base, IRQ, DMA, transceiver type
I am finalizing configuration of my network adapter. What has to connect to the transceiver on the network adapter to connect the medium or cable to it?	Connector
I am configuring a network adapter. What does the connector connect to in order to make the link from network adapter to the rest of the network?	Transceiver
I am connecting a network card that has an external transceiver. What type of connector will I be connecting to?	AUI or DIX
I want to connect a PC to a network that has a wireless NIC installed in the PC. What is needed to allow the PC to communicate with the rest of the network?	Wireless Access

CERTIFICATION SUMMARY

In this chapter you learned about the Physical layer of the OSI model, specifically the NIC, or network interface card. The NIC performs the following functions:

- It translates data from the parallel data bus to a serial bit stream for transmission across the network.
- It formats packets of data in accordance with protocol.
- It transmits and receives data based on the hardware address of the card.

There are many pieces to successful NIC implementation. You learned what defines and differentiates the various NICs available on the market, all of which are important when determining the appropriate NIC to use:

- The type of Data Link protocol they support, such as an Ethernet adapter or a Token Ring adapter
- The type of media to which they connect
- The data bus for which they were designed

The data bus is the internal communication channel the computer uses to communicate between devices. The types of buses include ISA, EISA, MCA, PCI, and PC Card. Each has its own distinct features. The EISA, MCA, and PCI are all 32-bit bus types. For the exam, the two you need to know are ISA and PCI. Most NICs today are designed to fit either the ISA bus or the PCI bus.

The Industry Standard Architecture, or ISA, bus is a 16-bit interface and was implemented on the earliest computers. Almost every computer today has ISA expansion slots in it. The Peripheral Component Interconnect, or PCI, bus, on the other hand, is a 64-bit bus, but it is implemented as a 32-bit bus, making it faster at communicating between the system and the interface cards. Most newer personal computers have a combination PCI/ISA bus in them, meaning that they have both kinds of slots.

You learned how to install a NIC. To prepare for the installation, you must ensure that the following things are in place first:

1. The card is compatible with the machine in which you will install it, including the bus, media, protocol, and operating system.
2. There is a slot available to install the card.

3. System resources, including IRQ, I/O base address, and DMA channel, are available to assign to the card.

4. You have the drivers you need for the operating system to which you are installing.

When you have accounted for all these things, you can go through the process of physically installing the card and configuring it.

The process of configuring a NIC differs depending on the vendor and model of the NIC. Some NICs are software configurable for all settings; others have jumpers you set to determine the configuration. Some cards have a flash able EPROM chip that may even boot to the network if the workstation does not have a diskette or hard drive.

Troubleshooting NICs can seem challenging, but if you take a structured approach to problem solving, the process is really pretty easy. The first thing to remember is to determine the problem and then isolate where the problem is occurring. The more you can narrow the source of the problem, the better off you will be when it comes to solving the problem. You can use different kinds of diagnostics to aid in the troubleshooting process. There are generic diagnostic programs and vendor-supplied diagnostic programs. One common test you learned about is the loopback test.

You learned about the types of resource conflicts that can occur when you are configuring a network card. There are three main ways for a device to communicate with components in a computer: the interrupt request (IRQ), direct memory access (DMA), and the I/O address. You have to be concerned with the settings for each of these when you are configuring a NIC. Plug and Play can assist in the configuration piece, but if you don't have a Plug and Play board you have to do some configuring of these resources first.

NICs must interact with other devices on the network. The various connectivity devices that link computers include hubs, MASS, switches, repeaters, and transceivers.

If your network layout exceeds the normal specifications of cable, you can use repeaters to build your network. This structure allows for greater cable lengths when you plan your cabling scheme.

Transceivers are that portion of the network interface that actually transmits and receives electrical signals across the transmission media and connects to the media. Transceiver types can be classified as being either onboard or external; DIX or AUI; coax, 10Base2, or BNC; or TP, UTP, or 10BaseT.

✓ TWO-MINUTE DRILL

Network Interface Cards

❑ Network interface cards (NICs) function by enabling computers to communicate across a network.

❑ The computer must have a software driver installed to enable it to interact with the NIC, just as it must for any other peripheral device.

❑ The Media Access Layer (MAC) address, or hardware address, is a 12-digit number consisting of digits 0 through 9 and the letters A through F.

❑ A *computer bus* is the term used for the speed and type of interface the computer uses with various types of interface cards and equipment.

❑ The Network+ exam will challenge you to know troubleshooting techniques and how to recognize the common issues that you will face as you work with NICs.

❑ Depending on the network operating system or the workstation, you might have to do some configuring of the NIC.

❑ EPROM stands for erasable programmable read-only memory and is a set of software instructions built into the interface card to perform its functions.

❑ Some network cards have jumpers on them to change the configuration.

❑ The premise behind Plug and Play software is to make configuration by the end user minimal if not nonexistent.

❑ When you are troubleshooting network problems, it is important to follow a logical troubleshooting methodology.

❑ There are three main ways for a device to communicate with components in a computer: The first and most commonly configured is the IRQ, or interrupt request. The second is the DMA, or direct memory access. The third is the I/O address, which is a specific memory address.

Network Components

❑ Hubs are the central location to which all cabling must connect in most topologies.

❑ When exam time comes, remember the difference between an active and passive hub: An active hub contains electronic components to boost the signal; a passive hub contains no power source or electronic components.

❑ A multistation access unit (MAU) is a device to which multiple workstations are connected in order to communicate on a Token Ring network.

❑ A common solution to traffic problems is to implement switches.

❑ Repeaters can be used in the Ethernet coaxial cable environment the same way they are used for UTP.

❑ Transceivers are the portion of the network interface that actually transmits and receives electrical signals across the transmission media.

❑ Wireless access points (WAS) are used to pickup the wireless transmissions from a PC wireless NIC and retransmit them on a backbone to which the servers are connected.

❑ WAS retransmit packets from a backbone to which the servers are connected to the wireless medium to be received by the PCs with the wireless NICs.

SELF TEST

The following questions will help you measure your understanding of the material presented in this chapter. Read all the choices carefully because there might be more than one correct answer. Choose all correct answers for each question.

Network Interface Cards

1. What does a network interface card add to a computer's functionality?

   A. It provides faster communication between the CPU and the hard disk.

   B. It provides the capability to communicate across a phone line to another computer.

   C. It provides the capability to communicate with other computers across a medium such as a CAT5 cable, with an RJ-45 connector connected to the computer to a hub.

   D. It provides the capability to save more information on a diskette than normal.

2. In order for a NIC to interact with the computer, what needs to be installed?

   A. The appropriate documentation for the user to take advantage of the features of the interface card.

   B. A driver, which is software that enables the NIC and the computer to communicate with each other.

   C. A bus, which enables the interface card to communicate through the various topologies of the Internet.

   D. Nothing.

3. Which of the following is a 16-bit computer bus?

   A. ISA

   B. EISA

   C. PCI

   D. MCA

4. Which of the following is a 32-bit computer bus?

   A. ISA

   B. EISA

   C. PCI

   D. MCA

5. Which of the following is a 64-bit computer bus?

   A. ISA

   B. EISA

   C. PCI

   D. MCA

6. Which of the following are methods that you can use to prevent electrostatic discharge when installing a NIC? (Choose all that apply.)

   A. Wear an antistatic wrist strap.

   B. Wear an antistatic ankle strap.

   C. Use antistatic spray on all components.

   D. Use an antistatic floor mat.

7. If the NIC is not software configurable, what is the most likely method of configuring the NIC with the appropriate IRQ?

   A. Diagnostics supplied by the manufacturer.

   B. Jumpers on the interface card itself.

   C. A setup utility from the manufacturer.

   D. Plug and Play will automatically set the IRQ.

8. Which of the following determines that a device can interrupt a process and request service?

   A. I/O address

   B. DMA

   C. IRC

   D. IRQ

9. Which of the following must be set to enable a device to directly access memory on the system, without the CPU's intervention?

   A. I/O address

   B. DMA

   C. IRC

   D. IRQ

10. If a card has the capability to connect to more than one kind of media, you might have to set which of the following in order to ensure connectivity?

    A. IRQ setting

    B. Link Light On/Off setting

    C. Transceiver type setting

    D. PCI setting

Network Components

11. Which of the following types of hubs does *not* regenerate the signal and therefore is not a repeater?

    A. Active

    B. Hybrid

    C. Passive

    D. Switching hub

12. What network component is used to extend the distance of the signal when transmitting over the normal specified distance?

    A. Passive hub

    B. NIC

    C. IRQ

    D. Repeater

13. What is the fourth step in troubleshooting, using the logical step-by-step plan presented in this chapter?

    A. Restart affected hardware.

    B. Segment the affected area.

    C. Identify any differences between the affected and unaffected areas.

    D. Get out additional tools, such as technical databases or diagnostics.

14. What does EPROM stand for?

    A. Enhanced programmable read-only memory

    B. Erasable programmable read-out memory

C. Enhanced permanent read-only memory

D. Erasable programmable read-only memory

15. If you are configuring a NIC in DOS, which of the following is the most likely extension for the file that determines the settings for the interface card?

A. .INF

B. .CON

C. .C.G.

D. .DOS

16. If you have a workstation that has no diskette drive or hard drive and you want to put the workstation on your network, what do you have to do?

A. Simply add any network card.

B. Add a network card that has a mini hard disk on it.

C. Add a network card that has an external connector for a diskette drive.

D. Add a network card that has a remote boot PROM chip.

17. What is an AUI connector?

A. A 9-pin DB male connector

B. A 15-pin D female connector

C. A 25-pin D female connector

D. Same as an RJ-45 connector

18. What type of network component enables each device to have the full bandwidth of the medium when transmitting?

A. Hub

B. Repeater

C. Switching hub

D. Transceiver

19. What does MAU stand for?

    A. Multisensing action unit

    B. Multistation access unit

    C. Multisplit addtransmission unit

    D. Multistation action unit

20. What type of hub enables more than one type of cable or media to connect to it?

    A. Passive

    B. Active

    C. Hybrid

    D. Multistation access unit

LAB QUESTION

You have been given the task of determining the requirements for a company that plans to implement a network in its office building. The executives require that at the present time a 10 Mbps network suffices, but it should be easily upgradable to 100 Mbps. The building has been purchased and was formerly owned by a company that dealt in selling stone, so the building is made of granite.

You have been told that the building does not allow for radio communication within it because the walls cause too much interference. The building is laid out as shown in Figure 2-9. There are five rooms of various sizes but of adequate space for the needs of the new business. There is a conduit to each room to allow for only two cables to be passed through to the next room. The rooms will be used as follows:

- Room 1 will be used by 22 employees with no extra requirements.

- Room 2 will be used as a type of storage room. Insurance regulations require no visible cabling due to the possibility of the cables becoming pulled and shorted by equipment used in the room. The equipment is used rarely and even then is used mostly after hours.

- Room 3 will be used by the existing employees of the company from the previous building they have outgrown. This network must be Token Ring since the executives prefer not to replace the equipment at this time.

- Room 4 will be used by the accounting and sales personnel who will share up-to-date information about sales and prices of products being sold to clients. The applications used by these employees will require at least 5 Mbps to 6 Mbps bandwidth at all times for the information to be as close to real time as possible.

- Room 5 will be the actual server room where the servers will reside.

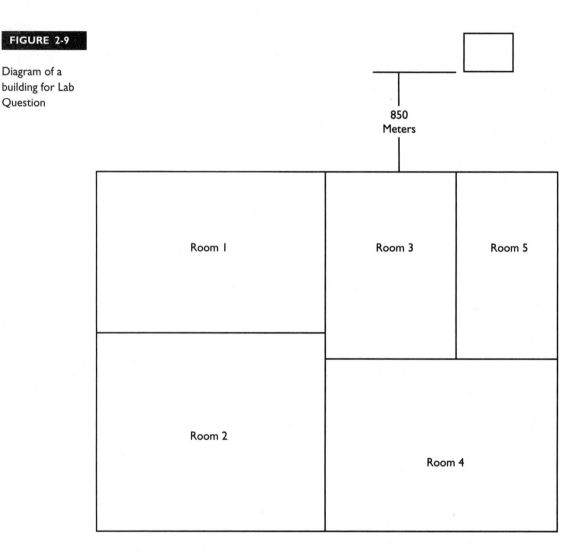

FIGURE 2-9

Diagram of a
building for Lab
Question

850
Meters

Room 1

Room 3

Room 5

Room 2

Room 4

There is also an outbuilding that is 850 meters from the main building. This building will require two PCs to be used to maintain inventory leaving the premises. The truck entrance is located next to the outbuilding and is used by the large semis to enter and exit the premises when delivering products to or from the building.

How would you cable this building to allow all the necessary requirements to be met?

SELF TEST ANSWERS

1. ☑ **C.** It provides the capability to communicate with other computers across a medium such as a CAT5 cable, with an RJ-45 connector connecting the computer to a hub. NICs are known by a variety of names, including network adapters, network cards, network adapter boards, and media access cards. Regardless of the name, they function by enabling computers to communicate across a network. NICs are often defined by the following criteria: 1) The type of Data Link protocol they support, such as an Ethernet adapter or a Token Ring adapter. 2) The type of media to which they connect. 3) The data bus for which they were designed.

   ☒ **A** is incorrect because a NIC does not help increase the bus speed between the CPU and the hard drive; that would require a different, faster system bus that is based on the system clock, which controls the bus speed. **B** is incorrect because a NIC does not provide communications on a phone line, which requires a modem. **D** is incorrect since the NIC has no bearing or connection to the diskette drive.

2. ☑ **B.** The computer must have a software driver installed to enable it to interact with the NIC, just as it must for any other peripheral device. These drivers enable the operating system and higher-level protocols to control the functions of the adapter. The NICs that exist in the various workstations on a network communicate with each other using their own unique addresses. The hardware address, or MAC address as it is commonly called, is unique on each network card on a network.

   ☒ **A** is incorrect because the documentation for a device or add-in card is for user reference only and has no bearing on the device's functionality. **C** is incorrect because all PCs must already have a bus for all internal components of the PC to communicate with one another. **D** is incorrect because the operating system does need to have instructions to communicate with a device, which requires a driver.

3. ☑ **A.** Industry Standard Architecture (ISA) was implemented on the earliest of computers. The ISA bus started in the IBM PC/XT and PC/AT models in the early 1990s. Almost every computer today has ISA expansion slots. The ISA architecture is a 16-bit interface.

   ☒ **B** is incorrect because the EISA bus is a 32-bit bus system. **C** is incorrect because a PCI bus is also a 32-bit system, or it can be 64-bit. **D** is incorrect because the MCA bus also has a 32-bit bus. Note that the EISA bus is backward compatible with 16-bit ISA cards, but the bus is 32 bits in size.

4. ☑ **B, C, and D.** EISA, PCI, and MCA are all 32-bit computer buses. EISA was brought about by companies like Hewlett-Packard and Compaq. The PCI bus was introduced by Intel; the MCA bus was introduced by IBM. All have different slot sizes, so each bus type has a specific connector on the card.

   ☒ **A.** ISA is incorrect because the bus size is only 16 bits. PCI has both 32- and 64-bit bus sizes.

5. ☑ C. PCI, or Peripheral Components Interconnect, is a 32-bit bus introduced by Intel. The bus is actually a 64-bit bus that is implemented as a 32-bit bus. The connector slots for PCI are shorter than ISA slots.

   ☒ A, B, and D are incorrect because the ISA bus is 16 bits and the EISA bus is 32 bits, as is the MCA bus.

6. ☑ A, B, and D. Wearing an antistatic wrist strap or ankle strap or using an antistatic floor mat are the methods that you can use to prevent electrostatic discharge when you are installing components. Electrostatic discharge can damage components inside the computer.

   ☒ C, using antistatic spray on all components, is incorrect.

7. ☑ B. The jumpers on an interface card can do many things. The most common things that they do are set the IRQ and the I/O address. Jumpers configure a card that is not software configurable.

   ☒ A is incorrect because diagnostic utilities are used to test the functionality of a NIC. C and D are incorrect because the setup utility provided by the manufacturer or Plug and Play are both forms of software configuration, not NIC configuration.

8. ☑ D. The device uses the interrupt request, or IRQ, to interrupt the processor and request service. There are 16 IRQ lines, many of which are routinely committed to devices such as the disk controllers and serial and parallel ports. A common configuration for a network card can use IRQ 3 (which is also used by the serial port COM2), IRQ 5, or IRQ 10. Like the I/O address, the IRQ must be chosen so that the card does not conflict with another device.

   ☒ A is incorrect because the I/O address is used by the system devices to designate the device being communicated with, just like a MAC address on a network. B is incorrect because DMA is the access used by devices to read and write data directly to memory (RAM), thus bypassing the processor. C is incorrect because IRC, or Internet Relay Chat, is a protocol used to perform Internet chats.

9. ☑ B. Direct memory access, or DMA, is a process whereby some devices can directly access memory on the system, without the intervention of the CPU. This feature offloads the processor from having to handle these data transfers and speeds the transfer process. Any device with DMA capability has a DMA channel, which it uses to control direct memory access. Since many hardware devices do not use this feature, there is more flexibility in configuring this setting.

   ☒ A is incorrect because the I/O address is used by the system devices to designate the device being communicated with, just like a MAC address on a network. C is incorrect because Internet Relay Chat (IRC) is a protocol used to perform Internet. D is incorrect because the IRQ is an interrupt a device uses to get the attention of the processor to allow it to be able to use the CPU to process information.

10. ☑   C. The transceiver type setting is required for network adapters that are capable of attaching to more than one media type. Typical cards of this nature include Ethernet cards that have both twisted-pair and coaxial connectors. This is one of the more common oversights in configuring a NIC and renders the card nonfunctional if configured for the wrong media connection. To alleviate this problem, some cards of this type have an Auto setting that causes the card to search for the transceiver that has media connected to it.

☒   A is incorrect because the IRQ setting allows you to specify that the IRQ is used to get the processor's attention, allowing the device to get some processing time. B and D are incorrect because the Link Light On/Off setting and the PCI setting do not exists.

Network Components

11. ☑   C. The function of a passive hub is simply to receive data from one port of the hub and send it out to the other ports. For example, an eight-port hub receives data from Port 3 and then resend that data to Ports 1, 2, 4, 5, 6, 7, and 8. It is as simple as that. A passive hub contains no power source or electrical components. There is no signal processing. It simply attaches the ports internally and enables communication to flow through the network.

☒   A is incorrect because the active hub does regenerate the signal, since it is powered. B is incorrect because, even though the hybrid hub is powered, the only difference between it and a regular hub is that the hybrid hub has connectors for different media types. D is incorrect because a switch is always powered and therefore will regenerate the data signals.

12. ☑   D. Repeaters can be used in the Ethernet coaxial cable environment the same way they are used for UTP. Thickwire can normally transmit a distance of 500 meters, which can be extended by introducing repeaters. Thinwire can normally transmit a distance of 185 meters and can also be extended by using a repeater. This, of course, is the advantage to using a repeater. If your network layout exceeds the normal specifications of cable, you can use repeaters to build your network. Doing so allows for greater lengths when planning your cabling scheme.

☒   A is incorrect because a passive hub does not regenerate signals, since it is not powered. B is incorrect because a NIC generates a signal but does not regenerate a signal. C is incorrect because the IRQ is used to get the CPU's attention by interrupting it to perform processing.

13. ☑   B. The fourth step is to segment the affected area by dividing the area in half. The best example of this is in thinwire coax. Determine the midpoint of the cable and place a terminator on each end. One half of the cable should now be working and is obviously not your problem.

☒   A, C, and D are incorrect because none of them is the fourth step of the process.

14. ☑ **D.** Erasable programmable read-only memory. Every interface card, whether it is a network card, a video card, or a sound card, comes with an EPROM. EPROM is a set of software instructions built into the interface card to perform its functions. An EPROM is sometimes *flash able*. This means that the software in the EPROM can be upgraded. This is done by downloading an update from the manufacturer and then using a utility to write the update out to the flash memory.

    ☒ **A, B,** and **C** are incorrect because they do not stand for EEPROM.

15. ☑ **C.** Depending on the network operating system or the workstation, you might need to do some configuring of the NIC. This is a definite if you have a DOS or Windows 3.1 workstation. The DOS-level drivers have either a configuration for (.C.G.) or an initialization file (.IN) that determines how the card functions.

    ☒ **A** is incorrect because .INF is used for information files in Windows. **B** is incorrect because .CON is used to redirect output with the console or video monitor. **D** is incorrect because DOS is not a valid standard extension.

16. ☑ **D.** The most common EPROM on a network card is the boot PROM. The boot PROM boots the workstation if there is no hard drive or diskette from which to boot.

    ☒ **A** is incorrect because a NIC requires a boot PROM. **B** is incorrect because a mini hard disk does not exist. **C** is incorrect because NICs do not have a hard drives or diskette drive connectors.

17. ☑ **B.** An AUI connector is a 15-pin D female connector. With an external transceiver, the actual media connection is made external to the NIC using a small device that attaches via an extension cable. These types of connections use an adapter unit interface (AUI) connector, also called a Digital-Intel-Xerox (DIX) connector, on the back of the NIC. The AUI connector is a female 15-pin D connector that looks very much like a joystick port.

    ☒ **A** is incorrect because a 9-pin male connector is found on the back of PCs and is the serial port. **C** is incorrect because a 25-pin connector is found on the back of a PC as the printer connection. **D** is incorrect because the RJ-45 is used with twisted-pair cable networks.

18. ☑ **C.** Switching is a fairly involved process and allows the device to have the full bandwidth when transmitting.

    ☒ **A** is incorrect because the bandwidth is divided among all used ports on a hub. **B** is incorrect because a repeater does not split bandwidth, since it is used only to receive signals on one cable and regenerate the signal on another cable. **D** is incorrect because a transceiver is the connection point on a NIC and does not allow for multiple users to send data through the transceiver. The bandwidth on the transceiver is dedicated to the PC in which the NIC is installed.

19. ☑   **B.** A MAU, or multistation access unit, is a device to which multiple workstations are connected in order to communicate on a Token Ring network. Sometimes a MAU is also referred to as a *hub*. Be careful not to confuse a MAU with a UTP hub; their actual functions are quite different.

    ☒   **A, C,** and **D** are incorrect because they are not the representation of MAU.

20. ☑   **C.** A hybrid hub is one that can use many types of cables in addition to UTP cabling. A hybrid hub is usually cabled using thinwire or thickwire Ethernet. A hybrid hub is the most common type of hub. Hybrid hubs are used to interconnect hubs that are farther than the 100-meter limitation of 10BaseT.

    ☒   **A** and **B** are incorrect because active and passive hubs have only one type of connector type; they differ only in that the active hub is powered and the passive hub is not. **D** is incorrect because a MAU is for Token Ring networks and does not support multiple connector types.

LAB ANSWER

Initially, the cabling will all be Category 5. The network needs to be a minimum of 10 Mbps to allow for the 5 Mbps to 6 Mbps bandwidth required by the sales and accounting departments. Category 5 cables allow for upgrading later to a 100 Mbps network when needed. The cabling to the outbuilding should be fiber optic to be able to cover the distance of the 850 meters. This could be a Thicknet cable with a repeater in between to allow for the distance over 500 meters but would require placement and a power source for the repeater. To be able to use fiber optic, the company needs a converter of some type to convert the fiber-optic cable to a Category 5 cable to allow for connection with the rest of the network. This could be accomplished by a special router that has both fiber-optic and RJ-45 connectors. There will also need to be a router with both fiber-optic and RJ-45 connectors in the outbuilding.

Now for the server room (Room 5). We should start here, since this will be the center of the network itself. There should be a switch in the room to allow for dedicated bandwidth to the sales and accounting departments in Room 4, which will also require a switch to allow for the connection of multiple computers. The server in Room 5 should have not only an Ethernet card but also a Token Ring card that is connected to a cable that goes to Room 3, which has a MAU in it for the Token Ring that was connected in the previous building.

Room 1 will need a standard hub or even a switch to allow for the employees here to have connectivity to the network.

A Category 5 cable will pass from Room 5 to Room 4 and through to Room 2, to be connected to a WAP device. This configuration negates the requirement for the Room 2 PCs for regular cabling of the sort the other rooms will have installed. This wiring configuration is shown in Figure 2-10.

FIGURE 2-10

Diagram of
a building for
Lab Answer

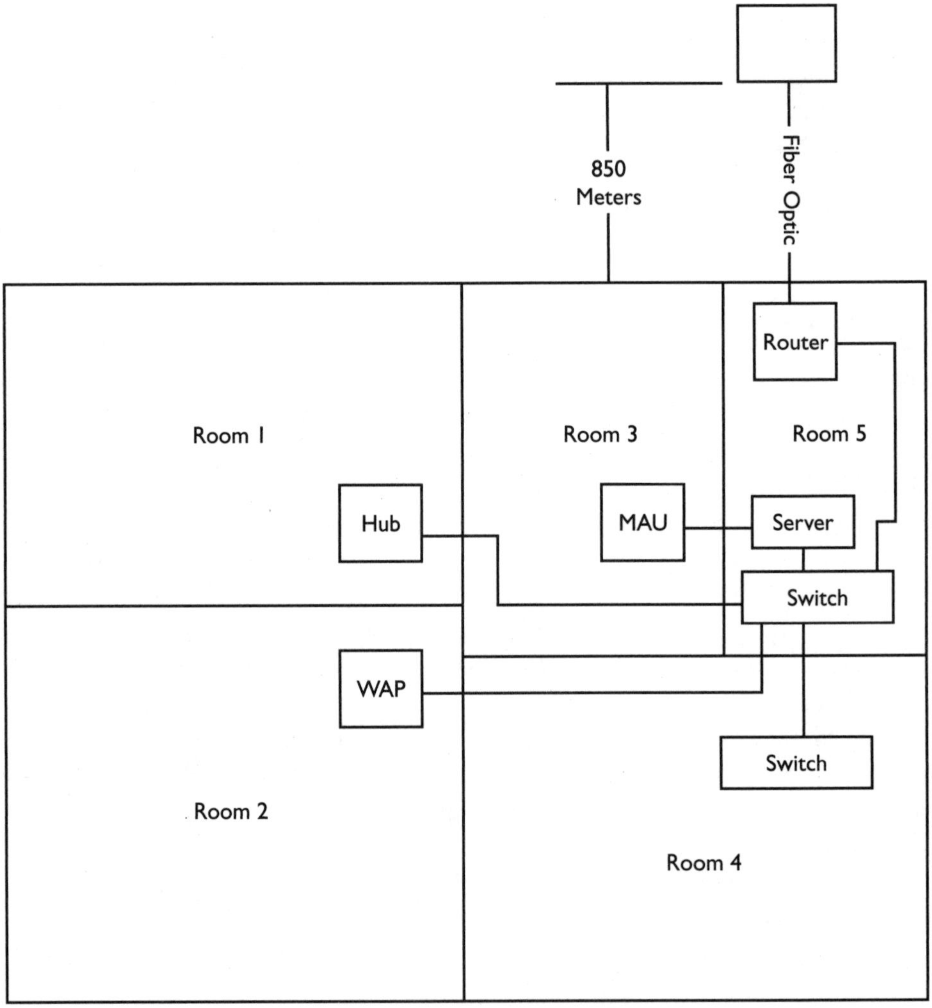

COMPUTING TECHNOLOGY INDUSTRY ASSOCIATION

3

Data Link, Network, and Transport Layers

CERTIFICATION OBJECTIVES

3.01   Data Link Layer Concepts

3.02   Network Layer Concepts

3.03   Transport Layer Concepts

✓   Two-Minute Drill

Q&A   Self Test

This chapter covers the intricacies of the three layers that reside north of the Physical layer of the OSI model: the Data Link layer, the Network layer, and the Transport layer. We begin with the Data Link layer, which packages data into smaller frames for easier routing across the network. Next, we cover the Network layer, which addresses these frames with the source and destinations, so the frames know where they are going. Finally, we cover the Transport layer, which has the function of making sure these frames are reordered correctly and that an acknowledgment is sent to the source computer confirming that the frame was received. Each of these layers performs a unique function, and work together, one continuing where the other layer leaves off.

This chapter also presents you with the network devices that are located within these layers, such as the bridge and router. This information is crucial for your exam. Of equal importance is the concept of routing. We discuss the topic in detail, including the differences between routable and nonroutable protocols, and when to choose one over another.

CERTIFICATION OBJECTIVE 3.01

Data Link Layer Concepts

The Data Link layer handles many issues for communicating on a simple network (the Network layer discussed in the next section performs the functions necessary to communicate beyond a single physical network). This layer takes the frames generated by the upper layers and disassembles the frames into bits for transmission. When receiving messages from the network, it reassembles this information back into frames to send to the upper layers. This layer actually does a lot more than just break apart and put together frames.

The IEEE 802 model (discussed later in this chapter) breaks the Data Link layer into two sublayers: *logical link control* (LLC) and *media access control* (MAC). The LLC layer starts and maintains connections between devices. When you send data from your workstation to a server on the same network segment, the LLC sublayer establishes a connection with that server. The MAC sublayer enables multiple devices to share the media. Most LANs have more than one computer (of course!), and the MAC sublayer determines who may speak and when.

Another important job of the Data Link layer is *addressing.* The MAC sublayer maintains *physical device addresses* for communicating with other devices (commonly referred to as *MAC addresses*). Each device on the network must have a unique MAC address; otherwise, the network will not know exactly where to send information when a node requests it. For example, how would the postal service know where to send your mail without your address?

Finally, the Data Link layer manages *flow control* and *error correction* between devices in a simple network. In more complex internetworks, it is up to the Network layer and other upper layers to perform these functions.

MAC Addresses

Most computer network interface cards (NICs) provide the MAC address as an address burned into the card. Some older network cards required an administrator to set the address manually using switches. Even with a permanent MAC address burned into the card, some protocols enable you to define this address via software, although this is unusual.

The MAC address is used to communicate only on the local network. When transmitting to a server on the same LAN segment, the protocol uses the MAC addresses to communicate between the two computers. If the server is located on another network segment across a WAN, the MAC address of the nearest router (we discuss routers later in this chapter) is used to send the information, and it is up to the router to forward the data.

EXERCISE 3-1

CertCam 3-1

Determining Your Local Machine's MAC Address

In this exercise, you will learn how to determine the MAC address of your computer. This can be helpful if you are having address resolution problems and need to investigate MAC address and IP address issues.

1. Open a command prompt window. In Windows 95/98, you can select Run from the Start menu, enter **COMMAND** in the space provided, and then click OK. In Windows NT, you can also select Run from the Start menu, but enter **CMD** in the space provided.

2. When the command prompt appears, type **WINIPCFG** and press ENTER if you are using a Windows 95 or Windows 98 machine. If you are using Windows NT, type **IPCONFIG /ALL**. Figure 3-1 shows the dialog box that appears when you are using Windows 95 or Windows 98.

WINIPCFG from
a Windows 95/98
machine

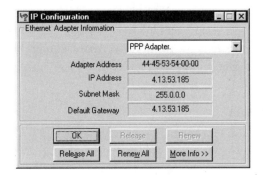

You can see that the adapter address, known as the MAC address, is present, as well as the IP address.

The following is the output from a Windows NT machine when the IPCONFIG /ALL command is issued:

```
Windows NT IP Configuration
    Host Name . . . . . . . . . : nevermore.dreamingneonblack.com
    DNS Servers . . . . . . . . : 172.18.160.224
    Node Type . . . . . . . . . : Broadcast
    NetBIOS Scope ID. . . . . . :
    IP Routing Enabled. . . . . : No
    WINS Proxy Enabled. . . . . : No
    NetBIOS Resolution Uses DNS : Yes
Token Ring adapter IBMTRP1:
    Description . . . . . . . . : IBM PCI Token-Ring Adapter
    Physical Address. . . . . . : 00-20-35-29-C5-29
    DHCP Enabled. . . . . . . . : Yes
    IP Address. . . . . . . . . : 172.18.193.104
    Subnet Mask . . . . . . . . : 255.255.252.0
    Default Gateway . . . . . . : 172.18.192.254
    DHCP Server . . . . . . . . : 172.18.160.242
    Lease Obtained. . . . . . . : Tuesday, January 19, 1999 7:29:32 AM
    Lease Expires . . . . . . . : Tuesday, January 19, 1999 7:29:32 PM
```

```
Ethernet adapter NdisWan5:
    Description . . . . . . . . : NdisWan Adapter
    Physical Address. . . . . . : 00-00-00-00-00-00
    DHCP Enabled. . . . . . . . : No
    IP Address. . . . . . . . . : 0.0.0.0
    Subnet Mask . . . . . . . . : 0.0.0.0
    Default Gateway . . . . . . :
```

As you can see, there is much more information with the IPCONFIG /ALL command than with the WINIPCFG command.

There is another little known way to get the MAC address from a Windows computer: the ARP command. ARP is an acronym for Address Resolution Protocol, which is the portion of the TCP/IP protocol that resolves an IP address to a MAC address. In order to send packets on a TCP/IP network, you need to resolve the IP address to a MAC address. A special packet will be broadcast on the network from the source computer that is trying to determine the destination computer's MAC address. Each host on the network will respond, indicating whether the address in question belongs to it or not. Every computer that doesn't match the address in question will disregard the message. The destination host will recognize its IP address in the request and send a response to the source host that contains the destination host's MAC address. When the source host receives the news, it will use the newly attained physical address to send the packet directly to the destination host.

You can view, add, or delete entries located in your ARP cache. You will not find much use for this utility; however, you should be aware of its existence. The –a switch is used to view the contents of the ARP cache. Before I initiated the ARP command on my machine, I verified that there were no entries in the cache. I then browsed through Network Neighborhood on a Windows NT machine and clicked on a couple of servers. I went back to the command prompt and typed the ARP –a command. The output from the command is shown here:

```
C:\arp -a
Interface: 172.18.193.104 on Interface 2
    Internet Address        Physical Address        Type
    172.18.192.249          00-06-29-87-d3-48        dynamic
    172.18.194.209          00-20-35-29-c5-d2        dynamic
```

A few minutes later, I did the same command and the ARP cache was empty. This is because on Windows NT, the entries in the ARP cache are purged if they are not used within two minutes. If they are used, the entries remain there for 10 minutes.

Now view the contents of the ARP command with the –g switch:

```
Interface: 172.18.193.104 on Interface 2
  Internet Address      Physical Address     Type
  172.18.192.249        00-06-29-87-d3-48    dynamic
  172.18.194.209        00-20-35-29-c5-d2    dynamic
```

Look familiar? That's because the output from the ARP –a and ARP –g command is identical; you use both commands to view the contents of the ARP cache.

Bridges

A bridge is a network connectivity device that connects two different networks and makes them appear to be one network. The bridge filters local traffic between the two networks and copies all other traffic to the other side of the bridge. Bridges operate at the Data Link layer. Bridges use the Data Link layer and its physical addressing to join several networks into a single network efficiently.

Network Segmentation

A bridge is a simple way to accomplish network segmentation. Placing a bridge between two different segments of the network decreases the amount of traffic on each of the local networks. Although this does accomplish network segmentation, most network administrators opt to use routers or switches, which we discuss later in the chapter.

Bridges segment the network by MAC addresses. When one of the workstations connected to Network 1 transmits a packet, the packet is copied across the bridge as long as the packet's destination is not on Network 1. A bridge uses a bridge routing table to calculate which MAC addresses are on which network.

Source Routing and Spanning Tree Bridges

Of the two primary types of bridges, source routing and spanning tree bridges, there is no major difference except for their applications. The result of both types of bridges is the same, even though the media they are used on are different. Spanning tree bridges are used for Ethernet networks, and source routing bridges are used to connect rings in a Token Ring network.

Building a Bridge Routing Table

Most bridges maintain their own bridge routing table dynamically and do not require an administrator to manage it unless he or she wishes to make a manual change to the table. To make a manual change to your bridge routing table, refer to the instructions that came with your bridge. Figure 3-2 illustrates a bridge with a bridge routing table.

OSI Data Link Layer

A bridge is constantly tracking the destination MAC addresses of all packets it receives. If the bridge determines that the packets should cross the bridge, it passes them across. Since the only information the bridge knows about the packet is the MAC address of the destination, the bridge is said to reside in the Data Link layer of the OSI model.

802 Project Model

The Institute of Electrical and Electronics Engineers (IEEE) is a large and respected professional organization that is also active in defining standards. The 802 committee of the IEEE defines one set of standards dear to the hearts of most network professionals. Twelve subcommittees of the 802 committee define low-level LAN and WAN access

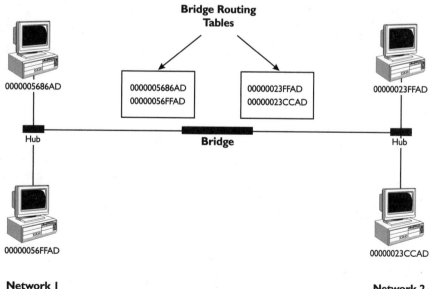

FIGURE 3-2

A bridge connects two local networks

Network I

Network 2

protocols. Most of the protocols defined by the 802 committee reside in the Physical and Data Link layers of the OSI model.

IEEE 802 Categories

As the use of LANs increased, standards were needed to define consistency and compatibility. The IEEE began a project in February 1980, known as Project 802 for the year and month it began. IEEE 802 is a set of standards given to the various LAN architectures such as Ethernet, Token Ring, and ArcNet by the LAN standards committee. The goal of the committee was to define more of the OSI's Data Link layer, which already contained the LLC and MAC sublayers. Several 802 subcommittee protocols are the heart of PC networking.

802.2

The LLC sublayer is used by other protocols defined by the 802 committee. This sublayer allows Network layer protocols to be designed separately from the low-level Physical layer and MAC sublayer protocols.

The LLC adds header information that identifies the upper layer protocols sending the frame. The header can also specify destination processes for the data (the *service address* discussed earlier).

802.3

Based on the original Ethernet network from DIX (Digital-Intel-Xerox), 802.3 is *the* standard for Ethernet networks today. The only difference between 802.3 Ethernet and DIX Ethernet V.2 is frame type. The two Ethernet networks can use the same physical network, but devices on one standard cannot communicate with devices on the other standard.

The MAC sublayer uses Carrier Sense Multiple Access with Collision Detection (CSMA/CD) for access to the physical medium. CSMA/CD keeps devices on the network from interfering with one another when trying to transmit; if they do, a *collision* occurs. To reduce collisions, CSMA/CD devices listen to the network before transmitting. If the network is "quiet" (no other devices are transmitting), the device can send its data. Since two devices can think the network is clear and start transmitting at the same time, resulting in a collision, all devices listen as they transmit. If a device detects another device transmitting at the same time, a collision occurs. The device stops transmitting and sends a signal to alert other nodes about the collision. Then, all the nodes stop transmitting and wait a random amount of time before they begin the process again.

CSMA/CD doesn't stop collisions from happening, but it helps manage the situations when they do occur. In fact, collisions are a normal part of Ethernet operation. It's only when collisions begin to occur frequently that you need to become concerned.

exam
ⓦatch

The exam leans quite heavily on Ethernet technology, because of its dominance in the marketplace. Pay attention to special characteristics of the various media types of Ethernet.

Ethernet has evolved over the years to include a number of popular specifications. These specifications are due in part to the media variety they employ, such as coaxial, twisted-pair, and fiber-optic cabling.

- The 10Base5 specification, commonly referred to as Thicknet, was the original Ethernet specification and has a maximum distance of 500 meters (approximately 1640 feet) with a maximum speed of 2.94 to 10 Mbps.

- The 10Base2 specification, commonly referred to as Thinnet, uses a thinner coaxial cable than 10Base5 does and has a maximum distance of 185 meters (approximately 607 feet) with a maximum speed of 10 Mbps.

- The 10BaseT specification uses twisted-pair cabling with a maximum distance of 100 meters (approximately 328 feet) with a speed of 10 to 100 Mbps.

802.5

Although Token Ring was first designed in the late 1960s, IBM's token passing implementation did not become a standard until 1985. It became IEEE standard 802.5 under the IEEE Project 802. The 802.5 standard was modeled after the IBM Token Ring network, which had been in use for many years before the standard was even developed.

The 802.5 network introduced a unique access method: token passing. The Token Ring IEEE 802.5 standard passes a special frame known as the *token* around the network. This token is generated by the first computer that comes online on the Token Ring network. When a workstation wants to transmit data, it grabs the token and then begins transmitting. This computer will send a data frame on the network with the address of the destination computer. The destination computer receives the data frame, modifies it, and sends it on to the network back to the destination computer, indicating successful transmission of data. When the workstation is finished transmitting, the token is released back on to the network. This ensures that workstations will not simultaneously communicate on the network, as in the CSMA/CD access method.

802.11

The IEEE 802.11 standard addresses wireless networking (discussed in Chapters 1 and 2).

This standard includes the wireless access point (WAP) devices and the wireless network interface cards (NICs) that are used to send and receive broadcasts from the cell or WAP device.

The WAPs and wireless NICs can be set to use different frequencies to allow for cell overlap. This technology does not include the same technology used by cell phones to manage movement of PCs or mobile devices. The wireless NIC is set to a specific frequency and must be changed manually to be able to communicate with another cell. This means that a PC cannot be moved from one cell area to another without changing frequency, unless for some reason the cells operate on the same frequency and have no overlap of coverage area.

FROM THE CLASSROOM

A Word about Fiber Distributed Data Interface (FDDI) Networks

FDDI is not actually an IEEE standard, but an enhancement to the Token Ring topology. FDDI is a fiber-optic network comprised of two rings instead of one. Each ring has a token which is circling in opposite directions, but only one ring is used at a time.

Since the topology is actually using fiber-optic cable, the network operates at 100 Mbps and is fault tolerant. Each PC and network device is connected to both rings. If one ring breaks, both rings are used in such a way as to make one continuous ring. If both rings break, the network fails.

Fiber-optic cable also allows for a much larger ring than other cable media do. Fiber optic also disallows electro-magnetic interference (EMI) or radio frequency interference (RFI), which is a possibility with copper media.

—*Jarret W. Buse, MCT, MCSE+Internet, CCNA, CNA, A+, Network+*

SCENARIO & SOLUTION

Which 802 standard separates the Network layer from the Physical layer?	802.2
Which standard defines Ethernet networks?	802.3
Which standard defines Token Ring networks and how they operate?	802.5
Which standard addresses networks that do not use physical cabling?	802.11

exam
ⓦatch

Expect to be asked about the IEEE standards, especially the four listed here. For example, know which 802 standard maps to Ethernet, which IEEE standard Token Ring maps to, and which one maps to wireless networks. Don't expect any questions on the less common IEEE standards; they have been omitted here for that very reason.

CERTIFICATION OBJECTIVE 3.02

Network Layer Concepts

The Network layer is one of the most complex and important layers. The Network layer manages addressing and delivering packets on a complex *internetwork*. This layer must determine a route by which to route the packet from the source to the destination computer. Factors such as network conditions, speed of the network, and priority of the packet determine the route to the destination computer through the internetwork. Internetworks are joined by devices known as *routers*, which use *routing tables* and *routing algorithms* to determine how to send data from one network to another.

The most obvious example of an internetwork is the Internet. The Internet is very large, spanning the entire globe, and consists of almost every conceivable type of computer, from palmtops to mainframes.

The Network layer must also take large packets and break them down into smaller units that are more conducive to traveling over many different complex routes. The packets must be broken into smaller pieces by the sending computer, and then reassembled by the Network layer of the destination computer once the packets arrive.

Unique Network IDs

In order to operate on an internetwork, each network that participates must be assigned a *network ID*. This address differentiates each network from every other network that forms the internetwork. When sending data from one network to another, the routers along the way use the network ID to determine the next step in the journey. Each host within this network ID uses the same network ID, much like each person or business within a zip code area uses the same zip code. The Postal Service sends your letter to the post office for your zip code first, and then your local post office uses your unique street address to determine where you are located within that zip code. In Chapter 4 you will see how the network ID portion of the IP address is crucial to routing IP packets effectively.

Routing

Routing protocols are quite different from bridging protocols. Bridging is designed to combine packets from multiple physical networks and consolidate them into one virtual network. Routing is designed to separate a physical network into multiple virtual networks.

The manner in which bridging and routing protocols operate also varies. A bridging protocol enables all traffic to cross that is not destined for the local network. A routing protocol enables traffic to cross that is destined for networks on the other side of the router.

Routing also requires intelligent devices that can determine the most effective path to the destination computer through a complex web of subnetworks. Routers can also remember the address of each segment, ensuring quicker delivery time without the need to "ask" other routers the address to a remote network.

Routers are also very popular because they filter unwanted traffic such as broadcasts from other network segments. Broadcasts are data packets that are sent to all PCs on the network. Broadcasts slow the network, since no other PC can transmit data until the network is clear of transmissions.

Traffic is also isolated so that one extremely busy segment, such as a high-bandwidth CAD department, will not overwhelm the users in another segment.

Figure 3-3 illustrates the concept of two distinct networks separated by a router or gateway. The central host has two network cards, each with an address for its respective subnets. As discussed earlier, each network must have a unique ID. In Figure 3-3, the network on the left has a network ID of 223.4.5, and the network on the right has a network ID of 223.4.6. On this TCP/IP network, the subnet mask is 255.255.255.0. Don't worry if you don't understand exactly what a subnet mask is; after reading Chapter 4, you will be versed in subnet masking!

Router and Brouter Differences

A brouter is a hybrid of both a bridge and a router and has a connection to more than two networks. When the brouter receives a packet from one segment of the network, it must first determine what the destination IP address is. If the packet is not destined for a port of the brouter, it sends it to the gateway address. If the packet is destined for a port of the brouter, it bridges the packet to the other port instead of routing it.

Remember, when you are making the decision to use either a bridge or a router on a network, you must consider whether you need to "isolate" or "consolidate" segments of the network. Routers are much more popular (and more expensive) than bridges because the most common network protocol is TCP/IP, which is used

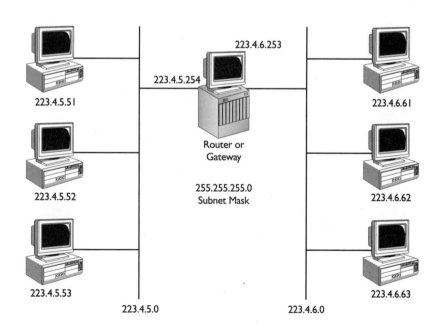

FIGURE 3-3

Subnetworks connected by a router or a gateway

to create many "logical" networks out of one physical network. A bridge is incapable of taking advantage of subnetting networks with the complex TCP/IP protocol, which requires a tremendous amount of routing. However, you can use a brouter when your network consists of both routable and nonroutable protocols, such as TCP/IP and NetBEUI. Brouting might provide a more cost-effective means of bridging and routing in one unit, rather than using two individual components.

Figure 3-4 illustrates the placement in the OSI model for both the router and the bridge.

Remember, the higher the network device is within the OSI layer, the more intelligent the device is. A router can make more intelligent decisions based on the address of the packet than the bridge can. Therefore, a router is used for more complex protocols, such as TCP/IP, which employs subnetting a network extensively.

Routable and Nonroutable Protocols within the Network Layer

An important difference between some protocols is their ability to be routed. A routable protocol is a protocol that can have packets transferred across a router. This section discusses exactly which packets are routable and which are not. It might seem that a routable protocol is the best solution for your network, but routable protocols require that additional information be included in the packet header for routing purposes; for example, a time-to-live (TTL) field.

If your company wants to route packets to remote networks, you will be dealing with routers to route these packets. You can see that the choice of protocol often makes the decision for you regarding which network device you will use to isolate or consolidate your network.

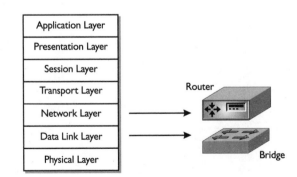

FIGURE 3-4

Where bridges and routers are located within the OSI model

| Application Layer |
| Presentation Layer |
| Session Layer |
| Transport Layer |
| Network Layer |
| Data Link Layer |
| Physical Layer |

Router

Bridge

TCP/IP

The Transmission Control Protocol/Internet Protocol (TCP/IP) is the protocol most used today. TCP/IP, a routable protocol, is very robust and is commonly associated with UNIX systems. TCP/IP was originally designed in the 1970s to be used by the Defense Advanced Research Projects Agency (DARPA) and the Department of Defense (DoD) to connect systems across the country. This design required the capability to cope with unstable network conditions. Therefore, the design of TCP/IP included the capability to reroute packets. You will learn much more about the TCP/IP protocol and routing in Chapter 4. Note: Only IP of the TCP/IP protocol resides in the Network layer. The TCP portion of the protocol is part of the Transport layer.

IPX/SPX/NWLink

Internetwork Packet Exchange/Sequenced Packet Exchange (IPX/SPX) is the protocol most commonly used with Novell NetWare and is the default protocol for NetWare versions before version 5. IPX/SPX, a routable protocol, is a very fast and highly established protocol, but it is not used on the Internet. Novell developed IPX/SPX for use in NetWare. The protocol NWLink IPX/SPX that ships with Windows 95 and Windows NT was written by Microsoft and is fully compatible with the Novell IPX/SPX protocol. Note: Only IPX of the IPX/SPX protocol resides in the Network layer. The SPX portion of the protocol is part of the Transport layer.

AppleTalk

AppleTalk is the proprietary protocol developed by Apple Computer, and is rarely found in network environments where Apple computers are not present. AppleTalk is a routable protocol.

NetBEUI

NetBIOS Extended User Interface (NetBEUI) is a transport protocol commonly found in smaller networks. NetBEUI is not frequently used in large networks and will become less used in the future because it is not a routable protocol. NetBEUI is an extremely quick protocol with little overhead because of its inability to route packets. NetBEUI is also very easy to configure; actually, you don't need to configure anything once you have the NetBEUI protocol installed and bound to the network adapter.

on the **Job**

On the first day of work at a new job, I sat down and attempted to log on with my newly created Windows NT account. After I entered my username and password, my workstation took an excessive amount of time to authenticate me. I commented on this to a coworker, who told me the network was very slow, and kept getting worse. I later learned that day that the company used TCP/IP and continued to use NetBEUI (a broadcast-intensive protocol) as a means of fault tolerance in case of a problem with TCP/IP. Having both of these protocols on every machine and bound to every adapter was saturating the network. Management knew this, but a standard is a standard. To solve this problem, every workstation will have to have the NetBEUI protocol removed, which will minimize broadcasts and increase performance.

exam **Watch**

Expect to have a question or two on the exam regarding the appropriate use of a bridge, brouter, or router. With the information we provide here, you should do just fine. Bear in mind that you will probably see a long, complex scenario with tons of information meant to confuse you.

Now that you know the differences between the network devices, here is a quick reference of possible scenario questions on the choice of one device over another, and the appropriate answers.

SCENARIO & SOLUTION

I need to minimize broadcast storms…	Don't use a bridge. They pass all broadcasts to the other network.
I use a routable protocol…	Don't use a bridge. Use a brouter or a router, which can route the protocol appropriately.
I only use NetBEUI…	There's your answer; NetBEUI is not routable, so you cannot use a brouter or router.
I need to separate or segment…	Use a brouter or a router. Routers isolate networks, not consolidate them.
I use a routing protocol and a nonrouting protocol…	Use a brouter. The brouter can route a routable protocol while it passes a nonroutable protocol.

Static and Dynamic Routing

There is a huge difference between the two types of routing: *static* and *dynamic*. Early routers had to be programmed exactly for which networks and interfaces they could route between, especially if there were many network interfaces. This is static routing, which consists of adding, maintaining, and deleting routes of the network routing devices by the network administrator. In a small company, this might not be much of a chore, but for medium to large networks, this can be nearly impossible. These larger networks usually employ many logical subnets, which requires you to update the route tables on each routing device. If these remote subnets are connected by routers with static route tables, you have to add the exact static route in order to communicate between the two subnets.

Table 3-1 is an example of what is contained in the routing table. In this table, you only specify the router to be used to reach your destination, not the actual destination itself. Also, notice the column for hops. This is what determines which route is the most efficient, similar to "Name That Tune." If a route claims it can reach the destination in one less hop than the next router can, let it prove it. If there are two identical routes to the same destination, the route with the fewest hops will be used.

One change to a network address means visiting every routing device that employs static routing and updating the entry. What do we do if our network is fairly large and complex? We must then use routing devices capable of dynamically updating the route tables.

Dynamic routing does not require the network administrator to edit complex routing tables in order to communicate with other networks or segments. These routers communicate with each other using a powerful routing protocol such as Routing Information Protocol (RIP) or Open Shortest Path First (OSPF). They can also query other routers for updated route information, which can create more efficient

TABLE 3-1	Destination	Adjacent Router	Hops
An example of a routing table	Network 1	Router A	1
	Network 1	Router B	2
	Network 2	Router B	2
	Network 2	Router C	3
	Network 3	Router D	3

paths for sending packets, or locate an alternative route if the original route fails. The routers can broadcast the routes they discover to neighboring routers, and, in turn, accept routes from other neighboring routers. The Internet is comprised of many dynamic routers. Can you imagine having to update a static routing table on thousands of static routers? I don't think so.

These dynamic routers, however, cannot update the route tables of static routers or nondynamic routers. There are a few situations in which integrating static and dynamic routers is acceptable:

- **When you have a router at either end of a slow WAN link**   This router will not increase traffic by broadcasting updated route information to the router on the other end of the link.

- **When you require a packet to travel the same path each time to a remote network**   Add the path you would like the packet to take to reach the destination network. You cannot enter the entire path over several routers, only the path to the first router.

- **When you want to configure a static router to point toward a dynamic router to take advantage of the dynamic router *indirectly***   This is the next best thing to using a dynamic router. You can hand off the packet to the dynamic router and let this router determine the most efficient path to the destination based on the paths it learned from neighboring dynamic routers.

Of course, dynamic routers cost much more. Although you can add static paths to a newer dynamic router, you cannot enable dynamic routing on an older static router. In addition, dynamic routing generates continuous traffic from the routers with route update information.

Comparing Static and Dynamic Routing

The static routing setup is more appropriate if you have only two networks. If your network has three or four parallel networks, then static routing might still be useful, although dynamic routing would be easier to set up.

However, the actual setup is far more complex. You cannot simply have the routers route to the other network by assigning the gateway addresses to the other NIC. This simply moves the packet to the other side, when the router actually needs to send the packet on to the specific gateway from that network to the next network.

Default Gateways and Subnetworks

Although we discuss the default gateway and subnetworks in detail in Chapter 4, it is appropriate to discuss the role of both of these concepts while we are on the subject of routing.

We learned that packets are routed to their destination through a web of routers. We discussed how these routers are updated, either statically or dynamically. What gets the whole process rolling when we are routing packets to remote subnetworks, or subnets for short, is the use of the default gateway. The default gateway is specified on each computer, and is what initially sends the packet on its way to the first router. When the packet hits this first router, the router must determine if the destination computer is on the local network, or send the packet to the next router that will get the packet to its destination. The default gateway is very important to the routing process, so expect to hear much more about it.

on the *Job*

When I was at one company, one of my coworkers was sent out to reconfigure the printers. These printers had their own IP addresses, which is what he was reconfiguring. He successfully entered the new IP address, but he couldn't get the printer to print on the network. I took a look, asked him what he configured, and he said "just the IP address and subnet mask." I asked him if he configured the default gateway. He said "no." Once we configured the default gateway, the printer started printing. We had forgotten that the printers were located on a different subnet from the rest of the computers, and without the default gateway the printers couldn't get information to the other subnet.

You have to be on your toes when you are administering a network with subnets, which is quite common today. Without that default gateway, you are stuck on the local network. The subnet mask, which you will learn about in the next chapter, is also very important. Without a properly configured subnet mask to determine which subnet your computer is on, you aren't going to be talking to anyone!

exam *Watch*

Since TCP/IP is so popular in the real world, expect the exam to lean heavily toward configuring TCP/IP; more specifically, the IP address, subnet mask, and default gateway—the three essential TCP/IP configuration parameters.

Figure 3-5 shows the IP address and subnet mask of a Windows 98 computer. To get there, open the Network applet in the Control Panel, double-click on TCP/IP on the Configuration tab (or select the TCP/IP protocol and then click Properties), and select the IP Address tab if it is not already selected.

Figure 3-6 illustrates configuring a Windows 98 computer with the default gateway. This tab is also in the TCP/IP Properties dialog box and can be reached by clicking the Gateway tab.

Figure 3-7 illustrates configuring a Windows NT computer with all of the critical TCP/IP information on one tab, also located in the Network applet of the Control Panel. This is also in the TCP/IP Properties dialog box and can be reached by clicking the Gateway tab.

exam
ⓌatcH

Make sure you know about the IP address, subnet mask, and default gateway for the exam. This knowledge will help you every day of your networking career! Want to know more about TCP/IP? Chapter 4 gives you everything you need to prepare for the exam.

FIGURE 3-5

Configuring the
IP address and
subnet mask on
a Windows 98
computer

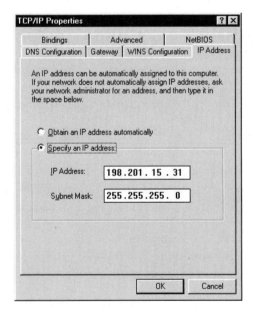

FIGURE 3-6

Configuring the
default gateway
on a Windows 98
computer

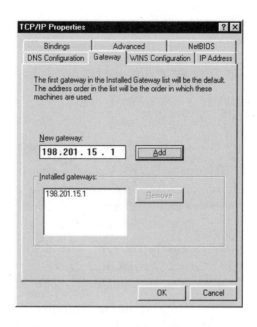

FIGURE 3-7

Configuring the
IP address, subnet
mask, and default
gateway on a
Windows NT
computer

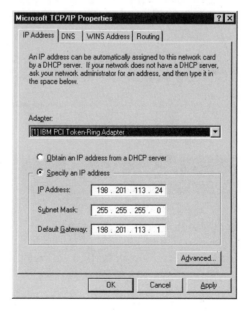

EXERCISE 3-2

Determining Your TCP/IP Configuration

This exercise will help you configure your TCP/IP configuration for a Windows 2000 PC.

1. On the desktop, right-click My Network Places and select Properties.

2. This opens the Dial-Up and Network Connections window that shows an icon for each dial-up session that has been configured, and an icon for each network card installed in the PC. Select the icon labeled Local Area Connection, right-click, and then select Properties.

3. This opens the Local Area Network Properties window. In the center box, the Clients, Services, and protocols are listed with a check mark next to the options that are installed. Highlight TCP/IP, and click Properties.

4. This opens the Internet Protocols (TCP/IP) Properties window, which allows you to specify the IP address, subnet mask, and default gateway to use. There is also a section to specify the primary and secondary DNS servers. If you need to specify other TCP/IP configurations, click Advanced... to set these options.

5. Click OK twice, and then close the Network and Dial-Up Connections window. The settings will take effect immediately.

CERTIFICATION OBJECTIVE 3.03

Transport Layer Concepts

The Transport layer works hard to ensure reliable delivery of data to its destination. The Transport layer also helps the upper layers (Application, Presentation, and Session) communicate with one another across the network, while hiding the complexities of the network.

The Transport layer also interacts with the Network layer, taking on some of the responsibilities for connection services.

One of the functions of the Transport layer is *segment sequencing*. Sequence switching is a connection-oriented service that takes segments that are received out of order and resequences them in the correct order.

Another function of the Transport layer is *error control*. It commonly uses acknowledgments (ACKs) to manage the flow of data between devices. Some Transport layer protocols can also request retransmission of recent segments to overcome errors.

exam
Ⓦatch

Be prepared for a few questions about the responsibilities of each of the layers of the OSI model. These can be quite tricky, so you have to thoroughly understand each. Make sure you understand the order of the layers; it helps when trying to memorize each layer, because each layer begins where the other layer leaves off.

Connection-Oriented Communication

Connection-oriented communication ensures reliable delivery of data from the sender to the receiver, without intervention required by either. Error correction and flow control are provided at various points from the source to the destination.

Handshaking and Data Reliability

Connection-oriented services must ensure that data is sent reliably across the network. When establishing these services, the protocol must perform some sort of *handshaking* function. Handshaking takes place at the beginning of a communication session. During handshaking, the two computers determine the rules for communication, such as transmission speed and which ports to use.

Handshaking also determines the proper way to terminate the session when finished. This ensures that communication ends in an orderly manner.

Sessions

A *session* is a reliable dialog between two computers. Because connection-oriented services can provide reliable communication, they are used when two computers need to communicate in a session. Sessions are maintained until the two computers decide that they are finished communicating.

A session is just like a telephone call. You set up a telephone call by dialing (handshaking), you speak to the other person (exchange data), say "Goodbye," and hang up when finished.

Virtual Circuits

Virtual circuits establish formal communication between two computers on an internetwork using a well-defined path. This enables two computers to act as if there is a dedicated circuit between the two, even though there is not.

The path the data takes while being exchanged between the two computers might vary, but the computers do not know this; they do not need to. Since the virtual circuit uses connection-oriented communication, all the points that comprise the circuit ensure that the data gets through unharmed, even if those points change while the virtual circuit is in place.

Connection-Oriented Protocols

Most network protocols have connection-oriented services. These protocols ensure a reliable connection across the network. They can handle errors on their own, independent of any higher-level protocols or applications.

The Internet's TCP/IP protocol provides this capability with the Transmission Control Protocol (TCP). In Novell's IPX/SPX protocol, the Sequenced Packet Exchange (SPX) protocol provides connection-oriented services.

Connectionless Communication

Connectionless communication is a form of communication in which the destination computer does not notify the source when the information is received. This type of communication can be unreliable because there is no notification to guarantee delivery. Connectionless communication can be faster than connection-oriented communication, because after information is sent, there is no second step to ensure proper receipt of information.

Datagrams

Datagrams, used by the User Datagram Protocol (UDP), are self-contained, independent pieces of data that contain enough information to be routed from the source computer to the destination computer without help from either. The network uses the self-contained information of the data to determine how to send the datagram.

A datagram is just like a piece of postal mail. You drop mail in the slot, and the stamp and address are enough for the postal service to route the mail to your recipient. However, the post office might lose a piece of mail, and there is no way to track when or where the mail was lost.

exam
Ⓦₐtₐcₕ *Remember, connectionless protocols in TCP/IP use the UDP protocol. Trivial File Transfer Protocol (TFTP) is one example of a connectionless-oriented protocol that uses UDP.*

Mailslots

Mailslots are an easy way for one computer to send information to many clients. A server can open a mailslot and write data to it. Other computers on the network can connect to the mailslot and read from it. The server sends the information out from the mailslot, but cannot be sure who is listening.

A mailslot is much like a bulletin board. Anyone can post a note to it and walk away, and anyone can read the note; you just don't know how many people might have seen it.

Lack of Reliable Delivery

Because all the nodes between the source and destination computers don't check to see that the data is unharmed, the computers must manage this function. A higher layer such as the Transport layer usually handles this, since it has error control, sequencing, and flow control capabilities.

Expanding the bulletin board example, you could ask people if they saw your message. This is one way to determine if your note was read, without actually having the note tell you. The Transport layer of the OSI model can act in this role, enabling even connectionless communication to have some degree of reliability.

exam
Ⓦₐtₐcₕ *It is important for the Network+ test that you understand the difference between connection-oriented and connectionless communication, and in which situations they are appropriate.*

Now that you understand connection and connectionless communication, let's look at some scenario questions relating to the two, and the appropriate answers.

SCENARIO & SOLUTION

My employees need to receive an audio broadcast every month on the network. What type of communication should I use?	Connectionless. It will not be necessary for all bits of the broadcast to be received. This is the same as an Internet broadcast and will only cause some possible "hiccups" in the audio.
I have employees who need to download an employee's manual from the Web server regardless of their location. What type of communication should I use?	Connection oriented. You will want the employees to have the entire manual and not have the file corrupted.
I need to know how servers send name resolutions to the network clients from the DNS server. What type of communication does the DNS server use?	Connectionless. As strange as it seems, the DNS responses are actually connectionless.

Name Resolution

In order to make it easier for humans, not computers, to remember things, we use friendly names for computers. In TPC/IP, these friendly names are resolved to an IP address, where they are then resolved to a MAC address by the computer. We, as humans, can still use the IP address, or, in some instances, the MAC address, when communicating with other computers, but it is much easier to remember and use the friendly name. For example, it is easier to remember the friendly name for the Syngress Web page as www.syngress.com, and not its IP address of 216.238.176.55. Two potential types of names need to be resolved when using a Windows-based computer: the NetBIOS name and the host name.

NetBIOS Name Resolution

The NetBIOS name is the computer name you specify in the Networking applet of the Control Panel in Windows 95/98, or NT. NetBIOS is a Microsoft solution only present in Windows-based operating systems. Since we are using NetBIOS names on the network, we need a way to resolve these NetBIOS names to IP addresses. There are two common ways of resolving a NetBIOS name: LMHOSTS and WINS. LMHOSTS is a text file located on each computer (sometimes located on a central server) that contains a list of NetBIOS name-to-IP address mappings. The LMHOSTS file is parsed when a NetBIOS name needs to be resolved to an IP address. The following is an example of the default LMHOSTS file sample provided by Microsoft:

```
# Copyright (c) 1993-1995 Microsoft Corp.
#
# This is a sample LMHOSTS file used by the Microsoft TCP/IP for Windows
# NT.
#
# This file contains the mappings of IP addresses to NT computernames
# (NetBIOS) names. Each entry should be kept on an individual line.
# The IP address should be placed in the first column followed by the
# corresponding computername. The address and the computername
# should be separated by at least one space or tab. The "#" character
# is generally used to denote the start of a comment (see the exceptions
# below).
#
# This file is compatible with Microsoft LAN Manager 2.x TCP/IP lmhosts
# files and offers the following extensions:
#
# #PRE
# #DOM:<domain>
# #INCLUDE <filename>
# #BEGIN_ALTERNATE
# #END_ALTERNATE
# \0xnn (non-printing character support)
#
# Following any entry in the file with the characters "#PRE" will cause
# the entry to be preloaded into the name cache. By default, entries are
# not preloaded, but are parsed only after dynamic name resolution fails.
#
# Following an entry with the "#DOM:<domain>" tag will associate the
# entry with the domain specified by <domain>. This affects how the
# browser and logon services behave in TCP/IP environments. To preload
# the host name associated with #DOM entry, it is necessary to also add a
# #PRE to the line. The <domain> is always preloaded although it will not
# be shown when the name cache is viewed.
#
# Specifying "#INCLUDE <filename>" will force the RFC NetBIOS (NBT)
# software to seek the specified <filename> and parse it as if it were
# local. <filename> is generally a UNC-based name, allowing a
# centralized lmhosts file to be maintained on a server.
# It is ALWAYS necessary to provide a mapping for the IP address of the
# server prior to the #INCLUDE. This mapping must use the #PRE directive.
# In addition the share "public" in the example below must be in the
# LanManServer list of "NullSessionShares" in order for client machines to
# be able to read the lmhosts file successfully. This key is under
# \machine\system\currentcontrolset\services\lanmanserver\parameters\nullsessionshares
# in the registry. Simply add "public" to the list found there.
```

```
#
# The #BEGIN_ and #END_ALTERNATE keywords allow multiple #INCLUDE
# statements to be grouped together. Any single successful include
# will cause the group to succeed.
#
# Finally, non-printing characters can be embedded in mappings by
# first surrounding the NetBIOS name in quotations, then using the
# \0xnn notation to specify a hex value for a non-printing character.
#
# The following example illustrates all of these extensions:
#
# 102.54.94.97 rhino #PRE #DOM:networking #net group's DC
# 102.54.94.102 "appname \0x14" #special app server
# 102.54.94.123 popular #PRE #source server
# 102.54.94.117 localsrv #PRE #needed for the include
#
# #BEGIN_ALTERNATE
# #INCLUDE \\localsrv\public\lmhosts
# #INCLUDE \\rhino\public\lmhosts
# #END_ALTERNATE
#
# In the example above, the "appname" server contains a special
# character in its name, the "popular" and "localsrv" server names are
# preloaded, and the "rhino" server name is specified so it can be used
# to later #INCLUDE a centrally maintained lmhosts file if the "localsrv"
# system is unavailable.
#
# Note that the whole file is parsed including comments on each lookup,
# so keeping the number of comments to a minimum will improve performance.
# Therefore it is not advisable to simply add lmhosts file entries onto the
# end of this file.
```

You can see a NetBIOS name-to-IP address mapping example in the following line:

```
102.54.94.97      rhino
```

First, this line is commented out (a line preceded by a # will not be parsed); therefore, the mapping will not work. If we removed the # sign from the line, we would be effectively telling the computer that the NetBIOS name of rhino maps to an IP address of 102.54.94.97. If the NetBIOS name were to change to kangaroo, we would have to visit each computer that uses an LMHOSTS file for name resolution and change the name from rhino to kangaroo. There has to be an easier way than updating a static LMHOSTS on every computer! Well, there is, and it's called the Windows Internet Naming Service (WINS).

FROM THE CLASSROOM

What Is NetBIOS?

You might be asking yourself, "What is NetBIOS? It's not a protocol, so what is it?" Well, in the working world you will hear many myths and rumors about what NetBIOS actually is and what it does for networking. The following are several aspects associated with NetBIOS that I have found helpful in understanding what NetBIOS means to your Windows NT networking career.

■ You might have heard that NetBIOS is the same as NetBEUI, but it is not.

■ NetBIOS is not a protocol or protocol stack.

■ When you install TCP/IP on Windows NT, you automatically get NetBIOS; there is no separating the two.

■ Since NetBIOS is not a transport protocol, it does not directly support routing, and depends on one of three transport protocols it can run on Windows NT: TCP/IP, NWLink IPX/SPX, or NetBEUI.

■ NetBIOS names can be a maximum of 16 bytes long; 15 bytes for the name, and 1 byte for the control character at the end.

■ NetBIOS is used for all the NET commands, such as NET USE.

■ The NBTSTAT command examines the contents of the NetBIOS name cache.

■ NetBIOS names can be resolved through broadcast, an LMHOSTS file, or a WINS server.

What does all this mean to you? If you don't thoroughly understand NetBIOS, you might have a difficult time understanding important concepts that rely on NetBIOS, such as WINS, LMHOSTS, and NetBIOS name resolution. It's very common for modern Windows NT networks to use WINS for NetBIOS resolution. If you are a Windows NT network administrator, you will be responsible for supporting, maintaining, and troubleshooting WINS. This can be a daunting task if you don't understand NetBIOS, because I believe WINS is one of the most difficult concepts to understand in Windows NT networking. I have a very experienced Windows NT network engineer sitting at the WINS server for hours trying to solve a WINS issue. Make sure you understand NetBIOS so you can solve any NetBIOS-related problems on your network.

—*Cameron Brandon, MCSE+Internet, CNE, A+, Network+*

exam
ⓦatch

Remember, a UNIX machine can use an LMHOSTS file to resolve machine names.

Using the WINS service on a Windows NT/2000/XP server eliminates the need for many network broadcasts, and therefore reduces network usage. Moreover, the need for manually updating tons of LMHOSTS files on every computer is eliminated. Enabling WINS on a Windows-based client uses a directed, or point-to-point, transmission for name resolution. WINS is dynamic, and is updated when machines are started or stopped, or when replicated with other WINS servers. When a name is registered, it is reserved for that one computer, further simplifying naming schemes. Each computer always has its own unique name. When a computer in a WINS-enabled network is started, it automatically registers all its NetBIOS names with the WINS server. If the computer's IP address has changed, the WINS server will know immediately. This is WINS' strength: its capability to keep an accurate IP mapping database in an ever-changing network environment. It is the best for NetBIOS name resolution in a routed network because it is designed to solve the problems that occur with name resolution.

When your computer is configured to use WINS for NetBIOS name resolution, you will query the WINS server directly when your computer is trying to determine the IP address of a computer with which you are communicating. Since WINS is dynamic, it will have up-to-date information on the current mapping for the computer you are trying to locate.

Host Name Resolution

Remember, NetBIOS name resolution is not the only form of name resolution. We also have host name resolution. The Internet is full of host names, such as microsoft.com. Also note that NetBIOS names are specific to Windows-based computers, whereas host names can be any type of operating system, from UNIX to Macintosh. As with NetBIOS name resolution, host name resolution can also use a static text file located on each computer. This file is called the HOSTS file, not to be confused with the LMHOSTS file for NetBIOS resolution. The premise is the same for the HOSTS file; it contains a list of host name-to-IP address mappings that are parsed when your computer is trying to resolve a host name to an IP address.

The following is an example of the HOSTS sample file provided by Microsoft:

```
# Copyright (c) 1998 Microsoft Corp.
#
# This is a sample HOSTS file used by Microsoft TCP/IP stack for Windows98
#
# This file contains the mappings of IP addresses to host names. Each
# entry should be kept on an individual line. The IP address should
# be placed in the first column followed by the corresponding host name.
# The IP address and the host name should be separated by at least one
# space.
#
# Additionally, comments (such as these) may be inserted on individual
# lines or following the machine name denoted by a '#' symbol.
#
# For example:
#
#      102.54.94.97     rhino.acme.com          # source server
#      38.25.63.10      x.acme.com              # x client host
127.0.0.1          localhost
```

As with the LMHOSTS file, the lines are commented out with a #, meaning they will not be processed. The only line that will be processed in the HOSTS sample file is the mapping for the localhost. If you needed to add an entry in this file, you would begin with the IP address, followed by a space or tab, and then the host name, such as:

```
143.67.119.31     gorilla
```

Does using the HOSTS file sound just as troublesome as the LMHOSTS file for maintenance? Yes, and like NetBIOS name resolution, there is another way to resolve a host name. This method is by using a Domain Name System (DNS), which is a server that provides a database and search algorithm for resolving the host name to an IP address. DNS is the service that takes a domain name and resolves it to an IP address for the TCP/IP hosts. The DNS server eliminates the need for the HOSTS file, but DNS is still not dynamic, like WINS. Therefore, all changes must be made manually for all earlier operating systems. However, instead of manually updating 492 hosts with a new HOSTS file, manually update the DNS server and have the 492 hosts point to the DNS server to resolve the host names. Understand that DNS is only used for the TCP/IP protocol; WINS was not tied to the TCP/IP protocol and can be used with NetBEUI.

Exercise 3-3 demonstrates how to edit the HOSTS file.

Editing the HOSTS File

This exercise shows you how to edit the HOSTS file.

1. Open a text editor such as Notepad or Wordpad. Select File | Open, and navigate to either C:\winnt\system32\drivers\etc or C:\windows\system32\drivers\etc, depending on your operating system.

2. Select the HOSTS file to open it. By default, you will only see some commented information at the top, and the last line should be:

   ```
   localhost
   ```

3. After this line, you can add more lines for name resolution and then save the file.

IP/IPX Addresses

There are a few differences between IP and IPX addresses. Chapter 4 focuses heavily on the IP address and many more aspects of the TCP/IP protocol, which is dominating the network industry.

Both the IP and IPX addresses are used to uniquely identify a host on a network. If this address is duplicated on the network, the packet will be confused about which computer is the actual destination for the packet. This is, of course, much like the real-world dilemma if you and your neighbor have the exact same address. This is remedied by using a Dynamic Host Configuration Protocol (DHCP) server to hand out addresses to clients when you are using the TCP/IP protocol (more about DHCP in Chapter 4). With Windows NT, if the system detects a duplicate IP address on the network, TCP/IP will refuse to initialize on this computer and an error will be generated. You must find the offending computer and determine who is at fault. Why did this second computer use an IP address that was already taken?

At one place I worked, we would get duplicate IP address conflicts every week, sometimes a few times a week. We were using TCP/IP with addresses assigned via a DHCP server. I would have to free the IP addresses (using the IPCONFIG or WINIPCFG commands) on both computers, release the IP address lease on the DHCP server, and then reboot the offending machines. We haven't figured out to this day what caused the storm of duplicate addresses. We did discover that although the IP address lease process is dynamic, the IP address was written to the Registry. We had to delete the Registry key that contained this IP address and reboot the computer to obtain a new address.

The second most common protocol is IPX, due in part to Novell NetWare's wide install base. With NetWare, you must also be sure you are not using duplicate IPX addresses. When you are installing your NetWare server, you will be asked for a one- to eight-digit IPX *internal network number*. This number will uniquely identify this server on the network. Most people accept the randomly generated IPX number. However, you should write this number down for future reference, or use a predetermined IPX number for this server to comply with company standards.

When I was installing NetWare servers at Intel, we could not accept the default IPX number that was generated during system installation. We needed to acquire a predetermined IPX address before we began the installation process. If Intel does it, then so should your company. Then again, your company might not have a zillion servers as Intel does.

Protocols within the Transport Layer

Just as the Network layer contains routable and nonroutable protocols such as TCP/IP and IPX, the Transport layer also contains its own protocols. As discussed earlier, IP and IPX are located in the Network layer, and the other components of these protocols, TCP and SPX, are located in the Transport layer. The protocols in this layer provide for communications sessions between computers to move data reliably.

I find it helpful to remember that the protocols that begin with I (IP and IPX) are located in the Network layer.

TCP

The TCP portion of the TCP/IP protocol is responsible for guaranteed delivery of data. The TCP protocol is a reliable, connection-oriented protocol that reorders the packets of information between two communicating devices for sending and receiving data. Note that the IP portion of the TCP/IP protocol works at a lower layer, forwarding and routing packets across the network.

SPX

The SPX portion of the IPX/SPX protocol is responsible for the sequencing of data during the communication session between two computers. Note that the IPX portion of the IPX/SPX protocol works at a lower level, just as IP does with TCP/IP, forwarding and routing packets across the network.

NetBEUI

NetBEUI is present in the Network layer, but is also considered a Transport layer protocol. NetBEUI is considered a Transport protocol because it establishes sessions between computers with the use of NetBIOS, and provides data transport services.

CERTIFICATION SUMMARY

In this chapter, you learned about the three important layers of the OSI model for addressing and forwarding packets of information: the Data Link layer, the Network layer, and the Transport layer. First, you learned how the Data Link layer packages data into smaller frames for routing across the network, and about the two sublayers of the Data Link layer: *logical link control* (LLC) and *media access control* (MAC). You discovered the importance of the MAC address, or hardware address, and how to retrieve the MAC address from a Windows 95/98 or Windows NT machine. You learned about the bridge, which resides in the Data Link layer and is used to consolidate networks. Finally, you learned about the IEEE 802 standards 802.2, 802.3, and 802.5 for the Data Link layer.

You learned how the Network layer addresses frames of information with the source and destinations so the frames know where they are going. Routing is very important in this layer, and you can expect more than a few questions about routing on the exam. Therefore, we spent plenty of time on routable versus nonroutable protocols, the default gateway, subnets, and the difference between bridges, brouters, and routers.

Finally, you learned about the Transport layer, whose job it is to make sure these frames are reordered correctly and that an acknowledgment is sent to the source computer confirming that the frame was received. You learned about connectionless and connection-oriented transport, which describes the two methods in which two computers transfer data. You discovered the need for name resolution, which makes it easier for us humans to use friendly names and not have to memorize IP or MAC addresses. Finally, you learned about the protocols within the Transport layer, such as TCP, SPX, and NetBEUI. These protocols create and maintain the session between two computers while the data is being transferred.

In the next chapter, you will learn about the TCP/IP protocol and what you will need to know to answer the TCP/IP questions on your Network+ exam. First, however, read through the Two-Minute Drill and take the Self Test to see just how well you understand the information presented in this chapter.

TWO-MINUTE DRILL

Data Link Layer Concepts

❏ The Data Link layer handles many issues for communicating on a simple network.

❏ The Data Link layer is divided into two sublayers: *logical link control* (LLC) and *media access control* (MAC). The LLC layer starts and maintains connections between devices. The MAC layer enables multiple devices to share the media.

❏ Another important job of the Data Link layer is *addressing*.

❏ The Data Link layer manages *flow control* and *error correction* between devices in a simple network.

❏ The MAC address is used to communicate only on the local network.

❏ A bridge is a network connectivity device that connects two different networks and makes them appear to be one network.

❏ Most of the protocols defined by the 802 committee reside in the Physical and Data Link layers of the OSI model.

❏ Carrier Sense Multiple Access with Collision Detection (CSMA/CD) keeps devices on the network from interfering with one another when trying to transmit; when they do interfere with each other, a *collision* occurs.

❏ The exam leans quite heavily on Ethernet technology because of its dominance in the marketplace. Pay special attention to special characteristics of the various media types of Ethernet.

❏ Expect to be asked about the IEEE standards, especially the ones presented in this chapter. Remember that 802.2 maps to the Logical Link Control layer, 802.3 is Ethernet, 802.5 defines Token Ring networks, and 802.11 deals with wireless networks.

Network Layer Concepts

❏ The Network layer manages addressing and delivering packets on a complex *internetwork*.

❏ The Network layer also enables the option of specifying a *service address* on the destination computer.

❏ In order to operate on an internetwork, each network that participates must be assigned a *network ID.*

❏ Routing protocols are designed to separate a physical network into multiple virtual networks.

❏ A brouter is a hybrid of both a bridge and a router and has a connection to more than two networks.

❏ A *routable* protocol can have packets transferred across a router.

❏ The Transmission Control Protocol/Internet Protocol (TCP/IP) is the protocol most used today. TCP/IP, a routable protocol, is very robust and is commonly associated with UNIX systems.

❏ Expect a question or two on the exam regarding the appropriate use of a bridge, brouter, or router. With the information provided here, you should do just fine. Bear in mind that the exam might give you a long, complex scenario with tons of information meant to confuse you. You learned in this chapter how to cut to the chase and quickly spot the keywords that will give away the answer.

❏ There is a huge difference between the two types of routing: static and dynamic. With static routing, the routing tables are manually entered, and with dynamic routing, the routers themselves learn of the routing table.

❏ The default gateway is specified on each computer, and is what initially sends the packet on its way to the first router.

❏ Without a properly configured subnet mask to determine which subnet your computer is on, you aren't going to be talking to anyone!

❏ Since TCP/IP is so popular in the real world, you can expect the exam to lean heavily toward configuring TCP/IP; more specifically, the IP address, subnet mask, and default gateway—the three essential TCP/IP configuration parameters.

Transport Layer Concepts

❑ The Transport layer works hard to ensure reliable delivery of data to its destinations.

❑ Expect a few questions on the exam about the responsibilities of each layer of the OSI model. These can be quite tricky, so you have to understand each thoroughly. Make sure you understand the order of the layers; I found it helpful when trying to memorize each layer, because each layer begins where the other layer leaves off.

❑ Connection-oriented communication ensures reliable delivery of data from the sender to the receiver, without intervention required by either.

❑ Connectionless communication is a form of communication in which the destination computer does not notify the source when the information is received.

❑ Remember, connectionless protocols in TCP/IP use the UDP protocol. TFTP is one example of a connectionless-oriented protocol that uses UDP.

❑ Two types of names have to be resolved when using a Windows-based computer, the NetBIOS name and the host name.

❑ Remember, a UNIX machine can use an LMHOSTS file to resolve machine names.

❑ I found it helpful to remember that the protocols that begin with I (IP and IPX) are located in the Network layer, and their counterparts (TCP and SPX) are in the Transport layer.

SELF TEST

The following Self Test questions will help you measure your understanding of the material presented in this chapter. Read all the choices carefully, as there might be more than one correct answer. Choose all correct answers for each question.

Data Link Layer Concepts

1. What happens when a server you are trying to reach is located on another segment of the network?

   A. You don't need the MAC address of this server.

   B. You still need the MAC address of this server.

   C. You need the MAC address of the nearest bridge.

   D. You need the MAC address of the nearest router.

2. At which layer of the OSI model does a bridge function?

   A. Data Link layer

   B. Network layer

   C. Transport layer

   D. Physical layer

3. Which IEEE 802 category uses Carrier Sense Multiple Access with Collision Detection (CSMA/CD) for access to the physical medium?

   A. 802

   B. 802.2

   C. 802.3

   D. 802.5

4. To which network topology does the IEEE 802 standard 802.5 map?

   A. ArcNet

   B. Token Ring

   C. Ethernet

   D. Twisted Pair

5. In order to operate on an internetwork, what must be assigned to each participating network?

    A. An IP address

    B. A network address

    C. A IPX address

    D. A default gateway

6. When should you use a brouter?

    A. When you are only using one protocol on the network.

    B. When you are using a routable and nonroutable protocol.

    C. When you have to subnet the network with the TCP/IP protocol.

    D. When you need to make other network segments visible to the entire network with a nonroutable protocol such as NetBEUI.

Network Layer Concepts

7. What will happen if we have a routing table with the same route to the same destination network?

    A. You cannot have the same route listed twice.

    B. You cannot have the same destination listed twice.

    C. The route with the closest router will be used.

    D. The route with the fewest number of hops will be used.

8. Which of the following is *not* true regarding a dynamic router?

    A. It can choose the most efficient path to a destination network.

    B. It can communicate and share information with neighboring routers.

    C. It cannot be configured with static routes.

    D. It can communicate with other routers using RIP and OSPF.

9. What will happen if the default gateway is not specified on your computer and you try to reach another network?

    A. The packet will ask every router if it knows the path to reach the destination.

    B. The packet will broadcast for the IP address of the nearest router.

    C. The packet will be forwarded to the DNS server.

    D. The packet will not be sent.

10. Which of the following is *not* true of the Transport layer of the OSI model?

    A. It is responsible for error control.

    B. It is responsible for encrypting session information.

    C. It interacts with the Network layer.

    D. It is responsible for segment sequencing.

Transport Layer Concepts

11. Which of the following is *not* a characteristic of connection-oriented communication?

    A. Datagrams

    B. Handshaking

    C. Virtual circuits

    D. Sessions

12. Why is connection-oriented data delivery faster?

    A. Because a session between the two computers is maintained for the entire duration of the transfer of data.

    B. Because you can quickly re-send data if it becomes lost or corrupt.

    C. Because the packets already know where they are going and don't have to find alternate routes.

    D. Connection-oriented data transfer is not quicker than connectionless-oriented data transfer.

13. Which are the best examples of a mailslot?

    A. A two-way telephone conversation

    B. A bulletin board

    C. An answering machine

    D. A specific port on a computer used for sending and receiving mail

14. The LMHOSTS file is a static file to resolve what types of names?

    A. UNIX

    B. NetBEUI

    C. HOSTS

    D. NetBIOS

15. What does DNS stand for?

    A. Directory Name Structure

    B. Domain Name System

    C. Domain Naming Service

    D. Directory Naming System

16. What will happen on a Windows NT Workstation if a duplicate IP address is detected during the boot process?

    A. An error will be issued and you can continue; just don't forget to fix the problem before it gets worse.

    B. An error will be generated and TCP/IP will not be working on your machine.

    C. You will be prompted to change your IP address to avoid an address conflict.

    D. Nothing will happen, at least until the first computer attempts to access the network.

17. Which of the following is a valid IPX internal network address?

    A. 00EE2210FF

    B. 112233ZZ

    C. ABACAB

    D. 1EF332001

18. Which two routable protocols are located in the Network layer?

    A. IPX and NetBEUI

    B. IP and SPX

    C. IPX and SPX

    D. IP and IPX

LAB QUESTION

You have been hired by a company to design a network layout to help increase efficiency on the network and keep bandwidth at a maximum.

The company is currently using switches, but has had many complaints that the network is too slow.

The network is comprised of five departments, each with different requirements. The company has decided that instead of having all servers managed by the IT department, department servers will be managed by the individual department employees themselves. The IT department will manage some troubleshooting of the servers, updating server hardware and some software, and managing network devices and cabling.

The fifth department is the IT department where the main server resides, providing security and authentication for Internet access. The IT department needs to allow all other departments to access the Internet.

Department 1 has a server, which has an intranet Web site for access by the department's employees to add and update database information, and print reports from the data entered.

Department 2 has an old program that was specifically written for their needs quite a few years ago. The program will only communicate with PCs using NetBEUI. The information that this program manages should not be accessible by any other department.

Department 3 has only Apple computers and uses AppleTalk to access other Apple computers and network devices within the department.

Department 4 has a NetWare 3.12 server that also has a specifically written application that requires it to be run on a NetWare server.

All departments have no need to access other servers in other departments except for Department 5, which will hold the e-mail server and provide access to the Internet.

What devices and changes are needed to meet all of these requirements and increase network efficiency?

SELF TEST ANSWERS

Data Link Layer Concepts

1. ☑ **D.** You need the MAC address of the nearest router. If the server is located on another network segment across a WAN, the MAC address of the nearest router is used to send the information, and it is up to the router to forward the data.

   ☒ **A** is incorrect because you always need a MAC address of any network device you are communicating with on the network. **B** is incorrect because you do not need the MAC address of the server, since the data packet will be sent to the default gateway to be sent on to the server. **C** is incorrect because data packets are not sent directly to bridges; the data packet is received by the bridge since the packets are broadcast, and the bridge forwards the packet onto the other segment if the MAC address of the server is in its routing list of the PCs on the other segment.

2. ☑ **A.** Data Link layer. The bridge filters local traffic between the two networks and copies all other traffic to the other side of the bridge. Bridges operate at the Data Link layer. Bridges use the Data Link layer and its physical addressing to join several networks into a single network efficiently.

   ☒ **B** is incorrect because the Network layer is the layer in which routers operate. **C** is incorrect because the Transport layer is where gateways operate (actually, all layers). **D** is incorrect because the repeater operates at the Physical layer.

3. ☑ **C.** 802.3. The MAC sublayer uses Carrier Sense Multiple Access with Collision Detection (CSMA/CD) for access to the physical medium. CSMA/CD keeps devices on the network from interfering with one another when trying to transmit; when they do interfere with each other, a *collision* occurs.

   ☒ **A** is incorrect; 802 represents the 802 project by the Institute of Electrical and Electronic Engineers. **B** is incorrect; 802.2 specifies the Logical Link Control (LLC) sublayer. **D** is incorrect; 802.5 specifies the requirements for the Token Ring network.

4. ☑ **B.** Token Ring. Although the first Token Ring design was developed in the late 1960s, IBM's token passing implementation did not become a standard until 1985. It became IEEE standard 802.5 under the IEEE Project 802. The 802.5 standard was actually modeled after the IBM Token Ring network, which had been in use for many years before the standard was even developed.

   ☒ **A** is incorrect because the ArcNet topology has no 802 project associated with it. **C** is incorrect because Ethernet is mapped to the 802.3 project. **D** is incorrect, and is also covered by the 802.3 project.

5. ☑ **B.** A network address. In order to operate on an internetwork, each network that participates must be assigned a network ID. This address differentiates each network from every other network that forms the internetwork. When sending data from one network to another, the routers along the way use the network ID to determine the next step in the journey.

☒ **A** is incorrect because each network device needs an IP address that falls within the range of IP addresses used by the internetwork segment to which the device is connected. **C** is incorrect because the network might not be using IPX/SPX, and by definition, an internetwork uses TCP/IP. **D** is incorrect because no network requires a gateway if you are not going to communicate outside the local network.

6. ☑ **B,** when you are using a routable and nonroutable protocol. You can use a brouter when your network consists of both routable and nonroutable protocols, such as TCP/IP and NetBEUI. Brouting might provide a more cost-effective means of bridging and routing in one unit, rather than using two individual components.

☒ **A** is incorrect. If you are using one protocol, then you can use either a bridge or router depending if the protocol is routable. **C** would require the use a router, and **D** would require a bridge. It is possible to use a brouter, but it would be slower. You only should use a brouter when you are using both routable and nonroutable protocols.

Network Layer Concepts

7. ☑ **D.** The route with the fewest number of hops will be used. If a route claims it can reach the destination in one fewer hop than the next router, then let it prove it. If there are two identical routes to the same destination, the route with the fewest hops will be used.

☒ **A** is incorrect since fault-tolerant routes are a main advantage of routers if one route is unavailable, which is the same reason why **B** is incorrect. **C** is incorrect because the cable distances aren't taken into account, only the number of hops.

8. ☑ **C.** It cannot be configured with static routes. There are times when you might want to use static routing; for example, when you have a router at either end of a slow WAN link. This router will not increase traffic by broadcasting updated route information to the router on the other end of the link.

☒ **A** is true about routers because they are supposed to choose the best route to use for sending data packets. **B** is true because dynamic routers are meant to share their routing tables with other routers making them dynamic and not static. **D** is true for routers because the two routing protocols used are either RIP or OSPF.

9. ☑ **D.** The packet will not be sent. Without that default gateway, you are stuck on the local network. The subnet mask, which you will learn about in the next chapter, is also very important. Without a properly configured subnet mask to determine which subnet your computer is on, you aren't going to be talking to anyone!

   ☒ **A** is incorrect because the PC will not know the addresses of the routers to send the data packets to, or even inquire about router addresses or destination addresses. **B** is incorrect for the same reasons. **C** is incorrect because the DNS server is used for name to IP address resolution and not IP addresses of routers.

10. ☑ **B.** It is responsible for encrypting session information. The Transport layer also interacts with the Network layer, taking on some of the responsibilities for connection services. One of the functions of the Transport layer is *segment sequencing*. Sequence switching is a connection-oriented service that takes segments that are received out of order and resequences them in the right order. Another function of the Transport layer is *error control*.

    ☒ **A, C,** and **D** are true. The Transport layer is responsible for error control, interacting with the Network layer as well as the Session layer, and is responsible for the sequencing of segmented data packets.

Transport Layer Concepts

11. ☑ **A.** Datagrams. Datagrams are not connection oriented because they contain everything they need to get from the source to the destination, such as the source and destination address. These are like pieces of mail that fly all across the country, but magically arrive intact.

    ☒ **B, C,** and **D** are incorrect because a virtual circuit is guaranteed connection-oriented session which is created first by initiating a handshaking sequence to create the virtual circuit.

12. ☑ **D.** Connection-oriented data transfer is not quicker than connectionless-oriented data transfer. Datagrams, used by the UDP protocol, are self-contained, independent pieces of data that contain enough information to be routed from the source computer to the destination computer without any help from the source or destination. When recommunicating via a connectionless-oriented session, the sending computer does not need to wait for a reply from the destination computer that the data arrived error-free; the source computer just sends the data out as fast as it can.

    ☒ **A** is incorrect because the session has no bearing on the speed of the communication. **B** is incorrect because resending data would take more time and make the session longer. **C** is incorrect because different routes could make the session faster.

13. ☑ **B** and **C**. A bulletin board and answering machine. A mailslot is much like a bulletin board. Anyone can post a note to it and walk away. Anyone can read the note; you don't know how many people have seen it. This is also true of an answering machine.

    ☒ **A** is incorrect because a two-way telephone conversation is like the standard communication on a network between PCs. **D** is incorrect because the port on a PC is used for transmitting data and not storage of data.

14. ☑ **D**. NetBIOS. There are two methods for resolving a NetBIOS name: LMHOSTS or WINS. LMHOSTS is a text file located on each computer (sometimes located on a central server) that contains a list of NetBIOS name-to-IP address mappings. The LMHOSTS file is parsed when a NetBIOS name needs to be resolved to an IP address.

    ☒ **A**, **B**, and **C** are incorrect. UNIX is an operating system, not a name resolution data file. NetBEUI is a protocol, and not name resolution. The HOSTS file is used to resolve host names to IP addresses, such as the same as a DNS server.

15. ☑ **B**. Domain Name System. DNS is a server that provides a database and search algorithm for resolving the host name to an IP address.

    ☒ **A**, **C**, and **D** are incorrect. DNS is the service that takes a domain name and resolves it to an IP address for the TCP/IP hosts. The DNS server eliminates the need for the HOSTS file, but DNS is still not dynamic, like WINS.

16. ☑ **B**. An error will be generated and TCP/IP will not be working on your machine. With Windows NT, if the system detects a duplicate IP address on the network, TCP/IP will refuse to initialize on this computer and an error will be generated. You must find the offending computer and determine who is at fault.

    ☒ **A** is incorrect because each network device needs to have a unique IP address, or there will be address issues when data is sent to either PC with the same IP address. **C** is incorrect because the user will not be given an option to change the IP address, only a message that the IP address is in conflict with an existing IP address. **D** is incorrect because the TCP/IP protocol will not bind to the NIC, and the second PC with the same IP address will not be able to use the TCP/IP protocol.

17. ☑ **C**. ABACAB. The IPX internal network address is a one- to eight-digit hexadecimal address. When installing your NetWare server, you will be asked for a one- to eight-digit IPX *internal network number*. This number will uniquely identify this server on the network. Most people accept the randomly generated IPX number.

    ☒ **A** and **D** are incorrect since they are longer than eight digits. **B** is incorrect because a hexadecimal number either is a number 0 through 9 or letters A through F.

18. ☑ **D.** IP and IPX. As discussed previously, IP and IPX are located in the Network layer, and the other components of these protocols, TCP and SPX, are located in the Transport layer. The protocols in this layer provide for communications sessions between computers to move data reliably.

☒ **A** is incorrect because the NetBEUI protocol is not routable. **B** and **C** are incorrect because the SPX protocol operates at the Transport layer.

LAB ANSWER

All departments need to be connected to the IT department (Department 5) by a router. If there is a router in the IT department and each department is connected to it with a switching hub or switch in the department itself, this will allow for the intra-department communications to stay within the department. It will also prevent any of the NetBEUI communications to be broadcast past Department 2.

Since all departments will need access to the Internet through the IT department, the IT department will require only TCP/IP protocol. The other departments will need TCP/IP in addition to the protocols already use. The main protocol for each department will be the protocol used for communication to the department server. This should increase network performance for all of the departments by segmenting them into individual networks with the routers and specifying in the router configuration to allow only TCP/IP to pass through it.

COMPUTING TECHNOLOGY INDUSTRY ASSOCIATION

4

TCP/IP
Fundamentals

CERTIFICATION OBJECTIVES

4.01   TCP/IP Fundamentals

4.02   TCP/IP Addressing

4.03   TCP/IP Configuration Concepts

✓   Two-Minute Drill

Q&A   Self Test

T
he most popular protocol in use today is Transmission Control Protocol/Internet
Protocol (TCP/IP). The Internet and most company intranets are currently using TCP/IP
because of its popularity, flexibility, compatibility, and capability to perform in both
small and large network implementations. TCP/IP can connect a diverse range of hosts, from
mainframes to palmtop computers. The popularity of this protocol makes it a likely culprit to
appear many times throughout your Network+ exam. Although TCP/IP is the most commonly
used protocol, it is not the easiest to configure or even to understand. This chapter gives you
a great understanding of TCP/IP, including the architecture, addressing issues, and configuration
involved with its use. The Network+ exam will test your knowledge of the protocol, but most
important, it will test your ability to configure the protocol on workstations. Real-world experience,
in addition to this chapter on TCP/IP, will ensure that you can easily answer any TCP/IP-related
questions presented to you on the exam.

CERTIFICATION OBJECTIVE 4.01

TCP/IP Fundamentals

TCP/IP stands for a combination of *Transmission Control Protocol (TCP)* and
Internet Protocol (IP). Don't let its name fool you; TCP/IP is a *suite* of protocols,
not just the two represented in the name.

As you learn in this chapter, each protocol in the suite has a specific purpose
and function. It is not important for the Network+ exam for you to understand
the evolution of TCP/IP, so we discuss here the details of the protocol on which
you are likely to be tested.

IP Addresses

TCP/IP's unique addressing mechanism provides for over 4.2 billion addresses. Each
host is referred to by its unique 32-bit address. These unique addresses are made up
of network and host identification. Let's take a closer look at the components of
these addresses.

Four-Octet Address

The 32-bit IP address is broken into four octets that can be represented in decimal or binary format. For example, the binary representation of an address could be:

```
11010100 00001111 10000100 01110101
```

The dotted-decimal representation of the same address might be:

```
212.15.132.117
```

Network ID and Host ID

The IP address is further fragmented into the network ID and the host ID. The network ID specifies a specific logical network on which resides the host that has the IP address. To further determine a specific PC on this logical network, part of the IP address is used for specifying the host ID that separates each PC from others on the network. The Internet is one large communication network that consists of multiple networks. Each machine uses part of the IP address to identify the network to which it belongs and the rest of the address to identify its host or local computer address.

Two PCs with different network IDs on the same physical network segment cannot readily communicate with one another. To have the ability for hosts on one network to communicate with hosts on another network (that is, with different network IDs), you need a router or gateway to allow this type of communication.

Dynamic Host Configuration Protocol

Configuring IP addressing on a large TCP/IP-based network can be a nightmare, especially if users move machines from one subnet to another without consulting you. The Dynamic Host Configuration Protocol (DHCP) can help with configuration problems in these, as well as in other situations.

Manual or Automatic Address Assignment

There are two methods of assigning an IP address to a client computer: An individual can configure the client manually, or a server computer can configure the client automatically.

We discussed assigning IP addresses manually in the previous chapter. This method is not recommended for the reason that it is very easy to assign a duplicate address to two PCs. Such duplication does not allow the second PC to come online to initialize

TCP/IP. Without the protocol initialized, the PC is not able to communicate on the network.

The process of dynamically assigning IP addresses is managed via a DHCP server. The DHCP server is configured with a set of usable IP addresses, called a *scope*. The scope can also include the IP addresses of the default gateway, DNS servers, WINS servers, and other necessary addresses. When a PC comes online and is set up to use a DHCP server, it requests an IP address by transmitting a broadcast request packet. The DHCP server responds with a valid IP address and other information. Then the PC assigns itself this address and configures TCP/IP with the other information that was sent. The PC then transmits an acknowledgment to the DHCP server that signifies that it will use the IP address sent by the DHCP server. The DHCP server marks the IP address in its database as being in use so that it is not assigned again and sends a final acknowledgment to the PC.

DHCP servers are recommended for use in medium-sized to large networks and can even be used in small networks. Within workgroups, IP address assignment is often handled manually.

Assigning Multiple Addresses

Suppose your boss tells you that 240 computers on your TCP/IP-based network were recently moved from one building to another and that you must reconfigure them all to work properly on the new subnet. This is a tedious process if you are using manual IP addressing. You will have to go to each machine and enter the correct IP address, subnet mask, and default gateway, along with the WINS and DNS addresses, if you are using those services on your network.

If you use manual IP address assignment, you should keep a database that contains the IP address used and the name of the PC or printer to which each address has been assigned. We stress that the database must be kept up to date, and no IP address should be used without first checking the database to see if it is in use. Furthermore, you should check the database after the IP address is assigned so that the address is not duplicated.

Errors in Manual Entry

Manually entering all this information is not only time consuming—the process is also vulnerable to human error. If the same IP address is configured for two or more computer systems, network problems will occur, and they can be difficult to trace. In addition, an error in entering any of the numbers for the IP address, subnet mask, or default gateway can lead to problems communicating through TCP/IP.

Looking back at the situation with the 240 computers, you are probably groaning, thinking of how long it will take you to accomplish this task manually. Fortunately, there is a better way to handle this situation: Use of DHCP. DHCP, as described in RFC 1541, provides a dependable, flexible option to manual TCP/IP configuration.

The DHCP server can assign to the client system all items normally configured manually. At a minimum, a DHCP server provides the DHCP client with the IP address, subnet mask, and usually a default gateway.

IP Addresses

The DHCP server issues an IP address to each DHCP client system on the network. Each system connected to a TCP/IP-based network is identified by a unique IP address. As you learned in Chapter 3, the IP address consists of four 8-bit octets separated by periods. The IP address is normally shown in dotted-decimal notation— for example, 127.10.24.62.

Subnet Masks

The IP address actually consists of two parts: the network ID and the host ID. The subnet mask is used to identify the part of the IP address that is the network ID and the part that is the host ID. Subnet masks assign 1s to the network ID bits and 0s to the host ID bits of the IP address.

For example, a subnet mask of 255.255.0.0 specifies the first two octets as signifying the network ID and the last two octets as the host ID. Another example is 255.255.255.0, which signifies the first three octets of the IP address as the network ID and the last octet as the host ID.

Default Gateway

A *default gateway* is required when the client system needs to communicate outside its own subnet. Normally, the default gateway is a router connected to the local subnet, which enables IP packets to be passed to other network segments. If the default gateway is not configured in the DHCP server, it defaults to 0.0.0.0.

FROM THE CLASSROOM

Understanding DHCP

You will find that nearly every site that uses Windows NT and TCP/IP in the real world also uses DHCP to automatically assign TCP/IP information to clients. This doesn't mean that you don't need to understand the fundamentals of TCP/IP. You still need to be knowledgeable about IP addressing, subnet masking, and default gateways for several reasons:

- Not every workstation or server on the network will be a DHCP client.

- You might have to manually configure TCP/IP on a workstation or server.

- You might need to evaluate the current DHCP settings and possibly modify them.

- You might need to configure TCP/IP on routers and hubs, which are not recommended DHCP clients.

- You might also have to coexist with a non-DHCP operating system or server, such as a mainframe or standalone server or workstation.

It is imperative that you understand DHCP from both the client side and the server side. Configuring the clients with DHCP is a no-brainer, but setting up the DHCP server with an address scope, subnet mask, default gateway, and other entries, such as DNS and WINS, can be very challenging. One incorrect setting and you could affect the entire network.

If you are in charge of a DHCP rollout, make sure that you spend time planning to ensure that the settings are correct from the outset. Ask yourself the following questions:

- Is the scope of IP addresses large enough to support our network's future growth?

- Do we also assign settings for WINS and DNS servers in the process?

- Will we be assigning DHCP information to clients across a subnet or segment?

- Do we need a backup DHCP server?

Answering these questions *before* the rollout will minimize growing pains during the life of your DHCP network.

If you are a new network administrator at a site with DHCP already implemented, make sure that you spend time taking note of the following information:

- The range of IP addresses your company uses.

- The subnet mask.

- The default gateway.

- Whether you are also assigning addresses for DNS or WINS servers.

- Which servers and workstations are not DHCP clients.

FROM THE CLASSROOM

Understanding Dynamic Host Configuration Protocol means that you understand how a TCP/IP network functions. If you gain this knowledge, you will be ready to troubleshoot any DHCP-related problem, whether server or client based, with ease.

—Cameron Brandon, MCSE+Internet, CNE, A+, Network+

Scope Options

A DHCP scope is a managerial arrangement that identifies the configuration parameters for all the DHCP clients on a physical subnet. As previously mentioned, the IP address and subnet mask are required items that the DHCP scope must include. Another requirement in the scope is the *lease duration*. It specifies how long a DHCP client can use an IP address before it must renew it with the DHCP server. This duration can be set for an unlimited time period or for a predetermined time period. You have the option of configuring a scope to reserve a specific IP address for a DHCP client or even for a system on the network that is not DHCP enabled.

In addition, many DHCP options can be configured by an administrator. You learn about DHCP options in more detail later in this chapter.

DHCP Server and Client Requirements

To successfully use DHCP on your network, your servers and clients must be able to support the protocol. In this section, our discussion centers on Microsoft products. To see if another product supports DHCP, refer to the documentation that comes with the product.

Exercise 4-1 shows you how to configure a Windows 95, 98, or ME OS to use DHCP when TCP/IP is installed.

EXERCISE 4-1

Configuring TCP/IP to Use DHCP

In this exercise, you learn how to enable your TCP/IP Windows 95/98/ME PC to use DHCP configuration when initializing TCP/IP. Do the following:

1. On the Windows 95/98/ME desktop, right-click **Network Neighborhood** and select **Properties**.

2. Select the **IP Address** tab.

3. In the middle of the page, select the option to **Obtain an IP address automatically** and select **OK**.

4. Reboot the PC when prompted.

Servers

Several versions of Windows NT Server, including versions 3.5, 3.51, 4.0, 2000, and XP, can act as DHCP servers on your network. But is it necessary to set up each of the servers on your network to support DHCP? Actually, the answer depends on your network's layout and needs. If your network is small, a single DHCP server might be adequate. The main factor to consider if you have multiple subnets is that your routers must comply with RFC 1542 so that the broadcast for an IP address from the DHCP client can be received by the single DHCP server. It is wise to keep in mind that, if your single DHCP server goes down and your DHCP clients cannot renew their lease, the clients will cease to function when their leases expire! Of course, this is assuming that TCP/IP is the only protocol used on your network.

One of the benefits of using multiple DHCP servers is redundancy. Redundancy can prevent your network from going down. If you decide to use multiple DHCP servers, you should place them on different subnets to achieve a higher degree of fault tolerance in case one of the subnets becomes unavailable. You can manage multiple servers on different subnets with the DHCP Manager, the graphical utility used to maintain and configure DHCP servers.

In most companies, two DHCP servers provide fault tolerance of IP addressing if one server fails or must be taken offline for maintenance. Each DHCP server has at least half of the available addresses in an active scope. The number of addresses on each DHCP server should be more than enough to provide addresses for all clients.

Supported Clients

The following Microsoft operating systems can perform as DHCP clients on your network:

- Windows NT Server, versions 3.5, 3.51, 4.0, 2000, and XP
- Windows NT Workstation, versions 3.5, 3.51, 4.0, 2000, and XP
- Windows 95, 98, and ME
- Windows for Workgroups, versions 3.11, 3.11a, and 3.11b, when using TCP/IP-32
- Microsoft Network Client, version 3.0 for MS-DOS
- Microsoft LAN Manager Client, version 2.2c for MS-DOS

Of course, DHCP clients are not limited to Microsoft operating systems. Any system that conforms to RFC 1541 can be a DHCP client.

Boot Protocol

The Boot Protocol, known as BOOTP, is used by diskless workstations. When a diskless workstation boots, it does so using an EEPROM on the network card to allow it to load basic drivers and connect to the network.

A BOOTP server, similar to a DHCP server, assigns the diskless workstation an address for the network to allow it to participate on the network.

The BOOTP server is usually the same as the DHCP server; the two are considered one and the same. Routers need to be BOOTP compatible to allow the DHCP requests to pass over the router to another segment.

Network Address Translation

Network Address Translation (NAT) is a process similar to DHCP and BOOTP, except for different reasons. Whereas a DHCP or BOOTP server is used to assign addresses to a client for access on the local network, the NAT server is used to assign or mask local addresses on a public network such as the Internet.

Another option for NAT arises when a company has a large number of employees—say, 300—who can access the Internet, but the company does not want to pay for 300 Internet addresses. The company can purchase one or more addresses and assign these to the NAT server, which will accept clients' requests to the Internet and translate their intranet TCP/IP to one of the Internet addresses assigned to the NAT server. This is accomplished by also assigning port numbers with the Internet address.

Let's look at an example. Say that you are on a company's intranet and you have been assigned the TCP/IP address of 10.0.0.25, which is a private address and cannot be used on the Internet. You make a request for the Syngress Web page. The request is sent on port 80, since this is an HTTP Web site, to the gateway, which is also the NAT server. The NAT server has been assigned an Internet address of 189.1.1.5 for use on the Internet. The NAT server has a conversion table by which it assigns addresses and makes an entry with your TCP/IP address and the new one you will be assigned. The entry is 10.0.0.25 and 189.1.1.5 port 5000. The NAT server then sends a request to the www.syngress.com port 80 with a return address of 189.1.1.5 port 5000. When the Syngress Web server receives the request, it sends the requested HTML page to the address of 189.1.1.5 port 5000 and sends it back to the NAT server, which receives the response. It then looks at the conversion table and changes the destination address from 189.1.1.5 port 5000 to 10.0.0.25 port 80 and sends it on the local network, which is received by your PC. At that point, you see the Syngress Web page.

NAT also provides for protection from Internet hackers. For instance, if your internal addressing scheme is made up of public addresses, this system prevents hackers from determining your internal network addresses to try to use a *spoof attack* to gain entry to the network.

Domain Name Service

One service that is used throughout the Internet is the Domain Name Service (DNS). All IP-based traffic requires the IP address of the destination. DNS is one method of resolving a hostname to a given IP address. As you learned in Chapter 3, when you are using friendly hostnames, such as eng001.engineering.microsoft.com, you need to resolve those hostnames to IP addresses. You also learned in Chapter 3 that the static HOSTS file was used before the advent of DNS. DNS is much more robust and reliable. Every domain name, such as microsoft.com, could represent a DNS zone containing the local hosts and their associated IP addresses. DNS provides a segmented service of small local databases that can pass, along a hierarchical chain, any requests for hostname resolution that cannot be resolved locally.

The hierarchical design of DNS is similar to a file tree structure. The root servers provide resolution to the same layer and the layer below. Any further layers provide localized data zone authorities. In a private intranet, the domain servers can have any names. In the Internet, the root server names have been around a long time and are frequently expanded to allow for the exponential growth seen in the past few years.

exam
ⓦatch

DNS was not a dynamic service, as WINS or DHCP are, but DDNS is dynamic and is now available in Windows 2000.

Domain Names in a Nutshell

A DNS host record consists of a name, record type, and an IP address. A set of these records can be associated with a grouping called a *domain*. The fully qualified domain name (FQDN) is the name of the host, suffixed by a period, and followed by the domain name.

An FQDN such as engineering.microsoft.com can be interpreted to mean that there is a root server somewhere that manages the .COM root zone. The next layer of zones is microsoft.com. The layer after that represents a zone within microsoft.com, in this case engineering, which is the leftmost part in the FQDN and thus represents the host. Note that the names are delimited by periods, similar to the format in a file system. All the hostnames are grouped into smaller, locally managed databases. Each of these databases knows about the parent servers above them, called *root servers*.

All DNS clients automatically use DNS when they request an IP address for a hostname that is not known locally. The hostname request is passed to DNS, which uses all known resources to try to resolve the hostname to an IP address. Optionally, you can configure the NT version of DNS to query any configured WINS servers. You learn more about WINS in the next section of this chapter.

Figure 4-1 shows the three basic levels of DNS. The root servers are named A, B, C, and so on. The top-level domains are .COM, .EDU, and .GOV, and there are many more.

The second level, or layer, represents the distributed DNS servers for each zone. Each zone maintains its own set of local host records. These are just the registered host records and might or might not be separate physical machines. These records are maintained on the DNS server that manages the microsoft.com zone.

DNS Server Location

The DNS server and the domain are not necessarily on one machine. A DNS server may support multiple domains or zones. The DNS hierarchy is simply the structure of how the data is supported. The actual DNS server machine is not indicated within the DNS hierarchy. Any machine could provide this DNS domain service for one or more zones.

DNS Search Pattern

DNS's hierarchical design provides an indexed search pattern that does not require looking at every host record. Each domain or zone database has records that point to at least the named root server and possibly other root servers. The local server provides an indexed search of its cached records or its database of records and passes the request up the hierarchy only if needed.

FIGURE 4-1

Small, selected DNS hierarchical structure from the internet

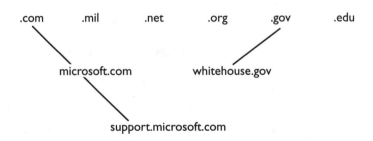

Internet Domain Name Server Hierarchies

Root domains represent the upper-indexed pointers to other DNS servers. These root domains represent the highest level of the DNS hierarchy and are the first to be consulted in the name resolution process. For example, if you are trying to connect to microsoft.com, the .COM root domain DNS server checks its database for an entry for *microsoft*. Once the entry is found, the root domain server passes your request to the microsoft.com DNS server.

The following is a description of the most popular DNS root domains found on the Internet:

- **.com** This is the commercial organizations group and is by far the largest. Almost everyone wants this domain because it is the first default extension for all commercial organizations such as DEC, Sun, IBM, and Microsoft.

- **.org** This is for noncommercial organizations.

- **.net** This is for networking organizations such as island.net and nfs.net as well as Internet service providers such as netzero.net.

- **.mil** This is for military organizations such as army.mil and navy.mil.

- **.gov** This is for U.S. government offices only.

- **.edu** This is for educational organizations.

Countries' Domain Names

The Internet started in the United States, so Internet-related organizations are normally located in this country. For the rest of the world, country servers are based on a two-letter shortcut. Every country, including the United States, has one. Here are a few of the most common country domain names:

- **.ca** Canada
- **.ie** Ireland
- **.uk** United Kingdom
- **.us** Unites States

Top-Level Domain Servers

Root servers are used to route a request to the next correct server. The root server for Canada, .CA, has another root server or subdomain for each province. A provincial server might or might not have further nested subdomain servers, as required. In other countries, the root servers might have city-based nested subdomains.

Within the .US and .CA root servers are additional sets of servers for each state, province, or region and possibly many cities—for example, dallas.tx.us for Dallas, Texas, United States, and vancouver.bc.ca for Vancouver, British Columbia, Canada. The hostnames are appended to these domain names. For example, a host called *info* in the city of Vancouver in British Columbia, Canada, could be reached with info.vancouver.bc.ca or www.vancouver.bc.ca. Normally, DNS names are displayed in lowercase. However, most DNS services are not case sensitive.

Root Servers

There are many root servers, but the .COM server is by far the largest and most overloaded. The other root servers offer local access with faster response for local users and make it easier to get a domain name that is not already used by another DNS service.

The root servers provide addresses to the domain servers associated with that root. For example, the .COM root server maintains IP address pointer records for all the *name*.com DNS servers. In turn, each *name*.com domain contains records for all of its local machines only. The root DNS database is maintained locally by a specific authority.

The .COM root server knows the .EDU, .MIL, and all other root server addresses. When a hostname request comes into a root server, the server simply looks at the root portion of the name and passes the name off to this root server. This second root server then looks up the domain name in its database and sends the packet on to that specific domain name service. This specific domain name then provides an answer or an error message if nothing is found.

Resolving Host and Domain Names

When a program requests a host by a single name, such as *sunsite*, the network protocol provides a sequence of steps to resolve the name. If the client is DNS aware, the DNS service request appends the local domain name to the end of the requested hostname and tries to resolve this within its database. If this first domain name fails and other suffix names are configured within DNS, the name is appended to each of them successively and tried within the specified DNS service again. If an FQDN is supplied, the DNS service is queried directly first.

Primary DNS Servers

Let's look at an example. The primary DNS server for arg.com first tries to resolve a request locally by checking its own records. The DNS server can have more than one zone database. If so, TCP/IP properties for alternate suffix search names must reflect these alternate domain names.

Some specialized servers are configured to maintain a cache of previous hits so that common requests do not have to repeat the longer full-request process.

Search DNS Servers

If the local DNS service cannot provide an address resolution for an FQDN, it passes the request "up the ladder" to the .COM server, which looks in its local databases. If it does not find the IP address for the host, it passes the record on to the root server of the remote hostname.

Return to Resolver

The .EDU server passes the request on to the unc.edu DNS zone server, which hopefully has the IP address. The found IP address then passes back through the same chain to the original host. At this point, the original host is finally able to send packets directly to the remote host.

DNS Files

All DNS information that is maintained in the registry can also be maintained in text file format if you select Update Data Files from the DNS Menu of DNS Manager. If you are using files from a UNIX BIND version of DNS, you can force the DNS server not to read the registry and simply use the files ported over from UNIX. Be aware that the UNIX BIND files could contain some commands that NT DNS will not understand. The files are located in: %systemroot%\system32\DNS.

For Windows 2000 and above, the DNS database can be integrated with Active Directory to allow for replication to all DNS servers when all domain controllers replicate the Active Directory structure. If the DNS database is integrated with Active Directory, it will not be located in the %systemroot%\system32\DNS directory.

Windows Internet Naming Service

The Windows Internet Naming Service (WINS) provides tools that enhance Windows NT to manage the NetBIOS names of servers and workstations in a TCP/IP networking environment. In order to understand WINS, you need to understand the precursor to it, NetBIOS. NetBIOS names are 15 characters long, with a 16th character used to signify the resource type. The NetBIOS name space is flat, meaning that names may be used only once within a network. These names are registered dynamically when computers boot, services start, or users log on. NetBIOS names can be registered as unique or as group names. All Windows NT network programs, such as Explorer, use NetBIOS names to access services.

A unique name has one associated address. A group name has more than one address mapped to it. NetBIOS is responsible for establishing logical names on the network, establishing sessions between two logical names on the network, and supporting reliable data transfer between computers that have established a session.

Before WINS, the LMHOSTS file was used to assist with remote NetBIOS name resolution. The LMHOSTS file is a static file that maps NetBIOS names to IP addresses. This file is similar to the HOSTS file in functionality; the only difference is that the HOSTS file is used for mapping hostnames to IP addresses.

If you are at a site that currently uses a WINS server but has used an LMHOSTS file in the past, make sure that the LMHOSTS file doesn't contain entries that are not updated. Some sites use the LMHOSTS file as a backup to WINS but forget to update the LMHOSTS file. I spent hours with another technician troubleshooting one computer that wouldn't connect to an application server. We finally figured out that the LMHOSTS file was still active and there was an incorrect entry for that server.

WINS Features

WINS includes many features that provide simplified networking. By enabling computers to register NetBIOS names in one location, we make easier the maintenance and management tasks. A WINS service eliminates the need for many network broadcasts, therefore reducing network usage. This is accomplished using directed, or point-to-point, transmissions for name resolution. WINS is dynamic and is updated when machines are started or stopped or by replication with other WINS services. When a name is registered, it is reserved for that one computer, further simplifying naming schemes. Each computer always has its own unique name.

Requirements for WINS

WINS works on any Windows NT server on a TCP/IP network. This server should also have a static IP address, not one obtained dynamically from a DHCP server. WINS maintains a database of mappings for IP addresses to NetBIOS names. When a WINS client requests an IP address, WINS checks its database and returns the address to the client. It is not required, but a secondary WINS service can be implemented for larger networks.

Dynamic Registration

WINS provides a distributed database for registering and querying dynamic NetBIOS names to IP address mappings in a routed network environment. When a computer in a WINS-enabled network starts, it automatically registers all its NetBIOS names with the WINS server. If the computer's IP address is changed, the WINS server knows immediately. This is WINS's strength: its ability to keep an accurate IP mapping database in an ever-changing network environment. WINS is the best choice for NetBIOS name resolution in a routed network because it is designed to solve the problems that occur with name resolution.

Even though DNS is dynamic on Windows 2000 servers and above, the Windows 2000 and above server can still use WINS for backward compatibility.

Table 4-1 outlines the differences between WINS and DNS.

TABLE 4-1	The Differences Between WINS and DNS

Feature	WINS	DNS
Purpose	Resolves NetBIOS names to IP addresses.	Resolves hostnames to IP addresses.
Names	Flat in structure and limited to 15 characters.	Hierarchical structure and limited to 255 characters.
Name Registration	Dynamic and automatic.	Static and must be done manually (is dynamic on Windows 2000 and XP servers).
Replication	Replicates changes.	Replicates whole database (Windows 2000 and XP servers can also replicate changes only).

HOSTS Files

In early TCP/IP networks, all known hostnames and their associated IP addresses were stored in a simple text file called *HOSTS*. In most UNIX installations, the HOSTS file is located in the /etc directory and is also commonly referred to as /etc/HOSTS.

The HOSTS file contained one line for each IP address and at least one associated name. The HOSTS file design allowed multiple names for the same IP address, all on one line, as shown in the following HOSTS file example:

```
206.197.150.11 bigsun BIGSUN ftp www
206.197.150.51 host51 HOST51 nevermore
206.197.150.52 host52 HOST52 icedearth
206.197.150.53 host53 HOST53 justinharvey
206.197.150.54 host54 HOST54 sanctuary
206.197.150.55 host55 HOST55 warrel
```

The HOSTS file provides a static lookup of a hostname for the associated IP address. Notice also that the HOSTS file is flexible in that multiple names can be associated with one IP address. In the first line of the HOSTS file example are four names associated with the one IP address on the left. This gives a network user the option of using bigsun, BIGSUN, ftp, or www as reference hostnames to reach the machine with the IP address 206.197.150.11.

Sharing the HOSTS File

Each isolated TCP/IP network must maintain its own HOSTS file and make it available, by some copy method, to every other host on the network. In a small network of less than 100 machines, this process can be managed centrally by paper and pencil. This design becomes cumbersome if the network is larger than a few hundred machines. You could not change a hostname or IP address without updating the HOSTS file on every other host in the network.

Limitations of the HOSTS File

As networks became more and more complex, not only topologically and geographically, a corresponding need to simplify name resolution arose. In small offices, a hostname might reflect the name of the user; the server could reflect the name of the company. But when there are hundreds of servers, spread out in many office locations, and thousands of users pressing the need for central management, the HOSTS file system reveals its limitations.

Internet Growth

As the Internet grew, every time a host was added, every other machine had to add that name to its host file. When this became too cumbersome, the host files were trimmed down to directly reachable hosts. These hosts then passed the requests on, if they were not destined locally, to the remote hosts of all the other networks that could possibly get the packet to the eventual host. This was like a raindrop falling on a pond, creating a wave of packets heading out in all directions from the server. Because some hosts knew about others who knew about them, the packets sometimes ended up routing in a circle. This routing loop was controlled via a *time-to-live (TTL) value* included in each packet.

TTL is the amount of time that a packet is allowed to be on the network before it is removed. This time is usually in seconds, but each router reduces the TTL by 1 when the packet passes through the router. Once a packet's TTL is 0, it is deleted from the router it passed through, and a packet is usually sent to the sending PC that the packet has not reached its destination.

The Main Protocols of the TCP/IP Suite

Contained within the TCP/IP model are several protocols that direct how computers connect and communicate using TCP/IP. Even though the protocol suite is called TCP/IP, many other protocols are available besides the TCP and IP protocols.

Transmission Control Protocol

Transmission Control Protocol (TCP) is one of the protocols for which the TCP/IP suite is named. TCP provides a reliable, connection-based delivery service. TCP guarantees successful delivery of packets. It uses a checksum to ensure that data is sequenced correctly. If a TCP packet is lost or corrupted during transmission, TCP resends a good packet. TCP's reliability is necessary for critical services, such as electronic mail. However, the reliability does not come cheaply, because TCP headers have additional overhead. The overhead is necessary to guarantee successful delivery of the data. Another factor to remember about TCP is that the protocol requires that the recipient acknowledge the successful receipt of data. Of course, all the acknowledgments, known as ACKs, generate additional traffic on the network, which causes a reduction in the amount of data that is passed for a given time frame.

User Datagram Protocol

User Datagram Protocol (UDP) offers a connectionless datagram service that is an unreliable "best effort" delivery. UDP does not guarantee the arrival of datagrams, nor does it promise that the delivered packets are in the correct sequence. Applications that don't require an acknowledgment of data receipt use UDP.

HyperText Transfer Protocol and HyperText Transfer Protocol, Secure

HyperText Transfer Protocol (HTTP) is the protocol used on the Internet to allow clients to request Web pages from Web servers and allow for client interaction with those Web servers. HTTP is a stateless protocol, meaning that the Web servers are not aware of what a client has or has not requested and cannot track users who have requested specific content. This system does not allow for good interaction with the Web server but does allow for retrieving the HTML pages stored on Web sites. To aid in tracking client requests, we use *cookies*—small files stored on the client computer that allow the Web server to send requests to the client and the client to respond with the information in the requested cookie. For this reason, when you visit certain Web sites, the page that is displayed has your name on it. When you visited the site for the first time, you probably filled in a questionnaire and it saved this information as a cookie, which is retrieved whenever you revisit the site.

HyperText Transfer Protocol, Secure (HTTPS) allows you to connect to a Web site and receive and send content in an encrypted format using Secure Sockets Layer (SSL). HTTPS is most commonly used on e-commerce sites to allow you to send personal information without worrying that an Internet hacker is viewing this information, especially credit card numbers and other confidential data. You can determine when HTTPS is being used because the address of the Web site starts with https:// and not http://, which is the regular HTTP protocol. Another sign that HTTPS is in use: In Internet Explorer, a lock appears in the status bar of a page; the lock is either closed, or locked.

HTTPS is not used for an entire e-commerce site because the encryption and decryption processes slow the connection time, so only the pages of personal information use HTTPS.

Network Time Protocol

Network Time Protocol (NTP) is used to synchronize the clocks of PCs on a network or Internet. This is accomplished by configuring a server to be the time server, which then is the server from which all other PCs on the network synchronize their time.

On a Windows network, you can manage time synchronization by placing a command in a logon script to synchronize the time with the time server. Use the following command:

```
NET TIME \\computername /SET
```

You do need to remember that the network's speed can cause some delay in the proper time being received by the client PC from the time server and can cause the time not to be exactly synchronized. The time sent from the time server can be off by as much as 50 milliseconds. This might not seem like much, but to a computer, it is quite a bit. However, this time difference should not cause problems.

Time servers on the Internet allow you to synchronize your PC's clock with the exact time kept by atomic clocks. The time synchronization takes into effect time zone settings of your operating system and allows you to synchronize with a time server even if it is not set for your local time zone.

Network News Transfer Protocol

Network News Transfer Protocol (NNTP) is used to send and retrieve news articles or news feeds on the Internet in newsgroups. NNTP uses TCP to send and receive news articles. NNTP allows the submission and retrieval of only the news articles that have not previously been sent or retrieved.

Internet Control Message Protocol

Internet Control Message Protocol (ICMP) enables systems on a TCP/IP network to share status and error information. You can use the status information to detect network trouble. ICMP messages are encapsulated within IP datagrams so that they may be routed throughout an internetwork. Two of the most common uses of ICMP messages are *PING* and *TRACERT*.

You can use PING to send ICMP echo requests to an IP address and wait for ICMP echo responses. PING reports the time interval between sending the request and receiving the response. With PING, you can determine whether a particular IP system on your network is functioning correctly. You can use many different options with the PING utility.

TRACERT traces the path taken to a particular host. This utility can be very useful in troubleshooting internetworks. TRACERT sends ICMP echo requests to an IP address while it increments the TTL field in the IP header by a count of 1 after starting at 1 and then analyzing the ICMP errors that are returned. Each succeeding echo request should get one further into the network before the TTL field reaches 0 and an "ICMP time exceeded" error message is returned by the router attempting to forward it.

Address Resolution Protocol

Address Resolution Protocol (ARP) provides IP-address-to-physical-address resolution for IP packets. To accomplish this feat, ARP sends out a broadcast message with an *ARP request packet* that contains the IP address of the system it is trying to find. All systems on the local network detect the broadcast message, and the system that owns the IP address for which ARP is looking replies by sending its physical address to the originating system in an *ARP reply packet*. The physical/IP address combo is then stored in the ARP cache of the originating system for future use.

All systems maintain ARP caches that include their own IP-address-to-physical-address mapping. The ARP cache is always checked for an IP-address-to-physical-address mapping before initiating a broadcast. You can see the contents of your ARP cache using the ARP utility you learned about in Chapter 3.

Simple Mail Transfer Protocol

Simple Mail Transfer Protocol (SMTP) is used to send and receive mail over the Internet. In the days of mainframes and terminals, workstations had continuous connections to the mainframe; therefore, electronic mail could be sent and received with great assurance. Because most computers today are standalone workstations and no longer terminal based, SMTP cannot provide a high degree of reliability between the nonpermanent connections.

Post Office Protocol 3

Post Office Protocol (POP) was designed to overcome the problem encountered with SMTP in which workstations were not confined to permanent terminal-based connections to a mainframe. (POP is on its third iteration, so now it's POP3.) A POP3 mail server holds the mail in a mail drop until the workstation is ready to receive it. When you set up a mail account with your Internet service provider (ISP), your ISP gives you the name of the POP3 server to which you can log in, with the correct username and password, to obtain your mail.

Internet Message Access Protocol 4

Internet Message Access Protocol (IMAP) is another protocol similar to POP that allows clients to retrieve messages from a mail server. (IMAP is on its fourth iteration, IMAP4.) IMAP allows e-mail retrieval for the purpose of storing the mail somewhere other than the mail server. IMAP is used with Microsoft Outlook to retrieve e-mail and store it in a data file on the local PC.

Simple Network Management Protocol

Simple Network Management Protocol (SNMP) is an Internet standard that provides a simple method for remotely managing virtually any network device. A network device can be a network card in a server, a program or service running on a server, or a standalone network device such as a hub or router.

The SNMP standard defines a two-tiered approach to network device management: a central *management system* and the *management information base (MIB)* located on the managed device. The management system can monitor one or many MIBs, allowing for centralized management of a network. From a management system you can see valuable performance and network device operation statistics, enabling you to diagnose network health without leaving your office.

The goal of a management system is to provide centralized network management. Any computer running SNMP management software is referred to as a *management system*. For a management system to be able to perform centralized network management, it must be able to collect and analyze many things, including the following:

■ Network protocol identification and statistics

■ Dynamic identification of computers attached to the network (referred to as *discovery*)

- Hardware and software configuration data
- Computer performance and usage statistics
- Computer event and error messages
- Program and application usage statistics

File Transfer Protocol

File Transfer Protocol (FTP) is a TCP/IP utility that exists solely to copy files from one computer to another. Like Telnet and PING, FTP can establish a connection to a remote computer using either the hostname or IP address and must resolve hostnames to IP addresses to establish communication with the remote computer. As you read in Chapter 1, Windows NT/2000 includes an FTP server in its Internet Information Services (IIS) software. Windows NT/2000 and Windows 95/98/ME computers each include a command-line FTP client with their TCP/IP protocol software. Although it is not widely known, the Windows FTP client supports scripting, which enables users to automate repetitive FTP tasks.

A number of third-party graphical user interface (GUI) FTP clients are available for all versions of Windows computers. If you use FTP a great deal, a GUI FTP client could save you a lot of time and frustration.

Internet Protocol

IP is the other protocol for which the TCP/IP suite is named. It is a vital link in the suite because all information that is sent using the TCP/IP protocol suite must use it. IP provides packet delivery for all other protocols within the suite. It is a connectionless delivery system that makes a "best effort" attempt to deliver the packets to the correct destination. IP does not guarantee delivery, nor does it promise that the IP packets will be received in the order in which they were sent. IP does use a checksum, but it confirms only the integrity of the IP header. Confirmation of the integrity of data contained within an IP packet can be accomplished only through higher-level protocols.

Now that you have seen some of the more confusing aspects of TCP/IP, take a look at the following quick reference of possible scenarios involving TCP/IP protocols and services and the appropriate answers.

SCENARIO & SOLUTION

I need to send e-mail from one server to another.	Use SMTP. The key to using SMTP is that, when servers are passing mail back and forth to each other, do not involve a client.
I need to download e-mail from my mail server.	Use POP3 or IMAP4. The POP3 and IMAP4 protocols were designed to store electronic messages for later retrieval by e-mail clients.
I need a protocol to use for my e-commerce site to protect the confidential information being sent by customers.	Use HTTPS. HyperText Transfer Protocol, Secure allows the encryption of data between a client and a server.
I need to resolve a hardware address.	Use ARP. Whenever you see *hardware address* and *resolve* in the same question, you are most likely talking about the Address Resolution Protocol (ARP).
The PCs on my network must have a common time to allow for proper logging of database updates by clients.	Use NTP. Network Time Protocol allows client PCs to synchronize time with the server so that the time is the same on all PCs.
I need to resolve a machine name.	Use LMHOSTS or WINS. These services are designed to resolve NetBIOS (machine) names to IP addresses. Note that a UNIX host uses the LMHOSTS file, not the WINS service.
I need to be able to connect to a Usenet group and send and retrieve news articles.	Use NNTP. Network News Transfer Protocol allows submission and retrieval of news articles in newsgroups.
I need to resolve a hostname.	Use HOSTS or DNS. These services are designed to resolve hostnames to IP addresses. Remember that the HOSTS file is located on each workstation and server, and the DNS service provides a central HOSTS file located on a server.
I need a connectionless protocol.	Use IP or UDP. UDP and IP are connectionless protocols, meaning that they don't establish connections between two computers. These protocols don't guarantee data will arrive at all, but they are very fast.
I need a connection-oriented protocol.	Use TCP. This protocol establishes a connection between the sending and receiving computers. Although slower than UDP, it can guarantee that data will arrive.

CERTIFICATION OBJECTIVE 4.02

TCP/IP Addressing

Many of the questions regarding TCP/IP on the Network+ exam will cover configuring TCP/IP, the architecture of TCP/IP, and TCP/IP addressing, which you learn about in this section. The following TCP/IP addressing topics are covered here:

■ The IP address

■ The address classes

■ Subnetting and the subnet mask

You learned a great deal about IP addresses in this chapter and in Chapter 3, so here we focus on the address classes and the subnet mask.

A, B, and C Classes of IP Addresses and Their Default Subnet Masks

A subnet mask is used to determine which part of the IP address is used for the network ID and which part is for the host ID. You must supply two required parameters to initialize TCP/IP:

■ **IP address**   A 4-octet address.

■ **Subnet mask**   A 4-octet value.

Every IP address belongs to a distinct class. The Internet community defined these classes to accommodate networks of various sizes. The class to which the IP address belongs initially determines the network ID and host ID portions of the address. The classes range from Class A to Class E; however, Microsoft TCP/IP supports only Class A, B, and C addresses assigned to hosts. This section details each class of addresses.

As you just learned, the IP addressing scheme can build fairly large networks. Table 4-2 lists the three types of network addresses, called *network classes,* that are assigned to a company or an organization.

Class A Addresses

As you can see in Table 4-2, Class A addresses are assigned to networks with a very large number of hosts. Table 4-3 illustrates the most important features of a Class A address, which you need to memorize for the exam.

Managing a Class A Network Address

When addressing classes first came into use, companies that received a Class A address had over 16 million host addresses at their disposal. With only 126 allocated Class A networks, many prime host addresses were wasted.

This is where subnetting came in. Breaking down one Class A network address into multiple subnetworks makes for better use of the available IP address pool.

TABLE 4-2	Network Class	Number of Hosts
TCP/IP Network Classes and Numbers of Hosts	Class A	Approximately 16,000,000
	Class B	Approximately 65,000
	Class C	254

TABLE 4-3 Class A Address Information

Class A Range	Number of Class A Networks	Default Subnet Mask
Class A addresses range from 1.0.0.0 to 126.0.0.0.	The Class A range has the possibility of 126 networks, with each network having the capability of 16,777,214 unique hosts when you use the default subnet mask.	The default subnet mask for a Class A network is 255.0.0.0 or, in binary representation, 11111111 00000000 00000000 00000000.

Class B Addresses

Class B addresses are assigned to medium-sized networks. Table 4-4 illustrates the most important features of a Class B address, which you need to memorize for the exam.

Class C Addresses

Class C addresses are usually assigned to small local area networks (LANs) and comprise most of the Internet and intranet sites available. Even the Class C addresses are quickly being used up due to the overwhelming popularity of the Internet. Table 4-5 illustrates the most important features of a Class C address, which you need to memorize for the exam.

TABLE 4-4   Class B Address Information

Class B Range	Number of Class B Networks	Default Subnet Mask
Class B addresses range from 128.0.0.0 to 191.255.0.0.	The Class B range has the possibility of 16,384 networks, with each network having the capability of 65,534 unique hosts when you use the default subnet mask.	The default subnet mask for a Class B network is 255.255.0.0 or, in binary representation, 11111111 11111111 00000000 00000000.

TABLE 4-5   Class C Address information

Class C Ranges	Number of Class C Networks	Default Subnet Mask
Class C addresses range from 192.0.1.0 to 223.255.255.0.	The Class C range has the possibility of 2,097,152 networks, with each network having the capability of 254 unique hosts when you use the default subnet mask.	The default subnet mask for a Class C network is 255.255.255.0 or, in binary representation, 11111111 11111111 11111111 00000000.

Class D Addresses

Class D addresses are used for multicasting to a number of hosts. Data is passed to one, two, three, or more users on a network. Only those hosts registered for the multicast address receive the data.

Class D Ranges

Class D addresses range from 224.0.0.0 to 239.255.255.255. Class D has the potential for 268,435,456 unique multicast groups.

Broadcast Examples

Currently, Class D addresses are used mainly for experimentation. Membership in an IP multicast group is dynamic. A host can join or leave a group at any time. You could see Class D addressing used for audio news multicasting, video presentations, or a music multicast.

Class E Addresses

Class E is an experimental address block that is reserved for future use.

Class E Ranges

Class E addresses range from 240.0.0.0 to 247.255.255.255.

exam
ⓦatch

It's guaranteed that you will see a question or two on the address classes on the Network+ exam. Make sure you know the ranges as well as the default subnet mask for each address class.

Subnetting

You might wonder how there can be so many people and places on the Internet if you are using 4 octets of numbers that are limited to 0–255 each, with some exceptions. This is where *subnetting* comes in. Subnetting allows for the existence of more usable numbers as addresses on the Internet.

Initially, the main point to remember is that each TCP/IP class has a default subnet mask: Class A has a subnet mask of 255.0.0.0, Class B a subnet mask of 255.255.0.0, and Class C a subnet mask of 255.255.255.0 (or basically, Class A uses 1 octet, Class B uses 2 octets, and Class C uses 3 octets).

The next thing to remember is that the part of the default subnet mask that is 255 designates the part of the IP address that is the network ID, while the rest is the host ID. Any two computers that have the same network ID and different host IDs will be able to communicate if they are on the same physical network. The network ID specifies the logical network to which the PC is communicating; the host ID specifies the ID of the PC or device on the logical network. For example, if you have a PC with an IP address of 10.0.0.1 and a subnet mask of 255.0.0.0, your network ID is 10 and your PC ID is 0.0.1.

Subnetting is the process of borrowing individual bits to add more network IDs. By using only the default subnet masks, we have only three possible networks. So, to borrow bits, we must convert the decimal number of all 4 octets to binary and start changing 0s to 1s, starting from the left and going to the right. Let's take a Class A address that we used in the last example and borrow 16 bits to make the subnet mask 255.255.255.0 for the address of 10.0.0.1. This now means that the network ID is 10.0.0 and the host ID is 1. If you have a PC with a TCP/IP address of 10.0.0.2 and a subnet mask of 255.255.0.0, your computer could not communicate with 10.0.0.1, since the logical network is different. Even if the second PC had an IP address of 10.0.0.1 and a subnet mask of 255.255.0.0, the two computers could coexist on the same physical network without causing a conflict of IP addresses, since they are logically on two different networks.

Most network administrators of large networks, especially WANs, must have a firm grasp of TCP/IP and subnetting. You can access many resources to understand subnetting in more depth; the old MCSE for NT4 had an exam specific to TCP/IP, which did originally require an understanding of subnetting. Another certification exam requiring a great understanding of subnetting is the CCNA certification from Cisco.

Special Internet Addresses

Now you need to learn about some special Internet addresses. You might wonder why a Class C address can have only 254 hosts and not 256, as would seem more likely, since an 8-bit number can have 256 values. The reason for this seeming discrepancy is that two addresses are lost from the available host pool. The first is an address that has all 0s in the host ID, which signifies "this host" and is normally used in a BOOTP process when a host doesn't yet know its IP address. The second is an address that has all 1s in the host ID, which signifies a broadcast address. So, for example, in the Class C network 200.158.157.x, the addresses 200.158.157.0 and 200.158.157.255 are not available to hosts, reducing the available number of hosts from 256 to 254.

A network ID that is all 1s is used for limited broadcasts. A network ID that is all 0s signifies "this network." The number of Class A networks is reduced by 1 for this situation.

Loopback Addresses

Network IDs cannot start with 127 because this address is reserved for loopback and is used mainly for testing TCP/IP and internal loopback functions on the local system. If a program uses the loopback address as a destination, the protocol software in the system returns the data without sending traffic across the network. In fact, 127 is technically a Class A address because the high-order bit has a value of 0. However, remember that 127 is reserved and is not in use for live networks. To determine that TCP/IP is initialized properly, PING the loopback address to PING your own PC; if TCP/IP is initialized, you will get a response. To try this on a PC with TCP/IP, perform Exercise 4-2.

Configuring TCP/IP to Use DHCP

In this exercise you learn how to determine if TCP/IP is initialized on your local PC. Do the following:

1. Using a Windows PC, select **Start | Run**. If you are using Windows 95/98/ME, type **command** in the Run box; if you are using Windows NT/2000/XP, type **CMD** in the Run window.

2. At the command prompt, type **PING 127.0.0.1**.

3. If the response is four replies, TCP/IP is initialized. If there are four messages that state "Destination host unreachable," TCP/IP is not initialized.

4. Type **Exit** to return to the Windows desktop.

Port Numbers (HTTP, FTP, and SMTP)

When you use TCP/IP, it is very common to hear the term *port*. An application or process uses a TCP/IP port to communicate between a client and a server computer. *Port numbers*, often called *well-known ports*, are preassigned TCP/IP port numbers on the server that do not change (although they can be changed); they are preassigned so that they can expect traffic on a corresponding port relating to the service that is using that port.

For example, FTP uses two ports, 20 and 21. The server has the preassigned ports of 20 and 21 set aside for FTP traffic and nothing else. Clients, however, do not have to use the preassigned well-known port numbers when they connect to a server with an application or process; clients can use any dynamically assigned port to connect to the server. This works something like telephone communication. You (the client) can pick up a telephone anywhere in the world and dial your friend's number (the server), and if your friend is home, he or she will pick up the phone.

Table 4-6 is a list of well-known port numbers that remain constant on all TCP/IP-based operating systems.

exam
⚠️atch

You don't have to memorize the entire contents of Table 4-6 for the exam. The most popular, and therefore most likely, exam choices to remember are the FTP ports (20 and 21), SMTP port (25), and HTTP port (80).

TABLE 4-6		Well-Known TCP/IP Port Numbers

Port Number	Process	Description
20	FTP-DATA	File Transfer Protocol—data
21	FTP	File Transfer Protocol—control
23	TELNET	Telnet
25	SMTP	Simple Mail Transfer Protocol
69	TFTP	Trivial File Transfer Protocol
70	GOPHER	Gopher
80	HTTP	HyperText Transfer Protocol
110	POP3	Post Office Protocol, version 3
119	NNTP	Network News Transfer Protocol
123	NTP	Network Time Protocol
443	HTTPS	HyperText Transfer Protocol, Secure

Now let's look at a few scenarios and solutions related to port numbers.

SCENARIO & SOLUTION

I need to know which port number to block on my Web server so that no one can gain access to my FTP site from the Internet.	Use port 21. This is the port used by FTP.
I need to know which port to block on my router that is located between the Internet and my Web server to prevent hackers from Telnetting into my server. What port should I block?	Block port 23. This is the port used by Telnet clients.
I need to make sure that all my employee PCs will synchronize their clocks with the main server on the network and not with a time server on the Internet. What port do I block on my Internet connection?	Block port 123. This is the port used to synchronize the times on PCs using the Network Time Protocol.
I need to block my employees from being able to participate in Internet newsgroups while at work. How can I do this?	Block port 119 from internal access to the Internet.

TCP/IP Version 6

Even with subnetting, the number of IP addresses is still finite with the current version of TCP/IP (version 4 or IPv4). With all the Web sites and Internet users on the Internet, the number of available IP addresses is almost depleted, and a new IP addressing scheme has been created. The new TCP/IP addressing scheme is IP the Next Generation (IPv6).

The new version of TCP/IP, IPv6, will support 16 octets, or 128 bits, as opposed to IPv4, which has 4 octets and 32 bits. The 128-bit addressing scheme will allow for almost a *trillion trillion* addresses!

IPv6 offers many variations of possible IP addresses, even those that allow backward compatibility to make possible the coexistence of IPv4 and IPv6. IPv6 will designate priorities of packets to allow for almost real-time communication on the Internet for video conferencing and other real-time needs.

CERTIFICATION OBJECTIVE 4.03

TCP/IP Configuration Concepts

Configuring TCP/IP on a workstation is a topic that will surely make its way onto your Network+ exam. Now that you have a good understanding of the main TCP/IP properties that must be configured for each workstation, we can go about configuring these workstations. The following sections involve configuring TCP/IP on the most popular client operating systems: Windows 95/98 and Windows NT Workstation.

Configuration Parameters for a Workstation

As indicated before, you have two options for configuring a workstation: You can configure it manually, or you can use a DHCP server. Configuring the DHCP server is beyond the scope of the Network+ exam, so we exclude coverage of the server-side of DHCP configuration and focus on manually configuring each workstation.

Although in your corporate jobs you are more likely to encounter a TCP/IP network using DHCP for the workstations, the servers will not be DHCP clients and will require manual configuration. The process of manually configuring TCP/IP properties for a Windows NT server is identical to configuring Windows NT workstation properties. In addition, the knowledge gained from reading this chapter will benefit you when you are the administrator who must install and configure the DHCP scope of IP addresses and the additional TCP/IP settings, such as the default gateway and address of the WINS servers.

IP Address and Subnet Mask

The single most important piece of information required for a TCP/IP-based workstation to operate is the IP address. This address must be unique on the network. If you use DHCP to assign the workstation's IP address, the DHCP server assigns the workstation an IP address that is not in use. When you are manually assigning an IP address to a workstation, it is imperative that you do not duplicate IP addresses on the network. You can avoid doing so by using a spreadsheet that contains workstation and server names and the corresponding IP addresses. This spreadsheet should also contain all static IP addresses, such as routers and printers, and should specify the range of IP addresses that are in the DHCP scope of addresses as well as the addresses that are not currently being used. You must update this information frequently.

The second most important piece of information is the subnet mask. With an improperly configured subnet mask, you won't communicate with anyone on a TCP/IP-based network. As you learned earlier, the subnet mask performs double duty by determining the host ID and network ID from the IP address.

exam
Watch

Expect more than a few questions on your exam regarding TCP/IP, especially the IP address and subnet mask. These two settings are the most important of any TCP/IP implementation and are guaranteed to find their way into your Network+ exam.

In Windows 95, 98, and NT, you can specify an IP address and subnet mask or specify the use of a DHCP service. From the Control Panel, double-click the **Network** applet, click the **Properties** button, and select **TCP/IP Protocol**. On the TCP/IP Properties dialog box, click the **IP Address** tab to bring it to the front. Select the **Specify an IP address** option button, as shown in Figure 4-2, to manually assign an IP address and subnet mask. If you use DHCP, simply select the **Obtain an IP address automatically** option button.

Use the IP address page of the TCP/IP properties dialog box to specify DHCP or manually assign an IP Address and subnet mask

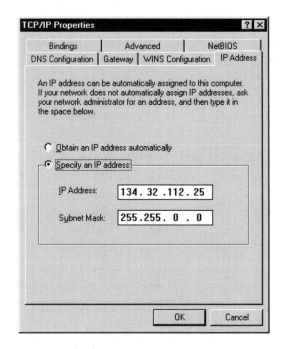

DNS

To configure a client to use DNS, you need to configure your TCP/IP settings to point to the DNS service and indicate the domain name that this DNS service provides. To do so, from the Control Panel, double-click the **Network** applet, click the **Properties** button, and select **TCP/IP Protocol.** In the Microsoft TCP/IP Properties dialog box, click the **DNS** tab to bring it to the front. If you are a client only of the DNS service, you need to enter the **Internet domain name** and the **IP address** of the DNS service. Click in the Domain text box and enter your **domain name**—for example, arg.com, as shown in Figure 4-3. Click the **Add** button and enter the **IP address** of this service in the DNS Service Search Order box. These are the minimum requirements to be a client of a DNS service.

Hostname

By default, your DNS hostname on a Windows-based machine is your computer name. In the example in Figure 4.3, the hostname is nt4. You can override this default by specifying a new hostname in the Host Name text box. There is a difference between

FIGURE 4-3

Use the DNS page
on the TCP/IP
properties dialog
box to configure a
client to use DNS

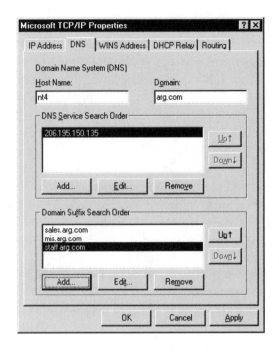

the hostname and the NetBIOS name, so don't get them confused. You will learn
how to change your computer name (your NetBIOS name) later in this chapter.

DNS Client Setup with Secondary Server

A secondary DNS server is a backup server with a copy of the zone information from
the master server. If this domain has one or more secondary DNS servers, you need
to enter one or more additional IP addresses in the DNS Service Search Order box
(the same way you did for the primary DNS service IP address). Click the **Add** button
within this box and then add the **IP address** of the secondary DNS server.

The DNS service search order is a failover list, not an additional location. Only if
the first service fails to respond after a nominal timeout period is the next DNS service
list tried with the same request, and so on. These secondary servers must have a valid
domain zone file for this system to work.

For the client, you need to add the domain name and IP address for the server that
is running the DNS service.

In the example in Figure 4-3, the arg.com domain is being managed. The IP address of the server managing arg.com is 206.195.150.135, the same IP address as the current host.

If your DNS service will split the domain information into subdomains, such as sales.arg.com, mis.arg.com, and staff.arg.com, you need to add these domain suffixes to the domain suffix search order list. The request for a single hostname with no domain qualification, no periods in the name, will iterate through the main domain suffix and then try each of these additional suffixes in an attempt to resolve the name to an IP address.

To add each additional domain suffix to the list, click the **Add** button in the Domain Suffix Search Order box on the DNS page. Enter each path with the full domain name structure. No leading period is required; the period will be supplied when the suffix is appended after the hostname.

There are far too many details associated with configuring a DNS server, so don't expect the exam to contain detailed questions in this area. Focusing on configuring client workstations to use DNS is much more important.

Default Gateways

The default gateway is needed only for systems that are part of an internetwork. Data packets with a destination IP address not on the local subnet nor elsewhere in the route table are automatically forwarded to the default gateway.

The default gateway is normally a computer system or router connected to the local subnet and other networks that knows the network IDs for other networks in the internetwork and the best path to reach them. Because the default gateway knows the network IDs of the other networks in the internetwork, it can forward the data packet to other gateways until the packet is ultimately delivered to a gateway connected to the intended destination. However, if the default gateway becomes unavailable, the system cannot communicate outside its own subnet, except with systems with which it had established connections prior to the failure.

Multiple Gateways   If the default gateway becomes unavailable, data packets cannot reach their destinations. You can use multiple gateways to prevent this situation.

To configure the default gateway for a client, click the **Gateway** tab in the TCP/IP Properties dialog box. Figure 4-4 illustrates the window interface used to configure the default gateway for a Windows 98 machine.

WINS

A WINS client is the machine that requests a NetBIOS mapping. This computer can use one of several operating systems. In addition to an acceptable operating system, a WINS client must be configured with the address of the WINS service. On computers running Windows 95 or Windows NT, this configuration is entered on the WINS Address page of the Microsoft TCP/IP Properties dialog box. (From the Control Panel, double-click the **Network** applet, click the **Properties** button, and select **TCP/IP Protocol**. Then click the **WINS Address** tab to bring it to the front.) In Windows 98, the WINS information is entered on the WINS Configuration page, as shown in Figure 4-5.

FIGURE 4-4

Use the gateway page on the TCP/IP properties dialog box to configure the default gateway for a client

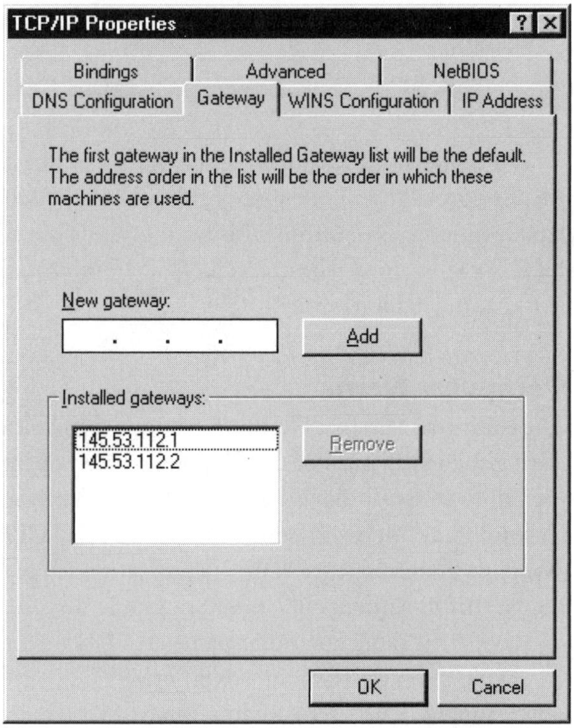

Use the WINS
configuration
page to configure
the WINS service
on a Windows 98
machine

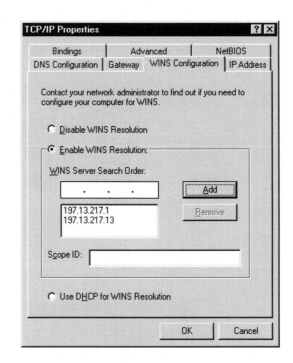

You can obtain the address of the WINS service dynamically from a DHCP server. In Windows 98, you can specify this address by selecting the **Use DHCP for WINS Resolution** option button. This button sends the address of the WINS server to the DHCP client, along with the vital TCP/IP information, such as the IP address, subnet mask, and default gateway.

Computer Name

The computer name, or NetBIOS name, is the name of the machine that you specified during the installation of the Windows-based operating system. NetBIOS names are used only with Windows-based machines. The NetBIOS name is specified in the Control Panel Network applet but not in the TCP/IP Properties dialog box. On a Windows 98 machine, click the **Identification** tab of the Network dialog box to change the NetBIOS name, as illustrated in Figure 4-6.

Having the same computer name and DNS hostname eliminates confusion. Changing the NetBIOS name won't override your hostname if you have specified one manually.

Exercise 4-3 shows you how to change the NetBIOS name.

Use the
identification page
to specify the
NetBIOS name
for the computer

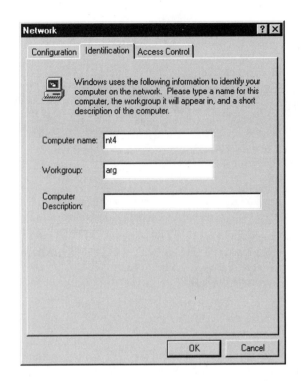

EXERCISE 4-3

CertCam 4-3

Changing the NetBIOS Name

In this exercise you learn how to change the NetBIOS name on your Windows
95/98/ME PC. Do the following:

1. On the Windows 95/98/ME desktop, right-click **Network Neighborhood**
   and select **Properties**.

2. Select the **Identification** tab.

3. The first option box is labeled Computer Name: and has the current NetBIOS
   name in the box. Select the name in the box and delete it, then retype your
   new NetBIOS name. Be careful to avoid duplicate names on the network.

Now let's look at some scenarios and solutions involving various aspects of TCP/IP use.

SCENARIO & SOLUTION

I need to be able to allow my network users to access my TCP/IP network. What utility can I use to assign them addresses?	Use DHCP.
If I have a router separating the intranet from the Internet and I want to allow access to the Internet, what do I configure?	Configure the default gateway. The IP address of the intranet side of the router should be designated as the default gateway.
I have a DNS server that I want internal users to query when trying to resolve a domain name. What should I configure to manage this task?	Configure the primary DNS server.
I have a WINS server that I want internal users to query when trying to resolve a NetBIOS name. What should I configure to manage this task?	Configure the primary WINS server.
I need to give each PC a friendly name and allow the WINS server to resolve these names when querying. What should I configure?	Configure the computer names.

CERTIFICATION SUMMARY

In this chapter you learned the fundamentals of TCP/IP and what makes this protocol so common in today's networking market. The following list summarizes what you learned about TCP/IP:

■ The IP address and subnet mask are the most important configuration settings and must be specified correctly in order to communicate on the TCP/IP-based network. Next in importance is the default gateway, which specifies where to route packets if you are communicating outside the local network.

■ Dynamic Host Configuration Protocol (DHCP) automatically configures a workstation with the correct TCP/IP settings, relieving you of the burden of manually configuring every workstation.

■ Domain Name System (DNS) is essential for Internet-based machines and company intranets that use DNS for hostname resolution. You learned about the hostname, domain name, resolution, and Internet domain name server hierarchies.

■ The Windows Internet Naming Service (WINS), which ironically has little to do with the Internet, enables workstations to resolve NetBIOS names to IP addresses rather than using a static LMHOSTS file on each machine.

■ TCP/IP is a suite of protocols, the most popular of which are TCP, UDP, IP, and ARP. (Your Network+ exam will definitely have several questions on some of these TCP/IP protocol suite members.)

■ TCP/IP addressing involves a strong knowledge of the IP address, subnet mask, network classes, and the special reserved addresses. (You should memorize each network class for the exam.)

■ The most important portions of TCP/IP as it relates to your Network+ exam is the TCP/IP configuration concepts. You need these to configure workstations with TCP/IP. The concepts include the IP address, the subnet mask, DHCP, DNS, WINS, the default gateway, the hostname, and the NetBIOS name.

With a strong understanding of the material presented in this chapter, you will have no problems with any TCP/IP-related questions on your exam. Not only is the material presented here important for the exam, but it will also be important after you ace the exam and continue on to a career as a networking professional.

✓ TWO-MINUTE DRILL

TCP/IP Fundamentals

❏ The popularity of TCP/IP makes the protocol a likely culprit to appear many times throughout your Network+ exam.

❏ TCP/IP is a *suite* of protocols.

❏ TCP/IP's unique addressing mechanism provides for over 4.2 billion addresses.

❏ Dynamic Host Configuration Protocol (DHCP) can help with configuring IP addressing on a large TCP/IP-based network.

❏ One service that is used throughout the Internet is the Domain Name System (DNS).

❏ DNS is one method of resolving a hostname to a given IP address.

❏ DNS is not a dynamic service like WINS or DHCP, except on Windows 2000/XP servers.

❏ The fully qualified domain name (FQDN) is the name of the host suffixed by a period and followed by the domain name.

❏ Root domains represent the upper-indexed pointers to other DNS servers.

❏ When a program requests a host by a single name, such as *sunsite*, the network protocol provides a sequence of steps to resolve the name.

❏ Windows Internet Naming Service (WINS) provides tools that enhance Windows NT to manage the NetBIOS names of servers and workstations in a TCP/IP networking environment.

❏ Before WINS, the LMHOSTS file was used to assist with remote NetBIOS name resolution.

❏ The LMHOSTS file is a static file that maps NetBIOS names to IP addresses.

❏ In early TCP/IP networks, all known hostnames and their associated IP addresses were stored in a simple text file called *HOSTS*.

❑ Even though the protocol suite is called TCP/IP, many other protocols are available besides the TCP and IP protocols.

❑ TCP provides a reliable, connection-based delivery service.

❑ User Datagram Protocol (UDP) offers a connectionless datagram service that is an unreliable "best effort" delivery.

❑ HyperText Transfer Protocol (HTTP) allows clients to request Web pages from servers.

❑ HyperText Transfer Protocol, Secure (HTTPS) is used the same way as HTTP, but the data is encrypted. HTTPS is used on e-commerce sites.

❑ Network Time Protocol (NTP) is used to synchronize the clocks on all PCs with a single PC or time server.

❑ Network News Transfer Protocol (NNTP) is used to view and update news articles on newsgroups.

❑ Internet Control Message Protocol (ICMP) enables systems on a TCP/IP network to share status and error information.

❑ Address Resolution Protocol (ARP) is used to provide IP-address-to-physical-address resolution for IP packets.

❑ Simple Mail Transfer Protocol (SMTP) is used to send and receive mail over the Internet.

❑ Post Office Protocol (POP) was designed to overcome the problem encountered with SMTP in which workstations were not confined to permanent terminal-based connections to a mainframe.

❑ Internet Message Access Protocol (IMAP), a protocol similar to POP, is used to retrieve messages from a mail server.

❑ Simple Network Management Protocol (SNMP) is an Internet standard that provides a simple method for remotely managing virtually any network device.

❑ File Transfer Protocol (FTP) is a TCP/IP utility that exists solely to copy files from one computer to another.

❑ IP provides packet delivery for all other protocols within the suite.

TCP/IP Addressing

❑ Many of the questions regarding TCP/IP on the Network+ exam will cover configuring TCP/IP, the architecture of TCP/IP, and TCP/IP addressing.

❑ A subnet mask is used to determine the part of the IP address used for the network ID and the part used for the host ID.

❑ Class A addresses are assigned to networks with a very large number of hosts.

❑ Class B addresses are assigned to medium-sized networks.

❑ Class C addresses, usually assigned to small LANs, comprise most of the Internet and intranet sites available.

❑ Class D addresses are used for multicasting to a number of different hosts.

❑ Class E is an experimental address block that is reserved for future use.

❑ An application or process uses a TCP/IP port to communicate between client and server computers.

❑ The most popular, and therefore most likely, exam choices to remember are the FTP ports (20 and 21), SMTP port (25), and HTTP port (80).

TCP/IP Configuration Concepts

❑ Configuring TCP/IP on a workstation is a topic that will surely make its way on to your Network+ exam.

❑ You have two options for configuring a workstation: You can configure it manually, or you can use a DHCP server.

❑ Expect more than a few questions regarding TCP/IP on the exam, especially the IP address and subnet mask. These two are the most important settings of any TCP/IP implementation and are guaranteed to find their way onto your Network+ exam.

❑ There are far too many details associated with configuring a DNS server, so don't expect detailed questions in this area. Focusing on configuring client workstations to use DNS is much more important.

SELF TEST

The following questions will help you measure your understanding of the material presented in this chapter. Read all the choices carefully because there might be more than one correct answer. Choose all correct answers for each question.

TCP/IP Fundamentals

1. TCP/IP's unique addressing mechanism provides more than how many IP addresses?

   A. 3.5 billion addresses

   B. 5.2 billion addresses

   C. 4.2 billion addresses

   D. 6.6 billion addresses

2. Which of the following will happen if the default gateway is not configured in the DHCP server for a client that is configured to use DHCP?

   A. An error will be issued.

   B. The default gateway will default to 0.0.0.0.

   C. The default gateway will default to 255.255.255.255.

   D. You must specify the IP address, subnet mask, and default gateway as a minimum for DHCP configured clients.

3. Which of the following is *not* true regarding DNS root servers?

   A. DNS root servers are not required.

   B. The root DNS database is maintained locally by a specific authority.

   C. The root servers are used to route the request to the next correct server.

   D. The actual DNS server machine is not indicated within the DNS hierarchy.

4. Where is DNS information stored?

   A. unix/bin/etc/DNS

   B. %systemroot%\system32\DNS

   C. unix/etc/bin

   D. %systemroot%\system32\etc\DNS

5. How are name registration and replication implemented in WINS?

   A. Name resolution is static, and replication is done manually.

   B. Name resolution is dynamic, and the whole database is replicated.

   C. Name resolution is static, and changes are replicated.

   D. Name resolution is dynamic, and changes are replicated.

6. How can you stop name resolution packets from endlessly looping around the network?

   A. Specify a lower TTL value.

   B. Specify a maximum number of hops in the HOSTS file.

   C. Specify a higher TTL in the HOSTS file.

   D. Specify a lower TTL in the DNS cache file.

7. Which of the following is *not* associated with the SNMP implementation?

   A. Network protocol identification and statistics

   B. Management system

   C. Packet routing

   D. Management Information Base

8. Which of the following is true regarding the IP protocol?

   A. The IP protocol guarantees timely and error-free delivery.

   B. The TCP protocol can be used to send information if the IP protocol is not configured correctly.

   C. The IP protocol is a connectionless delivery system.

   D. The IP protocol requires that the TCP protocol provide routing information.

TCP/IP Addressing

9. Which network address class supports more than 70,000 hosts?

   A. Class A

   B. Class B

   C. Class C

   D. Class D

10. What is the default subnet mask for a Class C network?

    A. 255.255.0.0

    B. 225.225.225.0

    C. 255.255.255.0

    D. 225.255.255.0

11. Which host is normally used in a BOOTP process?

    A. The local host

    B. The DHCP server

    C. 255.255.255.255

    D. 0.0.0.0

12. Which address is reserved for internal loopback functions?

    A. 0.0.0.0

    B. 1.0.0.0

    C. 121.0.0.0

    D. 127.0.0.0

13. What is the well-known port number for the HTTP service?

    A. 20

    B. 21

    C. 80

    D. 70

14. Which of the following methods would *not* be helpful when you are trying to stop the assignment of duplicate IP addresses on your network?

    A. Using two DHCP servers on the same network

    B. Using a spreadsheet to track in-use IP addresses

    C. Using PING to test for connectivity before you assign an IP address

    D. Using a DHCP server

TCP/IP Configuration

15. On a Windows 98 machine, which page of the TCP/IP Properties dialog box would you use to configure your workstation to use a DHCP server?

A. Identification

B. DHCP

C. IP Address

D. WINS

16. Which of the following is *not* on the DNS page of the TCP/IP Properties dialog box?

A. DNS Service Search Order

B. Domain Suffix Search Order

C. Use WINS for DNS Resolution

D. Domain name

17. Where can you specify a second DNS service for faster host and domain name resolution?

A. DNS Service Search Order

B. Domain Suffix Search Order

C. Domain Name

D. You can't specify a second DNS service for faster host and domain name resolution

18. You are having problems communicating with a remote network via the default gateway. Which of the following will *not* ensure fault tolerance if you have specified an incorrect default gateway on a client computer?

A. Obtain the default gateway entry from a DHCP service.

B. Configure the workstation to use the WINS service instead.

C. Implement a route table, which can be used to route packets to known networks before the default gateway entry is used.

D. Specify multiple gateways.

19. Which tab would you click on a Windows 98 machine to configure the gateway?

   A. IP Address

   B. NetBIOS

   C. Advanced

   D. Gateway

20. Which is *not* an available option on the WINS Configuration page of the TCP/IP Properties dialog box on a Windows 98 machine?

   A. WINS Suffix Search Order

   B. Scope ID

   C. Use DHCP for WINS Resolution

   D. WINS Server Search Order

LAB QUESTION

A company asks you to design a network scheme according to its requirements. The company wants to keep administrative overhead on its network to a minimum, and it will set TCP/IP as the only protocol for intranet communications and browsing the Internet.

The company is connected to a T1 line, which is connected to a special router that also has an Ethernet port for connection to the hub. This setup allows for easy access to the Internet as well as support. The company has been given a Class C address to use; this address is 200.10.0.0.

The network will have four subnets with client PCs, and the company is required to use the first TCP/IP addresses before others. Company management has decided that the first subnet will be reserved for the main application servers, while the four client PC subnets will use the next four subnets.

What things would you do to meet the company's requirements? Which addresses would you assign to the four subnets and the application server subnet?

SELF TEST ANSWERS

TCP/IP Fundamentals

1. ☑ **C.** TCP/IP's unique addressing mechanism provides over 4.2 billion addresses. Each host is referred to by its unique 32-bit address. These unique addresses are made up of network and host identification.

   ☒ **A, B,** and **D** are incorrect because the correct answer is 4.2 billion addresses.

2. ☑ **B.** The default gateway defaults to 0.0.0.0. A default gateway is required when the client system needs to communicate outside its own subnet. Normally, the default gateway is a router connected to the local subnet, which enables IP packets to be passed to other network segments. If the default gateway is not configured in the DHCP server, it defaults to 0.0.0.0.

   ☒ **A** is incorrect because a default gateway is not required and will not generate an error if the value is not configured. **C** is incorrect because the address 255.255.255.255 is a broadcast address. **D** is incorrect because the default gateway is not required.

3. ☑ **A.** DNS root servers are not required. When a hostname request comes in to a root server, it simply looks at the root portion of the name and passes the name to this root server. This second root server then looks up the domain name in its database and sends the packet on to that specific domain name service. This specific domain name then provides an answer or an error if nothing is found.

   ☒ **B** is incorrect because the root database is maintained by an authority. **C** is incorrect because the root server will redirect the requested domain name resolution request to the next DNS server in the hierarchy. **D** is incorrect because the DNS server will have the information for other DNS servers for its root. The root server does have the addresses to the next level of the domain hierarchy or domains such as .NET, .COM, or .EDU and so on.

4. ☑ **B.** Although DNS information can be supplied in the registry, it can also be supplied in the directory %systemroot%\system32\DNS on a Windows NT machine.

   ☒ **A, C,** and **D** are incorrect because DNS information is stored in %systemroot%\system32\DNS.

5. ☑ **D.** Name resolution is dynamic, and changes are replicated. You must remember that WINS is dynamic and DNS is static. Another major difference between WINS and DNS is that with WINS, changes to the database are replicated, whereas with DNS, the entire database is replicated.

   ☒ **A** and **C** are incorrect because WINS is dynamic, not static. **B** is incorrect because the WINS database, not the whole database, is replicated as changes are made.

6. ☑ A. Specify a lower TTL value. The time-to-live (TTL) value for a TCP/IP packet is the maximum number of hops, usually around 30, that a packet can travel in the course of the packet's lifetime. "Hopping" over a router designates a hop. This TTL value is not specified in the HOSTS or DNS cache file.

   ☒ B is incorrect because the HOST file does not specify hops. C is incorrect because a higher TTL will keep the data packet on the network longer. D is incorrect because the TTL is not specified in the DNS cache file.

7. ☑ C. The SNMP standard defines a two-tiered approach to network device management: a central management system and the management information base (MIB) located on the managed device. The management system can monitor one or many MIBs, allowing for centralized management of a network. From a management system you can see valuable performance and operation statistics of network devices, enabling you to diagnose network health without leaving your office.

   ☒ A, B, and D are incorrect because SNMP does not deal with packet routing but does deal with these options.

8. ☑ C. The IP protocol is a connectionless delivery system. IP does not guarantee delivery, nor does it promise that the IP packets will be received in the order they were sent. IP does use a checksum, but it confirms only the integrity of the IP header. Confirmation of the integrity of data contained within an IP packet can be accomplished only through higher-level protocols.

   ☒ A is incorrect because it is an explanation of TCP. B is incorrect because TCP works IP and there is no configuration for IP specifically. D is incorrect because TCP is not necessary since UDP can be used if the communication will be connectionless.

TCP/IP Addressing

9. ☑ A. Class A supports more than 70,000 hosts.

   ☒ B is incorrect because, in the Class B range, there is the possibility of having 16,384 networks, with each network having the capability of 65,534 unique hosts using the default subnet mask. C and D are also incorrect.

10. ☑ C. The default subnet mask for a Class C network is 255.255.255.0 or, in binary representation, 11111111 11111111 11111111 00000000. You can see how the first three octets of the IP address are masked by binary 1s to display the three-octet, or 24-bit, network address.

    ☒ A, B, and D are incorrect because the correct answer is 255.255.255.0.

11. ☑ **D.** Two addresses are lost from the available host pool of IP addresses. The first is an address that has all 0s in the host ID, which signifies "this host" and is normally used in a BOOTP process when a host doesn't yet know its IP address. The second is an address that has all 1s in the host ID, which signifies a broadcast address.
☒ **A** is incorrect because the local host address is unknown at that point, so it is not used. **B** is incorrect because the DHCP server is not known either. **C** is incorrect because a host cannot have the same address.

12. ☑ **D.** Network IDs cannot start with 127 because this address is reserved for loopback and is used mainly for testing TCP/IP and internal loopback functions on the local system. If a program uses the loopback address as a destination, the protocol software in the system returns the data without sending traffic across the network.
☒ **A** is incorrect because it is an unknown or invalid address. **B** and **C** are incorrect because these are valid Class A addresses.

13. ☑ **C.** The HTTP service uses a well-known port of 80 on the server. A client is not forced into using port 80 to contact the Web server with HTTP traffic; it will use any port number.
☒ **A** and **B** are incorrect because they are used for FTP. **D** is incorrect because it is used for the Gopher protocol.

14. ☑ **A.** It is not advisable to use two DHCP servers on one network, unless the network is separated by routers. The second DHCP can provide backup for the first DHCP server, but the IP address scope should *not* contain the same IP addresses.
☒ **B** is incorrect because duplicate IP addresses can be avoided using a spreadsheet that contains workstation and server names and the corresponding IP addresses. This spreadsheet should also contain all static IP addresses, such as routers and printers, and should specify which range of IP addresses is in the DHCP scope of addresses, and which addresses are currently not used. **C** is incorrect because using PING to test for IP addresses is not useful, since a PC can be turned off and will then not respond to the PING. **D** is incorrect because it is helpful to use one DHCP server when you are trying to stop the assignment of duplicate addresses on your network.

TCP/IP Configuration

15. ☑ **C.** In Windows 95, 98, and NT, you can specify an IP address and subnet mask, or specify the use of a DHCP service. From the Control Panel, double-click the Network applet, click the Properties button, and select TCP/IP Protocol. On the TCP/IP Properties dialog box, click the IP Address tab to bring it to the front. Select the Specify an IP address option button to manually assign an IP address and subnet mask.

☒   A is incorrect because the Identification page is used to specify the computer name as well as the domain or workgroup to which the PC belongs. **B** is incorrect because there is no page called DHCP. **D** is incorrect because there is no WINS page in the TCP/IP configuration pages; it is actually called WINS configuration.

16. ☑   **C.** On the Microsoft TCP/IP Properties dialog box, click the DNS tab to bring it to the front. If you are a client only of the DNS service, you need to enter the Internet domain name and the IP address of the DNS service. Click in the Domain text box and enter your domain name. Click the Add button and enter the IP address of this service in the DNS Service Search Order box. The check box for Use WINS for DNS Resolution is on the WINS configuration page.
☒   **A, B,** and **D** are incorrect because they are all on the DNS page of the TCP/IP Properties dialog box.

17. ☑   **D.** You can't specify a second DNS service for faster host and domain name resolution. The DNS Service Search Order is a failover list, not an additional location. Only if the first one fails to respond after a nominal timeout period is the next DNS service list tried with the same request, and so on. These secondary servers must have a valid domain zone file for this process to work.
☒   **A, B,** and **C** are incorrect because you can't specify a second DNS service for faster host and domain name resolution.

18. ☑   **B.** Configure the workstation to use the WINS service instead. When a system is configured with multiple gateways, data transmission problems result in the system trying to use the other configured gateways, enabling internetworking communications capabilities to continue uninterrupted.
☒   **A** is incorrect because obtaining the default gateway from the server should work if the default gateway entry is correct. However, to receive this information from the DHCP server, you need to use DHCP completely. **C** is incorrect because the route would specify the route to the default gateway, and if it is incorrect, it still will not work. **D** is incorrect because you can specify multiple gateways in Windows 95, 98, ME, and NT. You can specify multiple gateways in Windows 2000 and XP.

19. ☑   **D.** To specify the default gateway on a Windows 98 machine, click the Gateway tab on the TCP/IP Properties dialog box. You have the option of specifying more than one gateway on this page.
☒   **A** is incorrect since the IP address page is used to specify whether to use DHCP or not and if not, what IP address, Subnet Mask, and default gateway to use. **B** is incorrect because the NetBIOS page is used to configure NetBIOS if used. **C** is incorrect because the Advanced page lets you set the default protocol.

20. ☑ **A.** WINS Suffix Search Order is not found on the WINS Configuration page. In Windows 98, the WINS information is entered on the WINS Configuration page, DNS uses a suffix search order, but the WINS service uses a server search order. The DNS Service also uses a DNS service search order. Don't let all these services get you confused!

☒ **B, C,** and **D** are incorrect because they are all found on the WINS Configuration page.

LAB ANSWER

Since the company will use TCP/IP and wants to keep administrative overhead at a minimum, it will of course use WINS to manage name resolution on the network. If the company were using Windows 2000, the network would use DNS instead, or even both. Windows 2000 allows for a dynamic DNS server instead of static.

DHCP should also be employed to assign TCP/IP addresses. The server subnet will use the address range of 200.10.1.1 to 200.10.1.254. These addresses need to be statically assigned. The other four subnets will consist of the following:

- 200.10.2.1 to 200.10.2.254
- 200.10.3.1 to 200.10.3.254
- 200.10.4.1 to 200.10.4.254
- 200.10.5.1 to 200.10.5.254

The subnets have to be separated by a router to manage proper routing of information.

The router separating the Internet from the intranet could also employ a NAT server to do some address translation to higher numbers in the TCP/IP range to attempt to mask the addresses used on the subnets. This step is not necessary, but it could be taken for security reasons.

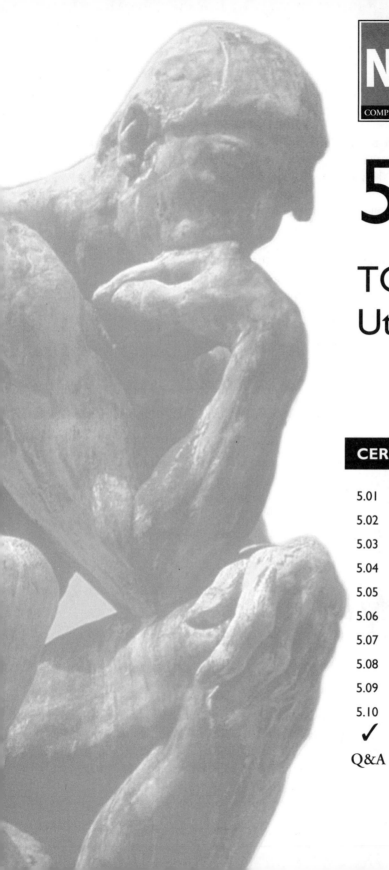

Network+

COMPUTING TECHNOLOGY INDUSTRY ASSOCIATION

5

TCP/IP Suite Utilities

CERTIFICATION OBJECTIVES

5.01	ARP
5.02	Telnet
5.03	NBTSTAT
5.04	Tracert
5.05	Netstat
5.06	IPCONFIG/WINIPCFG
5.07	FTP
5.08	Ping
5.09	NSLOOKUP
5.10	Troubleshooting with TCP/IP Utilities
✓	Two-Minute Drill
Q&A	Self Test

M

any utilities are available to troubleshoot TCP/IP connectivity problems. Most utilities are public domain and are included with the TCP/IP protocol stack provided with the operating system. This also means that they vary slightly depending on the implementation of these programs by the vendor. Although these utilities generally provide very basic functions, a proper understanding of the usage of these tools will enable you to effectively troubleshoot most problems.

We discuss the most commonly used TCP/IP troubleshooting tools in this chapter. Individual sections are further organized by tool. The final section identifies common problems, and how you can use the different tools to troubleshoot and resolve these problems. The following list provides a brief description of each utility discussed in this chapter and its core functions:

- **ARP**   Displays and modifies the local ARP cache.
- **Telnet**   Remote Terminal Emulation, administration, and troubleshooting.
- **NBTSTAT**   Checks the state of NetBIOS over TCP/IP connections.
- **Tracert**   Traces and reports on the route to a remote computer.
- **Netstat**   Displays statistics for current TCP/IP connections.
- **IPCONFIG/WINIPCFG**   Displays current IP configuration information.
- **FTP**   Enables file transfers between remote computers.
- **Ping**   Verifies hostname, host IP address, and physical connectivity to a remote TCP/IP computer.

CERTIFICATION OBJECTIVE 5.01

ARP

As discussed in Chapter 3, "Data Link, Network, and Transport Layers," network interface cards (NICs) have a hardware address or MAC address associated with them. Applications understand TCP/IP addressing, but network hardware devices, such as NICs, do not. For example, when two Ethernet cards are communicating, they have no knowledge of the IP address being used. Instead, they use the MAC addresses assigned to each card to address data frames. The *Address Resolution Protocol (ARP)* was designed to provide a mapping from the logical 32-bit TCP/IP addresses to the physical 48-bit MAC addresses.

Address resolution is the process of finding the address of a host within a network. In this case, the address is resolved by using a protocol to request information via a form of broadcast to locate a remote host. The remote host receives the packet and forwards it with the appropriate address information included. The address resolution process is complete once the original computer has received the address information.

ARP maintains the protocol rules for making this translation and providing address conversion in both directions within the OSI layers, as illustrated in Figure 5-1. A utility by the same name is available for Windows 95/98/ME and Windows NT/200/XP. This utility is used to display and modify entries within the ARP table. ARP is discussed in-depth in RFC 826.

exam
Ⓦⓐⓣ⓬⓱ *Remember that ARP translates IP addresses into MAC addresses. The Reverse Address Resolution Protocol, or RARP, is used to find a TCP/IP address from a MAC address.*

How ARP Works

When a data packet destined for a computer on a particular local area network (LAN) arrives at a host or gateway, the ARP protocol is tasked to find a MAC address that matches the IP address for the destination computer. The ARP protocol then looks inside its cache table for the appropriate address. If the address is found, the destination

FIGURE 5-1	
The logical data flow for the Address Resolution Protocol	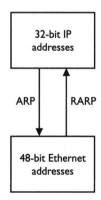

address is then added to the data packet and forwarded. If no entry exists for the IP address, ARP broadcasts a request packet to all the machines on the LAN to determine which machine maintains that IP address. If found, the host with that IP address will send an ARP reply with its own MAC address. If the destination is on a remote subnet, the address of the router or gateway used to reach that subnet is placed in the packet and forwarded. If the ARP cache does not contain an IP address for the router or gateway, it will use the same methods to resolve the address. The ARP cache is then updated for future reference, and the original data packets are then forwarded to the correct host.

As protocols go, ARP provides a very basic function. Only four types of messages can be sent out by the ARP protocol on any machine:

- ARP request
- ARP reply
- RARP request
- RARP reply

ARP Cache

To reduce the number of address resolution requests, thereby minimizing network utilization, a client caches resolved addresses for a short time. This table, known as the ARP cache, is used to maintain the mappings between each MAC address and its corresponding IP address locally. This is the most important part of this protocol. Since the size of the ARP cache is limited, entries need to be purged periodically. If they are not, the cache could become huge in size and could contain quite a few obsolete entries. Therefore, ARP cache entries are removed at predefined intervals. This process also removes any unsuccessful attempts to contact computers that are not currently running.

Entries in the ARP cache can be viewed, added, or deleted by using the ARP utility. Entries that are added with this utility manually are static and will not age out of the cache as the dynamic entries will. This can be helpful when trying to resolve address resolution problems. By displaying the current cache, you can determine whether a remote host MAC address is being resolved correctly.

Type the following command, and press **Enter** to view the ARP cache:

```
ARP -a
```

Figure 5-2 shows an example of an ARP cache.

Customizing the ARP Cache   Additional options are available to customize the information found in the ARP cache. For example, you can filter the entries displayed when you list them with ARP. By appending the appropriate IP address after the –a switch, the table will list entries only for that particular IP address, as shown in Figure 5-3. This can be useful when trying to isolate specific entries in a large table.

Type the following command, and press **Enter** to view the ARP cache for a specific IP address:

```
ARP -a <IP address>
```

Computers that contain multiple NICs, or multihomed computers have more than one network interface listed. The ARP cache maintains addresses for each interface within its tables. By using the ARP –a option, all interfaces will be listed. To filter the display address listing based on a specific interface, use the –n option. This enables you to specify which interface to display addresses for, as shown in Figure 5-4.

FIGURE 5-2	
Use the ARP –a command to view the ARP cache	

```
C:\>arp -a
Interface: 207.222.234.73
    Internet Address         Physical Address         Type
    10.37.14.92              00-60-08-72-43-d6         static
    198.70.146.70            20-53-52-43-00-00         dynamic
    199.182.120.2            20-53-52-43-00-00         dynamic
    199.182.120.202          20-53-52-43-00-00         dynamic
    206.246.150.88           20-53-52-43-00-00         dynamic
    207.211.106.40           20-53-52-43-00-00         dynamic
    207.211.106.90           20-53-52-43-00-00         dynamic
    208.223.32.77            20-53-52-43-00-00         dynamic
```

FIGURE 5-3	
An example of filtering a specific IP address within	

```
C:\>arp -a 10.37.14.92

Interface: 207.222.234.73
    Internet Address         Physical Address         Type
    10.37.14.92              00-60-08-72-43-d6         static
```

FIGURE 5-4

Use the –n switch
with the –a option
to specify a
particular
interface when
displaying the
ARP cache

```
C:\>arp -a -n 207.222.234.73

Interface: 207.222.234.73
    Internet Address        Physical Address        Type
    10.37.14.92             00-60-08-72-43-d6       static
    32.97.105.123           20-53-52-43-00-00       dynamic
    198.70.146.70           20-53-52-43-00-00       dynamic
    199.182.120.2           20-53-52-43-00-00       dynamic
    207.211.106.40          20-53-52-43-00-00       dynamic
    207.211.106.90          20-53-52-43-00-00       dynamic
```

Type the following command, and press **Enter** to view the ARP cache for a specific interface:

```
ARP -a -n <interface>
```

Once you understand these concepts, you can see what your ARP cache contains on your local PC in Exercise 5-1. Please note that this exercise does require the PC to be on a network.

EXERCISE 5-1

Using ARP to See Your Local ARP Cache

1. Connect to another PC by mapping to a shared directory.

2. Go to the Command prompt by selecting **Start | Run**, and then type **CMD** if you are using Windows NT/2000, or **COMMAND** if you are using Windows 95/98/ME.

3. At the command prompt, type **arp –a**.

4. You will get a list of all of the IP address to MAC address resolutions that have been made on this PC. This will list, at the very least, the information from the PC to which you made the connection in step 1.

Adding Static Entries   Static entries can be added manually when necessary. This can be especially helpful when you have a computer that transfers large amounts of data to a remote host continually. By adding a static entry for the remote host into the computer's ARP cache table, updates do not need to constantly occur. This option can also be used to test whether the local computer is receiving updates correctly.

Suppose that you are trying to connect to another computer on the same network. You are unable to find the remote computer; however, the other machines around you seem to work fine. First, display the local ARP cache to determine if the remote host has an entry present. If not, you can add a static entry into the ARP cache to allow you to determine whether the computer is properly receiving updates. With the entry in place, notice that you can now locate the remote computer. The cache was not updated correctly with the appropriate MAC address, and adding a static entry bypassed that problem.

You can manually add entries with the following command:

```
ARP -s <IP address> <MAC address>
```

Deleting Static Entries   You might need to delete any entries you have manually added, or manually remove any entries that have been dynamically added to the ARP cache. Use the following command to delete entries from the ARP cache:

```
ARP -d <IP Address>
```

ARP Cache Aging   Unlike static addresses, which never age out, dynamic addresses remain for only a predetermined amount of time. Windows NT adjusts the size of the ARP cache automatically. If entries are reused within two minutes, they remain for 10 minutes. A Registry parameter within Windows NT is also available to allow for more control over the aging parameters. The Registry parameter is located in the following directory:

```
Hkey_Local_Machine\System\CurrentControlSet\Services\Tcpip\Parameters\
ArpCacheLife
```

RARP

A little-known protocol exists to facilitate the reverse function of ARP. The *Reverse Address Resolution Protocol* (RARP) enables a machine to learn its own IP address by broadcasting to resolve its own MAC address. A RARP server containing these mappings can respond with the IP address for the requesting host. In most cases, a machine knows its own IP address; therefore, RARP is primarily used for situations such as diskless workstations, or machines without hard disks. Dumb terminals and NetPCs are good examples of diskless workstations.

Troubleshooting Duplicate IP Address Problems

During system startup and as the IP protocol initializes, an ARP request is broadcast containing its own MAC and IP addresses. This is done so that other computers can update their ARP caches with this information. If a computer already has this IP address, it will respond with an *ARP reply* containing its own MAC and IP address, indicating a conflict. Other computers will have already updated their own ARP caches, though. By having two computers with the same IP address, you can potentially cause problems with many different computers.

If a duplicate address is found, the TCP/IP stack for Windows NT 4.0 Service Pack 3 or higher is written to send out a new ARP broadcast to remap the ARP cache on all affected computers. The MAC and IP addresses of the original computer will be contained within this new ARP. Once this ARP has been broadcast, the TCP/IP protocol stack will shut down, and the computer will log the address conflict.

Although ARP is simple compared to most other protocols, it is just as important to TCP/IP for proper functionality. The utility included with this protocol will enable you to display and modify the ARP cache as needed. This enables you to effectively troubleshoot any issues that might arise with ARP. Table 5-1 details ARP parameters and their corresponding definitions.

TABLE 5-1	ARP Parameters	Definition
ARP Parameters	–a	Displays the entire current ARP cache or a single entry by allowing you to specify the IP address of an adapter
	–g	Same as –a
	–N	Shows the ARP entries for a specified IP address and allows for modification
	–d	Deletes specified entry
	–s	Adds an entry to the ARP cache by specifying a MAC address and IP address.

Telnet

Another utility commonly used is Telnet (telecommunications network). This utility was designed to provide a virtual terminal or remote login across the network. This enables the user to execute commands on a remote machine anywhere on the network as if he or she were sitting in front of the console. The term *Telnet* refers to both the protocol and the application used for remote logins.

Telnet was originally designed to allow for a single universal interface in a world that was very diverse. It was an efficient method of simulating a console session when very little else was available. It is still widely used today for remotely administering devices such as network equipment and UNIX servers. It can also be a great troubleshooting tool when used correctly.

How Telnet Works

The Telnet service uses TCP port 23 and is defined in-depth in RFC 854. It is connection based and handles its own session negotiation, which makes it very efficient and effective. By maintaining its own protocol, it can set up its own sessions and manage them accordingly. This keeps the remote host from spending too much time processing requests, and enables it to concentrate on its own processes. Usually, a client-based program is used to connect to the remote server. The remote server must also be running a Telnet service to enable the client to connect.

Telnet uses a concept known as network virtual terminal (NVT) to define both ends of a Telnet connection. Each end of the connection maintains a logical keyboard and printer. The logical keyboard generates characters, and the logical printer displays them. The logical printer is usually a terminal screen, and the logical keyboard is the user's keyboard.

Using Telnet

A Telnet client utility is included with Windows 95/98/ME and Windows NT/200/XP. To use Telnet, you must be connected to the network. You can run this utility by typing **TELNET.EXE** at a command prompt, or by selecting **Start | Programs |**

FIGURE 5-5

Connecting to a
remote host with
the Telnet client
application

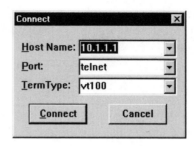

Accessories | Telnet. Select Connect | Remote System. The Connect dialog box appears, as shown in Figure 5-5. You can enter either an IP address or a hostname. To connect via a hostname, the client must be able to resolve the name to an IP address. You must also specify the port to connect to and the terminal emulation type. By default, this Telnet will try to connect to the Telnet port (port 23) on the remote server. VT100 is the default terminal emulation used for Telnet.

Telnet requires a username and password on the server to log in. Different functions and applications are available to assist you in performing remote administration. These are dependent upon what services are being offered by the remote host. Many external devices also offer Telnet capability, such as Uninterruptible Power Supplies (UPS), remote control server administration cards, and most networking equipment.

Customizing Telnet Settings

Due to the different environments that exist, Telnet offers multiple types of terminal emulation. Options include setting the terminal emulation, command buffer size, screen fonts, and cursor behavior. Some of these options are required to work on different types of remote hosts, but others are purely cosmetic. Figure 5-6 shows the available options for customization.

You can change screen fonts and cursor behavior to fit the screen output to your needs. These settings will not affect the server-based process. Some Telnet applications will not function correctly without particular cursor or font settings. The Local Echo option displays all of your keyboard input. The VT100 Arrows option specifies how cursor movement is handled. The Blinking Cursor and Block Cursor options adjust how the cursor is displayed on the screen.

The Buffer Size enables you to customize the amount of history that remains in memory. You can scroll through to see what commands or output have already been processed. The default is 25 lines, but you can set this value as high as 399. The Telnet application will not enable you to specify fewer than 25 lines.

FIGURE 5-6

Use the Terminal
Preferences
dialog box to set
Telnet
preferences

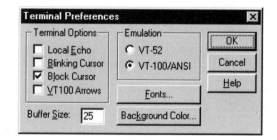

The Terminal Emulation option defines what type of remote terminal to use. This controls how commands are interpreted and displayed by the remote server. VT-52 is an older standard not commonly used anymore. VT100 is the default standard emulation used today.

Another function of Telnet is logging; it logs the console display to keep a record of all activity. To start or stop logging, select **Terminal** from the menu bar, and select **Start Logging** or **Stop Logging** from the menu. When you select Start Logging, the Open Log File window appears. You need to select the folder that you want Telnet to save the log files to. The log files are saved as telnet.log and are readable by any standard text editor.

Troubleshooting with Telnet

The primary use of Telnet is remote administration. If you are unable to connect to a remote server by other methods, depending upon the problem, Telnet might still work. This will enable you to troubleshoot and work with a remote server without being in front of it. If a server is inaccessible, you might still be able to contact its peripherals.

Suppose an NT server has crashed and is displaying a blue screen. Some servers include an option to have remote administration cards plugged in. In this case, you could Telnet to this card and possibly determine if there is a hardware failure, or reboot the server. Suppose you have a UPS attached to the server. This peripheral might have Telnet capability to enable you to power cycle the server. Both cases enable you to remotely troubleshoot the server without local interaction.

Another example of troubleshooting with Telnet is to connect to an applications service to verify that it is functioning properly. As discussed earlier, every TCP/IP service uses a specific TCP or UDP port. You can specify a particular port to connect to and test the connectivity and functionality of a service. For example, you can connect to a Windows NT server running Microsoft Exchange to verify that the Internet Mail Connector is transferring mail properly. Exercise 5-2 shows a trick to troubleshooting the Exchange Internet Mail Service.

EXERCISE 5-2

Connecting to an Exchange Internet Mail Service

1. Connect to the **IP address** of the Exchange server Internet Mail Service. Specify **port 25** to connect to.

2. Type **HELO test.company.com**.

3. Type the following to list who the message is from: **MAIL FROM** *<admin@test.company.com>*.

4. Type the following to list who the message is to: **RCPT TO:** *<user@hi.company.com>*.

5. Type the following command to tell the connector that you are ready to send data: **DATA**. You should now see the following: `"354 Send data. End with CRLF.CRLF."`

6. Type the following command to add a subject: **Subject: test**, and press **Enter** twice.

7. Enter the following as the message body: **This is a test message.** Press **Enter**, add a period to the next line, and press **Enter** again. This will end the data portion.

8. Type **QUIT** to end the connection.

When you have finished this exercise, you can check to see if the message was delivered. If the message arrives, the Internet Mail Connector is functioning properly.

exam
Ⓦatch

Make sure you can recognize the output from each of the TCP/IP utilities listed in this chapter. On your Network+ exam you will be presented with output from a command and asked which command produced the output.

NBTSTAT

The Microsoft TCP/IP stack uses an additional sub-protocol for its services, NetBIOS over TCP/IP (NetBT). This provides additional functionality, but it can make troubleshooting much more difficult. You must fully understand how it works and when it can be a factor in any issues that may arise. Because this is a Microsoft addition to the TCP/IP protocol, Microsoft created this utility to troubleshoot the problems that can arise.

How NetBIOS over TCP/IP Works

NetBIOS is a software interface and naming convention. It was used in the early days of local area networking in a communication protocol, known as NetBEUI. It was designed for use in small local environments, so it has no routing functions built in. It also primarily relied upon broadcast-based name resolution. This design does not port well to today's expanded wide area networks (WANs). Microsoft has taken this protocol and incorporated it into TCP/IP to enable it to be used in today's expanded environments. This helps to take advantage of the WAN environment, while allowing for interoperability with other operating systems.

NetBT Naming

The NetBIOS namespace is a flat structure, meaning that all names within its network must be unique. This means that all computers within a workgroup or domain must have unique names. Names are comprised of 16 hexadecimal characters. The first 15 can be set by the administrator or user, and the 16th specifies a resource type. This resource type is used to determine what services are available from a computer. Table 5-2 lists some common resource types.

NetBT Sessions

Because NetBT travels through TCP/IP, sessions are set up the same way. There is an additional overhead associated with this, but it is usually very small. When a service using NetBT attempts to access a resource, it first resolves the name to an IP

TABLE 5-2	Suffix	Usage
Common NetBIOS Resource Types	00	Workstation Service
	06	Remote Access Server
	20	File Server Service
	87	Microsoft Exchange Message Transfer Agent

address. Next, a TCP connection is established to port 139, designated for the NetBIOS Datagram service. When connected, the computer sends a NetBIOS session request to the server name over the TCP connection. If the server is listening, it will respond with the requested information.

When the session is established, the two computers negotiate a higher-level protocol to use over the connection. Microsoft networking uses only one session between two computers at any time. Additional services required between the two machines will travel through the same connection.

Using NBTSTAT

NBTSTAT is used to troubleshoot connectivity between two computers trying to communicate via NetBT. It displays the protocol statistics and the current connections to each remote host. You can also display the information about a remote host and the names stored in its local name cache.

Displaying the Local Cache

Every connection made via NetBIOS keeps the name in cache for a short period of time. You can display the local cache by using the NBTSTAT –c option. By using this option, each machine that remains in cache will be displayed. This listing will also include the type of connection, TCP/IP address of the remote connection, and the length of time the connection will be kept.

By using the –n option, you can display the services the local machine is advertising. This lists the registered names for the local machine as well. You can also reload the local name cache with the –R option. This will enable you to reload the LMHOSTS file after the name cache is cleared.

To determine the services on the local machine, perform Exercise 5-3.

EXERCISE 5-3

CertCam 5-3

Using NBTSTAT to Determine the Services Available on a Local PC

1. Go to the Command prompt by selecting **Start | Run,** and then type **CMD** if you are using Windows NT/2000, or **COMMAND** if you are using Windows 95/98/ME.

2. At the command prompt, type **NBTSTAT –n.**

3. You will get a list of all the services that are available on the local PC by network users. The suffix types were previously listed.

Connecting to Remote Machines

You can also display the cache of registered services on a remote machine by using the –a or –A option. The –a option enables you to specify a remote host by hostname, and the –A option specifies it by IP address. These options will enable you to determine what services the remote machine is offering. Core operating system services such as the Server service or Browse services are listed here. Applications such as Microsoft Exchange or Microsoft Internet Information Server might also list entries here as well. Figure 5-7 shows an example of a remote machine's cache table.

Displaying Registration Statistics

Services can register in two ways, via broadcast or with the WINS service. You can display the statistics of how many times you have registered, and with what method.

FIGURE 5-7

Use the –A option to display a remote machine's name table

```
C:\>nbtstat -A 10.10.10.1

         NetBIOS Remote Machine Name Table

    Name               Type         Status
    ---------------------------------------------
    WORKSTATION1   <00>  UNIQUE   Registered
    WORKSTATION1   <20>  UNIQUE   Registered
    WORKGROUP      <00>  GROUP    Registered
    WORKSTATION1   <03>  UNIQUE   Registered
    WORKGROUP      <1E>  GROUP    Registered
    WORKGROUP      <1D>  UNIQUE   Registered
    .._MSBROWSE_.  <01>  GROUP    Registered
    ADMINISTRATOR  <03>  UNIQUE   Registered

    MAC Address = 00-60-97-E4-D7-CB

C:\>
```

You can also display information on how remote NetBIOS names are being resolved. This can help you to determine whether you are using a WINS service correctly, or are broadcasting for services. Broadcasting can consume a lot of bandwidth and is generally not recommended except in the smallest networks. To view the registration statistics, use the –r option with NBTSTAT.

on the
job

The NBTSTAT utility can be crucial in defining problems with Microsoft computers. Since they use the NetBIOS naming standard, this utility is good at finding and isolating connectivity problems. It provides the extra information on NetBIOS statistics that you can't get out of regular TCP/IP utilities such as Tracert.

Displaying Session Information

Another option with NBTSTAT is to list the sessions that are currently open. You can see what you are connected to, and also list the open sessions that other computers have with your machine. Use the –s option to list names by IP address only. When you use the –s option, NBTSTAT will attempt to resolve the IP addresses to hostnames.

Statistics available with this option include number of bytes in, number of bytes out, current state, and whether the connection is inbound or outbound. Figure 5-8 shows an example of the sessions displayed with this option. Table 5-3 details the NBTSTAT parameters and their definitions.

exam
Watch

Make sure you know the options available with the NBTSTAT command, such as NBTSTAT –R and NBTSTAT –a. I was surprised when I received a question asking which option to use to accomplish a certain goal.

FIGURE 5-8

Local NetBIOS sessions listing. The lowercase –s option resolves the IP address to its hostname

```
C:\>nbtstat -s

                        NetBIOS Connection Table

Local Name              State     In/Out  Remote Host        Input   Output
-----------------------------------------------------------------------------
WORKSTATION2   <03>   Listening
WORKSTATION2          Listening
ADMINISTRATOR  <03>   Listening

C:\>
```

TABLE 5-3	NBTSTAT Parameters	Definition
NBTSTAT Parameters	–a	Lists a remote PC's name table by specifying a remote PC's name
	–A	Lists a remote PC's name table by specifying a remote PC's IP address
	–c	Displays contents of the name cache giving the IP address of each name
	–n	Displays local names
	–R	Deletes name cache and reloads LMHOSTS file
	–r	Displays name resolution statistics
	–S	Lists client and server sessions, listing the remote computers by IP address
	–s	Displays both client and server sessions attempting to convert the remote computer IP address to a name using the Hosts file
	interval	Specifies the interval to pause display

CERTIFICATION OBJECTIVE 5.04

Tracert

Network routing can quickly become very complicated, even in the smallest networks. There is an arsenal of public utilities and third-party products to help troubleshoot and isolate network-related problems. Many of these utilities require at least a moderate level of knowledge to understand how to use these tools and interpret the results of using them. A good example is a network sniffer. Using a network sniffer can become complicated quickly.

Tracert is a command-line utility that was designed to perform a very basic task: to determine the path taken by a data packet to reach its destination. This can be very helpful in determining at what point a network connection is no longer active. It can also be helpful in troubleshooting issues around network response times.

To see the path from your PC over the Internet to the www.syngress.com Web site, you can perform Exercise 5-4 if you are connected to the Internet.

Using Tracert to Determine Internet Paths

1. Go to the Command prompt by selecting **Start | Run**, and type **CMD** if you are using Windows NT/2000, or **COMMAND** if you are using Windows 95/98/ME.

2. At the command prompt, type **tracert www.syngress.com**.

3. You will get a list of all of the routers or gateways between your PC and the Syngress Web site. Note that some ISPs will not allow a Ping packet to pass through their gateway. This can also be performed on a network by typing **tracert <computername>**, where computername is the name of a PC or server on the network.

How Tracert Works

Tracert functions by sending out Internet Control Message Protocol (ICMP) echo packets to the destination specified by either an IP address or hostname. These packets are sent with varying IP Time To Live (TTL) values. Each router along the path is required to decrement the TTL on a packet by at least one before forwarding it, so the TTL is effectively a hop count. When the TTL on a packet reaches zero, the router should send an ICMP Time Exceeded message back to the source computer.

Tracert then determines the route by sending the first echo packet with a TTL of one, and incrementing by one on each subsequent transmission. This is done until the target responds or the maximum TTL is reached. The route is actually determined by looking at the ICMP Time Exceeded messages sent back by intermediate routers. Tracert then displays a list of the routers in the path that returned the ICMP Time Exceeded message.

When using the utility, you will notice several numbers in the display. Figure 5-9 shows an example of the tracert command.

Although a tracert might look rather confusing at first, it is fairly easy to understand. Each row gathers information about that hop three times. The first column shows the number of hops. The next three columns show the time it took for the router or gateway to respond for each attempt. The last column lists the router name and router address.

FIGURE 5-9

A tracert to a
local workstation

```
C:\>tracert 10.10.10.1
Tracing route to WORKSTATION1      [10.10.10.1]
over a maximum of 30 hops:
  1     1 ms     1 ms     1 ms  WORKSTATION1      [10.10.10.1]
Trace complete.
C:\>
```

Using Tracert

Let's say that you cannot access a particular Web site on the Internet. Your company is directly connected to the Internet via an ISDN line, which is used by approximately 35 people. You are able to hit certain Web sites consistently, but others are available only sporadically. Other users begin to notice that they are unable to connect to the same Web sites with which you are having a problem.

Tracert fits in well here to begin isolating where the problem is. Although you might have a good idea of what network equipment and options are used within your company, once packets enter the Internet, there is no telling what they might come across. Because routes can be so dynamic, this is a great tool for figuring out where the data is traveling to reach its destination.

You can begin troubleshooting this problem by typing one of the following commands:

```
TRACERT <hostname>
```

or

```
TRACERT <ipaddress>
```

After the utility has run, you might notice the following entry on one of the routers along the way:

```
Destination Net Unreachable
```

Although this utility is unable to determine why the error is occurring, it has effectively found at what point the problem exists. Armed with this information, that router or link can then be looked at by the owner to help him or her resolve the issue.

In the event a name resolution method is not available for remote hosts, you can specify the –d option to prohibit the utility from trying to resolve hostnames as it runs. Without this switch, the program will still work, but it will attempt to translate every hop's hostname, thereby slowing the process.

Maximum Number of Hops

One function of the Tracert utility is to provide the number of hops, or networks, the data is crossing. Because each network can use different devices and have varying bandwidth, this function can be very helpful. There are instances, however, in which you will need to limit the number of hops the program will make to search for the remote host. This means that a tracert will continue for 30 hops by default if it cannot reach its destination. This can be very time-consuming if you are working with a device four or five hops away. In the unusual case that you must surpass more than 30 hops, you can also specify a greater interval.

By using the –h option with Tracert, you can specify the maximum number of hops to trace a route to. Figure 5-10 shows an example of this option.

Adjusting Timeout Values

Another option associated with Tracert is to adjust the timeout value using the -w switch. This value determines the amount of time in milliseconds the program will wait for a response before moving on. Using this option will enable you to possibly understand a little more about the problem that is occurring. For example, if you notice that many responses are timing out, you can raise this value. If, after raising this value, remote devices are responding, this could be a good indication that you have a bandwidth problem.

FIGURE 5-10

An example of a tracert with the –d and –h options

```
C:\>tracert -d -h 15 www.syngress.com

Tracing route to www.syngress.com [146.115.28.75]
over a maximum of 15 hops:

  1     *        *        *        Request timed out.
  2    312 ms   325 ms   381 ms   165.236.51.1
  3    383 ms   272 ms   354 ms   163.179.232.194
  4    396 ms   354 ms   408 ms   163.179.220.182
  5    301 ms   354 ms   258 ms   192.41.177.74
  6    384 ms   325 ms    *       204.152.42.2
  7    366 ms   422 ms   353 ms   207.152.148.41
  8    301 ms   272 ms   299 ms   207.152.148.30
  9    268 ms   270 ms   268 ms   207.152.148.34
 10    383 ms  2030 ms   409 ms   207.152.148.37
 11    410 ms   382 ms   271 ms   198.32.178.13
 12    439 ms   272 ms   368 ms   146.115.17.125
 13    384 ms   381 ms   410 ms   199.232.56.39
 14    274 ms   382 ms   271 ms   146.115.28.75

Trace complete.

C:\>_
```

Loose Source Routing Options

An additional option is to use what is known as *loose source routing*. The –j option can be used to force the outbound datagram to pass through a specific router and back. This enables you to trace the round-trip route for a destination. A normal tracert follows the route until it reaches its destination or times out. When you specify this option, Tracert follows the path to the router specified and returns to your computer. To use loose source routing, enter the following command:

```
TRACERT -j <router name> <local computer>
```

Tracert can be a useful tool in determining why a remote host can't be reached. It can also be a good tool to notice other issues, such as bandwidth utilization problems. Its additional options and functionality make it a powerful tool. Table 5-4 lists the TRACERT parameters and the corresponding definitions.

CERTIFICATION OBJECTIVE 5.05

Netstat

Now that you've learned how to trace data packets throughout the network, another utility similar to NBTSTAT is available for troubleshooting TCP/IP-specific issues. Netstat displays protocol statistics and current TCP/IP network connections. TCP/IP can be a complicated protocol to understand, and therefore very difficult to troubleshoot. This utility can be used to display in-depth detail about protocol status and statistics for the different network interfaces as well as the current routing tables.

TABLE 5-4	TRACERT Parameters	Definition
TRACERT Parameters	–d	Do not resolve address to computer names
	–h	Specifies maximum number of hops
	–j	Specifies loose source route along computer-list
	–w	Specifies time in milliseconds to wait for reply
	–target_name	Specifies target computer

How Netstat Works

TCP-based connections use a three-step handshake method for establishing and disconnecting sessions. This forms the basis for TCP and its reliable data transfer methodology. This enables it to act as a message-validation protocol to provide reliable communications between two hosts. A virtual circuit is created via this handshake to appropriately handle the transport messages. Netstat displays information about these virtual circuits, the network interfaces, and how they are being used.

By default, Netstat lists the protocol type, local address and port information, remote address and port information, and current state. The information provided explains what connections are open or in progress, through what ports, and what their current state is. Figure 5-11 shows an example of the Netstat utility.

Perform Exercise 5-5 to see this output on your PC and determine connections you might have open to other systems.

EXERCISE 5-5

CertCam 5-5

Using Netstat to Determine Open Connections to Other Systems

1. Go to the command prompt by selecting **Start | Run**, and then type **CMD if you are using Windows NT/2000, or COMMAND** if you are using Windows 95/98/ME.

2. At the command prompt, type **netstat**.

3. You will get a list of all the connections open between your PC and any other. This is beneficial when on the Internet to see if you are connected to anyone, or someone is connected to your PC.

The State column displays the current status of TCP connections only. You can determine from the status in this column whether the connection is functioning properly. For example, if the connection stays at a form of wait state for a long period of time, you might need to look at the connection between the two hosts and verify that a network problem does not exist. Table 5-5 lists the available states.

FIGURE 5-11

Output from the
netstat command

```
C:\>netstat

Active Connections
  Proto  Local Address          Foreign Address          State
  TCP    workstation2:1192       207.211.106.40:80        TIME_WAIT
  TCP    workstation2:1201       207.211.106.90:80        TIME_WAIT
  TCP    workstation2:1218       www.syngress.com:80      ESTABLISHED
  TCP    workstation2:1219       www.syngress.com:80      ESTABLISHED

C:\>
```

Netstat Options

Different types of statistics are available depending upon the utility options used. You can display all connections and listening ports, because server connections are not displayed in the standard output. You can also display Ethernet statistics and per-protocol statistics. The routing table can also be displayed with this command.

You can use the –n option to display addresses and port numbers without resolving the names. This could take additional overhead if the listing is long, and it might not work properly if you have no form of name resolution set up. Suppose you want the information that is displayed to continually update. By default, the information is displayed once. You can specify an interval in seconds appended to the end of

TABLE 5-5

TCP Connection
States

State	Explanation
SYN_SEND	Indicates an active open
SYN_RECEIVED	Server just received a SYN from the remote client
ESTABLISHED	Client received SYN, and the connection is complete
LISTEN	Server is awaiting a connection
FIN_WAIT_1	Indicates an active close
TIMED_WAIT	Clients enter this state after an active close
CLOSE_WAIT	Indicates a passive close; the server has just received the first FIN from client
FIN_WAIT_2	Client just received acknowledgment of its first FIN from the server
LAST+ACK	Server enters this state when it sends its own FIN
CLOSED	Server received the ACK from the client, and the connection is closed

the command to have the utility update itself. The following is an example of the command line:

```
NETSTAT -a 5
```

This command will display the active connections every five seconds. Use CTRL-C to stop this program. This can be helpful when trying to actively monitor connections and their statistics.

Displaying Server Connections and Listening Ports

From the standard output, Netstat does not display the server-based connections and listening ports. This information might be necessary to understand who the computer is communicating with and its current status. Therefore, this information can be obtained by using the −a option with Netstat. This listing contains all local server services that are currently active or communicating.

Displaying Ethernet Statistics

Another option available enables you to display the Ethernet interface statistics. The information available with the −e option includes the number of bytes received and sent, the number of discards and errors, and unknown protocols. By understanding what this information means, you can monitor the amount of traffic that is being used in communications. Since this option also displays error, you can check here to see if there are communication-related problems occurring. Figure 5-12 shows an example of the Netstat utility with this option.

Displaying Per-Protocol Statistics

While the previous option shows Ethernet interface-specific information, protocol-specific information is also available. With the −s option, you can display statistics

FIGURE 5-12	

The −e option displays the Ethernet interface statistics

```
C:\>netstat -e
Interface Statistics

                            Received            Sent
Bytes                       1242591           302546
Unicast packets                2406             2568
Non-unicast packets             252              262
Discards                          0                0
Errors                            0              144
Unknown protocols                64

C:\>
```

for the communications protocols and how they are being used. The protocols include TCP, UDP, ICMP, and IP. Detailed information can be obtained with this option that can help you to isolate TCP/IP communications issues.

You can also filter by protocol to drill down to specific areas. The –p option can be used alone to filter the standard Netstat output by TCP or UDP or you can use it with the protocol statistics option to filter by TCP, UDP, ICMP, or IP. Figure 5-13 shows an example of this filtering.

Displaying the Current Route Table

Netstat offers another option that enables you to display the current route table using the –r switch. This enables you to see what routes are used, as well as display the active sessions and their addresses. Because routing tables are constantly updating, this can be a good reference as you troubleshoot with this utility to understand how the data is traveling across the network. For every route, it displays the network address, the net mask, the gateway address and interface, and the number of hops to the host.

Troubleshooting with Netstat

Using Netstat to monitor TCP protocol activity can enable you to troubleshoot TCP/IP-based connections. Netstat can be used in a variety of ways.

You can use the –a option to monitor active connections. The state of a good TCP connection is usually established with 0 bytes in the send and receive queues. If the state is irregular or the data is blocked in either queue, there is probably a problem with the connection. If not, you are probably experiencing network or application delay.

FIGURE 5-13

Use the –s option and the –p option together to display specific information about a protocol

```
C:\>netstat -s -p IP

IP Statistics

    Packets Received              = 2564
    Received Header Errors        = 0
    Received Address Errors       = 28
    Datagrams Forwarded           = 0
    Unknown Protocols Received    = 0
    Received Packets Discarded    = 0
    Received Packets Delivered    = 2564
    Output Requests               = 2801
    Routing Discards              = 4194332
    Discarded Output Packets      = 0
    Output Packet No Route        = 0
    Reassembly Required           = 0
    Reassembly Successful         = 0
    Reassembly Failures           = 0
    Datagrams Successfully Fragmented = 0
    Datagrams Failing Fragmentation   = 0
    Fragments Created             = 0

C:\>_
```

SCENARIO & SOLUTION

I need to see the MAC addresses of a PC to which I am connected. How can I do this?	Use the ARP utility to determine the IP address to MAC address resolution. If the ARP cache is empty, disconnect from the PC and reconnect to the PC to which you need the MAC address.
I need to access a UNIX system from my Windows PC. What utility can I use to do this?	Telnet will allow you to open a terminal session to a UNIX server if terminal emulation is enabled.
I need to determine the IP address of the company gateway and all routers between the company and a specific Web server on the Internet. How can I manage this?	Use Tracert to determine the data path between your PC and the destination PC. The company gateway should be one the first items listed in the Tracert listing. You can check the IPCONFIG/WINIPCFG utility for the default gateway address.
I need to determine the IP addresses of systems to which I am connected, as well as those connected to my PC. How can I get a listing of these IP addresses?	Use Netstat to see the IP addresses as well and ports to which you are connected and are connected to your PC.

You can also monitor the error counts for protocols and the Ethernet interface. These are a good indication that a problem might be occurring. In addition, monitor the route tables; if there is a network routing problem, you might be able to spot something here as well. Table 5-6 lists the NETSTAT parameters and corresponding definitions.

TABLE 5-6	NETSTAT Parameters	Definition
NETSTAT Parameters	–a	Displays all connections and ports
	–e	Displays Ethernet statistics
	–n	Lists addresses and ports in numerical form
	–s	Lists per-protocol statistics
	–p	Allows specification of protocol, can be tcp, udp, icmp, or ip
	–r	Lists routing table
	–interval	Specifies interval to pause display

IPCONFIG/WINIPCFG

IPCONFIG and WINIPCFG are utilities used to display the current TCP/IP configurations on the local workstations, and to modify the DHCP addresses assigned to each interface. IPCONFIG is a command-line utility for WINDOWS NT and later. WINIPCFG is a graphical interface used in Windows 95, 98, and ME. By default, they both display the IP address, the subnet mask, and the default gateway.

Table 5-7 lists the information available from these utilities.

TABLE 5-7	Item Displayed	Description
Parameters Displayed with IPCONFIG or WINIPCFG	Host Name	TCP/IP-based hostname
	DNS Servers	Configured IP addresses for DNS servers
	Node Type	NetBIOS node type
	NetBIOS Scope ID	Scope ID used to segment NetBIOS networks
	IP Routing Enabled	Displays if NT is set up as a TCP/IP router
	WINS proxy enabled	An advanced WINS feature
	NetBIOS resolution uses DNS	Enables NetBIOS name requests to query DNS for resolution
	Description	Network interface description
	Physical Address	MAC address of adapter
	DHCP Enabled	States whether the configured IP address was assigned via DHCP
	IP Address	TCP/IP address assigned
	Subnet Mask	Network subnet mask
	Default Gateway	Default router to send through
	Lease Obtained	Time and date DHCP address was obtained
	Lease Expires	Time and date DHCP address expires

IPCONFIG

IPCONFIG is used in Windows NT/2000 to display TCP/IP information from a command prompt. With this utility you can also display other related IP settings, such as DNS servers, WINS servers, and the network interface's physical MAC address. If you have more than one network interface, statistics are displayed about each one individually, or can be filtered to a particular one.

You can append /ALL to this command to display all TCP/IP information available. Figure 5-14 shows an example of IPCONFIG /ALL.

IPCONFIG DHCP Parameters

The IPCONFIG command-line utility enables you to control DHCP functions. Two switches are available to release and renew the addresses assigned to an interface. You can specify a particular adapter for these options, or allow it to work for all adapters that have DHCP-assigned addresses.

The /Release option removes the assigned IP address from all adapters configured for DCHP use. By specifying the adapter name after the switch, only that adapter will be affected by the command. This can be useful if you are experiencing problems associated with DHCP. It can also be used to release the address if an IP conflict occurs.

The /Renew option sends a request to the DHCP server asking for an address. It takes the last address DHCP assigned if it is available. If not, the computer is given the next available address in the pool. As with the /Release option, you can specify a particular adapter after the switch to renew the address. This will only work if the adapter has been set up to receive its IP address from a DHCP server.

FIGURE 5-14

The IPCONFIG /all command displays all TCP/IP information available

```
C:\>ipconfig /all

Windows NT IP Configuration

        Host Name . . . . . . . . . : workstation1
        DNS Servers . . . . . . . . :
        Node Type . . . . . . . . . : Broadcast
        NetBIOS Scope ID. . . . . . :
        IP Routing Enabled. . . . . : No
        WINS Proxy Enabled. . . . . : No
        NetBIOS Resolution Uses DNS : Yes

Ethernet adapter E190x1:

        Description . . . . . . . . : 3Com 3C90x Ethernet Adapter
        Physical Address. . . . . . : 00-60-97-E4-D7-CB
        DHCP Enabled. . . . . . . . : No
        IP Address. . . . . . . . . : 10.10.10.1
        Subnet Mask . . . . . . . . : 255.0.0.0
        Default Gateway . . . . . . : 10.10.1.1

C:\>
```

WINIPCFG

WINIPCFG is the Windows 95/98/ME-based graphical utility used to display TCP/IP information. The information displayed is the same as that in the Windows NT/2000 IPCONFIG utility. Microsoft has added a graphical interface for ease of use, but it can still be run from the command line with specific options.

WINIPCFG Options

As with the IPCONFIG utility, several features are available from a command-line prompt in the WINIPCFG utility. When you open WINIPCFG, the only information displayed is the TCP/IP address, the subnet mask, and the default gateway. There is a button at the bottom for more information, or you can use the WINIPCFG /ALL switch. Both present the same interface. A drop-down box is included to enable you to specify a specific adapter. Figure 5-15 shows WINIPCFG.

DHCP Options

The WINIPCFG utility includes buttons for releasing and renewing IP addresses for DHCP. It also contains information pertaining to the time and date the lease was

FIGURE 5-15

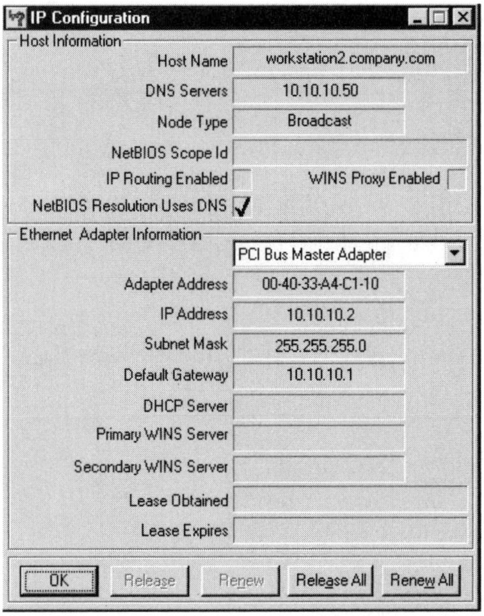

WINIPCFG/ALL displays all of the TCP/IP information available

obtained and when it expires. WINIPCFG does not, however, enable you to specify specific adapters for a particular function, such as releasing an address through the graphical interface. You can, however, use command-line options to specify certain or all adapters. The available options are listed here:

- **\Renew_All**   Renew all adapters
- **\Release_All**   Release all adapters
- **\Renew** *<adapter>*   Renew a specified adapter
- **\Release** *<adapter>*   Release a specified adapter

Batch Option

An additional option included with WINIPCFG is the /Batch switch. This enables you to forward the information in this utility to a text file. Be default, output is placed in the WINIPCFG.OUT file in the %WINDIR% directory. By appending a path and filename to the end of this switch, you can place this information wherever you prefer. The batch option can be used with any command-line option available for this utility.

Perform Exercise 5-6 to try this utility.

CertCam 5-6

EXERCISE 5-6

Using IPCONFIG or WINIPCFG

1. If you are using Windows NT/2000, go to the command prompt by selecting **Start | Run**, type **CMD**, and then type **IPCONFIG**. If you are using Windows 95/98/ME, go to **Start | Run**, and type **WINIPCFG**.

2. You will get a list of your TCP/IP protocol settings if you are using Windows NT/2000, or a window of TCP/IP settings if you are using Windows 95/98/ME.

FTP

The File Transfer Protocol (FTP) is designed primarily for transferring data across a network. FTP denotes both a protocol and a utility used for this purpose. It was created to transfer data files from one host to another quickly and efficiently without affecting the remote host's resources. You can also manage remote directories and even access e-mail; however, this program does not enable you to execute remote commands such as the Telnet utility.

How FTP works

FTP is unusual in that it uses two TCP channels to operate: TCP port 20 as the data transfer channel, and TCP port 21 for commands. The data transfer channel is known as the DTP, or Data Transfer Process, and the command channel is known as the PI, or Protocol Interpreter. The two channels enable you to transfer data and execute commands at the same time, and provide a more efficient and faster data transfer. FTP also works in real time. It does not queue up requests as most other utilities do; it transfers data while you watch.

Like Telnet, FTP requires a server-based program to facilitate client requests. The remote host FTP server application performs FTP processing and hands the data back to the client.

FTP enables file transfers in several formats based on the type of remote system. Most systems have two modes of transfer, text and binary. Text transfers are ASCII based and use characters separated by carriage returns and newline characters. The binary format uses a transfer method that requires no form of conversion. Because it requires no conversion or formatting, binary mode is faster. Most systems default to text mode, although many systems still use binary transfers. FTP is unable to transfer file permissions because they are not part of the protocol. Figure 5-16 shows an example of an FTP session.

FIGURE 5-16

An example of an
FTP session

```
C:\>ftp
ftp> open 10.10.10.2
> ftp: connect:10061
ftp> ls
Not connected.
ftp>
```

Using FTP

A command-line client utility is included with Windows NT/2000/XP and Windows 95/98/ME, and many third-party FTP server and client applications are available. Some add a graphical interface, while others add add-ons and functionality.

FTP is started by typing **FTP** at a command prompt followed by the name or address of the target machine. As with Telnet, the computer must be able to resolve the remote computer's name into an IP address for the command to succeed. Once logged on, users can transfer files, manage directories, and log in or log out.

There is a wide array of commands available in the FTP utility. These commands are used to control the FTP application and its functions. Table 5-8 lists some of the more common commands.

To use the FTP utility, perform Exercise 5-7 when connected to the Internet.

EXERCISE 5-7

CertCam 5-7

Using FTP to Display a Listing of Available Files

1. If you are using Windows NT/2000, go to the command prompt by selecting and type **CMD**. If you are using Windows 95/98/ME, go to Start | Run, and type **COMMAND**.

2. At the command prompt, type: **ftp ftp.hp.com**.

3. You will get a few lines of information and then a prompt to log in to the FTP server; just type **anonymous**.

4. You will then be prompted for a password; type your full **e-mail address**: user@provider.com.

5. You will then be notified that the password was accepted, and come back to an ftp> prompt.

6. Type **dir**, and press **Enter** to get a listing of files and directories available on the FTP server.

7. To change directories to the PUB directory, type **CD PUB**, and press **Enter**.

8. Type **dir** again to see the contents of the PUB directory.

9. Type **QUIT** to close the FTP session.

	Command	Description
TABLE 5-8	CD	Change working directory
Common FTP Commands	DELETE	Delete file
	LS	List current directory contents
	BYE	Log out
	GET	Download a file
	PUT	Upload a file
	VERBOSE	Turns verbose mode on and off

Configuring FTP

Users require a login ID to access FTP services. Most systems today enable an anonymous login, but you do not want to allow these users to have full rights to the system. Common problems with connecting via FTP are an invalid login or insufficient access rights. If you are having problems connecting to an FTP server, contact your FTP server administrator to verify that your ID is set up correctly.

FTP Options

Several switches are available for the command-line FTP utility. These options enable you to further customize the use of FTP to meet your needs. The –v option suppresses the display of remote server responses. This provides a more user-friendly interface to the utility. By default, when you start FTP, it attempts to log in automatically. You can disable this function by using the –n option.

The –I option turns off the interactive prompting that occurs during multiple transfers, which makes for a more automated approach to FTP. The –d option enables you to turn on the debugging functions. This feature displays all FTP commands that are passed between the client and server. The –g option turns off filename globbing. By disabling these functions, you are able to use wildcard characters in local filenames and directories.

Another option included with the FTP command-line utility is the capability to run a script of commands after the program is started. The script file is used instead of redirection, and can include any standard command. You must append the –s: switch followed by the path and filename of the script.

FROM THE CLASSROOM

The TCP/IP Suite of Utilities

I cannot stress enough how the TCP/IP suite of utilities presented here will help you in the field. I use these utilities almost daily in maintaining and troubleshooting the network. You will find yourself biased toward the most helpful utilities, such as Ping and IPCONFIG/WINIPCFG, but I recommend you learn when and how to use each utility. You never know when you will be placed in a situation where one of these lesser-used utilities can come in really handy. For example, FTP has been decreasing in popularity, so administrators don't get a chance to use it as much as we used to.

My FTP skills had dwindled, like those of many other administrators. One day, I received a call from another branch of the corporation that needed immediate access to a few spreadsheets that were temporarily unavailable because the WINS server was currently not replicating to remote sites. We figured the quickest way we could get these files to the remote site was through the FTP service. I placed the spreadsheets in the correct FTP drop box, and the remote administrator loaded up the FTP utility and downloaded the spreadsheets minutes later.

You can even enhance the effects of the TCP/IP utilities through batch files and programming languages. I recently worked on an automated Ping utility that would ping key servers on the network and report their status, in addition to the time required for the ping, and display the results in a spreadsheet or network diagram. Each network link to a key server would appear as a green line if the ping was successful, and a red line if the ping was unsuccessful. With a click of a button, any user on the network could determine if there was a network problem affecting their workstation. A user could call you and say "The link to the database server from my workstation appears to be down," rather than, "My computer is broken. Can you come and fix it?" This proactive approach on the user's part can save you time and effort when troubleshooting problems.

So, make sure you have these TCP/IP utilities committed to memory for the exam, and for real life, practice using them. I wish I had a nickel for every time I used the ping command!

—*Cameron Brandon, MCSE+Internet, CNE, A+, Network+*

Troubleshooting with FTP

One of the most common forms of troubleshooting with FTP is to use online services to obtain patches and documentation. For example, Microsoft provides an online FTP server from which you can obtain any public updates and fixes. You can find the information you need much faster this way; then you can contact Microsoft support. Most vendors provide online sites such as this for the same type of updates for their own products. Many companies also set up internal FTP sites to enable remote users to quickly access information.

If you need a way to efficiently get updates to your servers when a new patch is available, you can set up FTP services on each machine to copy the updates to. You can use the –s option to automate most of this process. Because FTP is much faster than a traditional file copy, it can save you a lot of time. Table 5-9 details the FTP parameters.

TFTP

The Trivial File Transfer Protocol (TFTP) is a slight variation on FTP. TFTP differs from FTP in two ways: It uses the User Datagram Protocol (UDP) connectionless transport instead of TCP, and you do not log on to the remote machine. Because it uses UDP, TFTP does not provide error-correcting services as TCP does. This has advantages, but it does have to use more complex algorithms to guarantee data integrity. Because users do not log in, user access and file permission problems are avoided.

TABLE 5-9	FTP Parameters	Definition
FTP Parameters	–v	Does not list remote server responses
	–n	Does not autologin on initial connection
	–i	Disables interactive prompting for multiple file transfers
	–d	Enables debugging
	–g	Allows use of wildcard characters
	–s	Specifies a text file of FTP commands to execute after FTP starts
	–a	Allows use of any local interface when binding data connection
	–w	Allows specification of transfer buffer size; the default is 4096
	–computer	Specify computer name or IP address of remote PC with which to connect

TFTP is generally not used for file transfers as FTP is; instead, it is used in scenarios such as diskless terminals or workstations. Typically, TFTP is used to load applications or for bootstrapping. Because the operating systems are not loaded at this point, the diskless machines cannot execute FTP. TFTP handles access and file permissions by imposing restraints from within the host operating system. For example, by setting the file permissions on the TFTP server, you can limit the security to areas inside the TFTP server.

on the
Ĵob

TFTP is commonly used when using Cisco routers. TFTP servers allow you to save the router information to the TFTP server and be able to reload the configuration information from the TFTP server. Cisco offers a TFTP service you can download and install on a Windows PC.

exam
Ẅatch

Please make sure you know what each TCP/IP utility is used for; for example, ARP is used to view and modify hardware (MAC) addresses. You will definitely receive a couple of questions testing your knowledge.

CERTIFICATION OBJECTIVE 5.08

Ping

The ping (Packet Internet Groper) command is the most basic TCP/IP troubleshooting tool available. This command is used to test a machine's connectivity to the network, and to verify that it is active. Usually, using this command is the first step to any troubleshooting if a connectivity problem is occurring between two computers. This can quickly help you to determine whether a remote host is available and responsive.

How Ping Works

Ping uses the ICMP to verify connections to remote hosts by sending echo packets and listening for reply packets. Ping waits for up to one second for each packet sent, and prints the number of packets sent and received. Each packet is then validated against the transmitted message. By default, four packets are transmitted containing 64 bytes of data. Figure 5-17 shows an example of a ping.

To use a PING command and see the results, perform Exercise 5-8.

FIGURE 5-17

Ping uses
ICMP to verify
connections to
remote hosts

```
C:\>ping 10.10.10.1

Pinging 10.10.10.1 with 32 bytes of data:

Reply from 10.10.10.1: bytes=32 time=1ms TTL=128
Reply from 10.10.10.1: bytes=32 time=1ms TTL=128
Reply from 10.10.10.1: bytes=32 time=1ms TTL=128
Reply from 10.10.10.1: bytes=32 time<10ms TTL=128

C:\>
```

EXERCISE 5-8

CertCam 5-8

Using PING

1. If you are using Windows NT/2000, go to the command prompt by selecting **Start | Run**, and then type **CMD**. If you are using Windows 95/98/ME, go to **Start | Run**, and type **COMMAND**.

2. At the command prompt, type: **ping <your hostname>**.

3. You will get a line showing the hostname to IP address resolution, and then four lines of information that determine whether the transmission was successful. Since you are trying to ping your own PC, you should get four lines of replies.

4. You can also type: **ping 127.0.0.1**.

5. If you receive four lines of information showing successes, the TCP/IP protocol is initialized and functioning. Four lines of failed transmissions will show that TCP/IP is not initialized and cannot be used to perform network transmissions.

   Note: 127.0.0.1 is a reserved address used as a loopback to test that TCP/IP is functioning on the local PC.

Ping Options

Additional options are available to customize the output that Ping provides. Options include changing packet length, type of service, and TTL settings. You can append the –a option to resolve an IP address to its hostname. The –f option will not enable the packets to be fragmented by a router or gateway. This can be used to further stress connections to see if they are failing.

The TTL settings can be specified with the –I option. In addition, the type of service option is available via the –v switch.

Setting the Length Option   By default, packets are sent in 64-byte chunks. You can modify the packet size to further test the response time. When larger packets are involved, you can see what larger loads will do to response time as well as responsiveness. To change the packet size, use the –I option followed by the packet length. The maximum packet length that can be specified is 8192 bytes.

Setting the Number of Echo Packets   You can specify the number of packets to send to the remote host. By default, only four packets are sent. You can specify any number of packets to send with the –n option. You can also use the –t option to specify a continuous stream of packets. This functionality is useful in monitoring trends in data transfers.

Timeout Intervals   Timeout intervals are used to interpret the time to travel between hops. A normal LAN usually lists devices as being less than 10 milliseconds away. By default, two seconds is the timeout before a "reply timed out" message is generated. You can use the –w option to raise this value for troubleshooting.

Loose Source Routing   Use Ping to specify intermediate gateways to test against. You can route packets through particular IP addresses or hostnames specified. The –j option enables you to specify the hosts to route through. The –k option enables you to exclude hosts from this route list. The maximum number of hosts you can specify with both options is nine.

Troubleshooting with Ping

Use the Ping utility to verify connectivity by IP address or hostname. You must be able to resolve the hostname to use this functionality. If you are unable to ping by hostname, but you can ping by IP address, you might have a name resolution problem.

If you are receiving "reply timed out" messages, you might try to bump up the timeout value with the –w option. Maybe the packets are arriving, but are timing out before two seconds. After bumping up the value, if the replies are returning, a bandwidth problem might be present. Contact the network administrator where the numbers seem to rise. Table 5-10 details the PING parameters.

TABLE 5-10	PING Parameters	Definition
PING Parameters	−t	Specifies to perform the PING command until interrupted.
	−a	Resolves addresses to computer names.
	−n	Specifies the number of ECHO packets; the default is 4.
	−l	Specifies amount of data to send in ECHO packet. Default is 32 bytes, maximum is 65,527 bytes.
	−f	Specifies to not fragment packets.
	−i	Sets TTL (Time To Live) value for packets.
	−v	Sets TOS (Type Of Service).
	−r	Records routes of packets.
	−s	Specifies timestamp for number of hops.
	−j	Specifies route for packets (loose source route).
	−k	Specifies route for packets (strict source route).
	−w	Specifies timeout interval in milliseconds.
	−destination-list	Specifies remote PC to PING.

CERTIFICATION OBJECTIVE 5.09

NSLOOKUP

The NSLOOKUP command is used to verify DNS name resolution from a DNS server. This is very useful for a Windows 2000 network, which depends immensely on the use of DNS. If DNS should fail or return improper information, network communication can slow due to name resolution not being done to allow data packets to be sent to the proper PCs. If DNS fails, the network PCs can start to perform name resolution using broadcasts, but this will cause a large overhead of traffic and use bandwidth. In a Windows 2000 network, Active Directory needs DNS, or Active Directory will fail and the domain will fail.

How **NSLOOKUP** Works

NSLOOKUP will query a DNS server to verify that name resolution is occurring, as well as to check that a DNS name registration has taken place. For example, if a server appears to be offline to client PCs because no one is able to reach the server's resources, you need to determine a few things:

- Determine that the server is online and is able to communicate on the network.

- Verify that the client PC is able to communicate with any PC on the server segment.

- Verify that the resource on the server is still shared and you do have rights to access it.

These items can be verified fairly quickly if you are located at the client PC. You can ping the server by the server IP address. If you can ping the server by IP address and not by the server DNS name, there is a DNS name resolution issue. You can then pursue the issue further by using NSLOOKUP to verify that the DNS server is operational, as well as having the server DNS name and proper IP address in the DNS database.

It is possible, but unlikely, that the name to IP address resolution is incorrect. The DNS name could be matched to an improper IP address. This can cause the data packets to be sent to a PC or network device other than the server, or even to a nonexistent IP address.

NSLOOKUP Options

There are two different modes in which you can use NSLOOKUP: interactive and noninteractive.

The type of information you require will determine which mode you use.

Interactive Mode   Interactive mode is used when you have more than one item in the DNS database you will be querying. Interactive mode will allow you enter a command-line state that will keep prompting you for more commands until you type **EXIT** at the NSLOOKUP command prompt to return to a standard DOS command prompt and exit the NSLOOKUP utility.

To enter interactive mode, perform Exercise 5-9. Otherwise, just type **NSLOOKUP** and the single parameter that you wish to query.

EXERCISE 5-9

Starting the **NSLOOKUP** Utility

1. Go to **Start | Run**.

2. In the Run window, type **CMD**.

3. In the window that opens you will see a DOS prompt; type **NSLOOKUP** to start the NSLOOKUP utility.

4. NSLOOKUP will display two lines of information: The first is the default DNS server name to which you are connected, and the second is the IP address of the DNS server. The prompt will be blinking next to a ">" symbol.

5. You can now issue commands to query the DNS database, or type **Exit** to quit the NSLOOKUP utility.

Table 5-11 lists the parameters available in NSLOOKUP.

TABLE 5-11	Command	Description
NSLOOKUP Commands	HELP	Displays a brief summary of NSLOOKUP commands.
	EXIT	Exits the NSLOOKUP utility.
	FINGER	Connects to the current finger server, and queries that server.
	LS (−t, −a, −d, −h, −s)	Lists information for a DNS domain: −t lists all records of a specified type −a lists aliases in DNS domain −d lists all DNS domain records −h lists CPU and OS information for DNS domain −s lists well-known services in DNS domain
	LSERVER	Changes the default DNS domain to a specified DNS domain.
	ROOT	Changes the name of the ROOT server to the specified domain.
	SERVER	Changes the server to a specified DNS domain.

TABLE 5-11	Command	Description
NSLOOKUP Commands (continued)	SET	Changes configuration settings for the NSLOOKUP utility.
	SET ALL	Lists current NSLOOKUP configuration values.
	SET CL[ass] = (IN, CHAOS, HESIOD, ANY)	Sets Query class as specified by the option setting: IN Internet class CHAOS Chaos class HESIOD MIT Athena Hesiod class ANY Any of the previously listed wildcards
	SET [no] DEB[ug]	Turns debugger mode off or on.
	SET [no] D2	Turns exhaustive debug mode off or on.
	SET [no] DEF[name]	Appends the default domain name to the request made.
	SET DO[mail]	Changes the default domain name to that specified.
	SET [no] IG[nore]	Ignores any packet truncation errors.
	SET PO[rt]	Changes port used by DNS name server.
	SET Q[uerytype] = (A, ANY, CNAME, GID, HINFO, MB, MG, MINFO, MR, MX, NS, PTR, SOA, TXT, UID, UINFO, WKS)	Changes type of query: **A** Computer's IP address **ANY** All types of data **CNAME** Canonical name for an alias **GID** Group name's group identifier **HINFO** CPU and operating system type of computer **MB** Mailbox domain name **MG** Mail group member **MINFO** Mailbox or mail list information **MR** Mail rename domain name **MX** Mail exchanger **NS** DNS name server for the zone **PTR** Computer name if the query is an IP address **SOA** DNS domain's start-of-authority record **TXT** Text information **UID** User identifier **UINFO** User information **WKS** Well-known service description
	SET [no] REC[urse]	Allows you to specify whether to recurse a query to other servers.
	SET RET[ry]	Set number of retries.

	Command	Description
TABLE 5-11		
NSLOOKUP Commands *(continued)*	SET RO[ot]	Changes the name of the ROOT server.
	SET [no] SEA[rch]	Specifies whether to append the domain name to a request.
	SET SRCHL[ist]	Changes default DNS domain name and search used in queries.
	SET TI[meout]	Sets the number of seconds to wait for a response before timing out.
	SET TY[pe]	Changes type of information queried.
	SET [no] V[c]	Specifies whether to use a virtual circuit when querying a server.
	VIEW	Sorts and lists output.

CERTIFICATION OBJECTIVE 5.10

Troubleshooting with TCP/IP Utilities

The two most common TCP/IP problems are network connectivity and name resolution. In this section, you will learn how to troubleshoot these problems and how to determine where the problems truly reside.

Given the following scenario, how do you troubleshoot the problem?

You are trying to use a third-party application to access a remote computer via TCP/IP. You are unable to connect to the remote server.

To properly troubleshoot this problem, you must know where to begin. A scenario which follows is very common in the TCP/IP world, and could be categorized by one of the following problems:

- Basic network connectivity problem
- Name resolution problem

It is very easy to determine which problem is occurring in a given situation. Start by trying to access the resource via the IP address rather than the hostname. For example, if the problem is related to name resolution, **PING** *<hostname>* might not work, but **PING** *<ipaddress>* will. This indicates that because the name cannot be resolved, the application does not know what the IP address is, and therefore cannot access the remote host. If you cannot access the local resource via the IP address, this indicates a connectivity problem.

SCENARIO & SOLUTION

I need to download a file from another PC on the Internet. What utility can I use?	If the other PC has FTP services installed, you can use the FTP utility.
I don't know what my DNS client settings are.	Use the WINIPCFG or IPCONFIG command with the /All option.
I can ping a server, but the NBTSTAT utility shows that its tables are empty.	The appropriate services on the remote computer are not started. The services broadcast are dependent on items such as the Server or Workstation services.
If I ping a remote server, it does not respond; however, every now and then I can connect.	Try increasing the timeout value for Ping. This might be an indication of a network problem between the client and remote server.
I need to find my computer MAC address.	Use the WINIPCFG or IPCONFIG command.
I need to find if a specific DNS name is being properly resolved after I have changed the IP address.	Use the NSLOOKUP command to verify that the DNS server has the proper DNS name matched to the new IP address.

Connectivity Problems

Connectivity problems can be difficult to isolate and resolve quickly, especially in complex networks. Let's use some of the tools you've learned about to troubleshoot the earlier problem of using a third-party application to access a remote computer via TCP/IP and being unable to connect to the remote server. You cannot ping the remote host by its IP address.

Check Your TCP/IP Configuration

Start by checking your TCP/IP configuration. TCP/IP requires several settings to be complete and accurate. When you use TCP/IP as your network protocol, an incorrect setting such as a mistyped subnet mask can keep your computer from talking with other hosts on the network. For example, if you have an incorrect default gateway setup, you might not be able to communicate with anyone on a remote network.

Use the IPCONFIG or WINIPCFG utility to determine your computer's basic TCP/IP settings. Verify that the IP address and subnet mask displayed by the IPCONFIG/WINIPCFG command are the correct values for your computer. Verify that your default gateway is set up with the correct address.

Ping the Loopback Address

Try pinging the loopback address. You can use the PING command to verify that TCP/IP is working properly. By pinging the loopback address, which is 127.0.0.1, you are actually verifying that the protocol stack is functioning properly. You should receive a reply like the one shown in Figure 5-18.

An error while pinging the loopback address usually indicates a problem with the TCP/IP protocol installed locally. If you do receive an error at this point, you should try uninstalling and reinstalling TCP/IP. You can remove and install TCP/IP from within the Control Panel.

Ping the Local IP Address

If you can successfully ping the loopback address, try pinging your local computer's IP address. If you do not know what you IP address is, remember that IPCONFIG/ WINIPCFG will display this information for you. By typing the following at a command prompt, you should receive a response similar to the one shown in Figure 5-18:

```
PING local IP address
```

If an error occurs at this point, there might be a problem communicating with the NIC. You can first try reinstalling the adapter driver for the card. If that doesn't work, try removing and reseating the card. This error might only be resolved by completely replacing the NIC.

Clear the ARP Cache Table

If the local IP address responds correctly, try clearing the ARP cache. If an IP address was errantly stored here, it could cause the client to attempt to contact the wrong computer.

Start by displaying the ARP cache. You can then see if there is an entry located for the remote IP address. If an entry exists, try deleting it with the –d option.

FIGURE 5-18

Ping the loopback address to test local connectivity

```
C:\>ping loopback
Pinging workstation2.company.com [127.0.0.1] with 32 bytes of data:
Reply from 127.0.0.1: bytes=32 time<10ms TTL=128
Reply from 127.0.0.1: bytes=32 time=1ms TTL=128
Reply from 127.0.0.1: bytes=32 time<10ms TTL=128
Reply from 127.0.0.1: bytes=32 time<10ms TTL=128
C:\>
```

Verify the Default Gateway

After removing any errant entries, the next step is to ping the default gateway. This will only be involved if the host is on a remote subnet. When trying to ping a host not located on the local subnet, the request is automatically forwarded to the appropriate route. If a route does not exist, the packet is forwarded to the default gateway. If the gateway does not respond, the packets will not be able to get to the remote host.

You can use IPCONFIG/WINIPCFG to display your default gateway. Once you have that address, try pinging that address or hostname.

Trace the Route to the Remote Host

After a packet leaves the default gateway, any route can be taken to reach a remote computer. The next step is to try to trace the route to the remote computer. The example in Figure 5-19 shows a tracert in action.

A wide array of problems could show up here. You may notice that when the utility gets to a certain point, it responds with "Request timed out." If this occurs, it could indicate a route problem or a device failure. It could also indicate bandwidth issues. Try raising the timeout value. If it responds, but with high values, your data transfers could be failing because the application does not wait long enough. Try reconfiguring your application or adding more bandwidth to your network.

Another error you might receive is "Destination Net Unreachable." This usually indicates a network routing problem. Contact the network administrator responsible for that network segment.

Check IP Security on the Server

The next thing to try is to verify the security and settings on the remote computer. Port settings for services on the other computer may be different from the port settings you are trying to use to connect. Table 5-12 lists the standard port settings for commonly used protocols:

You can use the Telnet tool to verify that the other computer is configured to permit connections on the same port you are using. If you do not receive an error

---

FIGURE 5-19

Use Tracert to help you troubleshoot this problem

```
C:\>tracert 10.10.10.1

Tracing route to WORKSTATION1    [10.10.10.1]
over a maximum of 30 hops:

  1     1 ms     1 ms     1 ms  WORKSTATION1    [10.10.10.1]

Trace complete.

C:\>
```

message, the other computer is configured to enable connections. If you do receive an error, try looking at the settings on the remote computer to verify that they are set up properly.

Name Resolution Problems

Suppose you are able to connect to a remote host but are unable to connect via its hostname. This indicates a name resolution problem. In the Microsoft world, there are two types of computer names: TCP/IP-based hostnames and NetBIOS names. These names can be resolved in several ways, including the Domain Name System (DNS), Windows Internet Naming Service (WINS), a HOSTS file, or an LMHOSTS file. Each method has its advantages and disadvantages.

Name Resolution Order

The two types of Microsoft computer names each work a little differently. They can use the other's services; however, they use their own resolution methods first. TCP/IP-based hosts use the following resolution method:

1. Check local name

2. Check local HOSTS file

3. Check DNS servers

4. Check local NetBIOS cache

5. Check WINS servers

6. Broadcasts

TABLE 5-12	Port	Protocol
Standard Port Settings for Common Protocols	80	HTTP
	20	FTP
	21	FTP
	23	TELNET
	25	SMTP
	110	POP3

NetBIOS resolution works in a very similar way. Name resolution for these services work in the following method:

1. Check its local NetBIOS cache

2. Check the WINS server

3. Broadcast for computer

4. Check LMHOSTS file

5. Check local hostname (if **Enable DNS for Windows Resolution** is checked in TCP/IP properties)

6. Check TCP/IP HOSTS file

7. Check DNS servers

By knowing the order of name resolution, you can better understand how these services work and effectively troubleshoot them.

Check the HOSTS File

You can start by checking the HOSTS file. A HOSTS file is a text file that can be configured with any standard text editor. It contains static mappings for remote TCP/IP hosts. Each computer has its own host file, HOSTS.SAM, located in %windir% for Windows 95\98, and HOSTS located in %SystemRoot%\System32\Drivers\Etc for Windows NT 4.0.

Because every machine maintains its own HOSTS file, they are not generally used in medium or large environments. If a modification or addition has to be made, each machine needs to receive this update. When you are talking about four or five machines, it's not that bad. When you have to modify 150 machines, it can become very difficult. Figure 5-20 shows an example of a HOSTS file.

To check your HOSTS file, open it and scan for the entry of the remote host. If this file is the method by which your computer is resolving addresses, verify that the entry exists and that it contains the correct information. If this is not the resolution method you are using, trying checking your DNS configuration.

Check Your Domain Name System Configuration

DNS provides TCP/IP name resolution services. This is a central server that computers can use to query for name resolution. The advantage over the host file here is that you only have to make the change on your server; all clients querying it will receive the update. This is much easier to administer than 150 or more workstations.

FIGURE 5-20

An example of
a HOSTS file

```
# This file contains the mappings of IP addresses to host names. Each
# entry should be kept on an individual line. The IP address should
# be placed in the first column followed by the corresponding host name.
# The IP address and the host name should be separated by at least one
# space.
#
# Additionally, comments (such as these) may be inserted on individual
# lines or following the machine name denoted by a '#' symbol.
#
# For example:
#
#      102.54.94.97        rhino.acme.com            # source server
#       38.25.63.10        x.acme.com                # x client host

127.0.0.1          localhost
10.10.10.1         workstation1
```

If you use DNS for name resolution, first verify that you have the DNS client set up correctly on the workstation. From a command prompt, type **IPCONFIG /ALL** or **WINIPCFG /ALL** to list the DNS servers. If they exist and are correct, try pinging the DNS server to see if it is online. If it responds, try changing your DNS server to another server. It is possible that one DNS server might have different information than another does. You also might need to contact your DNS administrator to verify that the name exists in DNS and has the correct information.

Check the LMHOSTS File

The LMHOSTS file is similar to the HOSTS file, but is primarily used for NetBIOS-based hostname resolution. It can be used to handle TCP/IP hostname resolution, but it is not recommended because it is low in the resolution order.

Like the HOSTS file, LMHOSTS is a text file that can be edited with any standard text editor. If your network uses LMHOSTS files for NetBIOS-based name resolution and you cannot connect to the remote computer using its NetBIOS name, there could be an invalid entry in your LMHOSTS file. Try scanning this file for the name of the remote machine. Verify that it exists and that it contains the correct information. If you are not using LMHOSTS, try checking your WINS server configuration settings.

Check Your Windows Internet Naming Service Configuration

A WINS server provides NetBIOS name resolution much like DNS servers provide TCP/IP hostname resolution. If you use WINS for NetBIOS name resolution and you cannot connect to the other machine with its NetBIOS name, there might be a problem with your computer's WINS configuration.

Start by verifying your WINS configuration. From a command prompt, type **IPCONFIG /ALL** or **WINIPCFG /ALL**. This will display the current WINS servers configured for your computer. If the correct servers are listed, try pinging the primary WINS server. This is the first server that your requests will go to. If the hostname is not located here, your computer will not try to get to the secondary WINS server. This second WINS server is used only if the primary cannot be reached.

If you cannot ping the primary WINS server address, try switching your primary with the secondary in the Control Panel. If you are able to resolve the name now, contact your WINS administrator to correct the problem. You might also need to verify that the remote host is registered with WINS correctly.

exam
ⓦatch *Make sure you understand the differences between hostname resolution and NetBIOS (machine) name resolution. The exam will quiz you on both name resolution scenarios.*

Check Your Domain Name Server Database

A Domain Name Server (DNS) will provide the DNS domain name to IP address resolution when trying to connect to services using domain names, such as on the Internet. If the name and IP address are not matched correctly in the database, you will be unable to access the proper PC for the services you are requesting.

For example, if you were on the Internet and wanted to access an FTP site, but the company has changed the IP address of the FTP server, you would type in the DNS name of the FTP server in the address bar, and this name would be matched to the old FTP IP address. The FTP utility would try to query the old IP address for the FTP service. If no FTP service exists on the old IP address, or a server is not currently using the old IP address, you would receive an error. Until the company updates the DNS servers on the Internet, the FTP server will be unreachable unless you can find the new IP address of the FTP server.

After querying the DNS server and getting an IP address for the DNS name, you should try to ping the IP address returned to verify that the server at the IP address is functioning.

It is also possible that the DNS server might be unavailable and you will receive no response to your request for the DNS name resolution. If this occurs, you will need to set your default DNS server to one that is functioning, or contact someone about the DNS server and report that it is not functioning.

SCENARIO & SOLUTION

I cannot access any other PC on the network, and no one can access my PC. What could be the problem?	Use IPCONFIG/WINIPCFG to make sure your TCP/IP settings are correct.
I added a static ARP entry to a server that I often access, but I have been unable to access the server since I added the entry. What's wrong?	You mistyped the MAC address of the server, and it is not using the correct MAC address.
The administrator has recently installed a new server and I cannot access it. What can be wrong?	The name resolution is not being managed properly check the DNS and WINS databases.
A new server has been added and I am unable to access any shared files. What's wrong?	The server services can be disabled, causing no resources to be shared. Use NBTSTAT to determine that the PC responds with a line that contains <20> in it.
I am unable to access any resources on the network. When I started my PC, I received an error message about duplicate IP addresses. What's wrong?	The TCP/IP protocol is not configured properly since two PCs have the same IP address, so your PC apparently did not initialize the protocol. You need to use IPCONFIG/WINIPCFG to release and renew the IP address if you are using DHCP, or get a new IP address and type it in manually.

on the
Job

Most companies will use a DNS server provided by their ISP for DNS name resolution. If DNS name resolution is failing, contact your ISP. For Windows 2000 networks, you will have a DNS server on your network and it will query the ISP DNS server. Therefore, you will need to verify that your DNS server can still access the ISP server when trying to resolve DNS names on the Internet.

CERTIFICATION SUMMARY

The ARP utility is used to display and modify the Address Resolution Protocol name cache. This protocol maintains the mappings between the 32-bit TCP/IP addresses and the 48-bit Ethernet addresses. Each time you access a remote computer, its entry is updated in the ARP cache. Entries can also be manually added and deleted. By default, the ARP cache maintains unused entries for two minutes, and entries in use for 10 minutes. RARP works in reverse to provide 48-bit Ethernet addresses to 32-bit TCP/IP address mappings.

The Telnet utility provides a virtual terminal to execute remote console commands. Telnet uses a TCP protocol connection to port 23. Telnet can also be used to connect to other ports set up to be interactive. The default line buffer size is 25 and can be configured to a maximum of 399 lines. The default terminal emulation for Telnet is VT100.

NBTSTAT displays NetBIOS over TCP/IP (NetBT) protocol statistics and connections. NetBT is a software standard and naming convention. Each workstation in a domain or workgroup must have a unique name. NetBIOS names are 16 characters. with the last reserved for a hexadecimal number used as a resource type identifier. You can display remote statistics, registration information, and session information.

Tracert is used to determine the route that data travels to reach its destination. It uses the ICMP protocol to display information such as hop count and timeout values. You can specify the maximum number of hops and timeout values to further customize the utility.

Netstat displays TCP/IP protocol statistics and session information. You can also display the local IP route table. Netstat can display Ethernet-specific statistics, subprotocol statistics, and session information, including listening ports.

IPCONFIG displays the current TCP/IP configuration for a Windows NT/2000 computer. WINIPCFG is a graphical interface used on Windows 95/98/ME computers to display information on DNS servers, WINS servers, default gateway, subnet mask, IP address, and DHCP leases. These utilities can be used to release or renew DHCP addresses assigned to an interface.

The File Transfer Protocol (FTP) is used for file transfers between two computers. FTP requires two TCP port connections: port 20 for data, and port 21 for commands. This allows for faster transfer speeds. A server-based FTP program is used to store files and process commands. Additional features include debugging, disabling auto-logons, and suppressing screen output.

Ping is used to verify a remote computer's connectivity to the network. Additional options for troubleshooting include setting packet lengths, changing the TTL values, and specifying host lists to return routing statistics for.

NSLOOKUP is used to query a DNS server for information in its database to verify that name resolution is working with DNS names.

✓ TWO-MINUTE DRILL

ARP

❑ The Address Resolution Protocol (ARP) was designed to provide a mapping from the logical 32-bit TCP/IP addresses to the physical 48-bit MAC addresses.

❑ *Address resolution* is the process of finding the address of a host within a network.

❑ Remember that ARP translates IP addresses into MAC addresses. The Reverse Address Resolution Protocol, or RARP, is used to find a TCP/IP address from a MAC address.

❑ Only four types of messages can be sent by the ARP protocol on any machine:

  ❑ ARP request

  ❑ ARP reply

  ❑ RARP request

  ❑ RARP reply

❑ The Reverse Address Resolution Protocol (RARP) enables a machine to learn its own IP address by broadcasting to resolve its own MAC address.

Telnet

❑ Telnet was designed to provide a virtual terminal or remote login across the network. It is connection based and handles its own session negotiation.

❑ The primary use of Telnet is remote administration.

❑ Make sure you can recognize the output from each of the TCP/IP utilities listed in this chapter. On your Network+ exam, you will be presented with output from a command and asked which command produced the output.

NBTSTAT

❑ The Microsoft TCP/IP stack uses an additional subprotocol for its services, NetBIOS over TCP/IP (NetBT).

❑ NBTSTAT is used to troubleshoot connectivity between two computers trying to communicate via NetBT.

❑ Make sure you know the options available with the NBTSTAT command, such as NBTSTAT –R and NBTSTAT –a.

Tracert

❑ Tracert is a command-line utility that was designed to perform a very basic task: to determine the path taken by a data packet to reach its destination.

Netstat

❑ Netstat displays protocol statistics and current TCP/IP network connections.

❑ Using Netstat to monitor TCP protocol activity can enable you to troubleshoot TCP/IP-based connections.

IPCONFIG/WINIPCFG

❑ IPCONFIG and WINIPCFG are utilities used to display the current TCP/IP configurations on the local workstations, and to modify the DHCP addresses assigned to each interface.

❑ IPCONFIG is used in Windows NT to display TCP/IP information from a command prompt.

❑ WINIPCFG is the Windows 95/98-based graphical utility used to display TCP/IP information.

FTP

❑ The File Transfer Protocol (FTP) is designed primarily for transferring data across a network.

❑ One of the most common forms of troubleshooting with FTP is to use online services to obtain patches and documentation.

❑ TFTP differs from FTP in two ways: It uses the User Datagram Protocol (UDP) connectionless transport instead of TCP, and it does not log on to the remote machine.

❑ Make sure you know what each TCP/IP utility is used for. For example, ARP is used to view and modify hardware (MAC) addresses. You will definitely receive a couple questions testing your knowledge of this.

Ping

❑ The PING command is used to test a machine's connectivity to the network, and to verify that it is active.

❑ Ping uses the Internet Control Message Protocol (ICMP) to verify connections to remote hosts by sending echo packets and listening for reply packets.

❑ Use the Ping utility to verify connectivity by IP address or hostname.

❑ The two most common problems with TCP/IP are network connectivity problems and name resolution.

❑ Make sure you understand the differences between hostname resolution and NetBIOS (machine) name resolution. The exam will quiz you on both scenarios.

NSLOOKUP

❑ NSLOOKUP displays information in the DNS server database.

SELF TEST

The following Self Test questions will help measure your understanding of the material presented in this chapter. Read all the choices carefully, as there may be more than one correct answer. Choose all correct answers for each question.

ARP

1. Which utility can be used to display and modify the table that maintains the TCP/IP address to MAC address translation?

   A. NBTSTAT

   B. Telnet

   C. ARP

   D. SNMP

2. Which format types are not valid for ARP? (Choose all that apply.)

   A. ARP reply

   B. ARP decline

   C. ARP response

   D. ARP request

3. How long will a dynamic ARP entry remain in cache if it is not in use?

   A. 10 minutes

   B. 5 minutes

   C. 2 minutes

   D. None of the above

4. Which protocols do not have statistics available with the Netstat utility?

   A. TCP

   B. ICMP

   C. ARP

   D. IP

Telnet

5. Which utility enables you to execute console commands remotely at a virtual terminal?

   A. FTP

   B. Ping

   C. Telnet

   D. NBTSTAT

6. Which protocol is defined to use TCP port 23?

   A. Telnet

   B. FTP

   C. HTTP

   D. SMTP

7. What is the default terminal emulation type for Telnet?

   A. DEC

   B. ANSI

   C. VT52

   D. VT100

NBTSTAT

8. Which protocol uses a 16-character name, with the last digit reserved as a resource identifier?

   A. TCP/IP

   B. IPX

   C. NetBT

   D. NBTSTAT

9. Which utility can be used to troubleshoot NetBIOS over TCP/IP connectivity issues?

   A. NetBT

   B. NetBEUI

   C. NBTSTAT

   D. NetBIOS

10. Which NBTSTAT switch enables you to display the computer's local NetBT name cache?

    A. –R

    B. –c

    C. –a

    D. –A

11. In what ways can a computer with a NetBIOS name register its services on the network?

    A. Broadcast

    B. HOSTS file

    C. WINS server

    D. Both A and C

Tracert

12. Which utility is used to determine the path that data takes during transport to a remote host?

    A. NBTSTAT

    B. ARP

    C. FTP

    D. Tracert

Netstat

13. Which utility is used to display TCP/IP-specific protocol and interface statistics?

    A. NBTSTAT

    B. ARP

    C. Netstat

    D. None of the above

IPCONFIG/WINIPCFG

14. Which items are not available for display in IPCONFIG?

    A. TCP/IP address

    B. MAC address

C. DHCP lease information

D. None of the above

15. Which option listed is not available with WINIPCFG?

A. /ALL

B. /Release

C. /Obtain

D. /Renew

FTP

16. Which utility is used to facilitate file transfers between two remote hosts?

A. FTP

B. Telnet

C. Ping

D. None of the above

17. What TCP ports are used by FTP services?

A. TCP port 20

B. TCP port 25

C. TPC port 21

D. A and C

PING

18. Which utility is used to verify network connectivity of a remote host?

A. Route

B. ARP

C. Ping

D. None of the above

NSLOOKUP

19. Which utility is used to verify the DNS database on a DNS server?

   A. Route

   B. ARP

   C. Ping

   D. NSLOOKUP

LAB QUESTION

A company has hired you to perform some maintenance on its network. They have been having problems with various systems. The network is shown in Figure 5-21, and the problems are as follows:

1. PC 1 cannot access the Internet or any PC on subnet B. It can access all PCs on Subnet A without problems. When you ping the configured default gateway, you receive no response.

2. PC 2 is unable to ping any PC in any subnet. When you look at its TCP/IP address, it is all 0s.

3. PC 3 has been trying to access PC 4 and transfer a file to PC 4. PC 3 can ping PC 4 and receive a response.

4. PC 5 is trying to access the Internet, but cannot connect to any Web site, ping any Web site, or use Tracert to get any information. PC 5 can access any other PC in Subnet A or B.

5. PC 6 receives no information when using WINIPCFG (it is a Windows 98 PC). It is also unable to connect to any other PC, or be connected to by any other PC. What do you think can be wrong with these systems?

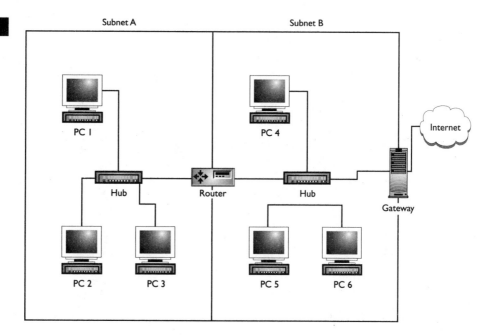

FIGURE 5-21

An example of
a HOSTS file

SELF TEST ANSWERS

ARP

1. ☑ C. ARP. ARP maintains the protocol rules for making this translation and providing address conversion in both directions within the OSI layers. A utility by the same name is available for Windows 95, Windows 98, and Windows NT. This utility is used to display and modify entries within the ARP table.

   ☒ A, B, and D are incorrect. NBTSTAT is used to determine services provided by PCs, Telnet is used to open a terminal emulation session with a terminal server, and SNMP is used for PC management.

2. ☑ B and C. ARP decline and ARP response. As protocols go, ARP provides a very basic function. Only four types of messages can be sent out by the ARP protocol on any machine: ARP request, ARP reply, RARP request, and RARP reply.

   ☒ A and D are incorrect because of the preceding explanation.

3. ☑ C. Two minutes. Unlike static addresses, which never age out, dynamic addresses remain for only a predetermined amount of time. Windows NT adjusts the size of the ARP cache automatically. Entries not used after two minutes are removed. If entries are in use, they remain for 10 minutes before they are removed. A registry parameter within Windows NT is also available to allow for more control over the aging parameters.

   ☒ A, B, and D are incorrect because a dynamic ARP entry remains in cache for two minutes if it is not in use.

4. ☑ C. ARP. Protocol-specific information is available with the ARP command-line utility. With the –s option, you can display statistics for the communications protocols and how they are being used. The protocols include TCP, UDP, ICMP, and IP. Detailed information can be obtained with this option that can help you to isolate TCP/IP communications issues.

   ☒ A, B, and D are incorrect because ARP is the correct answer.

Telnet

5. ☑ C. Telnet (telecommunications network) was designed to provide a virtual terminal or remote login across the network. This enables the user to execute commands on a remote machine anywhere on the network as if he were sitting in front of the console. The term *Telnet* refers to both the protocol and application used for remote logins.

☒ **A**, **B**, and **D** are incorrect because FTP allows for file transfers between two PCs; Ping is used to verify that connectivity can be established between two PCs; and NBTSTAT will allow you to verify the services available on a PC.

6. ☑ **A**. Telnet. To connect via a hostname, the client must be able to resolve the name to an IP address. You must also specify the port to connect to and the terminal emulation type. By default, this Telnet will try to connect to the Telnet port (port 23) on the remote server.
☒ **B**, **C**, and **D** are incorrect because FTP uses ports 20 and 21, HTTP uses port 80, and SMTP uses port 25.

7. ☑ **B** and **D**. VT100 and ANSI. The terminal emulation option defines what type of remote terminal to use. This controls how commands are interpreted and displayed by the remote server.
☒ **A** and **C** are incorrect. VT-52 is an older standard not commonly used anymore. VT100/ANSI is the default standard emulation used today. DEC is not an available option.

NBTSTAT

8. ☑ **C**. NetBT. The NetBIOS namespace is a flat structure, meaning that all names within its network must be unique. This means that all computers within a workgroup or domain must have a unique name. Names are comprised of 16 hexadecimal characters. The first 15 can be set by the administrator or user, and the 16th specifies a resource type.
☒ **A**, **B**, and **D** are incorrect because NetBT is the correct answer.

9. ☑ **C**. NBTSTAT. NBTSTAT is used to troubleshoot connectivity between two computers trying to communicate via NetBT. It displays the protocol statistics and the current connections to each remote host. You can also display the information about a remote host and the names stored in its local name cache.
☒ **A**, **B**, and **D** are incorrect. NetBT stands for NetBIOS over TCP/IP; NetBEUI is a nonroutable protocol; and NetBIOS is a software and naming convention.

10. ☑ **B**. –c. Every connection made via NetBIOS keeps the name in cache for a short period of time. You can display the local cache by using the NBTSTAT –c option. By using this option, each machine that remains in cache will be displayed. This listing will also include the type of connection, TCP/IP address of the remote connection, and the length of time the connection will be kept.
☒ **A**, **C**, and **D** are incorrect. –R will reload the LMHOSTS file. The –a parameter is used to list a name table of a remote PC by specifying the name of the remote PC, while –A does the same, but you must specify the remote PC by IP address.

11. ☑ **D. Both A and C.** Services can register in two ways, via broadcast or with a WINS service. You can display the statistics of how many times you have registered, and with what method. You can also display information on how remote NetBIOS names are being resolved. This can help you to determine if you are using a WINS service correctly, or are broadcasting for services.

 ☒ **B** is incorrect. The HOSTS file is used for local name to IP address resolution for the network.

Tracert

12. ☑ **D. Tracert.** Tracert is a command-line utility that was designed to perform a very basic task: to determine the path taken by a data packet to reach its destination. This can be very helpful in determining at what point a network connection is no longer active. It can also be helpful in troubleshooting issues around network response times.

 ☒ **A, B,** and **C** are incorrect. NBTSTAT is used to verify services on a remote PC. ARP is a cache to track IP address to MAC address resolution. FTP is used to transfer files between two PCs.

Netstat

13. ☑ **C. Netstat.** Netstat displays protocol statistics and current TCP/IP network connections. TCP/IP can be a complicated protocol to understand, and therefore be very difficult to troubleshoot. This utility can be used to display in-depth detail about protocol status, statistics for the different network interfaces, and the current routing tables.

 ☒ **A** and **B** are incorrect. NBTSTAT is used to verify services on a remote PC. ARP is a cache to track IP address to MAC address resolution.

IPCONFIG/WINIPCFG

14. ☑ **D. None of the above.** All of the options listed can be displayed in IPCONFIG by using the /ALL option. The following table is a list of the available settings you can view with the IPCONFIG /ALL.

Host Name	NetBIOS Scope ID	WINS proxy enabled
Node Type	NetBIOS resolution uses DNS	Description
Physical Address	IP Routing Enabled	DHCP Enabled
IP Address	Subnet Mask	DNS Servers
Default Gateway	Lease Obtained	Lease Expires

 ☒ **A, B,** and **C** are incorrect because all are available for display in IPCONFIG.

15. ☑ C. /Obtain. There is no /Obtain for the command WINIPCFG.

    ☒ A, B, and D are incorrect because they are all valid options for the command WINIPCFG.

FTP

16. ☑ A. FTP. FTP (File Transfer Protocol) is designed primarily for transferring data across a network. FTP denotes both a protocol and a utility used for this purpose. It was created to transfer data files quickly and efficiently from one host to another without affecting the remote host's resources. You can also manage remote directories and even access e-mail; however, this program does not enable you to execute remote commands such as the Telnet utility.

    ☒ B, C, and D are incorrect. Ping is used to verify communication between two PCs. D is incorrect because there is a correct answer.

17. ☑ D. A and C. FTP is unusual in that it uses two TCP channels to operate. It uses TCP port 20 as the data transfer channel, and TCP port 21 for commands. The data transfer channel is known as the DTP, or Data Transfer Process, and the command channel is known as the PI, or Protocol Interpreter. The two channels enable you to transfer data and execute commands at the same time, and provide a more efficient and faster data transfer. FTP also works in real time. It does not queue up requests as most other utilities do; it transfers data while you watch.

    ☒ B is incorrect. Port 25 is used by SMTP.

PING

18. ☑ C. Ping. The PING (Packet Internet Groper) command is the most basic TCP/IP troubleshooting tool available. This command is used to test a machine's connectivity to the network, and to verify that it is active. Usually, using this command is the first step to any troubleshooting if a connectivity problem is occurring between two computers. This can quickly help you to determine if a remote host is available and responsive.

    ☒ A and B are incorrect. Route is not a valid command in Windows. ARP is used to cache IP address to MAC address resolutions.

NSLOOKUP

19. ☑ D. NSLOOKUP. The NSLOOKUP utility is used to view and test the DNS database on the DNS server.

    ☒ A, B, and C are incorrect. Route is not a valid command in Windows. ARP is used to cache IP address to MAC address resolutions. Ping is used to verify communications between two PCs.

LAB ANSWER

The following answers correspond numerically to the preceding problems:

1. PC 1 has the wrong default gateway address. If you try to ping the address listed in the WINIPCFG/IPCONFIG utility, you will receive an error. Since the address is incorrect, the PC is unable to send packets to the router to be forwarded to subnet B. It will be able to access subnet A with no problems.

2. If the IPCONFIG/WINIPCFG utility shows all 0s, the TCP/IP protocol is not initialized. This could be due to an incorrect configuration or a duplicate IP address on the network. You should change the IP address using WINIPCFG/IPCONFIG by releasing the address and renewing a new one if DHCP is used. Otherwise, you need to go into the TCP/IP protocol properties and change the static address to a valid address.

3. Everything seems to be OK as far as connectivity is concerned. The most likely problem is that the FTP utility is not being used correctly.

4. PC 5 is configured with only one default gateway, and is sending all information to the router and not the gateway to the Internet. The other gateway needs to be added.

5. If WINIPCFG/IPCONFIG does not work at all, the TCP/IP protocol is not present and needs to be installed.

COMPUTING TECHNOLOGY INDUSTRY ASSOCIATION

6

Remote Connectivity

CERTIFICATION OBJECTIVES

6.01	Remote Connectivity Concepts
6.02	Dial-Up Networking
6.03	Terminal Services
✓	Two-Minute Drill
Q&A	Self Test

Due to the expansion of networks in the world today, user demands are increasing dramatically. They require additional functionality that has not existed before, and the industry is challenged to meet user demands. Many new advancements in the computing industry have come about this way. A very common example is remote connectivity, which came about as the need to interconnect networks and users became more and more prevalent.

As companies expanded and joined an increasingly global market, the need to interconnect offices became crucial to business operations. The Internet is now based on this concept: making information accessible to anyone in the world, from any location. To enable remote installations to communicate with each other and to provide redundancy in case of war, the U.S. government created ARPANET, the first truly remote network. As ARPANET began its transformation into what is now known as the Internet, universities began using it to interconnect and share information and resources. Now, a large portion of the world population uses the Internet for information exchange and research.

Today, companies use networks to interconnect remote sites. They also provide dial-up access to their users to enable them to connect from home or the road. This increased connectivity helps increase productivity and allows use of additional communication channels. Many technologies we take for granted today implement these concepts. For example, telephone systems use complex networks to enable us to call almost anyone in the world. E-mail is used to send messages and files through the Internet to reach anyone who has access to these services. As with any technology that we come to depend on, remote connectivity has become a part of our everyday lives.

Companies also use terminal services to allow them to use older PCs when they have upgraded to a newer version of a network operating system (NOS). Usually when a newer NOS is purchased, a company wants or needs to upgrade all the existing workstations and their OSs to take full advantage of the new NOS's functionality. A special version of an NOS or special licensing allows the NOS server to act as a terminal server and the clients to act as terminal workstations or dumb terminals. Terminal services allow us to recycle older PCs so that they can remain in use and save companies money.

CERTIFICATION OBJECTIVE 6.01

Remote Connectivity Concepts

Many technologies and functions are used for remote connectivity. One of the first networks—the telephone system—is still used today by almost everyone in the world. The telephone system concept was based on the idea of enabling two people in different physical locations to speak with each other. The same basic idea is used today for many different applications. Global networks have been created by corporations and institutions alike to enable remote communication and information sharing.

The basic functionality of remote connectivity is available in many different protocols and devices. For example, companies use network links such as Frame Relay and asynchronous transfer mode (ATM), which encompass many different technologies. More common applications include Point-to-Point Protocol (PPP) dial-up and the Public Switched Telephone Network (PSTN), which are used by the general public.

As technology has progressed, we've added features that allow for a more seamless and improved remote connection. Higher bandwidths and better media have made remote networking an effective tool in today's global market. Additionally, as more and more features are added, the new technologies must provide support or they will not be as effective. For example, the Serial Line Internet Protocol (SLIP) was designed to enable users to connect remotely to a TCP/IP network through a standard phone line. Some networks require additional protocols to function. PPP has replaced SLIP because PPP enables users to pass multiple protocols over a single connection.

Each type of technology has its uses and advantages over others; however, to make use of these advantages, you must first understand how these things work and the functionalities they offer. Let's take a closer look at some of these technologies.

Serial Line Internet Protocol and Point-to-Point Protocol

SLIP and PPP are two communications protocols that are used to connect a computer to a remote network through a serial connection using a device such as a modem. When the computer attaches to the remote network, it is treated as an actual node. This setup enables us to run network applications from home as though we were on the network. The most common use of these protocols is to connect to the Internet.

SLIP and PPP are fairly similar. They use some of the same underlying technologies, but PPP is newer and better suited for today's expanding networks. The following sections discuss each protocol, how it works, and some of its advantages.

SLIP

The Serial Line Internet Protocol, or SLIP, is a communications protocol used for making a TCP/IP connection over a serial interface to a remote network. SLIP was designed for connecting to remote UNIX servers across a standard phone line. This protocol was one of the first of its kind, enabling a remote network connection to be established over a standard phone line.

SLIP was designed when TCP/IP was the only network protocol commonly used by all UNIX platforms. TCP/IP was the protocol used to interconnect UNIX servers with the Internet and on a private network. It made sense to design a dial-up method that would use the same Network layer. Although it is still in use today, SLIP has primarily been replaced by PPP. SLIP services are still available with Windows 95, 98, and ME and Windows NT and 2000.

Windows NT and 2000 servers can use SLIP to connect to other servers, but Windows NT and 2000 do not support clients to connect to their Remote Access Services (RAS) using SLIP.

Using SLIP to Connect to a Remote Host   To set up SLIP, you must first set up a dial-up networking connection. Once a profile is set up, you can configure the dial-up protocol to use from within the properties of the connection. Figure 6-1 shows an example of the properties available for configuring a SLIP connection.

You might notice that many of the fields in the figure are grayed out. This is because SLIP provides no support for advanced features such as software compression, password encryption, or multiple network protocols. Click the TCP/IP Settings button to configure parameters such as the IP address, DNS server addresses, default gateway, and IP header compression.

SLIP is a very simple serial-based protocol. It does not provide the complexity that others, such as PPP, do. Although this can be an advantage, it unfortunately does not include the feature set of other protocols. For example, it does not support option negotiation or error detection during the session setup. It cannot be assigned a DHCP address. It also cannot negotiate the authentication method. Issues such as

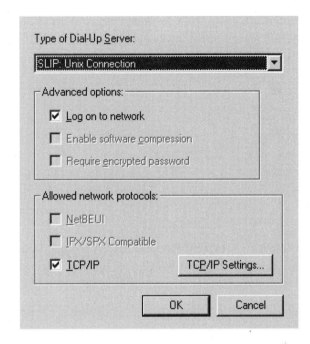

FIGURE 6-1

Configure the
Dial-Up protocol
for your SLIP
connection

these have helped define the new protocols that are emerging, because the functionality
does not exist in SLIP.

SLIP is an older technology that is, in effect, no longer in use. Many Internet
service providers (ISPs) still provide support for SLIP, but SLIP is quickly being
replaced by protocols with much more functionality, such as PPP or PPTP.

PPP

Point-to-Point Protocol, or PPP, is a Data Link layer protocol used to encapsulate
higher Network layer protocols to pass over synchronous and asynchronous
communication lines. PPP was originally designed as an encapsulation protocol
for transporting multiple Network layer traffic over point-to-point links. PPP also
established other standards, including asynchronous and bit-oriented synchronous
encapsulation, network protocol multiplexing, session negotiation, and data-compression
negotiation. PPP also supports protocols other than TCP/IP, such as IPX/SPX and
DECnet.

For PPP to transmit data over a serial point-to-point link, it uses three components. Each component has its own separate function but requires the use of the other two to complete its tasks. The following list explains the three components and their purposes:

- PPP uses the High-Level Data-Link Control (HDLC) protocol as the basis to encapsulate its data during transmission.

- PPP uses Link Control Protocol (LCP) to establish, test, and configure the data link connection.

- Various Network Control Protocols (NCPs) are used to configure the different communications protocols. This system enables you to use different protocols, such as TCP/IP and IPX, over the same line simultaneously.

Network Control Protocols   Although multiple NCPs are available, Microsoft products use three main protocols for PPP. Each NCP is specific to a particular Network layer protocol such as IP or IPX/SPX:

- The Internet Protocol Control Protocol (IPCP) is used to configure, enable, and disable the IP protocol modules at each end of the link.

- The Internet Packet eXchange Control Protocol (IPXCP) is used to enable, configure, and disable IPX protocol modules at each end of the link. Multiple versions of this NCP are available; however, IPXCP is the most common and is overtaking the other IPX NCPs in popularity.

- The NetBIOS Frames Control Protocol (NBFCP) is used to enable, configure, and disable NetBEUI protocol modules at each end of the link. This NCP is a Microsoft-proposed protocol and is in draft status with the Internet Engineering Task Force (IETF).

How PPP Works   PPP uses these three components together to enable it to communicate. It starts by sending LCP frames to test and configure the data link. This action establishes the link and negotiates any additional options required to facilitate the connection. Next, the authentication protocols are negotiated. Multiple types of authentication protocols are available; however, the most common are Challenge Handshaking Authentication Protocol (CHAP) and Password Authentication Protocol (PAP). They determine the type of validation performed for security. The client then sends NCP frames to configure and set up the Network layer protocols to be used during this session. When this step is complete, each network protocol can pass data through this connection. HDLC is used to encapsulate the data stream as it passes through the PPP connection. The link remains active until an LCP or NCP frame closes the link or until an error or external event, such as a user disconnecting the link, occurs.

A control mechanism is included in PPP to enable each protocol to communicate with each other. Finite-State Automation (FSA) processes status messages between each layer to coordinate communications. FSA does not actually participate in data flows; it works with the other protocols to keep them in sync and enable them to concentrate on their own jobs.

PPP Framing   *PPP framing* defines the format in which data is encapsulated before it crosses the network. PPP offers a standard framing solution to enable connections to any standard PPP server because all these vendors use the same format. PPP uses HDLC as the basis for its encapsulation framing for serial connections. HDLC is widely used in other implementations and has been slightly modified for use with PPP. The modifications were made to facilitate multiplexing NCP layers.

PPP Devices   PPP is capable of operating across any data terminal equipment/ data circuit terminating equipment (DTE/DCE) device. Many examples of these devices are available, including the most common, the EIA/TIA 232 standard, better known as a modem. PPP is able to use any DTE/DCE devices as long as they support duplex circuits. These can be dedicated or switched and can operate in an asynchronous or synchronous bit-serial mode. In addition, the limit on transmission rates is specified by the interfaces and is not controlled by PPP.

You need to remember that the DTE is the terminal or PC used to communicate with other systems, and the DCE is the modem that actually does the communicating.

Authentication Protocols   With PPP, each system could be required to authenticate itself. This can be done using an authentication protocol. The most common authentication protocols are PAP, CHAP, and the Microsoft adaptation of CHAP, MS-CHAP. When a connection is being established, either end node can require the other to authenticate itself, whether it is the remote host or the originator of the call. The LCP can be used to send information to the other node to specify the authentication type. Using the authentication protocols, you enable the capability to offer a level of security by requiring authentication to make a remote connection; you also have control over the level of security used.

PAP works very similarly to a regular network login. The client authenticates itself to a server by passing the username and password to it. The server then compares this information to its password store. Because the password is passed in clear text, this system would not work well in an environment in which security concerns are an issue. The system opens the door for anyone "listening" to the line, such as with a network sniffer, and to brute-force password-cracking attacks.

Alternatively, CHAP uses an encryption algorithm to pass the authentication data to protect it from hackers. The server sends the client a randomly generated challenge request with its hostname. The client then uses the hostname to look up the appropriate secret password and returns a response using a one-way hash with the client's hostname. The host now compares the result and acknowledges the client if it matches. CHAP also sends challenges at regular intervals to verify that the correct client is still using this connection. The challenge values change during each interval. Because CHAP is so much more secure than PAP, it is used widely on the Internet. PAP is usually used only in public FTP sites or other public areas.

MS-CHAP is a Microsoft adaptation of CHAP. It uses the same type of encryption methodology but is slightly more secure. The server sends a challenge to the originating host, which must return the username and an MD-4 hash of the challenge string, the session ID, and the MD-4 hashed password. This system enables the authenticator to store the passwords in an encrypted format instead of plain text. MS-CHAP also provides expanded functionality, such as more error codes and additional services.

EXERCISE 6-1

Creating a PPP Dial-Up Connection in Windows 9x

For this exercise, make sure that you have the Windows 9x CD in your CD-ROM drive, since the PC might require access to the source files to install Dial-Up Networking. Do the following:

1. To install Dial-Up Networking for Windows 9x, select **Start | Settings | Control Panel**. The Control Panel folder opens.

2. Double-click **Add/Remove Programs**. The Add/Remove Programs Properties dialog box appears.

3. Click the **Windows Setup** tab to bring it to the front. Highlight **Communications** in the Components box, and click the **Details** button. The Communications dialog box appears.

4. Place a check mark in the **Dial-Up Networking** check box in the Components box, and then click the **OK** button. Click **OK** to back out of the remaining dialog boxes and close the Control Panel. (If the Dial-Up Networking option is already selected, click the **Cancel** button, close the other dialog boxes, and go to Step 5.)

5. Select **Start | Programs | Accessories | Dial-Up Networking**. The Dial-Up Networking folder opens.

6. Double-click the **Make New Connection** icon. The Make New Connection dialog box appears. (If you do not have a modem installed, you will have to set one up prior to continuing.)

7. The Connection Wizard takes you through choosing the appropriate modem (if necessary) and entering the remote phone number to be used. When the process is complete, an icon for the new PPP connection appears in the Dial-Up Networking window.

8. To connect with the new PPP connection, double-click the **connection** icon in the Dial-Up Networking folder and click the **Connect** button.

Troubleshooting PPP   When you use PPP to connect to a remote network, you could encounter problems. These problems can range from no dial tone to a modem misconfiguration or connectivity problems with the remote PPP server. A log is included with PPP to enable you to monitor the steps in opening a PPP connection and to troubleshoot where the breakdown might have occurred. Exercise 6-2 shows how to set up a dial-up networking connection to enable the PPP log file.

EXERCISE 6-2

Enabling the Log File for a PPP Dial-Up Networking Connection for Windows 9x

1. Select **Start | Settings | Control Panel**. The Control Panel folder opens.

2. Double-click the **Network** icon. The Network dialog box appears.

3. On the Configuration page, highlight **Dial-Up Adapter**, and click **Properties**. The Dial-Up Adapter dialog box appears.

4. Click the **Advanced** tab to bring it to the front.

5. In the Properties box, select **Record a log file**; in the Value box, select **Yes**, and then click **OK**.

6. Click **OK** in the Network dialog box. You are prompted to reboot. Click **Yes**. Your system reboots.

When logging has been enabled, you can see the log file after the next attempt to connect to a PPP server. The log file, PPPLOG.TXT, is stored in the Windows directory by default. It can be viewed by any standard text editor and is appended to each time a new connection is attempted.

Figure 6-2 shows the beginning of a PPP connection to a remote network. It demonstrates the layout of the log file and how detailed it can become. Understanding how to read these log files enables you to troubleshoot almost any PPP problem that could occur.

Advantages of PPP Over SLIP

PPP offers several advantages over SLIP. First, PPP offers multinetwork protocol support. SLIP can be used only with TCP/IP. PPP can use myriad protocols, such as TCP/IP, IPX, AppleTalk, and DECnet, through one session. You do not have to use TCP/IP with PPP. Any of these protocols can be used. This enables you to connect to multiple types of systems on the remote network. The addition of NCPs allows for this functionality in PPP.

In addition, PPP offers the capability to negotiate IP addresses during the session setup. In other words, you can specify that PPP use DHCP and you won't have to

```
05-18-1998 20:10:30.83 - Remote access driver log opened.
05-18-1998 20:10:30.83 - Installable CP VxD SPAP     is loaded
05-18-1998 20:10:30.83 - Server type is  PPP (Point to Point
Protocol).
05-18-1998 20:10:30.83 - FSA : Adding Control Protocol 80fd (CCP) to
control protocol chain.
05-18-1998 20:10:30.83 - FSA : Protocol not bound - skipping control
protocol 803f (NBFCP).
05-18-1998 20:10:30.83 - FSA : Adding Control Protocol 8021 (IPCP) to
control protocol chain.
05-18-1998 20:10:30.83 - FSA : Protocol not bound - skipping control
protocol 802b (IPXCP).
05-18-1998 20:10:30.83 - FSA : Adding Control Protocol c029
(CallbackCP) to control protocol chain.
05-18-1998 20:10:30.83 - FSA : Adding Control Protocol c027 (no
description) to control protocol chain.
05-18-1998 20:10:30.83 - FSA : Adding Control Protocol c023 (PAP) to
control protocol chain.
```

manually set up an IP address during each connection. The addition of LCP made
options such as this available to PPP. PPP also handles higher-speed links better than
SLIP does. This easier use is due to the error-checking capability within the protocol.
SLIP does not check datagrams for errors as they pass through the connection.

Now let's examine a few possible protocol scenarios and their solutions.

SCENARIO & SOLUTION

I want to use serial-based dial-up access with TCP/IP and IPX.	You should use PPP, because SLIP does not support anything except TCP/IP.
I only need TCP/IP; should I use SLIP instead of PPP?	Most ISPs do not provide support for SLIP. PPP has replaced SLIP in most cases, with the exception of UNIX servers.
Can PPP be used for server data replication services?	Yes; however, if you plan to have much data, PPP through serial connection speeds can reach only 56Kbps. You should consider a faster solution, such as ISDN.
I need to have 50 users connect to the internal network from their laptops.	PPP can facilitate that, but a modem bank to support it could be costly. You might consider PPTP if the internal network is connected to the Internet or other public TCP/IP network.

Point-to-Point Tunneling Protocol

Point-to-Point Tunneling Protocol (PPTP) is a network protocol that provides for the secure transfer of data from a remote client to a private server by creating a multiprotocol virtual private network, or VPN. PPTP is used in TCP/IP networks as an alternative to conventional dial-up networking methods. This system enables multiprotocol secure communications over a public TCP/IP network such as the Internet. PPTP takes advantage of an additional level of security that is not currently available in other standard implementations.

PPTP is actually an extension of PPP. It encapsulates PPP packets into IP datagrams for transmission across a network. This system enables the functionality of PPP while taking advantage of the security features offered by the VPN technology. Using both options tied into one protocol, you get the best of both worlds.

A Brief History of PPTP

PPTP became recognized by the IETF (a standards committee) in June 1996. Many tunneling protocols have been created and implemented; however, this was the first standard tunneling protocol to become available. Many vendors have adopted it in an attempt to provide a secure method to connect across the public Internet into a corporate internal network.

How PPTP Works

VPNs are used to provide tunneling through a public network with a secure communications channel. Users can employ PPTP to dial into a public network, such as PSTN, to use the Internet to connect to their corporate offices. This system enables users to use the network infrastructure that is already in place; it negates the need for dedicated modem banks for users.

PPTP tunneling can be defined as routing packets through an intermediate public network to reach a private network. Only the PPTP-enabled client can access the remote network; other clients on the same segment cannot. The interesting thing about this process is that you can dial into a standard PPP server and use it to establish a PPTP connection to the remote network. No additional setup or options are required of your ISP; most offer PPP access already. You could also set up a PPTP server to dial into; this setup would enable you to only require PPP to be set up on the clients.

Once the PPTP server receives the packet from the client connection, it routes the data to the appropriate resource. This occurs by stripping off the PPTP and PPP overhead to obtain the addressing information originally applied to it. The PPTP server must be configured with TCP/IP to communicate with PPTP and whatever other protocols are being passed through this VPN tunnel.

A VPN works by encapsulating the data within IP packets to transport it through PPP. This enables the data to pass through the Internet and use the standards already in place. No configuration changes are required to your existing network stacks; they can be used as-is over the PPTP connection. Other protocols, such as NetBEUI and IPX, can also pass through this secure connection.

VPNs are virtual devices set up as though they were regular devices such as modems. In addition, PPTP must be set up on the client and the server. Host computers in the route between these two computers do not need to be PPTP aware. They need only provide an IP route to the remote server. Figure 6-3 shows the PPTP connection sequence.

PPTP mainly involves three processes to set up a secure communications channel. Each process must be completed prior to beginning the next process.

FIGURE 6-3   PPTP connection methodology

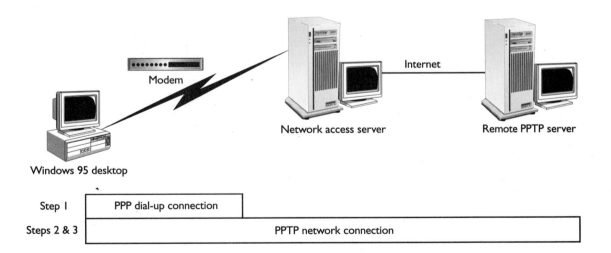

The following list identifies the processes involved:

- **PPP connection and communication**   PPTP uses PPP to connect to a remote network. When connected, PPP is also used to encrypt the data packets being passed between the remote host and the local machine.

- **PPTP control connection**   When the PPP session is established, PPTP creates a control connection between the client and the remote PPTP server. This process is referred to as *tunneling*.

- **PPTP data tunneling**   PPTP creates the IP datagrams for PPP to send. PPP encrypts the packets, which are sent through the tunnel to the PPTP server. The PPTP server is then used to decrypt the PPP-encrypted packets, disassemble the IP datagram, and route to the appropriate host.

exam
Ⓦatch   *Be sure that you know the three processes involved with PPTP and how PPP applies to each one.*

PPTP relies heavily on PPP to perform its job. PPP is used to enable multiple Network layer protocols to be used within the connection. PPP is also used to perform other functions such as establishing and maintaining a connection, authenticating users, and encrypting data packets.

Setting Up PPTP

There are three main components to setting up a PPTP connection:

- PPTP client
- PPTP server
- Network access server (NAS)

The components are equally important and must be configured properly to enable a user to access resources on a remote network.

Each component has its specified functions and requirements. Today, Windows 95/98/ME and Windows NT/2000 can be used as PPTP clients. Windows NT/2000 Server also supports PPTP server services through Remote Access Service (RAS). Exercise 6-3 explains how to set up Windows NT as a PPTP client. The exercise demonstrates using Windows NT as a PPTP client dialing into an ISP to access a remote PPTP server.

Setting Up Windows NT as a PPTP Client

1. Verify that the following are installed and configured:

   ■ TCP/IP

   ■ RAS with Dial-Up Networking

   ■ Analog modem or ISDN connection

   ■ ISP-based PPP account

2. Select **Start | Settings | Control** Panel, and then double-click the **Network** icon.

3. Click the **Protocols** tab to bring it to the front, and then click **Add**.

4. Select **Point to Point Tunneling Protocol** from the Network Protocol box, as shown in Figure 6-4, and then click **OK**.

5. Type the drive and path to the Windows NT source files. The appropriate files will then be copied to the local hard drive.

FIGURE 6-4

Choosing PPTP
during the set-up
process

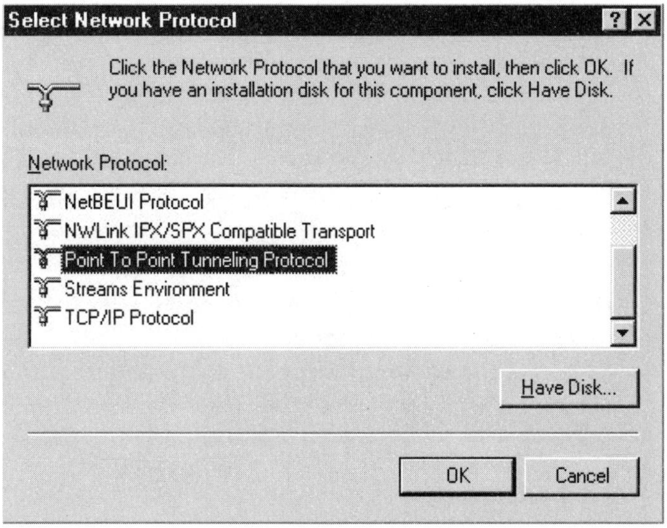

Select Network Protocol

Click the Network Protocol that you want to install, then click OK. If you have an installation disk for this component, click Have Disk.

Network Protocol:

- NetBEUI Protocol
- NWLink IPX/SPX Compatible Transport
- Point To Point Tunneling Protocol
- Streams Environment
- TCP/IP Protocol

Have Disk...

OK   Cancel

FIGURE 6-5

Setting up RAS to
use PPTP through
a configured VPN

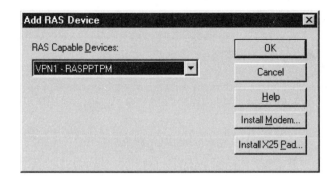

6. The Setup Wizard asks you to define the number of VPNs to use. For the
   client, typically this should be the default setting of 1. By default, Windows
   NT Server supports 256 VPNs. Choose **1** and click **OK**.

7. You must configure a VPN device for RAS in the Add RAS Device dialog
   box, as shown in Figure 6-5. By default, the RAS-capable device is shown.
   Click **OK** to accept this device.

8. To configure VPN settings, use the Remote Access Setup applet. Click the
   Network button to assign protocols. Click the **Configure** button to set up
   dial-in and dial-up settings.

9. When finished, close all applets and applications and reboot the computer.

Due to the popularity of PPP and the Internet, a more secure dial-in solution was
needed. PPTP grants you the capability to have a user log in to a remote, private,
corporate network via any ISP and maintain a secure, encrypted connection. This
concept is being implemented by more and more companies every year; its popularity
has exploded since its first draft was proposed in 1996.

on the
()ob

Most larger companies now have employees traveling for training, seminars,
and conventions and require a means for these traveling employees to be able
to access the company network. Remote access is becoming widely used,
whether via direct connections with modems or a virtual connection through
the Internet.

Integrated Services Digital Network and the Public Switched Telephone Network

In the past, the phone network consisted of an interconnection of wires that directly connected telephone users via an analog-based system. This system was very inefficient because it did not work well for long-distance connections and was very prone to "noise." In the 1960s, the telephone company began converting this system to a packet-based, digital switching network. Today, nearly all voice switching in the United States is digital; however, the customer connection to the switching office is primarily still analog.

ISDN

Integrated Services Digital Network (ISDN) is a system of digital telephone connections that enables data to be transmitted simultaneously end to end. This technology has been available for more than a decade and is designed to enable faster, clearer communications for small offices and home users. It came about as the standard telephone system began its migration from an analog format to digital. ISDN is the format portions of the digital telephone system now use to replace analog systems.

A History of ISDN   In the 1950s, the phone companies began looking at ways to improve communications. They began by sampling the analog signals that were passed during a phone conversation and attempted to convert them to digital signals. From this analog sampling, they determined that 64Kbps would enable a digital signal to properly handle voice communications through the telephone network. This concept became the foundation of ISDN.

Because a standard did not exist among the phone companies, the Consultative Committee for International Telephony and Telegraph (CCITT) began working on the Integrated Digital Network (IDN) in the late 1960s. IDN combined the functions of switching and transmission into one piece of hardware that could be set as the standard for all telephone companies to use. This initiative not only moved telephony services toward a standard, it also made the network much more efficient. It wasn't perfect, but was a step in the right direction.

The concept of ISDN was introduced in 1972. The concept was based on moving the analog/digital conversion equipment onto the customer premises to enable voice and data services to be sent through a single line. Telephone companies also began using a new kind of digital communications link between each central office. A T1 link could carry 24 of these 64Kbps voice channels, and it used the same amount of copper wire as only two analog voice calls. Throughout the 1970s the telephone companies continued to upgrade their switching offices. They began rolling out T1 links directly to customers to provide high-speed access. The need for an efficient solution was greater than ever.

When ISDN was recognized by the International Telecommunications Union (ITU), an initiative was begun to define its standards. The initial recommendations, published in CCITT Recommendation I.120 (1984), described some initial guidelines for implementing ISDN. In the early 1990s, an effort was begun to establish a standard implementation for ISDN in the United States. The National ISDN 1 (NI-1) standard was defined by the industry so that users would not have to know the type of switch they are connected to in order to buy equipment and software compatible with it.

Because some major office switches were incompatible with this standard, some major telephone companies had trouble switching to the NI-1 standard. This caused a number of problems in trying to communicate between these nonstandard systems and everyone else. Eventually, all the systems were brought up to standard. A set of core services was defined in all Basic Rate Interfaces (BRIs) of the NI-1 standard. The services include data call services, voice call services, call forwarding, and call waiting. Most devices today conform to the NI-1 standard.

A more comprehensive standardization initiative, National ISDN 2 (NI-2), was recently adopted. Now, several major manufacturers of networking equipment have become involved to help set the standard and make ISDN a more economical solution. The NI-2 standard had two goals: to standardize Primary Rate Interface (PRI), as NI-1 did for BRI, and to simplify the identification process. Until this point, PRIs were mainly vendor-dependent, which made it difficult to interconnect these. Furthermore, a standard was created for NI-2 for identifiers.

ISDN Channels   An ISDN transmission circuit consists of a logical grouping of data channels. With ISDN, voice and data are carried by these channels. Two types of channels, a B channel and a D channel, are used for a single ISDN connection. Each channel has a specific function and bandwidth associated with it. The *bearer channels*, or *B channels*, transfer data. They offer a bandwidth of 64Kbps per channel. In ISDN terminology, a *kilobyte* is equal to 1000 bytes. Many other computer-related functions using this term refer to 1024 bytes instead. Therefore, ISDN B channels operate at 64,000 bytes. A hardware limitation in some switches limits the B channels to 56Kbps, or 56,000 bytes.

The *data channel*, or *D channel*, handles signaling at 16Kbps or 64Kbps. This includes the session setup and teardown using a communications language known as DSS1. The purpose of the D channel is to enable the B channels to strictly pass data. You remove the administrative overhead from B channels using the D channel. The bandwidth available for the D channel depends on the type of service; BRIs usually require 16Kbps and PRIs use 64Kbps. Typically, ISDN service contains two B channels and a single D channel.

H channels are used to specify a number of B channels. The following list shows the implementations:

- **H0**   384Kbps (6 B channels)
- **H10**   1472Kbps (23 B channels)
- **H11**   1536Kbps (24 B channels)
- **H12**   1920Kbps (30 B channels, the European standard)

ISDN Interfaces   Although B channels and D channels can be combined in any number of ways, the phone companies created two standard configurations. There are two basic types of ISDN service: BRI and PRI. BRI consists of two 64Kbps B channels and one 16Kbps D channel, for a total of 144Kbps. Only 128Kbps is used for user data transfers. BRIs were designed to enable customers to use their existing wiring. This provided a low-cost solution for customers, so it is the most basic type of service intended for small business or home use.

PRI is intended for users with greater bandwidth requirements. It requires T1 carriers to facilitate communications. Normally, the channel structure contains 23 B channels plus one 64Kbps D channel, for a total of 1536Kbps. This standard is used only in North America and Japan. European countries support a different kind of ISDN standard for PRI. It consists of 30 B channels and one 64Kbps D channel, for a total of 1984Kbps. A technology known as Non-Facility Associated Signaling (NFAS) is available to enable support of multiple PRI lines with one 64Kbps D channel.

To use BRI services, you must subscribe to ISDN services through a local telephone company or provider. By default, you must be within 18,000 feet (about 3.4 miles) of the telephone company central office in order to use BRI services. Repeater devices are available for ISDN service to extend this distance, but these devices can be very expensive. Special types of equipment are required to communicate with the ISDN provider switch and with other ISDN devices. You must have an ISDN terminal adapter and an ISDN router.

ISDN Devices The phrase *ISDN standard* refers to the devices that are required to connect the end node to the network. Although some vendors provide devices that include several functions, a separate device defines each function within the standard. The protocols that each device uses are also defined and are associated with a specific letter. Also known as reference points, these letters are *R, S, T,* and *U.* ISDN standards also define the device types. They are NT1, NT2, TE1, TE2, and TA. The architecture for these devices and the reference points are shown in Figure 6-6 and are explained in the following section.

exam
ⓦatch *Be sure to know the device types and where each type is used. In addition, know the number of channels and speeds associated with a BRI and a PRI.*

ISDN Reference Points Reference points are used to define logical interfaces. They are, in effect, a type of protocol used in communications. The following list contains the reference points:

- ■ R Defines the reference point between a TE2 device and a TA device.
- ■ S Defines the reference point between TE1 devices and NT1 or NT2 devices.
- ■ T Defines the reference point between NT1 and NT2 devices.
- ■ U Defines the reference point between NT1 devices and line termination equipment. This is usually the central switch.

FIGURE 6-6

ISDN device
architecture

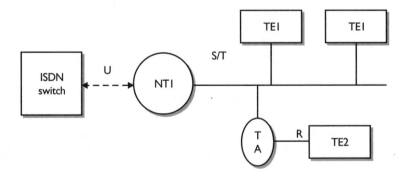

Network terminator 1 (NT1) is the device that communicates directly with the central office switch. The NT1 receives a U-interface connection from the telephone company and puts out a T-interface connection for the NT2. NT1 handles the physical layer portions of the connection, such as physical and electrical termination, line monitoring, and multiplexing.

Network terminator 2 (NT2) is placed between an NT1 device and any adapters or terminal equipment. Many devices provide the NT1 and NT2 device in the same physical hardware. Larger installations generally separate these devices. An example of an NT2 device is a digital private branch exchange (PBX) or ISDN network router. An NT2 device provides an S interface and accepts a T interface from an NT1. NT2 usually handles Data Link and Network layer functions, such as contention monitoring and routing, in networks with multiple devices.

Terminal equipment 1 (TE1) is a local device that speaks via an S interface. It can be directly connected to the NT1 or NT2 devices. An ISDN telephone or ISDN fax are good examples of TE1 devices.

Terminal equipment 2 (TE2) devices are common, everyday devices that can be used for ISDN connectivity. Any telecommunications device that is not in the TE1 category is classified as a TE2 device. A terminal adapter is used to connect these devices to an ISDN and attaches through an R interface. Examples of TE2 devices include standard fax machines, PCs, and regular telephones.

A *terminal adapter (TA)* connects TE2 devices to an ISDN network. A TA connects through the R interface to the TE2 device and through the S interface to the ISDN. The peripheral required for personal computers often includes an NT1 device. These are better known as ISDN modems.

on the job *ISDN modems are used in PCs to connect them to an ISDN. The term modem is used incorrectly here. ISDN passes data in a digital format. Conventional modems convert analog to digital and vice versa.*

Identifiers   Standard telephone lines use a 10-digit identifier, better known as a telephone number, that is permanently assigned. ISDN uses similar types of identifiers; however, they are not as easily used as a telephone number. ISDN uses five separate identifiers to make a connection. When the connection is first set up, the provider assigns two of these: the service profile identifier (SPID) and the directory number (DN). These are the most common numbers used because the other three are dynamically set up each time a connection is made. The three dynamic identifiers are the terminal endpoint identifier (TEI), the service address point identifier (SAPI), and the bearer code (BC).

The *directory number (DN)* is the 10-digit phone number the telephone company assigns to any analog line. ISDN services enable a greater deal of flexibility in using this number than analog services do. Unlike an analog line, where a one-to-one relationship exists, the DN is only a logical mapping. A single DN can be used for multiple channels or devices. Also, up to eight DNs can be assigned to one device. Because a single BRI can have up to eight devices, it can support up to 64 directory numbers. This is how offices are able to have multiple numbers assigned to them. Most standard BRI installations include only two directory numbers, one for each B channel.

The *service profile identifier (SPID)* is the most important number needed when you are using ISDN. The provider statically assigns the SPID when the ISDN service is set up. It usually includes the DN plus a few extra digits. The SPID usually contains between 10 and 14 characters and varies from region to region. SPIDs can be assigned for every ISDN device, for the entire line, or for each B channel.

The SPID is unique throughout the entire switch and must be set up correctly. If it is incorrect, it is like dialing the wrong phone number—you will not be able to contact the person you were trying to reach. When an ISDN device is connected to the network, it sends the SPID to the switch. If the SPID is correct, the switch uses the stored information about your service profile to set up the data link. The ISDN device will not send the SPID again unless the device is disconnected from the network.

A *terminal endpoint identifier (TEI)* identifies the particular ISDN device to the switch. This identifier changes each time a device is connected to the ISDN. Unlike the SPID or the DN, the TEI is dynamically allocated by the central switch.

The *service address point identifier (SAPI)* identifies the particular interface on the switch to which your devices are connected. This identifier is used by the switch and is also dynamically updated each time a device connects to the network.

The *bearer code (BC)* is an identifier made up of the combination of TEI and SAPI. It is used as the call reference and is dynamic, like the two identifiers included within it. It changes each time a connection is established.

exam
ⓦatch   *Before the exam, make sure that you understand the ISDN identifiers.*

Advantages of ISDN   ISDN offers several major advantages over conventional analog methods. First, it has a speed advantage over normal dial-up lines. Normal dial-up lines use a modem to convert the digital signals from a PC into analog. This enables data to be transferred over public phone lines. This technology does, however, have speed limitations. The fastest standard modem connection that is currently available is 56Kbps. Because this is an analog connection, many modems cannot reach this speed, since they are limited by the quality of the connection. This fact accounts for your connecting at different speeds each time you dial in to a remote network. Because phone lines cannot actually transmit at 56Kbps, a special kind of compression is used to enable these speeds. Two standards currently exist. For ISPs to appease everyone, they must support both standards, which quickly gets expensive.

ISDN enables you to use multiple digital channels at the same time to pass data through regular phone lines. The difference is that the connection made from your computer is completely digital instead of converting to analog. You can also use other protocols that enable you to bind channels together to get a higher bandwidth rate. In addition, ISDN makes a connection in half the time of an analog line.

In addition to speed, ISDN supports multiple devices set up in one link. In an analog system, a single line is required for each device that is attached. For example, a separate phone line is needed for a normal phone, a fax machine, or a computer modem. Since ISDN supports multiple devices, you can use each one of these items on a single line. The connection will also be clearer due to the fact that the data is being passed in digital format.

Because ISDN uses a separate channel—the D channel for signaling—it removes the administrative overhead. This means that the data is not hindered by the session setups and the communications required by the devices. The D channel keeps all this information off the datastreams. Due to this separation, the setup and takedown of each session is much faster. In addition, ISDN equipment is able to handle calls more intelligently.

PSTN

Almost everyone in the world has used a telephone at least once. Today, you can call anywhere in the world and get a direct connection almost instantly using this technology. The Public Switched Telephone Network (PSTN) was originally designed as an analog switching system for routing voice calls. Because it has existed for several decades and has been used by so many, it has come to be known as *plain old telephone service,* or *POTS.* Because PSTN is considered the first wide area network, it was the basis for many of the WAN technologies that exist today and has been instrumental in their evolution.

A History of PSTN   During the initial years of PSTN, digital technologies had not even been considered. The telephone network was based purely on analog signals traveling across copper wire to transport a human voice. The only repetitions of the signal that might have occurred were through one or two repeater devices. The term *via net loss (VNL)* was coined to calculate the signal degradation that occurred. This degradation was measured in *decibels (dB).* The only metering equipment needed to test connections was test tones, decibel meters, or volume unit (VU) meters. VU meters were used to measure complex signals such as the human voice. These meters simply measure the loss or gain of a specific circuit.

Prior to the 1960s, PSTN lines could handle nothing more than what they were originally designed for—voice communication. Since then, many great technology leaps have helped the network progress. The beginning of this era was marked by the advent of the Bell T1 transmission system. As T1s became more frequently used in the telephone network, bandwidth and quality increased. This advent also began the true migration from using human operators to route calls to switching these functions electronically.

In the 1970s and 1980s, the phone companies began to invest more resources in improving the quality of the PSTN backbone. This backbone, also known as the *Digital Access Cross-Connect System (DACCS),* was a combination of all the T1 and T3 lines. Although many problems were associated with DACCS during this time, it provided a technology upgrade to help improve services all the way around. Soon companies started looking at PSTN lines as an alternative to the dedicated point-to-point links they were using.

As the industry started to move in the direction of PSTN lines, manufacturers began to market modems for this purpose. As modems became more commonplace, the manufacturers began mass marketing them for everyday users. Today, using a modem to dial in to a remote computer network is quickly becoming as common as having a telephone in your house. More and more people are getting online, which has played a large part in the popularity of the Internet. Companies use PSTN lines today to enable remote users to dial in to private networks as well as back up data links for computer systems that require remote connectivity.

How PSTN Works   The POTS network originally began with human operators sitting at a switch, manually routing calls. The original concept of the Bell Telephone system was a series of PSTN trunks connecting the major U.S. cities. This was an analog-based system that met its requirements for human voice transmissions at the time. Since the inception of the telephone, the world has changed. PSTN systems still use analog from the end node to the first switch. Once the signal is received, the switch converts the signal to a digital format and then routes the call on. Once the call is received on the other end, the last switch in the loop converts the signal back to analog, and the call is initiated. Because the end node is still analog, modems are used in most homes to facilitate dial-up access. Faster technologies such as ISDN or T1s use a dedicated point-to-point link through a completely digital path. In this way, higher bandwidths are reachable. Currently, analog lines can reach only a maximum speed of 56Kbps. Using digital lines, speeds in excess of 2GB per second can be reached.

exam
ⓦatch

Remember that the maximum available speed with an analog modem is 56Kbps.

The telephone network works very similarly to the TCP transport protocol. It is connection based, and the connection is maintained until the call is terminated. This enables you to hear the other person almost instantaneously. Telephone networks also still use two copper wires run into most homes. The switching media, however, is mainly fiber. This allows for the high-speed switching in the back end but slow response in data communications because they generally attach to the end node.

Modem Types   *Analog modems* are used to connect to a remote network via a PSTN line. Although there are many different types and makes of modems, they can be categorized into three areas: single external, single internal, and multiline rack or shelf mounted.

The *external modem* is the modem most commonly used today. Many ISPs use pools of external modems to enable dial-in access. These modems are also common in server hardware. Many IT workers include modems in production systems to allow for a backup communications link or for remote access.

The *internal modem* conforms to the same type as the external modem. The only real difference is the fact that it is located inside the computer chassis. Most companies no longer use these modems, because externals are easier to replace and troubleshoot. For example, internal modems do not have the light-emitting diodes (LEDs) that external modems do. This translates into a headache if you have to figure out why the modem won't connect to a remote host via the dial-up connection. Some modem manufacturers provide software interfaces; however, these generally are not as full featured as those in external modems. A common use for internal modems is in laptop computers using PC (PCMCIA) Cards. Many laptop vendors still integrate phone jacks into the chassis of their computers. In addition, PC Cards can technically be classified as internal modems. These are used widely and do not include the LEDs or lamps an external modem offers. Quite a few businesses use external modems while home users use internal modems. The cost difference is almost negligible, but home users usually opt for the cheaper of the two.

These types of solutions are becoming increasingly popular. Many vendors offer solutions that involve a single chassis containing a certain number of modem cards that can be connected directly to the network. The modularity and size of these devices are much more efficient than trying to maintain a shelf with a stack of external modems sitting on it. These solutions have also been included in some new networking equipment. Manufacturers place analog modems in their equipment to facilitate redundancy features such as a backup network link.

Now let's take a look at some possible scenarios and their solutions.

SCENARIO & SOLUTION

I need a transmission medium that will allow for moderate speeds but is widely available. What should I use?	PSTN is the regular phone system that is available practically anywhere and provides for speeds under 56K. PSTN was one of the first true networks. It provided the foundation on which the digital age has flourished and exploded. It was a huge contributor to the popularity of public online networks such as the Internet. We use this network for many functions today because it has evolved into a truly global communications network.
I need a transmission medium that I can use from my business that provides for high-speed transmissions with no analog signals.	ISDN is a digital medium that allows for 64K per channel.
If I have an ISDN connection installed to my business, what is required for me to communicate on the ISDN medium?	ISDN modems are required to transmit local data packets onto the ISDN line, receive the data packets from the ISDN connection, and transmit them on the local network.

CERTIFICATION OBJECTIVE 6.02

Dial-Up Networking

Remote connectivity has had a huge impact on the world market. Many businesses everywhere use remote connectivity to interconnect sites to a single network. It is also used to connect users to the public Internet and to private corporate networks. Windows NT/2000 and Windows 95/98/ME include a Dial-Up Networking client. This client supports all the major flavors of dial-up connectivity and network protocols. Although it not installed by default, Dial-Up Networking is included with the operating systems. Exercise 6-4 explains the process of installing Dial-Up Networking on a Windows 95 desktop.

EXERCISE 6-4

Installing Dial-Up Networking

  1. Select **Start I Settings I Control Panel**, and then double-click the **Add/Remove Programs** icon.

  2. Click the **Windows Setup** tab to bring it to the front, select **Communications** from the Components box, and click the **Details** button.

  3. Place a check mark in the **Dial-Up Networking** check box, and then click **OK**. The appropriate files will be installed. If this is the first time Dial-Up Networking has been installed, you will be prompted to fill in the location information. Otherwise, click **Make a New Connection** to start the wizard.

e x a m
 ᗯa t c h

Make sure that you know how to install Dial-Up Networking as well as how to configure it.

Dial-Up Networking provides support for four types of line protocols. Each protocol can be used to connect to a subset of services on remote hosts. The line protocols are as follows:

- **NetWare Connect (NRN)**   Used to connect to NetWare services via IPX/SPX.

- **Remote Access Services (RAS)**   Used to connect to Windows NT/2000 RAS.

- **Serial Line Internet Protocol (SLIP)**   Used to connect to a SLIP server via TCP/IP.

- **Point-to-Point Protocol (PPP)**   Used to connect to a PPP server. Multiple protocols, including TCP/IP, IPX, and NetBEUI, can be used.

To use Dial-Up Networking, you can invoke the process by one of three methods. Each method can be carried out by a user:

- **Explicit**   A user can manually initiate a connection.

- **Implicit**   In some events, if Windows 95/98/ME cannot find a connection, it prompts you to try a dial-up connection.

- **Application invoked**   Some applications try to establish a dial-up connection when connecting to server resources. For example, Microsoft Outlook trying to contact an Exchange server can be set up to dial into the Exchange server.

Modem Configuration Parameters

Modems are data communication devices that are used to pass data through the PSTN from node to node. A modem—a word that combines *modulator* with *demodulator*— is used to convert a digital signal to an analog format to transmit across the network. It reverses the conversion process on the other end node to receive the data. Typically, the EIA/TIA-232 serial standard is used to connect the modem to a computer.

Modem communication can be of various types: asynchronous, synchronous, or both. In *asynchronous communication,* all data is sent separately, relying on the node on the other end to translate the packet order. *Synchronous communication* sends all data in a steady stream and uses a clock signal to interpret the beginning and end of a packet. Most users today employ synchronous communication in the modems that they buy.

FROM THE CLASSROOM

Establishing Foolproof Remote Access

Nearly every computer on a Windows NT or 2000 network also has some sort of remote access capability. Many employees have laptops that are configured to dial in to the network to download e-mail and upload information. Traveling salespeople are notorious for requiring a solid dial-in capability to perform their duties while they are on the road.

Accessing a network through Dial-Up Networking is usually much slower than accessing the network from the "inside," so users tend to complain more about the amount of time it takes to achieve everyday activities such as retrieving e-mail. They do not tolerate their computers failing to dial in correctly. Rest assured, you will be called when a user is having problems dialing in from a remote site.

Many users work from home at night, and if their Dial-Up Networking configuration is not working correctly 100 percent of the time, they cannot finish their work, causing them to miss deadlines and fall behind. This is not a good thing. I was once at a job interview with the owners of a company who were complaining that they just got back from Hawaii and had not been able to dial in to the network for a week. The previous administrator had assured them the system would work correctly. Is it any wonder why they were interviewing new administrators?

To ensure that you have configured the user's laptops correctly, find an analog phone line inside the building and test the Dial-Up Networking connection while the user is standing there. Demonstrate exactly how to access the network via the modem and what to do when he or she is dialed in. This process seems like second nature to you, but to a user it is another new computer task with which they are unfamiliar. After you have showed the user how to dial in once or twice, have the user do it. By testing the dial-up connection from inside the building, you are simulating a remote location. If it doesn't work in this situation, it probably won't work at the user's house. If there are problems, you will see them for yourself first hand during this test.

I have had users bring in their home computers for me to configure for remote access. If you give them a detailed list of instructions for configuring remote access, they will most likely not be successful. Working with them face to face until they get the hang of the process is the best way to ensure success when they're working on their own.

There is nothing more wonderful than a happy user, so you will feel good about getting the job done right. Maybe your users will get promotions for all the hard work they accomplish at night!

—Cameron Brandon, MCSE+Internet, CNE, A+, Network+

Various system parameters must be set up properly to enable a modem to work. These parameters define the system resources for the modem device to use during its operations. Common parameters include serial ports, IRQs, I/O addresses, and baud rates. Let's look at these parameters in more detail.

Serial Port

Serial communications send signals across a point-to-point link. Bits are transmitted one after another in a continuous datastream. Serial ports are the common method for connecting modems to personal computers. They are based on 9-pin (DB-9) and 25-pin (DB-25) connectors commonly known as COM1, COM2, COM3, and COM4. As we touched on earlier in the chapter, the computer side of the connection is known as the *data terminal equipment (DTE)* and the modem is known as the *data circuit-terminating equipment (DCE)*. Various pins are used for different functions inside these connectors. Some are used for transmitting data, others for receiving data, and the remainder for control signals.

You must specify the appropriate serial port when you set up a modem. Most modems attempt to use COM1 by default. Each COM port is assigned a specific set of address variables by default when you set up connections. To change the modem COM port after the setup is complete, select **Start | Settings | Control Panel**, and then double-click the **Modems** icon. Highlight the appropriate modem and click the **Properties** button. Select the appropriate port from the Port box, as shown in Figure 6-7.

Interrupt Requests and I/O Addresses

Interrupt request levels (IRQs) are hardware lines over which devices send interrupt signals to the microprocessor. IRQs are used to provide a communications channel to the computer architecture to request processing power. Every time a device sends a command to the computer, an interrupt interprets the signal. IRQs are an integral part of the modem setup.

Input/output (I/O) addresses are spaces in memory designated for memory's own use. The address spaces are used to exchange information between memory and the rest of the computer. This concept, known as *memory-mapped I/O*, uses hexadecimal notation to define the locations. You might notice that some of these addresses overlap each other. You can have multiple devices set up with different IRQs, such as COM1 and COM3 with the default settings. However, they cannot be used at the same time. The exceptions to this rule are if Plug and Play is enabled and you cannot share I/O addresses for a device at any time.

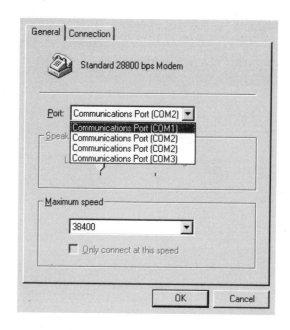

FIGURE 6-7

Using the modem
properties dialog
box, you can
adjust the
COM port

Table 6-1 shows default IRQs and I/O addresses. Figure 6-8 displays an example of IRQ3 and I/O address 2F8 set up in a configuration for COM2.

Maximum Port Speed

The *maximum port speed* is defined by the kilobytes per second that the modem can support. Maximum rates are defined primarily by the modem hardware; however, the current pubic telephone network has an upper limit of 56Kbps through an analog modem. Port speeds are defined by standards and features available to them.

TABLE 6-1   Default IRQs and I/O Addresses

COM Port	IRQ	I/O Address
COM1	04	03F8–03FF
COM2	03	02F8–02FF
COM3	04	03E8–03EF
COM4	03	02E8–02EF

FIGURE 6-8

An example of a modem set up to use COM2

Port Information
Port: COM2
Interrupt: 3
Address: 2F8
UART: NS 16550AN
Highest Speed :

Standard 28800 bps Modem
Identifier: MDMGEN288

OK

on the **job**

Note that the terms baud *and* port speed *are not identical. Port speeds define how fast data is traveling; baud measures the signal change per second. With encoding, 2 bits look like 1; therefore, the two terms will not match.*

Multiple modem standards exist to define the various features and bandwidths available. Various models provide different standards levels. Before you purchase any modem, verify that it fits your current needs and meets the appropriate standard. Table 6-2 illustrates the standards.

To configure the port speed in Windows 95/98/ME or Window NT/2000, select **Start | Settings | Control Panel**, and then double-click the **Modems** icon. Select your modem and click the **Properties** button. Select the appropriate port speed from the Maximum Speed list, as shown in Figure 6-9.

Unimodem

With Windows 95/98/ME, an additional subsystem is available to simplify dial-up networking. *Unimodem* provides an easy, centralized mechanism for installing and configuring modems, as shown in Figure 6-10. In installing the modem, the wizard

| TABLE 6-2 | Modem Standards That Define Speeds or Feature Sets |

Standard	Feature Set
V.22	1200bps, full duplex
V.22bis	2400bps full duplex
V.32	Asynch/sync 4800bps/9600bps
V.32bis	Asynch/sync 14,400bps
V.35	Defines high transfer rates over dedicated circuits
V.42	Defines error-checking standards
V.42bis	Defines modem compression
V.34	28,800bps
V.34+	33,600bps

enables you to specify configurations included with Windows 95/98/ME or to obtain the configuration from disk. Windows 95/98/ME ships with over 600 modem configurations included. The information obtained by this process is then accessible

FIGURE 6-9

Use the modems properties dialog box to set the maximum port speed for a modem

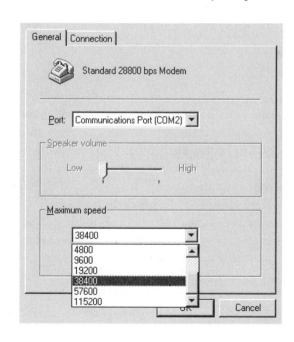

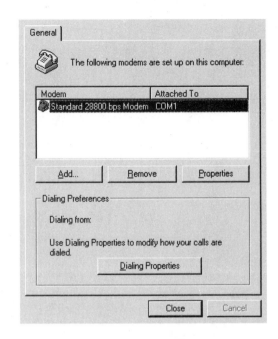

FIGURE 6-10

The unimodem
process enables
one interface for
configuring
modems

to any other applications. Many applications written today to run on Windows
95/98/ME specifically request information from this process if a modem is required.

Telephony API

The Microsoft Telephony API (TAPI) is an application interface used for accessing
communications features such as connection monitoring. This API is used to provide
services such as these without relying on the hardware to set them up. It ties in heavily
to the Unimodem mechanism. TAPI functions completely independently from the
device hardware. It is now used for modem data transfers; the COMM.API is used
for these operations.

When modems were first becoming popular, they could be difficult to configure.
You had to understand the settings to use such as which COM port to set up; the
system resources, such as IRQs and DMA channels; and modem baud rates. Each
application that was to use this device had to be set up separately. This process could
take a great deal of time and become complex quickly when you attempted to use
advanced modem initialization strings. TAPI replaced this requirement by providing

a standard interface with which the modem would communicate so that the interface could be set up once, and all applications could use it.

TAPI also provides other features, such as multiple calling locations. You can set up connection profiles for different dial-up access numbers. You can also customize how the number is dialed. For example, say that you set up two separate connection profiles, one with call waiting enabled and the second without it. This setup enables you to manage multiple connections without having to reconfigure your modem setup every time you need a variation.

To access the TAPI options, select **Start | Control Panel | Modems**. Click the **Dialing Properties** button. Figure 6-11 displays some of the options available for customization.

Requirements for a Remote Connection

Over the course of this chapter, we have addressed several different types of remote connectivity technologies. Each has its strengths and weaknesses as well as its core functions. Some technologies provide features or functionality that you might not need or want. Understanding how each one works and its benefits and disadvantages enables you to recommend solutions to fit business needs. It is now time to pull all

FIGURE 6-11

TAPI enables you to further customize your modem settings

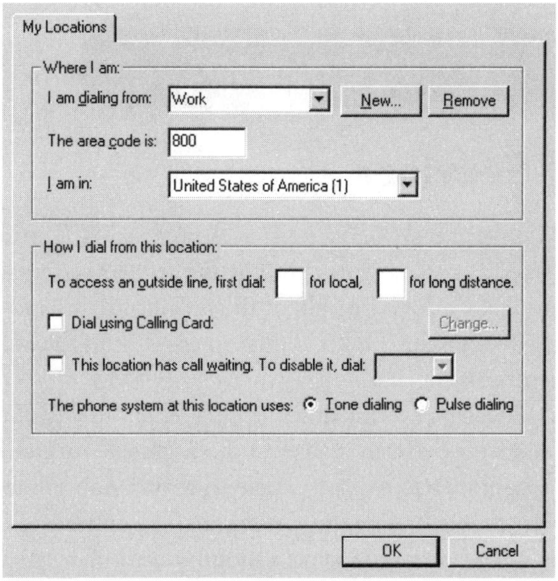

the information together to figure out what is required to make your remote connection work.

To provide access to a remote server or network, you must properly set up and configure several items. Each item depends on other items, and this connection will not work without them all. The following list contains the common components required to connect to remote resources:

- **Dial-Up Networking client** This client must be set up with the appropriate parameters defined.

- **Remote server** You must have a remote server to dial in to reach a remote network.

- **User account (PPP, SLIP, RAS)** You must maintain a valid ID and password on the remote server or network.

- **Modem/ISDN** You must have a hardware device that enables you to communicate with the remote host.

- **Access protocol** A Network layer protocol must be set up and configured properly to access resources on the remote server or network. Examples include TCP/IP, IPX, and NetBEUI.

CERTIFICATION OBJECTIVE 6.03

Terminal Services

With terminal NOSs, such as Windows NT Terminal Server or Windows 2000 Server, a company can employ the server as a terminal server. A *terminal server* is a server that does the bulk of the processing, instead of the workstation performing the processing. This is similar in concept to the older days of mainframes and dumb terminals.

Basically, a terminal server does all processing of data and screen images. The server passes these screen images to the terminal workstation. Terminal workstations are sometimes referred to as *dumb terminals*. A dumb terminal is a system with no internal devices such as disks and processors. The dumb terminal has only a keyboard on which to enter information and a monitor on which typed or processed data is displayed.

The data typed is sent to the terminal server and the screen information is changed, causing the new screen image to be sent to the dumb terminal, which then displays the new screen image on the monitor.

Advantages of Terminal Services

The advantage of using terminal services is they allow newer software applications to run on older PCs that might not have the necessary hardware. For example, we can have a Pentium 90 system running Windows for Workgroups that is acting as a terminal workstation. If the terminal server has a product such as Office XP installed on it, the Windows for Workgroups user will be allowed to use the Office XP programs, since those programs are run on the terminal server, even though the workstation does not have enough horsepower to execute Office XP.

Since we are allowed to use older PCs, we can keep costs down by not having to upgrade PCs to be able to execute the newer applications that will be required for users to perform their jobs. This will also keep down training costs because we won't have to train employees on new OSs when the systems must be replaced.

Terminal services can be employed over a dial-up connection, via a direct connection through a serial port, and via network connections, allowing for many possibilities of use.

Another advantage is that the administrator can view a user's session and actually take control of it to show the user how to perform some action. This is great in a help desk environment when a user is having difficulties. The administrator can actually watch the user's actions and see what he or she is doing incorrectly.

Disadvantages of Terminal Services

One of the disadvantages is that a terminal server must have quite a bit of processing power and RAM to be able to process all user requests and screen images and store the output as well as screen images in memory. The more users who are using terminal services, the more processors, processing speed, and RAM are required—all of which could require that you constantly upgrade the server for better performance.

The other problem with terminal services is that the network bandwidth must be adequate to process all data being passed from the terminal server to all terminal workstations. This might require a 100 Mbps network as well as switches to enhance throughput.

One of the main issues with terminal services is the cost of licensing. Each application, depending on manufacturer, must be licensed differently. These licenses can be costly compared with purchasing licenses and placing an application on individual workstations. Licenses are required for the clients connecting to the server not only from within the company but also outside the company if access is allowed through the Internet. If the terminal server runs out of licenses, it issues a temporary license that will be logged and required to purchase additional licenses to cover the temporary ones.

Another main issue is the consideration that not all applications will work with terminal services and must be written to be able to operate with terminal services.

Protocols

Depending on the type of terminal server OS, various protocols can be used. Here we look at two types of terminal server OS protocols: Windows NT/2000 Remote Desktop Protocol (RDP) and Citrix Independent Computing Architecture (ICA).

exam
ⓦatch

You need to understand the concepts behind terminal services as well as the difference between the RDP and ICA protocols.

Remote Desktop Protocol

Windows NT 4.0 has a special version of the NOS that acts as a terminal server; it is Windows NT Terminal Server. Windows 2000 Server and later have terminal services as an add-in to the NOS. A terminal service is added via Add/Remove Programs. A terminal service does require a special license to make it functional.

Windows terminal services use Remote Desktop Protocol (RDP), which is actually encapsulated inside TCP/IP packets and transmitted over the network media. This allows the network to be routable and requires no extra network devices to be able to manage RDP, since no network device will even "see" RDP, only TCP/IP.

Windows Terminal Servers allow clients to operate Windows CE, Windows for Workgroups, Windows 95/98/ME, and Windows NT/2000. Other operating systems require the Citrix ICA client.

Citrix Independent Computing Architecture Protocol

Citrix has a version of a NOS that is dedicated for terminal services and built on Windows NT 3.51. The company also offers an add-on for Windows NT 4.0 Terminal Server and Windows 2000 with terminal services installed.

The Citrix Independent Computing Architecture (ICA) client is a workstationside client that allows the workstation to simulate a terminal workstation and allow all the processing to be done on the server side. The local OS can still be used to run programs locally, as it normally would without ICA.

The ICA client uses the ICA protocol, which is the same as Microsoft's RDP. The main difference between the two is that the ICA protocol uses a special product called SpeedScreen 2 to transmit screen images, but only the portions of the screen that change. This method requires less overhead and provides better performance.

The OS on which ICA is operating determines the protocols into which the ICA protocol will be encapsulated before transmission. These can be seen in Table 6-3 and Exercise 6-5, which shows how to install the Citrix ICA client on a 32-bit Windows platform.

EXERCISE 6-5

CertCam 6-5

Installing a Windows 32-bit ICA Client

1. Run **Setup.exe** from the installation source (CD-ROM, server, etc.).

2. Click **Yes** to accept the license terms.

3. Change the default destination for installation on the next window or select **Next** to accept the default.

4. Click **Next** on the following window to allow the ICA icon to placed in the Start menu, or specify a different location and then select **Next**.

5. The following screen shows the NEtBIOS name of the local PC. You can accept this name by selecting **Next** or change it and then select **Next**.

6. Click **OK** to start copying the files from the source.

TABLE 6-3 Protocols for Specific ICA Clients

Client	Protocol
Windows 3.x, Windows 9x/ME, Windows NT/2000, DOS (16 or 32-bit)	IPX/SPX, TCP/IP
Windows CE, Web Clients, UNIX, Macintosh, Java	TCP/IP

7. Click **OK** again to finish the setup.

8. Reboot the PC to let the changes take effect.

Another difference between the Microsoft and Citrix clients is that the Microsoft client does not allow the remote application to access local devices, whereas ICA does allow local devices to be used. For example, if your PC had a locally attached printer on LPT1:, you would not be able to print to the printer using RDP, but you would be allowed to do so using ICA. The local devices include the printer, diskette drive, hard disk, and other such peripherals that can be installed on or in a local PC.

Now let's look at some scenarios and their possible solutions.

SCENARIO & SOLUTION

I need to access a terminal server using a protocol that provides security for the data. Which protocol should I use?	Use RDP. This protocol prevents users from saving the data to a local machine to save to a diskette and remove from the premises.
I need a fast protocol to access a terminal server from a dial-up connection. Which protocol should I use?	Use ICA. ICA requires less bandwidth because of SpeedScreen 2.
With which protocol can I use IPX/SPX for encapsulation?	ICA allows IPX/SPX and TCP/IP to encapsulate the ICA packets. RDP uses only TCP/IP.

CERTIFICATION SUMMARY

The concept behind remote connectivity is to provide access to a network from a remote location. Originally, the U.S. government used ARPANET to connect remote sites. From there, networks have drastically expanded in size over the past several decades. Many technologies have been spawned from the growing need for remote access.

Point-to-Point Protocol (PPP) and Serial Line Internet Protocol (SLIP) are communications protocols used to communicate with remote networks through a serial device such as an analog modem. SLIP was originally designed to connect to remote UNIX boxes. SLIP supports only the TCP/IP Network layer protocol. It is quickly being replaced by PPP.

PPP is a more robust protocol than SLIP. PPP was designed to handle multiple Network layer protocols, such as TCP/IP, IPX, and NetBEUI. It includes additional features such as encapsulation, network protocol multiplexing, session negotiation, and data compression negotiation. PPP uses three subprotocols: High-Level Data-Link Control (HDLC), Network Control Protocol (NCP), and Link Control Protocol (LCP). HDLC handles data encapsulation, NCP handles Network layer protocols, and LCP handles connection maintenance and testing. PPP uses three different NCPs: IPCP for TCP/IP, IPXCP for IPX, and NBFCP for NetBEUI. PPP uses authentication protocols such as CHAP, PAP, and MS-CHAP. PPPLOG.TXT is located in the Windows directory, which by default is C:\Windows and is used to troubleshoot PPP issues.

Point-to-Point Tunneling Protocol (PPTP) provides a secure communications channel through a public TCP/IP network such as the Internet. PPTP provides multiple Network layer support using PPP as the underlying structure. PPTP uses a technology called Virtual Private Networks (VPNs) to create the channel through which to tunnel. You can use a PPTP client to connect to a standard PPP server and create a tunnel to another PPTP server across the network. You can also use a PPP client to connect to a PPTP server and enable it to handle the tunneling. VPN devices are created to facilitate PPTP connectivity following a three-step process: PPP connection and communication, PPTP control connection, and PPTP data tunneling.

Integrated Services Digital Network (ISDN) is a system of digital telephone connections that enables data to be transmitted simultaneously end to end. ISDN developed as the standard telephone network progressed. ISDN uses channels to make up a logical circuit. Two types of channels are used: a B channel for data transfer and a D channel for circuit control functions. Each B channel equals 64Kbps; each D channel represents either 16Kbps or 64Kbps. H channels are used to specify a number of B channels. Basic Rate Interface (BRI) consists of two B channels and one 16Kbps D channel, totaling 144Kbps. Primary Rate Interface (PRI) consists of 23 B channels and one 64Kbps D channel, totaling 1536Kbps. ISDN device types define the type of hardware used and include NT1, NT2, TE1, TE2, and TA. Reference points are used to define logical interfaces. Identifiers label the connection and include the service profile identifier (SPID), the directory number (DN), the terminal endpoint identifier (TEI), the service address point identifier (SAPI), and the bearer code (BC).

The Public Switched Telephone Network (PSTN) facilitates voice communications globally. Also known as plain old telephone system (POTS), PSTN was the first telecommunications network of its size in existence. Wide area network technologies are all based to some degree on this network. Various analog device types, including external modems, internal modems, and multilane modem banks, are available to enable data communications.

Dial-Up Networking functionality is included with Windows 95/98/ME and Windows NT/2000. It enables users to connect to their internal networks or the Internet from remote locations. Dial-Up Networking supports four line protocols: NetWare Connect (NRN), Remote Access Service (RAS), SLIP, and PPP. Three methods exist to invoke a dial-up session: explicit, implicit, or application invoked. Because modems are used to connect to remote networks, you must know how to configure them. IRQs, I/O addresses, and serial ports all must be configured properly. Modems have a maximum port speed defined by the standards they meet. The Unimodem subsystem provides one interface for all applications to tie into the modem. Telephony API (TAPI) provides additional features such as connection monitoring and multiple-location support. Specific items are required to use Dial-Up Networking; you must have the appropriate network protocol set up, a line protocol set up, a server to dial into, and a properly set up modem.

✓ TWO-MINUTE DRILL

Remote Connectivity Concepts

❑ The basic functionality that remote connectivity uses is available in many different protocols and devices.

❑ Companies use network links such as Frame Relay and ATM that encompass many different technologies.

❑ Common applications include PPP dial-up and the Public Switched Telephone Network (PSTN).

❑ SLIP and PPP are two communication protocols that are used to connect a computer to a remote network through a serial connection using a device such as a modem.

❑ Serial Line Internet Protocol, or SLIP, is a communications protocol used for making a TCP/IP connection over a serial interface to a remote network.

❑ Point-to-Point Protocol, or PPP, is a Data Link layer protocol used to encapsulate higher Network layer protocols to pass over synchronous and asynchronous communication lines.

❑ The most common authentication protocols include Password Authentication Protocol (PAP), the Challenge Handshake Authentication Protocol (CHAP), and the Microsoft adaptation of CHAP, MS-CHAP.

❑ Point-to-Point Tunneling Protocol (PPTP) is a network protocol that provides for the secure transfer of data from a remote client to a private server by creating a multiprotocol virtual private network, or VPN. PPTP is used in TCP/IP networks as an alternative to conventional dial-up networking methods.

❑ A VPN works by encapsulating the data within IP packets to transport it through PPP. VPNs are virtual devices set up as thought they were regular devices such as a modem.

❑ Be sure to know the three processes involved with PPTP and how PPP applies to each one.

❑ Integrated Services Digital Network (ISDN) is a system of digital telephone connections that enables data to be transmitted simultaneously end to end.

❑ There are two basic types of ISDN service: Basic Rate Interface (BRI) and Primary Rate Interface (PRI).

❑ Be sure to know the device types and where each type is used. In addition, know the number of channels and speeds associated with BRI and PRI.

❑ Network terminator 1 (NT1) is the device that communicates directly with the central office switch.

❑ Network terminator 2 (NT2) is placed between an NT1 device and any adapters or terminal equipment.

❑ Terminal equipment 1 (TE1) is a local device that speaks via an S interface.

❑ Terminal equipment 2 (TE2) devices are common everyday devices that can be used for ISDN connectivity.

❑ The service profile identifier (SPID) is the most important number you need when you use ISDN.

❑ The directory number (DN) is the 10-digit phone number the telephone company assigns to any analog line.

❑ A terminal endpoint identifier (TEI) identifies the particular ISDN device to the switch.

❑ The service address point identifier (SAPI) identifies the particular interface on the switch to which your devices are connected.

❑ The bearer code (BC) is an identifier made up of the combination of TEI and SAPI.

❑ The Public Switched Telephone Network (PSTN) was originally designed as an analog switching system for routing voice calls.

❑ Remember that the maximum available speed with an analog modem is 56Kbps.

Dial-Up Networking

❑ Windows NT/2000 and Windows 95/98/ME include a Dial-Up Networking client.

❑ Dial-Up Networking provides support for four types of line protocols.

❑ Modems are asynchronous, synchronous, or both.

❑ The computer side of the connection is known as the *data terminal equipment (DTE)* and the modem is known as the *data circuit-terminating equipment (DCE)*.

❑ Interrupt request levels (IRQs) are hardware lines over which devices send interrupt signals to the microprocessor.

❑ Input/output (I/O) addresses are spaces in memory designated for memory's own use.

❑ Unimodem provides an easy, centralized mechanism for installing and configuring modems.

❑ Microsoft Telephony API (TAPI) is an application interface used for accessing communications features such as connection monitoring.

Terminal Services

❑ Terminal services allow applications to be run completely on the server.

❑ Older PC hardware can still be utilized with terminal services.

❑ Connections to a terminal server can be done over a dial-up connection, LAN connection, and even a direct connection.

❑ A terminal server requires more RAM and processor power.

❑ There are two terminal service protocols: RDP and ICA.

❑ RDP is used on Microsoft Window clients as well as Microsoft CE platforms.

❑ ICA can be used on DOS 16-bit PCs as well as any Microsoft OS released afterward, and even UNIX, Java and Macintosh systems.

❑ ICA allows the use of local devices on the local workstation.

SELF TEST

The following Self Test questions will help you measure your understanding of the material presented in this chapter. Read all the choices carefully, because there might be more than one correct answer. Choose all correct answers for each question.

Remote Connectivity Concepts

1. Which Network layer protocols can Serial Line Internet Protocol use during a dial-up session?

   A. TCP/IP

   B. IPX

   C. SLP

   D. None of the above

2. Which protocol supports multiple Network layer protocols over a serial link?

   A. SLIP

   B. PPP

   C. IPX

   D. NetBEUI

3. Which components are part of Point-to-Point Protocol?

   A. Network Control Protocol

   B. Link Control Protocol

   C. Internet Protocol

   D. Internet Packet eXchange Protocol

4. Which Network Control Protocol is used in PPP to facilitate the transport of TCP/IP?

   A. IPNP

   B. IPCP

   C. IPXCP

   D. None of the above

5. Which forms of validation can PPP use to authenticate users against a remote server?

    A. CHAP

    B. Domain Account

    C. PAP

    D. KPA

6. Where is the connection information for a PPP dial-up session stored?

    A. C:\Windows\ppp\PPPLOG.TXT

    B. C:\Windows\PPP.LOG

    C. C:\Windows\PPPLOG.TXT

    D. C:\PPP.TXT

7. What technology do virtual private networks (VPNs) offer to provide a more secure communications channel?

    A. IP header compression

    B. Tunneling

    C. Multiple network protocol support

    D. None of the above

8. Virtual private networks use which of the following kinds of devices as though they were modems inside the computer?

    A. Network interface cards

    B. Virtual devices

    C. Nonvirtual devices

    D. Modems

9. Which of the following is the process for setting up a "tunnel" for PPTP?

    A. PPP connection and communication

    B. PPTP control connection

    C. PPTP data tunneling

    D. PPTP data transfer

10. What is the maximum number of virtual devices a Windows NT 4.0 server can have?

    A. 10

    B. 50

    C. 256

    D. 1024

11. What was the first Integrated Services Digital Network standard to be published by the ITU?

    A. ISDN-1

    B. ISDN-NI

    C. NI

    D. NI-1

12. How many B channels are available in a typical ISDN PRI?

    A. 2

    B. 20

    C. 23

    D. 30

Dial-Up Networking

13. What line protocols are available with Microsoft's Dial-Up Networking?

    A. NetWare Connect

    B. Point-to-Point Protocol

    C. Serial Line Internet Protocol

    D. All of the above

14. What COM port is used by default when you set up a modem?

    A. 2

    B. 4

    C. 1

    D. 3

15. What is the default IRQ setting for COM2?

    A. 2

    B. 14

    C. 4

    D. 3

16. Which application programming interface is used to include features such as call monitoring and multiple localities?

    A. Unimodem

    B. COMM

    C. TAPI

    D. None of the above

17. Which items listed are required for a dial-up connection to a remote host?

    A. Modem device

    B. Line protocol setup

    C. Valid user ID and password

    D. All of the above

18. Which modem standard defines error-checking standards?

    A. V.42

    B. V.34

    C. V.52

    D. V.100

Terminal Services

19. What two terminal services protocols can be used in terminal services environment?

    A. RDP

    B. NetBEUI

    C. ICA

    D. Both A and C

20. What are some advantages of using terminal services? (Choose all that apply.)

    A. Use of older workstation PCs

    B. Higher-performance server is required

    C. Allows administrators to watch user sessions

    D. Less training required for employees

LAB QUESTION

A company needs traveling employees to be able to connect to the company network, even when they are away from the office. They need two means of remote access: one for employees who live or travel very far away and need access to the company network for extended periods of time without incurring a long-distance phone bill, and the other for employees who need to quickly check e-mail or the like and are not worried about the phone charges.

A special department within the company also requires a new server to allow execution of a new application. They do not have the funds to upgrade all PCs as well as the server. They need a solution that will not affect the rest of the network.

How would you meet these requirements for the company?

SELF TEST ANSWERS

Remote Connectivity Concepts

1. ☑ **A.** Serial Line Internet Protocol, or SLIP, is a communications protocol used for making a TCP/IP connection over a serial interface to a remote network. SLIP was designed for connecting to remote UNIX servers across a standard phone line. This protocol was one of the first of its kind, enabling a remote network connection to be established over a standard phone line.
   ☒ **B** and **C** are incorrect because SLP is not a protocol and IPX is not a Network layer protocol. **D** is incorrect because there is a correct answer.

2. ☑ **B.** PPP established other standards, including asynchronous and bit-orientated synchronous encapsulation, network protocol multiplexing, session negotiation, and data-compression negotiation. PPP also supports protocols other than TCP/IP, such as IPX/SPX and DECnet.
   ☒ **A**, **C**, and **D** are incorrect because SLIP was very limited in the protocols used. IPX and NetBEUI are standard network protocols, not protocols for asynchronous transfer.

3. ☑ **A** and **B.** The following explains the three components of PPP and their purpose: PPP uses the High-Level Data-Link Control (HDLC) protocol as the basis to encapsulate its data during transmission; PPP uses Link Control Protocol (LCP) to establish, test, and configure the data link connection; various Network Control Protocols (NCPs) are used to configure the different communications protocols. This enables you to use different protocols such as TCP/IP and IPX over the same line simultaneously.
   ☒ **C** and **D** are incorrect because they are not a part of Point-to-Point Protocol.

4. ☑ **B.** The Internet Protocol Control Protocol (IPCP) is the NCP used to configure, enable, and disable the IP protocol modules at each end of the link.
   ☒ **A**, **C**, and **D** are incorrect because none of them exists.

5. ☑ **A** and **C.** With PPP, each system could be required to authenticate itself. This can be done using an authentication protocol. The most common authentication protocols include Password Authentication Protocol (PAP), Challenge Handshake Authentication Protocol (CHAP), and the Microsoft adaptation of CHAP, MS-CHAP.
   ☒ **B** and **D** are incorrect because domain authentication is used to validate user, not the connection, and KPA does not exist.

6. ☑ **C.** When logging has been enabled, you can see the log file after the next attempt to connect to a PPP server. The log file, PPPLOG.TXT, is stored in the Windows directory by default. It can be viewed by any standard text editor and is appended to each time a new connection is attempted.

☒ **A, B,** and **D** are incorrect connection information.

7. ☑ **B.** PPTP is used in TCP/IP networks as an alternative to conventional dial-up networking methods. This enables multiprotocol secure communications over a public TCP/IP network such as the Internet. PPTP takes advantage of an additional level of security that is not currently available in other standard implementations.

☒ **A, C,** and **D** are incorrect because none of the other choices deals with providing a secure link.

8. ☑ **B.** VPNs are virtual devices set up as though they were regular devices such as modems. In addition, PPTP must be set up on the client and the server. Host computers in the route between these two computers do not need to be PPTP aware. They need only provide an IP route to the remote server.

☒ **A, C,** and **D** are incorrect because the physical hardware devices, modems and NICs, are used as transmission devices, but a special driver is loaded to make a virtual device of the physical device.

9. ☑ **B.** When the PPP session is established, PPTP creates a control connection between the client and the remote PPTP server. This process is referred to as *tunneling*.

☒ **A** is incorrect because PPTP uses PPP to connect to a remote network. When connected, PPP is also used to encrypt the data packets being passed between the remote host and the local machine. **C** is incorrect because PPTP creates the IP datagrams for PPP to send. The packets are encrypted by PPP and sent through the tunnel to the PPTP server. The PPTP server is then used to decrypt the PPP-encrypted packets, disassemble the IP datagram, and route to the appropriate host. **D** is incorrect because the transfer of data is not started until the tunnel is established.

10. ☑ **C.** By default, Windows NT Server can accommodate up to 256 VPNs. Workstations will require only one VPN; servers require as many connections as there are users attaching to it.

☒ **A, B,** and **D** are incorrect numbers of virtual devices.

11. ☑ **D.** The National ISDN 1 (NI-1) standard was defined by the industry so that users would not have to know the type of switch to which they are connected in order to buy equipment and software compatible with it.

☒ **A, B,** and **C** are incorrect because NI-1 is the term used for ISDN.

12. ☑ **B.** PRI is intended for users with greater bandwidth requirements. It requires T1 carriers to facilitate communications. Normally, the channel structure contains 23 B channels plus one 64Kbps D channel, for a total of 1536Kbps.

☒ **A, C,** and **D** are incorrect numbers of B channels.

Dial-Up Networking

13. ☑ **D.** NetWare Connect, PPP, and SLIP are all valid line protocols with Microsoft's Dial-Up Networking. NetWare Connect supports only IPX, PPP supports multiple network protocols, and SLIP supports only TCP/IP.

☒ **A, B,** and **C** are all incorrect: NetWare Connect (NRN) is used to connect to NetWare services via IPX/SPX; Remote Access Services (RAS) is used to connect to Windows NT/2000 Remote Access Service; Serial Line Internet Protocol (SLIP) is used to connect to a SLIP server via TCP/IP; and Point-to-Point Protocol (PPP) is used to connect to a PPP server. Multiple protocols can be utilized including TCP/IP, IPX, and NetBEUI.

14. ☑ **C.** You must specify the appropriate serial port when setting up a modem. Most modems attempt to use COM1 by default. Each COM port is assigned a specific set of address variables by default when you set up connections. To change the modem COM port after the setup is complete, select Start | Settings | Control Panel, and then double-click the Modems icon.

☒ **A, B,** and **D** are incorrect port numbers.

15. ☑ **D.** The default IRQ setting for COM2 is 3. COM1 uses a default IRQ of 4. IRQs 2 and 14 are usually taken by the system for other resources.

☒ **A, B,** and **C** are incorrect default IRQ settings.

16. ☑ **C.** TAPI also provides other features, such as multiple calling locations. You can set up different connection profiles for different dial-up access numbers. You can also customize how the number is dialed. For example, if you set up two separate connection profiles, one with call waiting enabled and the second without it, you can manage multiple connections without having to reconfigure your modem setup every time you need a variation.

☒ **A** is incorrect because Unimodem is a part of Windows that allows for a single installation and configuration of a modem. **B** is incorrect because COMM is not a valid choice, since it is not a common program name with Windows, it is a driver name. **D** is incorrect because there is a correct answer choice.

17. ☑ **D.** A modem device, a line protocol, and a valid user ID and password are all required to connect to a remote host.

☒ **A, B,** and **C** are incorrect because they are not complete answers.

18. ☑ **A.** The V.42 modem standard defines error-checking standards.

☒ **B, C,** and **D** are incorrect because the V.34 standard defines the standard for communications at the speed of 28Kbps. V.52 and V.100 are not valid modem standards.

Terminal Services

19. ☑ **D.** A terminal services environment uses both RDP and ICA to transmit screen images as well as mouse and keyboard entry.

☒ **A** and **C** are incorrect because they are not complete answers. **B** is incorrect because NetBEUI is a standard network protocol that is not used with terminal services.

20. ☑ **A, C,** and **D.** A terminal services environment allows for the use of older equipment and requires less training for users, who can continue to use their old OS. Administrators are also able to watch user sessions and determine what users are doing as well as be able to help users who are unable to perform some function.

☒ **B** is incorrect because a higher performance server being required is a disadvantage.

LAB ANSWER

The first solution for employees who don't care about phone charges and those who do not live too far away to be considered long distance requires setting up an array of modems. The modem pool allows these employees to dial directly to the company modem pool from their home PCs via their modems.

The second solution is to set up VPN ability to allow long-distance employees to be able to connect to an ISP and connect to the company network through a VPN. Since a local call is made to the ISP, these employees will incur no long-distance phone charges. For employees who travel, they can subscribe to a national ISP such as America Online (AOL) or Microsoft Network (MSN).

The final solution for the special department is to purchase a very good server and use terminal services so that they can continue to use their older workstations. The department should then be separated from the rest of the network by a bridge. Furthermore, the department should have a switch to allow for better bandwidth usage.

COMPUTING TECHNOLOGY INDUSTRY ASSOCIATION

7

Wide Area Network Technologies

CERTIFICATION OBJECTIVE

7.01	Packet-Switching versus Circuit-Switching Networks
7.02	Asynchronous Transfer Mode
7.03	Synchronous Optical NETwork/Synchronous Digital Hierarchy
7.04	Optical Carrier Level-X
7.05	Frame Relay
7.06	Fiber Distributed Data Interface
7.07	Tx/Ex-Carrier
✓	Two-Minute Drill
Q&A	Self Test

With companies becoming larger and more geographically diverse, wide area networks (WANs) have become more the norm for networks these days. With the expansion of the Internet have come advances in technology to allow other ways to get data from one place to another. The technology allows companies to create WANs and will overall improve the Internet itself.

Many companies will connect geographically distant WANs through the Internet. Doing so will allow a local company to pay only for a local connection to an ISP, rather than pay for the entire connection between offices. This will keep the costs down to help in the expansion of business.

Each company requiring a WAN will have different needs as far as available and required bandwidth, and the cost and availability of the connection. Some companies may only need a connection for a few hours a day, while others will require the connection 24 hours a day, 7 days a week. Some companies will even require a backup method in case the main connection fails.

Some WAN technologies will integrate well with existing topologies, while others might be chosen because of geographic location. When implementing a WAN or just taking the Network+ exam, you will need to understand the capabilities of the different WAN technologies. We will not list all the available technologies here, because technology is always improving and discovering new ways to do old things.

An Integrated Services Digital Network (ISDN) is also considered a WAN technology that can be used to connect local area networks (LANs) together to form a WAN. As we discussed in Chapter 6, some people have ISDN at home to allow for remote connectivity to the office. Other WAN technologies can be used to allow for remote connectivity of a single user rather than a remote office with multiple users.

CERTIFICATION OBJECTIVE 7.01

Packet-Switching versus Circuit-Switching Networks

Packet switching is used by the Internet and routed networks. The path that is used to send data packets from one point to another through routers is not predetermined if there are multiple paths. If you look at the routed network in Figure 7-1, you can see that from point A to point B, there exist many paths and ways for packets to travel between the source and destination PCs. If we assume that each router is a LAN, which is not shown, then it is possible for each LAN to experience different bandwidth usage.

When a user at PC A wants to copy a shared file from PC B, the data path is not a set path between specific routers. Packets will be sent from router to router based on the quickest or shortest path. If a router is extremely busy, it will not be used, and a different path will be chosen if one exists. Remember that other users are also sending data packets over the same media and routers as you are using.

Using Figure 7-1, let's now look at an example of how packet switching works. PC B will send its data to the router that is the least busy; for the first data packet, let us assume that it is Router 6. Now that Router 6 has the data packet, it will look at its routing table and determine that Router 3 might be the best way for it to reach PC A. Router 6 sends the data packet to Router 3, which in turn decides that the best path is to forward the packet on to Router 1. Router 1 will then send the packet to PC A. Now, the second packet might be sent to Router 7, because Router 6 has suddenly become very busy. Router 7 will receive the data packet and forward it to Router 4. Router 4 sends the packet to Router 2. Router 2 checks its routing table and sends the packet on to PC A. PC A will then start assembling the entire data file

FIGURE 7-1   Routed network

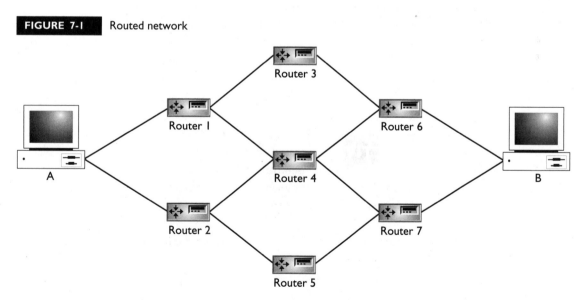

from the packets received. For the third data packet, let's say that it is also sent to Router 7, which will send it to Router 5 again. Now let's say that Router 2 has suddenly gone offline. Router 5 waits to contact Router 2, but eventually times out and sends the data packet back to Router 7, which then tries to send the data packet to Router 4. Router 4 has since determined that Router 2 is offline, and sends the data packet to Router 1. Router 1 sends the data packet to PC A. The fourth data packet is sent to Router 6, on to Router 3, then to Router 1, and finally delivered to PC A.

Let's look more closely at packets 3 and 4: While packet 3 was detained at Router 5 because of the failure of Router 2, packet 4 was able to be delivered to PC A before the arrival of packet 3. This shows that a packet-switched network is not dependent on packets being delivered in the order in which they were sent. Actually, if there are enough data paths, it is very common for packets to be received out of order. With routable protocols, data packets are numbered so they can be placed back in the proper order to create the original block of data that existed at the sending PC. It would do no good to receive a jumbled database or unreadable document.

Data packets are sent out of order on the Internet all of the time. The only time this is a problem is when the data being sent is streaming voice or video. If you have ever tried to use the Internet as a media for making telephone calls, you know that the sound quality is not very good on slow network links such as a 56K modem.

Circuit switching, on the other hand, is the foundation for the telephone system. When you make a telephone call from your home to someone next door or even 1000 miles away, a circuit is opened between your telephone and the telephone to which you are calling. The circuit is not usable by others, so it is 100-percent dedicated for your use. As you speak, your voice is sent over the media to the other telephone and is not broken up or rerouted. If the telephone system was a packet-switched network, telephone conversations could be very confusing.

One problem with circuit switching is when a circuit fails. If you are speaking with someone and the line you're using is broken because of a fallen tree, for example, your circuit is broken and the line will go dead. You will have to hang up and place the call again. The switches will determine that the circuit has been broken where the tree fell, and will route all calls around the point of failure. Therefore, when you place the call again, you will use a different circuit and be able to continue your conversation. The call cannot be placed if the circuit was broken at a point that has no fault tolerance, such as outside your home where the telephone line leaves your house, or at the other person's house.

The future should hold the possibility of the telephone circuit-switching network to eventually be part of the Internet. Technology is already at the stage to make it possible for sending voice over a packet-switched network. Voice over the Internet is usually referred to as Voice over IP (VoIP), and there are specialized routers available to aid in this pursuit.

Other technologies using packet-switched networks are Asynchronous Transfer Mode (ATM) and Frame Relay.

exam
ⓦatch
Know the differences between packet- and circuit-switching networks. In addition, remember that data networks are usually packet-switched, whereas telephone connections are circuit-switched.

EXERCISE 7-1

Packet-Switching Network Exercise

In this exercise, you are given a scenario and a network diagram to determine the path of a data packet.

Your company has a headquarters and 10 remote offices. All of the offices are connected by a packet-switching network to create a WAN. Look at Figure 7-2, and then answer the following questions.

PC A is at the main headquarters, and PC B is one of the remote offices. Each router in the diagram designates an office. You are sending data from PC A to PC B, and you want to try to determine the path the data will take on its route. If using a diagnostic utility, you determine that all of the even numbered outers are extremely busy and are actually sending out messages to slow transmissions from the local LAN and remote LANs to which they are transmitting.

1. What is the path that data packets could take from PC A to PC B?

2. Is it possible that the data packets could arrive out of order?

3. What are some reasons why Router 1 might be preferred over Router 3?

4. What path would be used if the odd-numbered routers were offline or busy, and the even-numbered routers were online and not busy?

5. What would occur if Routers 1, 2, and 3 were to become extremely busy or go offline?

FIGURE 7-2   Sample network

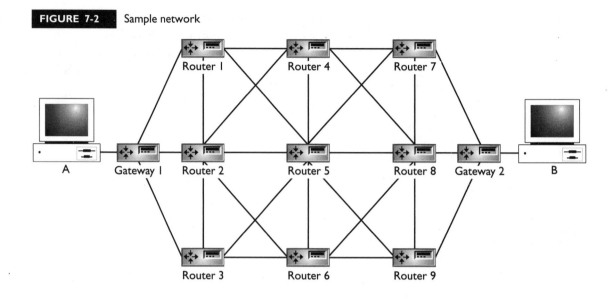

The answers are as follows:

1. The route would be from PC A to the default gateway, then to either Router 1 or Router 3. The packet will then travel from Router 1 or 3 to Router 5, and from Router 5 to Router 7 or Router 9. Then the data packet will go from Router 7 or 9 to the default gateway for PC B, and then to PC B.

2. Yes, since there are still multiple routes, one data path might be less busy than another at any given time. This could allow data packets to arrive before others. For example, if Router 1 should suddenly become a little busier than Router 3, any packets sent to Router 3 might arrive before those sent to Router 1.

3. Router 3 might be busier than Router 1, which will cause a packet to be delayed a little while. The routers might be configured to have a specific method to determine which route to use as a default, or to make one more used than another. This could cause one router to be used until it is too busy, at which point, another will be used. The specified method could be determined by hop counts or by some other configured means.

4. From PC A, the data packet would be passed to the default gateway, which would then be passed to Router 2. From Router 2, the data packet would be

sent to either Router 4 or Router 6. Router 4 or Router 6 would send the data packet to Router 8. Router 8 would send the data packets to the default gateway for PC B, and then the packet would be sent to PC B.

5. No data could be sent from PC A to PC B, since there is no open path from PC A to PC B.

CERTIFICATION OBJECTIVE 7.02

Asynchronous Transfer Mode

Asynchronous Transfer Mode (ATM) is a technology used mainly as a backbone in the Internet world. ATM technology is suitable for both LAN and WAN connectivity. Since ATM can be used for either a LAN or WAN, it can allow for a company LAN to be a fiber-optic network and will operate at very high speeds. With ATM technology in place for a LAN, it will be easy to extend the technology to cover a large area if needed, and make a WAN without loss of performance.

ATM can be used to enhance broadband ISDN to allow for the transmission of voice, data, and multimedia packets over the same media simultaneously. Whereas standard ISDN is digital, ATM and broadband ISDN use broadband, meaning that they are analog. Broadband media uses frequencies to be able to manage many "circuits" over one cable. Digital transmissions are electrical or light pulses of on or off, depending on the physical media over which it is transferred. Broadband is how cable TV works, with multiple channels on one cable using different frequencies for each channel.

ATM will provide for high bandwidth as needed if enough users are implementing the bandwidth. ATM bandwidth ranges from slow speeds, around 12.96 to 25 Mbps using copper media such as category 3 UTP cable, and high speeds around 622.08 Mbps using fiber-optic cable. With advances in technology, ATM speeds can reach 2.488 Gbps.

ATM can be used with physical interfaces such as FDDI and SONET/SDH, which we discuss later in this chapter. This means that in an FDDI or SONET/SDH network, ATM can be used on the network topology for data transmissions. When setting up a switched network similar to Figure 7-1, ATM can allow for parallel transmissions between nodes. This means that if data is being passed to and from PC A and PC B, the data packets can be passed between two routers (nodes) simultaneously. Data packets are referred to as cells, and each cell is a fixed length of 53 octets. There are no variable-length cells as with some transmission standards. This allows all of the devices to be optimized for the specified cell size, thereby providing better performance. Once in place, an ATM network will be transparent to users and will provide for high data transmission speeds that can grow into a WAN when needed.

exam
ⓌatcH

Remember the characteristics and speeds of ATM.

EXERCISE 7-2

ATM Network Exercise

In this exercise, you are given some questions that a manager might ask. We will assume that you are the person whom the manager is questioning about ATM technology for the purpose of possible implementation.

1. Is the ATM technology able to be used to replace our LAN?

2. Can the ATM network be in place with our existing category 3 network until we get the cables replaced with other type?

3. What cabling is preferred for optimum speed?

4. What is the top speed we can achieve if we replace the cabling to fiber optic?

5. Is ATM a digital technology?

    The answers are as follows:

1. Yes, ATM is usable as either a LAN or WAN technology.

2. Yes, the ATM network will operate at a speed lower than its capability. The network will operate at around 12.96 Mbps to 25 Mbps, depending on the network functionality and the devices purchased.

3. Fiber-optic cable is the preferred media.

4. With fiber-optic cable, the speeds of ATM could be as high as 622.08 Mbps, or with future technology advances as high as 2.488 Gbps.

5. No, it is a broadband technology similar to cable TV.

CERTIFICATION OBJECTIVE 7.03

Synchronous Optical NETwork/ Synchronous Digital Hierarchy

Synchronous Optical NETwork (SONET) is an American standard that allows the unifying of unlike transmissions into one single data stream. SDH is an international standard designed for the same purpose as SONET. Basically, SONET allows multiple companies to transmit their packets on their network onto a SONET backbone to be transmitted to a remote location. Since many companies might be using different network topologies and protocols, the data streams from each company will most likely differ. SONET allows these companies to transmit their information over SONET without having to conform to a network standard. For example, one company might have a 10-Mbps category-5 Ethernet network using IPX/SPX, while another is using fiber optic with TCP/IP. These can then be combined into a single data stream for transmission over one cable. More companies can be added for transmission over the SONET medium without making any changes to any of the company networks.

SONET can be used as a backbone between unlike systems. This architecture allows for different media types and transmission types to be combined into one stream and sent over a fiber-optic cable at a minimum speed of 54.84 Mbps for SONET-1. SONET is divided into electrical levels that have varying speeds, termed synchronous transport signals (STS). The highest level is SONET-192 with a speed of 9953.280 Mbps. SDH has no equivalent for SONET-1 at the speed of 51.84 Mbps, but has a low speed of 155.520 Mbps mapping to SONET-3. The different SDH levels are termed synchronous transfer mode (STM). Table 7-1 lists the different levels.

TABLE 7-1   SONET Levels and Bandwidth

Electrical Level	SDH Level	Bandwidth
STS-1	None	51.84 Mbps
STS-3	STM-1	155.52 Mbps
STS-9	STM-3	466.56 Mbps
STS-12	STM-4	622.08 Mbps
STS-18	STM-6	933.15 Mbps
STS-24	STM-8	1244.16 Mbps
STS-36	STM-12	1866.24 Mbps
STS-48	STM-16	2488.32 Mbps
STS-96	STM-32	4976.64 Mbps
STS-192	STM-64	9953.28 Mbps

The format for SONET is created by multiplexing all data signals into a single data stream called a synchronous transport signal (STS). The multiplexer is managed by the path terminating equipment (PTE) from various different media and transmission types, shown in Figure 7-3. Now that the STS signal is created, it must be transmitted on the SONET media. The STS transmission is managed by the line terminating equipment (LTE), also shown in Figure 7-3. The LTE will send and receive the STS signal on both ends of the SONET media. Remember that the STS signal is in the form of electrical pulses. The SONET link might not be a single connection from one point to another, and entire segment might be comprised of sections of SONET media. Therefore, to create the sections and have the entire segment appear as one physical link, you use section terminating equipment (STE) to begin and end a section as shown in Figure 7-3.

There can also exist a scrambling device to allow a transmission to be somewhat random, thereby allowing for privacy. This is the same as encryption of a single data stream that is integrated into the SONET data stream. The scrambling device must exist at both ends of the transmission to be able to descramble the stream back into usable data.

ATM signals can be sent over a SONET/SDH link as was discussed in the previous section. There is also the capability to transmit PPP over SONET/SDH.

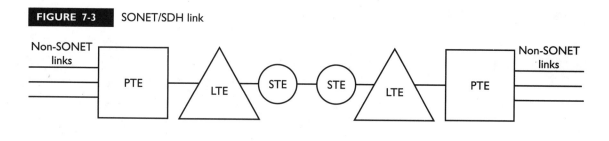

FIGURE 7-3 SONET/SDH link

exam
ⓦatch

Remember the characteristics and speeds of SONET/SDH.

EXERCISE 7-3

SONET Network Exercise

In this exercise, a company wishes to create a LAN with its existing four LANs. Figure 7-4 shows the LAN and how it will be connected. You need to determine which SONET will be required for each link.

Two main offices consist of a fiber-optic network operating at 1G bps. One office has a 100-Mbps network using Fast Ethernet and category-5 cabling. The last LAN is comprised of an ATM network operating at 622.08 Mbps.

Which SONET levels would you use for each connection to allow for the connected networks to communicate at the highest speed that will not slow network functionality for the users and be the most affordable?

The answers are as follows:

■ Connection 1: STS-3 at 155.52 Mbps

■ Connection 2: STS-12 at 622.08 Mbps

■ Connection 3: STS-24 at 1244.16 Mbps

■ Connection 4: STS-3 at 155.52 Mbps

■ Connection 5: STS-12 at 622.08 Mbps

Connection 1 must be at least 10 Mbps to equal the slower LAN. The SONET level that is at least 100 Mbps is STS-3 at 155.52 Mbps.

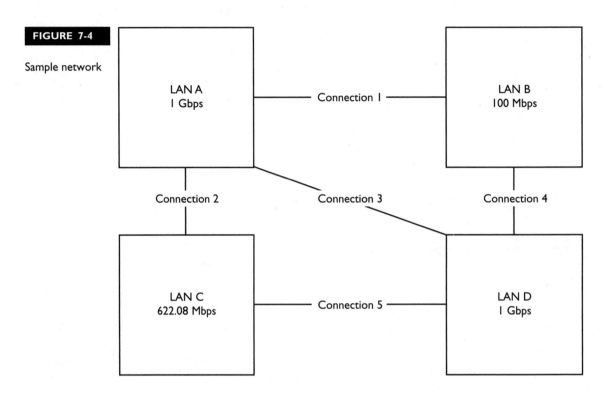

FIGURE 7-4

Sample network

Connection 2 must be equal to the slowest LAN, which would be LAN C at 622.08 Mbps. This means that the lowest SONET level would be STS-12 at exactly 622.08 Mbps.

LAN A and LAN D, connected by Connection 3, need a connection that is 1Gbps or better to allow for no delays when transmissions occur between the two LANs. This would require STS-24 at 1.24416 Gbps.

Connection 4 is connected to LAN B, which is the slowest LAN of the two and requires level STS-3 at 155.52 Mbps to cause no delays with the 100-Mbps network.

LAN C and LAN D are connected by Connection 5; LAN C is the slower LAN of the two at 622.08 Mbps. This would require a SONET level of STS-12 at 622.08 Mbps to connect the two LANs.

CERTIFICATION OBJECTIVE 7.04

Optical Carrier Level-X

The Optical Carrier (OC) standard is used to specify bandwidth for transmissions that are sent over fiber-optic cables. These standards are equivalent to the SONET/SDH standards and will correlate to the bandwidths available for SONET/SDH.

One OC channel (OC-1) is 51.84 Mbps, as is STS-1. When multiple channels are used, the bandwidth increases. For example, nine OC channels (OC-9) are comprised of nine OC-1 channels at 51.84 Mbps each. This results in a total bandwidth of 9 x 51.84 Mbps, for a total bandwidth of 466.56 Mbps. The OC levels can be matched to the SONET levels, and to the SDH levels as shown in Table 7-2.

TABLE 7-2 Optical Carrier and SONET/SDH Levels and Bandwidth

Optical Carrier Level	Electrical Level	SDH Level	Bandwidth
OC-1	STS-1	None	51.84 Mbps
OC-3	STS-3	STM-1	155.52 Mbps
OC-9	STS-9	STM-3	466.56 Mbps
OC-12	STS-12	STM-4	622.08 Mbps
OC-18	STS-18	STM-6	933.15 Mbps
OC-24	STS-24	STM-8	1244.16 Mbps
OC-36	STS-36	STM-12	1866.24 Mbps
OC-48	STS-48	STM-16	2488.32 Mbps
OC-96	STS-96	STM-32	4976.64 Mbps
OC-192	STS-192	STM-64	9953.28 Mbps

CERTIFICATION OBJECTIVE 7.05

Frame Relay

Frame Relay is one of the standards for WAN networking. It is a choice for WAN networking among ATM, Broadcast ISDN (BISDN), and Cell Relay. Frame Relay is an architecture that operates at the OSI Physical layer and is independent of all protocols being used over the medium.

Frame Relay is for transmitting data only because the transmission speeds are not always constant. Since Frame Relay is not a constant speed, real-time voice or video is impossible. The data packets, or frames, are sent through a packet-switching network with higher-level protocols managing error checking, such as IPX/SPX or TCP/IP.

Frame Relay is a highly efficient method of transmitting data using bandwidth at an optimum level, allowing for bandwidths as high as 2 Mbps. The nodes, which are used to route the frames in the packet-switching network, each use a routing algorithm that can help determine the efficiency of the Frame Relay network. Frame Relay does send frames as variable-length packets that are not all set at the same size before transmission.

If the bandwidth becomes too congested, Frame Relay will drop any frames that it cannot handle. This can include corrupted frames, as well as those that are unable to be delivered because the destination cannot be reached. Any dropped frames must be requested for retransmission by the protocols being used. Once the available bandwidth is at a minimum, the source or destination can be notified to slow the transmissions to avoid over-utilization of the bandwidth, which will avoid packets being dropped due to congestion. Although the source or destination is requested to slow the transmissions, the transmissions do not necessarily have to slow.

To determine which packets are dropped, we must first be aware of who is transmitting over the Frame Relay network. Multiple companies can share a Frame Relay backbone to the Internet or between office buildings. Each company will pay for a specific amount of the bandwidth on the Frame Relay medium. If the bandwidth is available, a company can use more bandwidth than for which they have paid. Once other companies start using their bandwidth, then all the companies will be limited to the bandwidth that has been committed to them. The bandwidth that each company pays for will be noted by their Committed Information Rate (CIR). The CIR will help determine whether frames can be dropped when the bandwidth becomes congested. The CIR will be included in all frames sent by any company on the Frame Relay network. The Frame Relay nodes will keep statistics on network bandwidth and usage by all companies. If a company is using less bandwidth than what they paid for, their frames will be sent on through the node. If the company is using more bandwidth than the CIR designates, the frames will be most likely dropped.

EXERCISE 7-4

Frame Relay Network Exercise

In this exercise, three companies are each using a Frame Relay connection to a remote office. Figure 7-5 shows the WAN and how it will be connected. You will need to determine the answers to some questions about the WAN.

Company A is larger than Company B or C is. Company A has many more users than the other two companies, so they have leased 50 percent of the Frame Relay connection to meet their needs.

Company B and Company C do not have the needs for bandwidth that Company A requires, so Company B leased 20 percent and Company C leased the remaining 30 percent of the connection.

The Frame Relay connection is 2 Mbps and is used strictly by these three companies. Other Frame Relay networks exist for other companies, but this connection is strictly for these three companies.

Answer the following questions:

1. On Monday morning, Company A is using only 30 percent of the leased connection. Company B is using 20 percent of the leased connection. Company C needs to transmit a large data file from the headquarters to the remote office. Company C is using 40 percent of the Frame Relay connection. After about 20 minutes have passed and only half of the data file has been sent, Company A starts using 15 percent more of the connection. What will this cause to happen?

2. On a Sunday afternoon, an administrator goes into the main office at Company B. No one is using the link at Company A or Company C. The administrator needs to perform a remote backup of a server at the remote office. How much of the bandwidth will be available for the backup?

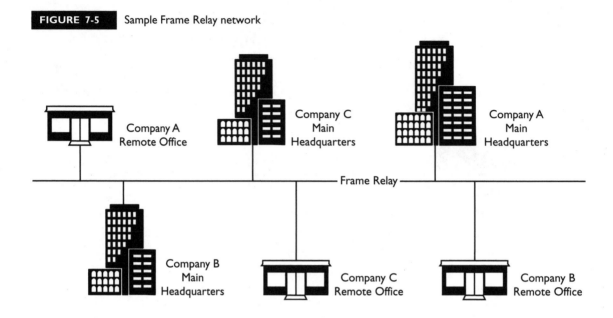

FIGURE 7-5 Sample Frame Relay network

3. Company C is closed on a specified day that the other companies, A and B, are still open. Company A is using 55 percent of the bandwidth, and Company B is using the remaining 45 percent. Later in the day, Company B starts trying to use more bandwidth. What will occur?

4. From Question 3, what would occur when data files are sent and their packets are dropped?

The answers are as follows:

1. The transmissions from Company C will start to be dropped if the transmission is not slowed when requested. This will cause the portion of the leased line for Company C to drop to 35 percent.

2. Although Company B has only leased 20 percent of the bandwidth, 100 percent can be used if no one else is using it.

3. Packets will start being dropped. Most likely, more packets will be dropped for Company B than for Company A, since Company B is more over their

leased limit than Company A. It is possible that the transmissions will decrease from Company B if the request to slow transmissions is not ignored.

4. The protocol being used would request packets to be resent. This allows any dropped packets to be resent so the data files will be complete and intact.

FROM THE CLASSROOM

One Company's Experience with Frame Relay

I once worked for a utility company that managed the electrical lines for a large portion of a state. They also had five power plants that produced electricity that were located in surrounding cities. There were remote offices located in various surrounding cities that were connected to the main headquarters by dial-up connections. The power plants were all connected by fractional T1 connections, with the headquarters connected to the Internet by a full T1 connection.

The company had a database of all customers within the state, which included customer information, power consumption, bill information, and other various items for that customer.

The department that managed the database was becoming too large to house in the main headquarters, so a building was purchased about 15 blocks away. The database department was moved to this building, but their database

server remained at the main office. Frame Relay was used to connect the database department to the main office. The Frame Relay network was shared by other various companies in the area.

One or two days a week, the database personnel had no problems accessing the database and were actually extremely pleased with the bandwidth available. The other three to four days, accessing the database was extremely slow and unacceptable. With the other companies using the bandwidth on specific days, the database personnel had very little available bandwidth. Their applications, which allowed them to access the database, would often time out and cause major problems.

Eventually, the Frame Relay was removed and the company put in place a dedicated connection to allow for full access at all times. The company finally determined that Frame Relay was not suitable for their needs.

—Jarret W. Buse, MCSE+I, MCT, CCNA, CNA, A+, Network+

Remember the characteristics and speeds of Frame Relay.

CERTIFICATION OBJECTIVE 7.06

Fiber Distributed Data Interface (FDDI)

The Fiber Distributed Data Interface (FDDI) topology is sometimes referred to as a fast redundant Token Ring network. FDDI is similar to a Token Ring network, but there are two rings and the media is fiber-optic cable operating at 100 Mbps. If copper cable is used, such as category 5 at 100 Mbps, the topology is termed Copper Distributed Data Interface (CDDI).

Two rings are used, the primary ring and the secondary ring. The primary ring is used at all times, and the secondary ring is only used if the primary ring fails. The token is passed on each ring in opposite directions; the reason for this will be apparent shortly.

FDDI is specifically for WAN use and not for LAN use. FDDI is used to connect multiple sites. Even if the individual LANs are using non-Token Ring topologies, they can still be connected by FDDI.

Each building or office will have a dual-attachment concentrator (DAC) that allows both rings to be connected to the DAC, or two single attachment concentrators (SAC). The SAC will connect to a single ring, allowing the SAC to be powered down without affecting the ring.

Now let's examine the FDDI redundancy and why the two rings operate in opposite directions. If any ring should break or if a SAC should be shut down as shown in Figure 7-6 part A, the network will still operate. Operation will continue because the broken section will be bypassed by using the secondary ring to allow the network to go back on itself and still be a continual ring. In Figure 7-6 part B, we can see that part of the ring is broken, so part of the secondary ring will be used to create a complete ring. The reason that the rings must operate in opposite directions is to continue the token from one ring to another and not cause the direction to change. This will allow for continuation if both rings are broken or if a DAC goes offline. If a DAC goes offline, then both rings are "broken."

FDDI redundancy

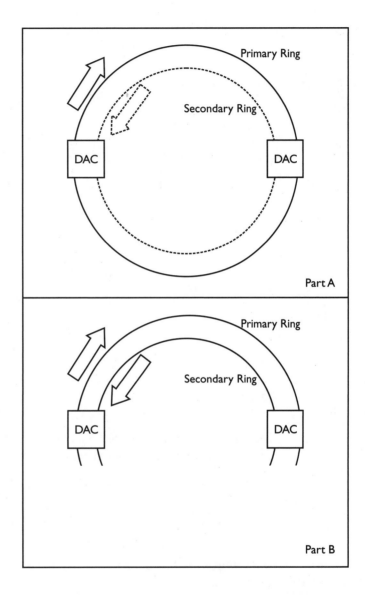

Each DAC will have two sets of connectors, one set for both rings coming in, and one set for both rings going out. Let us look at an example of three office buildings set up with FDDI, and how redundancy works to keep them online.

Figure 7-7 shows the three DACs or SACs, depending on which they will use. The three companies are all connected with dual rings.

FIGURE 7-7

Functional FDDI
example

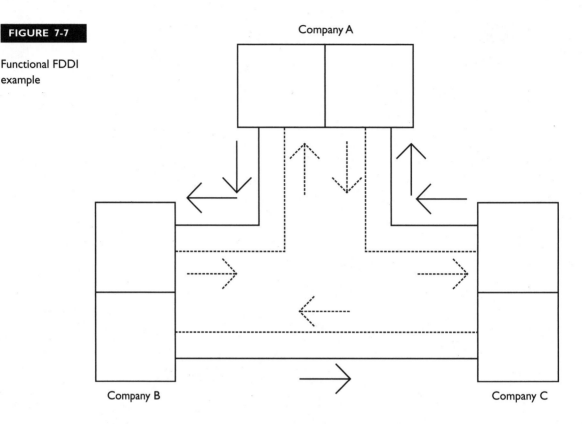

The grayed (inside) areas show the secondary ring, which is not in use. Now, let us assume that the fiber-optic cable is broken between Company B and Company C that was shown in Figure 7-5. Figure 7-8 shows what happens to the secondary ring when part of the primary fails, and how the ring is still complete, thereby allowing the WAN to continue operating.

Originally, the token was transferred from Company A to Company B, from Company B to Company C, and then from Company C to Company A. Once the token reaches Company A again, it will continue the process. After the break and the redundancy feature starts, the token will go from Company A to Company B, then to Company A again and on to Company C, and back to Company A. Once at Company A, the process will continue until the break is fixed, and the token will be passed as it originally was before the cable break. Multiple cable breaks can take down the entire network or even cause multiple WANs to be created.

FIGURE 7-8

FDDI redundancy
example

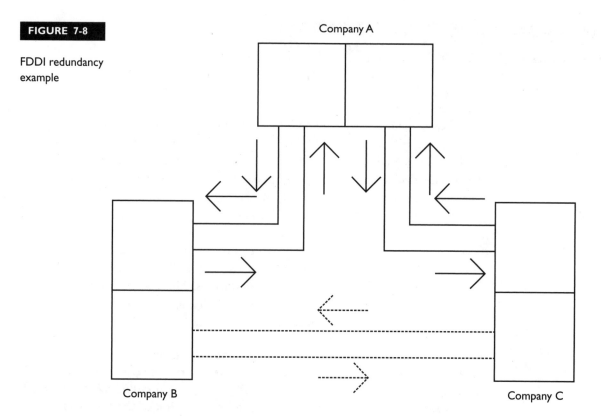

FIGURE 7-8

FDDI redundancy example

e x a m
ⓦ a t c h   *Remember the characteristics and speeds of FDDI and its capability to be redundant.*

o n t h e
ⓙ o b   *With FDDI, you need to remember that a company will have to have someone specialized in fiber-optic cable to install the cabling. The higher the quality of fiber cable, the longer the distances that can be achieved.*

CERTIFICATION OBJECTIVE 7.07

Tx/Ex-Carrier

The T-carrier and E-carrier are both digital media for which to transmit voice, data, or images. The T-carrier is used in the United States, Japan, and Australia, whereas the E-carrier is used in Europe, Mexico, and South America. The T1 is comprised of 24 channels that are made up of 64-Kbps bandwidth each, for a total of 1.544 Mbps. The 24 channels are referred to as digital signal level 0 (DS0), with the 24 DS0 channels making a digital signal level 1 (DS1). These lines can be multiplexed into faster links as shown in Table 7-3.

The E1-carrier is identical to the T-carrier, but differs in bandwidth. An E1-carrier is comprised of 30- to 64-Kbps data channels with 2 to 64 Kbps channels for signaling. The E1-carrier has a total bandwidth of 2.048 Mbps. The E3-carrier is comprised of 16 T1-carrier channels for a total bandwidth of 34.368 Mbps. The Ex-carriers are listed in Table 7-4 with their total bandwidth.

on the
Job

Most companies cannot afford a T-carrier line, so it is best for some companies to look into other means of connecting to the Internet or creating a WAN. If needed, a company can lease a partial T1 line, which is called a Fractional T1 at a lesser price. A Fractional T1 will also be a fraction of the bandwidth.

exam
Watch

Remember the characteristics and speeds of the T- and E-carriers, and where they are used.

TABLE 7-3	Tx-Carrier and Bandwidth

E-Carrier	Bandwidth
E1	2.048 Mbps
E2	8.448 Mbps
E3	34.368 Mbps
E4	139.264 Mbps
E5	565.148 Mbps

TABLE 7-4	Ex-Carrier and Bandwidth

T-Carrier	Bandwidth
T1	1.544 Mbps
T1C	3.152 Mbps
T2	6.312 Mbps
T3	44.736 Mbps
T4	274.176 Mbps

CSU/DSU

The Channel Service Unit/Data Service Unit (CSU/DSU) is device that allows a business to connect a high-speed data link from the telephone company to the business' router for access to and from the LAN or WAN. The high-speed connections are usually T1 or T3 connections as well as the European counterparts of the E1 and E3.

The CSU/DSU used will be specific to the line speed being connected to from the telephone company.

The CSU is the user end of the high-speed connection that will perform encoding and line conditioning as well as protect the LAN or WAN from electrical interference such as lightning. It can also provide statistics for the line use. There is also the capability of a loopback test to assure that the high-speed data connection is still intact.

The DSU portion is on the side of the telephone company and will support timing functions as well as data conversion.

EXERCISE 7-5

FDDI Network Exercise

In this exercise, a company is using FDDI to connect the main headquarters and four remote offices. Figure 7-9 shows the WAN and how it will be connected. You need to determine what will happen if a cable break occurs in certain areas.

Answer the following questions:

1. During the day, a connection fails between the Main Headquarters and Remote Office 4. How will the network operate after the break?

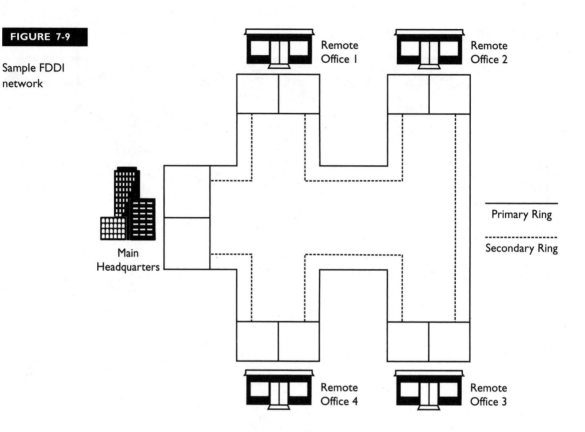

FIGURE 7-9

Sample FDDI
network

2. On another day, the connection is broken on the FDDI network between Remote Office 2 and Remote Office 3. How will the network operate after the break?

The answers are as follows:

1. Packets will be sent from the Main Headquarters in the following order:

Remote Office 1

Remote Office 2

Remote Office 3

Remote Office 4

Remote Office 3

Remote Office 2

Remote Office 1

Main Headquarters

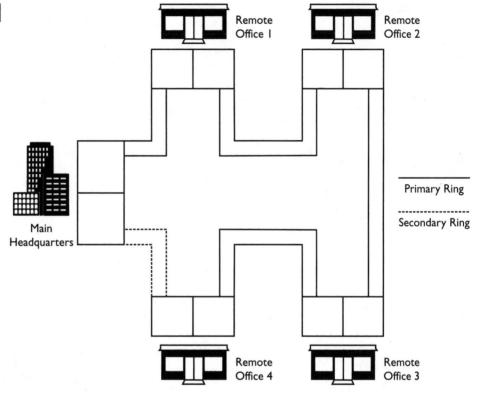

FIGURE 7-10

FDDI network
broken between
Main Headquarters
and Remote
Office 4

Figure 7-10 shows the network.

2. Packets will be sent from the Main Headquarters in the following order:

Remote Office 1

Remote Office 2

Remote Office 1

Main Headquarters

Remote Office 4

Remote Office 3

Remote Office 4

Main Headquarters

Figure 7-11 shows the network.

FIGURE 7-11

FDDI Network
broken between
Remote Offices 2
and 3

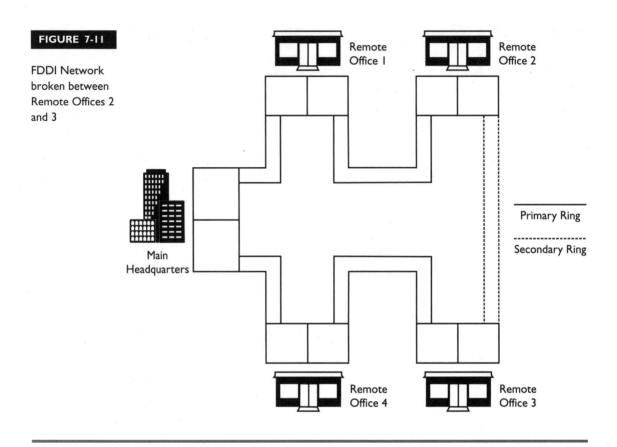

SCENARIO & SOLUTION

My company needs a WAN technology that will allow them to lease a specific bandwidth only and then pay only for that bandwidth and no more. What technology should they consider?	Frame Relay allows for the leasing of a specific amount of bandwidth.
A company wants to implement the same technology for both their LAN and WAN. What would you suggest they consider implementing?	ATM can be used as both a LAN and WAN technology. This allows a company to purchase all of the same networking devices for both the LAN and WAN.

SCENARIO & SOLUTION

Which technology would you suggest to a company that does not require a great deal of bandwidth as some technologies provide, but does provide redundancy?	FDDI provides only 100-Mbps bandwidth, but does provide redundancy.
A remote office in Europe wishes to connect to the Internet with a technology that will provide at least 500-Mbps bandwidth. What should they consider using?	An E5-carrier link will provide over 500 Mbps, and is a European standard.
A company on the West Coast needs to send data to the main headquarters on the East Coast. All of the companies have been purchased and taken over. They all employ different LAN technologies. What can be used to transmit this data to the main headquarters without changing the remote office LANs?	SONET will allow the different technologies to transmit data over the same link. For the headquarters to use the data, they will have to translate the data by using some type of gateway for conversion of the packet format into one usable by the network at the headquarters. This will be less expensive than converting the LAN networks.

CERTIFICATION SUMMARY

Networks have become such an important element in the business world that most businesses could not survive the loss of their network. Wide area networks (WANs) have evolved to allow for the connection of multiple local area networks (LANs) that are not within close proximity. WANs allow the multiple LANs to operate as a single large network for growing companies.

The Internet has brought about the evolution of technologies that allow WANs to exist. The Internet itself is a WAN, and uses the same technology as a WAN used by a company.

The different WAN technologies include Asynchronous Transfer Mode (ATM), which can also be used to create a LAN. ATM provides bandwidth on demand for users using an optical network. ATM can also use a copper network using category 3 or higher UTP cable. ATM also provides parallel transmissions so data can flow in both directions at once.

Another WAN technology is SONET/SDH, or even Optical Carrier (OC) levels. These use fiber-optic cables to transfer data from different mediums. Data streams can be taken from different mediums and combined into one data stream, allowing for transmission speeds from 51.84 Mbps to 9953.28 Mbps. The non-SONET media is connected to a physical terminating equipment (PTE) device, which converts the electrical signals into optical signals. The optical signal is sent to the line terminating equipment (LTE), which transmits the signal over different sections of fiber-optic cable. The many different sections of fiber-optic cable making up the SONET network are terminated by section terminating equipment (STE). The OC levels are standards to specify bandwidth over fiber-optic cable.

Another WAN technology is Frame Relay. Frame Relay is a leased-line situation where a company can share the medium and the cost with other companies. The amount of bandwidth available to a company will be determined by the amount of bandwidth for which they pay. Frame Relay networks can start dropping packets if the network is too congested.

FDDI is another WAN technology that is based on the Token Ring topology. It operates at 100 Mbps over fiber optic or category 5 cables. Using category 5 cables is known as a Copper Distributed Data Interface (CDDI). FDDI is comprised of two rings operating in different directions. The second ring is only used if the first ring fails.

A popular transmission method is the T-carriers or E-carriers. Each carrier is used in different countries with different bandwidths. The T- and E-carriers are completely digital and operate at speeds as high as 565.148 Mbps.

✓ TWO-MINUTE DRILL

Packet Switching versus Circuit Switching

- ❑ Packet switching is used with standard data networks. Circuit switching is used by telephone-based networks.
- ❑ Packet switching is faster than circuit switching.
- ❑ Circuit switching is meant more for real-time transfers such as voice communication.
- ❑ Packet-switching networks might not deliver packets in order they were sent.

Asynchronous Transfer Mode

- ❑ ATM uses broadband media.
- ❑ ATM allows for parallel transmissions between nodes.
- ❑ Data packets are referred to as cells.

Synchronous Optical NETwork/Synchronous Digital Hierarchy

- ❑ Used to unify unlike transmissions into one transmission data stream.
- ❑ Uses fiber-optic cable for transmissions.
- ❑ SDH is the international standard for SONET.
- ❑ Bandwidth ranges from 51.84 Mbps to 9953.28 Mbps.
- ❑ Data can be scrambled for user privacy.

Optical Carrier Level-x

- ❑ OC is used to specify bandwidth standards over fiber-optic media.
- ❑ The OC levels map to the same SONET and SDH levels.

Frame Relay

- ❑ Frame Relay is independent of all protocols used on it.
- ❑ Error correction is monitored by protocols.

❑ Data is transmitted at 2 Mbps.

❑ Frame Relay can drop packets if the network becomes congested.

Fiber Distributed Data Interface

❑ FDDI is based on the Token Ring topology.

❑ There are two rings operating in opposite directions.

❑ FDDI is for WAN, not LAN use.

❑ Two rings allow for redundancy.

Tx/Ex-Carrier

❑ Widely used and very popular.

❑ Used as a backbone by the telephone company.

❑ Very expensive.

SELF TEST

The following Self Test questions will help you measure your understanding of the material presented in this chapter. Read all the choices carefully, as there may be more than one correct answer. Choose all correct answers for each question.

Packet Switching versus Circuit Switching

1. Which switching technology is used by the telephone company?

   A. Packet

   B. Circuit

   C. WAN

   D. Hub

2. Which switching method will allow for data transmissions even when part of the network fails?

   A. Packet

   B. Circuit

   C. WAN

   D. Hub

Asynchronous Transfer Mode

3. In which area networking environments is ATM usable?

   A. Dial-up

   B. Workgroup

   C. WAN

   D. LAN

4. How are the signals sent on an ATM network?

   A. Digitally

   B. Infra-red

   C. Analog

   D. Sonar

Synchronous Optical NETwork/Synchronous Digital Hierarchy

5. How many streams does the SONET network transfer?

    A. 1

    B. 2

    C. 3

    D. 4 or more

6. Which of the following is in the form of electrical pulses on a SONET network?

    A. STM

    B. STS

    C. PTE

    D. LTE

7. What can be used in a SONET network to allow user's data to remain private?

    A. Multiplexer

    B. PTE

    C. LTE

    D. Scrambler

8. What is the speed of one SONET level?

    A. 32.24 Mbps

    B. 51.84 Mbps

    C. 64.08 Mbps

    D. 155.52 Mbps

Optical Carrier Level-X

9. What levels are the OC levels matched to?

    A. ATM

    B. SDH

    C. SONET

    D. T1

10. What is the highest OC level?

    A. 32

    B. 64

    C. 128

    D. 192

Frame Relay

11. How is error checking managed on a Frame Relay network?

    A. Network devices

    B. User at the sending PC

    C. User at the receiving PC

    D. By the protocol used

12. If the network is congested and the destination device requests that the source device slow its transmission, what will occur?

    A. The source will stop responding for 30 seconds, and then continue transmitting.

    B. The source will find a different route to send the data.

    C. The destination will drop all packets for 30 seconds.

    D. Possibly nothing.

13. What happens if a company uses more bandwidth than it has paid for?

    A. Its packets will be dropped no matter the state of the network.

    B. Its packets will be delivered even if the network is busy.

    C. Its packets will be delivered if the bandwidth is available.

    D. Its packets will be delivered no matter the state of the network.

Fiber Distributed Data Interface

14. If the primary ring fails, what is used for redundancy?

    A. The entire secondary ring.

    B. A portion of the primary ring that has not failed, and a part of the secondary ring that is equal to the primary ring that failed.

    C. A portion of the primary ring that has not failed, and a part of the secondary ring that is equal to the primary ring that has not failed.

    D. A portion of the primary ring that failed, and a part of the secondary ring that is equal to the primary ring that has failed.

15. How does the token pass on the rings when functioning normally?

    A. From one ring to the other.

    B. Randomly.

    C. Opposite directions.

    D. Same direction.

16. At what speed does FDDI operate?

    A. 10 Mbps

    B. 100 Mbps

    C. 1 Gbps

    D. 2 Gbps

Tx/Ex-Carrier

17. In what countries do E-carriers operate? (Choose all that apply.)

    A. Japan

    B. Europe

    C. Mexico

    D. South America

18. How many channels make up a T1?

    A. 6

    B. 12

    C. 24

    D. 48

LAB QUESTION

A company has asked you to suggest the connections they should use to connect their remote offices together. They have four offices in Los Angeles, with one acting as a type of headquarters, and want to connect them all with some type of redundant capability so the WAN does not go down. They also have four offices and the main headquarters in New York City, and want them connected by redundant means. They then want to be able to connect the Los Angeles and New York offices into one WAN using the Internet.

The company has just opened a new office in Europe to determine how business will fare there. They want to have this office also connected to the U.S. WAN. Executives have decided that all connections need be at least 100 Mbps or more, but no less than 100 Mbps. How can this be done?

SELF TEST ANSWERS

Packet Switching versus Circuit Switching

I. ☑ **B.** Circuit switching is used by the telephone companies for the network of telephone users.

☒ **A, C,** and **D** are incorrect. Packet switching is used by most data networks. WANs and hubs are not switching types of WAN technology.

2. ☑ **A.** With a packet-switching network, the failed portion will be routed around the point of failure to continue to deliver packets.

☒ **B, C,** and **D** are incorrect. In a circuit-switched network, the connection will be terminated. For example, if you are speaking with someone on the telephone and a telephone line breaks, the call is terminated and must be made again. WANs and hubs are not switching types of WAN technology.

Asynchronous Transfer Mode

3. ☑ **C and D.** ATM technology can be used to create LANs and connect them to a WAN.

☒ **A and B** are incorrect. Dial-up is a type of connection made from one PC to another, or even possibly a LAN to a LAN. Workgroup is a group of 10 or fewer PCs that are connected to share resources with no centralized administration point.

4. ☑ **C.** ATM is analog and sends the data as frequencies.

☒ **A, B,** and **D** are incorrect. Digital signals are off or on with no variance. Infra-red allows for point-to-point connectivity by line of sight using infra-red lights. Sonar is used to track objects underwater and has no bearing on networking.

Synchronous Optical NETwork/Synchronous Digital Hierarchy

5. ☑ **A.** The SONET network will multiplex multiple streams into one stream and transmit this single stream over the SONET network. Multiple streams can be combined to form the single SONET data stream.

☒ **B, C,** and **D** are incorrect amounts.

6. ☑ **B.** The synchronous transport signal (STS) is in the form of electrical pulses.

☒ **A, C,** and **D** are incorrect. The electrical pulses are converted by the PTE into one stream, and sent to the LTE as light pulses on fiber-optic cable. STM is used to term the different levels of SDH.

7. ☑ **D.** The scrambler is used to randomize the stream pattern to allow the data to be encrypted. This requires a descrambler on the other end of the connection to replace the data into a usable form.
☒ **A, B,** and **C** are incorrect. The multiplexer is used to generate one data stream from many data streams. The electrical pulses are converted by the PTE into one stream, and sent to the LTE as light pulses on fiber-optic cable.

8. ☑ **B.** One SONET Level is 51.84 Mbps. If more are added, the value is multiplied by the number of levels.
☒ **A, C,** and **D** are incorrect speeds.

Optical Carrier Level-X

9. ☑ **B** and **C.** The OC levels are standards for transmitting over fiber optic. The levels match to those of SONET and SDH, which require fiber optic.
☒ **A** and **D** are incorrect. ATM and T1 do not have the same standards.

10. ☑ **D.** 192 is the highest level currently set for OC.
☒ **A, B,** and **C** are not the highest OC levels.

Frame Relay

11. ☑ **D.** Frame Relay depends on the protocols used to manage error checking.
☒ **A, B,** and **C** are incorrect because Frame Relay depends on the protocols used to manage error checking.

12. ☑ **D.** Just because a device is requested to slow transmissions does not mean the device will perform the action.
☒ **A, B,** and **C** are incorrect and are not valid choices.

13. ☑ **C.** The packets will be delivered if the bandwidth is available; if it is not, they will be dropped.
☒ **A, B,** and **D** are incorrect. The state of the network must be taken into account.

Fiber Distributed Data Interface

14. ☑ C. The part that is used for redundancy is the portion of the primary ring that has not failed, and the same part of the secondary ring that has not failed.
☒ A, B, and D are incorrect. No part of the failed portion of the primary ring can be used, and neither can the same portion of the secondary ring.

15. ☑ C. The token is circulated in opposite directions. This helps to keep the flow of the token the same on both the rings even after a failure.
☒ A, B, and D are incorrect. The token only passes from one ring to the other when a failure has occurred. The token is not randomly moved, nor does the token move in the same direction on both rings.

16. ☑ B. FDDI operates at 100 Mbps, no matter if it is fiber or copper cabling.
☒ A, C, and D are incorrect speeds.

Tx/Ex-Carrier

17. ☑ B, C, and D. E-carriers are found in Europe, Mexico, and South America.
☒ A is incorrect. T-carriers are found in the United States, Japan, and Australia.

18. ☑ C. There are 24 channels that are 64 Kbps each to make one T1 for a total of 1.544 Mbps.
☒ A, B, and D are incorrect channels amounts.

LAB ANSWER

The offices in Los Angeles and New York City need to be connected by FDDI. This will allow for the redundancy needed as well as the speed of 100 Mbps.

The headquarters in New York City and the acting headquarters in Los Angeles will need a connection to the Internet to allow for a virtual private network (VPN) between the two. To allow for the speed of 100Mbps or greater, they will need a T4-carrier at both locations. Using a T4-carrier will give bandwidth just over 274 Mbps.

The European office will require a connection to the Internet of at least 100 Mbps. However, the European standard is not the T-carrier but the E-carrier, so they will require an E4-carrier connection to attain a bandwidth around 139 Mbps. This will allow them to create a VPN over the Internet to the New York main headquarters.

This will create one large WAN for all of the companies to be able to share information securely.

8

Network Security

CERTIFICATION OBJECTIVES

8.01	Selecting a Security Model— User-Level and Share-Level
8.02	Password Practices and Procedures
8.03	Data Encryption and Protecting Network Data
8.04	Uses of a Firewall
✓	Two-Minute Drill
Q&A	Self Test

I n today's world of ever-changing technology, information has become an essential asset for any corporation. As computers have become the standard for storing and manipulating this information, the need has arisen to share it with the appropriate parties. Networks have become commonplace to facilitate this need. The Internet has grown tremendously as more people and corporations harness the amount of information that this system provides. As a downside, if someone were able to obtain or modify this information, depending upon the content, it could be disastrous. Organizations such as the New York Stock Exchange or the United States Department of Defense (DoD) are interconnected with other networks to facilitate today's growing needs. If the information stored within these systems became accessible to the public, who knows what might happen. For example, the economy could be drastically altered if the New York Stock Exchange became infiltrated. Even though the DoD only has unclassified systems accessible via the Internet, if certain sensitive unclassified documents were accidentally made available to the wrong people, it could be detrimental to the nation.

The need for security in today's networks has become a requirement for any size organization. Many different products, processes, and policies can be used to maintain the information and its validity. Security is more of a mind set or way of thinking. It is important to understand that many things can be done to maintain a secure environment, but being 100 percent secure is not possible. The best any organization can do is to understand the security threats that exist and how to best control and react to them. In this chapter, you will learn what you can do to help prevent security breaches.

When designing a network, be sure to take into consideration the available options and the security impacts of each. When securing information, make sure to understand the default permissions created and how to modify those in the most secure manner. Understand the utilities available and create processes and procedures around these for users to follow. Be sure to enforce these standards, or else the tools in place provide no value. Additionally, understand what can be done to protect the individual data and how it is stored. Lastly, protect the network itself from outside intrusion. Connecting to the Internet is quickly becoming a necessity for companies today. Make sure that access from across this huge global network is monitored and locked down.

CERTIFICATION OBJECTIVE 8.01

Selecting a Security Model—User-Level and Share-Level

When you begin thinking about the security of your organization, you must first look at the security models you have in place or that you will use in the future. A security model is a generic term that describes methodologies used to secure a system. These can be anything from file versus share security or the underlying subsystem used by an operating system. Each model adds to the overall security architecture. Defining the model that you will use and deciding how it will be incorporated is important in any organization.

To understand the security mechanisms available for Windows NT and other operating systems, you must initially understand the security available. First, you will learn about security subsystems and file and directory permissions. Then you will learn about the workgroup and domain model, and finally, we will discuss the share-level security model available in other operating systems.

Windows NT Security Subsystem

It is important to understand the underlying security subsystem used by Windows NT. This subsystem ties into every other form of security available within the operating system. The Department of Defense class C2 security rating was a major influence in the security design that Microsoft put forth. They wanted Windows NT to be able to achieve this certification, and though Windows NT 3.5 with U.S. Service Pack 3 did finally meet the certification requirements, you could not network the server or have access to a floppy drive.

on the *job*

Some companies are using Windows 2000 systems instead of Windows NT. The security features implemented in Windows NT are still used in Windows 2000, but are contained in Windows 2000 Active Directory. You will need to remember that Active Directory is similar to the Windows NT Security Accounts Management database except that it is hierarchical and is distributed to all domain controller servers for both read and write ability.

There are four parts to the security subsystem in Windows NT, each playing an integral part in the security functions provided. Table 8-1 lists the security subsystems and gives a brief description.

The logon process uses each one of these four components. The following is the logon process for a domain user:

- Press CTRL-ALT-DEL. The username and password dialog is displayed.

- Enter a valid domain user ID and password and press ENTER.

- The LSA makes a call to an authentication package. This requires that a secure RPC connection be established with a domain controller's NETLOGON service from the client.

- The authentication package then compares the user ID and password to the domain SAM database. The process of comparing these is known as NT Challenge and Response.

- Once complete, the NETLOGON service returns the user's Security Identifier (SID) and the global SID obtained from the SAM. NETLOGON services on the client returns the user SID and global SID to the LSA.

- The local LSA accesses the local SAM to generate a local SID. All three SIDs are then used to generate an "access token."

- The access token is assigned and the explorer interface is started. The access token is used for any process started by this user.

TABLE 8-1 The Four Components that Make Up the Windows NT Security Subsystem

Security Subsystem Component	Description
Local Security Authority (LSA)	Handles local security policies and user authentication and generates audit log messages.
Security Accounts Manager (SAM)	Handles authentication services for LSA. Database of user, group, and machine accounts.
Security Reference Monitor	Verifies that a user has the appropriate permissions to access an object. It also enforces the audit generation policy provided by the LSA.
Logon Processes	User interface provided for interactive logon. Also provides an interface for administrative tools.

Access Tokens

When the Security Accounts Manager validates a user, an access token is created. This token is used in the future for all access validations that occur when a user tries to open a resource, and is utilized until the user logs out, whereby it is permanently destroyed. The token maintains all the information required for resource validation, and includes the following information:

- User Security Identifier (SID)
- Primary Group Security Identifier
- Group Security Identifier
- Access Rights

Security Descriptors and Access Control Lists

The security model is based upon objects. Every named object has security-related attributes associated with it that can be modified. The term used to describe these attributes is a *security descriptor,* which includes the Access Control List, or ACL, and the information about the object. The ACL is a list that provides the users and/or groups allowed to access the object as well as the level of permissions applied. Multiple groups or users can be associated to an object with the ACL. For example, a directory may be set up to allow the sales team read-only access while the marketing group may have read-write access. A user, John Doe, could be a member of both groups. Rules are set up within Windows NT to compare these and apply the appropriate set of permissions.

Security Descriptors are broken down into several components: the System Access Control List (SACL), the Discretionary Access Control list (DACL), an owner, and a primary group. Each term is listed in Table 8-2 with a brief description.

TABLE 8-2   Four Attributes for the Security Descriptor

Security Descriptor	Description
System Access Control List (SACL)	Controls the security auditing for the Windows NT object.
Discretionary Access-Control List (DACL)	Determines which users and groups have access to this object.
Owner	Maintains a record of the user who owns the resource.
Primary Group	Each user must be a member of a primary group. This is required for Macintosh support as well as the POSIX subsystem and is ignored by Windows NT.

Access Control Entries   Every access control list is broken down into access control entries, or ACEs. ACEs specify the access or auditing permissions assigned for a specific user or group. Three types of ACEs exist: one for system security and two for discretionary access control. The system access control is used to maintain and generate the security audit log messages that appear. This ACE is called "SystemAudit." The discretionary ACEs are known as "AccessAllowed" and "AccessDenied." These are used to specifically deny or grant access for a specific user or group.

User-Level Security

One method of security available for use is file and directory level permissions. These permissions are based upon user or group accounts. Effectively combining these two types of permissions enables you to delineate what access a particular user will have when working in Windows NT. You must understand the permissions available and how to apply them.

File and directory permissions are available on NTFS-formatted partitions only. Other file systems available with Windows NT, such as FAT, do not provide a mechanism to support permissions. In FAT file systems, only file attributes are available and any user can modify these.

In addition to the predefined permissions, you can custom specify certain access to a file or directory. Using individual permissions enables you to customize the files and directories to meet your security requirements. Predefined permissions use a combination of individual permissions to provide standard templates. Table 8-3 lists the predefined permissions available. This includes the individual permissions given by default. On a directory there will be two sets of parentheses. The first set is applied to any new file placed in this directory and the second set is applied to any new subdirectory created in this directory. It is important to note that both sets of parentheses apply for directories, but only the first set applies for file permissions. You will also notice that an additional category exists for directory permissions, labeled "Not Specified." By having this permission setup, users and groups do not have access to those files or directories unless it is applied through something else—for example, a group membership. A good example is the List permission, which enables users to list the contents. Unfortunately, they will not be able to see new files added. Table 8-4 lists the individual permissions available and their uses, while Figure 8-1 shows an example of a security configuration for the D:\Data directory.

| TABLE 8-3 | File and Directory Permissions Available |

Access Permission	Description
No Access(None)(None)	Directory and File permission. This provides a user with no access at all.
List(RX)(Not Specified)	Directory permission. Enables users to display contents of a directory along with permissions and attributes. This can include listing subdirectories if this permission is applied to all subdirectories as well.
Read(RX)(RX)	Directory and File permissions. Enables a user to open and read files and directories, and to run executable files. This also includes permissions granted by List.
Add(WX)(Not Specified)	Directory permission. Enables a user to add files to a directory and to create folders—they cannot, however, view the contents of the folders.
Add & Read(RWX)(RX)	Directory permission. Enables users to open and add files to a directory. This also includes displaying directory contents and information and executing files.
Change(RWXD)(RWXD)	Directory and File permission. Enables users to open, modify, and delete directories and files. This also includes displaying contents, navigating subdirectories, and executing and viewing files.
Full Control(All)(All)	Directory and File permission. Grants full rights to a file or directory. This gives a user all the permissions that are available by using or combining the previous items, as well as the right of taking ownership of the directory or file.
Special File Access	File permission. This can be used to customize file permissions. By using this access, you are creating individual permissions rather than using the predefined permissions.
Special Directory Access	Directory permission. This can be used to customize the directory permissions. By using this access, you are creating individual permissions rather than using the predefined permissions.

exam
ⓦatch   *Make sure you understand the different parentheses and what each set signifies as well as what they can contain and the meanings for each. (Shown in Table 8-4.)*

Users and Groups

Windows NT uses user and group objects, more commonly known as accounts, to delineate access permissions. Two types of user accounts exist: global accounts that are used throughout a domain, and local accounts that are used on a single Windows NT

TABLE 8-4 Individual Permissions and Their Abbreviations

Individual Permission Abbreviation	Description
(R)	Read
(W)	Write
(X)	Execute
(D)	Delete
(P)	Change Permissions
(O)	Take Ownership

computer. During installation of a Windows NT system or domain, several group objects and two user objects are created by default. Some domain implementations can contain thousands of groups and tens of thousands of user IDs. By properly designing a strategy, you can use these to provide effective security levels without getting too complex. Windows NT creates two user objects, by default, for a server, workstation, or domain: Administrator and Guest. The Administrator account is given full control access to the entire system or domain. This account acts as the equivalent of "root" on a Unix system. The Guest account is created with no password. This account is granted limited access permissions and is disabled by default. Most organizations leave this account disabled so users cannot gain access to any computers.

FIGURE 8-1

Permissions can be applied to files or directories

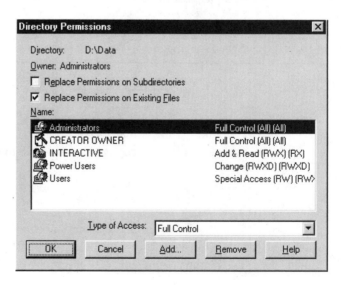

Windows NT creates several groups by default. Each group is used to provide access for specific types of users. Two types of groups exist: local groups and global groups. Global groups are used only in domain environments, but local groups can be used in domain, server, or workstation environments. Each group provides a method for delineating common groups of tasks to users. For example, an individual may be responsible for performing backups for a server. You can make this user a member of the Backup Operator group to give him permissions to perform this task. Table 8-5 lists the available groups and their primary functions and permissions.

TABLE 8-5   Default User and Groups Created During Installation of a Windows NT

NT Group	Description	Default Contents
Administrators	Local group found on servers, workstations, and domains. Provides full access to entire Windows NT computer or domain.	Domain Administrators (global group) and Administrator (user account)
Account Operators	Local group found in domains. This group is used to manage users and groups within a domain. It can only modify users or groups that have lesser security permissions.	None
Backup Operators	Local group found on servers, workstations, and domains. This provides privileges to perform functions of a backup operator, such as log on locally, shut down system, and back up and restore files.	None
Domain Admins	Global group found in domains. This group is set up in the Administrators local group on all member servers and workstations in a domain.	Administrator (user account)
Domain Guests	Global group found in domains. Provides guest privileges to a domain.	Guest (user account)
Domain Users	Global group found in domains. This provides access for a normal user.	Administrator (user account) and all new users created by default
Guests	Local group found on servers, workstations, and domains. This is used to provide limited guest access.	Domain Guests (in domains)
Print Operators	Local group found in domains. This privilege provides the capability to control printer resources, log on locally, and shut down the server.	None

TABLE 8-5	Default User and Groups Created During Installation of a Windows NT *(continued)*	
Power Users	Local group found on workstations and servers. This group provides additional access to install applications, manage printers and local users, and modify file permissions.	None
Replicator	Local group found on servers, workstations, and domains. These members can manage replication services for files and directories.	None
Server Operators	Local group found in domains. This privilege provides the capability to shut down the system, control shared resources, back up and restore files, and log on locally.	None
Users	Local group found on servers, workstations, and domains. On domains, the Domain Users global group is a member of the domain local Users group. This is set up for normal users.	Domain Users (in domains)

exam
ⓦatch

Make sure you know what each of the built-in groups have permissions to perform.

Computer or Domain Groups are created based upon whether they reside on a server or workstation or on a domain controller. A domain controller group list includes Administrators, Account Operators, Backup Operators, Guests, Print Operators, Replicators, Server Operators, and Users. A server or workstation group list includes Administrators, Backup Operators, Guests, Power Users, Replicators, and Users. By using a combination of global groups within a domain and local groups on computers, you can create a good strategy that enables access permissions to flow down to the servers or workstations in a domain. Figure 8-2 shows the User Manager screen which displays the standard users and groups created for a member server.

When you are adding users to multiple groups, you may have groups set up for different permission levels to a resource. Although Windows NT handles the rules for how these permissions are applied, they vary depending upon the type of resource. A few rules need to be noted:

■ File permissions override directory permissions.

■ Permissions are cumulative; however, the No Access permission will always override the others that are set.

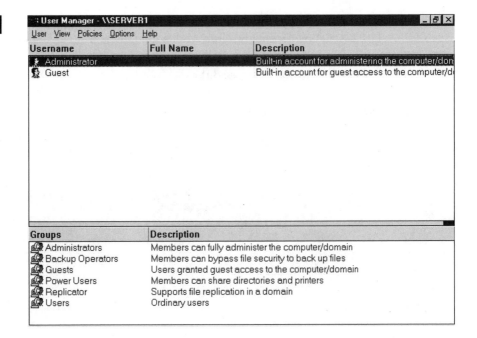

The User Manager screen shows the local users and groups available by default for a Windows NT member server

■ When creating files, by default they inherit the permissions granted to the directory.

■ When creating a file, that user is set as the owner. The owner always has control over permissions for a file. Administrators always have the capability to take ownership of any files.

Windows 2000 includes similar groups to Windows NT, but also has an additional group: universal groups. The Windows NT local and global accounts are now called Domain Local and Domain Global. Domain Local Groups are created in the domain in which they are used and are employed to assign permissions to the group. The Domain Local Group can contain any user account from any domain, global groups from any domain, universal groups from any domain, and other Domain Local Groups from the same domain. Domain Global Groups are created within the domain in which user accounts reside to group the users requiring the same permissions. The global group can contain user accounts from the same domain, Global Groups from the same domain.

Universal groups are used only when there are no Windows NT Domain Controllers left in the domain and you have manually changed to native mode. The nice thing about universal groups is that you can create a universal group just as you would a Domain Global Group, but instead of adding users from only a single domain, you can add users from all domains and use it anywhere in any domain.

Now that we have discussed the different permissions available in Windows NT, it's time for an exercise. Exercise 8-1 explains how to set up a share and to apply user-level security to it. Figure 8-3 shows an example of the share creation process.

SCENARIO & SOLUTION

I need to give the data center operators rights to monitor and modify backup jobs but not permit them to perform domain or server administration.	Make them members of the Backup Operators group.
I want a group to have rights to add computer accounts to the domain, but I do not want them to have access to shut down any NT system.	You have two choices: give a global group on the domain the advanced right "Add workstations to Domain," or make them a member of the Server Operators group and remove the "Shutdown system" advanced right from this group.
I need to give the HR group, list, read, and delete access to a directory.	These permissions are not available in a standard permission. You will have to give the directory special directory permissions to reach this level of granularity. This uses individual permissions rather than those predefined.
Users are connecting to a share and their NTFS permissions are set to Everyone Full Control. They still cannot delete files.	Check the share security. If the share permissions are set up for read-only access, they will be unable to delete any files found regardless of the file and directory permissions. This is because the share permission is more restrictive and overrides the NTFS permissions.
I changed the Everyone group to No Access and I have Full Control as an administrator. I get an "access denied" error message whenever I try to access that directory.	If you are a member of the Everyone group, the No Access permission overrides all others.

FIGURE 8-3

Use the Data
Properties dialog
box when
creating a share
to enable remote
access

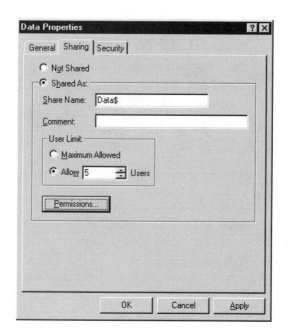

EXERCISE 8-1

CertCam 8-1

Creating a New Share Using User-Level Security

1. Log on to the computer with a user ID that has Administrator group membership.

2. Open Windows Explorer by selecting Start | Programs | Windows NT Explorer.

3. Create a new directory on your local hard drive called "Data." Highlight the drive and select File | New | Folder. Type **Data** as the name and press ENTER.

4. Highlight the Data folder and select File | Sharing. The Data Properties dialog box appears, as was shown in Figure 8-3. By default, the option is set to Not Shared.

5. Select the Shared As option and type **Data$** in the Share Name text box. (Appending the $ symbol hides the share from the browse listing.)

6. In the User Limit box, select the Allow option and enter 5 for the number of users. (The default is 10.)

7. Click the Permissions button to modify the permissions for this share. By default, Everyone has Full Control. Change Everyone to Read and add Administrators as Full Control.

8. When complete, click OK to set the permissions and then click OK to create the share.

Several shares are created by default whenever a Windows NT workstation or server is installed. These include Admin$ for the <systemroot>, Repl$ for directory replication, and <drive>$ for every logical drive, such as C$ and D$. The $ sign appended to these make the shares hidden. When creating a new share, this can be used to keep the share from appearing in the browser list of available resources. Effectively combining share permissions with NTFS permissions can provide a secure computing environment. User-level security is much more secure than the share-level security we will discuss in the next section.

Share-Level Security

It is important to not become confused between share permissions (which we just discussed) and share-level security since they are two totally different items. Share-level security is available on client operating systems such as Windows 95 and Windows 98 as shown in Figure 8-4.

Access to a resource in share-level security is determined by a password assigned to the resource and is not based on a user account or group membership. Any user that knows the share password can utilize the resource. Share-level security is easy to implement and maintain on small peer-to-peer networks, however, users must remember the password for each resource that is shared (unless password caching is in use). Access is very hard to control since anyone that knows the password can gain access. This is one reason user-level access is much more secure than share-level access.

Domains and Workgroups

In addition to its underlying security model, Windows NT provides an additional type of security model. If you have ever installed Windows NT with networking,

FIGURE 8-4

The Access
Control tab from
Windows 98

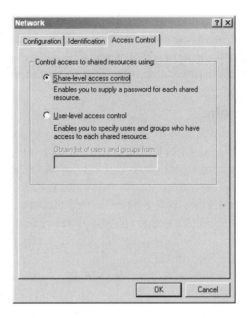

you noticed it always requires you specify a workgroup or domain to make it a member of. Each type of implementation has its advantages. You need to understand the fundamental differences between each, and the security architecture defined.

Workgroups

A workgroup can be defined as an organizational unit, or a way to organize a group of computers. Workgroups are primarily used in very small environments where users need to share information but do not have an NT server. A good example of this is a small office with a collection of Windows 98 computers that need to share information. Each computer in a workgroup maintains its own account information and these accounts are not shared or accessible elsewhere on the network. To access a remote resource on a Windows 98 computer, a share is created with a generic password. By entering this password, you have whatever permissions have been defined for everyone. This method does not enable you to audit to determine which users are accessing which resources. Any user with the one password has access to the resource. In addition, these installations can be dangerous because the authentication methods used are less secure than other environments.

on the **Job**

Home networks are growing in popularity as PC and network devices become more inexpensive. Home networks are mostly workgroups allowing for shared access to network devices and files such as disks, CD-ROMs, and printers. They also allow Internet connections to be shared by multiple people simultaneously.

Domains

A domain is used to share common user accounts and policies. It consists of one or more Windows NT servers acting as domain controllers. Each domain is composed of one primary domain controller and any number of backup domain controllers. The primary domain controller maintains the centralized accounts database and provides authentication services. The backup domain controllers provide authentication services and redundancy for the primary. In addition, member servers can be used to provide services such as file and print or application support while using this centralized database for authentication. Any Windows NT computer maintains a local SAM database and can use the domain accounts as well. The domain model also provides redundancy. The user account database is synchronized, and other functions, such as the logon scripts, can be replicated to additional Windows NT computers.

You can also link multiple domains to create an enterprise environment. This concept is known as a "trust relationship." From these trusts, different domain models can be created to fit almost any environment. Because a single user account can be utilized to access any resource, auditing can be employed to monitor what every user is doing; however, file and directory permission can only be audited on NTFS partitions. This additional level of security is used to meet the industry standards that the Windows NT security architecture was based upon.

exam
Watch

Be aware of the differences in security for the domain and workgroup models.

Windows 2000 manages domains differently than Windows NT. With Windows 2000, there is no primary or backup domain controllers. Windows 2000 uses Active Directory in domain mode, which is replicated to all domain controllers and is readable and writeable on all domain controllers. With Windows NT, the SAM database is readable and writeable on the primary domain controller only and readable on the backup domain controllers only.

Any change made to AD on a Windows 2000 DC is replicated to all other DCs. These critical changes consist of things such as password changes, user accounts being disabled or deleted, and other changes that can affect security. All other non-critical items are replicated by default every 5 minutes to all additional domain controllers.

Securing the Registry

You must secure the registry for any Windows NT computer. The registry contains the control parameters for the entire operating system. If this information were accessible to a malicious user, the results could be disastrous. Because of the risk involved in accessing the registry, Microsoft does not even list the utilities provided to do this with the rest of the administrative tools. These utilities, REGEDIT.EXE and REGEDT32.EXE, are located in the <systemroot>\system32 directory. Although both are included, only REGEDT32 contains the capability to modify the appropriate ACLs for the registry to make it secure.

There are two parts to securing the registry. First, the files that the registry information is stored in are located in <systemroot>\system32\config. This directory must have only the permissions required to enable the system to perform its job. If the partition that this directory is located on was created as NTFS, this is done by default. In addition, if you create an emergency repair disk (ERD) with the –S option, the files are updated and placed in the <systemroot>\repair directory. Although tampering with these files will not impact the registry, it will mess with the ERD process. This directory also contains the information that an intruder can use to compromise your system. For example, a copy of the SAM database is stored here that could be used to back out of a problem.

The second part to securing the registry includes applying permission directly to particular keys. The Registry Editor has the built-in functionality to connect to a remote computer and enable modification of certain keys. If these keys are not secured, you may find someone hacking away at your registry without you knowing. Be sure to test your security configuration carefully when modifying the registry because it can have some very adverse effects.

CERTIFICATION OBJECTIVE 8.02

Password Practices and Procedures

The most basic security mechanism is the password. We use passwords every day to access automated teller machines, to place calling card calls, and to access voice-mail systems. Because it is such a basic concept, many implementations use this method to provide a form of security for accessing systems or resources. This widespread use is a concern, because passwords are noted as one of the poorest forms of protection available. According to the Computer Emergency Response Team (CERT), more security breaches result from poorly used passwords than from all other methods combined.

A password is a series of characters that can be used to lock down anything from an operating system to an individual file or directory. The purpose of this technique is to ensure that the user trying to access this resource is authorized to do so. If the user does not know the password, he is not allowed to access the resource. However, if a super-user account is compromised, then the other passwords stored in the same database can be at risk. In addition, someone can use one system as a starting point to reach other systems on the same network.

Password Policies

Setting up password authentication is a good start; however, it will be useless against a knowledgeable intruder without solid policies and processes defined. Each environment will be different and should be studied carefully to determine what policies would work best in that organization. Some organizations, such as the Department of Defense, may require a very stringent security setup, while others may require very little security. Most network operating systems provide these policies as a part of their implementation. For example, Windows NT enables you to specify required security settings, such as the number of characters required for a password, the number of tries before an account is locked out, and the maximum password age.

RFC 1244 is a security guidelines handbook and can be a good start as well as offer some basic guidelines to use when implementing password policies. This document provides some standard options and can be used to start creating a security policy for any environment. This is only provided as a starting point; additional policies and process will need to be defined to create an effective security guideline for an organization. Some security guidelines from the handbook are listed here:

- Do not use your login name as your password. This includes reversing it, changing the case of the name, or any other variable.

- Do not use a familiar name such as your child's name, your spouse's name, or your pet's name.

- Do not use your first, middle, or last name. This includes any nicknames as well.

- Do not use a password of all single digits or the same letter. For example: 1111111 or AAAAAAA.

- Do not use easily obtainable information about yourself, such as date of birth, house number, or social security number.

- Do not use a word that can be found in a dictionary in any language.

- Use more than six characters in your password.

- Use a password with mixed-case characters. Use uppercase and lowercase randomly.

- Include non-alphanumeric characters, such as &#$@*.

- Do not write your password anywhere and do not give it to someone else for any reason.

on the job *Definitely be knowledgeable on these password guidelines when working with any company. These are standard guidelines that can be enhanced for any business need, but be aware of the initial rules.*

In addition to these guidelines, you can implement other policies to secure your installation. Require that users change their passwords at defined intervals. In addition, administrators need to understand that other systems can be used to compromise another installation. Most users will utilize the same password for multiple accounts. For example, if one network is compromised, the intruder can use the same ID and password to log on to another network if it exists. This is a common attack method. For example, if a user sets the same password for two different e-mail accounts or uses his network password to log on to an FTP site, a hacker can trace this activity and use the password to access more secure systems. This enables an intruder to start with one system and hop to others.

Many organizations set stricter password policies for Administrator accounts than for normal user accounts, due to the security level. For example, a user account may require a password with six characters and a password change every 60 days. Administrator accounts may require passwords with eight characters and password changes every 30 days. Although this cannot be defined within Windows NT, you can set up a process to help enforce this as a standard. This higher security is due to the amount of access Administrator accounts retain. You also may want to set up two accounts for an administrator: The main account would have limited permissions for normal day-to-day activity, while the second would have full administrator access. Most installations also include a single main account with full access privileges. On a Windows NT server, the account is labeled Administrator. You should rename this account to make it a little more difficult to hack into since every hacker knows that Administrator is the default name for the most powerful account in Windows NT. Do not use this account once an administrative equivalent has been set up, unless absolutely necessary.

You may also use special accounts that are not assigned to normal users. For example, you may have an application service account or backup account that requires a great deal of access to a server or even multiple systems. Be sure to require a strict standard policy for these accounts, such as ten-character passwords and a combination of alphanumeric and other characters. Remember that you cannot set up multiple policies within a single account database and these policies need to be implemented as part of your environment security handbook. In addition to administrator accounts, many systems create a guest level account, by default. This account usually has minimal permissions; nevertheless, you may want to disable this account outright.

Username and Password Guidelines

Policies and processes only begin to make an environment secure. Good guidelines should be developed around the username and password. Many users use a common word, name, or number as their password. With a little detective work, someone could quickly figure out several things users might employ as their passwords. In many cases, it would not take long to get a password for a regular user. Although this would provide limited access, administrators commonly use similar words or phrases as their own passwords. This can lead to a greater amount of access, even super-user access.

Many resources are available to help create guidelines to use when generating passwords. In addition, mechanisms have already been defined that will help you develop these guidelines.

Mechanisms for Creating Secure Usernames and Passwords

There are many different ways for creating usernames and passwords. Applications exist that will create a random series of characters based upon the guidelines you set; however, these usernames or passwords can be difficult to remember. This may work well for system accounts; however, a normal user needs something that can be easily remembered. This means that users must write the username and password down so they won't forget them, which creates another security problem. The trick to providing effective security is to create a username and password that is cryptic but easily remembered by an everyday user.

Because usernames are more easily obtainable, most organizations tend to use basic names for user login and rely more heavily on password security. A common strategy is to use the first initial, last name or the first name, last initial. For example, Joe Smith would be Jsmith or JoeS. These are easily remembered and can be identified quickly by an administrator. Some companies will also assign employees a company ID for the username. This will help in keeping the usernames somewhat secure from outsiders.

Another common strategy for usernames is to create a more cryptic name by using some combination of information. For example, you may choose the user's first initial, last initial, and the last four digits of his social security number. For example, Joe Smith with a social security number of 123-45-6789 would have a username of JS6789. More control is available when specifying usernames. These are created for the user; therefore, you can make sure it meets the criteria set. There are many different methodologies available, but it's best to evaluate your specific needs to determine what will work best.

When working with passwords, organizations tend to rely more heavily on securing their environment by requiring strict password policies. In most organizations, they generally rely upon the users to set up their own password. Here, it is more difficult to maintain policies since not every user can be monitored. Few organizations set up passwords for users and force them to keep these passwords. For good reason. This does not work well, because if they are cryptic, users have to write them down to remember them, and the administrator who set up the password also has access to their account. Generally, companies set up policies that are controllable and rely upon the user to choose a cryptic password.

There are many different tactics when it comes to creating passwords. You might suggest taking a well-known dialogue or phrase and deriving the first letter from each word. Try to use one that would use a myriad of alphanumeric characters intermingled to create a secure password. Try creating your own word that sounds like rubbish but is pronounceable. This makes it a little easier to remember. Consider taking several words and using different portions of each separated by a non-alphanumeric character. For example, you may take *Eat at Joe's* and turn it into *et$a#j's*.

These mechanisms can be used to design a method for creating passwords and usernames, but are useless if they are not followed and enforced.

Windows NT Security Policies

Because Windows NT provides an authentication method, it offers quite a few policies to help enforce password security. These can be set up to make sure users are maintaining a secure environment. Several of these policies are listed in this chapter and are included in RFC 1244. To set up policies, you must run the User Manager application. The policies can be set up differently depending upon whether you are using Windows NT Workstation, a domain controller, or a member server to fit your environment. To access User Manager, choose Start | Programs | Administrative Tools | User Manager For Domains. The User Manager window opens. Select Policies | Account.

Depending upon what policies you want to change, User Manager must be run locally or connected to a specific computer. If you want to set up policies on Windows NT Workstation, you must open User Manager on the individual workstation or type the command **MUSRMGR.EXE**. To access a domain policy, you must run User Manager for Domains (USRMGR.EXE). To access a specific member server, run User Manager for Domains on that server and when choosing a domain, type in the server name.

on the **J** o b *Be aware of the availability of the password policies in a Windows network to be able to control security issues and keep the employees within the specified business security rules.*

In addition to the password policies available, additional security can be defined through User Manager. Specific rights are delineated to users and groups when a domain is installed, but these options may need to be modified from time to time.

Options such as "Log on locally" might be required by specific users. These options are available from User Manager by choosing the Policies | User Rights option. Security for some of the more common tasks that can be defined include "Shutdown system," "Access this computer from network," "Log on locally," Change the system time," and "Back up files and directories." In addition, an advanced user rights option is available to control some of the more complex operations. Figure 8-5 shows the users set up for Shutdown system privileges by default. You can select an option from the Rights drop-down menu to set specific rights. Then check the Show Advanced User Rights check box to include more complex operations.

Auditing Password Usage

After you have set up password policies, you must audit the systems being accessed to ensure that the policies are being enforced. With these policies set up, if someone is attempting to violate the password security, you will see evidence in the computer security event logs. This information can be used to track down what accounts are being hacked against. In addition, you can audit what resources are successfully being accessed or modified. This information is vital to ensuring the security of your Windows NT systems. Auditing is set up with User Manager also. Exercise 8-2 walks you through setting up auditing within Windows NT, and Figure 8-6 shows an example of an auditing configuration for a domain.

FIGURE 8-5

The Rights drop-down menu

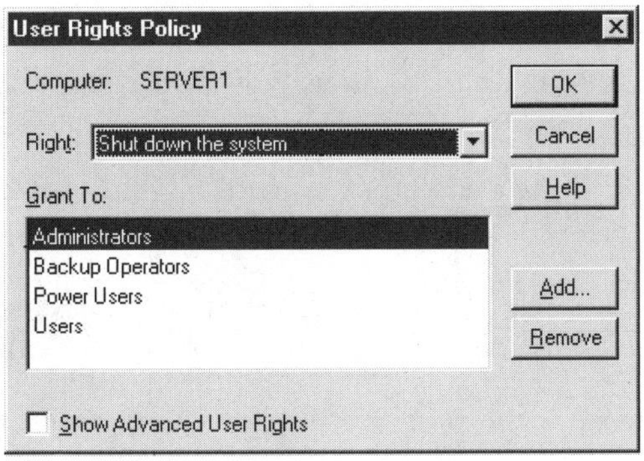

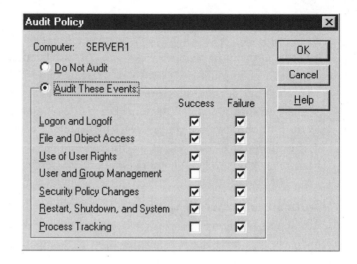

FIGURE 8-6

Auditing ongoing security activity in Windows NT is important to protect against intruders

---

EXERCISE 8-2

Auditing Setup

1. Select Start | Programs | Administrative Tools | User Manager For Domains. The User Manager window opens.

2. Select Policies | Audit. The Audit Policy dialog box appears.

3. Select the Audit These Events option. (By default, no objects are selected.)

4. Place a check in the Failure column for the following objects: Logon and Logoff; File and Object Access; Use of User Rights; User and Group Management; Security Policy Changes; Restart, Shutdown, and System; and Process Tracking.

5. Place a check box under the success category for the following objects: Logon and Logoff; File and Object Access; Use of User Rights; Security Policy Changes; and Restart, Shutdown, and System.

6. Click the OK button. The policies take affect immediately.

Each object has its own use and purpose. You must understand what each object shown in Figure 8-6 does and how it is used to tighten security. Table 8-6 displays each object and provides a brief description.

When setting up audit policies, the File and Object Access settings are dependent upon other portions of Windows NT. You can only use this function if the drive that data is stored on is on an NTFS-formatted partition. In addition, you must set the auditing attributes for specific files from within the Windows NT Explorer.

After you've set auditing up, you can monitor the server security event logs to ensure that no one is trying to compromise your system. It will display the information you have specified in your audit policy, such as file access, logon and logoff, and security policy changes. You can access the events logs by selecting Start | Programs | Administrative Tools | Event Viewer. The Event Viewer window opens. Select Log | Security. Figure 8-7 shows the Event Viewer with entries from the security event log. The security event log is used to monitor usage and activity of your users, and the information it displays is based upon the level of auditing set up by an administrator.

Passwords are the most common security authentication method used today. They can quickly become a point of access to an intruder if not set up and monitored properly, so be sure to set up strict guidelines and policies to secure your users' usernames and passwords. Several methods are available to help enforce and audit password policies, and by applying these techniques, you can effectively tighten the security of your network.

TABLE 8-6	Each Audit Object Handles a Specific Set of Events
Auditing Object	**Description**
Logon and Logoff	Maintains a record of local and remote resource logins.
File and Object Access	Maintains listing of all file, directory, and printer access.
Use of User Rights	User rights are monitored, excluding logon and logoff.
User and Group Management	Maintains record of changes made to any user or group, including additions. Password changes are also monitored here.
Security Policy Changes	Monitors changes made to auditing, policies, or trust relationships.
Restart, Shutdown, and System	Monitors events around system startup, shutdown, and the security log itself.
Process Tracking	Monitors application execution, process access, and process termination.

FIGURE 8-7

The security
event log

Event Viewer - Security Log on \\SERVER1

Date	Time	Source	Category	Event	User
1/1/90	1:29:29 PM	Security	Logon/Logoff	538	Administratc
1/1/90	1:29:28 PM	Security	Privilege Use	576	Administratc
1/1/90	1:29:28 PM	Security	Logon/Logoff	528	Administratc
1/1/90	1:29:28 PM	Security	Privilege Use	576	Administratc
1/1/90	1:29:28 PM	Security	Logon/Logoff	528	Administratc
1/1/90	1:29:17 PM	Security	Privilege Use	578	USER2
1/1/90	1:28:51 PM	Security	Logon/Logoff	538	Administratc
1/1/90	1:28:50 PM	Security	Logon/Logoff	538	USER2
1/1/90	1:28:50 PM	Security	Privilege Use	576	USER2
1/1/90	1:28:50 PM	Security	Logon/Logoff	528	USER2
1/1/90	1:28:50 PM	Security	Privilege Use	576	USER2
1/1/90	1:28:50 PM	Security	Logon/Logoff	528	USER2
1/1/90	1:28:42 PM	Security	Privilege Use	578	Administratc
1/1/90	1:28:30 PM	Security	Privilege Use	577	Administratc
1/1/90	1:28:30 PM	Security	Privilege Use	577	Administratc
1/1/90	1:28:27 PM	Security	Privilege Use	577	Administratc

SCENARIO & SOLUTION

I have employees in my company who are using their names as their password. Is this secure?	No. Passwords need to be non-intuitive; otherwise someone may be able to guess the password for that user.
Is there a way on my Windows NT network to specify specific rules on passwords?	Yes, password policies can be used to specify password length, password expiration, the time before the password can be changed, and even to track password history so the user cannot employ the same password over and over.
I have a user whom I trust implicitly, but I am not allowed to make him an Administrator on the Windows NT network. I need to allow him to shut down the server. What can be done?	Specify in the User Rights Policy that the individual can shut down the server. This does not require giving them Administrative rights.
I have a security issue in which I believe a hacker is attempting to log on to the network. How can I determine if this is happening?	Audit failed logon attempts. If the log shows that someone is attempting to log on continually and get the password incorrect, then you can approach the user with the username that is being used for logon attempts and verify that it is not he or she who is trying to get on the network.

FROM THE CLASSROOM

Don't Expect a User to Know as Much as an Administrator

When it comes to users, groups, rights, and permissions, it can get very confusing. It's even confusing sometimes for administrators who study this stuff and use it on a daily basis. Imagine what users with little experience are going through when they have to manage files, shares, rights, or permissions. When dealing with security issues such as assigning permissions to a directory tree, users must know exactly what they are doing. If they do not, they can give access to private information that is not intended for all users. This is especially the case when users assign rights or permissions. Many times I have had users call me and say they accidentally checked the Replace Permissions on Subdirectories dialog box, which modified the rights on every subdirectory below the specified directory. It can take hours to restore permissions that were wiped out in seconds.

In a small workgroup, it is imperative that everyone knows how to share and access files and directories on another person's computer. This sounds easy for administrators, but it can be quite difficult for a novice user. They need to share the directory, select share level security, enter the share name, determine a user limit, and then assign permissions to the share. There are too many chances for a user to make a mistake.

If you are an administrator in an organization where users are expected to take part in the daily administration of files, directories, and shares, then you should spend the time to make sure they are adequately trained. Spending a few minutes in advance can save headaches later when a user makes a costly mistake. Many won't even ask for help, so by training them beforehand, you will ensure they have the necessary skills to handle these administrative tasks. It may be more convenient for you to visit each user on an individual basis. Just the same, you should consider a classroom environment if many users require training at once.

Ensuring that users are thoroughly trained can make your job easier. Having many users fulfill small tasks that you would normally be required to do can free you up for higher-level projects that require your training and dedication.

—*Cameron Brandon, MCSE+Internet, CNE, A+, Network+*

Data Encryption and Protecting Network Data

As more companies go online with the Internet, the need to protect data becomes more prevalent. The industry has strived to provide a more secure data transfer mechanism. The idea is to protect the data during a transfer and guarantee that it makes it to its recipient unread and unmodified. From this need, encryption services have grown in popularity. Multiple encryption implementations have been published and are now available to the public. Several standards have also come about as the industry has grown.

To understand encryption, you must first learn how it works. You will also be introduced to some specific methods and algorithms used for encryption services. In addition, the main standards that have been defined will be explained, as well as a few other data protection methods.

Defining Data Encryption

Many different types of data encryption are available. Each methodology provides advantages and has a varying level of security. To date, some encryption standards have not been broken yet. Other more simple methods have been, but can still provide a level of security if used appropriately. Encryption can be defined as the process of taking plain text data and converting it to a meaningless format that is unreadable, better known as ciphertext. Once the data has been transferred, a mechanism exists to decrypt the data back to its original format.

A key of sorts is used during the encryption and decryption process to handle the data. This key is the algorithm that the data can be compared against. Only the persons who have obtained this key can encrypt or decrypt the data. Generally, a symmetric key contains a random number of bits that are used to encrypt the data. The longer the key, the more complex the encryption algorithm.

The most basic form of encryption is the *private-key encryption* or *symmetric* algorithm. This requires that each individual must possess a copy of the key. The problem is that you must have a secure way to transport the key to other people. If you do not, someone may intercept the key, which makes encryption useless. In addition, if you are using encryption techniques for multiple people, you may not want one person to have access to another's data. Now you must keep multiple single keys per person and this can get very cumbersome.

A second form of encryption available is the *public-key* or *asymmetrical algorithm.* This system requires two related but separate keys. You freely publish one key, the public key, to anyone you choose. You could even post it in public places for anyone. The second key, the private key, is kept in a secure location and is used only by you. Both keys are required to pass data with this encryption technique. For example, say you want to send data to a co-worker. You would retrieve his public key and encrypt the data. Once done, nothing but the private key can decrypt the message, not even the public key you have. Your co-worker could then reply by using your public key and you would be the only person able to decrypt that message. This system works well because it enables you to send the public key over an insecure communications channel and still maintain the level of security. You could even publish your public key on the Internet. Rivest, Shamir, and Adleman created the standard for how this method is used. It is known as the RSA standard and is discussed later in this chapter.

Encryption Methods

When encrypting data, different methods can be used. Each method provides advantages and drawbacks, and some work in cooperation with others to provide an overall solution. The more common methods are discussed and explained here.

e x a m
🐸 a t c h

Be aware of the different types of encryption and what they do.

Stream Cipher   Stream cipher algorithms encrypt data one bit at a time. Plain text bits are converted into encrypted cipher text. This method is usually not as secure as block cipher techniques, but they generally execute faster. In addition, the ciphertext is always the same size as the original plain text, and is a technique that is less prone to errors. If an error occurs during the encryption process, usually this only affects a single bit instead of the whole string. When block ciphers contain errors, at a minimum, the entire block is garbage.

Block Cipher   Instead of encrypting a bit at a time, block cipher algorithms encrypt data in blocks. Block ciphers also have more overhead than stream ciphers, which is provided separately depending upon the implementation and the block size that can be modified (the most common size being 64 bits). Because it handles encryption at a higher level, it is generally more secure. The downside is that the execution time takes longer. Additional cipher options (shown in Table 8-7) are available when using block cipher algorithms, such as Electronic Codebook (ECB), Cipher Block Chaining (CBC), and Output Feedback Mode (OFB).

Padding   When encrypting data, plain text messages usually do not take up an even number of blocks. Many times, padding must be added to the last block to complete the data stream. The data added can contain all ones, all zeros, or a combination of ones and zeros. The encryption algorithm used is responsible for determining the padding that will be applied. Multiple padding techniques are available and used depending upon the algorithm implementation.

Encryption Standards

As encryption has become more popular, the need for industry standards has arisen. Standards for different implementations and algorithms have been defined to move the industry in the same direction. The most popular standards are discussed here with a brief history and explanation.

DES   The Data Encryption Standard (DES) was created and standardized by IBM in 1977. It is a 64-bit block symmetric algorithm and is specified in the ANSI X3.92 and X3.106 standards for both enciphering and deciphering operations, which are based on a binary number. In addition, the National Security Agency (NSA) uses it as the standard for all government organizations. There currently exists 72 quadrillion

TABLE 8-7   Cipher Modes for the Block Cipher Encryption Method

Block Cipher Mode	Description
Electronic Codebook (ECB)	Each block is encrypted individually. If information reappears in the same text, such as a common word, it is encrypted the same way.
Cipher Block Chaining (CBC)	Feedback is inserted into each cipher block before it is encrypted. It includes information from the block that proceeded it. This ensures that repetitive information is encrypted differently.
Cipher Feedback Mode (CFB)	This enables you to encrypt portions of a block instead of an entire block.
Output Feedback Mode (OFB)	This works much like CFB. The underlying shift registers are used slightly differently.

(72,000,000,000,000,000) encryption keys for DES, in which a key is chosen at random. DES uses a block cipher methodology to apply a 56-bit symmetric key to each 64-bit block. An additional form of DES, known as triple DES, applies three keys in succession to each block.

RSA   Ron Rivest, Adi Shamir, and Leonard Adleman (RSA) were the individuals responsible for creating the RSA standard at MIT, which defines the mathematical properties in using the public-key encryption methodology. The algorithm randomly generates a very large prime number that is used for the public key, which is then consequently used to derive another prime number for the private key via mathematical computations. Many forms of RSA encryption are in use today, including the popular PGP. PGP, or Pretty Good Privacy, has worked well in the past. Some vendors have included implementations of RSA in their core application code. Novell NetWare, version 4.1*x* and 5.0 have RSA encryption built into the client and server to provide a secure communications channel.

Digital Signatures

Digital signatures are used to verify that a message that was sent is from the appropriate sender and that it has not been tampered with. When using digital signatures, the message is not altered, but a signature string is attached to verify its validity. Digital signatures usually use a public-key algorithm. A public key is used to verify the message, while the private key is used to create the signature. A trusted application is usually present on a secure computer somewhere on the network that is used to validate the signature provided. This computer is known as a *certificate authority* and stores the public key of every user on the system. Certificates are released containing the public key of the user in question. When these are dispensed, the certificate authority signs each package with its own private key. Several vendors offer commercial products that provide certificate authority services. For example, Microsoft Exchange Server can be set up to provide certificates to mail clients for using digital signatures. Employing this methodology doesn't mean you're protecting your data completely, but you will know if it has been tampered with.

On a Windows 2000 Server, certificates can be used to encrypt files on the NTFS partition—referred to as Encrypted File System (EFS). Since certificates are used to perform this encryption, only one user can decrypt the file and use it. The Administrator or another user can be set up as a recovery agent, which will allow them to decrypt the file if the original user is unavailable to open a file. The data file cannot be compressed and encrypted at the same time. To encrypt a file on a Windows 2000 partition, perform the steps in Exercise 8-3.

CertCam 8-3

EXERCISE 8-3

Encrypting Data Files with Windows 2000

1. Select the file to encrypt in Windows Explorer and right-click. Choose Properties.

2. Select the Advanced button on the General page.

3. Check the box next to the option to "Encrypt contents to secure data."

4. Select OK twice.

Internet Protocol Security

Internet Protocol Security (IPSec) is the basis for secure communications over the Internet, such as VPNs. IPSec uses authentication, integrity verification, and also encrypts the data packets sent during the session. IPSec can use other types of algorithms for encryption, but for connections to be functional, the algorithms must be interoperable on both sides of the connection. When the algorithms do not work together, the session cannot be created since the data packets to create the session cannot be decrypted and verified for authenticity.

Windows 2000 supports IPSec as the encryption protocol for creating a VPN between servers which allows the Internet to be used as a backbone.

Secure Sockets Layer

Secure Sockets Layer (SSL) is a Session layer protocol that encrypts data sent from any higher layer program such as FTP, HTTP, SMTP, and so on. It can only work with guaranteed transports, or basically anything using the TCP protocol that is connection-oriented and made up of the two different protocols: SSL Handshake and SSL Record. SSL Handshake is used to create a secure session between two systems. This includes all methods and parameters used for encryption and security measures. The SSL

Record protocol is used to encrypt all data packets including the SSL Handshake data packets.

SSL is mainly used on E-commerce Web sites during the exchange of personal information. This helps keep anyone on the Internet from seeing this information, including name, address, and most especially credit card information. SSL will cause the page load time to take longer and is denoted by a closed padlock on the bottom status bar of Internet Explorer.

Layer Two Tunneling Protocol

Layer Two Tunneling Protocol (L2TP) is a tunneling protocol similar to PPTP which creates a tunnel over the Internet between two points using PPP data packets encapsulated in TCP/IP protocol packets (for regular networks, you can also use IPX/SPX and NetBEUI). While using IPSec for encryption, the combination will create a VPN. L2TP is supported by Windows 2000 over a LAN or the Internet, but does not support implementation over ATM, X.25, or Frame Relay networks.

Kerberos

Kerberos is a distributed authentication security using private-keys that verifies the validity of a user during login, and will repeatedly do the same every time a request is made. This is useful when a user is going to access the network from a workstation that is not secure. A workstation could be in a public kiosk and anyone may be allowed to log in to the network as a guest, but a regular user may use the kiosk and log in using their individual user account.

SCENARIO & SOLUTION

Which encryption method is faster but less secure than others?	Stream Cipher functions at a faster speed but is less secure.
What method is similar to Stream Cipher but is more secure and takes longer?	Block Cipher encrypts a block of data at a time, not bit by bit like Stream Cipher.
What is done to make encrypted data be a specific length?	Padding
What can be used to verify that a message sent from a specific person is really from that person?	Digital signatures

Common Encryption Programs

Due to the popularity of encryption, several vendors and organizations have written and published cryptographic programs to provide security. Each works a little different from the others and can be applied in different ways. The most popular program in circulation is PGP. In addition, Microsoft provides an application-programming interface for encryption services, called CryptoAPI.

Pretty Good Privacy

A common implementation for encryption services is *Pretty Good Privacy*, or PGP, which is available for Windows, DOS, Amiga, UNIX, VMS, and Macintosh systems. It includes a full-featured tool set for encryption, digital signatures, and file compression. PGP has multiple encryption methodologies, including symmetric keys, asymmetric keys, and a random number generator. PGP is available for anyone to use and works well with most security implementations.

CryptoAPI

Microsoft foresaw the need to provide encryption services within applications. PGP and other implementations cannot work at the API level to provide these services to custom applications. Therefore, Microsoft created an API that enables you to add cryptographic services to your programs. This API contains a set of modules known as cryptographic service providers, or CSRs. CryptoAPI was included in Windows NT 4.0 Service Pack 3, Windows 95 OEM 2, and Internet Explorer 3.02. The API is used like PGP, but the encryption and decryption processes happen within the application.

CERTIFICATION OBJECTIVE 8.04

Uses of a Firewall

As the disadvantages of non-secure networks have become more apparent in today's business world, additional forms of protection have been devised. Because it seems to be a requirement today to connect to public networks such as the Internet, some form of protection from hackers must be provided at the network level. A *firewall* protects a secure internal network from being influenced by insecure public networks outside it. It can also be used to provide protection to a secure portion of a private network, such as a Human Resources physical network.

Although many vendors label products as firewalls, it is more of a network security strategy than a single product. A firewall is a collection of concepts used to protect one network from another. The most common implementation today is the use of a firewall between an organization's internal network and the Internet. Firewalls can be very complex, because they provide more features than just packet filtering. They also offer multiple layers of protection, including actually scanning the information stored in the packets to make sure no malicious data gets through. They do this by using advanced techniques to monitor connections, log potential intrusions, and then act upon these incidents.

Firewall Architecture

As mentioned earlier, a firewall is a combination of techniques and technologies used to control the flow of data between networks. A firewall enables all traffic to pass through to each network; however, it compares the traffic to a set of rules that determine how the traffic will be managed. If the traffic matches the rules for acceptable data, the traffic is passed on to the network. If the rule specifies that the data be denied, the traffic cannot continue and will be bounced back. Although some implementations may do this differently, the same basic functionality is used.

Dual-homed Host Firewalls

A *dual-homed host firewall* consists of a single computer with two physical network interfaces that acts as a gateway between the two networks. The server's routing capability is disabled so that the firewall can handle all traffic management. Either an application-level proxy or circuit level firewall software is run to provide data transfer capability. You must be careful not to enable routing within the network operating system or you will bypass your firewall software. Figure 8-8 shows an illustration of a dual-homed host firewall configuration.

Screened Host Firewalls

Screened host firewall configurations are considered by many to be more secure than the dual-homed firewall. In this configuration, you place a screening router between the gateway host and the public network. This enables you to provide packet filtering

An example of
a basic firewall
configuration

Internet   Firewall

before reaching the host computer. The host computer can then run a proxy to provide additional security to this configuration. As packets travel into the internal network, they only know of the computer host that exists. Figure 8-9 shows an illustration of a screened-host configuration.

Screened Subnet Firewalls

A screened subnet firewall configuration takes security to the next level by further isolating the internal network from the public network. An additional screening router is placed between the internal network and the firewall proxy server. The internal router handles local traffic while the external router handles inbound and outbound traffic to the public network. This provides two additional levels of security. First, by adding a link internally, you can protect the firewall host from an attack by an internal source. Second, it makes an external attack much more difficult because the number of links is increased. Figure 8-10 shows the screened subnet firewall configuration.

An example of a screened host firewall configuration

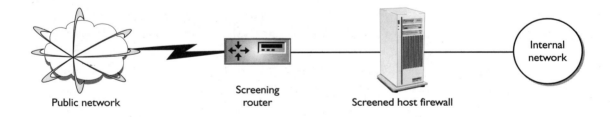

Public network   Screening
                        router   Screened host firewall   Internal
                                                                         network

FIGURE 8-10 An example of the screened subnet firewall configuration

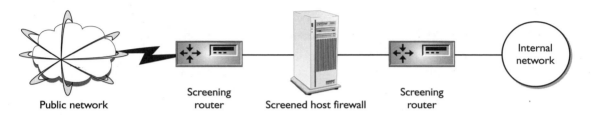

Public network   Screening   Screened host firewall   Screening   Internal network
                  router   router

Firewall Types

There are three types of firewalls that can be used: Packet Level firewall, Application Level firewall, and Circuit Level firewall. Each uses different security approaches, thus providing advantages over the others. One additional feature that was discussed earlier is encryption services. Most firewalls provide some sort of cryptographic services for data transfers.

When you have a complete understanding of the features and type of security needed from a firewall, you can determine the implementation that bests fits the environment.

Packet Level Firewall   A packet level firewall is usually a form of screening router that examines packets based upon filters set up at the network and transport layers. You can block incoming or outgoing transfers based upon a TCP/IP address or other rules. For example, you may choose not to enable any incoming IP connections, but instead enable all outgoing IP connections. You can set up rules that will enable certain types of requests to pass while others are denied. The information that rules can be based on includes source address, destination address, session protocol type, and the source and destination port. Because this works at only three layers, it is a very basic form of protection and is only a type of implementation. To provide security to another network properly, all seven layers must be protected by a full-featured conventional firewall.

Application Level Firewall   The application level firewall understands the data at the application level. Application layer firewalls operate at the application, presentation, and session layers. Data at the application level can actually be understood and monitored to verify that no harmful information is included. An example of an application level firewall is an Internet proxy or mail server. Many uses are available through some form of proxy, but these functions usually only provide security at that level. In addition, clients often must be configured to pass through the proxy to use it. Proxy servers are also used to mask the original origin of a packet. For example, an Internet proxy will pass the request on, but the source listed in the packet will be the proxy server address. The overall server doesn't just filter the packets, it actually takes in the original and retransmits a new packet through a different network interface.

Circuit Level Firewall   A circuit level firewall is similar to an application proxy except that the security mechanisms are applied at the time the connection is established. From then on, the packets flow between the hosts without any further checking from the firewall. Circuit level firewalls operate at the Transport layer.

Firewall Features

As firewalls have evolved, additional feature sets have grown out of, or been added to, these implementations. They are used to provide faster access and better security mechanisms. As encryption techniques have improved, they are being incorporated more into firewall implementations. Also, caching is being provided for services such as the World Wide Web. This enables pages to be cached for a period of time, which can dramatically speed up the user experience. New management techniques and technologies such as virtual private networks (VPNs) are now being included as well.

Proxy Servers Acting as a Firewall

By definition, a proxy server is a server that performs a function on behalf of another system. In most cases, this is a system that is acting as a type of gateway between the Internet and a company network. The employees who wish to access the Internet will perform actions as they normally would with their browser, but the browser will submit the request to the proxy server. The proxy server will then transmit the request on the Internet and receive the results, which are then sent to the original requester. A nice feature of the proxy server is that the Web pages which are not encrypted will be saved in a cache on the local hard disk. If another user requests the same page, the proxy server will not request the page from the Internet, but retrieve it from the hard disk. This saves quite a bit of time by not having to wait on Internet requests which may be coming from an overburdened Web server.

The proxy ability works both ways. Since we can cache requests going out, we can also act as a proxy for the Internet users making requests to the company Web server. This helps keep traffic minimized on the company network.

Another feature of the proxy server is that it can actually be used as the physical gateway between the Internet and the company network, which will filter out specific information, especially if we use the proxy server to act as a proxy between the Internet and the company Web server. Filtering can be configured for allowing or not allowing packets if they meet one or more of the following: specific port, direction of transfer, or source or destination of packets.

Specified Port   As we brought up in Chapter 4 in our discussion of well-known ports used with TCP/IP, we can filter the data transmissions on certain ports. For example, we can filter out port 21 so no one can access the FTP server from the Internet and will be allowed to access the FTP server only from the company network. We can also allow or disallow access for the ports, meaning we can allow only port 80 for our proxy server, and allow only requests for Web pages to the Internet from our intranetwork. This will disallow all other requests, such as FTP from the intranetwork.

Direction of Transfer   We can control access to and from the Internet by denoting whether specific data packets can be inbound to the intranetwork or outbound to the Internet. As with port filters, we could specify that port 80 is allowed outbound but not inbound. This would allow internal users to access the Internet, but no one from the Internet to access the company Web server.

Source or Destination of Packets   We can also filter out data packets going to or coming from a certain IP address, domain, or domain name. This would allow us to specify that a specific workstation within the company cannot send any requests on any port to the Internet. This could be a workstation that is in a public access kiosk within the company.

If we detect an intruder accessing the company network from the Internet and we have the IP address, we can block any data requests from this IP address. An example of allowing a domain name is to have a Web server set up within a company that is only accessible by anyone that uses a specific ISP. We can specify the ISP domain name or IP address range they use to assign to their clients and allow only those users to access the Web server. We can also offer special services to only those people we know are located in a certain geographical area. We could even do the opposite and allow access to a Web server that shows the benefits of the ISP, and not allow the existing clients of the ISP to access the site since we don't want them to see the special offers being offered to non-members.

EXERCISE 8-4

Setting Up Filtered Ports

A company wants you to determine what port filtering is needed to allow the access they wish. The requirements are as follows:

1. All internal employees need access to Web sites on the Internet.

2. The company employees need access to any FTP sites from which they may need to download files.

3. Another company requires access to the intranet Web server.

4. A third company needs access to accounting files placed on the intranet FTP server.

How can you configure this to meet the requirements of the company?

1. Enable port 80 outbound

2. Enable ports 20 and 21 outbound

3. Enable port 80 inbound from the specified domain of the company needing access, or by using the IP address range of the company.

4. Enable ports 20 and 21 for inbound for the specified domain of the third company, or for the IP address range of the third company.

CERTIFICATION SUMMARY

Information has increasingly become more important for organizations, and because of this, the securing of this information has become more of a priority. Organizations are using public communications channels such as the Internet to transfer data that must be secure.

Windows NT includes several different kinds of security models, which consist of four components: the Local Security Authority (LSA), Security Accounts Manager (SAM), Security Reference Monitor, and the logon process. After the Security Accounts Manager validates a user, an access token is created that includes the User Security Identifier (SID), Primary Group Security Identifier, and Group Security Identifier. Every named object includes a security descriptor containing information about the object and the Access Control List (ACL). The ACL catalogs the users and groups allowed to access the object as well as the level of permissions applied. The Security Descriptor is broken into four components: the System Access Control List (SACL), the Discretionary Access Control List (DACL), an owner, and a primary group. Access Control Entries specify the access or auditing permissions assigned for a specific user or group. Windows NT file and directory permissions are available on NTFS-formatted partitions. Various levels of security are available based upon your environment's requirements.

Two users, Administrator and Guest, are created by default for a server, workstation, or domain. In addition, functional groups are created that have varying rights levels. Shares are required to connect to remote directories on an NT computer. You can also append a $ symbol to the end of a share name to prevent its being listed in the browse list. A workgroup is an organizational unit, or a way to arrange a group of computers. In Windows 95/98 environments, accounts are not shared and resources are protected based upon a single password. In a Windows NT workgroup, user IDs and passwords are still used but are not shared among other computers. A domain is employed to share common user accounts and policies and consists of one or more NT servers. The registry needs to be secured in two ways: Set permissions on the registry keys themselves, and set up file and directory permissions for the directory in which it is stored.

A password is a series of characters used to authenticate a user's access permissions. Creating an effective password policy is critical to any organization sharing or protecting resources. Administrative accounts generally require a greater level of security than normal user accounts. Guidelines can be adopted to create secure passwords and usernames. Most organizations use a common scheme for creating usernames while depending upon the password to protect the resources. Windows NT includes several built-in policies that enforce password standards. In addition, auditing can be set up within User Manager to monitor usage and activity. You use Event Viewer to read the logs generated.

Data security has become more important as networks are becoming interconnected. Data encryption provides a way to ensure that the data is kept secure. Encryption is the process of taking plain text data and converting it into a meaningless format that is unreadable. A key is used to decipher the encryption code to return the data to a readable format. Two types of encryption types exist: symmetric (or private-key) and asymmetric (public-key). Two common encryption methods include Stream Cipher and Block Cipher. Two standards for encryption have been accepted: the Digital Encryption Standard (DES) and RSA. Both use different methodologies and are in wide use today. Digital signatures can be used to verify that a message arrived without being tampered with. Digital signatures do not encrypt a message. Instead, they just attach a signature that can be verified against a certificate authority. Windows 2000 uses certificates to encrypt files on an NTFS volume. Windows 2000 also uses Kerberos to encrypt logon authentication as well as Active Directory replication. Two common encryption-based products include PGP and Microsoft's CryptoAPI.

A firewall is a collection of methodologies for protecting one network from a second interconnected network such as the Internet. Firewalls compare the data passing through them to rules set up to allow or deny access. There are several architectures for firewalls, three of them are: dual-homed host, screened host, and screened subnet. A dual-homed host firewall has two network interfaces and acts as a gateway between the two networks. A screened host firewall has a screening router placed between the public network and the host. This provides an additional level of security against outside intrusion. A screened subnet firewall, meanwhile, puts a screening router on both sides of the firewall host. This provides protection on both sides of the host.

Three firewall types exist: packet level firewall, application level firewall, and circuit level firewall. The packet level firewall controls data at the network and transport layers. The application level type acts as a proxy and controls the top three layers of the OSI model. A circuit level firewall works similarly to an application level firewall but operates at the transport layer. Additional security features have been added to firewalls to provide better service, such as support for VPNs and caching and better management tools. Proxy servers can also function as a firewall and can also be used to enhance Internet access as well as function as a firewall by filtering ports.

✓ TWO-MINUTE DRILL

Selecting a Security Model—User-Level and Share-Level

❏ When designing a network, be sure to take into consideration the available options and the security impacts of each.

❏ A security model is a generic term that describes methodologies used to secure a system.

❏ There are four parts to the security subsystem in Windows NT. Each plays an integral part of the security functions provided.

❏ When the Security Accounts Manager validates a user, an access token is created.

❏ The ACL is a list that shows the users and/or groups allowed to access the object as well as the level of permissions applied.

❏ Security Descriptors are broken down into several components: the System Access Control List (SACL), the Discretionary Access Control List (DACL), an owner, and a primary group.

❏ One method of security available for use is file and directory level permissions.

❏ Windows NT uses user and group objects, more commonly known as accounts, to delineate access permissions.

❏ Two types of user accounts exist: global accounts that are used throughout a domain, and local accounts that are used on a single Windows NT computer.

❏ A domain group list includes Administrators, Account Operators, Backup Operators, Domain Admins, Domain Guests, Domain Users, Guests, Print Operators, Replicator, Server Operators, and Users.

❏ A server or workstation group list includes Administrators, Backup Operators, Guests, Power Users, Replicator, and Users.

❏ Share-level security is available on client operating systems such as Windows 95 and Windows 98.

❑ Share-level security is easy to implement and maintain on small peer-to-peer networks. However, users must remember the password for each shared resource (unless password caching is in use).

❑ Windows NT provides an additional type of security model. You need to understand the fundamental differences between domains and workgroups and the security architecture defined.

❑ You must secure the registry for any Windows NT computer. The registry contains the control parameters for the entire operating system.

Password Practices and Procedures

❑ The most basic security mechanism is the password.

❑ Setting up password authentication is a good start. Unfortunately, it will be useless against a knowledgeable intruder without solid policies and processes defined.

❑ Good guidelines should be developed around the username and password.

❑ Because Windows NT offers an authentication method, it provides quite a few policies to help enforce password security.

Data Encryption and Protecting Network Data

❑ As more companies go online with the Internet, the need to protect data becomes more prevalent.

❑ Multiple encryption implementations have been published and are now available to the public.

❑ Encryption can be defined as the process of taking plain text data and converting it to a meaningless format, better known as ciphertext, that is unreadable.

❑ Due to the popularity of encryption, several vendors and organizations have written and published cryptographic programs to provide security.

❑ Internet Protocol Security (IPSec) allows for encryption of data to create a VPN.

❑ Secure Sockets Layer (SSL) is used to encrypt Web pages and the information transferred between a user and the Web server (online credit card information is encrypted this way).

❑ Layer Two Tunneling Protocol (L2TP) is similar to PPTP, but has no built-in encryption and must use IPSec to create a VPN.

❑ Kerberos is a distributed authentication security used by Windows 2000 for user validation.

Uses of a Firewall

❑ A *firewall* protects a secure internal network from being influenced by insecure public networks outside it.

❑ A firewall enables all traffic to pass through to each network, comparing the traffic to a set of rules that determine how the traffic will be managed.

❑ Proxy server can be used as a firewall solution to allow or disallow traffic on a specific port, whether the data is inbound or outbound and the protected system is the destination or source of the data packets.

❑ Specific ports can be blocked, or allowed to let data pass through them.

❑ Data transfers can be allowed or disallowed, both inbound and/or outbound.

❑ Data transfers can be blocked or allowed whether it be to or from a specific PC or domain.

SELF TEST

The following Self Test questions will help you measure your understanding of the material presented in this chapter. Read all the choices carefully since there may be more than one correct answer. Choose all correct answers for each question.

Selecting a Security Model—User-Level and Share-Level

1. What portion of the Windows NT security subsystem handles both local security policies and user authentication, and generates audit log messages?

   A. Local Security Authority (LSA)

   B. Security Accounts Manager (SAM)

   C. Security Reference Monitor

   D. None of the above

2. What portion of the security reference model maintains the database used for storing user and group account information?

   A. Local Security Authority (LSA)

   B. Logon Process

   C. Security Reference Monitor

   D. Security Accounts Manager (SAM)

3. What access control list object determines what users and groups have permissions to this object?

   A. System Access Control List (SACL)

   B. Discretionary Access Control List (DACL)

   C. Owner

   D. User

4. Which of the following are valid, predefined file permission types?

   A. No Access

   B. List

   C. Add

   D. Change

5. Which groups are created by default for a stand-alone Windows NT server and workstation?

    A. Administrators

    B. Account Operators

    C. Backup Operators

    D. Print Operators

Password Practices

6. Which of these is a common rule for creating a secure password?

    A. Do not use a familiar name such as your child's name, your spouse's name, or your pet's name.

    B. Do not use your first, middle, or last name, or nickname.

    C. Do not use a password of all single digits or the same letter. For example: 1111111 or AAAAAAA.

    D. All of the above.

7. Which of the following is a common mechanism for creating passwords?

    A. Create a password that uses a myriad of intermingled alphanumeric characters.

    B. Take several words and use different portions of each, separating them with a non-alphanumeric character.

    C. Use a four-character password of non-alphanumeric characters.

    D. All of the above.

8. What policies are not available from within User Manager for Windows NT?

    A. Minimum password length

    B. Maximum password length

    C. Minimum password age

    D. Maximum password age

9. Within User Manager, what menu option lists additional user rights that can be added?

    A. Policies | Audit

    B. Users | Audit

C. Policies | User Rights

D. Users | User Rights

10. Which of the following options are available when setting up auditing?

A. Interactive Logon

B. Remote Resource Access

C. Logon and Logoff

D. System Process

Data Encryption and Protecting Network Data

11. What is the symmetric encryption algorithm better known as?

A. Digital Encryption Standard (DES)

B. RSA standard

C. Private-key algorithm

D. Public-key algorithm

12. Which of the following is classified as an encryption method?

A. Stream Cipher

B. Data Cipher

C. Byte Cipher

D. Block Cipher

13. What Block Cipher Mode encrypts each block individually during the encryption process?

A. Electronic Codebook (ECB)

B. Cipher Block Chaining (CBC)

C. Cipher Feedback Mode (CFB)

D. None of the above.

14. What encryption standard is based upon a fixed 56-bit symmetric key encryption algorithm?

A. RSA

B. DES

C. CPA

D. DSE

15. What technology uses certificate authorities to verify that a message has not been tampered with?

   A. RSA encryption

   B. Local Security Authority

   C. Digital Signatures

   D. None of the above

Uses of a Firewall

16. What technology provides a secure communications channel between an internal network and a public network such as the Internet?

   A. Encryption

   B. Firewall

   C. Router

   D. None of the above

17. What kind of firewall provides a single computer with two physical network interfaces?

   A. A dual-homed host firewall

   B. A screened host firewall

   C. A screening router

   D. A screened subnet firewall

18. What component(s) are included in a screened subnet firewall configuration?

   A. Single screening router

   B. Host firewall server

   C. Circuit application

   D. All of the above

19. What type of firewall is used to provide security based upon rules governing the network or transport layers?

   A. Packet level

   B. Application level

   C. Circuit level

   D. None of the above

LAB QUESTION

A company has the need to link several offices together that are in separate states, but to connect them with modems would end up generating a large phone bill. The company requires that the offices are linked 24 hours a day to allow for synchronization of data files to and from all offices.

The connections will most likely be used on a constant basis providing much intra-office communication. It's necessary the connections be secure.

Another option is that each office will need something to allow for faster Internet access. This is crucial since most data used by the employees will be taken from the Web sites of their clients. The same client Web sites may be accessed anywhere from 3 to15 times a day. The data on the client Web sites will not be changing much—maybe only once a week. Many employees will be accessing the same data.

It is also crucial that no unauthorized people have access to the intranet Web site. The only users able to access the intranet Web site are those working in the different offices. No access should be allowed by anyone other than the employees.

What would you do to meet these requirements in setting up this network?

SELF TEST ANSWERS

Selecting a Security Model—User-Level and Share-Level

1. ☑ **A.** Local Security Authority (LSA). The LSA handles these functions above the Security Accounts Manager and Security Reference Monitor. They are used to provide specific functions for the LSA.

   ☒ **B, C,** and **D** are incorrect. SAM is a database of users and groups. The Security Reference Monitor is used to validate a user right to access resources. This makes choices **B** and **C** incorrect.

2. ☑ **D.** Security Accounts Manager (SAM). The SAM maintains the database that users and groups are stored in. The LSA authenticates the logon processes and the Security Reference Monitor generates audit logs.

   ☒ **A, B,** and **C** are incorrect. The LSA handles these functions above the Security Accounts Manager and Security Reference Monitor. They are used to provide specific functions for the LSA. The Logon Process is applied in order to allow a user to log on and be verified. The Security Reference Monitor is used to validate a user right to access resources. This makes choices **B** and **C** incorrect.

3. ☑ **B.** Discretionary Access Control List (DACL). The DACL determines what users and groups have permissions to this object.

   ☒ **A, C,** and **D** are incorrect. SACL controls security auditing. The owner maintains ownership of the object and a user is not a valid ACL object type.

4. ☑ **A, C, D.** No Access and Change. List and Add are file and directory attributes.

   ☒ **B** is incorrect because List is used only in directory permissions.

5. ☑ **A, C.** Administrators and Backup Operators. These two groups are created on both member servers and domain controllers.

   ☒ **B** and **D** are incorrect because Account Operators and Print Operators are only created on domain controllers.

Password Practices

6. ☑ **D.** All of the above. Each one of these is a good rule of thumb when creating passwords. Other rules include using non-alphanumeric characters, randomly changing the capitalization, and using more than six characters in your password.

   ☒ There are no incorrect answer choices.

7. ☑ **A, B.** Create a password that uses a myriad of intermingled alphanumeric characters, and take several words and use different portions of each, separating them with a non-alphanumeric character. Both of these make an effective password.

   ☒ **C** is incorrect because using a four-character password is not recommended. **D** is incorrect because not all of the answer choices were correct.

8. ☑ **B.** Maximum password length. Windows NT does provide a maximum number of characters usable in a password; however, this cannot be modified through User Manager.

   ☒ **A, C,** and **D** are incorrect policies.

9. ☑ **C.** Policies | User Rights lists additional user rights that can be added.

   ☒ **A** is incorrect because the Policies | Audit option only supports auditing. **B** and **D** are incorrect because the Users tab does not have an Audit or User Rights option on its menu.

10. ☑ **C.** Logon and Logoff. This option is used to monitor the logon and logoff activity by users.

   ☒ **A, B,** and **D** are incorrect because Interactive Logon, Remote Resource Access, and System Process are not valid options.

Data Encryption and Protecting Network Data

11. ☑ **C.** Private-key algorithm. The symmetric algorithm is known as the private-key algorithm because both parties use the same key to encode and decode the encrypted data.

   ☒ **A, B,** and **D** are incorrect definitions.

12. ☑ **A, D.** Stream Cipher and Block Cipher. Both are valid encryption methods.

   ☒ **B** and **C** are incorrect because Data Cipher and Byte Cipher do not exist.

13. ☑ **A.** Electronic Codebook (ECB). The Electronic Codebook mode encrypts each block individually, but the Cipher Block Chaining and Cipher Feedback Modes do not.

   ☒ **B, C,** and **D** are incorrect because the Cipher Block Chaining and Cipher Feedback Modes do not encrypt each block individually.

14. ☑ **B.** DES. The Data Encryption Standard uses this algorithm.

   ☒ **A, C,** and **D** are incorrect because the RSA uses a different type of algorithm, and CPA and DSE are not valid encryption standards.

15. ☑ **C.** Digital Signatures. This technology does not encrypt the message—it only verifies that it arrived without being tampered with.

☒ **A, B,** and **D** are incorrect because RSA is an encryption standard and the Local Security Authority is a Windows NT subsystem.

Uses of a Firewall

16. ☑ **B.** Firewall. A firewall is used to provide a secure communications channel.

☒ **A, C,** and **D** are incorrect. Encryption service provides secure data. A router is used to provide a normal channel. Special types of router configurations are available for providing a secure channel.

17. ☑ **A.** A dual-homed host firewall. A dual-homed host firewall contains two internal physical interfaces.

☒ **B, C,** and **D** are incorrect because a screened host firewall passes data through a screening router first. A screening router is a secure configuration for a router; a screened subnet firewall provides two screening routers.

18. ☑ **B.** Host firewall server. However, this configuration requires two screening routers.

☒ **A** and **C** are not included in a screened subnet firewall configuration. **D** is incorrect because not all of the answer choices were correct.

19. ☑ **A.** Packet level. The packet level controls the network or transport layer within packets.

☒ **B, C,** and **D** are incorrect because the application level type controls the layers above the transport level and the circuit level type works at the Transport layer.

LAB ANSWER

First, connect all offices to the Internet through a local ISP. Once all are connected to the Internet, you can set up a VPN between all three, which will allow for secure connections over a public network.

Second, install and configure a proxy server at each office to act as the gateway to the Internet for the employees. This will allow for any Web sites that are visited to be cached, so later users who request the same page will retrieve it much quicker.

Finally, the proxy servers should be set to filter out all inbound traffic that is not part of the VPN, and allow port 80 outbound so the employees can access Web sites.

COMPUTING TECHNOLOGY INDUSTRY ASSOCIATION

9

Network Implementation

CERTIFICATION OBJECTIVES

9.01   Installing the Network

9.02   Environmental Factors That Affect
        Computer Networks

9.03   Common Peripheral Ports and
        Network Components

9.04   Compatibility and Cabling Issues

✓   Two-Minute Drill

Q&A   Self Test

Y ou'll find many questions concerning installing and maintaining computer networks located throughout the "Knowledge of Networking Technology" section of the Network+ exam. Knowing the concepts behind computer networking is very important and provides a strong foundation for other sections of the exam. When you work with computer networks, you need to know the components that make up the physical network as well as the theoretical terms used in computer networking as a whole.

Before you can begin connecting and shaping your network, you need to understand the concepts of computer networking. You might encounter problems with the computer network or the connection between two network segments and need to find and troubleshoot the network problem. Knowing the complete picture of how networking works and the components involved, from the cabling technologies to networking appliances such as routers and switches, will help you understand networking much more than you otherwise could.

In addition to knowing about the various networking areas for this exam, you need to know and understand PC fundamentals. This includes environmental characteristics of how PCs relate as well as basic troubleshooting techniques. When you couple knowledge of these computer technologies with "real-world" experience, you will be a force to be reckoned with in the information technology industry.

CERTIFICATION OBJECTIVE 9.01

Installing the Network

Installing a computer network might seem like a mindless task of simply connecting a few cables, but it's really much more complicated than that. You need to know how each independent component operates, and you need to learn many different terms. You have to think about many aspects of your computer network other than how you are going to physically connect the network cables to your PC.

When you first decide to hook up a network, you will encounter many things that you have probably never thought about before. Well, don't worry, because every person in the IT field has been in that situation before. Before you can consider yourself an expert on computer networking, you need to give your undivided attention to several important areas.

First, you need to plan how to configure your network. You have many choices. You must decide how to lay out your physical location. You have to choose between several network topologies, some of which work better than others, depending on the situation. As you have learned in the first chapter, each topology comes with advantages and disadvantages; you have to choose which will fit your environment the best. Choosing the best networking topology and implementing that technology correctly is what separates the good network administrators from the not-so-good ones.

Although the physical structure of the network is very important, you also have to provide for the administrative duties that need to be performed for your network to operate. These duties include setting up administrative and test accounts, passwords, IP addresses, IP configurations, connectivity requirements, and the necessary software so that once you have your network working, clients can communicate with one another. Without these ingredients, all that you end up with are a lot of very expensive computer components.

When you've built the physical architecture for your network, you still have a good deal of work in front of you to make sure that your network can function. As an administrator, you have total control over the layout and structure of your network as well as how each client will communicate with other clients or servers. It's up to you to decide which components to throw away and which technologies to utilize to the best of your ability. Note that in some companies, the administrator can suggest network topologies, but the final say is usually made by executives and the people who manage the money and will pay for the technology.

You have "administrative" control over the network, so in effect, you are in control. With the Administrator account rights for your network comes a big responsibility. You will be responsible for the security of your company's data, the efficiency of the network, and many other aspects that you might not have thought of yet, such as printing, file sharing, and e-mail. These specific areas of networking are probably not what you imagined when you first thought of creating a network. However, these are all very important factors in the big picture that you have before you.

Your most important duty as network administrator is to make sure that the clients on your network can communicate with one another at all times. Without this capability, your network is pretty much worthless. Besides supplying fundamental nonstop access to the network, you must try to make sure that the people who are using the network won't be interrupted during working hours. Sounds like an easy job, right?

Communication on a computer network is accomplished by the use of protocols. You can choose from hundreds of different protocols, but one of the most widely adopted standards in the computer industry is TCP/IP. You might be familiar with this protocol if you have ever surfed the Internet or downloaded a file.

An easy way to think of protocols is to consider them as you would a language. For example, for computers to talk to one another, they must speak the same language or use the same protocol. A French-speaking person and an English-speaking person might be able to hear one another speaking, but they are not able to understand each other, and that is where the importance lies. Communication between computers is actually a little more complicated than that, but that will do for now. You'll learn more of the subtleties of TCP/IP later in this chapter.

A computer network is all about sharing data and exchanging information. These fundamental practices on a network, however, pose certain security problems. You must be concerned with many types of security on a network, such as physical security, file and directory security, and Internet security, but one core area of security that is often overlooked is password security. When you share files or printers with other users, you sometimes are asked for a password. This password is a "key" that either admits or restricts your access to the data or peripherals on the network. Password security is the practice of making sure that the passwords are difficult to break. We use several fundamental practices to try to enforce password security on a network. You'll learn more about the practices of password security later in this chapter.

Standard operating procedures (SOPs) are the practices that you follow to enable your network to run smoothly and efficiently. SOPs typically consist of backing up the data on the network, making sure everyone can communicate, and fixing any problem that arises at a moment's notice. It doesn't get much simpler than that!

Administrative and Test Accounts

The network administrator holds the keys to the network castle. Any actions that the network administrator makes can ultimately affect users who are part of the network. The person who holds the Administrator account has complete, unrestricted access to all the files, folders, and shares on the network. He or she has complete power over the security of the network.

Because the Administrator account is a sensitive issue, people with system privileges to the account should be very careful and should restrict access to only those who truly need the account to complete their jobs. In no case should a person who has the capability to log in using the Administrator account use this privilege for day-to-day network use. That is a good way to inadvertently enable a virus or give unwelcome user complete access to the network. Remember that you are dealing with the sensitive nature of your data, and you should do whatever you can to protect it.

Basically, the Administrator account should be used to perform administrative duties only. All other duties should be completed when you are logged on with a personal user account. This practice allows for safe and restricted access to the sensitive areas of the network. The role of any network administrator is to protect the data on the network. With this role comes enormous responsibility. As the network administrator, you essentially hold the data in the palm of your hand. If by some chance the Administrator account accidentally becomes compromised, it could mean that you leave the safety of your network in the hands of others. This, of course, is not what you want to do.

on the job *Logging into a client's workstation as the administrator or with administrative privileges is commonly done by network technicians or administrators. Many times in business I have seen this done and the user forgets to log out when done with his or her task. The user sometimes takes advantage of the situation and accesses information he or she would normally not be allowed to access. I have even seen users install on their workstations applications that they would not normally have access to or even access Internet sites they would not normally have rights to reach. Some users could even start inadvertently deleting files on their system or the server and really cause problems.*

The administrative account is the most sensitive account on your network, so you have to be extra careful to use a password that is difficult to break. A password should consist of more than eight characters that include both upper- and lowercase letters as well as numbers or symbols. You should never use a simple phrase or word for the Administrator account.

Some operating systems, such as Windows NT Workstation and Server, allow some flexibility with the Administrator account. For example, a good practice to follow is to immediately rename the Administrator account to something other than "Administrator." If someone is trying to break into your computer network, the hacker needs two very important things: one, the name of the account, and two, the password for that account. If a potential hacker knows the name of an administrative account, he's already halfway to gaining access to your network. By renaming the Administrator account, you eliminate 50 percent of the problem right off the bat.

Another standard practice is to limit access to the Administrator account to those who have a justifiable need for the account. When the network administrator grants administrative access to too many people, there is no accountability on the network. Because so many people have access, you cannot be sure who is making changes on the network.

The worst-case scenario is when people have administrative access to important files that would normally be restricted to them under their personal accounts. With administrative access, they can roam and browse any files on the network without anyone being able to do anything to stop them.

Whenever you make a change to any part of your network, you should verify that the change didn't affect any other part of your network. You can accomplish this task using a test account to make sure that your change works. A *test account* is an account with normal rights within the network. If you used an administrative account to make the change, you should use a test account to test it. This practice is especially important when you make changes to file and directory permissions. When you have Administrative privileges, you have access to everything on the network, so you can't test to see your changes from the perspective of a normal user. Using a test account, you can make sure that you didn't give too much freedom on the network and that your changes went according to plan.

Consider this example of the consequences of not following the test account practice: A network administrator made a change to the Payroll folder and its subdirectories on one of the shares on a server. Instead of using a test account to verify that his changes went through as planned, he moved on to something else. What he didn't discover until later is that he accidentally gave everyone on the network access to the Payroll share. Through his error, anyone on the network could access the payroll files.

Table 9-1 lists the standard practices for administrative and test accounts on a network and will help you remember the advantages and purpose of having two separate accounts on the network. Usually, a network administrator has an account with administrative privileges and one without. During the course of the day, the network administrator uses her administrative account for making any needed changes. For normal day-to-day use, the network administrator uses her account that does not have administrative access to the entire network.

TABLE 9-1	Administrative and Test Accounts

Administrative Account	Test Account
Maintain exclusive permissions for all files and folders on the network.	Set with sample user rights; this account should have restricted privileges on the network.
Set and enforce tight security for anyone who has administrative rights on the network.	Set up your test account to resemble all other accounts on your network, including privileges and password security.
Assign a strong password with at least eight characters, using a mix of upper- and lowercase letters as well as numbers and symbols.	Assign a strong password.
Restrict access to the administrative account to those few people who need access.	Assign restricted privileges to the network.
Use this account to make any necessary changes to the network.	Use this account to test the changes that you made to the network. You are simulating a normal user with this account.

Passwords

Passwords are another form of computer security to ensure that users who aren't supposed to access certain files on the network don't do so. Passwords aren't a failsafe method of securing your network, but if they are implemented and enforced correctly, they can impose a level of security with which you should feel comfortable.

You can think of passwords in terms of a lock-and-key system. The user account is the lock and the password associated with that account is the key. If you have both the lock and the key for the network, you can have access to any files or data to which the user account has access. It's as simple as that.

It's your job as the network administrator to enforce strong passwords on the network and across your computing environment. A *strong password* is a password that is difficult to "crack," or break. With the intelligence, experience, and technology of today's hackers, it's getting easier and easier for them to gain access to our files. Your job is to keep them from doing so.

FROM THE CLASSROOM

The Importance of Having a Backup Administrator Account

I never realized the importance of having another account with administrative rights on the Windows NT network until I found myself in a particular bind one day. While logging on to my Administrator account, I was prompted that my password was set to expire soon. I changed my password, and that's where the trouble began. I had forgotten that I was currently logged on to another server in the server room. When I changed my password, Windows NT became confused that I was logged on to the network with a username that now had two different passwords assigned to it. The result is that I was locked out of my account —my *administrative* account! I couldn't figure out what had happened, until I discovered that I was logged on to the server in the server room.

I had no way to unlock my Administrator account, because you must have administrative rights in order to modify an account with administrative rights. Of course, I couldn't find my boss to ask him to unlock my account. When I paged my boss he told me to check the

filing cabinet for a sealed envelope containing the logon information for the backup Administrator account. I used this backup account to unlock my account and enclosed the logon information in another sealed envelope. (The sealed envelope helps us detect whether the account information has been tampered with.)

The moral of this story is to always have a backup Administrator account ready for emergencies. Another important lesson to be learned is: If you are using your account with administrative rights, always log out of machines when you are done. Someone could tamper with information while logged on as you, and it would appear that you were responsible. Finally, the last lesson to be learned is to never change your password on a Windows NT server or workstation if you are currently logged on to more than one machine. You will instantly be locked out of your account! Overall, be careful when you are using an account with administrative rights—it's very powerful!

—Cameron Brandon, MCSE+Internet, CNE, A+, Network+

e x a m
ⓦ a t c h *You should memorize what makes a secure and safe password. Make sure to eliminate the use of easily guessed words or phrases from your passwords!*

A good way to approach password security is to think like a hacker. If I were a hacker, I'd like to break into an account with a nice, easy password that resembles a common phrase or easily guessed word or group of words. For this reason, choosing such passwords is an absolute no-no for password security. If you want to enforce password security, you cannot, under any circumstances, allow your users to create passwords that include their names, the names of relatives, birthdays, or common phrases. Today's hackers use technology called "brute-force" attacks that run dictionary files against the user account in question in an attempt to break into that account. They are usually successful because the user decided to employ a commonly guessed word or phrase, such as their favorite baseball team or their spouse's birthday, as a password. Unfortunately, when you prevent users from choosing easily remembered passwords, some users are prone to compromise security even further by writing their password on a yellow sticky note and posting it on their monitor. You must educate your users about the need for password security and institute a policy that prohibits them from posting their passwords or sharing passwords with other users.

You should require users to change their passwords frequently, such as every three to four weeks. Even the most secure and seemingly unbreakable passwords are not impervious to some high-quality hacking programs. Some hacking programs run for a set period of time until the password is broken. On a standard Pentium 200MHz, it could take such a program roughly three or four weeks running nonstop to break the password. If you require frequent password changes, by the time the hacker can compromise a user's password it's time to change the password anyway, effectively stopping the hacker's progress. Exercise 9-1 shows you how to change a password on a Windows 2000 system.

CertCam 9-1

EXERCISE 9-1

Changing Your Password on a Windows 2000 System

1. Make sure that you are logged on to the system as yourself.

2. Press CTRL-ALT-DEL.

3. This action opens the Windows Security window, which includes a button marked Change Password.

4. Select the **Change Password** button and a new window appears that has five text boxes in which you can type information. The first line should be filled

in with your username under which you are currently logged in. The second line is for the domain or PC name to which you are going to change you password. The third line is for you to type in the old password; the fourth and fifth lines are for you to type in the new password and confirm the new password. Fill in all the text boxes with the appropriate information.

5. Select **OK** to change the password.

on the

①ob

With all the computer technology available to help secure your network, sometimes the weakest link in your network is the human factor. You can implement the strongest policies and use the latest technology available, but if your users fail to adhere to the rules and regulations regarding your network password policies, all your work is for naught. To combat this problem, you might want to encourage your users to become better trained on the technology that they are using.

The last standard practice for enforcing password guidelines on your network is to enable password lockouts. In particular, with the Microsoft Windows NT operating system, the network administrator can enable password lockout after a user makes x number of attempts to log in with an incorrect password. The network administrator specifies the duration of time that the account is locked. A reasonable amount of time is about 30 minutes. For example, if a hacker is attempting to break into the network via a certain user account and he doesn't know the password, after three unsuccessful attempts to log in, the user account that the hacker is trying to invade is disabled for 30 minutes. This practice severely limits the ability of a hacker to keep trying different passwords on the same user account.

Table 9-2 provides guidelines that will help you enforce strong passwords on your network.

exam

ⓦatch

It seems obvious to specify passwords with a mixture of upper- and lowercase letters and the use of at least one symbol. The exam will test your knowledge of safe password practices by having you select the most secure password from a list of choices.

IP Addresses

Transmission Control Protocol/Internet Protocol (TCP/IP) is an industry-standard suite of protocols designed for local and wide area networking. TCP/IP was developed in

TABLE 9-2	Strong password guidelines	

Guideline	Purpose
Password is at least eight characters long.	The more characters in a password, the more difficult it is to crack.
Password consists of both letters and numbers.	Passwords that contain a mix of letters and numbers defeat dictionary and "brute-force" attacks by disrupting the pattern that these programs look for.
Password includes symbols (!, @, #, $, %, ^, &, *,).	The use of symbols helps complicate the password and disrupts the pattern looked for by dictionary and "brute-force" programs.
Password does not consist of common words or phrases.	A dictionary program can easily crack passwords that consist of words or phrases.
Passwords are changed frequently.	Even a strong password can be cracked with time; changing a password frequently defeats any hacker that might have cracked the old password.
Lock user accounts after x number of attempts to log in with an incorrect password.	Account lockout prevents a hacker from running a program that repeatedly tries different passwords until finding the correct one.

1969, in a Defense Advanced Research Projects Agency (DARPA) research project on network interconnection. Formerly a military network, this global area network has exploded in popularity and is now referred to as the *Internet.*

TCP/IP gained most of its popularity through its wide use for Internet communication. Connecting computers throughout the world, TCP/IP is known for being both reliable and routable and for being able to "talk" to foreign networks.

Any PC with TCP/IP enables its user to connect to the Internet as well as to any machine running TCP/IP and providing TCP/IP services. This includes some applications that require TCP/IP to function. The following list summarizes the advantages of TCP/IP:

- It is the backbone of the Internet. If you need to connect to the Internet, you need TCP/IP.

- It is routable. This means that you can talk to other networks through routers.

- It is very popular. Think of all the computers on the Internet—they all use TCP/IP!

- Some applications need TCP/IP to run.

- TCP/IP provides connectivity across operating systems and hardware platforms. Windows NT can use an FTP client to access a UNIX workstation or server.

- TCP/IP provides Simple Network Management Protocol (SNMP) support, which is used to troubleshoot problems on the network.

- TCP/IP provides Dynamic Host Configuration Protocol (DHCP) support, which is used for dynamic IP addressing.

- TCP/IP provides Windows Internet Naming Service (WINS) support, which resolves Windows NetBIOS names on the network (mainly Windows systems).

To configure a TCP/IP address on a computer, you need specific TCP/IP parameters. These parameters consist of a static TCP/IP address, a subnet mask, and a default gateway (router), if you are connecting to the Internet or another network. You can use either a static or DHCP-assigned TCP/IP address to connect to the Internet. If you are using a server to connect to the Internet, a static IP address makes more sense, so you don't have to continue to update your DNS tables.

An IP address can be thought of as a "house" address that you might see on the side of a building. Just as every house has a street address, city, and ZIP code, every computer that uses TCP/IP has an IP address. A computer uses an IP address to identify itself on the network. Just as each and every house has an address associated with it, all computers on a network that uses TCP/IP must have an IP address. This address helps identify the computer on the network so that the computers can "talk" to one another. Each IP address can be configured for a separate subnet or network so that computers can communicate with one another. An IP address is a 32-bit address that is broken up into four parts, or *octets*. For example, an IP address of 10.11.12.13 is made up of four octets separated by decimals. The four octets are 10, 11, 12, and 13.

In order for one computer to communicate with another computer, there must be a dialog in place in the form of a network protocol. Due to its popularity on the Internet, TCP/IP has become one of the most widely adopted network communication standards within the entire computer industry. Because an IP address is actually a 32-bit address, a subnet mask helps separate the network from the host ID. The network ID identifies the network on which the computer resides (similar to the function of a ZIP code). The host ID identifies the specific computer (similar to a house address), as we discussed in Chapter 4.

IP Configurations

TCP/IP has many different uses and many possible IP configurations. Your TCP/IP parameters determine how and what your TCP/IP configuration will be. IP configurations are ultimately determined by the network operating system that you are running on your desktop. For instance, some operating systems do not recognize Dynamic Host Configuration Protocol (DHCP). DHCP is used to automatically hand out an IP address and configuration from an open pool of TCP/IP addresses.

Table 9-3 shows examples of the many TCP/IP parameters and the specifics of how they are used.

TABLE 9-3   TCP/IP configuration options

TCP/IP Parameters	Description
IP address	An IP address is a 32-bit network address that identifies a computer on a network. An IP address is made up of a network ID and a host ID. An IP address is a four-octet address—for example, 204.22.120.3.
Subnet mask	A subnet mask separates the network ID from the host ID. This mask can break down an individual IP address into different and separate logical networks, or subnets.
Default gateway	A default gateway is a router that is used to send packets to remote networks. A configured default gateway receives a packet from your computer and routes the packet to its correct destination. Without a default gateway configured, your computer cannot communicate with any remote networks.
Domain Name System	A DNS service is used to map IP addresses to fully qualified domain names (FQDNs). This form of name resolution is commonly used on the Internet to map IP addresses to popular Web sites.
Windows Internet Naming Service	Like DNS, WINS provides name resolution for computers, but it does so only for Windows computers and is normally "Microsoft centric." WINS maps IP addresses to NetBIOS names.
HOST file	A HOST file is an internal computer file that maps a computer's hostname to an IP address. This file is commonly used when a name resolution service such as DNS or WINS is not available.
LMHOST file	An LMHOST file maps NetBIOS names to IP addresses.
MAC address	A MAC address is the physical network address of a computer's network interface card. A MAC address is a 12-letter hexadecimal address that is broken up into two segments. The first six hex characters identify the vendor of the network card; the last six hex characters are the serial number that identifies the computer.

| TABLE 9-3 | TCP/IP configuration options *(continued)* |

TCP/IP Parameters	Description
Dynamic Host Configuration Protocol	DHCP is used to automatically allocate TCP/IP address information to a computer that is "DHCP enabled." This practice reduces the amount of administration necessary for large networks.
Hostname	A hostname uniquely identifies the computer on the network. A hostname or FQDN uniquely identifies a computer on the network or Internet, but a NetBIOS name is the computer name that is specified by the network administrator. These two names can be different, but unless they are changed, the hostname defaults to the NetBIOS computer name.

Name Resolution

Computers communicate with each other using network addresses, but people tend to want to communicate using computer names. It is much easier to remember a computer name than a set of four numbers. Therefore, a more intuitive solution has been introduced so that people can communicate using computer names instead of hard-to-remember network addresses.

Names must be resolved to their respective network addresses. The two main options associated with name resolution on computer networks are DNS and WINS. For name resolution on Windows networks, WINS resolves NetBIOS names to TCP/IP addresses. For computers that use hostnames, DNS resolves FQDNs to TCP/IP addresses. The Internet uses DNS to keep track of all of the different names found on the Internet.

WINS

Windows Internet Naming Service (WINS) was designed to eliminate the need for broadcasts to resolve NetBIOS names to IP addresses and to provide a dynamic database that maintains NetBIOS names to IP address mappings. (The computer name is just one of many NetBIOS names.) This type of name resolution was introduced by the IETF as an RFC for the use of NetBIOS Name Servers (NBNS) to resolve NetBIOS names to IP addresses. WINS is Microsoft's implementation of an RFC-compliant NBNS. The TCP/IP information is stored in a database on WINS. Instead of network clients broadcasting for name resolution, the client contacts WINS, which informs the client of the correct address.

Unlike Windows NT, Windows 2000 is dependent on DNS but still supports WINS for backward compatibility.

DNS

DNS (Domain Name System) maps TCP/IP addresses to hostnames. Normally, computers communicate on a network via their MAC addresses. To communicate by name, the TCP/IP address must be resolved to a hostname, which is not always the same as the computer name. DNS maps TCP/IP addresses to hostnames on the network. DNS uses a distributed database over hundreds of different computers to resolve computer hostnames. This helps us locate computers all over the Internet. We type the DNS name of the server we want to access, and DNS maps the correct TCP/IP address for us automatically. Sounds simple, right?

These DNS root servers used to be managed by the Internet Network Information Center (InterNic), but they are now managed by the Internet Corporation for Assigned Names and Numbers (ICANN). You are probably familiar with the DNS naming scheme: Microsoft.com, Cisco.com, Oracle.com, and Dell.com are all examples of DNS names.

Relevant Standard Operating Procedures

From network to network, many similar SOPs are maintained. No matter which network you visit, these procedures generally stay the same. The names of these procedures might change, but the duties that they involve are very similar. This section presents the most important SOPs that you should follow on your own network.

Keep the network up and running at all times. You can accomplish this SOP via many subprocedures, such as backing up the data on the network, monitoring the performance of your servers, and performing common administration duties for the network.

Back up network data every night. This is one of the most important duties that a network administrator can perform. No matter how secure and stable your computer network, events out of your control can bring down the network or accidentally destroy a server.

Monitor the performance of your servers and network infrastructure. Doing so helps you troubleshoot problems and work proactively to prevent problems. The best way to troubleshoot a bottleneck on a server resource is to have monitored the performance of that resource over time so that you have a *baseline* of the resource in day-to-day operation. The baseline measurement gathers statistics on network and resource usage under normal circumstances. You should also monitor the amount of traffic on the network. To do this, you can use a network *sniffer*, a network monitoring tool that analyzes the network's traffic and can help you solve infrastructure-related problems.

As a network administrator, you could have common duties such as securing the network, configuring network hardware, and managing users and permissions. The more comfortable you become with these daily SOPs, the more you can begin concentrating on other areas of network management, such as backing up your data and monitoring network performance.

Now let's take a look at some possible scenarios and their solutions.

SCENARIO & SOLUTION

I want to connect two LAN segments that use Ethernet and Token Ring.	Connect the two network segments with a switch. Switched ports are cheap, and they do a great job. Using a standard hub allows no separation of the two LAN segments.
I want to connect two LAN segments in different geographical locations.	To connect LAN segments in different geographical locations, you need a router. A router can find the destination address of a packet and send the packet accordingly.
A user wants to connect his PC, which has an RJ-45 connector, with a computer that has a BNC connection.	Connect the PC with the RJ-45 connector to a hub and the BNC connection to another hub that supports both connections.
I want to connect a TCP/IP network to an IPX/SPX network.	Use a gateway to connect networks that are using two different protocols.
I have 10 PCs that all connect to one server. What do I need to support the bandwidth requirements?	All that you need is a simple hub. Ten PCs do not require too much bandwidth unless you are doing video.
My client has over 2500 computers in one geographic location. What network appliance would be right for this large a network?	With a network of that size, you should use network switches and divide the computers into separate broadcast domains.
I want to connect two networks that are in the same location. Can I use a router?	A router can be used to connect networks that are in the same location, but for cost reasons, you might want to pick a less expensive solution relative to the number of ports that are required. Generally, routers are more expensive per port than switches or hubs.

Environmental Factors that Affect Computer Networks

Most networks have a centrally located area that can safely house all network appliances and servers. Within this room is a multitude of special features that can help protect the computers and other environmentally "sensitive" equipment from failing due to extreme temperatures.

Computers, like most other electrical hardware, are affected by temperature, moisture, vibrations, and electrical interference. If the computers are exposed to these elements, they can act irregularly and sometimes fail. Luckily, standards protect computer components from these situations.

Cables

Underneath the protection of most network cables lies a fragile layer of wire (or glass, in the case of fiber optic) that carries the data from one computer to another. Like most other computer components, this wire is not resistant to moisture, heat, or other electrical interference. To protect this cable from harm, a covering is placed over the wire to protect it from breaking or accidentally becoming wet. The main reason for the covering is to prevent cross-talk and electromagnetic interference (EMI).

Cables that bring data to networks come in many different forms, from copper to fiber optic. The type of cable determines the length that it can be. When a cable exceeds the recommended distance, the signal begins to fade. Table 9-4 lists the types of cables, their characteristics, and the distance they can carry a signal.

exam
ⓦatch

Make sure that you know the cable length limitations for each type of cable. You will be presented with scenario questions for which you are to determine if the configuration is valid; you must know whether the maximum cable length has been exceeded. These questions are challenging due to the complex scenario-based format.

| TABLE 9-4 | Cabling characteristics | |

Type of Cable	Characteristic	Length
10BaseT	Flexible; uses RJ-45 connector.	100 meters/328 feet
10Base2	Less flexible than 10BaseT; uses a BNC connector to hook computers together. Must be terminated at both ends.	185 meters/607 feet
10Base5	Rigid; does not bend well around corners. Not used often; AUI connector.	1640 feet
Fiber optic	Does not do well in tight changes of redirection. Carries data extreme distances. Easily broken; fragile.	2 kilometers

The Network Operations Center

Your *network operations center (NOC)* is the home base for all of the important servers on your network. The NOC enables you to centrally manage and keep a close eye on all your networked data.

An NOC, above all else, needs to be secure and able to house all the data and servers. Normally in a locked room, the NOC is a secured room that is equipped with different types of fire suppression (halon, foam), raised floors to place the cabling, and temperature control. You can't put a value on your data, so this room should never be compromised in any way.

The room conditions of your NOC should be cool, dry, and temperature controlled. Computers and other electrical equipment do not like humidity, heat, or extreme cold, so you should be very careful to regulate the temperature of your NOC. When a computer overheats, there is no guarantee that the data on your servers can be saved.

Because computer equipment is very sensitive to moisture, you need to use a form of fire suppression besides water. Putting out a fire in your NOS using a sprinkler system would ruin all your computer equipment. Many types of foams or halon are used to put out fires quickly and safely while minimizing the potential damage to your computer equipment. The laws of your geographical area could require that you not use certain types of fire control methods. Some states require older systems to be upgraded within a certain amount of time and consider older fire control methods dangerous.

exam
ⓌatⒸh

You will be asked to determine which environment of several scenarios is the most conducive to a server room. Just remember that servers need an environment free of dust, with plenty of ventilation and reasonable temperature and humidity. Placing servers near a window on a sunny day or in a dusty warehouse would not create an ideal operating environment.

Minimizing Electrical Interference

Electromagnetic interference (EMI) can wreak great havoc on any type of computer equipment. You might be aware of certain types of speakers that are magnetically shielded to prevent electrical interference. However, magnets and computers don't mix, so unfortunately this concept doesn't carry over to computer electronics. Your alternative is to keep all your computer equipment away from any electrical device that could interrupt the computing power of your equipment.

exam
ⓌatⒸh

For the exam, remember to make sure that you don't expose your computers or network equipment to any potential environmental hazards, such as moisture or extreme heat, or to electrical interference, such as generators and televisions. The exam might include questions pertaining to the location of equipment.

Computer Chassis

With the boom of today's technology, computers are faster than ever. Today there is more computing power on a single laptop computer than was used by NASA to place the first man on the moon. However, more computing power comes at a price. The price that we pay is heat. As processors become faster and faster, they become hotter and hotter as they perform billions of calculations. The scenario is the same for disk drives. The larger the drives become, the more work that needs to be done to find the data on the drive. The result is that the temperature within the PC's chassis becomes too hot for the computer to operate. When this happens, the overheating part fails or destroys the PC altogether.

To combat this problem, a cooling fan is placed inside the PC to circulate the air and prevent the PC from overheating. Some of the more inventive computer chassis help circulate the air inside the PC to keep the computer cool. The room where the servers are placed should also be air conditioned. The air in the PC chassis can only be as cool as the air it is circulating from the room in which it is placed.

Error Messages

Error messages carry a mixed blessing in the computer industry. It's great to know when an error arises, but some error messages are so vague and incomprehensible that they do nothing but confuse you further.

You will encounter many types of error messages in your day-to-day progress with computers. You will see syntax errors, general protection faults, memory dumps, Dr. Watson messages, error logs, .DLL conflicts, and several hundred others.

When using your computer, you might inadvertently generate an error message. When your computer gives you an error message, it is letting you know that it cannot understand the data input or that an unexpected error has occurred.

Some of the better-written and -coded programs go out of their way to let you know what exactly is happening when you generate an error message. Seeing "Error Code 12452" flash across the screen doesn't help you much unless you know exactly what "Error Code 12452" is. Chances are that you have no idea what that cryptic error message means.

If you are lucky, sometimes you can look into the Help file to find out what a vague error message means. It helps to check the vendor's Web site as well, because it might have an online support site specifically for those types of questions.

Some error messages are user friendly and tell you exactly what you did wrong. For instance, if you cannot print and you see the message "Incorrect Printer Driver, Please Install Correct Driver," you have a good idea as to what you might have done wrong and you know how to fix your problem.

Table 9-5 lists some common error messages and their meanings.

Now that you have an understanding of error messages, let's generate an error message in Exercise 9-2 so that you can see how they appear.

EXERCISE 9-2

Generating the "Deleting Files" Error Message

1. Place a CD in the CD-ROM (preferably a CD that came in a software package of some sort or a CD-R, not a CD-RW).

2. Close any windows that opened if the CD had some type of autorun code. Right-click **My Computer** on the desktop and select **Explore**.

3. In the left pane, select the **CD-ROM drive letter**.

4. In the right pane, select a **file** or **folder** and then press the **Delete** key on the keyboard.

5. Select **Yes** in the window that opens to verify the delete. If you selected a folder, you need to select **Yes to all** in the next window.

6. You should now get an error message that the file is read-only and cannot be deleted. Select **OK** in the error message window and then close Explorer.

TABLE 9-5   Common error messages

Error Message	Description
Syntax error	You have entered information that your computer cannot understand. This error is normally caused by a typo or an incorrect spelling of a desired command.
General protection fault	An overlapping memory block within your computer system causes a general protection fault. This error is less common with secure operating systems, such as Windows NT, because they can compensate by not giving any software direct access to the hardware and can run processes in separate memory spaces.
"Blue Screen of Death"	A common Windows NT error screen in which the computer crashes, reboots, and dumps the error logs into memory. If you see this screen, something major is wrong.
Bad command or file name	Your computer does not understand what has been entered. Make sure that you have the correct path and that the program or file that you want to access is in the specified directory.
File is listed as read only	With this attribute set, you can only see this error message when you try to write to a file that is listed as *read only*. With this permission, you can only have *read* access to the file; you cannot change the file.
Access denied	This error message is self-explanatory: Your permissions do not match the necessary permissions to access the file or directory.

Common Peripheral Ports and Network Components

What good is a computer without all the goodies that accompany it? There are literally hundreds of peripherals and network components to choose from in today's fun-filled world of computers. Here, you will learn the basics about the companion pieces you will likely encounter in your day-to-day experience.

All these ports and network components are mainly used to make the experience of using a computer easier and more user friendly. If you want to be an expert in networking technology, you should know and understand each component in case you have to troubleshoot a problem some day.

Network Interface Cards

Your *network interface card (NIC)* should be autodetected during setup, but if it is not, you must enter the NIC's IRQ, the I/O address, and the base memory address. If these settings are not correct, the network fails to start when you log on, and you receive a message while booting up that a service or driver failed to load. Usually the hardware vendor for your card provides you with a network configuration diskette that tells you exactly what the settings should be. To save time, verify these settings before you begin the setup process. As you configure your card, you'll be asked whether you are wired to the network or are connecting via the Remote Access Service (RAS). Make sure that you refer back to Chapter 2, "The Physical Layer," and review the lab for installing NICs.

Being Wired to the Network

Being part of a network is what networking is all about. Having access to thousands of files and applications that are just a click away is both convenient and efficient. In order for your Web server to communicate with other computers on the network, you have to install a NIC. This card also has to be configured correctly with TCP/IP. The NIC binds with TCP/IP to enable communication.

When you can communicate with other computes on the network, you are free to share files and information at the click of a button. This is what makes networking so special and one of the many reasons that computer networks are changing the face of business as we know it today.

Binding Protocols

Being wired to a network gives you connectivity to other computers and enables you to exchange information. However, each computer on a network generates a good deal of traffic, and when you have a large number of computers on the network, an awful lot of traffic is generated. If you have more than one protocol installed for your NIC, your computer will try to use each protocol that is installed. For best performance, you should have installed only the necessary protocols that you will use on your network. Having more than one protocol installed creates extra traffic and more overhead for your network than are necessary.

Network Connection

Connecting to the Internet with a networked server requires a large amount of bandwidth to provide connectivity for all users. The amount of bandwidth determines the number of users can access your site at once. A fast network connection enables easy access to your Web site, whereas a slow connection sometimes prohibits users from getting to your Web site. If you are on an intranet, you probably do not have to worry about the amount of bandwidth. A normal 10MB Ethernet network card should be sufficient.

To connect straight to the Internet, you need a router or default gateway so that others outside your network can access your site. If you do not want to use a dedicated router for your Internet connection, your Windows NT 4.0 Server can perform the same duties with proper configuration.

Network-Attached Storage

Network-attached storage (NAS) units are standalone devices, usually SCSI, which have a network interface but no PC. A NAS is a containment unit with a power supply, cooling fans, one or two SCSI controller cards, and bays to hold the storage units. The unit usually can also be locked to prevent anyone from opening it and removing its contents. The storage units are either CD-ROMs or hard disks.

With CD-ROMs, the unit is usually called a *CD tower* and allows you to share the CD on the network to allow users easy access to multiple CDs. CD towers can hold as many as 32 CD-ROMs.

With hard disks, a NAS allows for a large point of mass storage and can possibly include a built-in RAID controller to allow all the hard disks to be fault tolerant and be seen as a single volume.

You manage configuration of NAS by telnetting to the system and setting configuration options to allow sharing and setting up a unit name. The unit name allows you to use the Universal Naming Convention (UNC) to connect to the unit and its devices.

Advantages of NAS

One advantage of using NAS is that the units can be placed anywhere. Most of these units are a little larger than a tower PC and can be placed under a desk.

To add storage units, you don't need to purchase a PC and OS into which to place the required devices, such as the hard disks and CD-ROMs. In addition, the units take up less space and can be placed in a server room, even on a desk or table, or in another secure area, so you don't need a large amount of space.

Disadvantages of NAS

A disadvantage of NAS is that the interface requires some knowledge of Telnet and can require some training to use.

Administering these units also requires some monitoring to verify that the unit is still functioning properly with the proper share names. The administration might not be too difficult, but it will cause some overhead. Usually once it is set up, it won't need further administration for awhile. CD-ROM units usually require a little more administration because the CDs typically need to be changed, which changes some share names. Hard disk units are not too difficult to administer.

on the job

Network-attached storage units are very useful in a large network environment. It is easy to use a CD tower to share all the CDs required to install applications on new PCs. In a WAN environment during a mass upgrade, you can take the CD tower to the different locations at which the PCs are being upgraded. This portability allows for faster access without having to use slow WAN links.

Serial Ports

With a serial port like the one used by your keyboard or mouse, data can flow in only one direction. This makes for slow data transfer. Your keyboard and mouse are one-way devices that require only a serial interface and a line.

Parallel Ports

Parallel ports are the quicker of the devices that are connected to the outside of your computer. Parallel transmission works by sending data in both directions. (Serial transmission goes only one way.) Your printer, for instance, uses a parallel cable to speed up the printing process.

Universal Serial Bus

Universal Serial Bus (USB) is an innovation in computer peripheral technology that enables you to add devices such as audio players, joysticks, keyboards, telephones, and scanners to your computer without having to add an adapter card or even having to turn the computer off. Sounds like a good idea, huh? Well, USB can even transfer data up to 12 Mbps and works using the existing power of the computer, so you don't have to plug any of your USB devices into a wall socket.

Most PCs have only one or two USB ports. These ports can be extended using a USB hub which has four or more USB ports on it and can be connected by a USB cable to one of the PC USB ports.

on the **job** **One bad thing about USB is that it does not work with Windows NT. Windows 95, 98, ME, 2000, and XP do support USB.**

Small Computer System Interface

Small Computer System Interface (SCSI) is a standard interface that enables personal computers to communicate with peripheral hardware, such as disk drives, tape drives, CD-ROM drives, printers, and scanners. What makes SCSI devices so special is the improvement in data transfer over parallel devices. For example, the newest Ultra-Wide SCSI 2 devices can transfer data up to 80 Mbps. Another benefit of SCSI devices is the capability to daisy-chain up to 7 or 15 devices (depending on the bus width). SCSI devices are more important for high-performance computing systems such as servers than they are for the home PC.

Interrupts

The OS on your machine (probably a flavor of Windows) sets up the interrupt request (IRQ) lines that enable the OS to communicate with the various devices within your system, such as graphic cards, CD-ROM drives, network cards, and printers.

Your computer communicates to these peripherals using the IRQ hardware lines via which your computer sends input and output messages. These IRQs are assigned different priorities so that the microprocessor can determine which of the interrupts it's receiving is the most important.

To simplify matters, when your computer needs to use a device such as a network card, the network card signals the CPU via the IRQ so that it can use the processing power of the CPU to do its work.

Print Servers

Print servers can be either dedicated servers that are responsible for sending documents to various printer pools scattered around a corporation, or they can be used in tandem with file servers. These servers are used to send documents to a server that takes care of the printing process. This system makes much more sense than having a separate printer for each computer, and it gives you more control over administering the documents that are sent to each network printer.

Peripherals

With today's booming computer industry, you have many options in choosing peripherals for your computer. The standard I/O devices, such as keyboard and mouse, are the mainstays of computer peripherals, but you can choose many other peripherals to make your PC experience even better. Let's look at some now.

The Keyboard

A *keyboard* connects to the serial port of your computer and enables you to input data. Because the keyboard is the primary input device, you rely on the keyboard more than you realize. The keyboard contains certain standard function keys, such as the Escape key, Tab key, cursor movement keys, Shift keys, and Control keys, and sometimes other manufacturer-customized keys, such as the Windows key.

The serial port is actually a PS/2 port that is circular and is the same as the PS/2-style mouse port.

The Mouse

A *mouse* connects to the serial port of your computer and enables you to move a cursor around the GUI of your desktop operating system. The newer mice come standard with a PS/2 connector and sometimes have a PS/2-to-serial-port converter.

Printers

A *printer* outputs data on your computer to paper or other media, such as labels, transparencies, or envelopes.

Digital Camera

A *digital camera* is a new peripheral that enables the user to take pictures without film. The pictures are saved as digital images on a disk or card and can be transferred to a computer for manipulation, enhancement, and distribution through means such as e-mailing and printing.

Scanners

Scanners are used to import an image into a digital version for use by applications. Scanners usually plug into the PC using the parallel port, a USB port, or even SCSI connections.

Modems

A *modem* is a communications device that enables a computer to talk to another computer through a standard telephone line. The modem converts digital data from the computer to analog data for transmission over telephone lines and then back to digital data for the receiving computer. With the Internet boom, modems have increased in speed and have brought the power of millions of computers right inside your house.

Bridges

Bridges are intelligent devices used to connect LANs. A bridge can also forward packets of data based on MAC addresses. They can filter traffic on a LAN. They determine the source and destination involved in the transfer of packets. They read the specific physical address of a packet on one network segment and then decide to filter out the packet or forward it to another segment.

Hubs

Hubs enable you to concentrate LAN connections. You can connect devices using twisted-pair copper media (UTP) to hubs to concentrate computers together. The limitation of unshielded twisted-pair (UTP) network cable is that it has the capability to carry data only 100 meters before the signal begins to fade. To strengthen the signal, a hub is used. The type of hub depends on what type of technology you are using. You can have either Token Ring hubs, media access units (MAUs), or standard Ethernet hubs.

Because most modern networks use UTP for installation, you need to learn the standards relating to Ethernet hubs. If you have a network that has to cover a large physical location, you must remember that one piece of UTP cable can reach only 100 meters. This severely limits what you can do with your network unless you use hubs.

Table 9-6 describes some benefits of using hubs in a networked environment.

Switches

Switches offer full-duplex, dedicated bandwidth to LAN segments or desktops. You can think of a switch as an intelligent hub that guarantees a certain amount of bandwidth to the computer to which it is connected. The amount of bandwidth—

TABLE 9-6	Benefits of using hubs in a networked environment

Benefit	Description
Hubs centralize monitoring and administration.	Most "managed" hubs come with special monitoring and optimization tools that can be used to let you know if you are having a problem. You can also see the performance level of the throughput of your network.
Hubs enable easy expansion because you can daisy-chain several hubs to form one large hub.	If you want to expand your hub capacity, all you have to do is daisy-chain a separate hub to create one, large managed hub.
Hubs enable you to use several different ports that can connect to several different resources.	With hubs, you can utilize different ports for onsite administration and connect media, such as a coax segment with a UTP segment of your network.
Hubs provide a high level of fault tolerance.	When you have several wires coming into a hub, if one wire fails it will not affect any of the other wires that are linked to the hub.
Hubs expand the length of your network.	Due to the distance limitation of UTP (100 meters), you might have to use hubs to boost the strength of the signal to connect segments of your network.
Hubs enable you to connect multiple users to form one network.	This works with the star topology by which clients are connected to a hub in a star formation.

10, 100, or 1000 Mbps—of course depends on which port you are connected to. With a hub, you are guaranteed some of the bandwidth all of the time. This means that hubs are not intelligent enough to account for collisions on the network; you might be connected to a 10MB port, but you might be receiving only 4MB of data due to the amount of traffic on the network. With a switch, you are guaranteed the entire limit of your bandwidth because the switch is intelligent and can examine the packet and send it in the right direction.

on the job

Today's computer networks must support the combination of voice, video, and data, so many network administrators are beginning to favor intelligent switches over common shared hubs. Network switches enable you to have bandwidth on demand and ensure that you can use your network to its fullest capacity. If you have a switch that is capable of 100 Mbps, you are guaranteed that amount of bandwidth due to the way a switch can intelligently look at the packets. A shared hub, on the other hand, can sometimes supply only 40 percent of the network's potential bandwidth.

Routers

Routers route data packets across a network by opening the packets and making routing decisions based on their contents. As you learned earlier in this chapter, TCP/IP addresses enable communication between computers. In order for remote computer networks to talk to one another, a device is needed to guide the TCP/IP network traffic to its destination. This is where routers perform their duties.

Remember the OSI model that you learned about in Chapter 3? To understand better the functions of routers, you need a good understanding of the Network layer of the OSI model. The Network layer, or Layer 3, is responsible for addressing messages and translating their logical addresses into actual physical addresses. It is important to remember that a router is protocol dependent. That means that a TCP/IP router can connect to a TCP/IP network. In other words, this is the layer of the OSI model that is responsible for determining where to send the TCP/IP packets to get them to their destinations. Routers essentially separate broadcast domains from one another and route traffic based on the packets' destination, or Layer 3, addresses (the Layer 2 address is the MAC address).

When you want to communicate with another computer network, your computer essentially looks within the local network first before heading out to search for a remote address. For example, when your computer needs to access a file on another computer, your computer first checks its ARP cache to see if that computer has a recognizable MAC address. If it does not, your computer checks the local subnet by either broadcasting or asking a name server for help.

If the address is not found on the local subnet or network, your computer checks to see if you have a default gateway or router to which to send the information. Your computer sends this information to your router and the router routes the message accordingly. What happens is that the router receives the data with the address information and checks its routing tables to see where it should send your data. The type of router sometimes affects how quickly your data arrives at its destination.

Routers are either static or dynamic. Nine times out of ten, you have to deal with only a dynamic router—a router whose routing tables are populated automatically by receiving updates from other routers. Static routers have fixed routing tables that must be updated manually. These static routers are at a disadvantage because they cannot communicate with any type of router if a network route changes due to hardware failure or a change to the network layout.

The main benefit of a dynamic router is that, depending on which type of routing protocol is used, it attempts to route your network traffic to your destination as quickly as possible. For example, say that you have a network that is standardized on Cisco routers (dynamic) that all communicate with one another using the Open Shortest Path First (OSPF) routing protocol. All your routers are communicating with one another via broadcasts that they send whenever there is a change in their routing. This system comes in very handy and adds a layer of redundancy so that if a segment of the network fails, your routers will be able to route the network traffic to other paths. This way, no matter what happens to the network, your data will always arrive at its destination.

If you were using a static router and a segment of your network failed, your network traffic would cease until the segment was repaired or another static route was mapped on the router. This puts static routing at a severe disadvantage in a large, complex network environment.

Table 9-7 lists some of the characteristics of routers and what separates them from other network appliances.

Gateways

A *gateway* can link networks that have different protocols, such as TCP/IP to IPX/SPX. A gateway can change an entire protocol stack into another or provide protocol

TABLE 9-7   Router characteristics

Router Characteristic	Explanation
Protocol dependent	Routers are usually dependent on one protocol. A TCP/IP router cannot communicate with an IPX router.
Can communicate with other networks	A router works at the Network layer of the OSI model. It reads the destination of the packet and then sends the packet on its way to the destination network.
Used to connect to the Internet	Using a router, you can communicate with various remote networks, such as the ever-popular Internet.
Can connect to different types of media, such as Ethernet and Token Ring	Some routers can connect two different network types, such as an Ethernet to a Token Ring connection or an ATM to an Ethernet. Normally these routers work in the traditional way, but they might have one or two ports to connect to different media.
Works at the Network layer, or Level 3, of the OSI model	Routers work at the Network layer of the OSI model. This means that they can identify where the packet is coming from and then send the packet to the correct destination.
Two different types, static and dynamic routers	Static routers have fixed routing tables that must be updated manually. Dynamic routers work by sending out broadcasts of their routing tables to other routers. This way, routers can change the path of a packet dynamically to work around a "downed" link.

conversion and routing services between computer networks. Gateways examine the entire packet and then translate the incompatible protocols so that each network can understand the two different protocols. For example, protocol gateways can also be used to convert ATM cells to Frame Relay frames and vice versa.

Now that you have an understanding of the port types available, work through Exercise 9-3 to determine what ports you have an your PC that are recognized by your OS.

EXERCISE 9-3

CertCam 9-3

Determining Ports on a PC

1. On a Windows 9x or ME PC, right-click **My Computer**, select **Properties**, then click the **Device Manager** tab. On a Windows 2000 PC, right-click

My Computer, select **Properties**, select the **Hardware** tab, and then click the **Device Manager** tab.

2. In the Device Manager window, click the + sign next to the option you want to expand so that you can see the devices recognized by the OS.

3. Click the + next to Ports to see the detected ports.

4. Click the + next to Universal Serial Bus Controller to see the USB devices, if any.

5. Click the + next to SCSI to see the SCSI devices, if any.

Now that you have an understanding of some of the peripheral ports and network components, let's look at some possible scenarios dealing with these areas.

SCENARIO & SOLUTION

What type of device is required to allow a PC to communicate on the network?	You need a NIC.
What port allows for only a one-way link and sends data one bit at a time?	A serial port.
What port allows for bidirectional communication and sends data more than one bit at a time?	A parallel port.
What port type allows for transmission speeds of over 10 Mbps but does not work with Windows NT?	A USB port.
What port type allows for transfer speeds of up to 80 Mbps and can work with any type of OS?	Small Computer System Interface, or SCSI.
What does a device use to get the attention of the CPU?	An interrupt request (IRQ) line.
What are two peripherals required for a GUI OS?	A keyboard and a mouse.

CERTIFICATION OBJECTIVE 9.04

Compatibility and Cabling Issues

All network cables are not created equal. There are four different types of commonly used network cables: Thicknet (10Base5), Thinnet (10Base2), twisted pair, and fiber optic. For most of your networking needs, twisted pair is the cable of choice because it is relatively inexpensive and available. It is also easy to run in tight places, and many standards are adopted for its RJ-45 interface.

Twisted-pair cables come in many types with varying degrees of reliability. They are ranked in categories based on the proven level of data they can carry, as summarized in Table 9-8.

Basically, if you have two different types of cables and you need to connect them, you need a hub, a router, or a switch to insert your cable into the correct port.

Incompatibilities with Analog Modems and a Digital Jack

An analog modem and a digital jack will not work together, because they are two different technologies. An analog modem works over a standard phone line, and a digital jack for ISDN works with a digital PBX switch, not an analog phone switch.

on the **Job**

It is imperative that you do not plug an analog modem into a digital phone jack. Doing so can cause damage to the analog modem, which will most likely not work again.

TABLE 9-8		
	Cable Level	**Maximum Data Bandwidth**
Types of twisted-pair cable	CAT 1 or CAT 2	Less than 4 Mbps
	CAT 3	10MB compatible
	CAT 4	20MB compatible
	CAT 5	100MB compatible
	CAT 5 Level 7	1GB compatible

Uses of RJ-45 Connectors with Different Cabling

An RJ-45 connector is used to connect segments of twisted-pair cabling. To connect two different types of media cable, you need either a hub or a bridge that has a specific connection for this type of cabling. For example, you can connect a 10BaseT cable that plugs into a bridge that supports connectivity with a BNC connector for 10Base2. You must have the correct network hardware to connect the two different types of cabling media. There are no other options for connecting an RJ-45 connector to a BNC connector.

Patch Cables and Length of Cabling Segment

A patch cable of 10BaseT is normally a couple of feet long or however long you need. Commonly, a patch cable is used to "patch" the length it takes to get from your network card to the digital jack on the floor of your office.

Now let's take a look at some possible cabling scenarios and their solutions.

SCENARIO & SOLUTION

What type of copper cabling can I use to achieve speeds of 1GBps?	Use 10BaseT cable rated as Category 5 Level 7
What will happen if I connect an analog modem to a digital phone jack?	It will not work, and the modem might not work again.
I have two different LANs I need to connect. One LAN uses 10BaseT and the other still uses BNC. What can I do?	Use a hub or bridge that has both connector types to connect the two LANs.
What can I use to connect my NIC to the wall jack for network connectivity?	Use a patch cable.

CERTIFICATION SUMMARY

The information covered in this chapter is directly related to the material you will be tested on in the "Knowledge of Networking Technology" part of the Network+ exam. The detailed explanations in this book will make you better prepared to pass the exam. The information presented here is taken directly from the requirements listed for this exam; our approach is to explain what will be covered on the exam and summarize the key points you'll need to understand when you take the exam.

Becoming familiar with the networking components is one of the best ways to prepare for this exam. By understanding common networking practices, you will be better prepared to install your own network and troubleshoot problems that you might encounter in the process. Experience is the true test of knowledge; having a sound fundamental base of the networking basics is a great place to start.

Now that you have a firm grasp on networking fundamentals, you need to know more about network administration and how a network operates. Part of this process is becoming used to the standard procedures that make up most networks. Another part of networking of which you should be aware for the test is network administration. This involves making sure that you understand the day-to-day duties that a network administrator must deal with, from configuring TCP/IP to solving common network problems.

As well as understanding the networking tasks that an administrator must perform, you must gain a broader perspective of networking in general, including understanding the environmental factors that can affect computer performance, such as temperature, moisture, and electrical interference. You should also know and understand the standard operating procedures of a network operations center (NOC); these include backup procedures, handling user accounts, and managing users and groups.

Besides having a firm grasp on the fundamentals of computers, you also need to become well rounded in the realm of computers. Most likely you won't be sitting at a desk eight hours a day, so you'll need to know the insides of a computer—from IRQ settings to the various peripherals and why you need to use them.

As you gain more experience with computers and networking in general, you'll become more comfortable with the many concepts of troubleshooting, administration, and operating procedures.

✓ TWO-MINUTE DRILL

Installing the Network

❑ You'll find many questions concerning installing and maintaining computer networks throughout the "Knowledge of Networking Technology" section of the Network+ exam.

❑ Your most important duty as network administrator is to make sure that the clients on your network can communicate with one another at all times.

❑ Communication on a computer network is accomplished via the use of protocols.

❑ Standard operating procedures (SOPs) are the practices that you follow to enable your network to run smoothly and efficiently.

❑ The person who holds the Administrator account has complete, unrestricted access to all the files, folders, and shares on the network.

❑ Passwords aren't a failsafe method of securing your network, but if they are implemented and enforced correctly, they can impose a level of security with which you should feel comfortable.

❑ You should memorize what makes a secure and safe password. Make sure to eliminate the use of easily guessed words or phrases in your passwords!

❑ The exam will test your knowledge of safe password practices by having you select the most secure password from a list of choices.

❑ To configure a TCP/IP address on a computer, you need specific TCP/IP parameters. These parameters consist of a static TCP/IP address, a subnet mask, and a default gateway (router) if you are connecting to the Internet or another network.

❑ An IP address is a 32-bit address that is broken up into four parts, or octets.

❑ TCP/IP has many uses and many possible IP configurations.

❑ The two main options associated with name resolution on computer networks are Domain Name System (DNS) and Windows Internet Naming Service (WINS).

❑ WINS was designed to eliminate the need for broadcasts to resolve NetBIOS names to IP addresses and to provide a dynamic database that maintains NetBIOS names to IP address mappings.

❑ DNS maps TCP/IP addresses to hostnames.

❑ Keep the network up and running at all times.

❑ Back up network data every night.

❑ Monitor the performance of your servers and network infrastructure.

❑ As a network administrator, you could have common duties such as securing the network, configuring network hardware, and managing users and permissions.

❑ Computers, like most other electrical hardware, are affected by temperature, moisture, vibrations, and electrical interference.

❑ Make sure you know the cable length limitations for each type of cable. The exam presents you with scenario questions in which you are to determine if each configuration is valid; you'll have to know whether the maximum cable length has been exceeded. These questions are challenging due to the complex scenario-based format.

Environment Factors That Affect Computer Networks

❑ You will be asked to determine which environment is the most conducive to a server room. Just remember that servers need an environment free of dust, with plenty of ventilation and reasonable temperature and humidity levels. Placing servers near a window on a sunny day or in a dusty warehouse would not create an ideal operating environment.

❑ Make sure that you don't expose your computers or network equipment to any potential environmental hazards, such as moisture or extreme heat, or to sources of electrical interference, such as generators and televisions.

Common Peripheral Ports and Network Components

❑ Your network interface card (NIC) should be autodetected during setup, but if it is not, you must enter the NIC's IRQ, the I/O address, and the base memory address.

❑ Connecting to the Internet with a networked server requires a great deal of bandwidth to provide connectivity for all users.

❑ With a serial port such as that used by your keyboard or mouse, data can flow in only one direction.

❑ Parallel transmission works by sending data in both directions.

❑ *Universal Serial Bus (USB),* as it is typically called—is a new innovation in computer peripheral technology that enables you to add devices such as audio players, joysticks, keyboards, telephones, and scanners to your computer system without having to add an adapter card or even having to turn the computer off.

❑ *Small Computer System Interface (SCSI)* is a standard interface that enables personal computers to communicate with peripheral hardware such as disk drives, tape drives, CD-ROM drives, printers, and scanners.

❑ *Bridges* are intelligent devices used to connect LANs. A bridge can also forward packets of data based on MAC addresses.

❑ *Hubs* enable you to concentrate LAN connections.

❑ *Switches* offer full-duplex, dedicated bandwidth to LAN segments or desktops.

❑ *Routers* route data packets across a network by opening the packet and making routing decisions based on the contents.

❑ A *gateway* can link networks that have different protocols, such as TCP/IP to IPX/SPX.

Compatibility and Cabling Issues

❑ There are four different types of commonly used network cables: Thicknet (10Base5), Thinnet (10Base2), twisted pair, and fiber optic.

SELF TEST

The following Self Test questions will help you measure your understanding of the material presented in this chapter. Read all the choices carefully because there might be more than one correct answer. Choose all correct answers for each question.

Installing the Network

1. What hardware network components are needed to connect two computers with a standard eight-port hub on the same subnet? (Choose all that apply.)

   A. Network cards

   B. Category 5 UTP cable

   C. SCSI adapter card

   D. Router

   E. Network layer of the OSI model

2. Susan wants to make some changes to her file server so that the Accounting group only has permission to the \\Payroll and \\401K shares on her network. What two accounts should Susan use to make sure that she made the necessary changes and that an ordinary user won't gain accidental access to the share? (Choose all that apply.)

   A. Account Operator

   B. Root

   C. Her test account

   D. Backup Operator

   E. Administrator

3. Mike, a new employee at a large manufacturing company, needs to set a password for his account so that he can log on to the network. He is in charge of a large group of sensitive files, so he wants to make sure that he has a safe and secure password. What is an example of a strong password?

   A. BALONEY

   B. Fuh3H3manners!

   C. ilovethemets

   D. password

   E. cheesesandwich

4. Dave's computer is connected to his LAN. He wants to browse on his intranet to update his 401K information. However, he cannot connect to any of the Web servers on his intranet. Dave can, however, PING the computers using their IP addresses. The IP information is as follows:

```
Ethernet adapter:
Description . . . . . . . . .: 3Com Megahertz 10/100 Ethernet + 56K PC Card
Physical Address. . . . . . : 00-00-86-20-45-90
DHCP Enabled. . . . . . . . : No
IP Address. . . . . . . . . : 209.116.171.36
Subnet Mask . . . . . . . . : 255.255.255.192
Default Gateway . . . . . . : 209.116.171.65
Primary WINS Server . . . . :
Secondary WINS Server . . . :
Host Name . . . . . . . . . : USWEBCS
DNS Servers . . . . . . . . :
Lease Obtained. . . . . . . :
Lease Expires . . . . . . . :
```

What could be the problem?

A. Default gateway

B. Subnet mask

C. Name resolution

D. DHCP

E. Hostname

Environmental Factors That Affect Computer Networks

5. What are three adverse environmental conditions that would affect the performance and capability of a computer network?

A. Wind

B. Humidity

C. Extreme heat

D. Barometer

E. Moisture

F. pH balance

6. What is the technical computer term for a situation in which another system's electrical interference causes performance degradation of a computer?

   A. Attenuation

   B. EMI

   C. Cross-talk

   D. Plenum

7. Linda keeps getting the following error message every time she tries to start a program from the command line of her Windows 98 computer:

```
C:\program.exe
Bad command or file name
```

What could be the problem?

   A. Syntax error

   B. Wrong path for executable

   C. Typo

   D. Program does not exist

8. What environmental conditions are not recommended for housing network servers and other electrical equipment? (Choose all that apply.)

   A. Humid

   B. Wet

   C. Extreme cold

   D. Seventy degrees Fahrenheit

Common Peripheral Ports and Network Components

9. What two things you must make sure that you do before you can use any of your external SCSI components, such as backup devices or CD-ROM devices? (Choose two.)

   A. Make sure they are turned on before your computer is

   B. Reboot them twice

   C. Terminate them

   D. Use an IDE cable

10. Which computer peripheral is used to connect an ordinary computer to another computer via an existing telephone line?

   A. Network card

   B. Modem

   C. SCSI adapter

   D. Scanner

   E. Printer

11. Which network appliance is used to connect two computer networks that are separated by two different protocols?

   A. Router

   B. Bridge

   C. ATM switch

   D. Hub

   E. Gateway

12. On which layer of the OSI model does a network bridge work that is used to connect between TCP/IP networks?

   A. Physical

   B. Application

   C. Data Link

   D. Network

   E. Session

13. What two accounts should you use when you make a change on your network to ensure that the changes have been made?

   A. Root

   B. Backup Operator

   C. Normal

   D. Everyone

   E. Test account

   F. Administrator

14. At what level of the OSI model do network switches commonly work?

    A. Application

    B. Layer 8

    C. Network

    D. Physical

    E. Fiber Channel

15. Which type of NetBIOS name resolution is used to resolve Windows computer names to TCP/IP addresses on a local area network?

    A. DNS

    B. DSN

    C. WINS

    D. HOST file

16. What is used to separate the host ID from the network ID in a four-octet TCP/IP address?

    A. Default gateway

    B. Router

    C. Subnet mask

    D. WINS

    E. DNS

17. What account on a network server can have total control over the functionality of the server?

    A. Guest

    B. Test account

    C. Everyone

    D. Administrator

    E. Backup Operator

Compatibility and Cabling Issues

18. In an extreme case, how long can a standard fiber-optic cable be run from one end to the other?

   A. 100 meters

   B. 26.4 miles

   C. 2 kilometers

   D. 500 meters

19. What type of network cable can support data speeds up to 100 Mbps on a local area network?

   A. 10BaseT (Category 1)

   B. Phone wire

   C. 10BaseT (Category 5)

   D. TV cable

LAB QUESTION

You work for a company that implements a Windows NT network. You need to keep the network as secure as possible concerning usernames and passwords. You need to require that the users change their passwords on a regular basis and that the passwords are not reused within a one-year period. The passwords must be a minimum of seven characters and must be changed every 20 days. What would you do to implement these requirements for your company?

SELF TEST ANSWERS

Installing the Network

1. ☑ **A and B.** If you will use a hub, all you need to connect the two computers are a network card and the necessary unshielded twisted-pair, or UTP, cable.

   ☒ **C** is incorrect because a SCSI adapter card is normally used to connect SCSI components, so you wouldn't use it. **D** is incorrect because a router is used to connect two networks. **E** is incorrect because the Network layer of the OSI model is a logical layer that is used to help explain the concept of networking.

2. ☑ **C and E.** Whenever making changes to your network in any capacity, from changing permissions on a file server to implementing a new network policy, you should always make the changes with an Administrator account and then verify that you made the correct changes using a test account. With a test account that has "normal" privileges on the network, you can simulate an ordinary user. If you don't review your changes, you cannot guarantee that you made the correct changes.

   ☒ **A, B,** and **D** are incorrect because Account Operator, Root, and Backup Operator are all accounts that wouldn't have full access to the network.

3. ☑ **B.** Fuh3H3manners! Remember that when choosing a strong password, it should be more than eight characters and consist of both letters and numbers. To increase the strength of your password, you might even consider using the various keys such as !,@,#,$,%,^,&,*,(,). You should never consider using easily remembered passwords such as phrases, words, or birthdays. And remember—do not place any passwords on any yellow sticky notes stuck to your monitor!

   ☒ **A, C, D,** and **E** are not strong passwords because they could be detected by common hacker tools.

4. ☑ **C.** Name resolution enables computers with TCP/IP addresses to be mapped to logical names on a network. Two common name resolution techniques are WINS or DNS servers that automatically map these IP addresses to computer names. If Dave does not have any form of name resolution, he will not be able to map his computer to any computers using their names.

   ☒ **A, B, D,** and **E** are incorrect because they are not the problem.

Environmental Factors That Affect Computer Networks

5. ☑ **B, C,** and **E.** Humidity, extreme heat, and moisture adversely affect computer systems. At optimal conditions, your computer room should be air-conditioned, dry, and well lit and have

fire-suppression techniques. Extreme heat and moisture are detrimental to your computer. Air conditioning circulates the air and keeps it cool. Of course, this room should be locked at all times.

☒ **A, D,** and **F** are incorrect because wind has no effect on PCs that are placed inside a building. Barometer readings will not cause issues inside the building since the building interior should be temperature controlled and dry. The pH balance is not a factor since the acidic levels will affect users before they affect PCs and the network.

6. ☑ **B.** EMI, or electromagnetic interference, occurs when an electrical device interferes with a computer's normal performance. To fix this problem, you should move all your computer cables away from fluorescent lighting and other electrical appliances.

☒ **A, C,** and **D** are incorrect because attenuation occurs when the electrical signals in a network cable are eventually absorbed by the cable itself. Cross-talk occurs when one electrical pulse on a single wire is transferred to another wire within the cable. Plenum is a type of cable best known for not releasing poisonous gas when burned.

7. ☑ **B.** Normally, if you see a "Bad command or file name" message, you are not in the right path of your executable or program. You should make sure that you are in the correct directory and make sure that your program exists before calling tech support about this problem.

☒ **A, C,** and **D** are incorrect because they are not the source of the problem.

8. ☑ **A, B,** and **C.** Humid, wet, and extreme cold conditions are not ideal for computer systems. You should keep your servers and other electrical equipment away from extreme temperature, moisture, vibrations, and electrical interference. If computers are exposed to these conditions, they can act irregularly and sometimes fail.

☒ **D** is incorrect because it is a recommended condition.

Common Peripheral Ports and Network Components

9. ☑ **A** and **C.** Make sure they are turned on before your computer, and terminate them. Whenever using external SCSI devices, you need to make sure of a couple things before you can use them effectively. First, all SCSI devices must be turned on prior to starting your computer. Second, you need to make sure that you terminate the end of your SCSI adapter, which is located on your adapter card. Once you have these areas ironed out, you shouldn't have any problems with your SCSI devices.

☒ **B** and **D** are incorrect.

10. ☑ **B.** A modem is a communications device that enables a computer to talk to another computer through a standard telephone line. The modem converts digital data from the computer to analog data for transmission over the telephone line and then back to digital data for the receiving computer.

☒   **A, C, D,** and **E** are incorrect because network cards use network cables; SCSI adapters use SCSI cables; scanners have their own special connectors to connect to a SCSI port, parallel port, or USB port; and printers have a connection for a serial port, a USB port, a parallel port, or a network cable.

11. ☑   **E.** A gateway is used to connect two networks that are separated by two different protocols, such as TCP/IP and IPX/SPX. A gateway differentiates itself from a router in the sense that a router can connect two different networks that are separated by the *same* protocol, and a gateway can look at the packet and rebuild the protocol stack to the desired network.

    ☒   **A, B, C,** and **D** are incorrect because a router and bridge are used to join LANs, an ATM switch is used to join ATM networks, and a hub is used to join PCs that employ similar protocols.

12. ☑   **C.** A bridge works at Layer 2, or the Data Link layer, of the OSI model by forwarding packets of data based on MAC addresses. A bridge can be used to filter traffic on a LAN by determining the source and destination involved in the transfer of packets. A bridge reads the physical address of a packet on one network segment and then decides to filter out the packet or forward it to another segment on the network.

    ☒   **A, B, D,** and **E** are incorrect because they are not the correct layers.

13. ☑   **E** and **F.** To make any changes on your network, you need an administrative account. To ensure that your changes work under normal operating conditions, you should use a test account to verify that your changes are working.

    ☒   **A, B, C,** and **D** are incorrect because they are not accounts you should use when you change an account on your network to ensure that the changes have been made.

14. ☑   **C.** Network switches commonly work at Layer 3, or the Network layer, of the OSI model. Switches have the capability to look into the header of the packet, examine its contents, and transmit the packet according to its destination.

    ☒   **A, B, D,** and **E** are incorrect because they are not levels of the OSI model at which network switches commonly work.

15. ☑   **C.** A WINS, or Windows Internet Naming Service, server is used to resolve Windows computer names to TCP/IP addresses. Whenever a computer wants to communicate with another computer, it checks its local name cache and then contacts a configured WINS server to resolve the IP address.

    ☒   **A, B,** and **D** are incorrect because DNS is used for resolution of hostnames to IP addresses, DSN is used for ODBC configuration, and a HOST file is a static file stored on a PC for local resolution of hostnames to IP addresses.

16. ☑ C. A subnet mask is used to separate the host ID from the network ID in a TCP/IP address. This enables you to split an IP address into more than one configuration to scale to a new environment.

☒ A, B, D, and E are incorrect because the default gateway is used to connect two networks that are separated by different protocols, routers transmit packets destined for a different network.

17. ☑ D. Only the person who uses the Administrator account can manage and control the network to its fullest extent. The administrator is responsible for all changes to the network and should test all changes when they are made.

☒ A, B, C, and E are incorrect because they are not accounts on a network server that can have total control over the functionality of the server.

Compatibility and Cabling Issues

18. ☑ C. The maximum length a fiber-optic cable can be run is 2 kilometers. When that distance has been achieved, a device must be in place to boost the signal of the cable to continue.

☒ A, B, and D are incorrect because they are not the maximum distances.

19. ☑ C. 10BaseT network cabling that has been certified as Category 5 can support data transfer up to 100 Mbps for distances up to 100 meters.

☒ A, B, and D are incorrect because they are not cables that can support data speeds up to 100 Mbps on a LAN.

LAB ANSWER

To meet all the specifications of the question, you should do the following:

■ Create a password policy that requires a password change every 20 days and specify that passwords cannot be changed before 15 days.

■ Keep a password history of 25 passwords to make the user unable to reuse a password in a one-year period (25 passwords × 15 days = 375 days, or more than one year).

■ Set a minimum password length of seven characters and, if needed, educate the employees that the password is case sensitive. This will allow them to use both uppercase and lowercase characters. Also make sure that they try to use numbers and symbols as well as letters.

COMPUTING TECHNOLOGY INDUSTRY ASSOCIATION

10

Administering the Change Control System

CERTIFICATION OBJECTIVES

10.01	Documenting Current Status
10.02	Returning a System to Its Original State
10.03	Backup Techniques
10.04	Removing Outdated or Unused Drivers after a Successful Upgrade
10.05	Effects on the Network Caused by Local Changes
10.06	Drive Mapping
10.07	Printer Port Capturing
10.08	Changing or Moving Equipment
10.09	Adding, Deleting, or Modifying Users
10.10	User and Group Management
✓	Two-Minute Drill
Q&A	Self Test

I n this chapter, you will learn the techniques for managing a constantly changing network, as well as the recommended procedures for documenting current status, backing up and restoring data, and upgrading computers. You will also become acquainted with the most common user and group management issues you'll encounter in the real world when administering a network. Pay close attention, because, these same issues will appear on the exam.

CERTIFICATION OBJECTIVE 10.01

Documenting Current Status

Any good network administrator will tell you that it is very important you keep up-to-date records regarding the status and configuration of critical workstations and servers. Computers are usually upgraded or modified on an as-needed basis, which means you will have many systems with many different hardware and software configurations. This may or may not affect the network, but it *will* be a factor when you need to upgrade or reconfigure a computer.

You may have established a hardware standard, requiring, for example, that every computer have a minimum of 48MB of physical memory, a 4GB hard drive, a SCSI disk controller, and a 32x CD-ROM drive. By documenting the current status and configuration of these devices, you know exactly which computers are affected when a new standard arises. For example, if you determine that Windows NT servers now require 128MB of physical memory, by keeping adequate documentation on the configuration of each computer, you will immediately know which computers need to be upgraded.

With software, you may have also established a set of applications that each workstation will have installed by default. If this standard changes, you need to determine quickly which computers are affected without having to physically touch every computer on the network to determine which applications are installed on each computer. In addition to applications, it is also very important to document service packs and software updates. Often an application requires that a certain service pack be installed on the computer. These are known as *dependencies* because the application you wish to install is dependent on these additional applications, service packs, or software updates being present on the system.

The need to document the current status and configuration of a system is recommended when you are planning to deviate from this configuration in the future. If you are planning to retrofit (a fancy term for reconfigure) a large number of computers, it is helpful to have the configuration settings and application load documented should you need to return to a "known good" working condition. In an extreme situation, if the computer was to completely crash and need to be rebuilt, you would have the known good working condition documented, and you could quickly install and configure the operating system and applications according to this documentation with little or no guesswork.

An easy way to document current status and configuration of a Windows system is to use Windows Microsoft Diagnostics (WINMSD). The later versions of Windows will offer better diagnostics than the earlier versions. Later versions of DOS (6.x) also had a similar product called MSD.EXE, which performed similarly. The only issue with the DOS version is that devices would not be detected unless a driver was loaded for the device.

WINMSD allows you to print out a report or even save it to diskette for later printing, or to store it for a future need. It also displays information regarding BIOS dates, OS versions, OS service packs, devices, device driver dates, and many other items. Exercise 10-1 shows you how to run WINMSD.

EXERCISE 10-1

CertCam 10-1

Running WINMSD on a Windows 9x System or Later

1. Select Start | Run. The Run dialog box will appear.

2. Type **WINMSD** in the Run dialog box.

3. Select OK.

4. This will start the diagnostics software and allow you to view system information as well as save it to disk or print it out.

CERTIFICATION OBJECTIVE 10.02

Returning a System to Its Original State

If you do find yourself in a situation where you must rebuild a system, the use of existing configuration settings will come in very handy. Most times when you need to rebuild a computer, you can document the operating system version, application load, software patches, hardware configuration, and user settings *before* the computer is rebuilt. However, there are times when you have to rebuild a computer without any of this information. If a user's hard disk crashes and you have not documented what was installed on the computer in three years, you will have a difficult time rebuilding the computer to the user's specifications. The user would no doubt inform you that an application is missing, a printer is not configured correctly, or a shortcut on the desktop has disappeared. Then, just when you think you have a working rebuild, the user, once again, would undoubtedly inform you that something is still not quite right.

How can you return a system to its original state? As we indicated before, documentation is critical. Although it is impossible to document every computer on the network without third-party utilities, you should have documentation for every critical server and workstation on the network. Which computers on the network would be catastrophic if they went down suddenly? These are the computers you need to document thoroughly.

In addition to keeping documentation on these select systems on your network, you can also purchase third-party utilities that create images of these servers. If you create new, updated images every week or so, you can apply this image to a fresh rebuilt computer in a matter of minutes. You can go from a disastrous hard disk crash to being fully operational again in only thirty minutes. Time is everything in these situations. In addition to creating images with third-party utilities, you can use your unattended operating system installations with a predefined application load to restore the system to an operating state almost identical to its original. The server will have a fresh operating system with all of the applications installed, but the data may have to be restored from a recent backup. This is not as quick as the image, but it is a viable alternative to manually installing the operating system and applications.

If you are using an imaging program, you can rebuild your own computer in thirty minutes or more depending on how many applications you choose to load with the operating system. However, any data that was on the system will be lost. On the other hand, if you were backing up your data, you need simply restore the data to complete the rescue process.

Microsoft recommends you back up the Registry for each Windows computer. You must restore the Registry if you want to truly return a computer to its original operating state. The Registry contains current user and system information, which means the backup should be the most recent in order to rescue the latest changes to the system. In the Registry, user information changes much more frequently than system information changes. The Windows NT backup program and many third-party applications, such as Ghost, are able to back up the Registry information in the image.

Another method for returning a system to its original state is to manually reinstall and configure the operating system and all applications that previously existed, and then restore the Registry and/or data from the most recent backup. This is by far the most time-consuming method so far since the Registry on one system cannot be used on another. Many small companies are in this situation. Large companies have realized the need to engineer automated operating system installations because they can build hundreds of workstations a week for a gigantic rollout. A small company, on the other hand, can maybe produce ten to twenty systems a week using a manual installation method, depending on the number of technicians involved.

EXERCISE 10-2

Returning a System to Its Original State

After performing Exercise 10-1, use this information to restore a system to a state identical to that before the crash. This will require two semi-identical systems where one can be formatted. If the first is completely backed up, however, you should be able to format the hard drive and start over.

1. Use the information gained in Exercise 10-1 to restore the applications as well as the OS and service packs to the second system.

2. Follow the information gained from WINMSD and restore the second system to match the first.

3. Once finished, check the two to see how closely they match. You will also be able to determine what details are not included in the WINMSD report.

This will allow you to make a checklist which includes all the information necessary for keeping better documentation.

Backup Techniques

I hope you have realized the importance of the backup process by now. One of your most important tasks as a network administrator will be to guarantee the success of the backup process. It will take practice and effort to design, monitor, and test the backup process on a weekly basis.

The design process, if not already in place, will require you to develop a solution for backing up data on the network. You may have to evaluate several backup products in order to arrive at the product that is ideally suited for your organization. Features that are required for a Fortune 500 company might not be the features required for a small organization. The heart of the backup process is selecting which data needs to be backed up. You must communicate with others to determine which data is important enough to back up. What would happen if you suddenly lost that data today? Would anyone care? If not, then the data should not be backed up. You can't go back in time, so make sure you are backing up the critical data from the start. It's not a pretty sight when you have to tell someone that his or her project has just been lost forever.

Now that you have discovered which data needs to be backed up, you need to determine how often it should be done. Most companies do full backups every night. So, should a user accidentally delete a file, all you need to do is go back one day to retrieve the data.

After you have configured the initial backup process, you need to monitor it every day in order to catch errors. The backup program's error log is crucial for determining whether a backup job completed successfully or not. Keep in mind, too, that some errors are not as obvious as others. For example, if the tape was not able to load, you will get an obvious error and the backup job will fail to run. If the backup program could not attach to one user's computer because he shut his computer down at the end of the night, you will receive an error. Read through the error logs to determine where the job failed. If it fails every night trying to connect to another network server, remedy the situation before it's too late. The backup program should run successfully each night. If it doesn't, find out *why*. I've had many managers check the backup program event logs and then interrogate me as to why the backup job did not complete successfully.

When the backup process is configured and working relatively error free, you need to do test restores fairly often to ensure that the data is being backed up correctly. You may find yourself doing test restores once a week until you're confident of the backup process. You can then start doing the test restore once a month. However, you will most likely be restoring live data for users very often, so you can substitute that for your test restores.

In addition to doing test restores of data, you should make sure you understand how to restore programs and their data, such as when using Microsoft Exchange or SQL Server. These programs require more than just restoring the files from tape. Microsoft Exchange restores must be done on a server with the same name as the computer where they were backed up. This makes doing test restores difficult, because you cannot restore to a server with a different name.

It is a great feeling to guarantee you can restore a file at the drop of a hat. Management will love you, and so will the users!

Tape Backup

Backing up to tape is the most common form of backup done today, due to availability and price. Tape backup is slower, because of the sequential access of the medium. It's like a cassette tape, where you have to fast-forward or rewind to find your favorite song. This is the opposite of *random-access*. I have found myself frustrated during the backup and restore process because the tapes take so long to initialize and restore. Just verifying the label of a new tape can take a couple of minutes. Nevertheless, the price is right. For a few dollars a tape, you don't have to worry about reusing them. You can store every tape in an off-site storage facility. However, many companies still use tape rotation schemes to help circulate tapes for reuse, and permanently store a few select tapes in an off-site facility.

Multiple tape magazines are used for companies that back up large amounts of information every night. These backup jobs can even exceed a 24GB compressed tape. Thankfully, when one tape is full, the backup process will continue on the next available tape. The addition of extra tapes makes the backup process more likely to fail and the backup process more confusing. For example, you have one server that uses only one tape of a six-tape magazine; therefore, you can run the backup process every day for a week without reloading the tape magazine. One tape is used for the cleaning tape. You have another server that requires two tapes of a six-tape magazine. In this scenario, you can run the backup process every other day without reloading the tape magazine. Lastly, let's say you have a server that uses four tapes of a six-tape magazine, which must be reloaded on a daily basis. If this already seems confusing, imagine what its like for the person who has to swap tapes for you when you're on vacation!

Replicating a Folder to a Network Drive

Replicating a folder to a network drive is a viable means of backing up data. Although extremely fast and automated for the most part, this process does not guarantee you have a safe copy of data stored in an offsite location should an emergency occur. If both the workstation and the server where the data was replicated to were to fail, you would lose data, unless this data was also being backed up to tape or to another type of media. Replicating a folder to a network drive should be considered only as a temporary backup solution. To replicate means to copy data to another location. In the business world, duplicate data is very risky. What if Warrel and Jeff are working on the same project and they update the same document at the same time on different systems. Then Warrel goes on vacation. Which document becomes the master document? To solve this dilemma, you would have to merge both their updates into one document—not a pretty picture. If you are the only one in charge of the data being replicated, you may not have these updating problems. You may know exactly which copies are being updated and which aren't. However, if the data is important to you, it is wise to have a physical backup, such as a tape backup, of the data.

Windows NT provides a replication service to replicate data to other servers. This may sound like a means of backing up information, but the service is provided to replicate commonly used items such as logon scripts to backup domain controllers. This type of information can be duplicated. For example, a logon script for the San Francisco domain is replicated to the Seattle domain, so users in Seattle do not have to contact San Francisco to run the logon script.

EXERCISE 10-3

Backing Up Data to a Network Drive

This exercise will require a network connection and a share point on another system to allow for copying your local data to the remote system.

1. Map a drive to the shared directory on the other system. In a business environment, most users will have a personal drive they use to store data on the server for easier backup by the administrator. You can use this instead.

2. Copy important data files from the local hard disk to the mapped drive created in step 1.

3. When needed, the data can be retrieved from the remote system. This does require manual copying of data whenever the files are changed back to the share point, however. If the local file is corrupted or lost, you can copy the files from the share point back to the local hard disk.

Removable Media

Most backup systems employ removable media for the backup process, which can be removed (hence the name) and stored offsite in a safe location. There are many types of removable media—floppy disks, hard disks, tape cartridges, reel tapes, and optical disks—which vary in price, performance, and capacity. The type of removable media you require is based on the needs of your particular network, but many companies use tape backup for nightly backups, and then use writable CD-ROMs to create images or backup sets that can be used on any machine with access to a CD-ROM. If you are in charge of developing a removable storage solution, you need to determine how much money your company is willing to spend, the amount of data that needs to be archived, and the speed at which you require the data to be archived. Table 10-1 is a summary of most removable media solutions and their descriptions.

| **TABLE 10-1** | Comparison of Removable Media Technology |

Device	Description
Floppy disk	Floppy disks are slow with a small capacity. Some business computers have had the floppy disk drives removed for security reasons and to minimize viruses. Removable random-access.
Disk cartridge	Disk cartridges, such as Zip and Jaz, are growing in popularity as prices fall. Capacity is growing and the speed is increasing. Random-access.
Tape cartridge	Tape cartridges are slow, but are capable of holding large amounts of data. Sequential access.
Hard disk	Removable hard disks are dropping in price, while performance is gaining and capacity is growing. Random-access.
Reel tape	Reel tape is an older technology more commonly found on mainframe computers. Sequential access.
Optical disk	Optical disks are high quality, have a large storage capacity, and are increasing in popularity as prices drop. Random-access.

Multigeneration

There are a number of different techniques used to back up data. One of the most popular is the multigeneration tape rotation scheme, known as the Grandfather-Father-Son (GFS) scheme. This scheme became popular with mainframe computer tape rotation techniques many years ago, and is a method of maintaining backups on a daily, weekly, and monthly basis. The GFS rotation scheme is based on a seven-day weekly schedule, beginning on any day of the week, in which you create a full backup at least once a week. All of the other days you can perform full, incremental, differential, or no backups. The daily backups are called the Son, the last full backup in the week (the weekly backup) is called the Father, and the last full backup of the month (the monthly backup) is called the Grandfather.

You can reuse any of the daily tapes after six days, while the weekly tapes can be overwritten five weeks after they were last written to. Monthly tapes are saved throughout the year and should be taken offsite for storage. You can change any of these rotation defaults to suit your particular organization. To assist you, however, the GFS scheme does suggest a minimum standard for backing up the system and rotating and retiring the physical tapes.

Understand, though, that the GFS scheme is not the only tape rotation scheme on the block. You have the freedom to do as many or as few restores as needed. You can do full backups every night, or you can do a full backup once a week, with incremental and differential backups for the remaining days of the week. The choice depends entirely on the needs of your organization. Keep in mind that it's better to be safe than sorry.

CERTIFICATION OBJECTIVE 10.04

Removing Outdated or Unused Drivers after a Successful Upgrade

In any environment, computers are constantly being upgraded, and it's this capability to upgrade that is one of the most attractive features of the modern personal computer. It's simple to remove a device and replace it with a newer, faster, more powerful one, but when people upgrade their hardware, they often forget to remove the corresponding driver that goes with it. It's recommended you remove outdated or unused drivers on a system for the following reasons:

- So the drivers don't accidentally get loaded
- To conserve disk space
- To conserve memory
- To prevent any interference with new drivers

When you upgrade a device, usually you replace the driver with a more current version. However, when you *remove* a device from the system, you need to remove the device driver as well. If you don't remove it, the driver may still be loaded during system startup. In such cases, you may receive an error when loading the driver stating that the corresponding device could not be located.

Services, like drivers, are loaded into memory on Windows NT systems, and can be stopped and started. The chances are much greater you will forget to stop a service when a device is removed than forget to remove the unused driver.

Unused drivers, if not removed, can take up valuable hard disk space. Driver files are not very large, however, so don't worry about them too much. If you don't like the thought of anything wasting space on your hard drive, then make sure you locate these unused drivers and delete them. Remember though that Windows keeps a driver database of files on your hard disk, making it easier for you when you install a device. The corresponding driver will then be loaded if it is available.

Devices will not only have drivers, but some may also have applications used to access the device. Devices such as scanners will have a driver as well as an application used to read the image from the scanner and convert it into a digital image for use by the computer. If the driver is removed, the applications will usually not be needed anymore and can therefore be removed (they occupy much more space than the driver itself), freeing up a great deal of space. Sometimes removing the application will simultaneously remove the driver, but this isn't always the case.

Physical memory is something that can't be wasted on unused drivers. In the days of DOS and optimizing memory, we needed to remove these drivers from conventional memory in order to have enough memory to load applications. These drivers were loaded into memory using the CONFIG.SYS file. If you don't remove the lines that load the drivers, they will continue to be loaded into memory, and having one too many drivers loaded can make or break the performance of your system.

If you forget to unload and remove the previous drivers, they may cause problems during the subsequent loading of a new driver, possibly causing it to fail. If two drivers are expecting to have full control over a device, they both may fail when one tries to access the device. This was common when CD-ROM device drivers were loaded from the CONFIG.SYS file, and then Windows 95 also tried to load CD-ROM drivers later in the boot process.

exam
ⓦatch

Be sure you understand the reasons for removing unused or outdated drives from your system. The exam will present troubleshooting scenarios that include determining the cause of a system that isn't functioning correctly. When you understand how outdated drivers can affect a system, you're one step closer to answering these questions with ease during your exam.

Windows Update will automatically remove unneeded drivers and services, and if needed, will also update outdated drivers and system files. Some Windows OSs will have a program to start that will guide you through the Windows Update process.

Otherwise, go to http://windowsupdate.microsoft.com or http://www.microsoft.com/isapi/redir.dll?prd=windowsupdate. Both options require an Internet connection to be able to access the database containing a list of updated drivers and files. This procedure is outlined in Exercise 10-4.

EXERCISE 10-4

Using Windows Update on a Windows 2000 System

This exercise will require an Internet connection and a Windows 2000 system.

1. Open your Web browser and go to http://www.microsoft.com/isapi/redir.dll?prd=windowsupdate or to http://windowsupdate.microsoft.com.

2. Select the option for Product Updates.

3. A window will open stating that it is checking available updates.

4. Once the system is scanned, you will be presented with a list of available updates. Select those you wish to download and install, then select Download. NOTE: The Critical Updates will be selected automatically.

5. The next screen will show you the choices selected and the estimated download time. You can make final changes at this time and then select Start Download.

6. You will then be given a choice to open a download program and whether to agree to the license agreement of the drivers and files. Select Yes to continue.

7. A download window will appear and show the progress of the download. This window also displays the installation progress of the downloaded files. When the files are downloaded, they will be automatically installed.

8. Disconnect from the Internet if needed, then close all programs and reboot in order for the changes to take effect.

Effects on the Network Caused by Local Changes

Changes to a workstation or a server can have negative effects on the network. These changes include network hardware settings, protocol additions or modifications, or added or misconfigured applications or services. I wouldn't be paranoid of configuring a workstation, because chances are slim that you can down an entire network by misconfiguring a workstation.

However, with that in mind, make sure you use extreme caution when configuring a network adapter card. If you were going to crash the network from doing anything, it would be from misconfiguring a network card. Misconfiguring the speed on a network card will confuse and lock up a hub.

Another misconfiguration that will cause some network distress is accidentally configuring a workstation as the master browser. When this workstation initializes on the network, it will broadcast a message saying it is the master browser. If another computer is configured as a master browser, an election will occur between the two devices to determine who is the rightful master browser.

When a computer with a faulty network card is on the network, it can continuously chatter, eating up bandwidth. You need to use special software to analyze packets on the network in order to determine which computer is having problems. A Token Ring network will cease to function and the nearest active upstream neighbor (NAUN) to the failed computer will send out a beacon, alerting you as to which computer is not functioning correctly.

Version Conflicts

With companies continuing to update their products at a rapid pace, it may be difficult to keep up as a consumer. You may be finding yourself with version conflicts between software applications and your operating system. In many cases, version conflicts come from software applications designed to run on a specific operating system type. At the very worst, the application will not run. Or it may try to run, but fail, citing General Protection Faults or similar errors. Hopefully, the application will still run, but won't take advantage of some features until you upgrade the affected application.

In any version conflict situation, you would like to be informed from the software that such a problem is occurring. If you aren't aware of it, you may have no idea why an application is behaving erratically.

Lately, we've seen several applications that require a specific Windows NT service pack in order to perform. This was the case with the Y2K bug, which was said to be relieved by using Microsoft's Service Pack 4 for Windows NT. A few applications require that the operating system be patched with Service Pack 4 in order for the application itself to be Y2K-compliant. Other applications, such as Microsoft Office 97, require that Service Pack 2 or higher be installed prior to installing Office 97.

Some versions of software will issue warnings, but will still run. Microsoft applications such as Word can offer to save applications in a version that is compatible with all Microsoft Office versions. It is wise to save your applications in this version, in the event someone requiring access to the document does not have the version of the software you do.

Overwritten DLLs

One of the more complex situations to track down is the condition in which one application overwrites another application's dynamic link library (DLL) files. These files are used by one or more programs as libraries that contain functions called from the main software program. Most programs use their own DLLs, but some employ DLLs common not only to the operating system but to many different applications. This is a silent disaster waiting to happen. For example, let's say you have an application that installed a DLL dated 9-12-97, and that this DLL happens to overwrite a newer version of the same file needed by another application. One of the applications may work just fine, but the owner of the newer DLL that has just been back-leveled may not find the functions and routines within the DLL that he expects. The result can be lock-ups, General Protection Faults, or an application's refusal to run at all.

Overwritten DLLs become more of a problem as you add more applications to the system. It is nearly impossible to determine which applications' DLLs have been affected. You may have discovered that a DLL has been updated with a newer one, but which application was responsible? Even worse, you might have an older application that has written a much older DLL over a newer one on the system. The program you installed last should have no problems, but the existing application will most likely fail with the older DLL.

Many applications are smart enough to check the date and timestamp when installing, and prompt you when a file newer than the one being written is currently in use on the system. You have the opportunity to keep the existing newer file (recommended) rather than overwrite it with the version on the installation program.

Windows 2000 and XP have a feature called File Protection which helps prevent DLL and other files from being overwritten by older versions. If a program is unable to start due to an overwritten file, Windows attempts to reload the overwritten files from the installation source. The reinstallation occurs automatically if the source files are readily accessible. If they're not, Windows prompts you for the CD or a share point to connect to in order to gain access to the installation files. Each driver or file must have a signature from Microsoft, which is basically a certificate that states the file is not corrupted and that it is authentic and has been approved by Microsoft as being stable.

EXERCISE 10-5

CertCam 10-5

Setting Options for File Protection

This exercise will require a Windows 2000 system.

1. Select Start | Settings | Control Panel, then choose System.

2. Click the Hardware tab and select Driver Signing.

3. Now you will have three choices—Ignore, Warn, or Block—which are as follows:

   Ignore   Will allow any driver to be installed regardless of the driver signature.

   Warn   Prompts the user to choose whether or not to install the new driver.

   Block   Prohibits unsigned drivers from being installed.

CERTIFICATION OBJECTIVE 10.06

Drive Mapping

Drive mapping is the process of connecting network drives so you may use the resources located on them. On operating systems such as Windows 95/98 and Windows NT, you have the capability of mapping network drives through a command prompt or through a GUI interface. Figure 10-1 shows the Map Network Drive dialog box, the graphical utility for mapping network drives in Windows 95/98 and NT.

EXERCISE 10-6

CertCam 10-6

Mapping a Network Drive through the Graphical Utility with Windows 95/98 and NT

To map a network drive with the graphical utility, follow these directions:

1. Right-click the Network Neighborhood icon on the desktop.

2. Select File | Map Network Drive. The Map Network Drive dialog box appears.

3. Select the network drive you want to map to from the Drive list. In this example, we are using drive H.

4. In the Path text box, type the Universal Naming Convention (UNC) path for the shared network drive you would like to map to. In this example, we are using \\server\share. This will map to the share on the network drive called *share*, which is located on the server called *server*. You may also find the share you would like to map to in the Path drop-down list box if you have already made this mapping in the past.

5. If you want this drive mapping to remain consistent each time you log on, check the Reconnect At Logon box. If you only want the drive mapping to remain for this session, leave the box unchecked.

6. Click OK to save the drive mapping.

FIGURE 10-1

Use the Map
Network Drive
dialog box to map
network drives
on a Windows
95/98 or NT
system

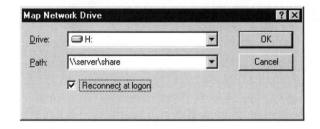

Although using the GUI interface is easier, if you learn to use the command prompt, you can create batch files with drive mappings that connect automatically.

It is imperative you understand the correct syntax for mapping to network shares. As indicated before, you are mapping to a specific share on a specific server. The mapping begins with two backslash characters before the server name. After the server name, a backslash precedes the share name. For example, the following command maps to the evacuation share on the safety server:

```
net use S: \\safety\evacuation
```

Notice that we are designating the drive letter S for the mapping in the net use command. If you forget the colon after the drive designator when mapping from the command prompt in Windows NT, an error will be issued.

exam
🖐️atch

Make sure you know the correct syntax for mapping network drives. It's very likely a question will show up on the exam asking which of the answers uses the correct syntax.

Printer Port Capturing

Just as you can connect network drives in order to use the resources located on them, you can also connect network printers in the same manner. In operating systems such as Windows 95/98 and Windows NT, you have the capability of mapping local and network printers through a command prompt or through a GUI interface. Figure 10-2 illustrates the graphical utility for mapping printers in Windows NT.

As with network drive mappings, you can use the command prompt to map network printers and place these mappings in batch files to connect automatically. You can also connect to multiple network drives and printers, as illustrated in this example of a batch file:

```
net use S: /delete
net use S: \\finance\July1998
net use U: /delete
net use U: \\Finance\YearlyReports
Net use lpt1: \\PrintServer\HPLJ3
```

FIGURE 10-2	

The Windows
NT Connect to
Printer utility
allows you to
map network
printers

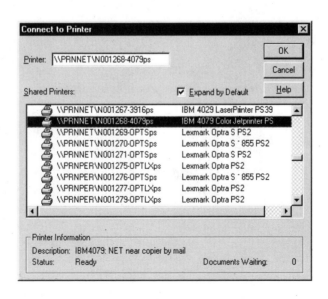

The preceding batch file commands will delete the share if it already exists and map the share again. The share is deleted before it is mapped to circumvent the error message that is received when you try to establish a drive mapping that is already in place, similar to Figure 10-3.

By deleting the share first, we ensure we'll never receive this error message. The final line in the batch file contains the network printer mapping. This batch file can be executed at logon or at anytime you want to connect all of these resources at once. Please note that when you are mapping a printer, you can omit the colon after lpt if you wish.

Do note that Windows does not do graphical port mapping. This requires the net use commands at a command prompt.

exam
ⓦatch

Make sure you are aware of the syntax for mapping ports.

EXERCISE 10-7

CertCam 10-7

Mapping a Network Printer

To map a network printer to a local printer port, follow these directions:

1. Double-click the Network Neighborhood icon on the desktop.

2. Browse for a PC or server that has a printer shared and double-click that PC or server.

3. Once the resources are shown on the next screen, double-click the Printers folder.

4. Select the printer you wish to connect to by right-clicking it. Choose Connect.

5. This should then create an icon for the printer in your Printers folder and allow you to print to it whenever the Print dialog box appears.

SCENARIO & SOLUTION

I need all users set up to have access to a network share automatically. The network share is the location of all applications and patches. How can I do this?	Set up a drive mapping in the logon script for all users.
I have a user who is using an old DOS program on his Windows 95 PC. The DOS program is set to print to printer port 1 and cannot be changed. It is against company policy to allow individuals to have their own printers. What can be done?	Map the LPT1: port to a network printer. In most cases, this should work for DOS programs unless they actually try to control the printer port.
I need users to run a batch file that is located on the network server in a shared directory. Once the batch file is run, the users should not have a drive letter mapped to the network share any longer. How can this be managed?	Map the drive in a logon script. Execute the batch file and then delete the mapping in the script.

FIGURE 10-3

Deleting a share prior to mapping it

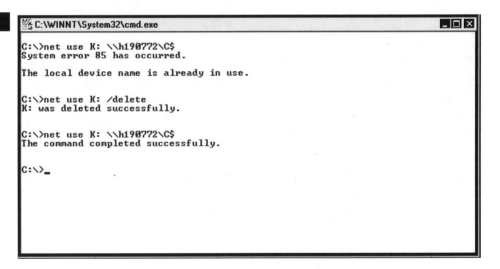

```
C:\>net use K: \\h190772\C$
System error 85 has occurred.

The local device name is already in use.

C:\>net use K: /delete
K: was deleted successfully.

C:\>net use K: \\h190772\C$
The command completed successfully.

C:\>_
```

CERTIFICATION OBJECTIVE 10.08

Changing or Moving Equipment

When you change equipment on a computer, to facilitate a smooth transition you need to test the newer equipment beforehand to make sure it works correctly. For example, if you are adding a SCSI controller and two SCSI hard disks to a network server, test the SCSI cards before placing them in the new server. If you don't test them, and you experience hardware failure, you may have difficulty determining which is the culprit amongst the additions: the SCSI controller, a SCSI hard drive, the SCSI cable, or the computer itself.

For Windows OSs, there is a table you can use to determine that a device will work with the OS called the Hardware Compatibility List (HCL). Before adding new devices to a Windows system, you should check the HCL. Just make sure you are using an updated HCL, which can be found at http://www.microsoft.com/isapi/redir.dll?prd=Win2000HCL&pver=1 for Windows 2000 systems. This process is performed in Exercise 10-8.

EXERCISE 10-8

Checking the Hardware Compatibility List

To check the Hardware Compatibility List (HCL), you need a connection to the Internet.

1. Open your Web browser and navigate to:
   http://www.microsoft.com/isapi/redir.dll?prd=Win2000HCL&pver=1

2. Scroll down and type in the manufacturers name in the Company box, then type in the model number of the device in the Model option box and finally select the device type in the Device Type box. Select All in the Device Type box if the device is not listed.

3. Select the Find button.

4. The next window shows the matches compatible with Windows 2000.

Moving a computer from one room to another doesn't sound like that difficult a process. However, there are hidden traps that can make this move more disruptive than it needs to be. You should test the area you are moving the computer to before the move. Most importantly, you should test the network connection. You may also need to determine if the network outlet supports the speed of the server or workstation. If this is a high-powered server, does the network drop in the room connect to a high-speed port on a hub or a switch?

Servers contain information and resources that must be available to users. Any disruption in these resources will affect how users work. You have to care for these servers differently than you do the average workstation. You should not place a server in a dusty, hot area, or in an area with little ventilation, such as a small closet. If you are moving a server to another location, make sure the spot is appropriately equipped to handle a network server. Your server room should be climate controlled, well ventilated, relatively dust free, and away from windows or direct sunlight.

CERTIFICATION OBJECTIVE 10.09

Adding, Deleting, or Modifying Users

When you are graced with administrative rights on the network, you can do anything. You can even delete the CEO's expense report if you wish. When given this extreme right, you have to be very responsible with it. Most problems occur when users are added, deleted, or modified without permission. I think many network administrators have been caught adding a new user without permission, or giving another user permissions they should not have. It's natural to want to be accepted as the computer techie in the organization. However, when it comes to giving other users permissions on the network that they shouldn't have, you are treading on thin ice. If a user were to obtain information they were not supposed to have and got caught, chances are it would come right back to you, the person that granted them the permissions in the first place. For this reason, companies develop forms that users must fill out and have signed by their supervisors. These forms document the permissions required when creating or modifying a user, such as the groups this user's account will be placed in. These forms are also used to give users Internet access, dial-up permissions, and permission to take software off the premises.

When users leave the company, their accounts must be deleted or disabled as shown in Exercise 10-9. Even though it's apparent the user will not be coming back, you should obtain permission before deleting his or her account. For example, a user named Jim Sheppard has left the company. Jim was in charge of the safety department and will be replaced soon. If you disable his account, you can rename the account to the new user that will take his place. If you delete his account immediately, however, you will have to re-create the account for the new hire and add that new hire to the existing shares Jim had access to. This can be an overwhelming task if Jim had explicit access to many files and folders.

EXERCISE 10-9

Disabling a User Account on a PC as a Workgroup

This process allows you to disable a single user account on a local computer as if it were a workgroup. These steps require a Windows 2000 system.

1. Select Start | Programs | Administrative Tools | Computer Management. This will open the Computer Management window.

2. In the left pane, select Local Users And Groups, then choose Users from the resulting drop-down list.

3. In the right pane, a list of all users will be shown. Double-click the user whose account you wish to disable.

4. This will show the user account information. The second option (the last one being grayed out) will be Account Is Disabled. Place a check mark next to this line and select OK. The account is no longer disabled.

Often the network administrator must fulfill the users' change requests, sign the documents, and submit the documents to his or her superior for approval. All this is aimed at establishing guidelines for network access and for deterring malicious behavior on the network. If you undermine this documentation process, you risk your job.

CERTIFICATION OBJECTIVE 10.10

User and Group Management

Let's face it, if not for the users, we wouldn't have much to do on the network as administrators. Everything we do revolves around the user in some way. Next time you are having fun configuring that RAID array, remember that its purpose is to increase the performance for the user. So, because everything does revolve around the user, it makes sense to begin the discussion of managing resources by talking about the user account.

The user account is what gives a user access to the network. If you do not have a user account, you aren't allowed to log on to the network. Since the account is based on the user, it makes sense that a new account must be created for each user. This can be time consuming, but is a necessity. After the user account is created and configured, you don't have to do much housekeeping with it, unless the user's situation changes or he gets locked out of the system. Just be sure to place the user account in the proper groups when you create it.

Group accounts are for grouping together users who perform the same function or require access to the same resources (shown in Exercise 10-10). If it were not for group accounts, you would have to grant access to resources on a per-user basis. It is entirely possible to use group membership for resource access without having to grant access on a per-user basis, but it's nice to know you can grant or deny access down to the user level.

EXERCISE 10-10

CertCam 10-10

Creating a Group Account and Adding Users to the Group

This process allows you to create a group and add users to it on a local computer as if it were a workgroup. These steps require a Windows 2000 system.

1. Select Start | Programs | Administrative Tools | Computer Management. The Computer Management window will open.

2. In the left pane, select Local Users and Groups, then choose Groups from the resulting drop-down list.

3. In the right pane, a list of all groups will be shown. Right-click in an empty area and select Create New Group.

4. This will show a window in which to create a new group. In the Group Name box, type in a name for the new group.

5. In the Description box, type an optional description for the group.

6. When done, select the Add button, which will show a list of all users. Select those users you wish to add to the group by highlighting the users and choosing the Add button.

7. When finished adding all the desired users, select the OK button.

8. In the Create A Group window, you will now see a list of all the users you selected to add to the group. Select the Create button to generate the group you made.

9. The Create A Group window will stay open to allow you to create another group, or you can select the Close button to stop creating groups.

Your grouping should mirror the way users are logically grouped in your organization. Say you have an organization with a sales force, support engineers, and technicians. If you group the users according to their job function, it makes it easier to complete such tasks as granting access to resources and sending notifications to group members. You can send a memo to the sales force informing them of sales-related information, which would not be of interest to your engineering staff. Plus, perhaps the Sales staff is the only group you would like to give Internet access to.

Groups can also be created geographically. If your company has a remote office in another state, then the Sales department in each office would have its own group and not one whole group of Sales people. This allows you to keep resource permissions separate for the two offices.

Although you can give rights, such as access to the Internet, to one group, it's a good idea to start a group called Internet, which will consist of users that have access to the Internet. As each user requires access to the Internet, you can place his/her account in this group. Even groups, such as the Sales group, can be placed in this same group to give every user in it access to the Internet.

exam
Watch *Make sure you understand the basics of user and group management for the exam. Placing users in groups makes assigning rights and permissions much easier. Whenever you are given a question about assigning rights to one user, consider if there is an alternative, such as creating a group and adding the user to the group.*

Profiles

A user profile stores user preferences like screen savers, last documents used, and network drive mappings, as well as environmental settings, such as program groups. When the user logs off, the changes are saved so that the next time the user logs on, the settings are just as he left them. The profile starts as the default user and then is saved in the user's logon name in the system root, which in Windows NT is usually C:\winnt\Profiles.

Figure 10-4 shows where Windows NT stores user preferences.

This directory structure is good for administrators to know, whether they make applications and files available to everyone on the system, or just to a select few. All Users is the default used as a model for all users who log on to the system. Just select the user you would like to have a program or shortcut for, and then copy it to the desktop or the Start Menu folder, whichever you prefer. Most NT administrators

---

FIGURE 10-4

The directory structure on a Windows NT computer for storing user preferences

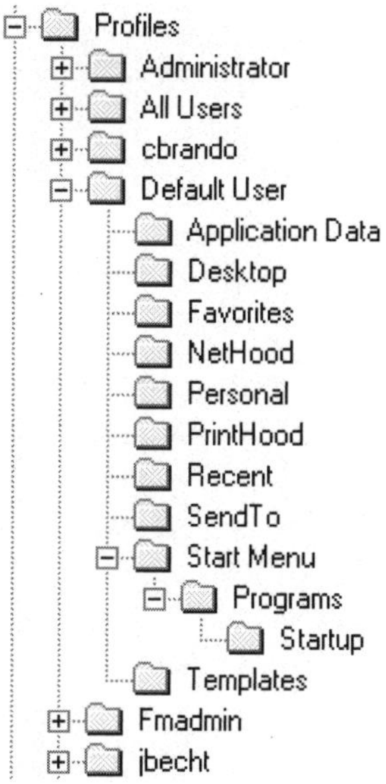

```
Profiles
├── Administrator
├── All Users
├── cbrando
├── Default User
│   ├── Application Data
│   ├── Desktop
│   ├── Favorites
│   ├── NetHood
│   ├── Personal
│   ├── PrintHood
│   ├── Recent
│   ├── SendTo
│   ├── Start Menu
│   │   └── Programs
│   │       └── Startup
│   └── Templates
├── Fmadmin
└── jbecht
```

do this kind of thing on a daily basis when installing software, so you may want to practice it.

You have the option of making a profile a *roaming profile*, which is stored on another computer (usually a server). The roaming profile enables you to keep your user preferences in one location so every change you make to the profile can be used on any computer you log on to. If you did not have a roaming profile, you would be forced to have a profile for each computer you log on to, and any changes you made to that profile would not be accessible on other computers. As you can see, it's a good idea to make your profile a roaming profile, so you can have shortcuts to commonly used areas available regardless of the user's machine. This way you don't have to browse the network to find everything you need while the user is watching impatiently.

Rights

You may be asking yourself what is the difference between a *right* and a *permission*. Rights are given to users, much like citizens in the United States are given the right to vote at a certain age. The user's profile carries around the credentials of the objects to which the user has rights. (Rights under other network operating systems are called system privileges.) Permissions are given to objects, and the object itself carries around a list of who is entitled to use the object.

You can assign access to resources in one of two ways: by giving the user *rights* to access the object, or by specifying which users have *permission* to access a specific resource. Just remember from which point of view you are assigning the rights or permissions—from the user's point of view or from the object's point of view.

When defining what permissions and rights a user will have on your network, it is best to make the user part of a group or groups that have the appropriate permissions to objects. In Windows NT, users should be added to global groups only. Global groups are specific to a domain. Local groups, on the other hand, are specific to a certain machine, such as a workstation or domain controller.

Very rarely do you want to give specific access to one user's account. If you find yourself giving rights to individual user accounts on a daily or weekly basis, you had better reevaluate your standards for assigning rights. It is very difficult to maintain standards when modifying individual user accounts.

Procedures/Policies

With your user accounts, there are account policies you can implement to help control the security of your network. Some items you can control with account policies include the minimum and maximum password age, minimum password length, and account lockout. The following is a list of the most popular policies available:

- **Maximum Password Age** Will the password expire? If so, in how many days?

- **Minimum Password Age** Can users change passwords immediately, or do they have to wait a certain number of days?

- **Minimum Password Length** Are blank passwords permitted? If not, how many characters does the password have to contain?

- **Password Uniqueness** Will you keep a password history? If so, how many passwords do you want the system to remember before enabling a password to be reused?

- **Account Lockout** Will accounts be locked out after a number of bad logon attempts? If so, how many bad logon attempts are allowed and how long before the account is reset, if at all?

- **Forcibly Disconnect Remote Users from Server When Logon Hours Expire** This goes hand in hand with logon hours. Logon hours can be specified for users and groups that restrict network access during a specified time period, such as 8:00 p.m. through 6:00 a.m. If a user is staying late, they can continue past the logon restriction as long as they do not log out. Once they log off, the logon restriction will be in effect, and they will be denied access. You can use the Forcibly Disconnect Remote Users option to log all users off when the logon hours are over. They will receive a warning a few minutes prior to the logon restriction informing them to save their data.

- **Users Must Log On in Order to Change Password** When a password expires, as the administrator you can allow the user to change it at his or her very next logon after the expiration time, or you can make the user come to you to reset it.

To set policies for user accounts, go to the Account Policy dialog box in Windows NT User Manager for Domains by selecting Policies from the pull-down menu, and then selecting Account. Figure 10-5 illustrates the Account Policy dialog box of User Manager for Domains.

Using these policies, you can fine-tune users' access and capabilities on the network. Although system policies are very effective in what they accomplish, they can add more work for the administrator of the network. Not only must the administrator learn the various utilities for system policy, he must also decide what to restrict, verify that the restrictions work, and explain to users why they have been restricted.

Most system policy restrictions are considered optional. You have to determine which settings are appropriate for your organization. The more policy restrictions you implement on your network, the more irritated users may become. Password restrictions, such as expiration and password uniqueness, are sure to upset users over time. For example, if your policy is that the system remembers an employee's last six passwords and passwords expire every month, you'll probably get daily complaints about the inconvenience of these restrictions. You'll just have to explain that those settings apply to everyone, from the president of the company right down to the hourly employees.

Use the Account Policy dialog box in User Manager for Domains to set policies for user accounts

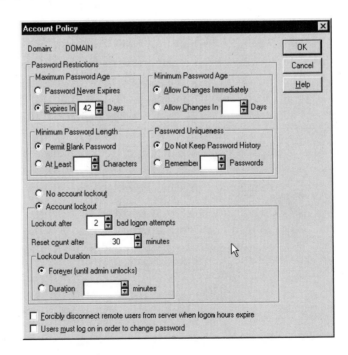

Administrative Utilities

Every network operating system has administrative utilities for managing users, groups, and resources. Microsoft Windows NT has User Manager for Domains; Windows NT Workstation has User Manager; Novell NetWare, version 3.*x* has SYSCON; and Novell NetWare, version 4.*x* has the graphical NetWare Administrator; and Windows 2000 has Active Directory Users and Computers for an Active Directory domain. Each of these administrative tools enables you to add, modify, and delete users and groups. Nearly everything you have learned about user and group management, policies, rights, and permissions are possible within these administrative utilities. Figure 10-6 shows the main screen of User Manager on a Windows NT workstation, which looks identical to User Manager for Domains found on Windows NT servers.

The User Properties dialog box enables you to configure settings for each user, as shown in Figure 10-7.

The User Manager utility on a Windows NT workstation enables you to manage users, groups, and resources

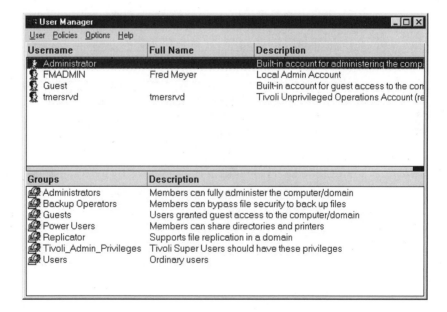

FIGURE 10-7

The User
Properties dialog
box in Windows
NT User
Manager enables
you to configure
a user's account

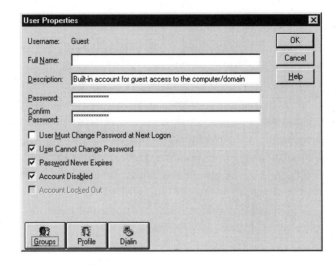

Login Accounts and Groups

Most operating systems provide two types of accounts that administrators have to
manage: user accounts and group accounts. A user account is the account for an
individual person on the network. A group account, on the other hand, is for a group
of users. You should place users in group accounts so you can assign permissions and
configure the users to take advantage of the features of the operating system.

When Windows NT Server is installed, there are two default user accounts created:
the administrator account and the guest account. The accounts set up during installation
are the basic accounts needed to administer the domain. Throughout the life of the
domain, users will come and go and a strong knowledge of how to maintain users is
a must in today's networking environment. By default, the guest account is disabled
so no one can access your network without being assigned a username and password.
It is up to the administrator to enable this account.

The administrator account is the most important account in the domain.
Administrators can complete a variety of tasks, which are not specific to one
operating system, including the following:

■ Create users and groups

■ Administer users and groups

■ Assign permissions and rights in the domain

- Share folders and printers
- Lock the server
- Format and manage drives on the server

It is a good idea to create a backup administrator account in the event the password is forgotten. This also helps if something happens to the administrator account that makes it unusable.

One other rule of thumb is to rename the administrator account. The administrator account cannot be deleted or disabled, but it can be renamed. Renaming it makes it more difficult for someone to hack into your network. In fact, the name of the account is 50 percent of the information a hacker needs to break in, so simply renaming the administrator account deprives the hacker of that 50 percent edge.

on the
job

It's a good idea for an administrator to have a second account with rights comparable to a regular user's. With this account, you can't surf the Internet or test installations and applications. In truth, you don't realize just how much power you have as an administrator until you log on as a regular user and find you can't do nearly as much to the system. Where I work, we are told to test the installs and applications as a regular user, in addition to testing them with our administrative accounts. We often find that shortcuts and applications we installed were only installed on the administrator's profile and did not appear for all users logged on to the system.

When Windows NT Server is installed, a series of built-in global groups are created:

- Domain Admins
- Domain Users
- Domain Guests

A series of default (built-in) local groups are also created:

- Administrators
- Users
- Guests
- Backup operators

- Account operators (domain controller only)
- Print operators (domain controller only)
- Server operators (domain controller only)
- Power users (non-domain controllers)
- Replicators

Administrators

The Administrators local group is the most powerful of all the groups. As you might expect, users in this group have full control of the system. For this reason, only trusted users should be members of this elite group. By default, the Domain Admins global group is a member of the local Administrators group.

Users

The Users local group has enough rights for users to get work done at their workstations, but not much else. Users don't have the right even to log on at a Windows NT Server. The Domain Users global group is a member of the Users local group by default.

Guests

The Guests group is even more limited than the Users group. It should be used for one-time or temporary access to resources. Either way, they are restricted in the tasks they can perform. The Domain Guests global group is, by default, a member of the Guests local group, but you can remove it.

Server Operators

The Server Operators group is intended to relieve the burden on the administrator. Members of this group can shut down servers, format server hard disks, create and modify shares, lock and unlock the server, back up and restore files, and change the system time. The Server Operators group is only available on a domain controller.

Print Operators

Users in the Print Operators local group have the capability to create, delete, and modify printer shares. These will most likely be on print servers, which the members of the Print Operators group can log on to and shut down if need be. The Print Operators group exists only on a domain controller.

Backup Operators

Members of the Backup Operators local group can back up and restore on the primary and backup domain controllers. They can log on to and shut down the server, if needed.

Account Operators

Users in the Account Operators local group have permissions to add, modify, and delete most user and group accounts in User Manager for Domains. They do not have the capability to modify any of the default groups, nor can they modify any member that belongs to any of these groups. They can also use Server Manager to add computers to the domain. The Account Operators group exists only on a domain controller.

Replicators

The Replicators group contains the Replicator user account for the replication services. This group should not be used for any other purpose. In other words, users other than your Replicator service account should not be added here.

Domain Admins

The Domain Admins global group is a member of the Administrators local group on every computer in the domain by default. (Actually, this is just for computers running Windows NT, because operating systems like Windows 95 do not use groups to administer the local machine.) Having the Domain Admins global group in the Administrators local group by default gives an administrator the capability to modify computers in the domain. You can revoke this right by removing the Domain Admins group from the Administrators local group on the machine.

Domain Users

The Domain Users global group contains all subsequent accounts created in the domain. This gives users the ability to access resources in other domains. The Domain Users global group is, by default, a member of the Users local group on every Windows NT computer in the domain. This gives users the ability to access non-domain controller computers and workstations in the domain. If you do not wish them to have this ability, remove the Domain Users group from the Users local group on the specific machine.

Domain Guests

The Domain Guests global group is intended to provide limited and/or temporary access to the domain. By default, the Domain Guests global group is a member of the Guests local group.

The Group Memberships dialog box, shown in Figure 10-8, reveals which groups the selected user is a member of.

FIGURE 10-8

The Group Memberships dialog box in the Windows NT User Manager utility enables you to assign membership to groups

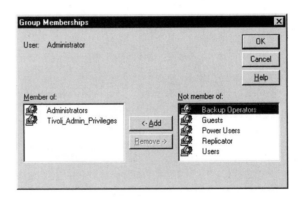

CERTIFICATION SUMMARY

In this chapter, you learned the importance of keeping current, detailed documentation for your network. Documenting important servers and workstations makes it easier to locate, upgrade, and troubleshoot these computers. This documentation is also helpful when returning computers to their original state in the event of an emergency.

You became acquainted with the backup routine and different tape-rotation techniques, as well as the various media on which to back up sensitive data, including tape, optical disks, floppy and hard disks, and network disks.

You also discovered that outdated and unused drivers can wreak havoc on a system and use up precious resources. Overwritten DLLs are also dangerous when it comes to application coexistence. One application may overwrite another application's DLLs and render the other application unstable or inoperable.

You learned about the network and printer drive mappings using the graphical and command-line utilities. It is imperative for the Network+ exam that you understand the syntax of these commands. The mapping begins with two backslash characters before the server name. After the server name, one backslash precedes the share name (\\server\share).

Finally, you became familiar with some of the user and group management techniques you'll encounter on the exam and in real life. These include the various user and group management utilities and the settings that are configured using these programs. A big part of being a network administrator is managing users and groups effectively.

TWO-MINUTE DRILL

Documenting Current Status

❑ It is very important you keep up-to-date records of the status and configuration of critical workstations and servers.

Returning a System to Its Original State

❑ In addition to keeping documentation on select systems on your network, you can also purchase third-party utilities that create images of these servers.

❑ Microsoft recommends you back up the Registry for each Windows computer.

Backup Techniques

❑ The heart of the backup process is selecting which data needs to be backed up.

❑ Backing up to tape is the most common form of backup done today, due to availability and price.

❑ Replicating a folder to a network drive is a viable means of backing up data.

❑ Most backup systems employ removable media for the backup process. There are many types of removable media: floppy disks, hard disks, tape cartridges, reel tapes, and optical disks.

❑ There are a number of different techniques used to back up data. One of the most popular is the multigeneration tape rotation scheme, known as the Grandfather-Father-Son (GFS) scheme.

Removing Outdated or Unused Drivers after a Successful Upgrade

❑ Be sure you understand the reasons for removing unused or outdated drives from your system. The exam will present troubleshooting scenarios that will include determining the cause of a system that is not functioning correctly. When you understand how outdated drivers can affect a system, you are one step closer to answering these questions with ease during your exam.

Effects on the Network Caused by Local Changes

❑ Changes to a workstation or a server can have negative effects on the network. These changes include network hardware settings, protocol additions or modifications, or added or misconfigured applications or services.

❑ Version conflicts may arise from software applications designed to run on a specific operating system type.

❑ One of the more complex situations to track down is the condition in which one application overwrites another application's dynamic link library (DLL) files.

Drive Mapping

❑ Drive mapping is the process of connecting network drives so that you may use the resources located on them.

❑ Make sure you know the correct syntax for mapping network drives. It is very likely you will receive a question on your exam asking which of the answers uses the correct syntax.

Printer Port Capturing

❑ Just as you can connect network drives in order to use the resources located on them, you can also connect network printers in the same manner.

Changing or Moving Equipment

❑ When you change equipment on a computer, in order to facilitate a smooth transition, you need to test the newer equipment beforehand to make sure it works correctly.

Adding, Deleting, or Modifying Users

❑ Most problems occur when users are added, deleted, or modified without permission.

User and Group Management

❑ Group accounts are for grouping together users who perform the same function or require access to the same resources.

❑ A user profile stores user preferences like screen savers, last documents used, and network drive mappings, as well as environmental settings, such as program groups.

❑ Rights are given to users. The user's profile carries around the credentials of what objects the user has rights to.

❑ Permissions are given to objects. The object itself carries around a list of who is entitled to use it.

❑ Some items you can control with account policies include the minimum and maximum password age, minimum password length, and account lockout.

❑ Every network operating system has administrative utilities for managing users, groups, and resources.

❑ Most operating systems provide two types of accounts that administrators have to manage: user accounts and group accounts.

SELF TEST

The following Self Test questions will help you measure your understanding of the material presented in this chapter. Read all the choices carefully, as there may be more than one correct answer. Choose all the answers that apply.

Documenting Current Status

1. Which of the following best describes the term *dependencies*?

   A. Applications that are required by another application in order to run correctly

   B. DLLs that are required by an application to run correctly

   C. Hardware resources that are required by another resource to run correctly

   D. Applications that are required for a software driver to work correctly

Returning a System to Its Original State

2. You have an e-mail server that has just lost a hard disk drive and needs to be up and running as quickly as possible. Which of the following is the fastest way to get the server operational using the most current data possible?

   A. Manually install the operating system, install the e-mail program, and then restore the data from the most recent tape backup.

   B. Use a third-party disk image program to bring down an image stored on a server, and then restore the data from the most recent tape backup.

   C. Use an unattended installation of the operating system, install the e-mail program, and then restore the data from the most recent tape backup.

   D. Manually install the operating system, and then restore the e-mail program and data from the most recent tape backup.

Backup Techniques

3. Which of the following items would restore a Windows NT system as closely as possible to the original configuration before a hard disk crash?

   A. A tape restore of the operating system and the user and system database

   B. A tape restore of the operating system, the Registry, and the user profiles

C. A tape restore of the full system, the Registry, and the most recent data

D. A tape restore of the operating system, the Registry, the most recent data, and the user profiles

4. You came to work this morning and discovered that the tape backup did not complete successfully. The backup job usually backs up around 13GB of data, but this time the backup was around 12GB of data. This job usually fits on one tape, rarely fails, and has not been changed lately. What is the most likely cause, and how should you remedy the situation?

A. The backup server most likely could not attach to a resource to complete the backup. Check the error logs to determine where the server could not connect. If a user has turned off his computer, make sure he leaves the system on at night.

B. The backup server could not load the tape. Check the contents of the tape to verify you are not trying to overwrite a write-protected tape.

C. The backup server could not append to the tape. Check the contents of the tape to verify you are not trying to overwrite a write-protected tape.

D. The backup server most likely could not attach to a resource to complete the backup. Verify the backup server has rights to the specific share. Grant the backup server rights to attach to the share.

5. Which of the following is not true concerning the tape backup?

A. It is the most expensive type of backup method.

B. It uses a sequential access method.

C. You can use multiple tapes in a tape magazine.

D. They are slower than most backup mediums.

6. What does Windows NT use to distribute logon scripts to multiple servers?

A. The distribution service

B. The domain controller service

C. The replication service

D. The backup process

7. You have a software development department with ten users, and you need to provide everyone in the department with a way to access data that has been backed up permanently. The users

will need to utilize this data at their computers to perform their jobs. What is the best way to accomplish this?

A. Install tape backup devices on each developer's computer and copy the nightly tape backups onto tape for each user to peruse.

B. Have a tape backup server holding the last five days worth of backups that each developer can attach to and peruse for information.

C. Archive the data on CD-ROM and copy the CD for each developer to peruse at their workstations.

D. Copy the backup data to the network, establish a share, and let the users attach to the share and look over the information.

Removing Outdated or Unused Drivers after a Successful Upgrade

8. Which of the following is not a good reason for removing an unused or outdated driver?

A. To conserve space

B. To conserve memory

C. So they don't accidentally get loaded

D. So they don't get corrupted

Effects on a Network Caused by Local Changes

9. Which of the following workstation settings can cause the most damage on a network?

A. An improperly configured binding order

B. An improperly configured speed on the network card

C. An invalid Token Ring address

D. A workstation configured as a master browser

10. Which of the following computers will send out a beacon on a Token Ring network indicating a fault?

A. The most active upstream neighbor

B. The nearest upstream station

C. The most active upstream station

D. The nearest active upstream neighbor

11. You just installed Windows NT Workstation on your machine and added a few applications, but while trying to add Microsoft Office 97, you received an error. What will this error most likely indicate?

A. That a DLL has been overwritten by a previous application install

B. That Office 97 has not been installed correctly

C. That your system requires Service Pack 2 or later

D. That a DLL could not be copied to the destination directory

Drive Mapping

12. Which of the following is the correct syntax for mapping to a share named HeatherCurtis on the server called PeaceCorp with a drive designator of L?

A. net use L \\PeaceCorp\HeatherCurtis

B. net use /L: \PeaceCorp\HeatherCurtis

C. net use L: \HeatherCurtis\\PeaceCorp

D. net use L: \\PeaceCorp\HeatherCurtis

13. You have created a batch file to map network drives and printers for each user in the department. The following is your newly created batch file:

```
net use R: /delete
net use R: \\Rhapsody\March99
net use S: /delete
net use S: \\Enertia\QuarterlyReports
net use lpt1: \\Sanvoisen\HPLJ4SI
```

Which line in the batch file is invalid or incorrect?

A. The second line is invalid.

B. The fourth line is invalid.

C. The fifth line is invalid.

D. There is no invalid or incorrect line in this batch file.

Changing or Moving Equipment

14. You are planning to move the Web servers from one location to another later tonight. The user support database is run from the Web server, so the move must be completed by the morning. What needs to be done to ensure a smooth move?

A. Migrate the user profiles to another server before the move.

B. Test the network connection in the new room.

C. Back up the data on the servers.

D. Back up the user profiles before the move.

Adding, Deleting, or Modifying Users

15. Van Williams, the supervisor for the A-crew in the Receiving department will be leaving the company. Jeff Loomis, the new supervisor, will replace him shortly. What should happen to Van's user account?

A. It should be deleted.

B. It should be disabled.

C. It should be moved to the temporary area.

D. It should be renamed to Jeff Loomis, the new supervisor.

User and Group Management

20. You need to give Internet access to eight users in the Sales department, but you don't want to give Internet access to the entire Sales department. How would you go about granting Internet access to these users?

A. Grant the sales group rights to access the Internet.

B. Grant each user rights to access the Internet.

C. Place each of the users into a group called Internet and give this group access to the Internet.

D. Grant the sales group rights to access the Internet, but revoke rights for those who do not need access to the Internet.

21. What is the difference between rights and permissions?

    A. Permissions are assigned to objects, while rights are given to user or group accounts.

    B. Permissions are given to user or group accounts, and rights are given to objects.

    C. Permissions are given to user accounts, and rights are given to groups.

    D. Permissions are given to groups, and rights are given to user accounts.

22. Tim Owens has come back this morning from a two-month sabbatical, and calls saying he can't access the network. You haven't disabled his account, however. He believes he is typing in the right password, because it's written on his monitor. What account policy is most likely causing the problem?

    A. Account Lockout

    B. Maximum Password Age

    C. Minimum Password Age

    D. Lockout Duration

23. What is the user and group management utility provided with NetWare 3.*x*?

    A. NetWare Administrator

    B. SYSADMIN

    C. SYSCONSOLE

    D. SYSCON

LAB QUESTION

Your company is starting out fresh in the IT field, and you are going to begin a whole new rollout that allows you to install all new PCs with a newer OS than before. There will be actual servers instead of everyone operating as a workgroup. Your task is to increase the efficiency in which the rollout is performed. Each technician involved is currently installing one PC a day. The following are the requirements:

    ■ All PCs will be the same make and model.

    ■ All PCs will require Windows NT Workstation.

    ■ All PCs will require the same patches for the OS.

    ■ All PCs will require the same applications. Few systems will have "extra" applications.

- All applications must be manually installed for the licensing software to be able to track the PCs which are running them.

- Each tech must be able to complete at least five PCs a day, if not more.

- All applications must be accessible form the network and not installed by using a local drive, such as a CD-ROM.

The following applications are to be installed:

- Microsoft Office XP

- Upgrade Web browse to IE version 6.0

- A specially written application for access to the company database

- A specially licensed training software for the Office XP products

All PCs will be connected to the network and will be running 100 Mbps NICs. What should be implemented to have a quick and efficient rollout?

SELF TEST ANSWERS

Documenting Current Status

1. ☑ **A.** Applications that are required by another application in order to run correctly. Many times an application requires that a certain service pack be installed on the computer. These are known as *dependencies* because the application you wish to install is dependent on these additional applications, service packs, or software updates being present on the system.

   ☒ **B, C, and D** are incorrect. DLLs are required by almost all programs and are not considered dependencies but libraries. Hardware resources required by other resources are going to be a complete device group, such as a printer that depends on the printer port. Applications are not really required to make a driver work; it is the other way around. Applications request information from the driver, which sends a request to the device for that information. The data is then directed back to the application by the driver.

Returning a System to Its Original State

2. ☑ **B.** Use a third-party disk image program to bring down an image stored on a server, and then restore the data from the most recent tape backup. In addition to keeping documentation on these select systems on your network, you can also purchase third-party utilities that create images of these servers. If you create new, updated images every week or so, you can apply this image to a freshly rebuilt computer in a matter of minutes. Given this type of updating, you can go from a disastrous hard disk crash to being fully operational again in thirty minutes.

   ☒ **A, C, and D** are incorrect. Manual restoration of an operating system and applications can take almost a whole day. An unattended install of the OS can take almost as long as a manual install. This makes choices **A, C,** and **D** incorrect.

Backup Techniques

3. ☑ **C.** A tape restore of the full system, the Registry, and the most recent data. Microsoft recommends backing up and restoring the Registry for each Windows computer if you truly want to return a computer to its original operating state. The Registry contains current user and system information, which means the backup should be the most recent in order to rescue the latest changes to the system. The most recent data will likely come from the tape backup done the night before. If the restore does not include the whole system, the applications will not be a part of the restore. This will not be a complete working system and will not be close to how the system was before the crash.

   ☒ **A, B,** and **D** will not restore a Windows NT system as closely as possible to the original configuration before a hard disk crash.

4. ☑ **A.** The backup server most likely could not attach to a resource to complete the backup. Check the error logs to determine where the server could not connect. If a user has turned off his computer, make sure he leaves the system on at night. If the backup program could not attach to one user's computer because he shut his computer down at the end of the night, you will receive an error. Read through the error logs to determine where the job failed. If it fails every night trying to connect to another network server, remedy the situation before it's too late.
   ☒ **B, C,** and **D** are incorrect. The tape should be good enough to load the tape and append to the tape, otherwise the 12GB of data would not have been backed up at all. This makes choices **B** and **C** incorrect. Rights rarely change and the Backup Operator should have rights to back up all files and folders no matter what rights are placed on a file or folder. This case is most likely a resource that is unavailable due to a PC being shut off or disconnected from the network.

5. ☑ **A.** It is the most expensive type of backup method. Backing up to tape is the most common form of backup done today because of availability and price. Tape backup is slower, due to the sequential access of the medium. It works like a cassette tape, where you have to fast-forward or rewind to find your favorite song. This is the opposite of *random-access*. Multiple tape magazines are used for companies that back up large amounts of information every night. These backup jobs can even exceed a 24GB compressed tape, but when one tape is full, the backup process will continue on the next available tape.
   ☒ **B, C,** and **D** are true concerning tape backup.

6. ☑ **C.** The replication service. Windows NT provides a replication service to replicate data to other servers. This may sound like a means of backing up, but the service is provided to replicate commonly used items such as logon scripts to back up domain controllers.
   ☒ **A, B,** and **D** are incorrect. There is no specific distribution or domain controller service. The backup process is used to copy or restore files to a specified folder location and not to distribute files to users.

7. ☑ **C.** Archive the data on CD-ROM and copy the CD for each developer to peruse at their workstations. The type of removable media you require is based on the needs of your particular network. Many companies use tape backup for nightly backups and then use writable CD-ROMs to create images or backup sets that can be used on any machine with access to a CD-ROM.
   ☒ **A, B,** and **D** are incorrect. Installing tape backup devices on all PCs would be a waste of money. A network is for sharing resources. It defeats the purpose to go out and purchase the same resources for every user. Data backed up by a tape backup is not readily accessible and must be restored to a hard disk for access by users. Copying the data to a network share allows for both the change of data and its possible loss. CD-ROMs, meanwhile, permit a more permanent and unchangeable media.

Removing Outdated or Unused Drivers after a Successful Upgrade

8.   ☑   **D.** So they don't get corrupted. There are a number of reasons why it is recommended to remove outdated or unused drivers on a system: so they don't accidentally get loaded, to conserve disk space, because loaded drivers consume memory, and because they can interfere with a new driver.

   ☒   **A, B,** and **C** are good reasons for removing an unused or outdated driver.

Effects on a Network Caused by Local Changes

9.   ☑   **B.** An improperly configured speed on the network card. However, with that in mind, make sure you use extreme caution when configuring a network adapter card. If anything can bring down the network, it will be misconfiguring a network card. Misconfiguring the speed on a network card, meanwhile, will confuse and lock up a hub.

   ☒   **A, C,** and **D** are incorrect. Binding order will not affect the network too much. When multiple protocols are configured on a computer, the first bound one is tried; and if it is not able to connect to the desired resource, the next bound protocol will be tried. Once a protocol works, it will be used to connect to the same resource. Token Rings do not have an address. The address is managed by the protocol and not the topology. A workstation that is configured as a master browser will not affect the network at all. An election will eventually be held and if any servers are online, the server will be used as the master browser.

10.   ☑   **D.** The nearest active upstream neighbor. When a computer with a faulty network card is on the network, it can continuously chatter on the network, eating up bandwidth. Usually you will need to use special software to analyze packets on the network to determine which computer is having problems. A Token Ring network will cease to function and the nearest active upstream neighbor (NAUN) to the failed computer will send out a beacon, alerting you as to which computer is not functioning correctly.

   ☒   **A, B,** and **C** will not send out a beacon on a Token Ring network indicating a fault.

11.   ☑   **C.** That your system requires Service Pack 2 or later. Lately, we've seen several applications that require a specific Windows NT service pack in order to perform. This was the case with the Y2K bug, which was said to be relieved by using Microsoft's Service Pack 4 for Windows NT. A few applications require that the operating system be patched with Service Pack 4 in order for the application itself to be Y2K-compliant. Other applications, such as Microsoft Office 97, require that Service Pack 2 or higher be installed prior to installing Office 97.

☒   **A, B,** and **D** are incorrect. Windows NT has no error services that prevent DLLs from being written over, as in Windows 2000. So choice **A** would be incorrect. The error message should relate to Office 97 not being installed properly, but there should be a more explicit message regarding the cause. This would make choice **B** incorrect. Windows NT could give an error message that a file couldn't be copied to the hard disk if certain rights are not granted to the logged in user for the directory where files will be copied. The only problem with this is that to start the setup, the program should determine if the user has rights to even attempt an application install. Additionally, most applications will try to determine first if it is compatible with the OS.

Drive Mapping

12.   ☑   **D.** net use L: \\PeaceCorp\HeatherCurtis. The mapping begins with two backslash characters before the server name. After the server name, one backslash precedes the share name.
☒   **A, B,** and **C** are not the correct syntax for mapping to a share called HeatherCurtis on the server called PeaceCorp with the drive designator of L.

13.   ☑   **D.** There is no invalid or incorrect line in this batch file. The preceding batch file commands will delete the share if it already exists and map the share again. The share is deleted before it is mapped to circumvent the error message received when you try to establish a drive mapping that is already in place. The last line in the batch file will map a printer to the local lpt1 port.
☒   **A, B,** and **C** are valid and correct.

Changing or Moving Equipment

14.   ☑   **B.** Test the network connection in the new room. Moving a computer from one room to another doesn't sound like that difficult a process. However, there are hidden traps that can make this move more disruptive than it needs to be. In order to complete a move without incident, you should test the area you are moving the computer to before the move. Most importantly, you should test the network connection.
☒   **A, C,** and **D** are incorrect. **A** would be incorrect since user profiles can be accessed as long as the PCs still have access to the server no matter what its location. Backing up the data on the Web servers will not assist in the move, but should be done on a constant basis despite what is happening with the servers. It doesn't matter if the user profiles are backed up independently; the whole server should be backed up on a regular basis.

Adding, Deleting, or Modifying Users

15. ☑ **B** and **D**. It should be renamed to Jeff Loomis, the new supervisor. You know the username of the new supervisor, so you should rename the account to his name. If you didn't know the name of the new user, you could have disabled Van's account and renamed the account when the new user arrived. If you delete his account immediately, you will just be forced to recreate it for the new hire and then add the new hire to the existing shares Jim had access to. This makes choice **A** incorrect. Keep in mind that the task could be overwhelming task if Jim had explicit access to many files and folders.

    ☒ **A** and **C** are incorrect. You should disable the account since no one will be using it until the new user arrives. Choice **C** is incorrect since there is no temporary area for user accounts.

User and Group Management

16. ☑ **C**. This is the best choice and also the one recommended by NOS manufacturers. Place each of the users into a group called Internet and grant this group access to the Internet. Although you can give rights, such as access to the Internet, to one group, it's a good idea to start a group called Internet, which will consist of users that have access to the Internet. As each user requires access to the Internet, you can place his account in this group. Even groups, such as the Sales group, can be placed in this group in order to give every user in it access to the Internet.

    ☒ **A**, **B**, and **D** are incorrect. Granting access to the whole Sales department (as in A) will give access to more than the specified eight users. **B** will work, but it is not recommended to grant rights to individual users. Groups should be created instead. **D** might work, but it will also cause more labor for the administrator and will require them to check two separate places for rights to access the Internet, rather than by just checking a group called Internet.

17. ☑ **A**. Permissions are assigned to objects, while rights are given to user or group accounts. The user account carries around the credentials of which tasks the user has rights to. Permissions are given to objects, which carry around a list of who is entitled to use it.

    ☒ **B**, **C**, and **D** are incorrect definitions.

18. ☑ **B**. Maximum Password Age. Some networks have a policy that passwords expire after a certain number of days. With your user accounts, there are account policies you can implement to help control the security of your network. Some of the items you can control with account policies include the minimum and maximum password age, minimum password length, and account lockout.

☒ **A, C, and D** are incorrect. Account Lockout occurs when someone types their password incorrectly a specified number of times. Minimum Password Age is the number of days that a password has to be kept before it can be changed. Lockout Duration concerns how long the account is locked out after a lockout has occurred. After the lockout duration has passed, the account will be re-enabled at this point.

19. ☑ **D. SYSCON.** Microsoft Windows NT 4.0 Server has User Manager for Domains; Windows NT Workstation has User Manager; Novell NetWare, version 3.*x* has SYSCON; and Novell NetWare, version 4.*x* has the graphical NetWare Administrator. Each of these administrative tools enables you to add, modify, and delete users and groups.
    ☒ **A, B, and C** are not the user and group management utility provided with NetWare 3.*x*.

LAB ANSWER

1. Install Windows NT Workstation and all patches for Windows NT Workstation to a test PC. Install all drivers needed for any special equipment that does not have drivers included in Windows NT Workstation. Create an image of this system using a third-party imaging tool and copy the image to a server directory called IMAGES, and then share the directory. Also copy the imaging software to the same directory (the DOS version).

2. Install all applications to the server in a directory called APPS. Share the APPS directory.

3. Create a network boot disk from the server and add the following line to the AUTOEXEC.BAT file:

    ```
    NET USE H: \\SERVER\IMAGES
    ```

4. Once the PC is connected to the network, boot the rest of the PCs with the boot disk. Verify login username and password (make sure you have rights to the shared directories).

5. Switch to the H: directory and run the DOS version of the imaging software loading the image to the local PC. (Note that this image and DOS file can be burned to a bootable CD-ROM and this could be used.)

6. Once done, reboot and log in as an administrator. Make sure the following line is included in the administrator login script:

    ```
    NET USE H: \\SERVER\APPS
    ```

7. Switch to the H: directory and run the setup program for all needed apps. Note that it may be easier to create an install directory and place a shortcut for all of the setup programs for all apps in the directory. This way you only have to navigate to one directory to run all of the required installs.

This will complete one machine, but a few machines can be completed simultaneously if the bandwidth is available. For better bandwidth, the best solution would be to have the OS image on a bootable CD and to only use network bandwidth for installing the applications.

11

Maintaining and Supporting the Network

CERTIFICATION OBJECTIVES

11.01	Test Documentation
11.02	Network Maintenance
✓	Two-Minute Drill
Q&A	Self Test

The two most important things you'll do in your job will be to maintain the network and support your users—functions that are vital to your success as a network administrator. If you don't keep your network up to date, you're headed for constant problems and possibly network failure. But if you keep your pieces current and stay on top of problems, the problems you face will be minor and the network will be a productive tool for your users.

In this chapter, you will learn some of the things you have to do to ensure your network is up more than it is down and that all your applications operate at peak performance. Documentation and learning are the biggest keys to success in maintaining and supporting your network. Alongside documentation come different maintenance components, such as patches, fixes, and general upgrades. When you change something on the network, you want to make sure the network continues functioning. This is where documenting what you did comes in handy, especially if you have to do it again.

CERTIFICATION OBJECTIVE 11.01

Test Documentation

When it comes to maintaining software on the network, it is important to know the details of what makes or breaks an application. If there is one thing I have learned while implementing and maintaining networks, it is to read the readme files. There isn't a patch I've seen in the past few years that doesn't come with a readme file or a text file of some sort with installation instructions. In fact, it's usually a good idea to read through the documentation and then afterward reread the documentation and any corresponding addendums.

It is more common today that new software installations require reading documentation from the CD or diskettes they come on. In order to do this, you must have the appropriate viewer installed on your workstation. Fortunately, the viewer usually comes on the software CD—for instance, Novell software has its own viewer for its documentation. Figure 11-1 shows an example of the Novell documentation viewer.

FIGURE 11-1

Novell software
comes with its
own viewer
for reading
installation
documentation
and readme files

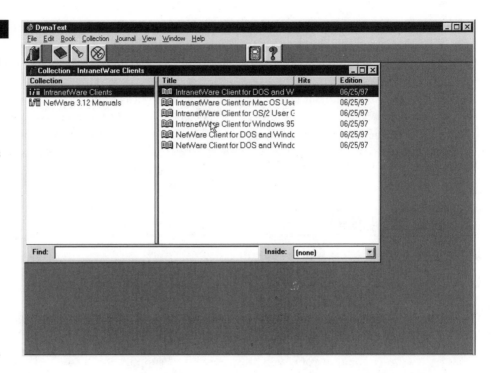

Not all vendor CDs will have a specialized viewer, of course. Some documentation may use standard word processor programs while others will use Adobe Reader as a standard, saving their documents in a PDF format.

Vendors' Software Patches

Part of maintaining your network is applying patches to your existing software to make sure you have the most current release. Vendors release updates or patches to their products when bugs are found or to simply make them run better. The main software vendors for network operating systems, Microsoft and Novell, have a service pack for the core network operating system. Applying these is a must when it comes to ensuring your network functions with third-party applications. You can access Novell service packs for their network operating systems by going directly to support.novell.com.

The vendor's Web site will most likely have the patches and service packs you need for your software. Microsoft, Computer Associates, APC, Compaq, Hewlett

Packard, and other vendors all have Web sites to support their customers, which include patches along with documentation on problems. For Microsoft patches and service packs, go to windowsupdate.microsoft.com or www.microsoft.com/download.

Sometimes it takes looking through the online support forums to figure out you need a patch. Thankfully, vendors have online support where you can perform a search for a particular error or problem, which may lead to the appropriate patch. The most popular place to access Microsoft's online support is support.microsoft.com.

Exercise 11-1 teaches you how to search for and download patches.

EXERCISE 11-1

Downloading a Patch from Novell

You are upgrading a server from NetWare 3.12 to NetWare 3.2. You call tech support and search the Web until you discover there is one patch you need to apply to NetWare 3.2 after the upgrade. Follow these steps to find, download, and extract a patch from Novell. (You should use Netscape in this exercise.)

1. Point your Web browser at http://support.novell.com.

2. On the Support Connection page, select the link for Minimum Patch List.

3. Scroll down to the Table of Contents and select Previous Product Versions.

4. Scroll down to the NetWare 3.12 section and find the patch named LIB312B.EXE.

5. Click the LIB312B.EXE link to go to the page where you can download the file and read about the patch.

6. Read through the Abstract, Issue, and Installation Instructions sections specifically.

7. Click the link at the top of the page and download the file to a temporary directory.

8. After the file is downloaded, go to the DOS prompt and change to the directory where you downloaded the file.

9. Type **LIB312B** to execute the patch. You will be prompted to continue the extraction. Press Y to answer yes.

10. A series of files will be extracted. One of these files is LIB312B.TXT. After the files are extracted, type **EDIT LIB312B.TXT** to open the text file.

11. Read through the text file to double-check any instructions for installation.

At this point, you apply the patch per the instructions on the Web page and in the text file; however, you probably do not actually have a NetWare 3.12 server to apply this patch to, so stop here.

Be sure to do the necessary research about the patch you are applying, so you know what you are doing. Applying a patch incorrectly can bring down the entire network. Be sure you have a good backup in case the patch crashes the server so badly you have to restore from tape. New patches and service packs are the riskiest. The newest ones have the most recent fixes, of course, but sometimes the service pack or patch may cause other problems. A good rule of thumb is to wait a few weeks after a patch comes out and then research what other users are saying. Let them be the guinea pigs, not your system. In fact, many vendors have forums that users can post information to in regards to items like patches. Vendors have been known to make patches and service packs available only to have to pull them off their Web site to modify them. The first service packs for NetWare 5 and Microsoft Office 97 were released, pulled, re-done, and then released again. The point is: sometimes waiting is not such a bad thing. If waiting is not an option, however, be sure to rename or backup the files that are being replaced. This is especially true if the files are copied manually, giving you complete control as the network administrator.

When installing service packs and patches, you should install them on one machine and test to verify that the updated files don't cause any problems with your applications. This is why some companies have test labs, allowing them to check out changes before implementing them on a companywide scale and having serious problems.

exam
ⓦatch

The exam touches on a lot of scenarios regarding troubleshooting and maintenance. Be sure to understand each component: patches, upgrades, virus signatures, backups, and so on.

Upgrades

Software manufacturers release upgrades for their products to improve them and make them more powerful. You should always install an upgrade on a stand-alone machine before distributing it to the network. This enables you to test the application and go through the upgrade process in a non-production environment.

Many minor upgrades are free and require a simple download similar to a patch. Upgrading from one version of an application or OS to another usually requires you pay a fee for the new product. Sometimes an application can have a minor version change, such as version 5.01 to 5.02, which may not require a fee, however. Other upgrades, meanwhile, can be ordered for free from the manufacturer, or may come at a minimal cost if you are a registered owner and user of the older version. Again, be sure to have a good backup before you install the upgrade in order to prevent data loss.

Hardware Upgrades

Does your company require hardware upgrades for maintaining the network? Lucky for you, firmware updates for the various ROMs are often contained in servers and workstations as well as in their devices. The main ROM that controls the computer is usually programmable and can be updated. I recommend getting the latest ROM updates for all components on your entire network. If there is an update, there is a reason for it, and if you can avoid the problem before it happens, you'll save yourself a lot of headaches.

Manufacturers devote an area on their Web sites to their hardware and allow you to update the components in your server and workstations. Figure 11-2 shows the Compaq Web site for downloading ROM updates for Compaq computers.

With the passing of the year 2000, ROM updates were especially important. The updates included readme files or other documentation, along with a version number and a date associated with the ROM revision. Figure 11-3 is the Hewlett Packard Web site showing a ROM revision with the version number and a link to more information.

If you were to click on the more info link, you would be taken to a page that shows the date of the ROM revision. This is helpful if the only thing you know is the date of your current ROM. The ROM dates are shown during the POST when the server or workstation is first turned on, so knowing just the date will usually tell

FIGURE 11-2

You can
download ROM
updates from
this Compaq
Web site

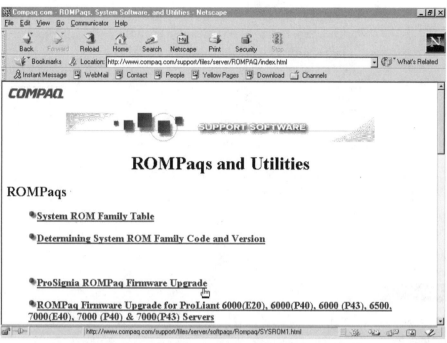

FIGURE 11-3

This HP Web site
shows a ROM
revision with the
version number

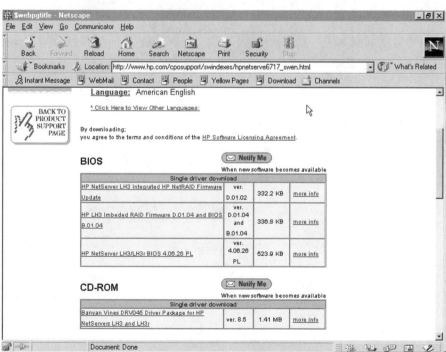

you whether your ROM needs to be updated. Figure 11-4 shows the Hewlett Packard page that appears when you click the More Info link.

Some hardware may not allow for ROM updates, while those that do may require a full hardware upgrade to meet the needs of the company. For example, if a company upgrades its network from 10 Mbps to 100Mbps Ethernet and the company had purchased only 10 Mbps Ethernet cards, then there won't be a way to just update the ROM to allow for 100 Mbps transfer speeds. This would require a full hardware replacement of the network card.

When new hardware is purchased, you must verify that the hardware will work with your existing PCs, as well as the OSs and current service packs.

FIGURE 11-4

This HP Web site gives the date of the ROM update

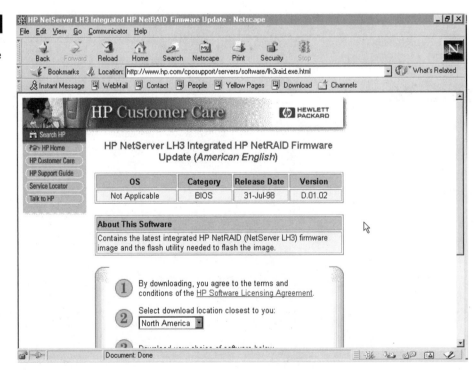

Be aware of how to perform a ROM BIOS flash upgrade. Remember that the power cannot be shut off during the upgrade, or else the BIOS will be corrupt and the system will not function. Also remember that after the upgrade is complete, the system must be shut off and turned back on for the changes to take effect.

CERTIFICATION OBJECTIVE 11.02

Network Maintenance

There is more to network maintenance than patches and updates. These include providing and testing a backup solution and providing and updating anti-virus software. You need to establish a backup routine, as well as a routine for applying updates of patches and virus signatures.

Standard Backup Procedures and Backup Media Storage Practices

Every network administrator should have a backup routine. Software packages are available for backing up network servers, and various types of tape drives are available for storing the backup. The software and the tape drive you choose determine how fast you back up and how much you back up to the media. This is determined by the storage capacity of the tape and the compression capability of the software.

Installing Backup Software

Before you install backup software, you need to take some preliminary steps:

1. Make sure the system you are installing meets all hardware and software requirements.

2. Physically install the tape drive and any adapter boards that are needed. Connect the cables between the tape drive and the adapter board, then make sure that the power is connected.

3. Make certain your backup software has everything in it before proceeding.

4. Refer to the instructions with your backup software for any unique preinstallation items.

This probably seems straightforward, but there are things about these steps to keep in mind. When ensuring that your system meets the hardware and software requirements, you have to know what devices are installed. Not just any tape drive or SCSI adapter will work in all cases. Also, there are things you can do with the network operating system to determine what you have available when it comes to resources. For example, Windows 9*x*, ME, and 2000 have the Device Manager available that lists all installed devices in the system detected by Plug and Play, as well as those manually added. There are also third-party utilities which give a listing of system resources such as the Norton Disk Doctor utility suite which has a program included with it that shows the specifications of the system on which it is run. Windows 2000 also includes Task Manager, which displays the available memory.

When installing the tape drive in a SCSI chain, you have to know if other devices are connected. If so, you must have a SCSI ID assigned to each device that is different. If you don't do this, your devices may not work properly.

After you install the software, you have to make sure it is loaded on the server. NetWare and Windows NT give you two distinct ways to check to see if the backup software is running. NetWare provides an NLM (NetWare Loadable Module) with a screen that you can switch to. With NetWare, you can press CTRL-ESC to get a list of available screens. Windows NT enables the backup software to run as a service. Select Start | Settings | Control Panel, and then double-click the Services icon. The Services dialog box lists the services available on that server. Check to see if your backup software is listed.

NetWare and Windows NT provide two different ways to get into the administrative utility that comes with the backup software. On Windows NT, everything can be done at the server. Computer Associates ArcServeIT, for example, has a utility that is the Manager for the backup software. This utility is run at the server on Windows NT and at a workstation on NetWare. Seagate's Backup Exec also has a management utility that runs on the workstation on a Novell network.

Tape Drives

The two most common types of tape drives are Digital Audio Tape (DAT) and Digital Linear Tape (DLT). This section looks at each drive in some detail. The exam will not delve into as many particulars, but understanding their backgrounds will help you remember the information about the drives, and in the end, help you on the test.

DAT (Digital Audio Tape) was developed in the mid-1980s by Sony and Philips to record music in a digital format, but has now become very popular as a medium for computer data storage. The DAT drive uses a helical scan, which means that the read/write heads spin diagonally across the tape. DAT uses the DDS (Digital Data Storage) format and a 4mm tape, and while the speed isn't as good as that of a DLT drive, the capacity can be quite large. Keep in mind, however, that the two systems, audio and computer, cannot share information.

Different DDS formats allow for different amounts of storage on a tape. Table 11-1 shows the breakdown of these different technologies.

As DDS-1 emerged, so did compression. That is why you'll notice that DDS-1 to DDS-3 have a second number associated with them which is always double the base storage capacity. Using this equation, standard 4mm tapes for DAT drives can hold up to 24GB of data. Other technologies have also emerged with the appearance of 8mm tapes, but you won't need to know these for the exam.

DLT (Digital Linear Tape) was introduced by Digital Equipment Corporation in the mid-80s, although Quantum Corporation owns the technology now. The DLT tape is a half-inch reel-to-reel magnetic tape, where the tape cartridge contains one reel and the DLT drive the other.

The standards for DLT are shown in Table 11-2. The main advantages are fast data transfer rates, higher storage capacity, and higher reliability. All this, of course, comes at a price to the customer.

TABLE 11-1   The DDS Formats for DAT Drives

Type of Format	Storage Capacity
DDS	2GB
DDS-1	2/4GB
DDS-2	4/8GB
DDS-3	12/24GB

TABLE 11-2   DLT Standards

OSI Layer	Protocols, Services, Methods, and Layers
Application	FTP, SMTP, Telnet
Presentation	JPEG, GIF, MPEG
Session	NFS, RPC

DLT drives store data on the tape differently than the DAT drives do. The data path is made up of parallel tracks recorded in a serpentine pattern. What this means is that the first track is written from one end of the tape to the other and then the heads are repositioned and the next track goes the opposite direction (again for the entire length of the tape). The drive continues to go back and forth, writing until the tape is full.

Tape Automation

When it comes to maintaining the network, you need to schedule a backup job and develop a routine for your backup schedule. Many companies do a tape rotation. They have daily, weekly, and monthly tapes, the rotation of which usually consists of 20 to 25 tapes, each with its purpose. Sometimes this is called an autopilot rotation. The backup software keeps a database and expects a certain tape on each day of the year. The most common one is a 21-tape rotation consisting of four daily tapes for Monday through Thursday, five weekly tapes for each Friday (some months have five Fridays), and 12 monthly tapes for the last weekday of the month. There are no backups on Saturday or Sunday. It is a good idea to store the monthly tapes offsite to keep fire or some other major catastrophe from ruining your data and your backups.

Along with tape rotations come tape libraries and tape arrays. Tape libraries are designed to have a series of tapes in a holder that is inserted into the tape mechanism to automate the rotation of tapes throughout the week. If the amount of data is very large, the tape library may be used on a daily basis to rotate multiple tapes in and out of the various drives to make sure all data fits onto a tape. Tape arrays, on the other hand, are similar to RAID technology with hard drives, where data is spread over a series of drives—for instance, there might be a parity drive for fault tolerance addition. Manufacturers claim that tape arrays increase the throughput because multiple drives are writing simultaneously.

Full, Incremental, and Differential Backups

Backup software enables you to run three different types of backups: full, incremental, and differential. These are the three you may see on the exam so we will focus on them. The key to backing up your data is to ensure that you can restore it in the event of a system failure. These three types of backup will function well if you use them together correctly.

A *full backup* backs up every file on the specified volume or volumes. Many companies run a full backup every day, no matter what. Under such a system, the restore process only requires the most recent tape. However, a full backup necessitates a large storage capacity and a lot of time. If you have a big system with a lot of data, running a daily full backup may not be practical.

An *incremental backup* backs up the files that have changed or were added since the last incremental or full backup. If you choose to run an incremental back up as your first backup, it will run as a full backup because there is no previous one to go by. Using a combination of the full backup and incremental backup is highly effective and less time consuming than running a full backup daily. However, to restore, you will need the last full backup tape and every incremental backup tape since the last full backup.

A *differential backup* backs up the files that have changed or were added since the last full backup. This can also be very efficient when you do not want to do full backups every day. Restoring requires only two tapes: the last full backup tape and the last differential backup tape.

Differential and incremental backups can make the restoration process a little more difficult, because you have to restore from the full backup first, and then restore from the incremental or differential backups to make sure any files that have changed since the last full backup are restored. If you have continuous full backup tapes, you can restore from the most recent backup and get all the files restored in one session. An important difference between differential and incremental backups is that incremental backups take less time to back up but more time to restore, while differential backups take more time to back up but less time to restore.

exam
ⓦatch

You will definitely see a question or two on the exam about the different kinds of backups. Be sure to know the differences between full, incremental, and differential, especially the last two, which can be the most confusing. You may be given a scenario and have to pick the backup plan and restoration process.

SCENARIO & SOLUTION

I want to be able to restore from one tape and get all the data. What type of backup do I need to run?	Run a full backup on a daily basis.
I want to have the quickest possible backup of only those files that have changed or were added since the last backup. Which backup method should I use?	Run an incremental backup.
I want to run a backup that will back up all files that have changed since the last full backup. What backup do I want to use on the days I am not doing a full backup?	Run a differential backup.
I want to be able to restore all my data with only two tapes. What tape backup scheme should I use?	Run a full backup with a differential backup.
If I am restoring data and need to use the full backup as well as every tape since the full backup. Which tape backup scheme am I using?	You are running a full backup with incremental backups.
If I run one full backup and then run a differential backup every day for three months, how many tapes will I need to restore the data entirely?	Two. You will need the full backup tape and the most recent differential backup tape.

Periodic Application of Software Patches and Other Fixes to the Network

Earlier in this chapter, you learned about patching and updating software on the server. There are a couple of details you should look at a little closer, however. First of all, you not only need to patch the software that runs on the server itself, such as the backup software and anti-virus software, but you also need to update any applications that run from the client workstations. Some applications may be located on the server but instead run on the workstation, while other applications are installed on the actual workstation. It may seem time consuming to have to update applications on every workstation; you need to have consistency throughout the network. A database application may have the client engine installed directly on the workstation and the data on the server—something very common among database applications.

The company I work for has a division that uses QuickBooks accounting software. The application is loaded on each workstation and the data is stored in a common directory on the server. One of the users downloaded an update from the Internet and updated his workstation. When the workstation software was updated, the database also was updated which caused a problem for the other users. When the other users tried to get into the database, they got an error because their workstations were not updated.

The other side to this piece of maintaining the network is logging the activity and documenting every change or update that is applied. If this isn't done, you may start seeing inconsistencies in your network with updates and patches. This leads to problems and then things can start to snowball.

Installing Anti-Virus Software on the Server and Workstations

Anti-virus software is a must on networks and workstations today, since viruses can destroy data on a hard drive in a matter of seconds. With more and more networks connecting to the Internet, the chance of getting a virus has increased significantly. Prior to offices being on the Internet, virus infections usually started from floppy disks brought from other offices or from home.

When you install anti-virus software in a networked environment, you must set multiple configuration items. There is usually both a workstation agent and a server application that run constantly, scanning for viruses and virus-like activity. Most people think of virus software as an application you use to scan your drives and files for viruses. This is one component of virus software, but the most important part is the memory-resident piece that scans files coming into the server from the workstations or the Internet. These files are considered incoming. It also scans any files that are opened on the server—considered outgoing files.

The installation of anti-virus software is different on the two major platforms for network OS: NetWare and Windows NT. The software we'll discuss in this section is Computer Associates' InoculateIT, but other popular virus protection suites include McAfee, Dr. Solomon's Anti-Virus Toolkit, and Norton Anti-Virus.

Though installations on both platforms have similarities, the end results can be a little different. The first few steps are similar to that of installation guidelines of just about any software.

1. Make sure the system meets all hardware and software requirements.

2. Check the workstation or server that you are installing from for viruses locally. With NetWare, you will be installing from a workstation, but from Windows NT, you will be installing at the server.

3. Install the software to your server's hard disk. Figure 11-5 shows part of the installation procedure. If you choose custom installation, you will have the option of installing the manager software. This is the workstation component for Windows and DOS.

4. Apply any patches or updates from the vendor's Web site. This includes updating the virus signatures, which we will look at in the next section.

Sounds pretty easy, right? Well, the installation piece is pretty easy anyway. It's the configuration that can be a bit challenging.

InoculateIT, as well as some of the other anti-virus programs, gives you three configuration options: Domain Manager, Local Scanner, and Critical Disk. These options are available regardless of whether you are running it on a NetWare network or a Windows NT network. Figure 11-6 shows the Quick Access dialog box. The Critical Disk option backs up the boot sector, BIOS information, and other important components that can be infected by viruses, and can be used to restore this vital information in case of failure.

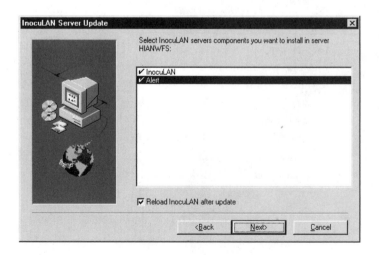

FIGURE 11-5

Installing InoculateIT from Computer Associates

The InoculateIT
Quick Access
dialog box gives
you three
configuration
options

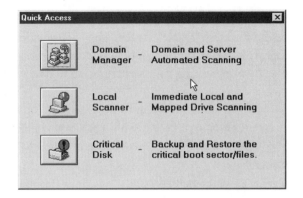

Domain Manager

The Domain Manager exists in both the Windows NT version and the Novell
NetWare version of InoculateIT. When InoculateIT is set up on a network, it is
possible to configure the servers as a domain within the virus software. This keeps
everything consistent throughout the network. A job can be set up and everything
can be managed at the domain level, which keeps it centralized.

Click the Domain Manager button on the Quick Access dialog box to open the
Domain Manager window, as shown in Figure 11-7.

The Domain
Manager window

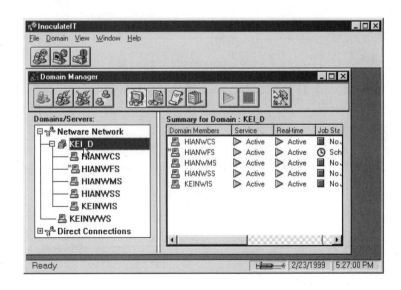

On the left is a list of possible servers or workstations to scan, while on the right are the currently scheduled jobs. There is also a listing with corresponding version number, along with the version and date of the virus signatures. This is very important in keeping your signatures up to date, which you will learn about in the next section.

Click the Add/Modify button to open the Job Properties dialog box. When you click this button to add or modify a job, you will get a window similar to Figure 11-8. The Job Properties dialog box enables you to add a new job, modify a current one, or delete a job.

When adding or modifying a job you have plenty of options available. This is where virus protection can get tricky if you are not careful. The Targets/Schedule page is pretty straightforward. It enables you to choose what you want scanned and what you want to exclude. It also enables you to choose when you want the scan to take place.

Select the Actions/Options tab to bring it to the front, as shown in Figure 11-9. The Actions/Options page enables you to choose what you want done with infected files and what file types you want scanned based on extension.

FIGURE 11-8

Use the Job Properties dialog box to add, modify, or delete a domain job

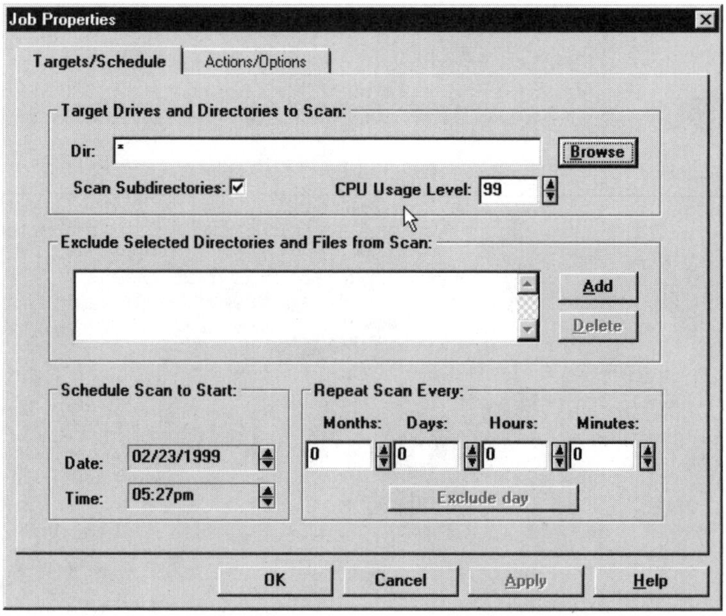

FIGURE 11-9

Use the
Actions/Options
page in InoculateIT
to choose the
types of files to
scan and what to
do with infected
files

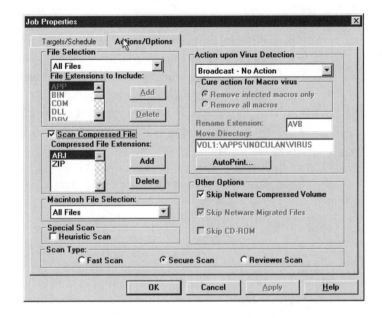

You can choose to have InoculateIT cure infected files, report the problem and
do nothing with the file, report and move the file to a special directory, or delete
infected files. Moved files are renamed with a special extension for easy recognition.
If you choose the cure option, and InoculateIT is unable to cure a file, the file will
be moved and renamed with the special extension. Other virus protection suites
have similar options.

The Actions/Options page has more options for scanning compressed files,
compressed volumes, CD-ROMs, as well as the type of scan. The types of scan
available with InoculateIT are Fast Scan, Secure Scan, and Reviewer Scan. Fast
Scan simply scans the beginning of the file for faster scanning. EXE and COM files are
scanned fully with this method, which does have a risk of missing infected files, though.

Secure Scan is the preferred scan to use, scanning every file fully. This takes more
time but also is more thorough. Reviewer Scan scans every file fully and scans for
virus-like activity within a file, but has the potential to raise false alarms.

Local Scanner
The local scanner option in the Quick Access dialog box is for immediate scanning
of local or mapped drives. This is good to do when you have a problem with a

workstation or particular volume on a server. This is also useful for a server that may not be part of the InoculateIT domain that is scanned regularly.

Click the Local Scanner button on the Quick Access dialog box to open the InoculateIT Local Scanner window. Select the drive you want to scan with the local scanner. The Local Scanner Options dialog box appears, as shown in Figure 11-10. Use this dialog box to specify what you want scanned and how you want it scanned.

The available options are similar to those for the Domain Manager, but are more concise and are contained on one screen. Local scanning can consume network bandwidth during peak periods, so it is better to do the scanning during off hours to keep from consuming the bandwidth on the network.

Log Files

When scanning is completed, the scan software writes the results to a log file, which you can review at a later time. The log file is useful when you want to determine where the viruses are originating. From time to time, you may have a user that is consistently infecting the network, or at least the user's workstation. The log file gives date and time stamps along with the drives that were scanned. All virus activity is logged, usually with the virus name and information as to whether the file or files were cured. Knowing the name of the infected file is good. This way you can do a

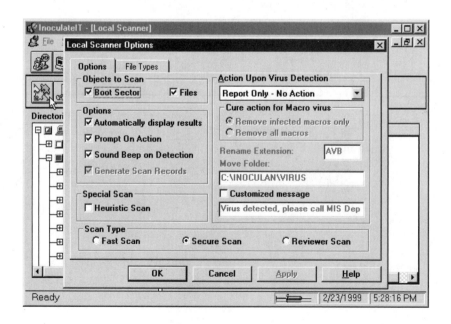

FIGURE 11-10

Use the Local Scanner Options dialog box to specify what to scan and how to scan it

search to see if the file was copied to anywhere else on the network. Figure 11-11 shows an example of the results logged for the past few scans.

Real-time Scanning

Virus scanning would not be very effective without *real-time scanning*, which scans every file that is accessed, opened, saved, or downloaded. This is especially critical when the Internet is available to users since numerous downloads of cached information and files can bring viruses to your network.

The Real-Time Monitor page in InoculateIT gives you the option to scan files either coming into the server or going out of the server. You can also specify both incoming and outgoing, which is the best scanning because it covers both angles of possible virus infection.

When you have a domain set up on the network, you can configure the Real-Time monitor settings from within the InoculateIT manager. Figure 11-12 shows the Real-Time Monitor configuration options.

The options are almost the same as they are for the local scanner and domain manager. The main difference here is that the chosen settings take effect

FIGURE 11-11

A virus scan results log lists the names of infected files, viruses detected, and whether the files were cured or deleted

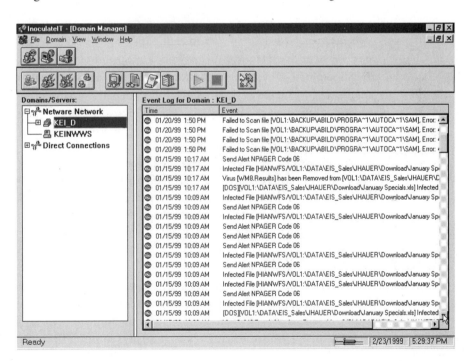

Real-Time
Monitor Options

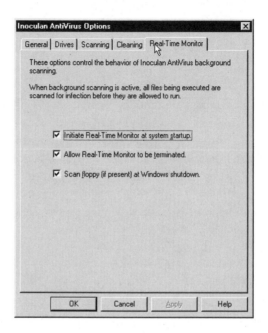

immediately. Real-time protection of your network is very important in keeping your network virus-free on a consistent basis. If you only do regular scans, viruses have a chance of infecting your network and spreading into other areas. With real-time monitoring, you should notice that the viruses are caught immediately upon entering the network. This, of course, depends on how up-to-date your virus signatures are.

exam
🕭 **atch**

The exam will test your knowledge of client- and server-side virus scanning implementations. Remember that in order to be fully secure from viruses, you need servers that continually scan files on the network for viruses on file servers, and workstations that scan for viruses on users' workstations. Users commonly bring in viruses through floppies and e-mail.

Update Virus Signatures

To ensure the integrity of the data on your network, you must keep your virus signature files up to date. A *virus signature file* is a database of known viruses that the anti-virus software uses when scanning files to eliminate viruses. These are updated monthly by the vendor, in most cases. Usually, you can download updates from the software vendor's Web site, some vendors even mail updates to registered users. Computer Associates' InoculateIT, for example, offers a couple of options for updating virus signatures: automatic updates and manual updates.

The automatic update feature takes advantage of the fact that more and more networks are linked to the Internet. Given this, InoculateIT automatically attaches via FTP to Computer Associates and downloads the most recent virus signatures—a convenient feature for network administrators. The one problem with this, of course, is that after the update is done, you don't know which files were updated. If there was a problem with the download, then a file could be corrupt and as a result corrupt your live software. I personally recommend downloading and applying the updates manually, which creates a much more controlled environment. This way, you can see what files are being updated and back up those that are. Should there be any problems, you can revert to the previous version.

Along with updating the servers, you have to update the workstations. InoculateIT comes with a feature that enables automatic synchronization of the workstations with the virus patterns off the server. This is a little more controlled, but I still recommend manually updating one workstation first each time you update to ensure that the update goes smoothly. After it is tested, you can automate the process from there. There is also a process to automatically update other servers on the network, which you can put in place after updating the first server. The documentation included with InoculateIT gives step-by-step instructions on how to configure and set this up, but you do not need to know this for the exam. To download and install virus signatures, perform Exercise 11-2.

EXERCISE 11-2

CertCam 11-2

Downloading and Installing a Virus Signature

You are upgrading the virus signatures for Inoculan. Follow these steps to find, download, and extract a virus signature update from Computer Associates.

1. Point your Web browser at www.computerassociates.com.

2. On the home page for Computer Associates, select the link to the Virus Information Center.

3. Choose the option to Download Signature Files in the far-right column under Support.

4. The resulting Web page allows you to select the version of Inoculan for which you're updating the Virus Signatures.

5. You will be directed to another section allowing you to find the row that corresponds to your processor type (Intel or Alpha) and also the language (English, Korean, and so on). Select the file in the appropriate row.

6. The download starts after you select a storage location to place the file.

7. Once the file is downloaded, extract the virus signature from the compressed Zip file. Place the extracted file in a similar location to execute it.

8. Once extracted, double-click the extracted file to execute the program. This extracts more files and starts the Inoculan Virus Signature Update process. Select Yes to update your files.

9. Continue with the Installation Wizard and the files will be updated.

At this point, you would restart the Inoculan program and let it scan the hard disk and files you previously configured.

CERTIFICATION SUMMARY

Network maintenance is a never-ending process. Because of this, certain procedures and practices must be followed on a daily basis to keep the network running. It's your job as network administrator to keep everything up to date and running in top shape.

To keep the network up to date, you need to apply patches and updates from software vendors. After software is released, the vendor will usually release bug fixes and improvements, called patches and service packs, which you can download from the vendor's Web site. These patches and service packs will not necessarily jump out at you as being needed. You may need to use the vendor's Web site to search through support forums to find out which patches you need to install.

These updates come with documentation in the form of text files, or readme files, which you should be sure to read before implementing the patch or update. Each patch or service pack usually has certain steps that must be followed in order to complete a successful install. It's also a good idea to print out the readme file so you can easily refer to it during installation.

Vendors release any necessary patches and service packs in between full upgrades. Upgrades, meanwhile, sometimes cost the customer money, while other times they are available for downloading from the vendor's Web site. In addition to keeping your network current with the latest software upgrades, you need to upgrade your firmware (software programmed into the hardware). More and more often, firmware updates are becoming available at manufacturers' Web sites.

In addition to updating and maintaining your software and firmware, you have to perform routine daily and weekly tasks to keep your network up and running. These tasks include backup routines, configuring anti-virus software and updating it, and maintaining and updating non-server software.

The two most common types of media used in backup tape drives are DAT (Digital Audio Tape) and DLT (Digital Linear Tape). DAT, originally used for recording audio, was ported into the computer field for storing data as a backup. DLT drives, however, support faster performance and larger capacities than DAT drives. Whichever tape software is used, it has to be loaded on the server in order to run on a regular schedule. On Windows NT, the tape software runs as a service, while on NetWare it is a loaded module and can be seen in the loaded list of modules when the CTRL-ESC keys are pressed.

There are three main types of backup: full, differential, and incremental. A full backup backs up all data on the drive, while an incremental backup backs up any files that have changed or were added since the last incremental or full backup. (This means the first incremental backup is actually a full backup.) A differential backup, meanwhile, backs up any files that have changed or were added since the last full backup.

Another part of network maintenance is updating and patching any business-driving applications that run at the workstation. One good example of this is a database that is stored on the server even though the application is resident on the workstation hard disk. Each workstation must be updated individually.

In today's networks, there is a serious threat of data loss from virus infections. To protect from this, you must install anti-virus protection on the network. Installing a virus protection suite such as InoculateIT or McAfee is vital to safeguarding against data loss.

Anti-virus software has different components that must be properly configured to protect your network from any serious threats. First, is the component that runs at the server level doing routine scans to ensure data is not infected with a virus; second, is the workstation component that scans the workstation to ensure data is protected from infection; third, and probably most important, is the real-time protection that can be loaded on the server and the workstation to constantly monitor all files that are opened, saved, copied, or accessed in any way? This component keeps the workstation, the server, and the entire network protected by monitoring in real time versus scanning at scheduled intervals.

To ensure each of these components works the way you want them to, you have to choose which drives to scan, what types of files to scan, and what to do with infected files. You can choose to exclude certain types of files from scanning, and to cure an infected file or simply report on it in the activity log.

Because the threat of new viruses is with us every day, anti-virus software vendors continually update their virus signature files. A virus signature file is a database of known viruses that the anti-virus software uses to detect and cure viruses. These updates are available usually monthly from the software vendors and can be retrieved automatically by the software, or implemented manually to keep from corrupting the database or any files in the live software.

✓ TWO-MINUTE DRILL

Test Documentation

- ❏ It's usually a good idea to read through the software documentation and then afterward reread the documentation and any corresponding addendums or readme files.

- ❏ Vendors release updates or patches to their products when bugs are found, or to simply make them run better.

- ❏ Microsoft and Novell have a service pack for the core network operating system.

- ❏ The vendor's Web site will most likely have the patches and service packs you need for your software.

- ❏ Applying a patch incorrectly can bring down the entire network.

- ❏ You should always install an upgrade on a stand-alone machine before distributing it to the network.

- ❏ There are firmware updates for the various ROMs that exist in servers and workstations.

Network Maintenance

- ❏ There is more to network maintenance than patches and updates. This includes providing and testing a backup solution and providing and updating anti-virus software.

- ❏ Every network administrator should have a backup routine.

- ❏ The two common types of tape drives are DAT and DLT.

- ❏ A *full backup* backs up every file on the specified volume or volumes.

- ❏ An *incremental backup* backs up the files that have changed or were added since the last incremental or full backup.

- ❏ A *differential backup* backs up the files that have changed or were added since the last full backup.

❑ You will definitely see a question or two on the exam about the different kinds of backups. Be sure to know the differences between full, incremental, and differential backups—especially the last two, which can be the most confusing. You may be given a scenario and have to pick the backup plan and restoration process.

❑ The other side to maintaining a network is logging the activity and documenting every change or update that is applied.

❑ When you install anti-virus software in a networked environment, you must set multiple configuration items.

SELF TEST

The following Self Test questions will help you measure your understanding of the material presented in this chapter. Read all the choices carefully, as there may be more than one correct answer. Choose all correct answers for each question.

Test Documentation

1. What is a key component of installing an update or patch successfully on your network?

    A. Reading competitors' documentation to see whose is better, and then selecting the better package.

    B. Reading the readme files and documentation to make sure you have the information you need to install the application successfully.

    C. Reading the documentation on the server to see if the software is compatible with the server.

    D. Reading the Web site home page to see if the product is still in production.

2. To make sure you have the most up-to-date files and version of the software, you need to go to the vendor's Web site and download the most current version of what?

    A. Software packs

    B. Network packs

    C. Software patches

    D. Readme files

3. Network operating systems, such as NetWare and Windows NT/2000/XP, use which of the following to update the operating system itself?

    A. Update packs

    B. Service calls

    C. Serial packs

    D. Service packs

4. Where can you go to search for information regarding network errors, in order to see if you need a patch or service pack?

    A. A vendor's online support forums

    B. The Excite search engine

    C. The Control Panel under System

    D. The Help section under the Start menu

5. When software vendors want to update their software in a major way and bring out a new version, this is known as a what? (Hint: This is sometimes free and sometimes costs money.)

    A. An update

    B. An upgrade

    C. An upload

    D. A patch

6. Along with updating the software, a particular hardware-related item may need to be updated. What is it called?

    A. RAM

    B. ROM

    C. Formware

    D. Adapter

7. To keep a consistent approach to network maintenance, it is important to do what?

    A. Format one hard disk per month on your network to clean up hard disk space.

    B. Get into the routine of downloading patches that are not for your network just so you have a grasp of everything out there.

    C. Get into the routine of applying updates and patches on your network on a regular basis.

    D. Delete and reconfigure system volumes on your servers on an annual basis.

Network Maintenance

8. What is the first thing you need to do to install backup software on your network server?

    A. Physically install the tape drive and any adapter boards necessary. Along with this, connect the cables between the tape drive and the adapter board. Also, make sure power is connected.

    B. Make certain your backup software has everything in it before proceeding.

    C. Refer to your backup software's specific instructions for any unique preinstallation items.

    D. Make sure the system you're installing meets all hardware and software requirements.

9. You are running a Windows NT Server and want to know if your backup software service is running. Where do you go to get this information?

 A. Go to My Computer and select the tape drive.

 B. Go to the Control Panel and select Backup.

 C. Press CTRL-ESC and select the screen for the backup software.

 D. Go to the Control Panel and select Services.

10. What are the two most common types of tape drives in today's networks? (Select two.)

 A. DDS

 B. DAT

 C. DLT

 D. DET

11. What available options are there for taking care of viruses? (Choose all that apply.)

 A. Move file

 B. Cure file

 C. Delete file

 D. Copy file

12. If you want to scan local or mapped network drives with InoculateIT, which of the following options should you choose?

 A. Network Scanner

 B. Local Scanner

 C. Real-Time Scanner

 D. Disk Recovery Option

13. How often are virus signatures generally updated by the vendor or manufacturer?

 A. Daily

 B. Weekly

 C. Monthly

 D. Annually

14. What are the main advantages of DLT tape drives compared to DAT tape drives? (Choose all that apply.)

    A. Faster data transfer rates

    B. Greater storage capacity

    C. Greater reliability

    D. Greater availability

    E. Greater accuracy

15. When DAT tapes were emerging as a popular storage media for computer data, a format name was given to the storage of computer data. What is this format known as?

    A. DDS

    B. DDT

    C. DAT

    D. DLT

16. You installed a tape drive in your server. The server has an existing SCSI controller and other SCSI devices in the system. Since adding the SCSI tape drive to the SCSI chain you get errors from two devices. What is the most likely cause of this type of problem?

    A. The tape drive is not compatible with the system.

    B. The SCSI ID is unique, not enabling the tape drive to communicate in the SCSI chain.

    C. The SCSI ID is the same on the two devices, causing a conflict.

    D. The IDE connector is not hooked up on the tape drive.

LAB QUESTION

A company wishes to perform daily backups of their server. The backup time does not matter, but the restore time is a major issue. If the server should crash, they wish to restore the server in the shortest time possible while still only using the least amount of tapes when performing a backup.

There are also worried about viruses being downloaded from the Internet. What can the company do to catch possible viruses when they are introduced to the network?

In addition, the company is concerned about keeping all applications up to date. What can an administrator do to keep on top of all the different applications used, especially if each department is responsible for purchasing their own applications?

SELF TEST ANSWERS

Test Documentation

1. ☑ **B.** Reading the readme files and documentation to make sure you have the information you need to install the application successfully. If there is one thing I have learned while implementing and maintaining networks, it is to read the readme files. There isn't a patch I've seen in the past few years that doesn't come with a readme file or a text file of some sort with installation instructions. In fact, it's usually a good idea to read through the documentation and then reread the documentation and any corresponding addendums.

   ☒ **A, C,** and **D** are incorrect. Updating to a different package is not an option here. Current documentation won't be found on the server, but instead on the manufacturer's Web site, CD, or in the product documentation. Most manufacturers will still support a product (at least for a little while) even after it's no longer being produced.

2. ☑ **C.** Software patches. Part of maintaining your network is applying patches to your existing software to make sure you have the most current release. Vendors release updates or patches to their products when bugs are found or to simply make them run better. The main software vendors for network operating systems, Microsoft and Novell, have a service pack for the core network operating system.

   ☒ **A, B,** and **D** are incorrect. There are no software or network packs. Readme files will only contain information on the actual update such as the files being updated, the bugs being fixed, and installation notes.

3. ☑ **D.** Service packs. The main software vendors for network operating systems, Microsoft and Novell, have service packs for the core network operating system. Applying these is a must when it comes to ensuring your network functions with third-party applications.

   ☒ **A, B,** and **C** are incorrect. Update packs do not exist. Service calls are calls to technical support when answers are needed for a specific problem. It is not an actual update to the NOS. Serial packs also do not exist.

4. ☑ **A.** A vendor's online support forums. Vendors have online support where you can perform a search for a particular error or problem, which may indicate whether you need a patch, and if so, where to find it.

   ☒ **B, C,** and **D** are incorrect. Web search engines may not get you to the information you need for an error code or message, since many manufacturers use similar codes. Control Panel options do not have any online help for error codes specific to an OS or application either.

The OS Help files, meanwhile, will not have up-to-date information on the newest service packs or patches available.

5. ☑ **B. An upgrade.** Software manufacturers release upgrades for their products to both improve them and make them more powerful. You should always install an upgrade on a stand-alone machine before distributing it to the network. This enables you to test the application and go through the upgrade process in a non-production environment.

   ☒ **A, C, and D are incorrect.** Updates are not a valid option because they are usually just technical news about new items to be added in a future release or about new patches already in existence. An upload, meanwhile, is a file you send to a Web site, while a patch is a minor upgrade, not a major upgrade.

6. ☑ **B. ROM.** Hardware upgrades for maintaining the network. I know this may sound wrong, but there are firmware updates for the various ROMs that exist in servers and workstations. The main ROM that controls the computer is usually programmable and can be updated. I recommend getting the latest ROM updates for all components on your entire network.

   ☒ **A, C, and D are incorrect.** RAM is the physical memory in a PC. Formware is not a valid choice, since it is actually called firmware. An adapter would replace the whole piece of hardware, not just its software portion.

7. ☑ **C.** Get into the routine of applying updates and patches on your network on a regular basis. There is more to network maintenance than patches and updates, including providing and testing a backup solution and providing and updating anti-virus software. You need to establish a routine of backing up the system, and of applying updates of patches and virus signatures.

   ☒ **A, B, and D are incorrect.** Formatting a disk will most likely destroy data on the hard disk, so this is not a viable choice. It's not necessary to download updates for applications you don't even use on the network. Deleting and reconfiguring the server volumes shouldn't be done unless the volumes crash or the server is being migrated to another NOS.

Network Maintenance

8. ☑ **D. Make sure the system you're installing meets all hardware and software requirements.** The first thing to do is make sure your system can run the software you're installing. If this step isn't successful, none of the other steps matter. Checking compatibility is the first step in installing any software on any system—stand-alone or networked.

   ☒ **A, B, and C are incorrect.** Installing the hardware may not work if the system you are installing the tape drive into is not compatible with the tape device. The backup software may be of no use if it will not operate on the OS, or if the tape device isn't compatible with the OS or PC. Even though you may get some installation notes regarding what to do prior to installation, you still won't be sure if both the tape device and software will be compatible with the OS and PC.

9. ☑ **D.** Go to the Control Panel and select Services. NetWare provides an NLM (NetWare Loadable Module) with a screen you can switch to. With NetWare, you can press CTRL-ESC to get a list of available screens. Windows NT enables the backup software to run as a service. Select Start | Settings | Control Panel, and then double-click the Services icon. The Services dialog box lists the services available on that server.

    ☒ **A, B,** and **C** are incorrect. **A** will not show that the services are running, only that the tape device is installed. In fact, the tape device may not show up under My Computer (this depends on the manufacturer). There is no Backup choice under the Control Panel. **C** will not show the actual backup service either. The program could be running strictly as a service in the background and will not have a window to allow for user intervention.

10. ☑ **B** and **C.** DAT and DLT. The DAT and DLT tape drives are the most common tape drives in today's networks. The DAT drive uses small Digital Audio Tapes with helical scanning, while the DLT drive uses large tapes that are faster and have more capacity (similar to the old reel-to-reel tape system).

    ☒ **A** and **D** are incorrect. DDS is a digital service and DET is a directory table. These are not backup tape media types.

11. ☑ **A, B,** and **C.** Move file, Cure file, and Delete file. You can choose to have InoculateIT cure infected files, report the problem and do nothing with the file, or report and move the file to a special directory, or delete infected files. Moved files are renamed with a special extension for easy recognition. If you choose the cure option, and InoculateIT is unable to cure a file, the file will be moved and renamed with the special extension. Other virus protection suites have similar options.

    ☒ **D** is incorrect. Copying the file is an invalid choice since this will leave the original file intact and in place to be used. Using an infected file can cause the virus to infect more files.

12. ☑ **B.** Local Scanner. The Local Scanner option in the Quick Access dialog box is for immediate scanning of local or mapped drives. This is good to do when you may have a problem with a workstation or particular volume on a server. This is also useful for a server that may not be part of the InoculateIT domain that is scanned regularly.

    ☒ **A, C,** and **D** are incorrect. There is no network scanner. The real-time scanner is used to scan files as they are opened or received by a system. Disk Recovery Options are for recovering the OS if the boot files are corrupted by a virus.

13. ☑ **C.** Monthly. To ensure the integrity of the data on your network, you must keep your virus signature files up to date. A *virus signature file* is a database of known viruses that the anti-virus software uses when scanning files to eliminate viruses. In most cases, these are updated monthly by the vendor. Usually you can download updates from the software vendor's Web site.

☒ **A, B,** and **D** are incorrect.

14. ☑ **A, B,** and **C.** Faster data transfer rates, greater storage capacity, and greater reliability. Along with the advantages of faster data transfer rates, higher storage capacity, and higher reliability, comes at a higher cost. The DLT technology is more expensive. The DAT drive, meanwhile, uses the old reel-to-reel system where the tape cartridge holds one reel and the other reel is contained in the tape drive.

☒ **D** is incorrect because both tapes use linear technology, so availability is the same for both tapes. **E** is also incorrect. Since the media are identical, the accuracy is therefore the same as well.

15. ☑ **A.** DDS. DDS format stands for Digital Data Storage. DAT (Digital Audio Tape) was developed in the mid-1980s by Sony and Philips to record music in a digital format. It is now very popular as a medium for computer data storage. The DAT drive uses a helical scan, which means that the read/write heads spin diagonally across the tape. DAT uses the DDS (Digital Data Storage) format.

☒ **B, C,** and **D** are incorrect. DDT is not a valid option, and DLT uses a different format than DDS.

16. ☑ **C.** The SCSI ID is the same on the two devices, causing a conflict. When installing the tape drive in a SCSI chain, you have to know if other devices are connected. If so, you must have a SCSI ID assigned to each device that is different. If you don't do this, your devices may not work properly.

☒ **A, B,** and **D** are incorrect. If the tape drive were incompatible, it would not work at all. The SCSI ID must be unique and not be the same on two or more devices on the same chain. Since the tape device is SCSI, the IDE controller is not used, therefore no IDE connector is needed.

LAB ANSWER

To perform quick restores and use the least amount of tapes, the company will need to perform differential backups every day, as well as a full backup at the beginning of the week. This will require only the restoration of the full backup and then the last differential tape.

To catch viruses immediately when introduced to the network, you will need to enable real-time scanning. This will scan all files as they are opened or received.

To track all applications, the administrator has two choices. One is to have every department make a list of all their applications as well as the version numbers and other pertinent information. This will allow the administrator to keep a database on all the applications. Once every month or so, the administrator can check the Web sites of the application manufacturers for updates. The second choice is to make some standards and require that every department goes to a smaller list of applications. This will allow the whole company to use the same applications for better compatibility, and will also require less update checking by the administrator.

COMPUTING TECHNOLOGY INDUSTRY ASSOCIATION

12

Identifying, Assessing, and Responding to Problems

CERTIFICATION OBJECTIVES

12.01	Handling Network Problems
12.02	Prioritizing Network Problems
✓	Two-Minute Drill
Q&A	Self Test

T he Network+ exam is very good at mimicking the problems you will be faced with in the real world. Passing the Network+ exam means you are well on your way to becoming a successful network professional. You will need to prioritize network problems, because you will often have more than one at a time. In the real world, there is not enough time, money, or employees to fix every network problem that arises. You will need to apply "Band-Aid fixes" sometimes to temporarily fix problems until you have spent enough time researching the problems and determining solutions. This chapter will help you in the real world just as much as it will help you to ace the Network+ exam.

CERTIFICATION OBJECTIVE 12.01

Handling Network Problems

It is nearly impossible for a network to run smoothly without problems. Networks are in a constant state of flux and change, and they grow bigger and more complicated as the days go by. More computers are being added to the network and the amount of available bandwidth slowly decreases. These new computers chew up precious bandwidth, and require one or more network cards, more cables, ports on the hubs, and, if you are using TCP/IP, these new computers must consume another IP address. In addition to the hardware, you must make sure the network interface card (NIC) is correctly configured, and that the correct network protocols are loaded and configured. TCP/IP is the protocol that requires more planning, configuration, and troubleshooting than all other protocols combined. Incidentally, that is why you will see many questions on your exam regarding TCP/IP. Not only do you need the required hardware and software to get these devices functioning on the network, you also need the knowledge and experience. This is the most important piece of the networking puzzle. Without you, the network professional, a network device such as a hub is just a useless, expensive box with wires and blinking lights. The hub needs you to make it come to life and function. You must understand how this device works, and how to diagnose and resolve problems related to this device and to every other device on your network. One mistake in any of the hardware or software configurations will cause a problem. It's your job to determine what to do in the event of one of these problems.

exam
<watch>**W**atch</watch>

Make sure you understand as much as you can about TCP/IP. With the Internet relying solely on TCP/IP, the protocol is very important on many exams.

How do you know that you are having a network problem? The symptoms can be anything from strange, reoccurring problems, to a workstation that is not able to access network resources, or even worse, an entire department unable to log in. Identifying the symptoms of the problem is the first step in diagnosing and solving it. This is the information-gathering phase. The more time you spend during this phase, the quicker the problem can be solved. This is also the most stressful phase for you. You will encounter problems that are mind numbing, but the more time you spend identifying the symptoms, the more the cause will be revealed. This is also where you draw on your real-life experiences. Have you ever encountered a situation such as this before? If so, how did you handle the problem? You might also draw on your studies and the books you have read during this phase. Have you read of a problem such as this before?

exam
Watch

I was surprised at the number of troubleshooting-related questions on the exam. Whenever you are faced with a troubleshooting-related question, remember that identification of the symptoms and cause is the first step in the troubleshooting process.

After you have enough information concerning the symptoms of the problem, you need to determine the nature of the action required to solve it. This is where the road to recovery can take several different paths. The path you take will depend on the severity of the problem and the amount of time and energy required to fix it. Once you are aware of a network problem, the path you take will always involve working together as a team to solve the problem, asking for help, or escalating the problem. To determine the nature of the action required, you need to understand the circumstances involved with choosing one path over another. On more severe network problems, you might find yourself going down every path, searching for the answer. The good news is, no matter what the problem, you will eventually find the solution.

Information Transfer

The computer industry is built on the transfer of tons of information. This information transfer refers to the exchange of data from one computer to another, and to the exchange of data between human beings. Just as in school, where the teacher is teaching the students, you might find yourself as a network professional learning from others, or you might find yourself teaching others. This communication is essential for diagnosing and resolving network problems, or any problem for that matter. The saying, "Two heads are better than one," is absolutely applicable to the process of troubleshooting a network problem. A team of professionals can distribute the load of solving network problems by assigning a different diagnostic task to each person, or by every member of the team collectively investigating the problem.

on the **job**

It is very important to get correct information from the user. Most times, users will not readily admit what they have done if they think they have caused a problem. They feel they might get into trouble or look stupid, so they will claim that the problem just started for no apparent reason. Talking to the users to get information from them is sometimes an art in itself.

Task Assignment

In attempting to resolve a network problem, you can assign each person on the team a different task for diagnosing the problem. When you distribute the load between many people, one person is not burdened with the overwhelming task of solving the problem alone. However, one person's load might still be larger than another person's load. The point of distributing the work involved with troubleshooting is to enable one person to spend quality time in one area, so that this person can thoroughly understand the complexities of the task. Bringing an entire group up to speed on a concept such as routing can be challenging. Picking one specialist to investigate the possible routing issues and report his findings to the group can be very beneficial.

Another method of assigning tasks could be to have one person call technical support, one person read through Knowledge Bases and Resource Kits, and one or more people work with the hardware or software to determine where the problem is. Everyone can then report his or her findings in a team meeting.

Team Collaboration

While attempting to resolve a network problem, you can have every member of the team collectively investigate the problem. Having the entire collective experience and knowledge of a group of people guarantees that a problem will be solved.

Highly experienced professionals can quickly determine where a problem lies and the best solution for solving it. Chances are good that someone in your group has experienced a problem such as this in the past.

This approach, as well as the first approach, requires a tremendous amount of communication. In troubleshooting, it often takes another person to stimulate the thoughts of a person who is on the verge of discovering the problem. This method also works in reverse. One person can be banging his head against the wall trying to solve the problem, and someone who is not immersed in the problem can ask a simple question from an outsider's perspective that can shed some new light on it.

on the job

Within some companies, there might be a few IT technicians who cannot work on problems as a team and must attempt to fix things themselves. They usually are still able to contact the other technicians to ask questions, but the steps used to troubleshoot problems can still be used.

An essential aspect of communication, one that some technicians are lacking, is knowing when to ask for help. Many of us feel embarrassed when we have to stop to ask for help. You should feel proud that you are stopping to ask for help. Would you rather stop and ask for help, or just continue reconfiguring things until the network completely breaks? Some technicians will never ask for help; these are not the type of technicians you want on your team. You need a team that can communicate effectively.

Do not feel that you are any less of a technician because you are asking for help. You will be admired by your peers and bosses as someone who is concerned with finding the problem as a team. Another saying comes to mind: "There is no "I" in TEAMWORK."

on the job

At the last job I interviewed for, the manager said there was no place for hot shots on his team. He said that he has been burned by technicians who do not adhere to standards and spend time reconfiguring a workstation any way possible until it works. Rather than escalate the problem, they sit there and play around until the problem fixes itself. This often causes more problems, especially in a tightly run ship where settings are configured for a reason.

FROM THE CLASSROOM

Everyone Can Contribute to Solving a Problem

At one of my first network jobs, my boss and I were sent out to network separate branches of a corporation to the company headquarters. My boss, who knew more than I did, was taking complete control of the situation, and I didn't feel very much a part of the process. He felt it was better for him to spend the time and work on the problem without having to explain every step to me as he went. Therefore, I felt unaware of what was going on.

He had me do simple tasks to keep me busy while he focused on the much more complicated issues, such as routing and the WINS Service. It was obvious he was having problems, but he did not want to ask for help. As the hours passed, he slowly began revealing the problems he was having. "I know we are having a WINS replication problem. I can just tell." Although he didn't have the answers, he was headed down the right track.

Not knowing as much about WINS as he did, I could offer little help on the technical complexities of WINS. However, I contributed in a different way. I would ask him, "How do you know it's a WINS problem?" He would then try to explain the situation, but before he could finish his explanation, a light bulb would go off in his head and he would continue down another path.

"It could be routing, because we can't replicate with the WINS server on the other side of the router," he said. "How did you configure the routing?" I would ask him, and once again, before he finished his explanation, he would get another idea and investigate it. At times, I would also try talking highly technically with him, just to fuel his troubleshooting process.

Eventually, we solved the problem, which was just a router that needed to be reset before changes would take affect. After feeling very happy that we fixed the problem, I admitted that I didn't really have any idea of what was going on, but I felt the more I stimulated his mental process, the further he would get, and he agreed.

The more you can verbalize the problem, the clearer your mind becomes. You will find that teachers have a great understanding of concepts, because they are able to verbalize complicated issues with ease. Once you begin explaining problems to others, you will find yourself thinking of the problem in a new light and you will be further down the road to solving the problem. There is no better feeling than solving a problem that has been challenging you for hours, or even days. All it takes is working together.

—Cameron Brandon, MCSE+Internet, CNE, A+, Network+

Handholding

It's just a matter of time before you encounter a problem that you and your team are not knowledgeable enough to solve. This is quite common in this fast-moving computer industry. You are not expected to know everything; however, you *are* expected to know when and where to look for answers. If you and your team are not able to solve the problem, you need to find additional information and resources to solve it. These can take the forms of Resource Kits, online help, and telephone technical support.

Resource Kits

Resource Kits are a valuable way of educating yourself. These are helpful for planning, implementing, configuring, and, most of all, troubleshooting. Microsoft includes the Resource Kits on the same TechNet CD as the Knowledge Base. The Resource Kits are more for reading and planning, whereas the Knowledge Base is loaded with information on symptoms, causes, and solutions to problems. If you are having a problem with a Microsoft product, you should consult the TechNet CD for more information. You should read the Resource Kits and verify that you have implemented and configured the software correctly. If you are still having problems, query the Knowledge Base to see if you can find a posted solution to the same problem you are having. These solutions are often comprised of step-by-step actions that must be taken to solve the problem.

EXERCISE 12-1

CertCam 12-1

Checking for a Resource Kit

Let us assume you are working in a company that has standardized software for all of the users. The company mainly uses Microsoft products. You need to get a Resource Kit for a particular product.

1. Connect to the Internet, and go to **www.microsoft.com/downloads/search.asp?**

2. In the **Search** area, select to perform a **Keyword Search**.

3. In the **Operating System** box, select the OS you are using.

4. In the **Show Results For** box, select **All Downloads**.

5. In the **Key Words** box, type **Resource Kit**, and click **Find It**.

6. This will reopen the same window with a list of available Resource Kits to download.

Online Help

The Internet is the most helpful resource for researching network problems. If you believe you are having a problem with a particular product or device, you should begin your search with the manufacturer's Web site. You will find information such as updated drivers and patches, detailed installation instructions, troubleshooting tips, and possibly a Knowledge Base of common problems. You should never feel embarrassed that you need to search on the manufacturer's Web site for answers to a problem. There is too much software with bugs, and too many incompatible software drivers out there to not find updated software. You should always find the latest patches and drivers if you determine that you are experiencing problems with this software. Updated patches and drivers are there for a reason: they fix bugs and improve functionality. If the software were right the first time, there would be no need for a second version of the driver or a software patch.

exam
ⓦatch

Remember that this is probably the biggest assistance you have access to when troubleshooting problems. The Internet is also very useful for downloading patches and drivers. The exam does focus on this as a solution once all inhouse avenues have been pursued, such as documentation or other people.

Telephone Technical Support

Most technicians feel that telephone tech support is the very last resort—I disagree. Who would know more about solving a problem with a product than the people who spend eight hours a day on the telephone solving problems with that particular product? They encounter every type of problem possible with their product, from small 10-node networks, to the largest companies in the world. They also troubleshoot their product on many different operating systems. These telephone support personnel have a database of known problems and resolutions that they can query if they don't have the immediate answer. They can also delegate the problem to more knowledgeable engineers. I have found that almost all my problems were answered within minutes on the first call. Their response can be as simple as, "Yes, we know about that problem. Download the newest patch to fix it."

I agree that sometimes telephone support can lead down a dead-end road, but that shouldn't deter you from at least calling and seeing whether there has been a similar problem reported. These support personnel can also lead you step by step through installing, testing, and configuring their product. This will often reveal details that you didn't adhere to during the initial installation that was giving you problems. The support personnel can also provide you with troubleshooting steps to get at the cause of the problem quickly. When you are troubleshooting a complicated problem, don't ignore telephone technical support, because they might have a quick and easy answer.

Unfortunately, telephone technical support is not free. Some companies charge steep prices per incident, which might be out of the reach of some companies' budgets. Large corporations usually have no problems opening telephone support incidences, as long as the problem gets resolved. I have worked for companies that run the gamut of philosophies for using telephone technical support. Some companies prefer that you exhaust every possible resource first, such as Microsoft TechNet, Resources Kits, online help, and documentation, before you open a support incident. The telephone support call would be the last resort, mostly because of the cost involved. Other companies do not hesitate to call telephone support as the first line of defense. Many times, you can save yourself hours of frustration if you just call for help beforehand. Sometimes the answer is quite simple; sometimes as simple as downloading a new driver. However, if you have spent hours, or even days, on a particular problem, have involved many of your highest-level onsite support personnel, and still haven't solved the problem, you should consider calling technical support. By solving the problem more quickly, your company can save money in the long run. In this situation, the initial cost of opening up a telephone support incident was outweighed by the resolution of a challenging problem.

Technical Service

Often it is not possible to determine the cause of a network problem with conventional tools. Networks have become so complicated that you need advanced tools to determine some complex network problems. These tools happen to be very expensive, which puts them out of reach for the average network administrator.

Network monitors and analyzers can inspect the packets traveling over the network and determine if any problems are occurring, such as broadcast storms.

on the **!** o b

One site I worked had ongoing bandwidth issues. The network seemed to be more congested than it should be. We didn't have the tools or knowledge to test for complex network problems, so we called in Bay Networks. They brought in a network analyzer and quickly determined that we had NetBEUI, AppleTalk, and IPX/SPX packets traveling the network. This was strange because we only used TCP/IP. We discovered that some print servers were also using NetBEUI, AppleTalk, and IPX/SPX protocols in addition to TCP/IP, because someone didn't disable these protocols during installation of the print server. Bay Networks also determined that we had a bottleneck in one area of our network that most packets had to travel. We had been unaware of this bottleneck, and armed with this information, we replaced the affected area, and the network was back to its full potential.

Not only do you sometimes need professional equipment to monitor your network, you also need professionals who are trained on the tools to analyze and identify possible afflicted areas based on the results. A network capture of hundreds of packets might make no sense to you, but these professionals are trained to interpret the results.

Even more common than having professionals come in to analyze the network is the need to contract the telephone company for wiring issues. You do not have the tools such as tone generators and time domain reflectometers (TDRs) to analyze possible cable problems. Incidentally, both tone generators and TDRs are discussed in more detail in Chapter 13.

At my last job, it was very common to see the telephone company in the wiring closet, server room, and everywhere around the site connecting new areas. For the average administrator, this will not be your job. The lines are blurring between the telephone company and network engineers, who both can be responsible for wiring. The telephone company is usually subcontracted to do wiring work. This means that you should stay in close contact with them, because they might be your best allies in the event you are troubleshooting a network-related problem. Take advantage of their knowledge and tools for troubleshooting.

Documentation

In order to maintain a smoothly running network, it is imperative that you keep adequate documentation of computer specifications, recent upgrades, future projects, and a list of known issues and resolved problems with each server on your network. This documentation is important for a number of reasons:

- You have something to refer to if it is determined that the computer was configured incorrectly.
- You can provide instructions for the next administrator or engineer.
- You can keep accurate inventory or records for each device on the network.
- Year-end inventories are made easier with documentation.

Incorrect Configuration

Documentation is essential in the event a computer was configured incorrectly. With a large group of support personnel, it might be difficult to determine who was the last to configure a certain server that is no longer functioning or is not working to its fullest potential. Determining who is responsible is not the same as finding someone to blame when something goes wrong. Support personnel often configure servers and network devices in a unique way, without sharing that information with the rest of the group. By documenting the modifications to the server, you can determine what has changed and whether that change is adversely affecting the server. If the person responsible for configuring this server or network device no longer works at your company, you have the existing documentation to determine what was changed, without the need to contact the person.

The documentation must include the technician's name, and the date the upgrade or modification took place. This is helpful in determining the order of chronological events that can be traced in case of an emergency.

With any company, it is best for the IT staff to document all tasks. Even tasks that are supposed to be done once, such as configuring a router, should be documented. These devices can fail and must be replaced. When replaced, they will need to be configured the same way the other device was configured. If documentation exists, this can be a very easy process. Some very simple troubleshooting techniques can be for the users themselves, such as how to change their own password. This can help keep the number of calls to the help desk to a minimum.

Future Administrators or Engineers

Documentation provides a set of instructions for the next administrator or engineer. Almost all network administrators or engineers have countless secrets they keep inside for the networks they support. Every day they are configuring, adding, and modifying servers, workstations, printers, and devices on the network. Each of these experiences might require custom configuration or troubleshooting in order to be installed correctly. Network support personnel can spend hours, if not days, getting something to work correctly, yet they rarely spend the time to document their findings for future use. If they leave the company, this information goes with them. The next administrator or engineer might find himself spending as much or more time than the original person trying to get the same problem resolved. If the previous person had documented his findings, it would have made the second person's job much easier. This is very important when one person goes on vacation and the other technicians are unaware as to how that person fixed items before he left.

Device Inventory

Proper documentation includes an accurate inventory or record for each device on the network. Documenting devices on the network gives you a current record of countless details about these devices. For example, you can document the amount of physical memory, the hard disk capacity, the IP address, the processor speed, the MAC address, and the serial numbers. This information can be stored in a centralized database for all computer support personnel to use. Many companies are very strict about keeping accurate, up-to-date information for their network. It is strongly recommended that you adhere to these documentation standards. If no standards currently exist, it is recommended that you start a project to inventory the network with as much information as possible. You will be surprised at how often you consult this information when it comes to locating devices, determining which devices need to be upgraded, and performing remote managing and software distribution.

Although IP addresses are not a device, they are part of the network card device configuration. If your company does not use DHCP to manage IP addresses, you will need to keep a spreadsheet of used and available IP addresses so no duplicates are used. This is one area in which some companies have found themselves running out of IP addresses. I know of one company that had to implement DHCP just to solve the problem.

Year-End Inventories

Proper documentation makes year-end inventories easier. These inventories also help companies which have leased or bought computers from the corporation and need to report their inventory at the end of the year. I have had to visit nearly every workstation and server on a network when corporation requested an audit of all machines that were purchased from the corporate computer fund. If we had kept better documentation, I could have used this information and saved hours. If you don't currently have serial number information in your hardware inventory database, now is a good time to start.

SCENARIO & SOLUTION

You are asked to help troubleshoot an issue with an older software package that monitors the network devices. No one in the IT department has experience with the product. You can find no documentation on the product. What can you do?	The first step might be to try to find some online manuals that might be included with the product, or to find a manual on the manufacturer's Web site.
A user has a problem with a hardware device communicating on the network. You have looked through the documentation and searched the Web site for resolutions. What should you most likely try next?	Call the manufacturer for technical support.
Your company has purchased a product to allow monitoring of network devices. The software is not performing as expected because it seems to be missing a utility to convert the logs into a usable format. What could you do to possibly find the utility?	You could search the manufacturer's Web site for the utility, or look for a Resource Kit. Resource Kits usually contain extra utilities and information.
A manager has purchased a device for his department to monitor their database and act as extra protection for the users accessing the database to keep it secure. The manager attempted to install the device himself. The device is still not working; what should he do?	Consult the installation manual to ensure the installation is performed properly.

CERTIFICATION OBJECTIVE 12.02

Prioritizing Network Problems

You can expect to find yourself in a situation with more than one network problem at a time. This is not uncommon in the real world. Sometimes, smaller problems are put on the back burner while the larger, more urgent problems are investigated. If you encounter more than one network problem, you need to prioritize them based on their severity. This often comes down to which problem is affecting users the most. If users are not able to do their work, then, of course, this becomes a major priority. You must do everything you can to get the users up and running as quickly as possible, because they could be at a standstill until you solve the network problem. When users are at a standstill, managers become impatient with the lack of work being done. Users feel the stress from management and become impatient with you to fix the problem. Performing under this stress can hamper your ability to think clearly.

Another important factor to consider when prioritizing network problems is the estimated amount of time required to solve the problem. If you have a network problem that will require 25 hours to complete by two support personnel, you might opt to rank this lower than a job that requires three hours for one person. Quick network problems, such as resetting a user's password, are often higher on the list of priorities because they can be fixed in a matter of minutes.

You should not use the estimated amount of time required to solve the problem as the only means of prioritizing network problems. For example, if you have a project that will take an estimated five hours to complete in order for the entire network to finally be up and running, this should take precedence over a 30-minute job restructuring the directories on the file server. The amount of time required to complete the job is now overshadowed by the extremely high priority of getting a failed network operational again.

When disaster strikes, you will notice how everything gets put on the back burner while all available resources are used to solve the network problem. Many projects are dependent on the network functioning correctly anyway, so it might be impossible to complete these tasks if the network is down.

High-Priority Problems

Any network problem that affects a large number of users should receive a high priority. Of course, you have to determine which network problems affect functions the users can live without for a period of time. If users cannot access important servers, you should make that a very high priority. You will receive many calls about problems that affect a large number of users. As stated previously, any network problem that affects a user's ability to do his work should receive a high priority. Any problem that affects a large number of users or any of the functions listed here should be ranked high on the list of prioritized network problems:

- Logging on and becoming authenticated
- Accessing e-mail
- Printing
- Accessing a database

Obviously, if users cannot log on to the network, they have no access to network resources. Users might be able to work with local resources, such as a word processor, but will not be able to retrieve or store any information on a network server.

Users complain most about the inability to receive e-mail and the inability to print. It is becoming very common for companies and departments to share reports, orders, meeting information, and announcements via e-mail. If users cannot access e-mail, they will not be able to do their jobs. Moreover, users print everything, and when they can't, you will find out very quickly. The problem could be major, such as the downing of a print server, or it could just affect one printer, such as a hardware malfunction.

on the
job

At one site, the e-mail server went down for a day. I didn't realize how many users relied on e-mail until that day. One user received time-sensitive requests every day from another company for orders to be filled, and without access to e-mail, the user could not fill these orders for the company. You will be surprised how e-mail is being used in your company to exchange schedules, reports, and announcements.

Databases are the reason why most companies use computers and networks. Databases contain critical information, such as employee records, distributor and client information, and any information related to the company's products. If users cannot access a database to add, modify, or delete records, you will know.

exam
ⓦatch

In business and on the exam, you will need to pay attention to company politics. For example, if the CEO of the company is having a printing problem that is not related to any other issue, then it will take priority. If the printing problem is related to a downed server, then the CEO will take precedence anyway.

Low-Priority Problems

When you have more than one network problem at a time, it will be fairly evident which problem takes precedence. The problems discussed in this section are important conditions that should be resolved soon, but if you are experiencing more than one network problem, these should receive a lower priority. The following is a list of problems that affect users but do not warrant a very high priority:

- Annoying or nagging prompts
- Slow network access
- Inability to access less-used information
- Inability to print to a *desired* printer

Users will call you when they receive unusual system prompts, and when printing or network access has slowed. The system prompts usually do not indicate a critical condition. It is common to see errors, or mild problems, with logon scripts that appear to the user as an error. Usually, these prompts are just informational or a warning. Slow system access might be annoying to the users, but it is not a high priority if you have another problem to resolve.

If users cannot access less-used information, but can still work, you should resolve other network problems before addressing this one.

If a user cannot print to a desired printer, but can print to a different printer, or if a user cannot print to any printer and does not need to print in order to work, this problem receives a low priority.

The following items are system maintenance and do not affect users directly. They should receive a low priority when you have a high-priority network problem to resolve:

- Updating a version of software or driver
- Applying a patch to a program
- Changing or disabling a protocol

Installing updates to software or drivers is never a high priority, unless the updated version of the software fixes a critical bug. Remember, you should test the patch or version update on a test machine before implementing it in the field.

Migrating from one protocol to another, such as from NetBEUI to TCP/IP, is not a high priority, unless you have workstations that cannot access the network until the migration takes place. Some companies run NetBEUI under TCP/IP as a backup, just in case TCP/IP doesn't work correctly. This type of migration takes planning, which automatically drops it to a lower priority.

Now that you have seen some of the possible network conditions that can exist, the following is a quick reference to test your ability to prioritize conditions based on their seriousness.

exam
Ⓦatch

Expect a question or two similar to the ones in the following Scenario and Solution. The Network+ exam is trying to test your ability to determine which condition is the most serious, based on a given scenario.

SCENARIO & SOLUTION

Some users are experiencing problems accessing the color printer. Another department is having trouble logging on.	Logging on is more important than accessing the color printer.
One user cannot access the materials database, while a number of users are receiving a message that the database is currently busy.	Accessing a critical database is a higher priority than warning or information messages.
A few users are noticing that the network is slow. One user's password no longer works.	A user's inability to gain access to the network is a higher priority than a mild decrease in network performance.
A bridge is currently locking a couple of times a week and needs to be replaced.	A bridge locking up can render an entire network segment useless, so this is definitely a higher priority.
A power surge has downed the messaging server, the database server, and two printers.	Although users' access to the messaging server (e-mail), the database server, and the printers is very important, the database server is most likely the more critical of the two servers, and the printers can wait until the critical servers are online.

You will find that with experience you don't even need to think about where to begin the process of prioritizing. When you receive a call from a user, you will instantly know where it ranks with your current projects.

CERTIFICATION SUMMARY

In this chapter, you have learned how to handle one or more network problems. You need to gather as much information as possible during the diagnosing of a network problem. You need to determine the nature of the action required to solve the problem. This involves several resources, such as communication with team members, Resource Kits, Knowledge Bases, online help, and telephone technical support. With these resources, you can determine where the problem lies and how to go about solving it. Notice that you didn't learn anything about actually *solving* the problem; that is for Chapter 13.

You have learned about the method of prioritizing network problems when one or more conditions exist at the same time. This can be a stressful time, but with the understanding of which problems require a higher priority, you can line up tasks in your queue based on priority to efficiently manage all your tasks at once.

✓ **TWO-MINUTE DRILL**

Handling Network Problems

❏ TCP/IP is the protocol that requires more planning, configuration, and troubleshooting than all other protocols combined. That is why you will see many questions on your exam regarding TCP/IP.

❏ Identifying the symptoms of the problem is the first step in diagnosing and solving the problem.

❏ There are a number of troubleshooting-related questions on the exam. Whenever you are faced with a troubleshooting-related question, remember that identification of the symptoms and cause is the first step in the troubleshooting process.

❏ Communication is essential for diagnosing and resolving network problems, or any problem for that matter.

❏ A team of professionals can distribute the load of solving network problems by assigning a different diagnostic task to each person, or by every member of the team collectively investigating the problem.

❏ If you and your team are not able to solve the problem, you need to find additional information and resources to solve the problem. These can take the form of Resource Kits, online help, and telephone technical support.

❏ Microsoft includes the Resource Kits on the same TechNet CD as the Knowledge Base.

❏ Internet is the most helpful resource for researching network problems.

❏ Network monitors and analyzers can inspect the packets traveling over the network and determine if any problems are occurring, such as broadcast storms.

❏ It is imperative that you keep adequate documentation of computer specifications, recent upgrades, future projects, and a list of known issues and resolved problems with each server on your network.

Prioritizing Network Problems

❏ If you encounter more than one network problem, you need to prioritize them based on their severity.

❏ Any network problem that affects a large number of users should receive a high priority.

❏ When you have more than one network problem at a time, it will be fairly evident which problem takes precedence.

❏ The Network+ exam tries to test your ability to determine which condition is the most serious, based on a given scenario.

SELF TEST

The following Self Test questions will help you measure your understanding of the material presented in this chapter. Read all the choices carefully, as there might be more than one correct answer. Choose all correct answers for each question.

Handling Network Problems

1. Which of the following is most likely *not* a problem when adding another workstation to the network segment?

    A. The workstation is not able to find a domain controller on the network.

    B. The bridge can no longer handle the amount of traffic on the network and begins to lock up.

    C. The workstation is not able to receive an IP address.

    D. The workstation has an error concerning the network card on boot up.

2. What is the first step in solving a problem?

    A. Replicating the problem

    B. Calling telephone technical support

    C. Gathering information

    D. Establishing a baseline

3. Why is it best to assign tasks to team members while you are troubleshooting a network problem?

    A. To keep them separated

    B. To avoid them working on the same problem

    C. To put a person in his or her area of expertise

    D. To minimize duplicate information

4. Why would you want to brainstorm the problem as a group?

    A. To keep everyone interested

    B. To not isolate anyone

    C. To see if anyone has changed anything recently that you don't know about

    D. To see if anyone has experienced this problem before

5. You are working on a user's computer that cannot access the employee database. You have tried everything on the workstation, but the user still cannot connect. What is the next logical step in arriving at a solution to the problem?

   A. Reboot the user's machine

   B. Call the database administrator to see if anything has changed

   C. Open a telephone incident with the manufacturer of the product

   D. Check the Resource Kits for a possible solution

6. You are not expected to know everything in your position as network administrator or engineer. However, what *are* you expected to know?

   A. The technical support telephone numbers for every manufacturer of devices that you have on the network.

   B. The version of every piece of software currently being used on the network.

   C. The answer to nearly every user-related problem.

   D. Where to find information.

7. What is the difference between a Resource Kit and a Knowledge Base?

   A. The Resource Kits are free; the Knowledge Bases are not.

   B. The Knowledge Base contains fixes to known problems and the resource kit contains self education information.

   C. The Resource Kits are for advertising third party products and the Knowledge Base is just basic concepts.

   D. The Knowledge Base comes with the product; the Resource Kit does not.

8. Where can you go to obtain the latest driver for a device?

   A. The CD that came with the product

   B. The Resource Kit

   C. The manufacturer's Web site

   D. The Knowledge Base

9. You are having a problem with the Shiva LANRemote dial-up networking server. Which of the following will most likely *not* be of any help in solving the problem?

   A. The Shiva Web site

   B. TechNe.

   C. The documentation that came with the product

   D. Telephone tech support

10. You are getting continuous errors when running IBM's Personal Communications terminal emulation software. You have been in contact with IBM technical support already, and they have advised you to try their new .dll file that they e-mailed you. You are not exactly sure how to test the new bug fix. What should you do in this situation?

    A. Put the .dll in the Windows directory

    B. Check their Web site for instructions

    C. Call IBM technical support

    D. Put the .dll in the Windows\system directory

11. A company released a service pack for their product, but quickly released a notice that the service pack should not be applied. The notice instructed administrators to uninstall the service pack and wait for the newest release. You have already upgraded a few servers with this service pack. How would you determine which servers have this service pack applied and which do not?

    A. Consult the documentation that is continually updated with the server.

    B. Ask everyone in the department if they installed the service pack.

    C. Check the event log for the date the service pack was installed.

    D. Check the operating system version for the new service pack.

12. Unfortunately, your current network supervisor is moving and must quit the company. What is the best way to ensure that the next administrator has enough information concerning the network configuration?

    A. Have the two administrators overlap in employment for at least a month.

    B. Have the new administrator call the old administrator.

    C. Have the old administrator spend his last week documenting everything he can about the network.

    D. Do nothing. The old administrator most likely has bad habits that you do not want to pass on to the next administrator.

Prioritizing Network Problems

13. Which of the following appears to be the most important condition and should warrant the highest priority?

    A. A user cannot log on.

    B. One of the printers is jammed.

    C. Several users are receiving a message that their hard drives are full.

    D. The network is slower than normal accessing the Internet.

14. Which of the following appears to be the most important condition and should warrant the highest priority?

    A. Several users are receiving a message that their hard drives are full.

    B. Several users are receiving a message that their e-mail inbox limit has been exceeded.

    C. The network is slower than normal accessing the Internet.

    D. A printer is down in the accounting department.

15. Which of the following appears to be the most important condition and should warrant the highest priority?

    A. A few users cannot access the employee time-reporting database.

    B. A printer is down in the accounting department.

    C. Several users are receiving a message that their e-mail inbox limit has been exceeded.

    D. A user cannot access his personal drive on the network.

16. The personnel department is having trouble accessing their corporatewide database system for checking job postings. Why does this warrant a higher priority?

    A. Because they are handling job postings.

    B. Because they are in the personnel department.

    C. Because the problem is affecting a large number of users.

    D. Because they are using an older system.

17. McAfee has just announced they have a new version of their virus-checking software available on their Web site. Why should this not be the highest priority; or should it be?

    A. It should be the highest priority, because it is virus-scanning software.

    B. It should be the highest priority, because it is a new release of a program.

    C. It should not be the highest priority, because patches and fixes are not a priority unless they address issues that affect your network.

    D. It should not be the highest priority, because virus scanning is not very important compared to other issues on the network.

18. Which of the following appears to be the least important condition and should warrant the lowest priority?

    A. A printer is down in the accounting department.

    B. Several users are receiving a message that their hard drives are full.

    C. The network is slower than normal accessing the Internet.

    D. A user cannot log on.

19. You just arrived at work this morning and you have four new voice messages. Which of the following messages appears to be the least important condition, and should warrant the lowest priority?

    A. "I'm getting an error that says I cannot access my personal drive on the network."

    B. "I'm trying to load a Web page, and it says the page is outdated."

    C. "Steve and I can't print to the LaserJet over here in accounting."

    D. "It's telling me my password is expired."

LAB QUESTION

Your company recently installed Office XP on all systems. Your company has a connection to the Internet, allowing for clients to send and receive mail and files from Internet users.

After installing Office XP to all of the systems, the users are no longer able to send mail from Word. When sending a message from Word as the editor using Word Mail, Outlook crashes and generates the following message:

```
Microsoft Word has encountered a problem and needs to close. We are
sorry for the inconvenience.
```

The e-mail is not sent and Outlook closes. You have been asked to find the problem. Where would you look, and what is the solution?

SELF TEST ANSWERS

Handling Network Problems

1. ☑ **B.** The bridge can no longer handle the amount of traffic on the network and begins to lock up. These new computers chew up precious bandwidth, and require one or more network cards, more cables, ports on the hubs, and, if you are using TCP/IP, another IP address. In addition to the hardware, you must make sure the network interface card (NIC) has been correctly configured, and the correct network protocols have been loaded and configured.
    ☒ **A, C,** and **D** are incorrect. If no changes are made to the protocol settings and the settings are not dynamically allocated, the workstation might not be able to communicate with any other system let alone the domain controller. This can also cause an issue of the workstation not receiving an IP address if the settings were static, or if TCP/IP was not used on the PC before. The network card might generate an error if the network cable has not been connected to the network card.

2. ☑ **C.** Gathering information. Identifying the symptoms of the problem is the first step in diagnosing and solving the problem. This is the information-gathering phase. The more time you spend during this phase, the quicker the problem can be solved. Always know what you are dealing with before you attempt to fix the problem.
    ☒ **A, B,** and **D** are not first steps to solving a problem.

3. ☑ **C.** To put a person in his or her area of expertise. The point of distributing the work involved with troubleshooting is that one person can spend quality time in one area, and this person can thoroughly understand the complexities of the task. Getting an entire group up to speed on a concept such as routing can be challenging. Picking one specialist to investigate the possible routing issues and report findings to the group can be very beneficial.
    ☒ **A, B,** and **D** are incorrect. The technicians should never be completely separated, so they can learn from each other and help each other. Large network issues might require having several people work on the same issue. When troubleshooting, information cannot be really duplicated. Documentation from the technicians is always valuable.

4. ☑ **C** and **D.** To see if anyone has experienced this problem before. It would be nice to know if anyone has changed anything recently, and to see if anyone has experienced this problem before. Having the entire collective experience and knowledge of a group of people guarantees that a problem will be solved. Highly experienced professionals can quickly determine where a problem lies, and the best solution for solving the problem. Chances are that someone in your group has experienced a problem such as this in the past.

☒　A and B are not valid reasons for brainstorming the problem as a group.

5.　☑　**B.** Call the database administrator to see if anything has changed. Maybe something has changed that you are not aware of yet. Would you rather stop and ask for help, or just continue reconfiguring things until the network completely breaks? Some technicians will never ask for help. This is not the type of technician you want on your team. You need a team that can communicate effectively.

☒　**A, C,** and **D** are incorrect. A technical incident will usually require the company to pay a fee. This is not always the case, but usually should be done after all other network issues are ruled out. The network issues are going to be the first thing that the technical support person will want to make sure is working.

6.　☑　**D.** Where to find information. You are not expected to know everything; however, you *are* expected to know when and where to look for answers. If you and your team are not able to solve the problem, you need to find additional information and resources to solve the problem. These can take the form of Resource Kits, online help, and telephone technical support.

☒　**A, B,** and **C** are incorrect.

7.　☑　**B.** The Knowledge Bases contain fixes to known problems. Resource Kits are a valuable way of educating yourself. These are helpful for planning, implementing, configuring, and, most of all, troubleshooting. Microsoft includes the Resource Kits on the same TechNet CD as the Knowledge Base. The Resource Kits are more for reading and planning, whereas the Knowledge Base is loaded with information on symptoms, causes, and solutions to problems.

☒　**A, C,** and **D** are incorrect definitions.

8.　☑　**C.** The manufacturer's Web site. If you believe you are having a problem with a particular product or device, you should begin your search with the manufacturer's Web site. You will find information such as updated drivers and patches, detailed installation instructions, troubleshooting tips, and possibly a Knowledge Base of common problems.

☒　**A, B,** and **D** are incorrect. The CD that came with a device might not be a newly created CD and might have an older outdated driver.

9.　☑　**B.** TechNet. TechNet is Microsoft's technical information database. Telephone support personnel have a database of known problems and resolutions that they can query if they don't have the immediate answer.

☒　**A, C,** and **D** are incorrect. The Web site, in addition to the product documentation, will also have information such as updated drivers and patches, detailed installation instructions, troubleshooting tips, and possibly a Knowledge Base of common problems.

10. ☑ **C.** Call IBM technical support. These support personnel can lead you step by step in installing, testing, and configuring their product. This will often reveal details that you didn't adhere to during the initial installation that was giving you problems. The support personnel can also provide you with troubleshooting steps to get at the cause of the problem quickly. When you are troubleshooting a complicated problem, don't ignore telephone technical support, because they might have a quick and easy answer to the problem.
    ☒ **A**, **B**, and **D** are incorrect.

11. ☑ **A.** Consult the documentation that is continually updated with the server. Determining who is responsible is not the same as finding someone to blame when something goes wrong. Support personnel often configure servers and network devices in a unique way, without sharing that information with the rest of the group. By documenting the modifications to the server, you can determine what has changed, and whether that change is adversely affecting the server.
    ☒ **B**, **C**, and **D** are incorrect. Depending on the memory of others to remember exactly which systems have been updated might lead to a system or two being missed and not having the update removed. Updates will not always update the event log or even the version of the OS. These cannot be relied upon to determine that the updates were made.

12. ☑ **C.** Have the old administrator spend his last week documenting everything he can about the network. Network support personnel can spend hours, if not days, getting something to work correctly, yet they rarely spend the time to document their findings for future use. If they leave the company, this information goes with them. The next administrator or engineer might find himself spending as much or more time than the original person trying to get the same problem resolved. If the previous person had documented his findings, it would have made the second person's job much easier.
    ☒ **A**, **B**, and **D** are incorrect. Having two administrators overlap their time would be beneficial, but this might not be the best solution, especially from the perspective of the person doing payroll. This will require having two people on staff doing the same thing. The old administrator might not be able to take technical telephone calls from the previous business at his new job. It might be a complicated situation if the old administrator is now with a consulting business and they would wish to have the time paid for while the old administrator is helping the new one. Each person will have his or her own habits, but this is not an issue since the new administrator will most likely stick with his or her habits rather than pick up new ones.

Prioritizing Network Problems

13. ☑ **A.** A user cannot log on. Any problem that affects a user's capability to log on and become authenticated should be a high priority. This means a user will not be able to log on to gain access to the network resources. The user might be able to work with local resources, such as a word processor, but will not be able to retrieve or store any information on a network server.
☒ **B, C,** and **D** are *not* the most important conditions.

14. ☑ **D.** A printer is down in the accounting department. Users complain most about the inability to receive e-mail and to print. Users print everything. When they can't print, you will find out very quickly. The problem could be major, such as the downing of a print server, or it could just affect one printer, such as a hardware malfunction.
☒ **A, B,** and **C** are not the most important conditions.

15. ☑ **A.** A few users cannot access the employee time-reporting database. Whenever a database issue arises, it usually takes precedence over anything else, especially if it is the employee time-reporting database. After that, you would begin working on the printer in the accounting department.
☒ **B, C,** and **D** are not the most important conditions.

16. ☑ **C.** Because the problem is affecting a large number of users. Although some problems affect a large number of users, you have to prioritize which functions the users can live without for a period of time. Problems such as access to important servers that are affecting many users should be very high priority.
☒ **A, B,** and **D** are not valid reasons.

17. ☑ **C.** It should not be the highest priority, because patches and fixes are not a priority unless they address issues that affect your network. Unless the updated version of the software fixes a critical bug, this condition does not warrant a high priority. You should test the patch or version update on a test machine before implementing it in the field. The updated program is the actual scanning software, not the signature files.
☒ **A, B,** and **D** are incorrect reasons.

18. ☑ **C.** The network is slower than normal accessing the Internet. Conditions in which the network is slower than usual do not warrant a high priority, unless the network is significantly slower. This can be expected in most networks at certain times of the day, such as in the morning when users are logging on to the network, or at lunch time, when some users are browsing the Internet.
☒ **A, B,** and **D** are not the least important conditions.

19. ☑   B. "I'm trying to load a Web page, and it says the page is outdated." The message most likely refers to a user having problems accessing a page on the Internet. Since this condition is not highly critical, it can be set to a lower priority if you have more than one problem you are working on.

   ☒   A, C, and D are not least important conditions.

LAB ANSWER

The best place to start is Microsoft TechNet or support.microsoft.com. This would require a search under Office XP for such words as *Word Mail* and *"Outlook*. This will give a list of possible problems. The one to look for is titled "OAER: Outlook Quits Unexpectedly After You Send a Message Using Word Mail (Q300935)."

   The solution is to install the "Microsoft Word 2002 Update: June 21, 2001."

Network+
COMPUTING TECHNOLOGY INDUSTRY ASSOCIATION

13

Troubleshooting the Network

CERTIFICATION OBJECTIVES

13.01	Managing Network Problems
13.02	Troubleshooting Network Problems
13.03	System or Operator Problems
13.04	Checking Physical and Logical Indicators
13.05	Network Troubleshooting Resources
13.06	Other Symptoms and Causes of Network Problems
13.07	Network Tools
13.08	Selecting Appropriate Tools to Resolve Network Problems
✓	Two-Minute Drill
Q&A	Self Test

One the most important parts of operating a network is knowing how to deal with network problems when they arise. Hopefully, during your tenure as a network administrator, you won't often need to apply the skills you learn here. Besides, you cannot learn how to resolve every problem that exists. You can, however, learn a methodology to find and diagnose nearly every problem in a systematic and logical manner. Teaching you that methodology is the goal of this chapter.

CERTIFICATION OBJECTIVE 13.01

Managing Network Problems

Data communication is still not "bullet proof." Many things can go wrong when you are networking several different types of computers, mainframes, printers, and network devices using different operating systems, protocols, and data transfer methods. When problems occur, you need not only an understanding of each of the devices on your network—you also need an understanding of the network as a whole. Learning how each device coexists and contributes to the network provides you with a strong foundation for understanding how and why network-related problems occur and how to resolve them. For example, if you don't understand how a router works, you will be quite overwhelmed when one segment of your network cannot communicate with another segment. If you have a very good understanding of routers and routing, and one segment of your network cannot communicate with another segment, you will immediately know that there is a problem with routing— that, possibly, a router is malfunctioning. It is helpful to classify the types of problems you are having and to ask yourself questions concerning the problem in order to stimulate your network problem-solving abilities.

Does the Problem Exist Across the Network?

When you first encounter a problem, it is very important to determine its scope. Does this problem occur with a specific machine, or does the problem exist across the network? You need to narrow the problem as soon as possible. If more than one computer is having the same problem at one time, it is obvious that you have a network problem, not a computer-specific problem. This phase of the problem-solving process often requires you to check the status of other computers on the network to determine whether they are having the same problem.

If you are having a network-related problem, the problem's symptoms are helpful in determining its cause. In the example of one segment of the network not being able to communicate with another segment, you quickly determined you had a routing problem. Another symptom is that everyone on the coaxial-based bus network is unable to communicate. The cause of this situation is most likely a problem with the network bus backbone, which requires terminators on each end. If the network backbone becomes severed, the end points will not be terminated and the data will echo through the network, rendering the entire network unusable. Another symptom is that one department of the company on a twisted-pair Ethernet network can no longer communicate with the rest of the network. The cause of this problem is most likely a problem with the hub used to connect this group. As you know, a hub connects groups of computers. The hub itself is then connected to the network backbone, and in this case, the connection to the network backbone might have been severed.

As you can see, quickly determining the scope of a problem is the first step in gathering information about the nature of the problem.

Workstation, Workgroup, LAN, or WAN Problem?

To continue the discussion on determining the scope of a problem, larger networks present even more possibilities for error. Not only are you faced with computer-specific problems, but you can have problems within your workgroup, your local area network, or even the wide area network.

For example, say that accounting department users employ a terminal-based order-entry system to transfer orders to corporate headquarters. This system operates through terminal sessions on user computers across the WAN to the corporate mainframe. One day the connection on a user's computer is not working. How can you diagnose such a complicated issue? First, you need to determine whether the problem is occurring with a workstation, workgroup, LAN, or WAN. You continue by going over to another computer and trying the connection. You find that this computer is having the same problem. Therefore, the problem is not computer specific. Luckily, the same order-entry program can be used to acquire the monthly sales orders from another terminal session, this time at the regional headquarters. You find that the user is able to connect to the regional headquarters mainframe with no problems. Therefore, you have proved that you can at least get out to another remote location, but you still haven't determined the true cause of the problem.

As it stands now, you could be having a routing problem with the corporate headquarters, a name resolution problem, or a mainframe connectivity problem. You can test the routing problem theory by trying to communicate with another computer on the corporate headquarters' network. For example, you could PING another computer on this network or use a program that connects to a computer on this network. You get the IP address for another computer on this network and PING it. You receive a response from this computer. This response determines that you don't have a routing problem to this remote network.

Next, you get the IP address of the mainframe and attempt to PING it:

```
Pinging 207.149.40.41 with 32 bytes of data:
Request timed out.
Request timed out.
Request timed out.
Request timed out.
```

You have found your problem. The mainframe at corporate headquarters is down. You're sure that corporate is aware of the problem, so you decide not to pester them. You can check back every so often to determine if the problem has been fixed. Luckily, it's their problem, not yours!

on the job

I can't tell you how many times I have benefitted from carrying around a list of computer and network device IP addresses. If I need to PING a server on another network, I can simply consult my table of IP addresses rather than call someone or go back to my cube and look up the information. Another method is to label the PC with the IP address it was assigned. This can help if you do not have the list or even the current list of IP addresses.

See how quickly you can determine the scope of the problem? It took only a few minutes to determine whether you had a workstation, workgroup, LAN, or WAN problem. Unfortunately, all problems won't be this easy to fix, but armed with the troubleshooting methodology presented here, you are on your way to solving any network problem that occurs.

Is the Problem Consistent and Replicable?

Sometimes you are faced with weird problems that are not so easy to solve. These problems require you to gain more information beyond the scope of the problem. You might already know you are having a LAN or WAN problem, for example, but you need more information to get you down the road to solving the problem. Next, you need to ask yourself, "Is the problem consistent and replicable?" To answer this question, you need to determine a way to replicate the problem.

For example, let's say that when someone in the purchasing department sends a job to the printer, it takes over five minutes for the job to print. As we did in the preceding section, we need to learn if more than one computer is having this problem. We send a print job from another computer, only to discover that the print job once again takes five minutes to print. We now have a consistent problem that is replicable. The problem is not computer specific because we were able to replicate the problem on another computer.

When we take a look at the print server, we discover that there are many jobs in the print queue, including one 120MB Excel document with 340 pages that is currently being printed in the finance department. We have found the source of our problem. Chances are, if we attempted to print after the print queue was empty, we would not have such a problem.

Once again, notice how quickly we narrowed the problem to a possible source. Furthermore, notice how we used logic to determine the cause of the problem. We went to the next logical source in our printing problem: the print server. We didn't immediately go to the router and check to see if it was routing correctly, and we didn't go to the domain controller to check whether the user had rights to print to this printer. We used logical troubleshooting methodology to arrive at the conclusion to the problem.

Standard Troubleshooting Methods

As you learned in the previous section, it is very important to isolate the subsystem involved with a problematic process. When you work with a problem internal to one computer, you learn to isolate the subsystem involved. For example, say that your system is not detecting your primary hard drive. What subsystem do you check? You check the disk subsystem, which includes the hard disk drive, the drive controller, and the drive cable. You wouldn't begin your troubleshooting by removing the video card and the CD-ROM drive.

You must apply this methodology to solving network-related problems, too. In the previous section, you knew you had a printing problem, so your troubleshooting remained on the printing subsystem. You could have been led to a problem outside the printing subsystem if you researched the problem and found out that *everything* you did on the network, not just printing, took five minutes.

EXERCISE 13-1

CertCam 13-1

Checking Device Manager

If you have installed a device on a PC and you want to see its status in Windows 2000, you need to check the Device Manager to verify it is working. Do the following:

1. Right-click **My Computer** and select **Properties**. The System Properties window opens.

2. Select the **Hardware** tab.

3. Select the **Device Manager** button.

4. The Device Manager window opens and displays a listing of all major resource areas of the PC that are configurable or require a device driver.

5. Choose the plus sign (+) next to the category you want to check. For example, to check the network card, you would select the + next to the category Network Adapters.

6. You will see a drop-down list of all of the devices that fall under the chosen category. Once the list is dropped down, you will see a red *X* on any devices not functioning properly and a yellow exclamation mark (!) that shows there is a minor issue with the device.

7. Double-click the chosen device to open its Properties and see information about the problem with the device.

CERTIFICATION OBJECTIVE 13.02

Troubleshooting Network Problems

When you are troubleshooting network problems, it is important to follow a logical troubleshooting methodology. Always assume that the problem will be simple. It might sound counterintuitive, but the simple solutions are most likely to elude you. As your experience grows, you can easily find yourself caught in a web of always assuming the problem is more complicated than it actually is. When that happens, it can result in an excessive waste of troubleshooting time. Don't forget to ask yourself three basic troubleshooting questions:

1. Did the device ever work?
2. When was it last known to be working?
3. What has changed since then?

Remember this: As an administrator, you are a "doctor." Your patients are computers and networking equipment. As with any doctor, your first step to finding a cure is making a proper diagnosis. Use logic and the scientific method, and do not forget to use one variable at a time. To put it in plain English: Fix one thing at a time!

Always remember to start with the simplest things first before checking the more complicated items. The majority of the time, the problem will be caused by something simple. It's easier to check simple items than complicated ones, and doing so can save a great deal of time. Complicated items can take hours to check, whereas simple items can take seconds or minutes to check.

exam
ⓦatch

The eight steps to becoming an effective troubleshooter are listed here. It would be wise to tape these steps to your monitor or to draw them on the white board in your office because they are important to your success as a network professional. (Plus, they are pretty heavily tested during the exam!)

1. *Establish the symptoms*
2. *Identify the affected area*
3. *Establish what has changed*
4. *Select the most probable cause*

5. *Implement a solution*

6. *Test the result*

7. *Recognize the potential effects of the solution*

8. *Document the solution*

Before we continue, let's look more closely at the steps to determine the symptoms and causes of a problem and the process of solving the problem in more detail.

First, establish the symptoms. Doing so allows us to know the exact effects the problem is causing. You'll use this information later to determine that the problem is resolved because these symptoms will disappear. For example, we need to know what the network users are experiencing—if this is a matter of not being able to connect to a specific server or all servers.

Second, determine which areas of the network are affected. For example, you need to determine if the problem is with one protocol, if it is with everything on one side of a router, or if all the machines are connected to the same cable. No matter what, the affected areas will always have something in common. This "something" could, of course, be your entire network, but that is something that the affected components have in common.

Third, identify any differences between the affected areas and the unaffected areas by determining what has changed since the last time there were no problems. For example, if you are unable to get a network connection with all your workstations that are connected to a thinwire coax cable, but all other workstations are functioning, it's more than likely that your problem resides in that thinwire coax cable.

Fourth, after narrowing down the list of effects caused by the problem, pinpointing the scope of the problem, and determining what has changed, we can then most likely come up with a few things to check. We choose the most probable problem and determine a solution. For example, if we have a whole segment of the network unable to connect to the server even though all other users can connect to the server, we know we have an issue with a specific segment. We can then say that the segment has been disconnected from the rest of the network.

Fifth, once a specific problem has been determined, we need to find a solution to that problem and implement that solution. For example, in the previous step we had a segment that was unable to connect to the rest of the network. If we think the problem is that the segment is disconnected from the rest of the network, our solution is to reconnect the segment at the router.

Sixth, once we have implemented a solution, we need to verify that the problems we found in Step 1 have all disappeared. For example, we could go back to the PCs that could not contact the server and make sure they can do so now.

Seventh, we need to make sure that our solution will not cause other problems. One thing that a technician or administrator needs to realize is that at times there could be multiple solutions to a single problem. Some solutions could cause other problems. For example, when installing service packs on a NOS, you need to determine what items the service packs will fix. You might have previously circumvented a problem on the server that the service pack will undo and cause a problem again.

Finally, you need to document the solution you implemented. This information will assist others working with you and those who might take your place someday so that they can fix the problem, benefitting from your experience rather than having to perform all the same troubleshooting techniques and waste a lot of time trying to find the same solution.

Later in this chapter you will learn about the various tools available for diagnosing and correcting network problems.

Establish the Symptoms

Establishing the symptoms is always the first step to resolving a problem. Whether you are an administrator or a technician, this part is usually the easiest. This portion of the problem-solving process is usually brought to your attention by network users. They will contact you and tell you what they are experiencing, but you need to be careful about taking at face value what they say about the effects they are seeing.

Sometimes people who have little or no technical knowledge about computers and networks give explanations for the problems they are experiencing that are completely opposite of what is really occurring. Always remember that user error is always a possible cause of the problem.

Working a help desk is usually a bad situation since most problems require a person to actually see the problems to be able to determine solutions and the scope of the issue. Some help desks are set up to actually assign problems to a specific technician. If each technician has a specific area of issues that they take care of or a specialty, this situation will cause problems.

For example, I once received a call from a user who could not access the server. The user's explanations were that the PC was disconnected from the network or the server was down. I was able to determine that the server was online and running fine, but after looking at the user's PC, I found out that they had not logged on to the network. The user had been using Windows 98, which allows you to press the Escape key at logon and have access to the local computer only. This was no real network issue, just an issue of the user failing to properly log on to the network.

Once someone is present to see the problem, the user needs to make sure that the problem still exists and that he or she is sure the problem is a network issue and not a user error. A technician or administrator should try to see the problem first-hand to make sure the information they have about the problem is correct.

Identify the Affected Areas

Once you have found the exact issues that are occurring due to the problem, you need to find out how many and which users are being affected. This step helps you not only determine the scope of the problem so you can narrow it down to specific segments or devices—it also enables you to determine the priority to place on the issue.

Sometimes this portion of the troubleshooting process allows you to find the problem's source, especially if it is something like a failing router or a broken hub. The scope of the issue can point to the exact cause of the problem, since the affected area will be controlled by a single network device or cable.

Knowing the scope of the problem will let you determine the priority of the problem and how long it can wait to be fixed. This is very important when there are other problems that also need to be considered and you will need to fix the crucial problems first.

Same Line, Different Computer

One method to isolate the network problem is to replace the problem workstation with a workstation that is known to be working. You could even use a laptop in place of the workstation to verify the connections, since a laptop would be easier to carry around. If the workstation or laptop that is known to be good has difficulties, the problem cannot be isolated to the original workstation. You should then begin troubleshooting network components such as the cable, hub, repeater, or network backbone, because the problem is not computer specific.

Same Computer, Different Line

In a similar method, the workstation having difficulties is moved to another line. If the workstation is able to function correctly in the new line, the problem is on the original line, not with the workstation itself. This method can also be tested using a network cable from a workstation that is close by without having to move any PCs. Technicians should always try to carry an extra patch cable that can be used to swap with the cable to make sure that the cable is not bad and that the wall jacks are all working fine. This can be done easily if you carry a laptop in a case and place the extra patch cable in a pocket of the case.

Swapping Components

Swap the components that are between the failing workstations. These components include hubs, cables, terminators—anything that can possibly go bad. This is a quick way to return the network to a functioning state. After the network is functioning, you can test the components that were replaced to determine which component failed. A lightning strike or some other type of electrical problem can sometimes cause a NIC to behave unpredictably. By swapping components, this problem can be solved quickly and efficiently.

Isolating Segments of the Network with Terminators

If you are using a thinwire coax network, isolating your network is easy. Simply choose a workstation to act as the dividing line for the isolation. Next, unplug the network cable from the T-connector and replace it with a terminator. You have now quickly isolated the network trouble.

Steps for Problem Isolation

Table 13-1 shows the steps you should take to isolate network problems.

Establish What Has Changed

Establishing what has changed since the last time all components worked correctly can be a very important step, depending on the problem. In some situations, the step may not have any bearing on the issue. On the other hand, if something has changed recently and everything worked before the change, you know the change has possibly had an adverse effect.

This is the step that will help determine the problem that has occurred when a network device has been reconfigured and the settings are not the same as before. For example, let's say that a network printer has its network interface card replaced and the new card is not given the same IP address as the previous configuration. This mistake will prevent anyone who could previously print from printing.

This step can also point to server upgrades of not only hardware but also software—drivers, software patches, and even application installation. Settings can be overwritten on the server, .DLL files can be replaced or removed, and many other things can happen to cause adverse affects for users.

This step can be easily determined from documentation kept by the network administrators and technicians. If a problem arises that is affecting a large number

TABLE 13-1 Techniques for Problem Isolation

Step	Action
Determine which workstations are and are not experiencing symptoms.	Separate the working and nonworking workstations from each other using a hub or terminator.
Rule out simple problems.	Reset all major components that are affected by unplugging the devices and plugging them back in.
Further determine which workstations are and are not experiencing symptoms.	Separate the nonworking network segment in half and determine which half is not working properly.
Eliminate simple cable problems.	Examine the cable for any physical damage.
Eliminate complicated cable problems.	Examine cables with a TDR to find any problems.
Get more help.	Consult TechNet, resource kits, or vendor Web sites for further information.

of network users or whole segments of the network, you can check the documentation and see if anyone has made any major or minor changes to network devices or servers.

Select the Most Probable Cause

Once they've gotten this far, most technicians and administrators formulate a few ideas as to the problem that has occurred and what has caused it. There is no definitive manual to assist someone in determining a problem's cause from a given set of issues; this kind of insight is mainly gained from experience. The more issues you resolve, the easier this step will be for you.

Selecting the most probable cause not only draws on your knowledge of networks in general—it also draws on your knowledge of the specific network you are working on at the time. Most employers do not realize that being onsite full time helps a technician or administrator know and understand their specific network better than a technician brought in from a computer repair shop. You will draw on past experiences and be able to determine the causes of problems that might be similar to other problems you've repaired in the past. If a technician is around a network long enough, he or she will know the ins and outs of the specific network and be able to notice a problem before it becomes too major and thus noticeable to users.

If a technician or administrator has not formulated any ideas about the problem by this point in the problem-solving process, he or she will at least have an idea where to look or whom to ask. This type of knowledge can be as important as determining the cause of the problem itself. If you have no idea of the cause, you need to have a backup way of determining the cause.

Implement a Solution

As noted in the last section, an administrator or technician will have an idea as to a problem's cause and will most likely also have a solution or multiple solutions in mind to repair the problem. Again, this step comes with experience and knowledge.

You not only need to determine the problem's cause—you also need to come up with a solution that might or might not be easily known. You might need to consult other people on how to fix the problem, requiring access to the Internet or technical support telephone numbers for specific manufacturers.

Once you have a solution in mind that seems as though it will fix the problem, you need to implement the solution. Again, you might not be able to implement the solution in a timely manner, since the problem could be a low priority.

Test the Result

Testing the result of your solution is a more important step than previous ones. Still, some technicians and administrators forget to take this step when troubleshooting problems. There is nothing more frustrating to a network user than contacting a tech support person to fix a problem and that person arrives to say that the problem is fixed, but instead of testing the solution, the support person leaves the user's office. The network user then resumes work and finds that the problem still exists.

Once you have implemented a solution, make sure that you return to the user to attempt to perform the task that was exhibiting the problem and make sure that the problem no longer exists.

Recognize the Potential Effects of the Solution

Once you have implemented and tested the solution, you need to make sure that the solution has not adversely affected anything else on the network. In some cases, you should consider this step *before* implementing the solution.

In some cases, when a service pack or patch is installed, certain .DLL files that are used by other programs could be overwritten. This will cause other programs to stop functioning.

Most implementations of a solution will not be a major concern in terms of adverse effects, but this does not mean that you don't need to consider the possibility of such effects. For example, Microsoft released Service Pack 6 for Windows NT 4.0 and then removed the Service Pack from the Web site because it caused more problems than it fixed. Later, Microsoft released Service Pack 6a, which fixed the issues that the original Service Pack was to fix, but it did not help repair the systems on which Service Pack 6 had been installed.

Once you fix a problem via a solution and have tested that solution, make sure you also test other network issues that could be affected by the fix. For example, if you make a change to a router configuration, make sure that you do some testing from all segments of the network that are joined by the router.

Documenting the Solution

The final and most important step in the troubleshooting process is documenting the solution. This step helps avoid wasted time later as you or someone else tries to resolve the same problem, going through all the steps you have already performed to come to the same solution.

Every help desk technician and administrator needs to have some type of database that is used to store all the problems and solutions that are found. In a company in which all hardware and software are standardized, the same problems can keep recurring. If time has passed since the last time you solved a particular problem, you might not remember the solution and will have to perform all the same steps again. Or a problem could be sporadic, appearing only every few months. Keeping up-to-date documentation helps you be sure of the solutions you have tried so that you do not implement that same solution multiple times with no effect.

Documentation is also important for anyone who is hired later to assist or replace you. If you are on vacation and return to find that your assistant has spent a week trying to solve a problem for which you already found a resolution months ago, you will not be too happy (and neither will your assistant!). Other work has been put aside in favor of working on a problem that's already been solved.

Documentation is also needed if you retire or leave a company. This documentation will help future technicians and administrators keep the network running smoothly.

Sample Troubleshooting Situations

To follow up on the troubleshooting steps, let's look at two examples of network issues and troubleshooting steps.

Example One

In this example, you get a call from a network user who says she cannot print to the laser printer in her department but has no problem accessing the servers or any other PC. She was able to print to the printer yesterday but is unable to print to it today. In fact, no one in the department is able to print to the printer, which is a network printer. The user verifies that the printer is turned on; she has even powered off the printer and turned it back on. No error messages are displayed on the front panel. What do you do?

The first step of troubleshooting is to establish the symptoms, which has just been reported by your caller. The second step is to determine the affected area; in this case, the whole department that uses the laser printer is affected.

The third step is to determine what has changed. You would consult the documentation of what has been performed on the printer or the print server since they worked yesterday. While searching, you might find that the network interface card in the printer was changed at the end of yesterday. You check the printer and determine that the NIC was improperly configured.

In Step 4, you would determine that the most probable cause of the problem is that the NIC was not configured correctly, so it cannot be contacted by the print server to receive print jobs.

For a solution in Step 5, you would want to configure the NIC correctly. After consulting the documentation for the printer configuration, you change the settings as they should be to allow proper connectivity.

For Step 6, you would test the result by waiting to see if the print jobs that have been sent to the print server will start spooling to the printer. After about a minute, the printer starts printing all the spooled print jobs.

Step 7 would dictate that you determine any adverse effects, but if there were none before the NIC was changed (except the problem for which the NIC configuration was corrected), all should be fine.

The last step is to add to the printer's documentation that the configuration was done improperly and has been redone. You might also document the settings that are correct again to make sure that this problem does not occur again.

Example Two

In this example, you are informed that the users in the accounting department are unable to access anything on the network.

To fulfill Step 1 of the problem-solving process, you go to the accounting department to see what the exact problems are and when they occurred. The accounting personnel tell you that they have been unable to access any PC or network printer anywhere. They have been trying all morning to do their work, and they can only access local files and programs that are located on the PCs at which they are sitting.

Step 2 has already been answered: The affected area is the accounting department only.

In Step 3, you ask if anything has changed. The accounting personnel answer that nothing has changed except that a PC was removed yesterday at closing time. You do not check the documentation since no one at the company has ever kept documentation.

You figure that the removed computer would have no bearing on the problem. You think the problem could reside at the router, which connects all the segments in the company. At the router you find that all connections are fine, but you notice that the connection from the accounting department is Thinnet. You had forgotten that this was an older segment that had never been upgraded to 10BaseT. You now have to go back to Step 4 and come up with another possible solution. You decide that maybe the PC being removed caused the problem. Removal of the PC might have left a break in the bus topology, causing the whole segment to stop functioning.

You return to the accounting department and ask where the PC that was removed had been located. You find out that the T-connector was removed and that the two ends of the cable are just lying on the floor.

To fix the problem, you get a barrel connector and connect the two cables. This action immediately allows all the accounting personnel to connect to the server and other network devices.

The potential side effects are none, since the cable was simply disconnected and rejoined.

Now you decide to keep some documentation and make some notes. Starting documentation after the network is in place takes some time and effort, but it will pay off.

CERTIFICATION OBJECTIVE 13.03

System or Operator Problems

In some cases, it is very apparent whether a system or operator error has occurred. A system error can be classified as an error on the part of a computer or network device or process that was not associated with a user's direct actions. This error can be hardware failure or an error involved in the process of transferring or manipulating data. An operator problem is the result of a user's action, such as not logging on correctly, connecting to the wrong server, or printing to the wrong printer. The source of most operator-related problems are obvious. However, operator problems can stem from misconfiguration of a device, program, or service by the initial operator: the network administrator. If a device is misconfigured, it might not be apparent until the device is promoted to a production area and fails in the process. For the Network+ exam, you need to understand the various ways a system or network device error occurs, the symptoms of such an error, and how to go about resolving the problem. First, you need to learn the areas that will provide you with a clue as to the problem's nature.

CERTIFICATION OBJECTIVE 13.04

Checking Physical and Logical Indicators

When you begin troubleshooting a network-related problem, you have several indicators that will help you determine the problem. These indicators are a combination of physical and logical elements. From a physical level, you can determine many things about the nature of the problem from the device in question by looking at its various indicator lights, error displays, and monitors. Let's look at these tools now.

Link Lights

Link lights are invaluable in determining whether a network connection is present. A link light is a green or amber light-emitting diode (LED) that shines if the networking device detects a network connection. Many network devices, such as routers, hubs, and network cards, are equipped with link lights for this very reason. Most network cards have two lights—a link light, which remains on for the duration of the network connection, and a light that displays the current activity of the network card and that pulses as data is transferred to and from the computer or device. This second light can be an obvious indicator that the device is functioning on the network. If you are troubleshooting a network-related problem, it is best to start by examining the device's link light to determine if a network connection is detected.

Collision Lights

Troubleshooting network issues can also be determined by *collision lights* on a hub. Collision lights show whether a specific connection is having problems caused by packets colliding with one another. Collision lights can sometimes be the same as activity lights; the activity light is green when sending or receiving data, and it turns yellow or orange when a collision occurs.

A collision results in the loss of the packet being received and the packet being sent. Sometimes a faulty cable or hub can cause packets to be generated from other packets or electrical interference. Sometimes called *chatter*, these disruptive packets can cause major collisions and can even halt an entire network due to collisions of all packets. Administrators and technicians need to watch these lights to verify that network chatter is not occurring.

Power Lights

Even more rudimentary than the link light in the network troubleshooting area is the *power light*. Simply put, absence of a power light means no power is present in the device or the power light is burned out. If the power light is not present, check that the device is receiving proper power. If it is not, you should check the power supply, the power cable, or the wall connector. If you have verified that all these are working, the device could literally be dead. In this case, you will have to replace it.

Error Displays

An *error display* is a means of alerting you to a malfunction or failure in a device. This display can be a visual error dialog box on a computer when the error occurs or an LED error display on a network device. Such error messages should describe the problem that is occurring; however, they might not provide the necessary course of action required to solve the problem.

The error display might refer to an error code that you must look up in order to determine the cause of the problem and the ways to resolve it. Referring to documentation for the device is very helpful when you're troubleshooting a network device, because each manufacturer has its own special procedure to resolve a physical or logical problem. Sometimes you must check the error codes on the manufacturer's Web site because they cannot easily or immediately be deciphered.

FROM THE CLASSROOM

Collision Light Experience

Working at a consulting firm, I was asked to look at the network because no PC or server could communicate. The firm's owners were concerned that hackers might be trying to access the company network and bring it down.

I first looked at the router activity lights to see what was coming in or going out to the Internet. No lights were blinking at all, but the connection light was on, showing that the company network was still connected to the Internet.

I then looked at the hub and saw a collision light on solid. I unplugged the network cable that was in that port and the network started functioning again. I removed the patch cable I had just unplugged and replaced it with a new one. This caused the same result as

before—the network stopped again due to collisions.

I unplugged the patch cable again and plugged it into a different port on the hub, and all was well. This series of steps showed that the port on the hub was bad and causing chatter. I then placed a piece of tape over the faulty port so that it would not be used again.

Even though hubs, routers, bridges, and other network devices are usually not to blame for network faults, you should never wholly discount these devices as the source of a problem. Remember that these devices have their own ways to let you know about network problems; make sure that you use them.

—*Jarret W. Buse, MCSE+I, MCT, CCNA, CNA, A+, Network+*

Error Logs and Displays

Similar to the error display is the error log, which maintains a listing of errors encountered on a device. This error log should contain the time the problem occurred, the nature of the problem, and quite possibly the procedure for resolving the problem. Unfortunately, error logs usually don't contain enough information to solve a problem, and you must consult documentation to diagnose and resolve it. However, error logging is very important because it can help you determine when the problem occurred, what might have caused the problem, and what other processes are affected by this problem. Often, error displays signal a visual alert of the problem and log the error into the error log for future reference. Many entries in the error log are not critical-stop errors. Some entries are warnings that do not currently indicate a problem but are worthy of your attention. Other entries, such as those indicating when the computer was restarted or when a service started or stopped, are purely informative.

Microsoft Windows NT Server and Workstation each have an error log mechanism called Event Viewer that is critical to the diagnosis and resolution of problems. It is recommended that you consult Event Viewer during the troubleshooting process, being cognizant of critical, red-stop error entries that have occurred.

The Event Viewer is an application that reads the binary log files. The log you open depends on the type of items you need to view:

- The *System log* contains events that are provided by the Windows NT internal services and drivers.

- The *Security log* contains all security-related events when auditing has been enabled.

- The *Application log* contains events that have been generated by applications.

EXERCISE 13-2

Checking Event Viewer

If you are having a problem with an application on a Windows 2000 PC, you can check Event Viewer to see what errors are being generated by the application. Do the following:

1. Select **Start | Programs | Administrative Tools** and select **Event Viewer**.

2. The Event Viewer window opens and shows the various logs in the left pane and the contents of the selected log in the right pane. In the left pane, select **Application Log**.

3. View the contents of the right pane to see what application errors have occurred.

Performance Monitors

Network Monitor is an outstanding tool for monitoring your system's network performance. Network Monitor that comes with Windows NT Server displays only the frames that are sent to or from your system. It does not monitor your entire network segment. To monitor the entire segment, you need to use the version of Network Monitor that comes with Systems Management Server (SMS).

Another useful tool is Performance Monitor, which is Performance Logs and Alerts in the Windows 2000 OS. Performance Monitor tracks system component and application resource use. Tracking different components of your system can help you see what is degrading performance. You can use Performance Monitor for a variety of reasons, including the following:

- Identifying bottlenecks in CPU, memory, disk I/O, or network I/O
- Identifying trends over a period of time
- Monitoring real-time system performance
- Monitoring system performance history
- Determining the system's capacity
- Monitoring system configuration changes

CERTIFICATION OBJECTIVE 13.05

Network Troubleshooting Resources

Once you have determined the cause of your network problems, the battle is only half over. You still have to figure out how to fix the problem. In many cases, the solution, such as replacing a bad cable, might be obvious. However, in other cases, additional solutions could be required. Resources are available to help in your search for the solution to your problems. Let's look at a few of those resources now.

TechNet

TechNet is a Microsoft product that is distributed on a monthly basis. TechNet is a searchable database of all Microsoft's articles and documentation on nearly all its products. Because there is a really good chance that someone else has already had the same problem that you are having, TechNet is likely to contain some documentation about how they solved the problem that can help you solve yours.

Manufacturer Web Sites

The World Wide Web has simplified network troubleshooting tenfold. The Web enables us to find up-to-the-minute information on both hardware and software. If you are having a problem with a NIC that is not properly communicating on the network, a good place to start is the Web site of the NIC's manufacturer. Most sites provide troubleshooting information, suggested steps to resolve common problems, phone numbers via which you can contact technical support, and the latest updated drivers. Figure 13-1 illustrates the Microsoft Technical Support Web site's interface.

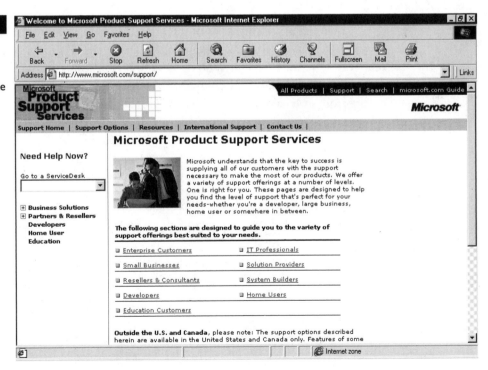

FIGURE 13-1

The Microsoft Technical Support Web site

Resource Kits and Documentation

Resource kits are a wealth of information about your operating system that provide technical information that is not available anywhere else. Resource kits contain additional documentation on your operating system that was too comprehensive to cover in the standard documentation. Whenever you are faced with a problem that you cannot solve, check the resource kit—your problem could already have been solved.

Trade Publications and White Papers

Other excellent sources of information are trade publications and white papers. These documents provide valuable information on current techniques and new practices that cannot be acquired anywhere else. In the event of actual network problems, these publications will probably be of little direct use to you, but the information you absorb over time from reading them will become one of your greatest tools.

Telephone Technical Support

Often, after you have exhausted your resources—vendor Web sites, resource kits, and documentation—it is common to open up a technical support incident with the vendor to solve the problem. Who is better to solve your problem than highly skilled technicians who work for the company that makes your equipment and who field similar requests on a daily basis? Chances are, the support personnel have already encountered the specific problem with their own software or hardware and have documented fixes. A problem that boggles you could be a very common tech support call for these professionals.

To improve the speed and accuracy of your technical support incident, make sure you have the following ready to assist the support technician when you call:

■ Hardware and software environment information, such as the operating system you are running

■ Version numbers of affected hardware or software

■ Serial numbers

■ Detailed account of the problem

■ Troubleshooting steps taken so far and their results

■ Contract number for your maintenance contract

Vendor CDs

Vendor-provided CDs that come with hardware and software are very important references for installation, configuration, and troubleshooting. Many technicians overlook these CDs and spend countless hours troubleshooting on their own or head straight to the phone for technical support. These CDs should be the first consultation, even before the product is installed, because usually the CDs provide preinstallation tips and warnings that are critical for a smooth installation. A vendor-provided CD also can include a technical information base, similar to Microsoft's TechNet, with a number of problems and their resolutions. Other CDs have tutorials, documentation, and software patches. Whatever these CDs contain, they should not be overlooked, whether you are planning to implement, support, or troubleshoot the product.

CERTIFICATION OBJECTIVE 13.06

Other Symptoms and Causes of Network Problems

It sounds obvious, but you need to closely examine the symptoms of a network problem in order to determine the cause. Now that you have seen the various causes for network problems, let's look at some network-related problem scenarios and the appropriate solutions.

You've seen some examples of the most common problems you will encounter in your networking professional journey. You are beginning to see that the same problems will continue to arise, but the causes and solutions could be a bit different.

Recognizing Abnormal Physical Conditions

The key to recognizing abnormal physical conditions on the network is knowing what a *normal* physical condition is. Such a condition could be different from one network to another. For example, it could take your network only three seconds to spool up a print document, but it could take another network one minute to spool up a document of the same size. This doesn't mean that the second network has a

SCENARIO & SOLUTION

I cannot connect to a computer on a remote network.	This sounds like a routing issue. Check to see if you can connect to a computer on your local network. If you can connect, try to PING the router or another host on the remote network. You need to determine whether the host or the link to the host is down.
No one can communicate on the entire network.	If this is a coax-based network, make sure that the bus has not been accidentally segmented, meaning that a connection came loose somewhere. If this is a twisted-pair network, ensure that the hub is operational. If this is a Token Ring network, make sure a computer is not beaconing, indicating a problem.
It takes way too long to connect to a network resource.	Make sure that the network is not being overloaded. Most network devices, such as hubs and routers, display a percentage of bandwidth being used; check this display to determine if the network is not being saturated. You can also use network monitor software to do the same thing. You should also determine who and what is being affected. Maybe you are experiencing a broadcast storm on one segment and not another.
A domain controller cannot be found.	Is anyone else receiving this error? This is most commonly a local workstation issue, either with an incorrect TCP/IP configuration or a problem with the network adapter or cable. Ensure that the network card has a link light and the cable is firmly plugged in. You should also try replacing the cable to the workstation.
A device in my system is not functioning and I can't connect to the network.	This sounds like a network card configuration error. Make sure that the NIC is configured correctly. Be sure to use a free IRQ and I/O address when configuring the card. In addition, the driver might not have loaded correctly. What has changed since this adapter worked correctly?

SCENARIO & SOLUTION

No one in this department can communicate, but other departments can.	Make sure that the hub is not locked up. Resetting the hub usually fixes this problem. Sometimes an incorrectly configured network adapter causes it. The speed of the network card is usually incorrectly set differently from other cards on the network. For example, a Token Ring network can use speeds of 4MB per second or 16MB per second. If a workstation is set to 4MB and the entire network is set to 16MB, the network could go down. On an Ethernet network, setting a NIC to 10 Mbps on a 100 Mbps network could cause the network to lock up.
No one can access the Internet.	This problem can be caused by many things, but make sure that there is no problem with the Internet gateway, if you are using one; this gateway is a computer that acts as an intermediary between the Internet and your local intranet. This problem also could be a routing issue if you are using a dedicated connection to the Internet. Verify that the router or gateway is functional and try PINGing key computers on remote networks and the Internet.
I can't reach the mainframe using its hostname.	Make sure that you are not having a name resolution problem. Did this problem just start occurring? Test for connectivity by PINGing the host. If you can connect to the host using an IP address instead, you definitely have a name resolution problem. If you can't connect with an IP address, try PINGing another computer on that network. Maybe you are having routing problems.
Our Token Ring network suddenly locked up.	Someone on the network is beaconing. Therefore, the nearest active upstream neighbor (NAUN) is having a problem. The network cannot continue until the problem is fixed. Sometimes the problem is because a bridge locks up, too.

problem; it could be merely a normal physical condition for that network. The following are things to look for when you attempt to determine whether an abnormal condition is occurring on your network:

■ Printing takes longer

■ Authentication takes longer

■ You are receiving more errors than usual.

■ Connecting to remote resources takes longer, if you can connect at all

■ You are losing connections to resources

■ Network applications are not running

To determine if these situations are abnormal occurrences on your network, you need to ask yourself a few questions:

■ How many users are affected by this problem?

■ Is the problem consistent?

■ Is the problem replicable?

■ Was there a recent upgrade to the network or computer?

■ Has any of the equipment been moved?

■ Have we encountered this problem before?

■ Has anyone else attempted to fix the problem?

■ How many applications is this problem affecting?

■ Are there new users or computers on the network?

■ Is this a busy or congested time of day?

■ Which products are involved?

Your mind should be going at top speed, thinking of what could have contributed to the problem. With knowledge of what constitutes a normal network environment, you can determine rather quickly what is not normal.

Isolating and Correcting Problems in the Physical Media

Experienced network administrators know that cabling is one of the most common causes of network failure. For this reason, you should check cabling first during your network troubleshooting process. Most often the cable that is damaged is the cable from the workstation to the wall jack. This cable receives the most abuse. Sometimes you can fix the problem by simply plugging the cable back in, if it has become loose or fallen out.

If you have determined that a cable could be the culprit of a network-related problem, the most logical step is to test your hypothesis by replacing the cable with a known good cable. The results are simple to assess: If you can communicate once again, the old cable was bad. If you cannot communicate again, you need to continue troubleshooting or find another cable to test.

There are devices you can use to determine whether cables have gone bad, but these devices can be expensive. Most of the time you can swap out the cables to determine if cables are bad.

Table 13-2 is a listing of some common cable-related problems and their solutions.

exam
ⓦatch

The information in the preceding section is important for the exam. Make sure that you know the symptoms of cable problems and how to correct them.

TABLE 13-2   The Most Common Cabling-Related Network Problems and Their Solutions

Cable Problem	Likely Solution
None of the workstations on the network are able to communicate with each other. They use a thinwire coax Ethernet to connect to each other.	The backbone has been severed. Find the point at which the bus became severed and reconnect it.
You have a brand-new UTP cable, but the workstation is still not able to communicate on the network. The workstation worked with your test cable.	The brand-new UTP cable might be a crossover cable. Obtain a regular UTP cable.
A workstation was just moved to a new location and is no longer able to communicate on the network. There is nothing wrong with the workstation's configuration.	Cables were damaged in the move. Replace each cable one at a time to find the problematic cable.

Checking the Status of Servers

A great many network administrators don't take enough time to check the status of their servers. Checking server status is critical because servers can be plagued with ongoing problems that are not so obvious, and if the problems are not corrected, they can become worse. There are many ways to continually monitor the status of your servers, and each is operating-system specific. Some general monitoring tasks are listed here:

- Check error logs
- Check services
- Verify connectivity
- Monitor the performance and the network
- Verify backup logs, including test restores
- Test alerts

The error logs can give you an indication of a failed device or service and a good idea of how to fix the problem. The errors listed vary from critical to informational. Some errors, such as a service failing to start, warrant immediate action. A service failing to start can be critical, and it often has dependencies that require the running of another service in order for the services themselves to run.

At one job I had, every Monday I had to check the Event Viewer logs on the Windows NT servers for possible errors of which we were not aware. It was a tedious task, but you would not believe how many problems we uncovered by inspecting the error logs. I recommend you do the same.

You can test for connectivity with a server using utilities such as PING to determine if the server is responding to network requests.

Performance and network monitoring can determine if the server is overloaded or is broadcasting unnecessarily. An overloaded server can increase the length of time needed to fulfill network requests.

If you are backing up a server, which is always recommended, you need to verify that the backups have finished successfully. This is imperative because in the event of an emergency you will need to recover data from the backup tapes. You must also do test restores to make sure that the data can be restored correctly and that you understand the restore process. A disaster is the worst time to discover that your backup routine hasn't been working correctly.

Finally, you can configure your server to send alerts to specific computers or users in the event of emergencies or when the system encounters thresholds that you have predefined. A *threshold* is a peak in the rate of activity, about which you would like to be notified so that you can correct the situation. Setting thresholds includes baselining your system so that you know the normal rate of activity.

Checking for Configuration Problems

When you are bringing a new server online or configuring a server with a new service such as DNS or WINS, it is imperative that you begin on the right foot by verifying that the configuration is correct. Often, you will incorrectly configure a server and it will continually deteriorate the server or the server will not work at all. You must make sure that the base operating system, such as TCP/IP, networking, error logs, and memory allocation, is configured correctly. You also have to correctly configure the additional services that will run on top of the operating system. You will frequently have an application or database server that also runs a backup service, such as ARCserve or Backup Exec. When you are configuring the backup server, you might have to reboot the machine for changes to take effect. This means downing a critical server for a few minutes, thus breaking connections with all users and services that are currently using that machine. You might have to do this during off-hours; be very careful about configuring services for mission-critical machines during business hours.

It is very important that the following services be correctly configured, because they have the capability to affect the entire network, not just the local server, which is a catastrophe waiting to happen: DNS, WINS, and the HOSTS file.

DNS

Configuring DNS requires planning. You need to gather the following information prior to installing the service:

- Your domain name
- The IP address of each server for which you want to provide name resolution
- The hostname of each server

This information must be correct; otherwise, your network will experience ongoing name resolution problems that will be difficult to diagnose. This is especially the case with hostname-to-IP address mappings. DNS entries can be entered manually, so you must be very careful not to enter a wrong IP address or hostname. You will not be prompted with an error message informing you that you have entered an incorrect IP address.

WINS

WINS is another service that can run over the base operating system. WINS is much like DNS in that it provides name resolution; however, DNS resolves hostnames to IP addresses, and WINS resolves NetBIOS names to IP addresses. Unlike some DNS, WINS does not require you to manually enter mappings before you begin. This is because WINS is a dynamic service that can add, modify, and delete mappings dynamically, saving valuable time for the network administrator. At times you will want to add a static mapping for important clients or servers.

WINS, like DNS, has many configuration possibilities, but most WINS configuration parameters will not be covered on your Network+ exam. A few of the WINS configuration settings are the duration of the client renewal and extinction of names as well as the replication partners with which this WINS server will replicate. You can strategically replicate with other WINS servers based on frequency and location.

The HOSTS File

As you have learned, when you use DNS you must manually add hostname-to-IP address mappings in order to resolve hostnames. With the HOSTS file, you also have to manually configure a database with these exact mappings. Unlike DNS, which uses a centrally located database of hostname mappings, the HOSTS file resides on every computer. This makes the process of updating the HOSTS file very difficult. The HOSTS file is usually located under the Windows directory (WINDOWS or WINNT) and then system32\drivers\etc. The default location can be changed in the registry, but usually people don't move it.

All the DNS rules apply to the HOSTS file: You must be very careful to enter the correct host-name-to-IP-address mappings. A helpful tip for configuring the HOSTS file is to copy to the remaining hosts the newly created file that you have guaranteed to be accurate. This step ensures that you don't make any more clerical errors on each of the remaining machines.

e x a m

ⓦa t c h

Make sure that you know the definition of WINS, DNS, the HOSTS file, and the LMHOSTS file. You won't be expected to know any in-depth information about each, just the purpose for each. For more information, review Chapter 4, "TCP/IP Fundamentals."

Checking for Viruses

If you have ever been a network administrator in the midst of a virus attack, you know how frustrating the situation can be. Once the virus gets in from the outside, whether from the Internet, a user's home computer, or from the local intranet, it poses a huge problem. But how can you eradicate the viruses before they come into the network? A server running a virus-scanning program can make all the difference in applying "preventive maintenance."

Many companies engage in multipronged attacks against viruses, including continually scanning for viruses on the file and messaging servers and installing virus-scanning software on every workstation. Both precautions are critical for stopping the spread of viruses. The server can catch viruses coming in from the messaging servers, such as Microsoft Exchange, and from files stored on the file servers. The workstation virus-scanning programs can catch viruses on users' machines before they get a chance to replicate to the servers and to other users' computers on the network. In any case, the virus-definition files must be updated on a continual basis. Many virus-scanning utilities enable workstations to automatically update the virus definition files from a central server, which means you, the network administrator, do not have to visit every workstation once a month to apply the new definition files.

Checking the Validity of the Account Name and Password

Usually you configure services or applications to log on with a certain account in order to perform their functions. The services usually use the built-in system account, but if the service requires logging in to a remote computer, it requires an account name and password. Some services require administrative privileges or membership in certain groups on the network to accomplish their tasks. You must document these special system and service accounts and remember not to delete or tamper with their accounts in any way. If you mistakenly disable, delete, or affect the account details, you could find yourself with a service that fails to start—a problem is often very difficult to diagnose.

I have seen network administrators install applications and specify their own administrator account for the service to use. When the network administrator leaves the company, his account is disabled or deleted, and, mysteriously, some of the programs fail. If the other members of the department were not aware of this configuration, they could be scratching their heads for days wondering why this program or service will not work anymore.

Rechecking Operator Logon Procedures

The most obvious problems often involve logging on. The ordinary user is not nearly as computer savvy as you are; even the process of logging on can boggle such a person. You usually have a number of domains you can log on to. If a user mistakenly tries to log on to a domain in which he doesn't have an account, he will be denied, and he will call you, the network administrator. Users often forget their passwords or the fact that the password is case sensitive. After three strikes (or however many times you have configured the system to accept guesses), the user will be locked out and disgruntled, and her next step will be to phone you.

Sometimes users return from vacation to find that their accounts have been disabled or their passwords have expired. You need to intervene to correct the situation.

Figure 13-2 illustrates the user password information in Windows NT.

Selecting and Running Appropriate Diagnostics

To build a strong network, you need to run diagnostics to determine bottlenecks or problematic situations. These diagnostics may reveal problems or limitations that you can fix before they get too bad.

You need to choose diagnostic programs that correlate with your specific network needs. For example, you can purchase extensive protocol-analyzing and packet-sniffing products, but they would be an overkill for a 20-node network. Often the free diagnostic products, such as Performance Monitor and Network Monitor, are capable of determining computer and network problems.

Whichever tool you choose, you must spend plenty of time with the product to determine the most effective way to deploy it. You must also be trained to analyze the results and determine what needs to be adjusted in order to remedy the situation. It will take more than one trial to establish a reliable baseline of activity for your testing.

FIGURE 13-2

Configuring user accounts in Microsoft Windows NT User Manager for domains

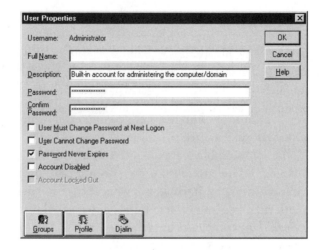

For example, running the diagnostics at 8:00 AM, when all the users are logging on, gives entirely different results from running the diagnostics at noon, when everyone is at lunch. Taking snapshots of activity from various periods of the day, week, and month gives you the most accurate assessment of your network. The longer you spend baselining your network, the more accurate the results. From there, you can begin assigning thresholds to chart and alert for abnormal activity. Furthermore, you are training yourself to read the various diagnostics so you can quickly determine how, why, and where a problem is occurring. The following section gives you more examples of devices that can help you troubleshoot your network.

CERTIFICATION OBJECTIVE 13.07

Network Tools

In most network troubleshooting sessions, there is a time at which a simple isolation of problems is just not feasible. In that situation, it's time to use some electronic tools to determine your problem and its source. This section discusses the most common network tools and how they are used.

Crossover Cables

A *crossover cable* appears to be just another twisted-pair cable, but two wires are crossed, which makes the cable not fit for plugging into a computer and a hub for normal use. The crossover cable is used to directly connect two computers to each other, without the use of a hub. To connect the two computers, you must use a small, inexpensive hub that both computers plug into or go directly through the crossover cable to each computer.

A crossover cable is also used to connect hubs in the event you need to cascade hubs. If you were to substitute a crossover cable for a regular twisted-pair cable to connect two hubs, it would not work correctly. Therefore, it is important that you mark your crossover cables or use a different color cable to designate a crossover cable. Many companies use yellow or black cables for regular cables and blue for crossover cables. You will not need many crossover cables, and you can make them yourself if you have the correct pinout.

Hardware Loopback

A *hardware loopback adapter* is a way to test the ports on a system without having to connect to an external device. For example, you can use a serial loopback adapter to verify that a transmitted signal is leaving your serial port and returning through the loopback adapter, ensuring that your serial port is working correctly.

Tone Generators

A *tone generator* is used to perform tests on phone and network lines in what is referred to as a *fox and hound* process. The device clips to a wire, terminal panel, or standard modular jack and aids in the identification of wires during the wire-tracing process. You begin by attaching the "fox" to the cable, jack, or panel that you would like to trace, and you continue with the "hound" on the other end of the cable to find the fox's tone. When you find the tone, you know that you have correctly tracked the cable. This is very helpful for determining which cable in a group of many cables, such as a wiring closet, has gone bad and needs to be replaced.

Time Division Reflectometers

A *time domain reflectometer (TDR)* sends a signal down the cable, where it is reflected at some point. The TDR then calculates the distance down the cable that the signal traveled before being reflected by measuring the amount of time it took for the signal to be returned. If this distance is less than your overall cable length, a cable problem exists at that distance from your location. (Yes, this means that it is in the most inconvenient location possible. It is a law of networking that when something breaks, it will be in the worst possible place to fix it.)

Oscilloscopes

An *oscilloscope* can determine when there are shorts, crimps, or attenuation in a cable. An oscilloscope formats its output in a graphical format. Oscilloscopes are commonly used to test cables that have been recently run through walls to ensure there are no problems with the cables before you use them.

Network Monitors and Protocol Analyzers

Network monitors and protocol analyzers monitor traffic on a network and display the packets that have been transmitted across it. If a particular type of packet is not being transmitted across the network, your problem could lie with that particular packet type. Note that a network monitor enables you to view the contents of *all* packets on the network. In many cases, viewing the contents of these packets is considered unethical or even illegal. Figure 13-3 shows some data obtained using the Microsoft Network Monitor utility.

CERTIFICATION OBJECTIVE 13.08

Selecting Appropriate Tools to Resolve Network Problems

You have seen the tools available for troubleshooting a network; now you'll learn the appropriate time to use each tool. Each of the following scenarios describes a

FIGURE 13-3

Capturing
network data
with Microsoft's
Network
Monitor

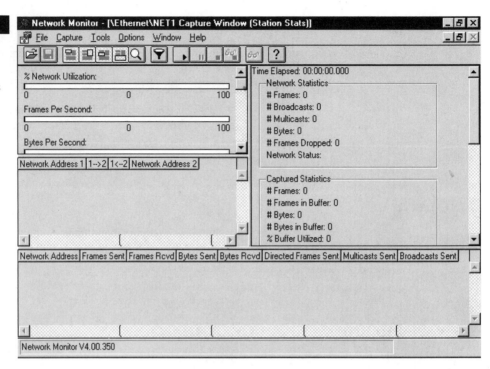

symptom of a network problem and then gives the likely tool to use to solve the
problem or to help gather additional information about it.

SCENARIO & SOLUTION

I need to create a baseline of network performance.	This is a job for Network Monitor or a similar product that can determine trends on the network and calculate the average utilization to provide a baseline of network activity. Use this baseline to determine if an abnormal network situation is occurring.
I have a cable that appears to be broken somewhere.	Use a TDR or an oscilloscope to find the exact spot where the cable is broken. If you don't have access to such a tool, you might be able to replace the cable without determining the exact area of breakage. However, it might be helpful to call in a networking company with access to a TDR or oscilloscope if the cable is long and the network is complex.

SCENARIO & SOLUTION

I need to find one end of a wire in a giant bundle of wires.	Definitely use a tone generator. Without it, it's virtually impossible to know which cable is the cable that you have singled out on the other end of a bundle of cables.
I need to look at the packets as they travel the network.	Use Network Monitor. It has the capability to capture packets so that you can analyze them.
I need to add another hub to increase the number of ports.	You can use a crossover cable to connect two hubs to each other. This is often helpful when you are adding a hub to a zone to increase the number of available ports.
I need to determine a baseline for my computer.	Use Performance Monitor. This tool is perfect for finding trends on your local computer. It can also be used to determine network-related information, such as the number of bytes sent and received.

CERTIFICATION SUMMARY

In this chapter you have learned quite a lot that will not only help you on the Network+ exam but has given you a troubleshooting methodology that you will use for the rest of your career. You have learned the general model for troubleshooting, which involves establishing the problem symptoms, identifying the affected area of the network, determining what has changed, selecting the most probable cause, implementing a solution, testing the result, recognizing possible side effects of the solution, and documenting the solution.

You have learned to ask yourself questions such as these:

- Does the problem exist across the network?
- Is this a workstation, workgroup, LAN, or WAN problem?
- Is the problem consistent and replicable?

You have learned the physical and logical indicators of network problems, such as link, collision, and power lights and error messages and error logs, which give you a good indication of the problem that is occurring.

You have discovered network troubleshooting resources such as TechNet, manufacturers' Web sites, and vender CDs. Each of these resources is invaluable for solving network problems; they are highly recommended.

Finally, you have learned about the various network tools that are available to you to obtain more information about the problem, to solve the problem, or simply to make your networking life a little bit easier.

With the lessons you have learned here, you should be on your way to becoming an invaluable network troubleshooting resource for your company. With experience in solving network problems, you will add more and more to your network troubleshooting repertoire, and you will be appreciated and sought out by your peers to help them with their network problems!

✓ TWO-MINUTE DRILL

Managing Network Problems

❏ Learning how each device coexists and contributes to the network will provide you with a strong foundation for understanding how and why network-related problems occur and how to resolve them.

❏ When you first encounter a problem, it is very important to determine its symptoms.

❏ You need to determine whether the problem is a workstation, workgroup, LAN, or WAN.

❏ Determine if the problem is consistent and replicable.

❏ It is very important to isolate the subsystem involved with the problem process.

Troubleshooting Network Problems

❏ When you troubleshoot network problems, it is important to follow a logical troubleshooting methodology.

❏ Having others troubleshoot the problem as a team will give you many different perspectives and theories as to the cause of the problem.

❏ Sometimes it is possible to recreate the problem, learning exactly why and how the problem occurred.

❏ The most important step of network troubleshooting is isolating the problem.

❏ Often there is more than one way to correct a problem, each with its own set of related issues and consequences.

System or Operator Problems

❏ In some cases, it is very apparent whether a system or operator error has occurred.

Checking Physical and Logical Indicators

❏ When you begin troubleshooting a network-related problem, you have several indicators available that will help you determine the problem.

❏ Link lights are invaluable in determining if a network connection is present.

❏ Collision lights can help determine if a network element has failed and is causing chatter.

❏ Even more rudimentary in the network troubleshooting area than the link light is the power light.

❏ An error display is a means of alerting you to a malfunction or failure in a device.

❏ Similar to the error display is the error log, which maintains a listing of errors encountered.

❏ Network Monitor is an outstanding tool for monitoring the network performance of your system.

❏ Performance Monitor tracks the use of resources by the system components and applications.

Network Troubleshooting Resources

❏ There are some resources available to help in your search for the solution to your problems. For instance, TechNet is a searchable database of all Microsoft articles and documentation on nearly all its products.

❏ The Web enables us to find up-to-the-minute information on both hardware and software.

❏ Resource kits are a wealth of information about your operating system that provide technical information that is not available anywhere else.

❏ Other excellent sources of information are trade publications and white papers.

❏ It is common to open up a technical support incident with the vendor to solve a problem.

❏ Vendor-provided CDs that come with hardware and software are very important references for installation, configuration, and troubleshooting.

Other Symptoms and Causes of Network Problems

❑ Experienced network administrators know that cabling is one of the most common causes of network failure.

❑ Make sure that you know the symptoms of cable problems and how to correct them.

❑ There are many ways to continually monitor the status of your servers, and each is operating-system specific.

❑ When you are bringing a new server online or configuring a server with a new service such as DNS or WINS, it is imperative that you begin on the right foot by verifying that the configuration is correct.

❑ Make sure that you know the definition of WINS, DNS, the HOSTS file, and the LMHOSTS file. You won't be expected to know any in-depth information about each, just the purpose of each. For more information, review Chapter 4, "TCP/IP Fundamentals."

❑ A server running a virus-scanning program can make all the difference in keeping viruses out of your network.

Network Tools

❑ To build a strong network, you need to run diagnostics to determine bottlenecks or problematic situations.

❑ A hardware loopback adapter is a way to test the ports on a system without having to connect to an external device.

❑ A TDR is a device that sends an electronic pulse down a cable. The pulse then travels until it is reflected back and the distance traveled is calculated. This process is similar to the way sonar works.

❑ An *oscilloscope* can determine when there are shorts, crimps, or attenuation in a cable.

❑ Network monitors and protocol analyzers monitor traffic on the network and display the packets that have been transmitted across it.

Selecting Appropriate Tools to Resolve Network Problems

❑ You need to know each network tool and how it can be used in troubleshooting the network.

SELF TEST

The following Self Test questions will help you measure your understanding of the material presented in this chapter. Read all the choices carefully because there might be more than one correct answer. Choose all correct answers for each question.

Managing Network Problems

1. A few computers on the engineering segment are having problems reaching the AutoCAD design segment on the network, but they can access all other segments. What is your initial diagnosis of the problem?

    A. It's a default gateway issue.

    B. It's a routing issue.

    C. The computers are having cable problems.

    D. A hub is locked up.

2. All users on a coaxial bus topology network have suddenly complained that the network is not functioning and they can no longer access resources on the local or remote networks. What is your initial diagnosis of the problem?

    A. It's a routing issue.

    B. It's a default gateway issue.

    C. The network is no longer terminated.

    D. A hub is locked up.

3. You think you are having problems with the UNIX server in another region. Two users have already complained this morning. What would be the next logical step in your troubleshooting methodology?

    A. Check the router.

    B. Check the hub.

    C. PING the UNIX server by name.

    D. PING the UNIX server by IP address.

4. You have a workstation that you moved from one cubicle to another. Nothing on the workstation was changed, but the computer refuses to connect to the network. Which of the following is a likely cause?

A. The network drop has not been activated in the wiring closet.

B. The cable was damaged in the move.

C. The TCP/IP configuration is incorrect.

D. The network adapter was damaged in the move.

Troubleshooting Network Problems

5. You are experiencing problems on a coax bus network. How can you quickly determine where the problem is occurring?

A. Divide the network in half, terminate it, and find which side is still not functioning. That is the affected area. Continue this process until the break is found.

B. Use a network packet sniffer to determine where the packets eventually stop responding. This will tell you which computer is the closest to the break.

C. Use a fox-and-hound process to determine the location of the break in the network backbone.

D. Use Network Monitor to determine what is causing the broadcast storm. One computer's faulty network card is the likely culprit and must be found.

System or Operator Problems

6. Steve, a user on your network, just got back from a two-week vacation. He calls you first thing Monday morning. Which of the following is most likely the reason for Steve's call?

A. He forgot his password.

B. His account has been disabled.

C. His password has expired.

D. A co-worker changed Steve's password while he was on vacation.

Checking Physical and Logical Indicators

7. You came to work on Monday morning only to notice that you are having network problems. Your domain controller, which also functions as a database server, appears to be having problems. How can you further investigate the situation?

   A. Check the error log.

   B. PING the server to see if it responds.

   C. Run diagnostics on the server.

   D. Restart the computer and then begin troubleshooting.

8. You have made system configuration changes to one of your servers. How can you tell if the changes have made a difference?

   A. Watch the server closely for a few hours, especially during peak usage.

   B. Run Network Monitor to perform an assessment of the current system activity and compare that with your previous baseline, taken before the configuration change took place.

   C. Run Performance Monitor to perform an assessment of the current system activity and compare that with your previous baseline, taken before the configuration change took place.

   D. Check the Event Viewer for errors, warnings, or any indicators that system degradation has occurred.

9. Which of the following is the most reliable indicator that a network server could be overloaded?

   A. The activity light on the network card is constantly lit.

   B. Performance Monitor shows network requests are backing up in the queue.

   C. Network Monitor shows too many packets are leaving this server.

   D. The computer is very slow to respond when you log on.

10. Which of the following is *not* a good recommendation when it comes to performing a baseline of your network?

   A. Monitor traffic at different times of the day.

   B. Configure the snapshots to take place at midnight each night.

   C. Monitor traffic for days, even weeks.

   D. Take as many traffic snapshots as possible.

Network Troubleshooting Resources

11. You feel you are having driver incompatibility problems with your network adapter. What is the best resource for finding another network adapter driver?

    A. TechNet

    B. Resource kit

    C. Vender Web site

    D. Documentation CD

12. You are instructed to migrate the DHCP service from a Windows NT 4.0 server to a Windows 2000 server. What is the best resource to begin preparing for the migration?

    A. A Windows magazine

    B. Telephone tech support

    C. Vendor CDs

    D. Resource kits

13. You are experiencing lockup problems with a new version of the virus-scanning utility that you just implemented. Which of the following is probably not needed when you open a technical support incident?

    A. The version of affected software or hardware

    B. The number of users on the network

    C. Troubleshooting steps taken so far and their results

    D. Current operating system

14. You have a user receiving the error message, "A domain controller cannot be found." Assuming that no one else has called you with this error, which of the following is *not* likely to be the problem?

    A. The TCP/IP configuration is not correct on the computer.

    B. The domain controller could be down.

    C. The network card is not functioning correctly.

    D. A cable might be faulty or not plugged in.

15. Which of the following is *not* likely to be an abnormal condition on a network?

    A. It takes a long time to print a large document that contains images.

    B. It takes longer to become authenticated.

    C. Users are having problems connecting to the SQL database.

    D. You continually lose connection to the mainframe.

16. Which of the following will you *not* need prior to installing DNS?

    A. The DHCP address scope

    B. Your domain name

    C. The hostnames of each server

    D. The IP address of each server for which you want to provide name resolution

17. Which of the following is *not* true regarding WINS?

    A. It resolves NetBIOS names to IP addresses.

    B. You must replicate with all other WINS servers.

    C. You must manually enter the address mappings.

    D. WINS dynamically updates the WINS database.

Network Tools

18. How can you eliminate complicated cable problems in your troubleshooting process?

    A. Visually inspect the cables.

    B. Use a "fox and hound" to find cables in a tangled mess.

    C. Examine cables with a TDR to find any problems.

    D. Swap suspect cables with known good cables.

19. What is the best tool to determine where a break has occurred in a cable?

    A. A tone generator

    B. A spectrum division analyzer

    C. A time domain reflectometer

    D. A fox and hound

LAB QUESTION

This lab might seem a bit backward, but take a network like the one shown in Figure 13-4. Assume that Router B fails. What kind of problem exists, and how can the problem be resolved without fixing Router B?

FIGURE 13-4 Network model for Lab Question

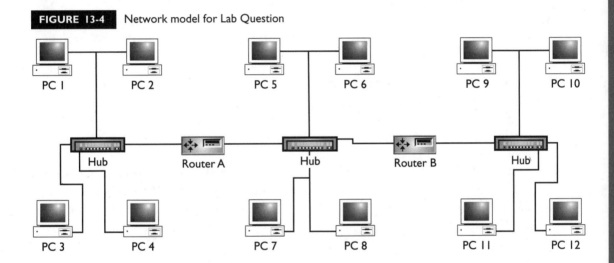

SELF TEST ANSWERS

Managing Network Problems

1. ☑ **B.** It's a routing issue. If you have a very good understanding of routers and routing, and one segment of your network cannot communicate with another segment, you will immediately know that there is a problem with routing—possibly a router is malfunctioning.
   ☒ **A, C,** and **D** are incorrect. Segments are usually created by routers or bridges, and one of these will be the issue when one segment has problems contacting another. Default gateways are used to connect to the gateway or router that is used to contact other segments. Since some segments in the question can be contacted, the default gateway is fine. Since some PCs can be contacted, the hub is not locked up.

2. ☑ **C.** The network is no longer terminated. One segment of the network is not able to communicate with another segment; therefore, you should quickly determine that you have a routing problem. Another symptom is that everyone on the coaxial-based bus network is not able to communicate. The cause of this problem most likely lies with the network bus backbone, which requires terminators on each end.
   ☒ **A, B,** and **D** are incorrect. The terminator is a problem with bus networks and should be checked whenever the whole network is the issue. If none of the PCs on the local segment can be contacted, the problem is not a router or gateway. Hubs do not simply lock up, so this is not the issue.

3. ☑ **D.** PING the UNIX server by IP address. You can test the routing problem by trying to communicate with another computer on the corporate headquarters network. For example, you can PING another computer on this network or use a program that connects to a computer on this network. Name resolution is usually not an issue when using terminal-type programs. They usually use the IP address, not the name of the server, when contacting the server.
   ☒ **A, B,** and **C** are incorrect. PING allows you to determine whether the problem is the hub, a router, or another network device.

4. ☑ **A, C,** and **D.** The network drop was not activated, TCP/IP is not configured correctly, or the network adapter was damaged in the move. When new cable drops have been run, sometimes they are not correctly connected in the wiring closet to a hub and therefore will not allow connection to the network. If TCP/IP is statically configured, the configuration needs to be updated, especially if the PC is on a new segment. Sometimes cards or other PC hardware become damaged if proper care is not taken in handling the PC.
   ☒ **B** is incorrect because cables are not usually moved with a PC.

Troubleshooting Network Problems

5. ☑ **A.** Divide the network in half, terminate it, and find which side is still not functioning. The best example of this is in thinwire coax. Determine the midpoint of the cable and place a terminator on each end. One-half of the cable should now be working and is obviously not your problem. Repeat this step until you find the problem.

☒ **B, C,** and **D** are incorrect because using a sniffer or fox-and-hound tool would require about as much work, but moving the terminator would allow you to find the problem with no extra tool other than the terminator, which is readily available. These tools might not be available to all technicians. Network Monitors might not always determine which computer is causing the problem. If the problem is a cable and not a computer, Network Monitor will be no help.

System or Operator Problems

6. ☑ **A, B,** and **C.** He forgot his password, his account has been disabled, or his password has expired. You need to intervene to correct the situation.

☒ **D** is incorrect because a co-worker can not change Steve's password while he is on vacation.

Checking Physical and Logical Indicators

7. ☑ **A.** Check the error log. Error logs usually don't contain enough information to solve a problem, and documentation must be consulted to diagnose and resolve it. However, checking the error logs is very important because you can determine when the problem occurred, what might have caused the problem, and what other processes are affected by this problem.

☒ **B, C,** and **D** are incorrect. PINGing the server verifies that TCP/IP is running and functional on the server, and with no calls from users who are unable to contact the server, this is not an issue. Running diagnostics can help, but you are not sure what diagnostics to run. Diagnostics can be run on all the physical hardware, the database, or the network. Restarting the computer and troubleshooting the system still require you know where to start troubleshooting.

8. ☑ **C.** Run Performance Monitor to perform an assessment of the current system activity and compare that with your previous baseline, taken before the configuration change took place. Performance Monitor can be used for a variety of purposes, including the following: identifying bottlenecks in CPU, memory, disk I/O, or network I/O; identifying trends over a period of time; monitoring real-time system performance; monitoring system performance history; determining the capacity the system can handle; and monitoring system configuration changes.

☒ **A, B,** and **D** are incorrect. Visual inspection of system performance is not a very good measure. It is hard to visually determine CPU and hard disk performance as well as other system resources. Network Monitor does not show system degradation or problems. Event Viewer shows only system-generated errors, not performance issues from configuration changes.

9. ☑   **B.** Performance Monitor shows network requests are backing up in the queue. Performance and network monitoring can determine whether the server is overloaded or broadcasting unnecessarily. An overloaded server can increase the length of time needed to fulfill network requests.

   ☒   **A, C,** and **D** are incorrect. A constant network light shows that the network or even the server network card is overburdened. Network Monitor is used to check for an overburdened network, not a server. When logging on, if you do not give the system enough time to start, services could still be in the process of being loaded, which can cause slow logon issues but not mean that the server is overburdened.

10. ☑   **B.** Configure the snapshots to take place at midnight each night. Taking snapshots of activity from various periods of the day, week, and month gives you the most accurate assessment of your network. The longer you spend baselining your network, the more accurate the results. If you are taking network activity snapshots only at midnight, you are not getting an accurate assessment of the normal network activity that occurs throughout the day.

   ☒   **A, C,** and **D** are incorrect because they are all good recommendations.

Network Troubleshooting Resources

11. ☑   **C.** Vendor Web site. If you are having a problem with a NIC not properly communicating on the network, a good place to start is the Web site of the NIC's manufacturer. Most sites provide troubleshooting information, suggested steps to resolve common problems, phone numbers with which to contact technical support, and the latest updated drivers.

   ☒   **A, B,** and **D** are incorrect. TechNet offers specific issues dealing with the Microsoft Windows OSs and applications, not hardware drivers. Resource kits provide more information and tools for a software product. The documentation CD does not have the most up-to-date driver, if it contains drivers at all.

12. ☑   **D.** Resource kits. Resource kits contain additional operating system documentation that was too comprehensive to cover in the standard documentation. Whenever you are faced with a problem that you cannot solve, check the resource kit—your problem might already have been solved by someone else.

   ☒   **A, B,** and **C** are incorrect. Windows magazines have information on various topics, and it could require some searching to find an article on migration, if any exist in a specific magazine. Telephone tech support is for problematic issues, not migration strategies. Vendor CDs contain documentation and drivers for specific products.

13. ☑ **B.** You probably don't need the number of users on the network. To improve the speed and accuracy of your technical support incident, make sure that you have the following ready to assist the support technician: hardware and software environment details, such as the operating system you are running; version numbers of affected hardware or software; serial numbers; a detailed account of the problem; and troubleshooting steps taken so far and their results.

☒ **A, C,** and **D** are incorrect because they are needed for your session with tech support.

14. ☑ **B.** The domain controller could be down. If no one else is receiving this error message, it is probably a local workstation issue, either with an incorrect TCP/IP configuration or a problem with the network adapter or cable. Ensure that the network card has a link light and the cable is firmly plugged in. You should also try replacing the cable to the workstation.

☒ **A, C,** and **D** are incorrect because they are valid potential causes of the problem.

15. ☑ **A.** It takes a long time to print a large document that contains images. For example, it might take your network only three seconds to spool up a print document, but it could take another network one minute to spool up a document of the same size. This doesn't mean the second network has a problem; it could be a normal physical condition for their network.

☒ **B, C,** and **D** are incorrect. Authentication is a process that requires information sent to a server for verification, which could take awhile if the network is busy. This is a common problem in the morning, when many users are attempting to log on at the same time. Sometimes portions of a database can be locked out when one user is updating the information. Mainframes can cause issues; users being kicked off the mainframe can be a common occurrence at those times.

16. ☑ **A.** The DHCP address scope. You need to gather information prior to installing the service. This information includes your domain name, the IP address of each server for which you want to provide name resolution, and the hostname of each server. Otherwise, you will not know how to configure the service for proper use on your network.

☒ **B, C,** and **D** are incorrect because they are all needed to install the DNS Service.

17. ☑ **B** and **C.** WINS does not require replication with all other WINS servers. You must manually enter the address mappings. A few of the WINS configuration settings are the duration of the client renewal and extinction of names and the replication partners with which this WINS server replicates. You can strategically replicate with other WINS servers based on frequency and location.

☒ **A** and **D** are incorrect. WINS does resolve NetBIOS names to IP addresses. The WINS database is dynamically managed by WINS.

Network Tools

18. ☑   C. Eliminate complicated cable problems by examining cables with a TDR to find any problems.
     ☒   A, B, and D are incorrect. Visually inspecting a cable cannot determine whether the cable is faulty. You need more advanced tools to determine if a cable is faulty. Using tools saves time and money if you catch a potentially faulty cable before it is put into production.

19. ☑   C. A time domain reflectometer. Use a TDR or an oscilloscope to find the exact spot where the cable is broken. If you don't have access to such a tool, you might be able to replace the cable without determining the exact area of breakage.
     ☒   A, B, and D are incorrect. A tone generator is used to determine the two ends of a specific cable within a large bulk of cables. A spectrum division analyzer is used with fiber-optic cables to determine its quality. A fox and hound is the same as a tone generator.

LAB ANSWER

The problem that exists is that PCs 1 through 8 are not able to connect to PCs 9 through 12. PCs 1 through 8 are able to connect to one another, and PCs 9 through 12 are able to connect with each another.

To fix the problem, the simplest is to fix Router B. For redundancy, the hub for PCs 1 through 4 can be connected to Router B, and the hub for PCs 9 through 12 can be connected to Router A. This setup allows for two routes between all segments. The routers require configuration if they are not set up for dynamic configuration.

Sometimes when you are diagnosing a problem, you need to make sure that you think of the components that will be affected. In this case, if we think Router B is the problem, we need to determine the issues that will be experienced by network users and then to see if those issues exist. This practice helps you avoid implementing an incorrect solution. You need to take care when doing this, since at times you might be seeing the issues created by several network problems and trying to find a single solution to fix all the issues when multiple solutions, one for each problem, are likely needed.

A

About the CD

Thois CD-ROM contains the CertTrainer software. CertTrainer comes complete with ExamSim, Skill Assessment tests, CertCam movie clips, the e-book (electronic version of the book), and Drive Time. CertTrainer is easy to install on any Windows 98/NT/2000 computer and must be installed to access these features. You may, however, browse the e-book directly from the CD without installation.

Installing CertTrainer

If your computer CD-ROM drive is configured to autorun, the CD-ROM will automatically start up upon inserting the disk. From the opening screen you may either browse the e-book or install CertTrainer by pressing the *Install Now* button. This will begin the installation process and create a program group named "CertTrainer." To run CertTrainer use START | PROGRAMS | CERTTRAINER.

System Requirements

CertTrainer requires Windows 98 or higher and Internet Explorer 4.0 or above and 600MB of hard disk space for full installation.

CertTrainer

CertTrainer provides a complete review of each exam objective, organized by chapter. You should read each objective summary and make certain that you understand it before proceeding to the SkillAssessor. If you still need more practice on the concepts of any objective, use the "In Depth" button to link to the corresponding section from the Study Guide or use the CertCam button to view a short .AVI clip illustrating various exercises from within the chapter.

Once you have completed the review(s) and feel comfortable with the material, launch the SkillAssessor quiz to test your grasp of each objective. Once you complete the quiz, you will be presented with your score for that chapter.

ExamSim

As its name implies, ExamSim provides you with a simulation of the actual exam. The number of questions, the type of questions, and the time allowed are intended to be an accurate representation of the exam environment. You will see the following screen when you are ready to begin ExamSim.

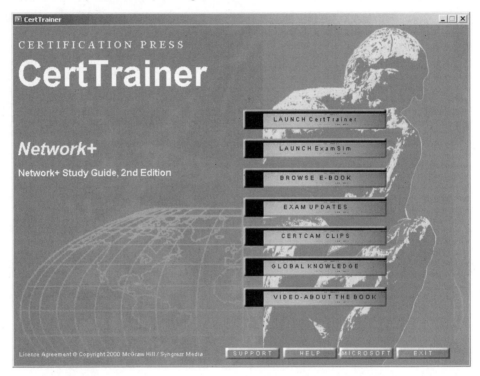

When you launch ExamSim, a digital clock display will appear in the upper left-hand corner of your screen. The clock will continue to count down to zero unless you choose to end the exam before the time expires.

Saving Scores as Cookies

Your ExamSim score is stored as a browser cookie. If you've configured your browser to accept cookies, your score will be stored in a file named *History*. If your browser is not configured to accept cookies, you cannot permanently save your scores. If you delete this History cookie, the scores will be deleted permanently.

E-Book

The entire contents of the Study Guide are provided in HTML form, as shown below. Although the files are optimized for Internet Explorer, they can also be viewed with other browsers including Netscape.

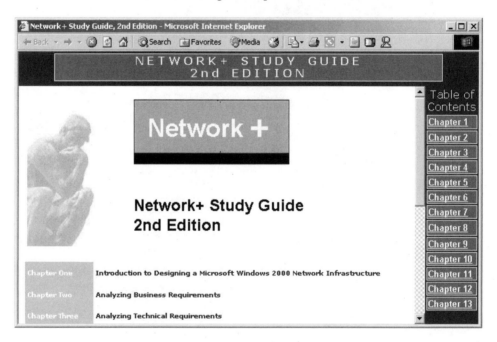

CertCam

CertCam .AVI clips provide detailed examples of key certification objectives. These clips walk you step-by-step through various system configuration. You can access the clips directly from the CertCam table of contents (shown on the next page) or through the CertTrainer objectives.

The CertCam .AVI clips are recorded and produced using TechSmiths Camtasia Producer. Since .AVI clips can be very large, ExamSim uses TechSmiths special AVI

Codec to compress the clips. The file named **tsccvid.dll** is copied to your Windows\System folder when you install CertTrainer. If the .AVI clip runs with audio but no video, you may need to re-install the file from the CD-ROM. Browse to the "bin" folder, and run TSCC.EXE.

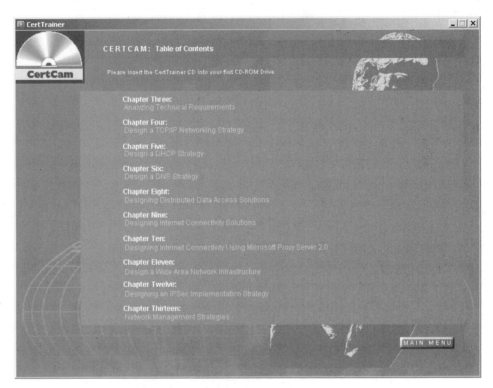

DriveTime

DriveTime audio tracks will automatically play when you insert the CD-ROM into a standard CD-ROM player, such as the one in you car or stereo. There is one track for each chapter. These tracks provide you with certification summaries for each chapter and are the perfect way to study while commuting.

Help

A help file is provided through a help button on the main CertTrainer screen in the lower right hand corner.

Upgrading

A button is provided on the main ExamSim screen for upgrades. This button will take you to www.syngress.com where you can download any available upgrades.

Network+
COMPUTING TECHNOLOGY INDUSTRY ASSOCIATION

B

About the Web Site

A t Access.Globalknowledge, the premier online information source for IT professionals (http://access.globalknowledge.com), you'll enter a Global Knowledge information portal designed to inform, educate, and update visitors on issues regarding IT and IT education.

Get *What* You Want *When* You Want It

At the Access.Globalknowledge site, you can do the following:

- Choose personalized technology articles related to your interests. Access a news article, a review, or a tutorial, customized to what you want to see, regularly throughout the week.

- Continue your education, in between Global courses, by taking advantage of discussion groups with other users or instructors. Get the tips, tricks, and advice that you need today!

- Have instant course information at your fingertips. Course calendars show you the courses you want, and when and where you want them.

- Obtain the resources you need with online tools, trivia, skills assessment, and more!

All this and more is available now on the Web at http://access.globalknowledge.com. Visit today!

INDEX

A

Access Control List. *See* ACL
Access permissions
    file and directory, 384-385
    share, 391-392
    users and groups, 385-390
Access tokens, how they work, 383
Account names, troubleshooting, 635-636
ACL, 383, 419
Active Directory, 17
Active hubs, 89-90, 102
Adapter unit interface. *See* AUI
Address classes, IP addresses, 188-191, 209
Address Resolution Protocol. *See* ARP
Address resolution, definition, 223
Addresses
    assignment methods, 165-167
    IP, 164-165
    loopback, 193
    special Internet, 193
Administrator account
    functions, 512
    permissions, 386
    usage, 436-439
Administrator functions
    adding users, 503-504
    applying patches, 537-539, 548-549,
      558-559
    checking HCL, 502

    creating group account, 505-506
    documenting network, 482-483, 518
    making backups, 486-491, 518, 543-547
    mapping, 497-501
    network policies, 509-510
    planning an installation, 434-436
    preventing crashes, 494-496
    rebuilding systems, 484-486, 518
    removing drivers, 491-493, 518-519
    SOPs, 447-448, 469
    upgrading hardware, 540-542
    using administrator account, 512-513
    utilities, 511
    virus scanning, 549-556
Analog modem, 311, 330
Anti-virus software, installing, 549-556
AppleTalk protocol, 129
Application layer, OSI model, 37
Applications
    downloading patches, 548-549, 559
    version conflicts, 494-495
ARP
    cache, 224-227
    clearing cache, 265
    definition, 184, 208
    how it works, 223-224, 271, 273
    parameters and definitions, 228
    troubleshooting, 228
ARPANET, 288
Array controller, 25

Asymmetric algorithm encryption, 407
Asynchronous communication, 314
Asynchronous Transfer Mode. *See* ATM
ATM, 347-349, 369
Auditing, password usage, 401-404
AUI connector, 95
Authentication protocols, PPP, 293-294, 329

B

Backbone, cable, 3, 4, 56
Backups
    administrator account, 512
    installing software for, 543-544
    methods of, 486-491, 518
    tape drives for, 545-546
    tape rotation, 546-547, 559
    strategies for, 28-29
Bandwidth
    ATM, 347
    E-carriers, 362
    Frame Relay, 354
    OC, 353
    SONET, 350
    T-carriers, 363
Baseband network, definition, 53, 58
Baud, speed, 318
Bearer channels, ISDN, 304-305
Block cipher encryption, 407-408
BNC connectors, 44-45
Boot disk, creating, 15-16
Boot PROM, 80-81
Boot protocol, 171-172
BOOTP, 171-172

Bridge
    brouter, 127-128
    defined, 150, 459, 470
    types of and how they work, 120-121
Bridge routing table, building, 121
Broadband network, definition, 52, 58
Broadcasts, what they are, 126
Brouter, vs. router, 127-128
Browser service, 33
Bus, common types of, 71-73, 99
Bus network. *See also* Bus topology
Bus network, how to install cabling, 5
Bus topology, how it works, 3-5

C

Cables, types of connectors, 43-46
Cables, different names for, 3
Cabling
    backbone, 3, 4, 11-12
    characteristics, 450
    compatibility issues, 465-466
    distance per segment, 43, 46
    for hubs, 89-90
    in a bus topology, 3
    in wireless topology, 9-11
    installing in bus network, 5
    segment, 3, 11-12
    types of, 39-41, 470
    when to use different types, 41-43
Cabling requirements
    ATM, 347
    FDDI, 358
    SONET, 349

Cache, ARP, 224-227

Carrier Sense Multiple Access with Collision Detection. *See* CSMA/CD

CAT3 cable, 40

CAT5 cable, 40

Cells, in wireless networks, 9

CertCam, 660-661

Certificate authorities, 409-410

CertTrainer software, installing, 658

Challenge Handshake Authentication Protocol. *See* CHAP

Chanel Service Unit. *See* CSU/DSU

CHAP, 292, 329

CIR, 355

Circuit switching, 344-345, 369

Citrix Independent Computing Architecture. *See* ICA

Classes, IP addresses, 188-191, 209

Client software
    Novell NetWare, 18
    Windows NT, 16-17

Clocks, synchronizing with NTP, 183

Coax. *See* Coaxial cable

Coaxial cable, 39-40

Collision lights, checking, 621

Collisions, 122, 150

Committed Information Rate. *See* CIR

Communication, types of between computers, 137-140

Computer bus
    definition, 101
    types of, 71-73, 99

Configuring
    default gateway and subnet, 133-135
    modems, 314-321

NICs, 80-84, 100

TCP/IP configuration, 136

TCP/IP for workstation, 196-204, 209

transceivers, 97

Connectionless
    communication, 138-140
    protocols, 188

Connectivity. *See also* Remote connectivity
    network devices, 88-98
    troubleshooting, 264-267, 234-236
    verifying with Ping, 258

Connections, high-speed, 363

Connectors
    different types of, 43-46
    using, 94-97

Credit card adapters, for PC Card bus, 73

Crossover cables, 638

CSMA/CD, 122, 150

CSU/DSU, 363

D

DACL, 383-384

Daily backup, 28

Daisy-chaining, 4

DAT tape drive, 545-546, 559

Data channels, ISDN, 305

Data delivery issues, 137, 139

Data encryption
    definition, 406-407, 420
    industry standards, 408-409
    methods, 407-408

Data Link Control. *See* DLC

Data Link layer

concepts, 150
how it works, 116-125
OSI model, 34-35
Data loss, methods of avoiding, 23-29
Data Service Unit. *See* CSU/DSU
Data transmission
using ATM, 347-349
using circuit switching, 344-345
using Frame Relay, 354-357
using packet switching, 342-347
using SONET, 349-352
using T- and E-carriers,362-366
Datagrams, 138-139
DECnet protocol, OSI model, 32
Default gateway, 166
configuring, 133-135, 200-201
verifying, 266
Device Manager, checking, 608
DHCP
configuring, 170
fundamentals, 165-171, 207
scope, 166
scope options, 169
servers, 170-171
supported clients, 171
Diagnostics programs
NICs, 84-85
selecting and running, 636-637
running WINMSD, 483
Dial-up networking, installing, 313
Differential backup, 8, 547, 561
Digital Audio Tape. *See* DAT
Digital camera, 459
Digital Linear Tape. *See* DLT
Digital signatures, 409-410

Digital-Intel-Xerox. *See* DIX
Direct memory access. *See* DMA
Directory permissions, 384-385
Directory services
Novell NetWare, 19
UNIX, 20
Windows NT, 17
Discretionary Access Control List. *See* DACL
Disk striping, with and without parity, 26-27
Diskless workstations, boot protocol, 171-172
DIX connector, 95
DLC protocol, OSI model, 32
DLL, overwriting, 495-496
DLT tape drive, 545-546, 559
DMA, 86
DNS, 447, 469
checking configuration, 268-269
components and structure, 173-174, 207
configuring client, 198-200
Internet root domains, 175
name resolution, 145, 176-178
troubleshooting, 633-634
DNS database, checking, 270-271
DNS name resolution, verifying with
NSLOOKUP, 259-263
Documentation, importance of, 583-585
Domain
definition, 173, 394
root, 175
Domain Admins group account, 515
Domain controller, 17
Domain Name System. *See* DNS
Domain names
by country, 175
resolving using DNS, 176-178

Drive mapping, 497-498, 519
Driver
    definition, 78
    installing network adapter, 76-77
    removing after upgrade, 491-493, 518-519
    updating, 78-80
DriveTime audio, 661
Dumb terminal. *See* Terminal services
Duplexing, 48
    to avoid data loss, 25
Dynamic Host Configuration Protocol.
  See DHCP
Dynamic link library. *See* DLL
Dynamic routing, 131-132

E

802 committee standards, 122-125
802 committee, IEEE, 121-122
E-book, 660
E-carrier transmissions, 362-366, 370
E-commerce
    security methods, 410-411
    use of HTTPS, 182-183
EISA bus, 71-72
Electromagnetic interference. *See* EMI
E-mail protocols, 184-185
EMI, minimizing, 451
Encryption
    industry standards, 408-409
    methods of, 407-408
    software, 412
    what it is, 406-407, 420

Environmental issues, networks, 449-453, 469
EPROM, 80, 101
Equipment, moving, 502-503
Erasable programmable read-only memory.
  See EPROM
Error control, 137
Error displays, checking, 621
Error logs, checking, 622-623
Error messages, types of, 452-453
Errors, sharing of information, 184
Ethernet, displaying statistics with Netstat, 243
Ethernet name jargon, 45
Ethernet networks, 802.3 standard, 122-123
Event Viewer, checking, 623
ExamSim, exam simulator, 659
Extended Industry Standard Architecture.
  See EISA
External modem, 311
External transceivers, 95

F

Fault tolerance, methods of, 23-29
FDDI, 358-361, 370
    networks, 124, 363-366
Fiber Distributed Data Interface. *See* FDDI
Fiber-optic cabling, 40-41
    connecting, 97
Fiber-optic connectors, 46
File permissions, 384-385
File Protection, setting options for, 496
File transfer process, OSI model, 38
File Transfer Protocol. *See* FTP

Firewalls
    defined, 412-413, 420
    features of, 416
    how they work, 413-414, 420
    types of, 415-416, 420
    using proxy servers, 416-418
Firewire, 457, 470
Fox and hound process, 638
FQDN, 173, 207
Frame Relay, 354-357, 369-370
FTP
    configuring, 253
    definition, 186, 208
    how it works, 251, 272, 274-275
    options, 253
    parameters, 255
    port numbers, 194-195, 209
    troubleshooting, 255
    using, 252
FTP protocol, OSI model, 32
Full backup, 28, 547, 561
Full-duplex dialogs, 36, 58
Fully qualified domain name. *See* FQDN

G

Gateway, 462-463, 470
    configuring default, 133-135, 200-201
    definition, 53, 58
GFS, backup method, 490-491
Gigabit cabling, 44
Global Knowledge Web site, 664
Group account
    creating, 505-506

defaults, 513-516
defined, 512
Guest account, permissions, 386

H

Half-duplex dialogs, 36, 58
Handshaking, 137
Hardware, resolving conflicts, 86-88
Hardware address, resolving, 187
Hardware Compatibility List. *See* HCL
Hardware loopback adapter, 638
Hardware upgrades, 540-542
HCL, checking, 502
Help
    CertTrainer, 662
    online, 580
Hops, tracert, 240
Host
    definition, 49
    name resolution, 144-145
Host ID, 165
Hostname
    configuring, 198-199
    troubleshooting problems, 267
HOSTS file
    editing, 146
    name resolution, 144-145, 179-181, 207
    troubleshooting, 634
    verifying, 268
HTTP
    definition, 182, 208
    port numbers, 194-195, 209
HTTPS, definition, 182-183, 208
Hubs

definition, 459-460, 470
switching, 90-92
types of, 88-90
Hybrid hubs, 90
HyperText Transfer Protocol. *See* HTTP
HyperText Transfer Protocol, Secure.
　See HTTPS

I

I/O addresses, 316, 331
I/O base address, 86
ICA, installing, 325-326, 331
ICMP, definition, 183-184, 208
Identifiers, ISDN, 307-308, 330
IEEE 802 categories, 122-124
IEEE standards, 122-125
IMAP, definition, 185, 208
Incremental backup, 28, 547, 561
Independent Computing Architecture. *See* ICA
Industry Standard Architecture. *See* ISA
InoculateIT software, installing, 549-556
Installing
　dial-up networking, 313
　network adapter drivers, 76-77
　NICs, 74-76, 99-100
Institute of Electrical and Electronic Engineers.
　See IEEE
Integrated Services Digital Network. *See* ISDN
Internal modem, 311
Internet, 125
　DNS root domains, 175
　domain name resolution methods,
　　176-181

mail protocols, 184-185
news articles, 183
online help, 580
security methods, 410-411
use of, 288
Internet addresses, special, 193
Internet Control Message Protocol. *See* ICMP
Internet Message Access Protocol. *See* IMAP
Internet Protocol. *See* IP
Internet Protocol Security. *See* IPSec
Internetwork Packet Exchange/Sequenced
　Packet Exchange. *See* IPX/SPX
Internetwork, concept of, 125
Interrupt request. *See* IRQ
Inventory, maintaining, 584-585
IP, definition, 186, 208
IP addresses, 146-147
　classes of, 188-191, 209
　components, 164-165
　configuring, 133-135, 197
　methods of assignment, 165-167
　network considerations, 442-444, 468
　pinging, 265
　subnet masks, 189-190, 192
　troubleshooting, 228
IP packets, address resolution, 184
IPCONFIG utility, 248, 271, 274
IPSec, 410
IPX addresses, 146-147
IPX protocol, OSI model, 31
IPX/SPX protocol, 21, 57, 129
IRQ
　modem, 316, 331
　settings, 86-87
ISA bus, 71

ISDN
  devices, 306, 330
  history of, 303-304
  reference points, 306-307, 330
  types of service, 305, 330

J

Jumpers, 81-82

K

Kerberos, 411
Keyboard, 458

L

L2TP, 411
LAN, definition, 48
Layer Two Tunneling Protocol. *See* L2TP
Layers, OSI model, 33-37, 58
Link lights, checking, 620
LLC layer, 116, 150
LMHOSTS file
  name resolution, 140-142
  verifying, 269
Local area network. *See* LAN
Local Security Authority. *See* LSA
Logical link control. *See* LLC
Logon
  process, 382
  troubleshooting, 636
Loopback address, 193
  pinging, 264

Loopback test, NICs, 85
Loose source routing, 241
LSA, 382

M

MAC address, 150
  determining for your computer, 117-120
  what it is, 71
MAC layer, 116, 150
Machine name, configuring and changing,
  202-204
Mailslots, 139
Mainframe system, use of star topology, 6
Mapping
  network drives, 497-498, 519
  network printers, 499-501, 519
MAU, 90, 102
MCA bus, 71
Media Access Layer. *See* MAC
Mesh topology, how it works, 7
Microchannel Architecture. *See* MCA
Microsoft
  troubleshooting computers with NBSTAT,
    236
  Web site, 538
  Windows NT network operating system,
    14-17
Mirroring, to avoid data loss, 24-25
Modem, 459
  configuration parameters, 314-318
  configuring with TAPI, 320-321
  configuring with Unimodem, 318-320
  definition of, 314

port speed, 317
serial ports, 316
types of, 311-312
Mouse, 458
Multigeneration, backup method, 490-491
Multiport bridges. *See* Switches
Multistation access unit. *See* MAU

N

Name resolution, 446
DNS, 176-178
procedures, 140-147
troubleshooting problems, 267-271
using NSLOOKUP, 259-263
WINS, 178-179
NAS, 455-456
NAT, how it works, 172
NBSTAT, 233-237, 271, 274
parameters, 237
troubleshooting, 234-236
NCP protocol, OSI model, 32
NetBEUI, network protocol, 22, 57, 129, 148
NetBIOS
configuring name, 202-204
hosts, 268
name resolution, 140-142, 144, 178
what it is, 143
NetBIOS Extended User Interface.
See NetBEUI
NetBIOS over TCP/IP. *See* NetBT
NetBT
how it works, 233
naming convention, 233
port number, 234

Netstat
how it works, 242, 271, 274
options, 243-245
parameters, 246
troubleshooting, 245-246
NetWare, testing backup software, 544
Network
adding users, 503-504
administrative account, 436-439
components of, 2, 56
choosing components, 92-93
data routing options, 342-347
documenting status of, 482-483, 518
environmental issues, 449-453, 469
peer-to-peer vs. server-based, 50-52
planning an installation, 434-436
test account, 436-439
types of components, 88-98
Network Address Translation. *See* NAT
Network administrator, password guidelines,
437-441
Network classes, 188-191, 209
Network connections, troubleshooting,
620-621
Network crashes, causes of, 494-496, 519
Network devices, management using SNMP,
185-186
Network drives, mapping, 497-498, 519
Network File System. *See* NFS
Network ID, 126, 165
Network interface card. *See* NIC
Network layer
concepts, 151
how it works, 125-136
OSI model, 35

Network monitors, 639
Network News Transfer Protocol. *See* NNTP
Network operating system. *See also* NOS
Network performance, using switches, 91-92
Network printers, mapping, 499-501, 519
Network problems
    assessing, 575-578, 604-608
    prioritizing, 586-590, 592
    troubleshooting steps, 609-617
Network protocols, types of, 20-22
Network routing, troubleshooting using
    tracert, 237-241
Network Time Protocol. *See* NTP
Network transmission
    circuit switching, 344-345
    packet switching, 342-347
    using ATM, 347-349
    using FDDI, 358-361, 363-366
    using Frame Relay, 354-357
    using SONET, 349-352
    using T- and E-carriers, 362-366
Network-attached storage. *See* NAS
News articles, use of NNTP, 183
NFS protocol, OSI model, 31
NIC
    configuring, 80-84, 100
    definition, 52, 58
    functions, 71, 99
    hardware address, 71
    installation steps, 74-76, 99-100
    installing network adapter drivers, 76-77
    network component, 454-455
    other names for, 70
    resolving hardware conflicts, 86-88
    testing installation, 77-78
    transceivers, 94-95

    troubleshooting steps, 84-85
NNTP, definition, 183, 208
Nonroutable protocols, 128-129
NOS
    Microsoft Windows NT, 14-17
    Novell NetWare, 17-19
    types of, 14, 56-57
    UNIX, 19-20
Novell
    NetWare, 17-19
    service packs, 537
    Web site, 538
Novell NetWare Core Protocol. *See* NCP
NSLOOKUP utility, 259-263, 272, 275
NTP, definition, 183, 208

O

100MB connectors, 43-44
OC standard, 353, 369
Onboard transceivers, 95
Online help, 580
Open Systems Interconnect. *See* OSI
Operating systems, to use as DHCP clients,
    171
Operator errors, troubleshooting, 619-620
Optical Carrier. *See* OC
Oscilloscopes, 639
OSI model
    definition, 29, 57
    layers, 33-37, 58
    protocols used, 30-33
Overheating, how to avoid, 451

P

Packet Internet Groper. *See* Ping
Packet switching, 342-347, 369
Packets
    customizing with Ping, 257-258
    defined, 20
Padding encryption, 408
PAP, 292, 329
Parallel ports, 457, 470
Passive hubs, 89, 102
Passive topology, definition, 4
Password Authentication Protocol. *See* PAP
Passwords
    auditing usage, 401-404
    basic guidelines, 396-398, 419-420
    creating and changing, 439-441
    creating secure, 399-400
    troubleshooting, 635
Patches, downloading, 537-539, 548-549
PC Card bus, 72
PCI bus, 71
Peer-to-peer networks, described, 50
Performance Monitor, using, 624
Peripheral Component Interconnect. *See* PCI
Peripherals, 458-459
Permissions
    file and directory, 384-385
    individual, 386
    share, 391-392
    users and groups, 385-390
Personal computer. *See* PC
Physical layer, OSI model, 2-30, 33
Piercing tap, 40
Ping
    how it works, 256-257, 272, 275
    ICMP message, 184
    options, 257-258
    parameters, 259
    troubleshooting, 258
Pinging, 265
Plain Old Telephone Service. *See* POTS
Plug and Play software, 82-84
Point-to-Point Protocol. *See* PPP
Point-to-Point Tunneling Protocol. *See* PPTP
Policies, network security, 509-510
POP, definition, 185, 208
Port number
    NetBT, 234
    Telnet, 229
    protocols, 267
    well-known, 194-195, 209
Port speed, modems, 317-318
Ports
    determining, 463-464
    parallel, 457, 470
    serial, 456, 470
    setting up filtered, 418
Post Office Protocol. *See* POP
POTS, 310
Power lights, checking, 621
PPP
    creating dial-up connection, 294-295
    how it works, 291-297, 329
PPP framing, 293
PPTP, how it works, 298-304, 329
Presentation layer, OSI model, 37
Print servers, 458
Printer, 459
Printers, mapping, 499-501, 519

Private-key encryption, 406
Problems
    assessing, 575-578, 591
    prioritizing, 586-590, 592
    troubleshooting steps, 609-617
Profiles, user, 507-508
Protocols
    connection-oriented, 138
    dial-up networking, 314, 330
    displaying with Netstat, 244-245
    implementing, 22-23
    PPP authentication, 293-294
    routable and nonroutable, 128-129
    TCP/IP suite, 181-188
    terminal server, 324-325, 331
    Transport layer, 147-148
    types of, 20-22
Proxy servers, acting as firewalls, 416-418
PSTN, how it works, 309-311
Public Switched Telephone Network.
    See PSTN
Public-key encryption, 407

R

RAID, 57
    levels of, 23-27
RARP, 223, 227-228
RDP, 324, 331
Readme files, 536
Rebuilding systems, 484-486, 518
Redundant Array of Inexpensive Disks. See
    RAID
Reference points, ISDN, 306-307
Registry

rebuilding system, 484-485
    securing, 395
Remote administration, troubleshooting,
    231-232
Remote connectivity
    general concepts, 289, 329-330
    requirements for, 321-322
Remote Desktop Protocol. See RDP
Removable media, backup method, 489-490
Repeaters, using, 94
Replicating data, for backup purposes, 488-489
Resource kits, 579-580, 626
Reverse Address Resolution Protocol. See
    RARP
RG-58 cabling, 39
Rights, vs. permissions, 508
Ring topology, how it works, 7-9
RJ-11 connectors, 44
RJ-45 connectors, 41, 45, 96
Routable protocols, 128-129
    types of, 33, 58
Router, 461-463, 470
    definition, 52, 58
    vs. brouter, 127-128
Routing
    concept of, 126-127
    different types of, 131-132
    network ID, 12
    protocols, 131
    table, 131

S

SACL, 383-384
SAM, 382

Scanner, 459
Scanning, virus, 553-556
Scope
    defined, 166
    options, 169
SCSI, 457, 470
SDH, 349-352
Secure Sockets Layer. *See* SSL
Security Accounts Manager. *See* SAM
Security
    changing passwords, 439-441
    creating passwords and usernames,
       399-400
    environmental issues, 449-453, 469
    network policies, 509-510
    password guidelines, 396-398, 419-420
    protocols, 410-411
    setting up auditing procedures, 401-404
    system components, 382, 419
    user-level, 384-392
    Windows NT policies, 400-401
Segment, cable, 3, 11-12
Segment sequencing, 137
Serial Line Internet Protocol. *See* SLIP
Serial ports, 456, 470
    using with modem, 316
Server
    checking IP security, 266-267
    definition, 49
    DNS, 174-176
    print, 458
    to use with DHCP, 170-171
Server-based networks, 50-52
Server Message Block. *See* SMB
Session
    definition, 137-138

    displaying open, 236
Session layer, OSI model, 36-37
Shielded twisted-pair. *See* STP
Simple Mail Transfer Protocol. *See* SMTP
Simple Network Management Protocol.
    See SNMP
Simplex dialogs, 36
SLIP, how it works, 290-291, 329
Small Computer System Interface. *See* SCSI
SMB protocol, OSI model, 32
SMTP
    definition, 184, 208
    OSI model, 32
    port numbers, 194-195, 209
SNMP, definition, 185-186, 208
Software
    downloading updates, 537-539
    installing anti-virus, 549-556
SONET, 349-352, 369
SOPs, network administrator, 447-448, 469
Source routing bridges,, 120
Spanning tree bridges, 120
Specifications, 10Base, 123
Spoof attack, 172
SPX protocol, 138
    Transport layer, 148
SSL, 182, 410-411
Standard operating procedure. *See* SOP
Star topology, how it works, 6
Startup boot disk, creating, 15-16
Static routing, 131-132
Storage, using NAS, 455-456
STP cable, 41
Stream cipher encryption, 407
Stripe set, creating on Windows 2000 server,
    27

Striping, to avoid data loss, 26-27
STS transmission, 350
Subnet mask
    components, 167
    configuring, 133-135, 197
    IP addresses, 189-190, 192
Subnetting, 192
Subnetwork. *See* Subnet
Suffixes, domain names, 175-176
Switches
    definition, 460-461, 470
    to improve network performance, 91-92
Symmetric algorithm encryption, 406
Synchronous communication, 314
Synchronous Digital Hierarchy. *See* SDH
Synchronous Optical NETwork. *See* SONET
Synchronous transport signal. *See* STS
System Access Control List. *See* SACL
System crashes, causes of, 494-496
System errors, troubleshooting, 619-620
System requirements, for CertTrainer
    installation, 658

T

10Base cabling, distance per segment, 43
10Base specifications, 123
10Mb connectors, 43
T1 links, 304
Tape backup, 546-547
    how to, 487-488
    using, 28-29
Tape drives, 545-546, 559
Tape logs, options available, 29
TAPI, 320-321, 331
T-carrier transmissions, 362-366, 370

T-connectors, using in bus topology, 3
TCP protocol, 138
    definition, 182
    Transport layer, 148
TCP/IP
    configuration options, 445-446
    configuring for workstation, 196-204, 209
    configuring to use DHCP, 194
    determining open connections, 242
    enabling to use DHCP, 170
    port numbers, 194-195, 209
TCP/IP addresses, using NAT, 172
TCP/IP configuration, 136
    checking, 264
TCP/IP hosts, name resolution methods,
    267-268
TCP/IP protocol, 21, 57, 129
    definition, 164, 207
    OSI model, 31
TCP/IP suite, main protocols, 181-188
TCP/IP utilities, 254
    ARP, 222-228
    FTP, 251-253, 255-256
    IPCONFIG, 248
    NBSTAT, 233-237
    Netstat, 242-246
    NSLOOKUP, 259-263
    Telnet, 229-232
    Tracert, 237-241
    WINIPCFG, 249-250
    Ping, 256-259
TDR, using, 639
TechNet, 625
Technical support, 580-581
    telephone, 626
Telecommunications network. *See* Telnet

Telephone services
    circuit switching, 344-345
    ISDN, 303-309
    POTS,310
Telnet
    customizing settings, 230-231
    description, 229, 271, 273
    port number, 229
    troubleshooting, 231-232
Terminal. *See* Workstation
Terminal services, 322-324, 331
Termination, in bus topology, 3-4
Terminators
    bus topology, 3-4
    ring topology, 8
Test accounts, usage, 436-439
Testing, NIC installation, 77-78
TFTP, 139, 255-256
TFTP protocol, OSI model, 32
Thicknet
    cable, 39-40
    specifications, 123
Thickwire coax
    connecting, 95-96
    transmission distance, 94
Thinnet
    cable, 39
    specifications, 123
Thinwire coax
    connecting, 96
    transmission distance, 94
Timeout values, adjusting, 240-241
Time-to-live. *See* TTL
Token ring networks
    802.5 standard, 123-124
    FDDI, 358-361
Tone generator, 638

Tools, troubleshooting, 638-639, 641
Topology
    bus, 3-5
    defined, 2, 56
    mesh. 7
    ring, 7-9
    star, 6
    wireless, 9-11
Tracert
    fundamentals, 237-241, 271, 274
    ICMP message, 184
    parameters, 241
Traffic problems, implementing switches,
    91-92
Traffic routing, 126-127
Transceivers
    configuring, 97
    types of, 87-8894-95, 100
Transmission Control Protocol/Internet
    Protocol. *See* TCP/IP
Transmission
    distance for thickwire and thinwire, 94
    speed FDDI, 358
Transmitters, in wireless networks, 9
Transport layer
    concepts, 152
    how it works, 136-148
    OSI model, 36
    protocols, 147-148
Trivial File Transfer Protocol. *See* TFTP
Troubleshooting
    account names, 635-636
    assessing network problems, 604-608
    assessing problems, 575-578
    available resources, 624-627
cable problems, 631
    configuration problems, 633-635

documentation, 583-585
eight steps, 609-617
examples, 617-619
help options, 580
lights and displays, 620-623
logon procedures, 636
name resolution problems, 267-271
network connectivity problems, 264-267
network tools, 638-639
NICs, 84-85, 100
operator and system, 619-620
passwords, 635-636
physical conditions, 627, 630
PPP, 295-296
prioritizing problems, 586-590, 592
resource kits, 579-580
scenarios and solutions, 628-629, 641
selecting the right tools, 641
servers, 632-633
using ARP, 228
using Event Viewer, 623
using FTP, 255
using NBSTAT, 234-236
using Netstat, 245-246
using Performance Monitor, 624
using Ping, 258
using technical equipment, 581-582
using Tracert, 237-241
viruses, 635
with Telnet, 231-232
Trunk, cable, 3
TTL, 128, 181
Twisted-pair cabling
connecting, 96
specifications, 123

U

UDP, 138
definition, 182, 208
Unimodem, 318-320, 331
Universal serial bus. *See* USB
UNIX
name resolution, 144
network operating system, 17-19
Unshielded twisted-pair. *See* UTP
Updating drivers, how to, 78-80
Upgrades, removing drivers, 491-493, 518-519
Upgrading hardware, 540-542
USB, 457, 470
Usenet groups, connecting to, 187
User accounts, defined, 512
User Datagram Protocol. *See* UDP
User Manager, Windows security application,
    400-401
Usernames, creating secure, 399-400
Users
    adding and deleting, 503-504, 519
    assigning rights, 508
    grouping, 505-507
    profiles, 507-508
Utilities, administrative, 512
UTP cable, 41

V

Vampire tap, using, 95-96
Vendor CDs, 627
Virtual circuits, 138
Virtual local area network. *See* VLAN
Virtual private network. *See* VPN
Virus scanning, 553-556

Virus signatures, downloading and installing, 556-558

Viruses
   checking for, 635
   software for, 549-556

VLAN, definition, 48

Volume, definition and use, 27-28

VPNs, how they work, 299, 329

WAN, definition, 48

WAPs, what they are, 97-98, 102

Web
   Global Knowledge, 664
   troubleshooting resource, 625
   use of HTTP, 182
   use of HTTPS, 182-183

Wide area network. *See* WAN

Windows Internet Naming Service. *See* WINS

Windows NT

default users and groups, 387-388
   logon process, 382
   security policies, 400-401
   security system components, 382, 419
   setting up PPTP, 301-302
   testing backup software, 544

Windows Update, using, 493

WINIPCFG utility, 249-50, 271-272, 274

WINS, 446, 469
   configuring, 201-202, 269-270
   features, 178-179, 207
   name resolution, 144
   requirements, 179
   troubleshooting, 634

Wireless access points. *See* WAPs

Wireless network. *See also* Wireless topology

Wireless networks, 802.11 standard, 124

Wireless topology, how it works, 9-11

Workgroups, what they are, 393

Workstation
   definition, 49
   booting diskless, 80-81

INTERNATIONAL CONTACT INFORMATION

AUSTRALIA
McGraw-Hill Book Company Australia Pty. Ltd.
TEL +61-2-9417-9899
FAX +61-2-9417-5687
http://www.mcgraw-hill.com.au
books-it_sydney@mcgraw-hill.com

CANADA
McGraw-Hill Ryerson Ltd.
TEL +905-430-5000
FAX +905-430-5020
http://www.mcgrawhill.ca

**GREECE, MIDDLE EAST,
NORTHERN AFRICA**
McGraw-Hill Hellas
TEL +30-1-656-0990-3-4
FAX +30-1-654-5525

MEXICO (Also serving Latin America)
McGraw-Hill Interamericana Editores S.A. de C.V.
TEL +525-117-1583
FAX +525-117-1589
http://www.mcgraw-hill.com.mx
fernando_castellanos@mcgraw-hill.com

SINGAPORE (Serving Asia)
McGraw-Hill Book Company
TEL +65-863-1580
FAX +65-862-3354
http://www.mcgraw-hill.com.sg
mghasia@mcgraw-hill.com

SOUTH AFRICA
McGraw-Hill South Africa
TEL +27-11-622-7512
FAX +27-11-622-9045
robyn_swanepoel@mcgraw-hill.com

**UNITED KINGDOM & EUROPE
(Excluding Southern Europe)**
McGraw-Hill Education Europe
TEL +44-1-628-502500
FAX +44-1-628-770224
http://www.mcgraw-hill.co.uk
computing_neurope@mcgraw-hill.com

ALL OTHER INQUIRIES Contact:
Osborne/McGraw-Hill
TEL +1-510-549-6600
FAX +1-510-883-7600
http://www.osborne.com
omg_international@mcgraw-hill.com